# What a Fellowship

# Gracia Grindal

# *What a Fellowship*

Remembering
Augsburg Seminary
and the
Lutheran Free
Church

FORTRESS PRESS
Minneapolis

WHAT A FELLOWSHIP

Remembering Augsburg Seminary and the Lutheran Free Church

Copyright © 2025 Fortress Press. All rights reserved. Except for brief quotations in critical articles or reviews, no part of this book may be reproduced in any manner without prior written permission from the publisher. Email copyright@fortresspress.com or write to Permissions, Fortress Press, PO Box 1209, Minneapolis, MN 55440-1209.

30 29 28 27 26 25     1 2 3 4 5 6 7 8 9

All Scripture quotations, unless otherwise indicated, are from the New Revised Standard Version Bible, copyright © 1989 National Council of the Churches of Christ in the United States of America. Used by permission. All rights reserved worldwide.

Library of Congress Cataloging-in-Publication Data

Names: Grindal, Gracia, author.
Title: What a fellowship : remembering Augsburg seminary and the Lutheran Free Church / Gracia Grindal.
Description: Minneapolis : Fortress Press, [2025]
Identifiers: LCCN 2024058617 (print) | LCCN 2024058618 (ebook) | ISBN 9798889834045 paperback | ISBN 9798889834052 ebook
Subjects: LCSH: Lutheran Free Church–History | Augsburg College and Theological Seminary–History | Norwegian Americans–History | United States–Church history
Classification: LCC BX8055.L8 G75 2025 (print) | LCC BX8055.L8 (ebook) | DDC 284.1/776579–dc23/eng/20250414
LC record available at https://lccn.loc.gov/2024058617
LC ebook record available at https://lccn.loc.gov/2024058618

Cover image: Decorative filigree from the cover page of an Augsburg Seminary course catalog, 1907–1908

Cover design: Kris E. Miller

Print ISBN: 979-8-8898-3404-5
eBook ISBN: 979-8-8898-3405-2

*To the blessed memory of my grandmothers, Helga Marie Kivle and Anda Jacobson Tinseth, and my foster grandmother, Anna Kathinka Watne Grindal; my mother, Jonette Torbjør Tinseth, and my father, Harald Kivley Grindal; and Uncle Fred Tinseth, whose letters, diaries, and stories helped me write this book*

# CONTENTS

*List of Figures*   ix
*Introduction*   xiii

Chapter 1: Leaving Norway   1

Chapter 2: Augsburg Moves to Minneapolis   49

Chapter 3: The Early Years   87

Chapter 4: Teaching the Faith in a New Land   117

Chapter 5: Mergers, Disputes, and the Founding of the Lutheran Free Church   139

Chapter 6: Passing the Torch   201

Chapter 7: Coeducation at Augsburg   251

Chapter 8: A New Augsburg President and War on the Horizon   299

Chapter 9: A World at War   329

Chapter 10: Postwar Ecumenism and Its Problems   379

Chapter 11: A Decade of Merger Talk   403

Chapter 12: Merger   461

*Epilogue*   491
*Notes*   515

# LIST OF FIGURES

| | | |
|---|---|---|
| Figure 1.1 | Harald Grindal by the family DeSoto. | 2 |
| Figure 1.2 | The Grindal family in 1948. | 4 |
| Figure 1.3 | Hans Nielsen Hauge (1771–1824). | 6 |
| Figure 1.4 | Bishop Erik Pontoppidan (1698–1764). | 8 |
| Figure 1.5 | August Weenaas (1835–1924). | 20 |
| Figure 1.6 | The Jacobson family ca. 1910. Front row, left to right: Hilda, Anda, Ole, Jonette, Lindor, and Sylvina; back row, left to right: Johan, Mathilda, Octer, Richard, Emma, and Peter. | 26 |
| Figure 1.7 | The seminary in Paxton. | 37 |
| Figure 1.8 | Gisle Johnson. | 40 |
| Figure 2.1 | Johan Arndt Bergh (1847–1927). | 52 |
| Figure 2.2 | Valborg Iversen Weenaas. | 56 |
| Figure 2.3 | Hans Paludan Smith Schreuder (1817–1882). | 57 |
| Figure 2.4 | Augsburg Seminary professors and students, ca. 1870. | 59 |
| Figure 2.5 | Faculty of Augsburg Seminary ca. 1874. | 60 |
| Figure 2.6 | Text and music of "I Am a Pilgrim Here" / *"Jeg er en vandringsmand."* | 61 |
| Figure 2.7 | Milwaukee Road train station, Minneapolis. | 62 |
| Figure 2.8 | Ole Paulson. | 64 |
| Figure 2.9 | Sven Oftedal (1844–1911). | 74 |
| Figure 2.10 | Georg Sverdrup (1848–1907). | 75 |
| Figure 2.11 | C. F. W. Walther (1811–1887). | 82 |
| Figure 3.1 | Old Main lit up at night. | 89 |
| Figure 3.2 | The Sverdrups. | 91 |
| Figure 3.3 | Period illustration of the grasshopper menace. | 97 |
| Figure 3.4 | Masthead of *Folkebladet* newspaper. | 99 |
| Figure 3.5 | Botolf Botolfsen Gjeldaker (1837–1885). | 104 |
| Figure 3.6 | Peter Andreas Torgersen Nykreim (1839–1924). | 106 |
| Figure 3.7 | M. Falk Gjertsen. | 107 |
| Figure 3.8 | Augsburg Seminary faculty wives, ca. 1874. From left to right: Elise Gunnersen, Katherine Sverdrup, and Marie Oftedal. | 113 |

| | | |
|---|---|---|
| Figure 4.1 | The Brønø Church. | 121 |
| Figure 4.2 | Haakon and Torbjør Tinseth, ca. 1899. | 126 |
| Figure 4.3 | Tinnosett Hotel in Norway. | 128 |
| Figure 4.4 | Tinseth homestead near Lamberton. | 129 |
| Figure 4.5 | Ole Gulbrandsen (1855–1914). | 132 |
| Figure 4.6 | Sverdrup teaching an Augsburg Seminary class. | 136 |
| Figure 5.1 | Friedrich August Schmidt (1837–1928). | 141 |
| Figure 5.2 | Peter Andreas Rasmussen (1829–1898). | 142 |
| Figure 5.3 | Gjermund Høyme. | 143 |
| Figure 5.4 | Main building at Augsburg Seminary. | 146 |
| Figure 5.5 | The Jacobson brothers. Right to left: Peder, Octer, Lindor, Richard, and Johan. | 168 |
| Figure 5.6 | M. Falk Gjertsen. | 170 |
| Figure 5.7 | Octer and Hilda (Hendrickson) Jacobson. | 175 |
| Figure 5.8 | Gustav Oftedal. | 178 |
| Figure 5.9 | The Oftedal brothers, Lars, Ommund, and Sven. | 179 |
| Figure 5.10 | Bernt and Sylvina (Jacobson) Sundal. | 183 |
| Figure 5.11 | Bernt Sundal as a young man. | 190 |
| Figure 5.12 | The second Trinity Lutheran Church building in Minneapolis. | 195 |
| Figure 5.13 | The Tinseth boys ca. 1899. Left to right: Theodor, Ole, Anton, and Fritjof. | 197 |
| Figure 6.1 | A young Anda Jacobson's growing musical skill was recognized in the *Minneapolis Daily News*. | 206 |
| Figure 6.2 | Anda reading a letter with a friend. | 209 |
| Figure 6.3 | Svein and Helga Kivle. | 220 |
| Figure 6.4 | F. A. Schaffnit. | 236 |
| Figure 6.5 | Mrs. Schaffnit. | 238 |
| Figure 6.6 | George Sverdrup Jr. (1879–1937), the second generation of Sverdrups to serve Augsburg. | 243 |
| Figure 6.7 | Theodore and Anda (Jacobson) Tinseth. | 246 |
| Figure 6.8 | Fred Tinseth during his time in the US Army. | 247 |
| Figure 6.9 | Jonette Jacobson with granddaughters Borghild (left) and Jonette (right). | 249 |
| Figure 7.1 | Mildred Jacobson on the family farm. | 251 |
| Figure 7.2 | Mildred Jacobson as a young woman. | 252 |
| Figure 7.3 | John Evjen. | 256 |
| Figure 7.4 | Mildred (third from right) as a member of the Augsburg women's basketball team. | 261 |

List of Figures   xi

| | | |
|---|---|---|
| Figure 7.5 | Mildred with nieces Jonette and Borghild. | 263 |
| Figure 7.6 | The Women's Missionary Federation Board ca. 1916. | 267 |
| Figure 7.7 | Sister Milla Pederson, missionary in Madagascar. | 267 |
| Figure 7.8 | Gerda Mortensen ca. 1933. | 271 |
| Figure 7.9 | Morton Hall at Augsburg Seminary. | 277 |
| Figure 7.10 | Harald Grindal at ten. | 284 |
| Figure 7.11 | Jonette Tinseth's first-grade class in Cyrus, Minnesota. Jonette is third from right. | 286 |
| Figure 7.12 | Gerda Mortensen in her Augsburg office. | 287 |
| Figure 7.13 | Jonette Tinseth in high school. | 289 |
| Figure 7.14 | Borghild and Jonette Tinseth. | 290 |
| Figure 7.15 | George Sverdrup ca. 1937. | 292 |
| Figure 7.16 | Breaking ground for a new dormitory at Augsburg. | 296 |
| Figure 7.17 | Bernard Christensen as a young professor. | 297 |
| Figure 8.1 | The inauguration of Bernard Christensen as president of Augsburg. From left to right: T. O. Burntvedt, Kristofer Hagen, Bernard Christensen, and H. N. Hendrikson. | 300 |
| Figure 8.2 | LFC President Thorvald Burntvedt preaching. | 302 |
| Figure 8.3 | Harald Grindal's uncle and aunt Ed and Mary Kivley—the former a descendant of the Kivles portrayed in *The Boy from Telemark*. | 306 |
| Figure 8.4 | Crown Prince Olav of Norway and his family. | 319 |
| Figure 8.5 | Harald Grindal and Jonette Tinseth. | 321 |
| Figure 8.6 | Augsburg Seminary's 1942 graduating class and their wives. From left to right: Helen and Luther Strommen, Olive and Alfred Sevig, Jonette and Harald Grindal, Marian and Lester Dahlen, and Fern and Larry Gudmestad. | 325 |
| Figure 8.7 | Newlyweds Harald and Jonette (Tinseth) Grindal. | 326 |
| Figure 9.1 | Ludvig Watne. | 331 |
| Figure 9.2 | The backyard of the Tioga, North Dakota, parsonage after a frost. | 334 |
| Figure 9.3 | Christian Ytrehus. | 347 |
| Figure 9.4 | Jonette Grindal and baby Gracia. | 350 |
| Figure 9.5 | Donald Ronning and Harald Grindal with babies Donald and Gracia. | 356 |
| Figure 9.6 | P. A. Strommen. | 361 |
| Figure 9.7 | Four generations of Tinseths and Grindals, pictured: Jonette, Gracia, Theodore, and Haakon. | 365 |

| | | |
|---|---|---|
| Figure 9.8 | Bernard Christensen. | 366 |
| Figure 9.9 | Fritjof Monseth. | 369 |
| Figure 9.10 | Gracia Grindal's debut appearance at an LFC annual meeting. | 372 |
| Figure 10.1 | The parsonage at Rugby, North Dakota. | 380 |
| Figure 10.2 | The Tunbridge church. | 383 |
| Figure 10.3 | A map of Lutheran Free Church congregations published in *Our Fellowship*. | 386 |
| Figure 10.4 | Anna Grindal and nurse. | 387 |
| Figure 10.5 | Elise Andersen. | 394 |
| Figure 11.1 | The newly rebuilt Bethany Church in Rugby, North Dakota. | 405 |
| Figure 11.2 | Merton Strommen (1919–2019). | 408 |
| Figure 11.3 | Rugby youth at a Luther League Convention. | 409 |
| Figure 11.4 | A Luther League Convention at Medicine Lake. | 418 |
| Figure 11.5 | The Grindal and Ronning cousins: Gracia, Donny, Merrill, LaRhae, Ruth Ann at Fosston, Minnesota, in 1954. | 427 |
| Figure 11.6 | The Christmas program at Berwick in 1954. | 430 |
| Figure 11.7 | Central Lutheran Church in Salem ca. 1955. | 432 |
| Figure 11.8 | Forrest Monson. | 444 |
| Figure 11.9 | Luthard Gjerde. | 450 |
| Figure 11.10 | T. O. Burntvedt and John M. Stensvaag on the cover of the *Lutheran Messenger*. | 453 |
| Figure 12.1 | Mario Colacci (1910–1968). | 464 |
| Figure 12.2 | Seth Pierre Andrianarivo. | 468 |
| Figure 12.3 | Rosalyn Holte. | 469 |
| Figure 12.4 | Augsburg Seminary graduates in 1960. | 475 |
| Figure 12.5 | Clarence Larson. | 481 |
| Figure 12.6 | Gerda Mortensen pouring tea ca. 1967. | 484 |
| Figure 12.7 | The Grindal family at Christmas, 1964. | 488 |
| Figure E.1 | The final issue of the *Lutheran Messenger*. | 494 |
| Figure E.2 | Gracia leaving for Norway with the Augsburg choir. | 497 |
| Figure E.3 | Harald Grindal in vestments with Jonette Grindal. | 505 |

# INTRODUCTION

This is a love story. Love for Augsburg, the Lutheran Free Church, and my family, who taught me to love the church and our tradition. I once thought it would be a love story with a betrayal, but as I began writing the epilogue, I realized it was a love story ending in the death of the beloved, a death caused by forces rampant in the West that a small communion like ours could not resist. That is what historians do: they set small stories into a larger context and see what happens. This love story, as I discovered, did not end with the merging of the LFC and the American Lutheran Church. It continued. It is not the church invisible that I love, the one ecumenical officers spend months in the air pursuing, leaving family and friends behind, to sup with other officials in world centers, where they express their love for the universal church while quaffing rare liquors and delicacies. After years in the ecumenical movement, with its high (and low) points, where the perks were almost irresistible, I came to think ecumenical officers had trouble with intimacy, like those who love humanity but hate people.

I love the church visible. When I walk into a church building—from Valamo, Finland, where the Russian Orthodox tradition from 1215 lives, celebrating the Assumption of the Virgin in a sanctuary with pungent Orthodox priests, local women in babushkas smiling to their neighbors and bowing in worship for a moment; to the Olav church in Seljord, Norway, from 1150, where my grandfather Svein Kivle was baptized; to the little Norwegian Methodist church in Kragerø, where my grandmother Helga was saved; to the little St. Petri church in Cyrus, Minnesota, where my mother was baptized; to old believers in Jutland, Denmark, where we used Pontoppidan's hymnal from 1740 and the preacher put his hands on our heads pronouncing the absolution; to being served slivovitz by the ladies of an ancient church in Romania; to the great cathedral in York, into which all the church buildings from my childhood could easily fit; to the unbearably ugly home mission start in Salem, Oregon, where I spent my adolescence in the presence of simple, warmhearted farmers from Iowa who had moved out West after World War II and would spend Sunday nights and Wednesday evening studying the word of God in the King James Version of the Bible and whose language began to sound Elizabethan, salted with *vouchsafe* and *gainsay*; to the Tunbridge Lutheran Free Church in North Dakota on the prairie, where the incense of egg coffee, ham dinners, dill pickles, and human sweat wafted through the sanctuary; and somber Lenten services in Rugby, where people came into the service after milking, snowflakes still pearling on their wool coats—in every one of these places and every other Christian church in the world, I feel at home. These places are home, not because of the way they look but because of what happens in them with the people there. We are all gathered as brothers and sisters in Christ. We share a Lord, and we share a rootedness that one can feel. And I love that, the same way I love home because Jesus, whose body is the visible church, is our home, as Augustine says in his *Christian Doctrine*, the country where we belong. As we know from the biblical story, God's temple is now in his people, no matter the grandeur of the building.

I know and love this not because the congregation is perfect—far from it. It is like all sacred love, given by Christ and brimming out of me helplessly and foolishly, but there it is. Growing up in the parsonage, I have seen people changed and turned from dissolute wrecks into new, joyful individuals; I have also seen people turning things that are penultimate, like the color of the kitchen walls, into something ultimate for which they will fight to the death, leaving ruin and destruction in their wake. I have watched my father and mother enjoy the people they served and also suffered terrible pain from members of the church who seemed to be the devil's warriors and wanted blood revenge for something. These struggles have not soured me or my siblings toward the faith or the church. Our mother and father taught us to understand that all congregations are made up of sinners, and a church full of sinners could be wonderful, edifying, funny, nasty, evil, and mean. But we did not reject our faith because of that. Hardly. We simply understood it as part of the fabric of life to which one grows very close in the parsonage, where births, marriages, divorces, terminal illnesses, deaths, joys, and sorrows walk together as brothers and sisters.

So, in this love story, I begin with the coming of my mother's maternal grandparents, Ole and Jonette Jacobson, to Minneapolis in 1868. Their pastor, Ole Paulson, at Trinity, the grandfather of Augsburg, started their love affair with Augsburg and what became the LFC. They raised their ten children to be faithful members of their local congregation in Montevideo, Minnesota. Next is the story of my mother's paternal grandparents, Haakon and Torbjør Tinseth, and their eight children, also faithful members of their congregations and supporters of local churches in Lamberton and Cyrus, Minnesota, as well as activities like ladies' aid, choirs, young people's society, and working together for orphanages and missions, both at home and foreign, and always Augsburg. Then the story of my father's birth parents, Svein and Helga Kivley—married by an LFC pastor, George Larson, in Sylvana, Washington—and his foster parents, Sjur and Anna Grindal, farming in Ferndale, Washington, all of whom were deeply rooted in the Augsburg tradition and later the LFC. Then I tell about my parents, their childhood, youths, time as students at Augsburg, and their serving

## Introduction

LFC congregations in North Dakota, Oregon, and Minnesota. All these stories played out against the history of Augsburg as well as the LFC and its progress toward merger with the ALC.

That larger story was something I expected to tell but not quite in the way it ended up. The leaders of most American Lutheran churches in the twentieth century were working for a Lutheran church merger. It was the grand climactic story of the histories of American Lutheranism, a fulfillment of Henry Melchior Muhlenberg's wish for "one book; one church." Historians loved to track the progress of such negotiations because they involved theological debates and political strategizing, ending in a grand convention for which Jesus's prayer in John 17 "that they might be one" was the slogan, displayed on billboards and flapping banners all around the convention center, where they met to make the merger official. While that story gave church officials at the time a sense of what they should do in their offices, historians are now coming to see in that version of the story that most of the other activities of the congregations that brought life to people—Bible study, ladies' aids, Luther Leagues, confirmations, local charity, the building of local orphanages, old people's homes, hospitals—were all subsumed and hidden under the great triumphalist arc of the progress toward merger.

Ironically enough, given my disagreement with that great arc, this book focuses on the merger story as well while trying to give the context of how that larger story affected the lives of the congregations and individual believers, which were shaped by the dailiness of the faith, not the story of a small, parochial group ultimately coming together with other small bodies in a merger. In the epilogue, I briefly summarize my life after the merger, when I fell in love with some of the opposing traditions of my childhood, from which, in most every case, I have received many blessings.

Loving institutions is complicated. Once in the mid-1970s, after an awful meeting of the faculty at Luther College, I was walking home with a colleague with whom I disagreed on absolutely everything and didn't much care for. There had been a terrible blizzard the night before, and the wind had packed the snow into drifts that were as hard as rock. As we were parting, standing on a drift in front of the Koren Library, he turned to me and said, "Gracia, you should never love an institution. It will always break your heart." I can still hear the snow crunching beneath my feet as I turned to go home. Was that true? I had loved Augsburg, Luther, the LFC, and the ALC with all my heart. I had seen how students, now alumni—coming back to their alma mater, filled with love for it, shaped by it, and happy to send their children there—had flourished because of those institutions. Much of the story of the twentieth century makes what he said true simply because of the inexorable tide of history, especially modernism, in which the seeds of destruction lurk in every new structure. My experience fits with his observation. The institutions of the church that I loved, led by people who were mostly against me, have broken my heart, but the people gathered around are still precious and to be loved. And this book taught me both truths. A good thing is that I can now, in my eighties, facing my end, rest in that knowledge, happy to have told a part of our story that has not quite been told.

This book would not have been possible without the diaries and letters of my grandmother Anda Jacobson Tinseth, who died in childbirth one hundred years ago on November 23, 1924. Her letters and brief diary gave me many insights into her life and the LFC that I would never have gotten without them, given her early demise. My foster grandmother Anna Grindal's frequent letters to her son—my father, Harald—while he was at Augsburg showed me also how involved she was in the workings of the LFC. My mother, Jonette Torbjør Tinseth Grindal (1919–1999), kept daily diaries from 1935 to 1999, which were invaluable, as was her short book, *Lots of Sky*, based on her diaries. I also vividly remember moments when she would tell me something about the LFC, with her comic and serious sense for storytelling, as though she expected me to be the scribe who would remember and tell the story, as I have tried to do here. My father, Harald Daniel Kivley Grindal (1916–1997), would also tell me about events in the history of both school and church that I would remember, as did my great-uncle Fred Tinseth.

In writing this book, I have received support and critiques from many friends and family members. I am most grateful to Dr. Mark Granquist, professor of church history at Luther Seminary, whose constant encouragement and support have been invaluable and gave me the heart to proceed. Without his help, this book would not have appeared, especially his support for the grant from the Publication Committee of the Lutheran Historical Conference. Many thanks! Pastor Brian Lunn of the Association of Free Lutheran Congregations, and current president of the Georg Sverdrup Society, has been a faithful colleague who very helpfully discussed with me my thoughts about Sverdrup and the Twelve Principles and how they played out in the Lutheran Free Church (LFC) and into the Association of Free Lutheran Congregations (AFLC), which is not my story to tell but that I need to be clear about.

My good friend and colleague Walter Sundberg has also reminded me of things I should have remembered in the telling of the story, and his critique and guidance have, as always, been vital. My brother, H. Theodore; several cousins; and other friends and colleagues have read various chapters of my drafts and also encouraged me. My cousin Randy Ellingboe helped me find pictures of his great-grandmother and -grandfather, Sylvina and Bernt Sundal, and others, as did archivists Kristen Anderson and Stewart van Cleve, at University Archivests and Paul Daniels at Luther Seminary. So did the late Kari Bostrom, who toured

Introduction    xvii

graveyards and lost homes in the Twin Cities for traces of people I mention in the book.

Marilyn Preus, an old friend, a bishop's widow, has also read the manuscript looking for howlers and places where I assumed too much of my readers, an old failing. Although deeply embedded in the Luther College and Norwegian Synod story, she had to get to know the LFC tradition while her husband led the Eastern North Dakota District of the ALC, where there were many strong former members of the LFC. They gave her a granular picture of its merits and faults. She once said to me that she understands the Free Church because she played the saxophone in her high school band. I cannot explain to anyone, including myself, why that is true and terribly funny, but I know what she means. Thanks to all.

Without question, I am grateful that Fortress Press under the leadership of Ryan Hemmer and the Editor-in-Chief, Laura Gifford, had taken on the project. That they considered the project and accepted it was a kind of benediction to my career and life as a thinker and writer about what I have loved so dearly. Many thanks, also, to Chantelle Gibbs who guided me through the final tasks of getting the manuscript ready for publication.

All translations are mine, if the footnote is in Norwegian, as are all the errors.

CHAPTER 1

# Leaving Norway

"There's the ALC. Germans. They drink beer, but they are fine people." I looked at my father beside me in the driver's seat. His hand scraped at the five o'clock shadow growing on his chin.

"Then there are a few Danes—the UELC. The others are Norwegian. The ELC. They are arrogant."

It was June 1951. The powder-blue 1951 DeSoto coupe rode west into the evening through South Dakota. We were on our way to the annual conference (*Årsmøte*) of the Lutheran Free Church (LFC) in Seattle. We were going there to vote against a merger. This year it was in the far west, not exactly at the center of the LFC population. To be sure, a significant number of Norwegian immigrants had made it to Puget Sound after failing on their farms during the Depression. Many who could not bear the upper Midwestern flatlands and harsh climate ended up there as well.

The issue was whether our little fellowship should continue "to explore the possibilities of union with the other members of the American Lutheran Conference."[1] These included the American Lutheran Church (ALC), centered in Ohio, Michigan, Texas, and Iowa; the Evangelical Lutheran Church (ELC), centered in the upper Midwest and Pacific Northwest; and the United Evangelical Lutheran Church (UELC), a small Danish American church body associated with Dana College in Blair, Nebraska. The wounds from a split some fifty years before were still fresh, even unto the third and fourth generations. Now, as I sat beside my pastor father in the hot, dusty car, I was drinking that liquor undiluted and strong.

That morning, June 5, 1951, we had gotten into the cramped car, packed with enough for a month away, and drove south-southwest out of Rugby, North Dakota, the geographical center of North America, where my dad served a three-point parish of the LFC: Bethany (the largest) in Rugby and Tunbridge and Berwick, small country churches—all named for English towns by James J. Hill, the owner of the Great Northern Railroad, as was the town of our first parish in Tioga, North Dakota.

Many families in our little fellowship looked forward to these yearly festivals. They would assemble the family and drive off to Minneapolis, Fargo, Willmar, Thief River Falls, or Minot, LFC congregations able to host large gatherings. This meeting in Seattle, unusual as it was, gave families the opportunity to go on

**Figure 1.1.** Harald Grindal by the family DeSoto. Used by permission of the Grindal family.

a longer trip. These conferences were highlights of the year for the pastors and the laity who were involved. They would enjoy seeing their old friends and colleagues at the meetings, usually four days from Thursday to Sunday or Sunday to Thursday. They were mostly just plain fun—eloquent sermons, testimony meetings, and good singing mixed in with church business and banquets and the telling of old jokes, well known and repeated, like favorite old songs.

Among the best raconteurs were the leaders of the church: Thorvald Olsen Burntvedt, president of the LFC; Bernhard Christensen, president of Augsburg; Clarence Carlsen, pastor at St. Olaf's Lutheran Church in North Minneapolis; and my mother, Jonette. They specialized in hilarious stories about the church, frequently in a mixture of Norwegian and English, or at least in a rich Norwegian brogue.

We looked forward to seeing missionaries, old friends back from exotic places like Madagascar, such as the deaconess Sister Milla Pederson, whose garb was redolent with her own body fragrance and tropical agricultural odors; or Malvin Rossing, who had recalibrated his own clock to fit Malagasy time, to the great consternation of his hosts in this country as they squired him around to his speaking engagements on time;[2] or Dr. Kristofer Hagen from India, who could diagnose illnesses in long lines of people just by hearing their voices. These missionaries would reacquaint the people there with their work using glass slides, the latest technology. And then there were the discussions of one or another serious matter, always Augsburg and merger. Always merger. Always Augsburg.

The conference, after 1916, usually included a meeting of the Women's Missionary Federation (WMF), in which relatively large amounts of money sent in from local ladies' aids would be designated for various mission causes. We knew everyone, or knew of most everyone, from small villages, to Minneapolis, to the farthest reaches of the globe: Madagascar, the Santal Mission in India, the China mission (now relocated, after the closing of the Bamboo Curtain, to Hong Kong or Formosa), and the mission just beginning in Japan. In some ways we were much less parochial than today. We knew these people from far away, the geography where they lived, and even the names of many of the native leaders of these far-flung churches.

The Dakota prairies sped by, a verdant green of summer stretching on toward what would be, depending on the time of day, either a glorious sunrise or a sunset—scarlet, pink, orange, and blue spreading out before us across the wide horizon. Every June when the fields are green and the skies over the prairies are bright blue, those of us raised in this tradition get the feeling we are missing something if we are not in a car speeding past the bountiful fields to an annual meeting.

Scandinavian immigrants, used to mountains and seascapes, thought of the prairies as an empty landscape with very rich soil. One pioneer woman told my mother, when she first lamented the bare landscape in Tioga, "But Mrs. Grindal, we have lots of sky!"[3] Another old salt told her, "Yes, Norway was beautiful, but Nord Dakota, she been good to us, and you can't eat scenery."

Because our father had grown up in Ferndale, Washington, a little Norwegian settlement near Bellingham, we were also going home. His widowed foster mother, Anna Watne Grindal (1886–1959), had recently moved to the LFC's Bethany Old People's Home in Everett. We would visit her and my dad's biological father, Svein Kivle (1879–1961), and his second wife, Ethel, who lived on a farm in Ferndale. We usually took the most direct route to Ferndale, Highway 2, a straight shot from Rugby, almost without a turn until Glacier Park. Then over the mountains.

That part of the trip frightened many Norwegian Americans who now knew only flatlands. Mrs. John (Kristine) Hjelmeland, the pastor's wife in Ferndale during Dad's teenage years, was said to have walked nearly the entire way across Glacier Park. She did not trust the Model T Ford they were driving on their way to Ferndale from the Midwest. Every time she saw a new mountain pass, one she feared the car could not make, she would say, "Nei, let me walk; you will never make it!" and followed after the car on foot. Others going through the mountains for the first time would make out their wills in case the brakes did not hold or a flat would send them hurtling over the side of the road to certain death.

This time, however, we planned to take the southern route west—through Denver, Salt Lake City, the Rocky Mountains—as many Americans did during

**Figure 1.2.** The Grindal family in 1948. Used by permission of the Grindal family.

that decade. World War II was still vivid in our minds, and the interstates, designed to connect the country as Hitler had done with his autobahn in Germany, had not yet been promised by Eisenhower. Harry Truman was the president.

We headed toward South Dakota on our way to Denver, Colorado, where we would stay with relatives of some of our members in Rugby. Although there were motels, they were still not so common. People on long trips at this time arranged to stay with friends on the way to save money but also renew acquaintances. Many did not even make arrangements but just showed up unannounced at the house, especially parsonages, expecting room and board for the night. We were no strangers to this practice. Many times, pastors' families would appear at the door just before noon, when we ate our big meal, and expect dinner.

Once a big family stopped by and brought their Irish setter in for dinner with us. He sat beside his master, who fed him a pork chop. He noisily gobbled it down as we looked on, minus a pork chop we had been counting on. On Mother's clean kitchen floor, no less.

The open windows roared with the dry, hot wind—this was long before air conditioning in automobiles. I was just eight. Mom, from whose breasts I had drunk the pure ecclesiology of the Free Church, and my three-year-old sister, LaRhae, were sleeping in the back seat. Soon we would have to find a place for the evening. We found a small motel outside of Belle Fourche, South Dakota. It was not very fancy and not clean enough for Mother's standards. I remember the cost was a major factor, and this less than fancy place was a dollar cheaper—four dollars instead of five?—than another one we had looked at. We were hot and thirsty and drank lots of water. Later, we found out it was contaminated. One after another, we succumbed to the germ and what the Belle Fourche papers called the "Belle Fourche flu."[4] Was it an omen?

There were other infections around us, too, not physical but ideological. We were fighting the idea of merger, rather like an endemic infection that broke out among Lutherans in America every so often.

The journey to this annual conference had begun at least a century before. Our family, going back to its beginning in this country, and earlier in Norway, had roots in a movement that began in Norway and replanted itself in the United States. It was especially strong in my great-grandparents Ole and Jonette Jacobson, who had left Sømna, Norway, in April, sailing on the *Neptunus* from Trondheim to Quebec and arriving at Minneapolis in July 1868.

## Jonette Adrianna Martinusdatter and Ole Jacobson (Bjørge)

Ole Henrik Kvitle Jacobson (Bjørge; 1833–1913) and Jonette Adrianna Martinusdatter (1842–1922), my mother's maternal grandparents, had left their homes in the region of Sømna, Norway, and the village of Vik in Helgeland, Norway, with a large group of relatives, neighbors, and friends bound for Minnesota.

That year in Helgeland had been rough. The previous summer had been unusually cold. Frost in June 1867 had ruined many crops in the region. Food was scarce through the winter. Worst of all, the herring did not appear, a basic foodstuff in the region. Families, now with more surviving children, felt pushed off their meager livings in Sømna and pulled to the United States, which promised rich farmland unimagined in Norway with opportunities they could only dream of.

Nearly all of them were devoted followers of the movement begun sixty years before by Hans Nielsen Hauge (1771–1824).[5] Whether they agreed with Hauge or not, every Norwegian at the time of the emigration—from high church to low

Figure 1.3. Hans Nielsen Hauge (1771–1824). Public domain.

or nothing—had had some experience of the Haugean movement. It is difficult to understand Augsburg or LFC without knowing his story, as it intersected with ours.

## Hans Nielsen Hauge (1771–1824)

Most of the large number of immigrants from Sømna, Norway—in all, 1,035—were deeply affected by Hauge's work. It began after Hans Nielsen Hauge's experience of salvation while he was plowing the fields on the family farm near Sarpsburg, Norway, on April 5, 1796. At the time, Norway's clergy was affected by the rationalism of the Enlightenment, and spiritual life was deemed dead by many. The pietism of the previous century, in which one's personal relation to Jesus Christ was primary, had cooled, although it was remembered by the devout, whose home devotions were still influenced by the pietist Erik Pontoppidan's explanation of the catechism (forklaring), *Truth unto Godliness* (Sandhed til Gudfrygtighed), and Hans Adolph Brorson's hymns.

Hauge, who had grown up on his pious father's farm in Rolvøy, near Sarpsborg, Norway, had been singing an old German hymn in translation, a

Jesus hymn, "Jesus, I Long for Your Blessed Communion" ("*Jesus din søte forening at smage*"), as he was plowing a field on the family farm. When he reached the second stanza, he was struck as if by a lightning bolt from heaven, almost like St. Paul on his way to Damascus. According to his account, he lay in a trance for some time before he came to. When he awoke, he wrote later,

> My heart was so uplifted to God that I don't know nor can express what took place in my soul. As soon as my understanding returned, I regretted that I hadn't served the loving and all-gracious God, now I felt that no worldly thing was of importance. It was a glory which no tongue can explain; my soul felt something supernatural, divine, and blessed... I had a completely transformed mind, a sorrow over all sins, a burning desire that others should share the same grace, a particular desire to read the Scriptures, especially Jesus' own teachings, as well as new light to understand them and the teachings of godly men; toward the one goal that Christ has come to be our Savior, that we should be born again by his spirit, be converted, and be sanctified more and more in godliness to serve the triune God alone in order to improve and prepare our souls for eternal blessedness.[6]

After this utterly transforming experience, Hauge went into a time of reflection. He emerged from it with the urge to write books and travel the country sharing his faith with others as he had been prompted by his experience. Like all pietists, he understood these stages to be the first steps of the *ordo salutis* (order of salvation): *electio*—believer is elected; *vocatio*—believer is called; *illuminatio*—illumined; *conversio*—converted; *regeneratio*—regenerated; *justificatio*—justification to grow in sanctification.[7] These traditional topics came up when Haugeans talked about their spiritual lives and would be used as sections in their hymnals.

Although Hauge had not attended university, the primary education of young Norwegians at the time was rather rigorous. In order to be confirmed, all boys and girls had to learn to read, as Martin Luther had endorsed in his letter to the German nobility two centuries before.[8] In 1737, Christian VI, king of Denmark and Norway, and the bishops asked Bishop Erik Pontoppidan (1698–1764), one-time bishop of Bergen, to prepare an explanation of the catechism, which all confirmands were expected to memorize before they could be confirmed. It was a daunting puberty rite, but passing it was crucial to the success of any young person in the society. Without being confirmed, one would have trouble marrying and finding work.

Its center was Luther's *Small Catechism*. Pontoppidan added more than seven hundred questions to the topics of the catechism, which confirmands in Norway were expected to know by heart. Over time, it came to be called

Figure 1.4. Bishop Erik Pontoppidan (1698–1764). Public domain.

*børnelærdom*, or *children's teaching*, which would become an issue in the church debates of the Norwegian American Lutheran churches. It was at the heart of Norwegian piety for nearly two hundred years. Usually, the lay assistant (*klokker*) was the teacher, but the pastor or more often the bishop catechized the students. Only the cruelest pastor would insist the confirmands learn them all—which no one really could do. Most pastors would kindly indicate prior to the ordeal which questions he would ask a student during catechization.

While the examination understandably struck terror into the hearts of the young, for those who wanted to learn, it gave most of them a rich understanding of both biblical truths and dogmatic concepts—for example, question no. 229, "What is Sanctification? Sanctification is the gracious work of the Holy Spirit whereby He day by day renews the believer more and more after the image of God."[9] These answers became the stuff of arguments Norwegian Americans would prosecute for over a century.

Somewhat memorable, it was accompanied by Bible verses that could be studied and discussed with the pastor. These Bible verses were part of an old dogmatic tradition the church had followed for millennia, and attentive students would be very well educated in biblical and theological things when they emerged into adulthood.[10] Hauge drank deeply of this work, the Bible, and the hymnal that were the tripod of Norwegian Lutheran piety, the børnelærdom, in his day.

In Pontoppidan's explanation, dancing, drinking, and playing cards were proscribed. These rules kept teenagers in Norwegian American Lutheran congregations, which all used a shortened version of the explanation, arguing with Pontoppidan and their pastors about dancing until the 1960s and the advent of the birth control pill. One might have tried, in vain, to explain the proscription to the protesting teenage girl in my father's congregation who said once that she had never had a dirty thought about dancing until she read the tract *The Dangerous Dance*. The best way to explain it might be the Jewish notion of the fence around the law. If misusing the name of God was a sin, then one should never say it, keeping one from carelessly breaking that law.

Most pastors would not have argued that dancing was in and of itself a sin. The pastors urged their teenagers not to dance and drink because, as they said, "it is what it leads to." Keeping away from the dangerous dance kept one somewhat safer from consequences that could be ruinous, saving many a young girl from an unwanted pregnancy that could destroy her life unless the young man married her immediately, and those marriages were not always the happiest.[11] It was the combination of liquor and dance that made pastors inveigh against these entertainments, all for the good of their young people, who might have thanked them later.

Hauge was not against drinking. He kept a still and served wine at his table, but he knew its dangers. Once when he was a teenager, before his ecstatic experience, his companions in town had gotten him drunk, and his parents had to come and take him home. There was no question that he thought he had broken a rule and regretted it, but drinking per se did not seem to bother him, while his followers were probably fiercer on this than he. There were many debates about this and many people who think, wrongly, that Hauge was a killjoy. Pontoppidan was probably more of a killjoy in that regard than Hauge.

As a young man, Hauge was what the Catholic tradition would call scrupulous. His scrupulosity terrified him. Joseph Shaw calls Hauge "one of history's rare souls who, like Luther, had the spiritual perception to understand the first commandment and the honesty to let it speak to him. It was the awful claim of the first commandment [you should fear, love, and trust in God above all things] which sent terror sweeping over his soul as the cold waters of the Glomma River enveloped him [when Hauge was thirteen, he had almost drowned in the Glomma River] that unforgettable day in his thirteenth year. 'I feared hell's darkness because I hadn't loved God as I should have.'"[12]

After Hauge's experience that April while plowing, which stunned him and made him almost incommunicado for some weeks—not eating, staring about, and worrying his mother—he finished writing two manuscripts. He walked the nearly sixty miles to Oslo from his home farm to get them published. The publisher he brought them to was at first not inclined to print them but then realized that Hauge had the means to publish them. Hauge, the son of a landowning farmer, and a budding entrepreneur in his own right, had resources that became obvious to the printer. He may also have been convinced by the unusual earnestness and obvious intelligence of the young man.

They were simple books, roughly written, burning with his righteous fervor to cleanse the church and bring people to a "sound conversion, a changed heart, and a holy life."[13] The first, *Meditation on the Folly of the World* (*Betragtning over Verdens Daarlighed*), was a youthful attack on Norwegian pastors for their dead spiritual lives and teachings.[14] The second was a tract, *Career* (*Løbebanen*), a spiritual autobiography that had a profound effect on people throughout the country. With its simple story of Hauge's finding peace with God, it caused thousands of Norwegians in almost every nook and cranny of the country to wonder whether they were saved and how to find personal salvation.

During the next eight years, until 1804, Hauge walked the length and breadth of Norway, bringing his message wherever he went. He held meetings in farm homes, where he preached, sang, read Scripture, and sold his books; he wrote edifying letters to his friends throughout the land to keep the movement going. The secret to the rapid growth of his movement was not only his travels and writings but that many of his followers, both men and women, became preachers and writers, traveling the country gathering people together in small groups to study the Bible, hear witnesses, and pray. As Hauge walked through the country, he saw entrepreneurial possibilities for sawmills, paper mills, and saltworks in various localities. All of these would give the locals a better income and improve their life situations.

Later, he had his followers build a paper mill in Eiker to manufacture paper so his books could be more easily printed in Norway. He began a shipping company to sell his books, establishing trade routes for the salt cod from Northern Norway to Bergen. Through his ministry, revival swept the small country and changed it.

His meetings soon attracted the unwelcome attention of the ecclesiastical leaders. He was a clear threat to their authority. Because he was a layman and proscribed from holding meetings without the presence of a state church pastor, he was accused of violating the Conventicle Law of 1741. This law had forbidden such lay activities as a way to stop the Moravian movement out of Herrnhut, Saxony, led by Nicolaus Zinzendorf (1700–1760), a pietist of royal blood, from taking hold in the twin kingdoms of Denmark and Norway.

During Hauge's journeys, this law, along with the one against vagrancy—being in a *fylke* (county) without legal permission—would land him briefly in prison several times, but he continued walking the countryside and having religious meetings with people. A shrewd businessman, he was sensitive to the people he met. As he walked along with others, he would feel whether he should talk about business or religion with them. His deep sense for the other person was no small part of his success.

In many respects, his was a young people's movement. Young people would hear that he was walking through their valley and run to follow him on his way. They brought him all their questions, both spiritual and worldly, receiving good counsel from him and singing together as they tramped through the countryside. The authorities watched closely, fearing rebellion and revolt. All the courts in Europe had watched this closely and, given the recent French Revolution, wanted to squelch (*stanse*) such movements in the bud.[15]

Hauge's flashing blue eyes and strong, expressive voice made a deep impression on his listeners as he preached or spoke. He was a humble man, the picture of good health, and now getting to know the Norwegian people and countryside on his extensive travels. When he came to a farm where a meeting had been announced, he would help with the chores both in the barn and in the kitchen. People loved him for that. He was even a good matchmaker, suggesting to young followers, whom he had come to know, that they marry and run the businesses he helped them establish. And they did, often very successfully. Sometimes, like the paper mill at Eiker, these businesses included places for workers to receive room and board, giving very needy people around them good jobs and places to live.

Hauge moved to Bergen and began a successful business of shipping salt cod from Nordland to Bergen, where it was sent in great quantities to Catholic countries for their Lenten fast. When his boats returned, he could ship his books north to sell. His business acumen was so well known, even in the middle of his long imprisonment from 1804 to 1814, that the government let him out of prison briefly in 1808 so he could build saltworks. Because of the English blockade of Norway during the Napoleonic Wars, salt was at a premium, and people needed it to live.

In addition, the land in Norway could never produce enough food for its growing population. Conditions were so bad during the war, not only because of the blockade but also from bad growing conditions at the time. Parents tried to relieve their children's hunger by feeding them bread made from tree bark. Adding it to the available flour from barley and rye stretched the dough. Usually made from the inside phloem of a deciduous tree dried and ground into flour, it served as a stomach filler, but it was unappetizing and difficult to digest. After the potato came to Norway in the early 1800s, Norwegians never again used bark bread. When the potato blight broke out in the mid-1840s in Ireland and the early 1850s in Norway, it dramatically increased emigration from both countries because once again people were starving. Given the lack of much arable land in Norway—under 5 percent is arable—many foodstuffs had to be imported. Some have said that until the discovery of oil in the 1970s, Norway was the poorest country in Europe except for Albania. That may be an exaggeration, but the land simply could not support its growing population in the 1800s.

Hauge's business sense helped him to change not just Norway's religious life but also turn it from a mercantilist economy—that is, an economy tightly regulated by the government for the economic benefit of the rich—to a more capitalistic one, open to the work of small entrepreneurs. His business savvy made him, over time, one of the richest men in Norway, so much so that his opponents accused him of fleecing his followers and depositing his money in a secret holy treasury (*Hellige Kasse*) for his own use, an unfounded accusation. Those who knew Hauge considered him one of the most honest men in Norway, behavior his followers also tried to emulate.

## Hallstein Gaupen and Ragnhild Gjærtsdatter
### Hauge's Friends

While Hauge was on one of his trips to the north during the spring of 1803, he spent time in Sømna and the surrounding areas in the Nordland county (*fylke*). There he held meetings that attracted many followers and created a group of friends (Hauge's friends/Hauges Venner). Among his most active friends were the maternal great-grandparents of Jonette Martinusdatter Tenfjord Jacobson: Hallstein Ingebrigtsen Gaupen (1761–1837), a lensmann (something like a local sheriff or policeman), and his wife, Ragnhild Gjærtsdatter (1763–1836).

Hallstein came from the upper class or *conditionert*. His father, Ingebrigt Taraldson, and his grandfather, Tarald Olsen Gaupen, were both officials (*lensmand*) in Bindalen, near Sømna. It was a pious family. Tarald Olsen Gaupen (1691–1773) wrote a book of hymns, *A Simple Layman's Sunday Pastime* (*Eenfoldig Lægmands Søndags Tidsfordriv*), in 1742. These were hymns like many Lutherans wrote for morning and evening devotions in the home. They became known as *Tarald's Poems* (*Taralds Digte*) and were well regarded by his peers. The collection was dedicated to the Hersleb family, a strong pietist family of pastors in Norway, among the most well-known pietists of their time within the Dano-Norwegian clergy.

Bishop of Oslo at the time, Peder Hersleb (1689–1757), was a strong proponent of pietism as it was coming out of Germany. His writings, such as *A Christian's Life, as a Battle* (*En Christens Liv, som en Strid*; 1731), was a marker of his thought, not dissimilar from the *Pilgrim's Progress* of John Bunyan. Ole Hersleb, Tarald's pastor in Brønnøysund and brother of Peder, came into conflict with the Trondheim bishop Eiler Eilersen Hagerup (1718–1789) on the theology of absolution. He resigned his position as pastor in protest because he like "many pietists thought it was wrong to give absolution to people who did not show any sorrow for their sins or any desire to amend their lives."[16] This would not be the last time this conflict would arise among Lutherans—or in my family. My Jacobson great-grandparents were well aware of this controversy in their own history and church lives, and it became a defining one in my own. The arguments were almost always the same, using the same resources back to Luther and Osiander.

Ingebrigt's son Hallstein, Jonette's great-grandfather, was a promising young boy who grew up to be sheriff (*lensmand*) in Bindalen as well. He and his wife, Ragnhild, also gifted, did much to further living Christianity in their area. They made their home a center for Christian work in the region, hosting testimony meetings, small groups for Bible study and edifying conversation. To the community, they were living examples of the pietist Christian life.

According to Per Øverland, who wrote biographies of many of Hauge's Friends, they were "light and salt" to their region. Both supported Hauge. When he came to Nordland, he stayed with them. They scheduled meetings in their home before Hauge appeared, which helped to create interest in him so the meetings would go well when he came. The meetings in homes on a Sunday often ended with Hauge leading the group into church for its regular worship. Øverland concluded his note on them by saying that "this special couple worked their entire lives in beautiful unity for their children's Christian rearing and education and for the spreading of Christian life in the parish. They had the joy to see the fruits of their labors in their lifetimes."[17]

Although Hauge sharply criticized the church, especially its spiritually dead pastors, he was careful not to create a separatist group wanting to leave the state church. His movement resulted in what became the *bedehus* (prayer house), where small groups would gather to sing, pray, and hear sermons. It came to be called the inner mission movement, which worked to evangelize the church from within, not leave it behind. This was consistent with Hauge's "Last Will and Testament."[18] In it, he urged his friends to faithfully attend the state church for the sacraments and life passage events, such as baptisms, confirmations, weddings, and funerals, while at the same time meeting in what would become the prayer house nearby for edifying meetings, hymn singing, Bible study, testimonies, and mission work. This is where Ragnhild Gjærtsdatter, Jonette's great-grandmother, known as a good preacher, had her ministry as a preacher and leader.

When Hauge was imprisoned in 1804, the government had to build a case against him. In 1807 and 1810, local officials arranged for hearings into Hauge's work throughout the country. A government official, Alexander Holst of Sømna, confiscated all the Hauge works he could find in people's homes and called on many citizens to testify against Hauge's activities in the area. The hearings were lengthy and tedious: in 1807, Holst questioned thirty-seven witnesses from the area and in 1810, forty-eight. They each had to answer twenty-four questions about Hauge's activities. Hallstein was the first witness at both hearings. Both Ragnhild and Hallstein courageously gave true reports of Hauge's activities and made clear that they supported him and his ministry.[19] Tor Mathisen, historian of the Sømna area, named them as among the most influential people in the region at the time. Their testimonies were especially important.

Many others, especially pastors and other church and government officials, could not say enough bad against Hauge. He had, among other things, encouraged women, if they had the gift, to preach the word. His opponents gossiped about his many women followers, his holy treasury, and his anticlerical stance and criticized him for going against St. Paul's statements against women speaking in church. Hauge had argued that if women could preach the Gospel faithfully, they should, although becoming a pastor was not something he said much about. In a way, it was not his fight. He was interested in the gifts of the Spirit as they manifested themselves in people, not the structures of something as traditional as the Erastian Dano-Norwegian church.[20]

Hauge consistently argued for the spiritual leadership of women throughout his life. When he chose leaders to help him with the movement, women were included in the group. In his 1802 book *A Reflection on the Society of the Orthodox* (*En Betænkning om den Rettroendes Samfund*), he wrote, "I have written to you before about Supervisors and stated that the one who searches the most for humility and love, and who humiliates and hates him or herself, they should be every place, whether they are young or old, rich or poor in the world, female or male sex."[21]

Later, Hauge wrote clearly on the way women had been treated in Norway in civil society. As a boy, he had learned from his father and brothers how to work outside on the farm as well as learning from his mother and sisters how to do women's work, keeping house but especially handwork, knitting, embroidery, and other fine sewing. While he walked through Norway, he frequently could be seen knitting. His work became highly desirable, not only because it was his work but also because it was so fine. During his time in prison, to earn money for the books he was finally allowed to buy, he would knit fine gloves, which outraged some of his plain followers! It shows, among other things, his ability to work and profit from his work caused him to see:

> that it is held as an (*sic*) dishonor if women work on diverse tasks, especially in cultivating the land and preparing the fruit, which they according to custom say are only the job of male persons.... Was it not well that women were accustomed, especially those who have less domestic work to do? ... and all energies should be used, especially during times of harvest, men and women, since the bread is common to the whole State. It is likewise with the proudly accepted custom and contempt for the domestic life among some of male sex, who either do not want to or are ashamed of working with clothing etc., Which they say only belong to the female sex and is a disgrace for male persons, since they though highly need to make clothes and many moments are idle.... And both sexes should be careful to teach and drive themselves ... each according to their gifts and strengths.[22]

When Hauge was apprehended by the authorities in 1804, he was treated cruelly. Accused by the bishop of Kristiansand, Peder Hansen (1746–1810), of being like Muhammad Ibn Abdul Vechab (1703–1792), the reformer of Islam who created the Wahhabi movement still regnant in Saudi Arabia and was feared by European monarchies, Hauge was bound in chains, forbidden to have books in his cell, and prevented from going outside into the sunlight and air.[23] His health began to fail almost immediately. Within three months, he lost his teeth. Doubt and attacks from the devil almost overwhelmed him. His friends could do nothing for him except pray and try to make the government proceed with his case.

One of the most affecting stories of him suffering in jail was when a loyal friend came to the prison and tried to communicate with him. They could not hear each other, but Hauge recognized the man and brought his candle to the window, which the man could see. It flickered, and then the man saw Hauge reach toward the wick and trim it. Then the candle flamed up brightly. It became an edifying story with deep religious significance for his followers. Not only did they get the message that Hauge was alive and able to respond but also that the wicks of their faith had to be trimmed through suffering so that the light would shine brighter. Egil Hovland in his opera on the life of Hauge. *Fange og Fri* (*Captive and Free*), sets the scene as the high point, with his choral anthem "Stay with Us" ("*Bli hos oss*") to be sung as Hauge's friends gather outside the prison to encourage him.[24]

The Napoleonic Wars had affected both civil and religious authorities in Denmark and Norway. The dilatory judicial processes they followed meant that Hauge suffered cruel and unusual punishment in prison for ten years, languishing there until Christmas Eve 1814. Although after 1808 he had been given a better cell, his health by that time was ruined. After his release, he was really an invalid for the rest of his life. His movement continued, however, stoked by his letters and friends.

Hauge's followers turned out to be something like Wesley's Methodists in England—honest, hardworking people who lived sober lives. It was Hauge's movement that gave the Norwegians who left Norway the grit and moral character to do well in the rough western lands where they would pioneer. They expected very little from this world, but like the Puritans, they had the right character for the frontier.

## The Emigration

It is difficult for people today to fathom the massive number of immigrants from Norway to America. At least one-third of Norway's population at the time, over 800,000 people, would emigrate to America. (No other country but Ireland had sent such a large percentage of its population there.) Since, for the most part, they came to the Upper Middle West, at the time a large open territory, they could create something like a Norway in America or, if not that, at least a Norwegian church in America.[25]

As they founded congregations, the first buildings they built after their homes, they tended to establish the kind of Lutheranism they knew from Norway. These emphases would be reflected in the various schools they built.[26] Their differences in this country became somewhat more pronounced as they sought to define who they were, now no longer under the umbrella of the state church in Norway.

Although there are records of Norwegians in America as early as 1624 in New Amsterdam, the emigration is officially regarded as beginning in 1825 with the coming of *Restaurationen*, a slooper—a small ship with one mast—bearing fifty-three immigrants, many of whom were Quakers from Stavanger.[27] Not many Norwegians followed until after 1838, when they began reading books and letters from America (*AmerikaBrev*) about the possibilities there.[28] By the end of the 1840s, the trickle became a steady stream, later a flood. There were thirteen thousand Norwegian immigrants in the United States by 1850. That next decade brought around thirty-six thousand. During the Civil War, the immigration slowed, but from 1870 to 1890 ca. 346,477 came. As the immigrants built their homes and established a society with churches, schools, and so on, their numbers exploded. While not all of them desired church membership, a good many did. The church was the one institution that to some extent could emigrate with them, and it felt like a home away from home with its language and customs.

Norway's society was divided into three classes. The upper class, educated professionals, was called the *conditionert* or people of condition: lawyers, doctors, pastors, businessmen. Second were the peasants, or *bønder*, who owned land their ancestors had very likely lived on it for generations, and a third, the cotters, or *husmen*, were those who worked on the land but did not own it. Many were younger sons who could not inherit the land since Norway practiced primogeniture. This assured that the farm remained one rather than being broken up into smaller and smaller plots of land for each son, but it also meant there were many strong, healthy young men who were without means. The landowning farmers' sons tended to be the first to come to America because they had some means to buy tickets; the poorer cotters came later. From the *conditionert*, generally only the clergy emigrated since they could use their education and professional training to serve congregations in Norwegian. It was much harder for lawyers or other professionals to establish themselves in another country for reasons of education and language.

## New Churches in America

The immigrants began founding congregations and calling pastors to serve them almost as soon as they arrived. Elling Eielsen (1804–1883), a Haugean layman, began his work in the Fox River, Illinois, settlement around 1839. There he helped form a congregation but moved to Wisconsin in 1843. On October 3, 1843, he was ordained in Chicago by Francis Alexander Hoffmann (1822–1903) of the Northern Illinois Synod. It was a ceremony that many other Norwegian American pastors regarded as illegitimate since Eielsen had had no formal theological education. He argued, however, that his ordination had been legitimate. The fourteenth Article of the Augsburg Confession stated, "It is taught among us that nobody should teach or preach or administer the sacraments in the church without a regular call."[29] His call made him a pastor, Eielsen maintained, language even Herman Preus, who could hardly defend Eielsen, would use on receiving his call from the Spring Prairie congregation in Wisconsin.[30] Eielsen argued that he had been rightly called by members of a congregation and thoroughly examined, so he was a pastor as well.

Eielsen was no picnic; it was said of him that when he entered a room, all the joy disappeared from it. But as a founder, he needed that kind of gristle. These stories are remembered. They are not buried in the past; they still live.

In 1987, the Committee of 70, which was planning the structure of the ELCA, could not agree on a practice or theology of ministry. As a compromise, it established a Task Force on the Study of Ministry (TFSM) to hammer out a theology and practice of ministry for the new church. I had been appointed to represent my tradition in the confab. From the very first meeting, I would be accused of holding to Eielsen's theology of ministry. He appeared to be sitting next to me. Often, when I spoke, I would be taunted for being an Ellingian.

The same month of Eielsen's ordination, a mild-mannered Dane, Claus Lauritz Clausen (1820–1892), was ordained to serve the Muskego parish near Milwaukee. Clausen had come as a layman and teacher. He soon realized he needed to be ordained to satisfy his parishioners' longing for a "real" pastor. On October 18, 1843, in a barn near Milwaukee, a German pastor from the Buffalo Synod, Lebrecht Friedrich Ehregott Krause (1804–1885), ordained Clausen after the traditional examination. His ordination was also viewed with some suspicion by other Norwegian American pastors.

Clausen and his wife, Martha Rasmussen (1815–1846), were much appreciated by the congregation, despite lingering doubts about his and Eielsen's ordinations. Several ladies' aids in the area called themselves the Martha Clausen circles. She is thought to have written the first hymn by a Lutheran woman in America, "And Now We Must Bid One Another Farewell" ("*Så nu må vi sige hverandre farvel*").[31] Unfortunately, she died not long after leaving Muskego.

In 1848, after the Clausens left, the Muskego congregation called a pastor from the Bergen area in Norway, Hans Andreas Stub (1822–1907), to serve them. When the Stubs arrived, the pioneers wept to realize they now had a "real" pastor from Norway to serve them. His son, Hans Gerhard (1849–1931), was the first pastor's son born in America to a Norwegian American Lutheran pastor. He lived up to his nativity. A member of the first graduating class of Luther College in 1866, he had studied in Norway at the Bergen Cathedral school from 1861 to 1865; he attended Missouri's Fort Wayne Seminary from 1866 to 1869; and he graduated from Concordia Seminary in St. Louis in 1872. A student of the Old Testament, he taught at Luther Seminary from its founding in 1876, serving as president for several terms until 1917. He was then elected the first president of the Norwegian Lutheran Church in America (1917–1925).

In 1851, Pastor Herman Amberg Preus (1825–1894) and his wife, Linka (1829–1880), set up housekeeping in DeForest, Wisconsin. Preus had been called to serve the Spring Prairie congregation there, just north of Madison, in Dane County. Two years later, Ulrik Vilhelm (1826–1910) and Elisabeth Koren (1832–1918) came to serve the Little Iowa Congregation in Washington Prairie near Decorah, Iowa. As the Norwegian population grew and moved west, these pioneer pastors followed them, founding congregations across the entire region from Michigan to the Dakotas.

These immigrant congregations had had little success calling pastors from Norway. All realized quickly that they needed to establish colleges and seminaries to appropriately prepare their own pastors to serve American congregations they had established in the new land. They founded church bodies and soon were building schools to educate their young—not just future pastors but schools for all their children desiring a higher education. Preus and Koren were fundamental in founding the Norwegian Synod in 1853, centered at Luther College in Iowa; Eielsen and his followers created the Eielsen Synod, which in 1876 became the Hauge's Synod, with a seminary in Red Wing, Minnesota.

The Norwegian Synod opened Luther College in 1861 as something of a preparatory school to educate future pastors before they went to seminary. It dedicated its new main building on October 14, 1865, to great fanfare. It was the largest such institution Norwegians had built up to that time in America. Because Norwegian Synod pastors had established a strong relationship with Missouri Synod pastors, they had, after some deliberation, agreed to send their theological students to Fort Wayne or Concordia Seminary in St. Louis to receive seminary training.[32] In 1876, the Norwegian Synod built Luther Seminary in Madison, Wisconsin. It would later move to Robbinsdale, Minnesota, then Hamline in Saint Paul, Minnesota, and finally to Como Avenue in St. Paul.

The Eielsen Synod had earlier opened a school for three students in Lisbon, Illinois, which lasted from October 1854 to May 1855. Peter Andreas Rasmussen (1829–1898) was both president and professor. In 1870, the Eielsen Synod voted to build a school in Chicago, which it finished in 1871. An imposing building three stories high, it cost almost $34,000, a large sum at the time (in 2017 dollars, $683,060). They called it Hauge's College and Eielsen's Seminary. It ultimately could not be supported by the small synod, and the building was turned over to the Hauge's Synod's Trinity congregation in the city. Later, the reformulated Eielsen Synod, now Hauge's Synod, would build a school, Red Wing Seminary, in 1883 in Red Wing, Minnesota, for its seminary students and others of its own flock interested in an education.

## The Middle Group

In the middle of these two wings of Norwegian American churches was a group of Norwegians who had joined with the Swedish Lutheran immigrants and others in the Northern Illinois Synod. In 1851, this synod also founded a seminary. They called it Illinois State University, a misleading name since it was neither owned by the state, nor was it a university. It included a mixture of Lutherans without regard to ethnic identities and traditions. Located in Springfield, Illinois, it was led by Lars Paul Esbjörn (1808–1870) from 1858 to 1860. He would soon come to disagree with the direction of the seminary. Esbjörn had been the leader of one of the first groups of Swedish immigrants and is still considered to be the pastoral pioneer of Swedish Lutheran immigration. With his concern for the future of Swedish Lutheranism in America, he had participated in establishing this school and was present when the Northern Illinois Synod was formed. But it did not last. The different ethnic and theological strains joined in this effort simply could not work together. Esbjörn got all the Scandinavian students to resign from this school and leave with him for Chicago, where he opened a school called Augustana Seminary.

When the Scandinavians left the school and the Northern Illinois Synod, the question was immediately before them: Should they organize a synod to support the new school? A group of Scandinavians met to discuss the matter on June 5, 1860, in Jefferson Prairie, Wisconsin, right on the border of Illinois and Wisconsin, near Clinton. Ole Andrewson (1818–1885), a Norwegian pastor, served as convener. The meeting established the Scandinavian Lutheran Augustana Synod. The Swedish pastor Tufve Nilsson Hasselquist (1816–1891) was elected president. Their school, the Scandinavian Augustana Seminary, would leave Chicago in 1863 for Paxton, Illinois. At the time, the Synod included probably twenty-six Norwegian and Swedish pastors, compared to sixteen pastors in the Norwegian Synod.

## August Weenaas

From its founding, the Scandinavian Augustana Seminary had known it needed to include Norwegian teachers for the growing number of Norwegian students. Not until 1868, however, and the coming of August Weenaas (1835–1924), did the Norwegian students at Augustana Seminary have a permanent teacher who spoke Norwegian and had been educated in Norway.

August Weenaas appeared to be a good candidate. He had been part of a group of students at the University of Christiania who had been converted during the Johnsonian revival led by Gisle Christian Johnson (1822–1894), professor of dogmatics at the University of Christiania (now Oslo). Johnson was known as a confessional pietist. He had led many pastors and his colleagues in a revival that in many ways brought the Haugean revival to all of Norwegian society, including the educated theologians and the upper-class laity.[33] Weenaas came highly recommended by his professors and fellow students at the University of Christiania. Augustana Seminary issued a call to him in the spring of 1868. Weenaas accepted it. Like most of these founders, he was a crusty, uncompromising man with a moody temperament.

As part of his preparation to assume the professorship, in the winter of 1868, he traveled to Germany for further theological schooling. He attended lectures at Erlangen University, hearing some of the luminaries of Lutheran theology at the time, among them Gottfried Thomasius (1802–1875), a confessional pietist

**Figure 1.5.** August Weenaas (1835–1924). Public domain.

somewhat like Weenaas's favorite professor, Gisle Johnson. Weenaas described Thomasius as still possessing his full powers and giving sparkling lectures, especially on dogmatics.[34]

Leaving Erlangen over its extended spring break, Weenaas visited Johann Konrad Wilhelm Löhe (1808–1872) and the Deaconess Motherhouse, founded in 1849, in Neuendettelsau. Weenaas admired, as most everyone did, the charismatic leadership of Löhe, now in his later years. This visit may have given Weenaas leanings toward a higher view of liturgy than his compatriots. He would later be accused of being too high church. In early May, he traveled back to Norway, visiting along the way the great cities of Germany—Eisenach, Leipzig, Berlin, Potsdam, Hamburg, Kiel—and taking in the sights and sounds of the bustling continent.

When Weenaas arrived back in Norway in late May 1868, he had hoped he and his family could leave immediately for America. Because the money for their passage had not yet arrived—a recurring problem with this group—their departure was delayed until the middle of July. After sailing to Hull and then taking a train across England to Liverpool, a very common route for immigrants from Norway, he and his mother, Inger Kristine; his wife, Valborg Iversen; and their three daughters, Agnes Marie (four), Valborg Karoline (two), and Ragna (one), boarded the steamship *Pennsylvania*. They arrived in New York some two weeks later. After seeing the sights, they took the train through Philadelphia and Pittsburgh to Fort Wayne, Indiana, and then Chicago. There they met Samson Madsen Krognæs (1830–1894), pastor of Trinity (*Trefoldighet*) church.

A learned graduate of the University of Christiania, and, like Weenaas, an admirer of theological professor Gisle Johnson, Krognæs was a leader in the Scandinavian Augustana Synod. He had visited the Weenaas family in Norway and knew them fairly well. They stayed with the Krognæs family for eight days as they got acclimatized to the vast American continent, where they would be living for the next eight years. While the Weenaas family was staying in Chicago, my great-grandparents Ole and Jonette traveled through the city on their way to Minneapolis.

Post-Civil War America was booming. Immigration had resumed now that hostilities had ended. Ulysses S. Grant was running for president. The country had just passed the Fourteenth Amendment, guaranteeing, among other things, citizenship to former slaves. Reconstruction was embroiling both Republicans and Democrats, but very little of this seems to have engaged these immigrants. They were busy making a place for themselves and a growing number of their countrymen flooding into the new land.

From Chicago, the Weenaas family traveled about one hundred miles southwest to Paxton and Augustana Lutheran Seminary on the Illinois prairie. In the blistering heat of an Illinois August, they arrived at the small town and tiny school.³⁵ Weenaas met the "praiseworthy and highly esteemed" Dr. Tufve Nilsson Hasselquist. Weenaas never forgot his kindness. He was not pleased, however, when the sainted, now older, professor showed him the four-room house they were expected to share, briefly, with two or three other families. Weenaas did not accept the offer.

With the help of Hasselquist, Weenaas found a small two-room house at the edge of town on the prairie. They could rent it until the church body finished a new building with two lecture halls and an apartment, where the Norwegian professor and his family would live. With some difficulty, the young couple managed to survive in these primitive conditions. They marveled at the fruitfulness of the land around them with its wild grapes, apple trees, and flowers. For them, it was a completely new world, which Weenaas described in his memoirs:

> The nature around us was foreign and new. For a newcomer there was much to see and take in. Around us lay the endless prairies spread out before our eyes. For now, they were unoccupied, but ready for cultivation. In the midst of this monotony, there was a large and stirring creation with a life so new and colossal that one would stand there, realizing one had truly come into a "New World." Imagine a summer night on the endless prairies hearing a person's voice accompanied by choirs in the swamps, the creeping singers: frogs, grasshoppers, turtles, lizards, and snakes that swarmed about. As soon as night fell until light returned, there was a cohesive chorus of these animals, clear evidence of the mighty life that moved about in these grassy fields. After this performance, when you looked, of an evening, west at the wide western horizon, you would see flashes and flashes like distant mighty canon explosions.³⁶

## Ole and Jonette Jacobson

Ole and Jonette Jacobson were of hardy Haugean stock. Ole Bjørge Kvitle Jacobson was thirty-five and Jonette Adrianna Martinusdatter Tenfjord twenty-six when they left for America in 1868. Both were committed Haugean Christians and knew how to work. They had heard about America from letters sent back by recent immigrants. Life in Norway on the farms, especially given the high taxes at the time, had become unendurable to many who had to fight simply to keep themselves afloat on long-standing family farms. In his extensive chronicling of the Sømna area, Tor Mathiesen notes that although things in Nordland had improved significantly from the previous generation—farmers could both fish and farm—1867 had been difficult for the people in the region. And, as one scholar wrote, Nordlanders' experience of fishing and the sea made them different from many Norwegians who only farmed the land: "Fishing had given them cash, and the land had given them support and certainty. Together with their farms and the great fisheries available to them Norlanders developed a taste for experiences and hazard that created more balance than that of the more tradition bound farmworker."[37]

The Homestead Act of 1862 of the United States of America had opened the West for European settlers. The Civil War was over, as were the 1862 battles with Native Americans in Minnesota. Ole and Jonette could see a future for themselves and their family in America that simply did not exist in Norway. Nothing could improve the climate, their land, the little they had, or their lack of opportunity. In the classic push/pull theory of immigration, they felt pushed out of Norway even as they felt the pull of America. It was irresistible to them and their relatives and friends who came with them.

The couple left Trondheim on April 15, 1868, bound for Quebec on the *Neptunus*, a barque, and arriving on July 15. Barques were three-mast ships that were less expensive to sail; they required a smaller crew than a fully rigged sailing vessel. Ole and Jonette arrived in Minneapolis on July 25. Like many such Norwegian couples at the time, and rather like Per Hansa and Beret in *Giants in the Earth*, who also hailed from the area near Vik, Jonette came from landowning farmers, while Ole was a *husman*, a younger son who could not inherit the farm.[38] She had the richer heritage and lineage, which could be traced almost back to the Vikings. Like Beret, she had more to lose, culturally, than Ole. Still, her prospects in Norway were bleak.

Unlike the Weenaas family's two-week steamer trip, the Jacobsons' journey had taken about two months. Steamboats, however, were not within financial reach of these immigrants. (Steamboats often did have full riggings as well but not always.) From what we can tell, the journey went about as well as any, but it was still rough on the Atlantic. Sailing vessels were not stable, responding to both the winds and the waves and making it difficult for people prone to nausea to travel on them. Many of the immigrants who wrote letters back home about the journey via sailing vessels could not recommend it to their compatriots who were awaiting their reports. Unendurable conditions were described to those left behind: food that became moldy and was barely edible, the overcrowding in steerage, the terrors of icebergs abundant during the favorable summertime for the voyage, and the constant battle with seasickness, which plagued many so memorably that they never wanted to sail again.

Jonette, long admired for her strong will, said she never, not even once, wished to return to Norway. The reason—her granddaughter, Theolina Hanson, added many years later—was that she would never return unless she could walk. Apparently two months of seasickness on the *Neptunus* had cured any desire she may have had to set sail ever again, even if it meant going home. That may not have been the only thing that kept her from longing to return. Because of the poor conditions in Norway when they left, most immigrants were not romantic about going back after a few years in America. They made this clear in their letters home. While they admitted that the journey and first years were difficult, they did not appear to long for Norway. In some ways, they felt betrayed by their native land and its inability to feed them or make it possible for them to flourish.

The following ballad by Pastor Johan Olsen (1834–1911), a fellow immigrant from Jonette's region, described the feeling well. He had emigrated in 1866 from Vik in Helgeland. His father, Ole Johan Jacobson (1803–1873), and stepmother, Ragnhild Johannesdatter (b. 1810), traveled to America about the same time as Ole and Jonette, sailing from Trondheim to Quebec. Olsen, a fine poet, would later become president of the Norwegian Danish evangelical Lutheran Church (Norsk-dansk Konferentsen—hereafter Conference), the church to which the Jacobsons would belong.

**Emigrants Visa**
Johan Olsen

Can it live, the love I carried
For my fatherland,
Since I traveled a new pathway
To a foreign strand?
Over Norway, I have fretted,
My dear mother's son,
When she locked the door behind me,
Just when I had gone.

People said I should feel guilty
That I went away
Far away from all her troubles
All for better pay.
Norway's loss is much regretted:
For each one that leaves
From her all the best is taken,
Losses she should grieve.

If I've lost the love I bore her
Greater is my loss,
Though I left for something better
I have borne the cost.
I have left behind my country,

> For my daily bread,
> Better danger on the ocean
> Than to suffer need.
>
> For I now do not regret it,
> I love liberty.
> Therefore I will live my own life,
> Norseman, I am free,
> It has always been our custom
> To be on our own
> When some others want to rule us,
> All our anger shows.
>
> Norway's mountains, Norway's dwellings
> I cannot forget.
> Thousands had to the leave the country
> Flee their homes and debt.
>
> Lovely place—let God be prais-ed!
> Here I built a home,
> Worked to build it, did not slumber,
> To God's praise alone.
> I have built my home,
> Worked to build it, did not slumber,
> The glory his alone.[39]

The third generation, and those following it, tended to be more romantic about Norway, a truth stated by Marcus Hansen, a Danish American scholar. The third generation of immigrants wanted to remember what the second generation wanted to forget.[40]

The route from Quebec to Minnesota for the earliest immigrants had been via the Great Lakes. By the time Ole and Jonette arrived, the train seemed preferable. During these transfers from ship to boat to train, many an immigrant suffered confusion and loss at the hands of swindlers who gave false information or took money for accommodations or travel that were either nonexistent or execrable. Bernt Hanson, Ole's grandson, tells of his Hanson grandfather, who came two years after Ole and Jonette. He had been misled to take the train, not to his intended destination of Montevideo, Minnesota, but to another place. Things got figured out, but he arrived in Montevideo with $1.35 in his pocket.

Many of the letters home give the impression this was the most trying leg of the journey—mostly because, for the first time, they were among people whose

**Figure 1.6.** The Jacobson family ca. 1910. Front row, left to right: Hilda, Anda, Ole, Jonette, Lindor, and Sylvina; back row, left to right: Johan, Mathilda, Octer, Richard, Emma, and Peter. Used by permission of the Grindal family.

language they did not understand and who did not understand theirs. From the little I know, the Jacobsons traveled through Port Huron and then to Chicago.

When they left Norway, Ole and Jonette were engaged but not yet married. Engagement at this time was tantamount to marriage. To break an engagement was almost as serious as divorce. It is a bit surprising that they did not marry before they left home, but long engagements were not unusual at the time.

It turned out to be a wise decision for the couple. A long trip across the ocean and needing time in the new land to get settled would have been much more difficult had she become pregnant and then had to care for a newborn. She needed to be able to work hard before they could settle in. The ship's manifest lists Jonette's name immediately after Ole's as they disembarked. Her parents, Nicoline Hansdatter (1819–1891) and Martinus Johanneson Tenfjord (1817–1908), who emigrated to Minnesota in 1871, would have felt comforted that Ole accompanied her. By all accounts, he was a good man.

They would remain in Minneapolis for the next year and a half. The local Norwegian paper, *Nordisk Folkebladet*, featured small articles and letters from visitors or settlers in the western regions of Minnesota. Chippewa County was highly recommended by several writers. One settler described life there in the summer of 1869, just when the Jacobsons were getting ready to move. The area had available land, which cost five to fifteen dollars an acre and was largely prairie with some woods by a river.[41] This was a good thing since most of the pioneers needed timber to build log houses after their dugouts had served as a temporary shelter. A new sawmill had just been built near Montevideo, and that same year a Norwegian doctor had moved to the county to open a drugstore. It would not be long until the railroad would come to Montevideo, the writer supposed. He figured that over one hundred Norwegian families had moved to the county the summer of 1869. Many had homesteaded in the townships just north of Montevideo, where the Jacobsons would settle in November.[42]

Although we do not know this for certain, we can suppose that Ole and maybe Jonette had gone to Chippewa County scouting out the land before they settled there. The requirements of the Homestead Law, the time of year they moved to Montevideo, and the sketchy legal documents available to us suggest that. Chippewa County history describes this as a common practice: "the home seekers sought out the sites in most cases selected before they ventured to bring their families."[43] The requirements of the law meant that one had to file a claim to the land by setting down a stake, apply for it at the nearest land office (which, in Ole's case, was Litchfield, Minnesota), and then prove the claim by living there for five years, improving it with a home and other buildings. The second winter of 1871–1872, after he had raised some corn on the farm that summer, he cut timber for logs near the Minnesota River, which he used to build a new house, sixteen by twenty-two feet. The family says it was the largest in the county for a time. The application Ole made is recorded in June 1871, with a second plot registered on June 6, 1872. The completion of the claim occurred in 1880 when he bought the land.

Meanwhile, Ole worked in the sawmill at Saint Anthony Falls in Minneapolis, and Jonette probably found work as a maid or servant some place among the Norwegians and Swedes in the neighborhood. One reason to think they had sufficient means is that they bought several expensive necessities on their way to Montevideo, a kind of team—an ox and a cow—and even a cookstove for their sod dugout. Not every family in the new settlement had one. Many women probably used the old methods of cooking over a hearth. Many would use their prairie schooners as they camped along the way, employing them as temporary homes when they arrived at their chosen site and built their dugouts or sod huts.

Minneapolis was booming at the time. It was still a very young city, incorporated in 1867, with about fifteen thousand residents. Ole Paulson (1832–1907) wrote some years later that he went out on the prairie to the east to look for a place to build Augsburg, which will soon become central to our narrative. The place he chose, where Augsburg is now, was empty land. All that could be seen to the east was one home, that of Judge Atwater near the river, and a small hut of a newcomer to the south.

Minneapolis boasted of having world-class sawmill operations on St. Anthony Falls. Northern Minnesota had large stands of virgin timber that, when cut, could be floated down the Mississippi River to Minneapolis. There, St. Anthony Falls made the milling of lumber very productive. For a time, Minneapolis was the world center for timber production.

Where the young couple stayed is not part of the record, but there were growing numbers of Norwegians in the city. Carl Hanson in *My Minneapolis* notes that Norwegians from Trøndelag (Trønders) created a lively neighborhood on the north side of the falls.[44] The Jacobsons might have found that group more compatible as their dialects were closer. However, we do not know. Their close association with Paulson, pastor of Trinity Lutheran Congregation, over the years makes me think they stayed on the south side, closer to Trinity, but that is pure speculation.

Paulson officiated at Ole and Jonette's wedding on December 27, 1868, in Minneapolis. Paulson had arrived in Minneapolis in July 1868, the same month as the Jacobsons, to serve Trinity, which had been meeting since April of that year. This connection with Paulson and his denomination would remain dear to the Jacobsons over their lifetimes.

## Ole Paulson

Paulson, a well-regarded graduate (1868) of Paxton Seminary, had completed his schooling there the spring before the arrival of Weenaas.[45] He had been called by the Scandinavian Augustana Synod to establish congregations west of the Mississippi. The call said that if needed, however, he could work only in Minneapolis, which he did.

Remembered now as the Grandfather of Augsburg, Paulson had a life worth mentioning, if only to see what kind of man he was and examine his brand of piety, which is essentially the piety of all of my forebears. This piety persisted in the Augsburg and LFC traditions until the end. In addition, his life on the western edge of the settlements tells a colorful story few know today.

Paulson had emigrated with his family from Finnskog in Norway, a region in Hedemark reaching all the way east to the Swedish border. They were descendants of Finns who had immigrated into Norway from Sweden, maintaining their language and traditional farming methods for centuries. Weenaas believed Paulson to be Finnish or Kvensk and thought maybe that he spoke a Finnish dialect.[46] The record does not say whether Paulson could speak Finnish or Kvensk, but there was a small contingent of pastors from Augsburg who ministered to the Finnish, reading Finnish sermons to those scattered congregations.[47]

Paulson was a rough and ready pioneer from landowning peasants in Norway. He tells in his memoirs how his family came to Muskego, Wisconsin, in 1850, when he was still a young man. There he experienced the first theological skirmish among Norwegian American Lutherans between Johannes Wilhelm Christian Dietrichson (1815–1883) and Elling Eielsen. Dietrichson had been called to establish congregations among the immigrants by Norwegians concerned for missions in Africa and America. A crusty, opiniated and capable administrator, he began his work in Koshkonong from where he worked to establish other congregations. In some sense Dietrichson was the founding pastor of the Norwegian Synod, serving Koshkonong for four years.[48] A fiercer set of combatants is hard to imagine. Compromise was not in the makeup of either Eielsen or Dietrichson. Paulson had heard the story, which he judged to be apocryphal but still had the ring of truth, that Eielsen had grabbed Dietrichson by the beard and screamed, "Listen, to me, you Pope! I intend to plague you as long as I live."[49] It did not attract Paulson to either side of the argument that these two men embodied. He did come to know Eielsen and would later write that Mrs. Sigurd Eielsen was a better preacher than her dour husband.[50]

Muskego, near Milwaukee, was often the first stopping point for the early Norwegian immigrants. They usually knew of someone there who could keep them until they found their way further west. Paulson's parents lived there for a bit, but the young Paulson needed work. He sailed from Muskego east across Lake Michigan to work in Manistee, Michigan, in a sawmill. After a disaster at the mill, which meant none of the workers received their pay, he returned to Muskego. He soon left with a group of settlers on their way to Decorah, Iowa, frequently the second stop for immigrants from Norway who were looking for a place to find land.

Outside of Dodgeville, Wisconsin, Paulson was bitten by a rattlesnake. At first, he thought nothing of it and treated it with folk remedies, none of which worked. His friends finally found him a doctor, who excoriated them for their stupidity in not immediately getting medical help. He then proceeded to cut out the infection in Paulson's foot, which hurt so much that two grown men had to hold him down.

As Paulson was fighting for his life, he heard Signe, the wife of his friend John Waa, praying for him. He began to realize that he needed to think of his own salvation. Although he did not come to the knowledge of salvation immediately, it did awaken his heart to his need for God.

He and John Waa tried to lay claim to property in the Big Canoe area, near Decorah, but they could not find good land that was available. They searched farther south and found land with both woodland and prairie beside the Turkey River. Waa bought a claim for fifty dollars, and Paulson bought one beside his. He then had to return to Muskego to bring his parents and siblings to the place he had just purchased.

While in Decorah, he observed a revival sweeping the area similar to the revival in Norway at the time. A colporteur, Peter Asbjørnson (Mehus), had brought tracts from the American Tract Society to the community. They had had a telling effect. Paulson and the farmer he worked for finished their chores early so they could attend a meeting led by Asbjørnson. Paulson admitted to being gripped by the messages and the meeting. He noted that in his agitation, he felt like Christian in John Bunyan's *Pilgrim's Progress (Pilegrims Vandring)*, a book that many of these people had read. Other than the Bible, Pontoppidan, and the hymnal, Bunyan's book would have probably been the only other one in the homes of Christian laypeople at the time.

Paulson was suffering from ague, probably from malaria contracted in Muskego.[51] It was taking him some months to recover. As he improved, he attended a prayer meeting. There he had a "shake" from the illness, he said. His prayer partners asked him if he would pray, and he agreed to, falling to his knees in a dark corner. While he could not remember what he prayed, he wrote years later, he did remember the joy that suddenly overcame him: "It was as if I had entered Paradise. The joy that overwhelmed me I took as the Spirit's witness that I had been reborn in God."[52]

As he continued traveling and attending prayer meetings with his friends, he especially enjoyed the singing. He had a good voice and was a capable song leader. He began assisting Asbjørnson with his tract ministry. One day as they were speaking, Asbjørnson told Paulson that he had noticed that while he had given his heart to God, he needed one thing more: faith in Jesus.

This confused Paulson. Asbjørnson recommended he read David Hollatz's (1730–1771) book, *The Evangelical Order of Grace*.[53] Hollatz, the grandson of a theologian in the last generation of orthodox Lutheran theologians, had become popular with Lutheran pietists in the north.

In April 1854, Paulson returned to Muskego and heard of better land in Minnesota. One of his sisters was working for a man in Hastings, Minnesota, so he thought he might take a look there as well. He took a steamboat from Lansing, Iowa, to Hastings and met her employer, Dr. Foster. Foster urged them to scout the land near Cannon Falls. They wanted land that had some woods, some prairie, and a fresh spring. Although they liked the area, they found nothing available that met their needs. A few days later, they returned to Foster and decided to take the steamboat to St. Paul, where another of Paulson's sisters and a brother lived and worked. At that time, St. Paul had about four thousand inhabitants.

On the boat, a Mr. Jørgensen heard them talking and understood that they were Norwegians. He recommended they scout for land in the area of St. Peter, Minnesota, not far from Mankato. The man was from a nearby area he had originally called Gothenborg but soon renamed Carver. Paulson and his partner,

Ole Hendrikson, decided to have a look. They were traveling with several Swedes also looking to lay claims to land. They took a flatboat from St. Paul to Shakopee and Chaska. The man had bragged about the new town Gothenborg, but when they got off the boat and asked where it was, he said, "Here" and pointed to an empty space with a little log shanty where Jørgensen had his blacksmith shop. He also used it for a watch repair shop, a hotel, and his own dwelling. They felt a bit cheated but stayed the night, planning to set out for points west in the morning.

They left early the next day with the Swedes, hoping to stake a claim. The Swedes found suitable land a bit before Paulson and his colleague did. Jørgensen urged them on until they came to a place with two brooks, between which there was good land, and a forest of maple trees. They took to it and made their claim, pleased with their choice.

From there, Paulson had to return to the Turkey River settlement and take his parents to the new claim. When they returned to Minnesota two months later, in the middle of summer, they found it to be overrun with weeds and swarming with mosquitoes. For Norwegians, mosquitos were a new trial. They were not used to them in Norway. Without screens, which were not invented until the 1870s, the hot, steamy Minnesota summers were miserable. Paulson suggested they go back to Iowa. His mother put her foot down. "Nei," she said, "I will go no further. I have traveled enough." That settled it. They decided to obey her and build a house for her as quickly as they could. She stayed there until she died some twenty-nine years later at age eighty.

The settlement grew quickly. It was soon in need of a Lutheran pastor. There were none to be had. For a while, a Baptist, Pastor Brown, served them—a good preacher, said Paulson, when he was not completely drunk. After a few scandalous appearances by Brown, Erik Norelius (1833–1916), the Swedish Augustana pastor central to the founding of Gustavus Adolphus College in St. Peter, came to the small settlement and acknowledged Brown's failures. The need for a Lutheran pastor trained in an American Lutheran school was becoming obvious. For many reasons, including the growing Scandinavian population in the area, the lack of Lutheran pastors was a deeply felt issue. The people needed shepherds.

Paulson struggled with his faith as the awakening spread. As he had noted before, his conversion had been to God but not to faith in Jesus. As the decade progressed, he became aware of the problem, but as he said, his taste for the things of the world had progressed in him as well. He thought of going to communion, at that time a most serious encounter, but he could not confess his sins to his own satisfaction. As he said about himself, quoting Revelation 3, "Oh that you were either cold or warm." His heart was troubled, but nothing seemed to be right. He even began to worry he had sinned against the Holy Spirit, a great concern among many at that time who had not finally come to the assurance of salvation.

They feared that because the Spirit was not helping them come to assurance, they had done something to make the Spirit unable to work in them.

The paragraph Paulson wrote describing his plight and his enlightenment is worth quoting in full. In it, one can read some of the same themes Hauge used to describe his experience:

> One evening we were together, many of us, as brothers. We stood together in a circle, sang, prayed and testified. It was with these disciples that it was said, "Then the disciples were glad for they had seen the Lord." But there was one among them who was not glad. That was me. I sat there alone by the table and read in the book, "Come to Jesus!" The dawning light began to shine clearer before me and I remembered the song, "Just as I am without one plea, / But that thy blood was shed for me / And that thou bidd'st me come to thee / O Lamb of God, I come, I come." I read further and came to the verse, which described my discontent thus: "So cold and dead and pained to seek all that I need in blessed joy from you. O Lamb of God, I come, I come!"[54] So amazingly simple! The blinders fell from my eyes. I said to myself, How could you be so dumb. You have not seen this before! All that you need to find union with Jesus is this. I found him and believed in him, God's Lamb, who had shed his blood for me, to cleanse me. The dark that had covered my soul vanished and there was light. God's peace which passes all understanding poured down into my soul and gave me a foretaste, "It is good to taste and see that the Lord is good" Psalm 34... Now my slavery is over! Jesus is mine!"[55]

The experience made Paulson one with the Haugean disciples whom he was to serve. His long period as a soul searching for salvation made him understand the people he would serve in this country. It was what he lived and taught in his long ministry in the Augsburg community.

Soon Paulson was looking for brothers in Christ who could continue to educate him and feed his hungry soul. He found a Swedish man, Carl Hedengran, a neighbor, who shared with him Johann Arndt's *True Christianity* (1604), the one book he had taken with him when he left Sweden.[56] Hedengran had come to faith through reading it; for some reason, he had fallen into a terrible season of doubt and anxiety. He could no longer believe. Paulson watched him pace back and forth in his house, wringing his hands and sighing. No one in the group could help him. Then a man with some more understanding spoke with Hedengran and read Psalm 68:19— "Blessed be the Lord, who daily bears us up. God is our salvation. Selah!" On hearing it, Hedengran was freed of his darkness and restored to his former joy.

Peter Carlson (1822–1909), another colporteur who later become a pastor in the Swedish Augustana Synod and founded East and West Union Lutheran churches in Carver County, Minnesota, visited Hedengran and asked him to help with the revival. He agreed and soon began giving edifying talks. He asked Paulson to come with him. Paulson studied as Hedengram began to preach and sing for the people who flocked to hear him. The houses were too small to hold all who came, so they split up.

Paulson went out on his own. At the meetings, he read Luther's sermons called *postils* and Scripture and sang spiritual songs. They continued their meetings through the winter. Each meeting was packed; the houses could not hold the gatherings. People came even when the snow, which was plentiful in the winter of 1859, piled so high that they could barely get through it. One woman walked three miles carrying her children on her back through deep snow to hear him. One of the most amazing things about it, said Paulson, was that even with the obvious presence of the Spirit, no *schwarmerei* (enthusiasm or excessive emotional experiences) broke out.

Paulson continued his work as colporteur, now on his own, through that summer and into the next winter. Carlson had promised the American Tract Society that he would not leave his post until he had found someone to take his place. He told Paulson that he was the one. Now Paulson, a layman, should begin to preach on his own, not just read postils. This was a challenge for the young man with no seminary training. The issue of lay preaching, which had been an issue with the Haugeans in Norway, had come along with the immigrants and would become a sore point from Eielsen onward to the ELCA's TFSM (1988–1993).

Paulson regarded Carlson's call as a real call from a brother in Christ. What should he do? When he told his family, they all agreed he should take it, except for his wife, Inger Lovberg (1840–1918), whom he had married in 1858. She said, "Absolutely not!" After a long night of talk, during which the family promised to help her with the farm, she finally agreed.

When he got the approval of the tract society, and the official papers, it was winter. To set out, he needed a horse, a sled, and a case that would keep his printed matter dry in rainstorms or other inclement weather. When he finally got that all in order, he lacked one thing: any notion of how to preach! His only comfort was that he could sing. What he sang were songs by Lina Sandell (1832–1903) and the composer Oskar Ahnfelt (1813–1882). The Swedish pastors whom Paulson was getting to know in the school had come from Småland, the area in Sweden where Lina Sandell lived with her parents. Many knew her father, Jonas, and were eager disseminators of these new songs. When Hasselquist began editing the church paper, *Den rätta Hemlandet*, he included psalmodikon versions of the tunes with texts on the first page of each issue. These would later be printed in songbooks that became treasured resources of the Augustana Synod, ending up in the 1892 *Hemlandssånger*. It included five hundred spiritual songs, over one hundred by Lina Sandell. It was from this relationship with the Swedes that several Norwegian pastors—Paulson, M. Falk Gjertsen (1847–1913), and Andrew Wright—learned these Swedish spiritual songs; they printed Norwegian versions of them, many during the 1870s to 1916.[57] These songbooks informed the editors of the *Concordia* in 1916 and later in its 1932 revision.

As Paulson rode around the area, he met revival everywhere. After his visits to Lakeville and Christiania, he went to Goodhue County, where he met Pastor Bernt Julius Muus (1832–1900) and his family. They had just arrived in 1858. Paulson wrote of Mrs. Muus that she was a gifted young woman, educated, and as far as he was concerned, a serious Christian.[58]

When he asked Pastor Muus if he could hold meetings for his people, Muus responded enthusiastically, "Yes, as long as what you preach is pure Lutheran doctrine." Paulson then noted that Muus loved to hear him sing Oskar Ahnfelt's songs. Muus could not himself sing but was a grateful listener.

As Paulson traveled through the area that January, it was bitterly cold, sometimes as low as thirty or forty below zero. His horse could manage, but Paulson remarked that he had no fur coat or sheepskin to keep him warm enough. Sometimes he came close to perishing. He would have died several times of cold if not for the goodness of people in the homes he would drive by in the bitter weather. Paulson called the early pastors and colporteurs "spiritual Vikings" for their courageous exploits, all in the name of bringing the Gospel to the immigrants.[59]

Paulson continued his travels throughout the region, serving Swedes and Norwegians wherever he found them: selling books, praying, singing, and preaching. From Wisconsin near St. Croix Falls to Marine-on-St. Croix, to Carver County, Kandiyohi, Chisago Lake, and St. Paul, back and forth he went, sometimes with a colleague but frequently by himself. His work was probably more with Swedes than Norwegians, given the former's larger settlements in that area at this time.

Unable to join with the Ellingians, and finding the Norwegian Synod too much like the state church in Norway, Paulson and other Norwegians were attracted to Swedish and Danish Lutherans who realized they needed a seminary and a church body. At a meeting in Jefferson Prairie, on the Illinois/Wisconsin border, in 1860, a gathering of Scandinavian Lutherans founded the Scandinavian Augustana Synod and Augustana College and Seminary, which Esbjörn had moved to Chicago from the Northern Illinois Synod's school, Northern Illinois University in Springfield, Illinois, which had included Swedish, Norwegian, and English-speaking Lutheran students.

Paulson attended that meeting as a delegate from his congregation and also as a colporteur. Very few people knew the participating congregations, pastors, and members of this group as well as Paulson, whose constant travels had brought him into contact with many who would likely want to belong to such an association.

With the establishment of the Scandinavian Augustana Synod, the seminary would remain in Chicago under the leadership of Esbjörn until it moved to Paxton, Illinois, in 1863. Paulson felt his call to become a pastor growing stronger. He wrote to Esbjörn in the fall of 1860, asking to be admitted to the seminary. That January 1861, he left Mrs. Paulson at home and set out for Chicago through deep snow and bitter cold on a horse-drawn sled, getting to Prairie du Chien to take the train to Chicago. He arrived in Chicago and was met by Pastor Erland Carlsson (1822–1893), another of the founders of the Augustana Synod. Carlsson had confirmed Mrs. Paulson, so they knew each other well.

The next day, he began his studies, five classes with Esbjörn and others. The next year, he returned, this time with his wife.[60] Together they ran something of a boarding club for the students. It was, Paulson wrote, like one big family. They had twelve students at the time. He would sometimes travel out in the country to preach. While there, he would ask for help to feed the students and return with fresh eggs, meat, milk, and many other necessities of life.

In the spring of 1861, the Civil War had broken out. It was not long before student numbers fell as students answered the call to fight for the Union, or "blue trousers," as Paulson called them. The war became increasingly pressing. After the school year ended in May 1862, Paulson and Inger left for Minnesota after staying with the Erland Carlsons for several days. Paulson had thought he could become a pastor in the Swedish church, but, more and more, he began to feel that he could not for reasons he did not explain, though most likely it was that the Swedish Lutheran polity, which included the historic episcopate, did not attract him. He and Carlson had long talks about it. After hearing Paulson's concerns, Carlson advised him to obey his conscience and not be ordained with them.

By 1862, the Civil War completely dominated everything in the country. Lincoln had ordered 600,000 men drafted. The country rang with the song lyrics "We are coming, Father Abraham, 600,000 strong." At first, Paulson thought he would not catch the war fever and even told his long-suffering wife that he was not going to enlist. He had promised "to take care of you, my little girl, I have a higher goal than to be a soldier."[61]

The promise lasted until Paulson appeared in Chaska, where the recruiting was going on. He heard the officer shouting out that they would not meet their quota until twelve more men volunteered. Paulson resisted the call until the very end, when someone asked him whether he would go. He said no, he could not go. Then someone shrieked, "Are you a coward?"

Another noted that they had listened to him preaching day after day, and he had said that the nation needed men of courage to fight and save it: "Are you a coward? Are you afraid?" This got to him, and very soon he volunteered. He feared telling his wife what he had done. But now it was too late. He got on the steamboat from Carver County to Fort Snelling. A man came on board and yelled, "You know as much as anyone else in this company. We have enough Yankees in the leadership. We need Scandinavians in the officer corps. You should be a second lieutenant."[62] Paulson did not know what that rank of officer meant. When the men were told to caucus and decide on officers, he was named second lieutenant and began serving his adopted country.[63]

Immediately, his service was required, not in the south but fighting the Sioux uprising, or Dakota War of 1862 in western Minnesota. Paulson's report is extensive and vivid. The uprising created a panic among white settlers in the Minnesota counties of LacQuie Parle, Yellow Medicine, Kandiyohi, and Carver, especially in the towns of Glencoe and Young America. In less than thirty-six hours, ca. five hundred settlers had been killed. Paulson was no friend of Native Americans, and what he said about them is racist. But he was an eyewitness to the after effects of the uprising, the worst of its kind in Minnesota history. His are first-person accounts of the panic in Hutchinson, Eagle Lake, and Willmar; the hanging of the thirty-eight Sioux in Mankato in December 1862; and a stint in the Sibley expedition to Devil's Lake.

On their return, Paulson's regiment was sent south for the conclusion of its Civil War service. After his discharge, Paulson returned to farming and thought for some time that he might remain as a farmer, but the call to ministry grew stronger and stronger as he plowed his fields. He began to think of continuing his education. In 1866, he decided he should return to school, this time in Paxton, Illinois, where the Scandinavian Augustana Synod now had its seminary. His brother, still in the army, found him plowing in his fields that summer. After some talk, Paulson sold him the farm and left farming forever.

The school year 1867–1868, which Paulson spent at the seminary in Paxton, began with several new students, some of whom would go on to become leaders for the Augsburg contingent: Johan Olsen (1834–1911), who would serve as president of the Conference for some years; Melchior Falk Gjertsen (1847–1913), the eloquent pastor who would later serve at Trinity Congregation in Minneapolis; his brother, Gerhard Ludvig Mølderup Gjertsen (1853–1896); Nils Christian Brun (1846–1919), a leader in the United Church; and Theodor Halvorson Dahl (1845–1923), who would become president of the United Church after the untimely death of Gjermund Høyme (1847–1902).

Paulson describes many events and practices we now think of as unremarkable for schools, among them the beginning of the Lutheran college choir tour. From the beginning, the school had a choir. He believed it was the first of such organizations among the Norwegians.[64] The choir would travel around the area singing and raising awareness of the school. Hasselquist, himself a fine singer,

**Figure 1.7.** The seminary in Paxton. Used by permission of Augsburg University Archives.

went with them to preach and talk about the needs of the school and raise money. Paulson, also a musician and choir leader, wrote several hymns, one of which, *"Jeg er en vandringsmand"* ("I Am a Pilgrim"), became the Augsburg Seminary song.[65]

The life at the Augustana Seminary in Paxton was almost monastic but typical of schools at the time: The bell would ring at five o'clock in the morning, and at five thirty, the custodian would check the beds to make sure everyone was up. Devotions were at eight, classes from nine until dinner at noon. Classes resumed at one and continued until five and supper. After this, the students were expected to study until ten. Then lights out, and they were to be in bed.

Paulson graduated in the spring of 1868, just before Weenaas arrived. He had expected a call from one congregation, but it had suffered a conflict and dissolved. At the Scandinavian Augustana Synod meeting in the spring of 1868, Paulson received a call to be a mission pastor: "It was then decided that Candidate Ole Paulson would be called to be a mission pastor in Omaha, Nebraska, with the express understanding that he first use a time to work in Minneapolis. If he should find that he should continue the work there, he should feel free to stay there."[66] With that call in hand, Paulson was ordained by Professor Hasselquist on June 14, 1868, at the Synod convention in Andover, Illinois.

On July 4, 1868, Paulson arrived in Minneapolis. He was met by Eberhard Titterud, a member of the congregation and a shoemaker with a store on Washington Avenue. His family lived above the shop. Another member, Aron Hendrick Edsten (1838–1917), one of the earliest Norwegians in Minneapolis, owned a little house on 12th Avenue between 3rd Street and Washington

Avenue. Of the Scandinavians in the city, only a very few owned their own homes. These men would be leaders in Trinity Congregation and other churchly efforts, such as the Deaconess Institute and Hospital in the city.

Edsten had also begun the work of organizing a congregation in the summer of 1867, which later became Trinity Congregation. Edsten was born in Sweden but had grown up in Sarpsborg, Norway, so he could speak both languages. When he came to the Twin Cities and inquired if there were divine services in a Scandinavian language, he was directed to Augustana Lutheran Church, which had been founded in 1866. When he saw that the Sunday school and catechism classes were conducted in Swedish, he realized the four Norwegian children in the class needed to be instructed in Norwegian, so he began to teach them.[67]

When the congregation declared itself to be Swedish, the Norwegians realized they had to have their own congregation. They began meeting together in Lars Erickson's Scandia House, a hotel. On April 6, 1868, they organized what became Trinity Congregation, known as the Norwegian Danish Church, during a meeting in the Episcopal schoolhouse on Sixth Street and Seventh Avenue South. Edsten donated some land on Twelfth Avenue South and Third Street where a church could be built. It was finished by that fall, soon after Ole Paulson's arrival in July 1868. As a leader in the congregation and in the neighborhood and a prosperous businessman with a furniture store on Washington Avenue, Edsten would have been hard to avoid, and the Jacobsons probably knew him well.

In July 1868, Ole and Jonette settled in Minneapolis and came to know Ole Paulson as their pastor. People were beginning to realize the new city was going to be a boomtown, one fueled in part by the Scandinavian immigrants flooding the country after the Civil War. Jobs were plentiful, especially in the sawmills and flour mills built to take advantage of the river's power.

As the immigrants arrived in Minneapolis, usually on their way to homestead in the west, they frequently lived for a time in the area bounded by Washington Avenue from 11th Avenue to where Cedar and Riverside Avenues meet. There were boardinghouses and saloons aplenty for the immigrants. One place known as Noah's Ark rented apartments for eight to thirteen dollars a month. Boarding could be had at cheap hotels that could be rented for a night or longer. Along Washington Avenue, a shopping area grew up. One could buy anything one needed to set up housekeeping—from groceries to shoes, furniture, and hardware—in the neighborhood. Later, the area would be known as the Gateway.

Ole and Jonette probably gravitated to this part of town. Everybody there would understand their rich Nordland dialect, and they would be able to talk with the clerks and understand and read all the signage of the shops in the burgeoning neighborhood. While they lived there, they could also take part in church activities under the direction of Ole Paulson.

They could also read in *Nordisk Folkebladet* about Paulson's plan to invite what became Augsburg to come to Minneapolis. Paulson realized from the first that Minneapolis would grow quickly and be filled with Norwegians. Already by the fall of 1868, he had found forty-two grown men and women to be charter members of the new congregation. Most of them were young, unmarried men, he said, and many were on their way out of the city to find land. Ole Jacobson would have been in that number, although he was not as young as many. For some reason, they did not join the congregation, probably thinking they would soon be building their home on the prairie.

Paulson expected that in the next few years, a thriving Norwegian American press would grow up in the city and region. A Scandinavian bank run by a Norwegian had been built on what is now Cedar and Riverside. Although the Jacobsons would be learning to speak and read some English, except for their dealings with the government and official things like citizenship, the buying of property and taxes, and a marriage license, their surroundings in Cedar and Riverside would have made it possible for them to speak only Norwegian. Minneapolis felt to them like a Norwegian city.

Chief among the Jacobsons' interests would have been the Trinity congregation. The congregation had finally settled on a name: *Den norsk-danske evangelisk lutherske Trefoldigheds Menighed af Minneapolis, Minnesota. The Norwegian Danish evangelical Lutheran Trinity Congregation of Minneapolis, Minnesota.* Paulson found it to be cumbersome and dull and noted it soon became simply Trinity Congregation, a name it has maintained for the past 150 years.

\* \* \*

## Weenaas Begins Teaching

Despite the privations in Paxton, Weenaas happily began teaching the Norwegian students under his care in September 1868. In October, the Weenaas family moved into the new home the synod had built for them. In *Memoirs: Eight Years in America* (*Mindeblade: Otte Aar i Amerika*), Weenaas tells how he came to love his Swedish colleagues. Tufve Nilsson Hasselquist and Anders R. Cervin (1823–1900), Hasselquist's brother-in-law, were among his closest colleagues.

When Weenaas came, there were already strong, even bitter, disagreements among Norwegian American pastors, which he knew well. One of the most scathing was an accusation made by B. J. Muus of the Norwegian Synod against the Scandinavian Augustana Synod concerning Weenaas's colleague Hasselquist. In December 1866, probably after he had been more influenced by his colleagues in the Norwegian Synod than when he first arrived, Muus wrote an article in Gisle Johnson's journal, *Lutherske Kirketidende*. He excoriated the Scandinavian

Figure 1.8. Gisle Johnson. Public domain.

Augustana Synod and especially the saintly Hasselquist for his preference for peace rather than truth: "A remarkably well meaning, cozy and godly man who seems to fear resentments and strife among people much more than the Lord; he is the president of the Synod and strives to keep everything quiet and peaceful—a good union man."[68] This harsh judgment did not escape the notice of the leaders, faculty, and students at Augustana College and Seminary.

Some months later, four seminary students at the Augustana Seminary answered Muus in the April 7, 1867, issue of *Luthersk Kirketidende*. Calling it the "Wisconsin" Synod because its leadership and majority of congregations at the time were in Wisconsin, they noted that in their experience of the Norwegian Synod, they had found it even more filled with dead orthodoxy than they had previously thought.

They wrote in their article that "sterile literalism, prejudice, intolerance and thoughtless polemics present themselves quite early in this church."[69] They ridiculed the Synod's conviction that slavery was not a sin in and of itself, but on the other hand, lay prayers and preaching were sin. The Norwegian Synod's teaching on absolution was also too much for them. They believed that "no man is justified before he has faith . . . while Synod pastors emphasized that the atonement of Christ alone (without faith) is the basis for forgiveness."[70] The strong defense of Augustana Lutheran Seminary and Synod against the accusations of Muus was signed by four students at the seminary: Johan Olsen (1834–1910), Johannes Müller-Eggen (1841–1913), Tobias Wilhelm Hanson Wald (1830–1913), and Theodor Halverson Dahl (1845–1923). All of them would become leaders in the Conference and then the United Norwegian Lutheran Church of 1890. Olsen and Dahl would both serve as presidents of the Conference. Müller-Eggen would serve as pastor in Chippewa County.

The older and more practiced Norwegian Synod pastors were, among other things, offended at these younger upstarts. The Synod leaders certainly treated them as such. Soon after, Preus, replying to the article by these recent graduates of Augustana Seminary, asked, impatiently, how reasonable it is that these "young men," still students, could enter these debates: "How reasonable indeed is it for mere beginners in theological studies to think they could be impartial referees in these matters, no matter how much they wanted to be? How reasonable is it that they have gotten the little understanding that they could have gotten of these circumstances substantially from their new teachers in Paxton and their judgment of the strife, which is nothing more than prejudice and, in many cases, false portrayals by the Augustana Synod teachers and leaders."[71]

He then went on to attack the frequent accusations by these students that Synod congregations were spiritually dead in their orthodoxy. How could that be, he protested, when the Synod congregations had supported these arguments:

> Come and see, how it is with us, and the judgment that our wish to have the pure teachings is "dead orthodoxy;" if our struggle to enhance church discipline, our struggle at the Synod and congregational meetings to teach congregations on that issue and our asking them to support our needy causes: ask about our congregations' sacrificial giving to support congregational schools, the school in Decorah, support for the teachers, for needy students, for our mission among the Indians, for our help to the needy congregations in New York, and others; I ask, if these endeavors deserve the name of "dead orthodoxy."[72]

These comments, however, seemed to fail to change anybody's mind. They only increased the rancor. They were published in 1867 in the *Kirketidende*, just after Preus, who was in Norway at the time, had given his "Seven Lectures on the Norwegian Lutheran Churches in America."[73] These included two fairly critical lectures on the Augustana Synod, plus his defense again of the Norwegian Synod's position on slavery. Although the Civil War had settled the question, Preus insisted on defending the Synod's position that slavery was not a sin because the Bible did not say so, even if it was a moral evil. This won him no credit. His answer to the students and his lectures were widely read by pastors both in Norway and America. Norwegian seminarians planning to answer the call to America knew of these arguments and would find their place among them with little trouble.

We should bear in mind these ripostes were not merely between theologians and pastors. The leaderships of both sides made clear to their people what was at stake. The church papers bristled with sharp language. The letters home to Norway revealed how well instructed their people were in these beliefs. Families might suffer conflict when two factions ended up on different sides, rather like political parties today.

Weenaas had barely moved into Paxton to teach at the Augustana Lutheran Seminary before he was pounding away at what he would call "Wisconsinism." Weenaas did not coin the moniker *Wisconsinism*, but he used it to great effect, later writing a book in 1873 explaining his side of things. There would be no dead orthodoxy taught in Marshall.

It is difficult today for us to fathom the venom in the arguments of both sides. After the disagreements on the above questions, the slanderous accounts of the controversies between the Conference and the Norwegian Synod in their newspapers and annual reports seem libelous. There was no love lost among any of these parties, and the rhetoric used by either side was sharp and unremitting, surprising to people unused to such conflicts. The Norwegian Synod leaders held the ordination of Clausen suspiciously as he had waffled on the slavery issue and finally would leave them. And the notion of lay preaching being a sin was a scandal to Preus's young critics.

The caricatures held steady and were repeated so often that the letters of the immigrants speak like mantras, word for word, whichever side they are on. In 1871, Gunder Larson Graven, a settler in Wanamingo, Minnesota, wrote home to his family about a pastor who had been a lay preacher in Norway: "[N. T.] Ylvisaker had joined the Norwegian state church pastors in the Wisconsin Synod and is opposed to us. Not long ago he complained that I held meetings in his congregation and tried to stop me. It seems he is an enemy of believers and opposed to the work of the believers and opposed to the work of lay preachers so we are at odds and he no longer has the support of believers."[74]

As one who grew up among critical Haugeans, and relished it some, I know this rhetoric well. One of our best family stories is of an old lay evangelist from Iowa who came to my father's Bible study in Salem, Oregon. As my father wrote his outline on the chalkboard, Ole commented in his most stentorian voice, one that could cut through diamonds, "That's just what the preacher in Forest City does, and he's going straight to hell along with all the rest of them!"

As Weenaas began teaching and feeling his way into the American academic context, he reacted strongly against Professor Sidney Levin Harkey (1827–1901), an American teaching at the school from 1868 to 1870. Harkey's classes in the academy, or college program, included what Weenaas called humbug.[75] He did not think the students needed to learn what we would call the liberal arts: languages, mathematics, philosophy, biology, chemistry, and physics.[76] For Weenaas, it was more important to educate students in theology and homiletics.

Harkey retorted that Weenaas seemed to want the school to be a mission school. Weenaas answered that "a good school of missions was exactly what we needed to build."[77] Many leaders felt the same way. The Stavanger School of Missions, established over two decades before in 1843, served as a positive model for many of the Norwegian American leaders as they sought to build seminaries that could produce effective, mission-minded pastors. Weenaas argued for a final year of seminary that included only theology and homiletics. His teaching included systematic theology, practical theology, and symbolics in Latin and Norwegian, the languages in which he was called to teach.

When Weenaas, something of a novice, began teaching, he decided he would use the methods and topics of his beloved teacher at the University of Christiania, Gisle Johnson. Johnson, a confessional pietist, had been professor for most of the university-trained pastors who came to America after 1850—Preus and Koren and all those who followed. As we saw earlier in the chapter, Johnson was something of a leader of the revival that swept Norway in the 1850s. He had enormous appeal to the laity in Norway as well. Every Saturday, he would lead a Bible study for his friends and interested people wherever he was that day. These sessions were extremely popular and won him praise from his devoted followers. Cervin, the Swedish professor at Paxton, translated Johnson into Swedish for the students, something Weenaas thought salutary.

Weenaas would later describe this year in Paxton (1868–1869) as a happy one. His class of some twenty Norwegian students did well. Over the next months, however, there began to be a growing recognition that the Norwegians (and Danes) needed to have their own school and leave the Swedes to theirs.

During a Missions and Pastoral meeting of Norwegian pastors in the early spring of 1869 at Bostwick Valley, near Lacrosse, Wisconsin, the Norwegians began talking about a national school for their own countrymen. Weenaas wrote up a plan for such a school, and it was presented to the Scandinavian Augustana Synod meeting in Moline, Illinois, in April 1869. The proposal was approved. The Norwegians should begin a school, a seminary—the first Norwegian Lutheran seminary in America. Weenaas would be its first president. Ole Paulson served as a delegate from Trinity at these meetings, along with others of his congregation.

After some conversation and at the suggestion of a delegate, the synod moved to establish its school in Marshall, Wisconsin, where there was an abandoned school building, still quite new, which they could purchase for $3,500. It would serve well for the new seminary as well as an academy. Marshall was some miles northeast of Madison, not far from DeForest, Wisconsin, where Preus had served since 1851, and Koshkonong, founded by Dietrichson. It was now Jakob Aall Ottensen's (1825–1904) parish. This was the heart of Norwegian Synod territory in Wisconsin.

Weenaas now, as president of the fledgling school, had responsibilities far more extensive than he had dreamed of when he and his young family sailed out of Christiania harbor. Now he had to prepare to run both a seminary and an academy. Making people aware of the mission of the school took time. Not least of all, raising money to support the school was an onerous but necessary task. He made several trips to areas where there were Norwegian American congregations who would be interested in their mission. He would preach, talk about the school, and raise money for it. He started in Chicago, visiting the church of Samuel Krognæs, a member of the Scandinavian Augustana Synod. Later that spring, he was called to help the congregation in Christiania, Minnesota, near Northfield. During his trip there, he took the opportunity to visit many in the area, making contacts and interesting people in Augsburg Seminary. When he returned to Paxton from his tour, to his great grief, his little daughter, Ragna, had contracted whooping cough and died. Ragna's dust lies in the Paxton churchyard. She would not be the last of Weenaas's losses in America.

After the meeting in the spring of 1869 where he was named president of the new seminary, and before the move to Marshall, the Weenaas family had taken a pleasure trip on a boat up the Mississippi, from Moline to McGregor, with some time in Springfield, Iowa, near Decorah, with Pastor Martin Peterson Ruh (1841–1923). Ruh was an accomplished early graduate of the Scandinavian Augustana Seminary. While in that region, Weenaas could take stock of the work of the Norwegian Synod and the large college building in Decorah that had been built in 1865. From Decorah, they went to Minneapolis.[78] There they would connect with Paulson, a recent graduate and now pastor of Trinity Congregation. Paulson was already talking with leaders in Minneapolis about bringing the school to the booming city. Weenaas understood Paulson was someone he needed to get to know, and he did. He also took the time to investigate western parts of Minnesota that were being settled by Norwegians but were still fairly empty after the evacuations of the Indian War in 1862 that had emptied the frontier of many settlers.

Ole and Jonette may well have met Weenaas when he visited Minneapolis and Paulson that summer of 1869. They surely knew about him and Augsburg from Pastor Paulson. Weenaas may even have seen the settlements in western Minnesota, as he suggested when he marveled at how much things had changed when he visited their congregation in Chippewa County in 1874 and noticed the many improvements and increased population.[79]

## Dedication of Augsburg Seminary in Marshall

As the school in Marshall was beginning its life, in the fall of 1869, Ole and Jonette were packing for their trip west. *Nordisk Folkebladet* kept its readers apprised of the new school being established in Marshall, so members of Trinity would have been aware of the situation. It began its work on September 1, 1869. Ten students enrolled on the first day, and eight more would come that same week. By the middle of the semester, there were twenty-one students. Their average age was twenty-seven.

On November 10, 1869, Martin Luther's birthday, Norwegian Lutheran pastors from the area around Marshall gathered, and singers from Milwaukee came to sing. Pastor Hattlestad, who later would become president of the Norwegian Danish Augustana Synod, opened the festivities with prayer. Several other pastors gave speeches, including Weenaas. The local school superintendent in Marshall, F. Craig, spoke as well, welcoming the school to the local area. The women of the small town provided a festive dinner, after which M. Falk Gjertsen, a recent graduate of the Scandinavian Augustana Lutheran Seminary in Paxton, serving at the time as pastor in Stoughton, Wisconsin, preached the sermon. Johan A. Bergh in a speech fifty years later noted that its beginning showed the poverty of the school.[80] The celebrants, however, were young and hopeful. The school needed much—even a name.[81] Very soon it received the name Augsburg. For the moment, things were stable and going well.

## The Jacobsons Move to Chippewa County

In late November 1869, Ole and Jonette left Minneapolis for their claim in Chippewa County. By then, she was heavily pregnant with their first child, Peder Hegge Norman. She would give birth at the end of December in a sod dugout dug into a small hill. Ole had probably built it before they arrived in November, as sod cannot be dug up when the grass is dormant.

It is an easy thing for historians to say that the young couple built a dugout and then go on as though this were a minor thing. For Ole and Jonette to have been able to set up housekeeping in such a home, many things would have had to be in place before they were able to live there. They could not just arrive and build a dugout, especially given her condition. They would have had to have money to buy an ox and a cow—one that was still fresh and could give milk for the food they would desperately need. These details are not in the family lore, but one can imagine them planning how to bring the materials with them on the train from Minneapolis or buy them in Willmar. They had needed time in Minneapolis before they could begin to farm. That same year, James J. Hill's railroad company had finished laying the first train tracks west of Minneapolis. By the time the couple left for Montevideo, the trains went as far as Willmar. The couple took the train to Willmar. It usually left Minneapolis at about nine o'clock in the morning and got to Willmar at about five. From there, they could have taken stages to a closer destination, but they had their own transportation arranged. Their one ox and one cow served as a team. (For those innocent of farm language, an ox is a castrated bull, tame and easy to manage. Bulls would not be suitable draft animals, as anyone growing up near farm animals knows. The bull was to be avoided at all costs.)

From there, they went by oxcart to Chippewa County. The average speed of an oxcart was about ten miles a day, so it would have taken them about four days to get to their chosen claim. Given that it was November, they did not have as long a day as they would have had in the summer. They would have used their cart like a prairie schooner—the utensils tied to the outside, banging away, to make room for other possessions inside the cart.

What were they thinking as they traveled west in November, the rolling landscape before their eyes so different from their home country surrounded by the roaring North Sea? Ten years later, Sven Oftedal would describe the fall in the Minnesota Valley with his poetic sensibilities:

> Spring and summer are fine, but if you want to see the prairies in their noblest dress, it is not unreasonable to travel out on a clear fall morning. A translucent pure air rests over the landscape as blue as in Greece. We approach the banks of the Minnesota River; an easy sound climbs up from the valley like a pure morning dress around the half sleeping woods. Each thing comes forward as clear and transparent and nobly formed under the river's steam. The woods themselves unfold all their colors in wonderful and gripping richness and harmony from single dark green leaves to light green, golden, crimson, purple and the deepest brown—it is the swansong of light and color: for soon it will be winter.[82]

All their faith and hope rode with them as they slowly made their way west toward the setting sun, which in late fall on the prairies can be stunning—red, pink, and blue swirling in majestic lines across the broad horizon, fallow now in the late fall. Given their past economic privations, they could only see opportunity before them, but they were no strangers to troubles either. Little did they know that the next decade would bring some of the worst economic conditions of the century, not just for them but also worldwide.

The land they chose, eighty acres on section 30 in Rosewood Township, was right at the western edge of the township, an ideal setting not far from the Minnesota River with its verdant stands of timber. Ole, as a farm boy and fisherman, knew how to build things and would use the knowledge he had from Norway as to how one could build a log house or a dugout. The couple was well equipped for their task.

Claims under the 1862 Homestead Act were quite simple: The homesteader had to be the head of a family or twenty-one years old. He or she had to live on the land and build some kind of primitive dwelling, make improvements, and farm the land for at least five years. Immigrants, women or men, and former slaves all qualified. While citizenship was not required to stake the claim, one had to be in the process of applying for citizenship in order to own it.

When the dugout was livable and Jonette could stay there alone with the baby, Ole returned to work at the sawmill in Minneapolis. A good way to get a richer sense of what the Jacobsons had to do to succeed is to read Laura Ingalls Wilder's book *On the Banks of Plum Creek*, not far from Chippewa Crossing. The Wilders were in that region about the same time as the Jacobsons. Wilder describes the life the Jacobsons would have been living at the time, surviving blizzards, grasshoppers, drought, and any of the harsh weather conditions that were common on the prairies, especially during that decade.

While the sod house may seem to us extremely primitive, and it was, good builders could make them relatively comfortable. Centuries of experience had given people a good sense of how to construct one: face the front south and build it on a dry elevation, into a little hill. The roof had to be thick enough to absorb the rain and snow. Sometimes the house could have as many as three or four rooms. Before they settled into a log or frame house, they could whitewash the dirt walls, so it was not so dark inside, as Per Hansa did for Beret in *Giants in the Earth*.[83] If well built, it kept the family dry and warm. When the pioneers became wealthy enough to afford log cabins and then frame houses, they sometimes would move back into the sod houses, briefly, because they were warmer in the winter than the other houses.

That Jonette dared to live alone on the open prairie, with a baby, in a hole dug into the side of a dirt hill, while Ole was working in Minneapolis or on the railroad from Minneapolis to Benson, is a tribute to her courage. Her son-in-law Bernt Sundal wrote in her obituary, "Mrs. Jacobson and other of the new settlers' housewives lived in wretched sod houses alone out on the wild prairies while their husbands were away for several months. And it can be said that life the first several years and a long time afterwards was filled with need and suffering, but also rich with experiences and hope for the future."[84]

She was said to have owned the only cookstove in the neighborhood, so many women in the settlement used it to bake their bread for the week. As Wilder explains in her book on Plum Creek, the cookstove was purchased in sections so it could be assembled at the home of the buyer. Where did they buy it? How did they install it? All we can do is read stories of how others like the Wilders managed. All that information and lore has now disappeared.

When Ole returned to work in the sawmill in Minneapolis, he may have stayed in the Erikson Hotel on Washington and Huy Streets. When he came home, he walked to Rosewood Township from Willmar. Family lore says he broke the land with a team made up of the ox and cow. The summer of 1871, to be closer to his family, Ole worked on the railroad that was being built from Minneapolis to Benson. While he was closer, it was still a good way away. The family had no way of knowing anything about his whereabouts until they would see a black dot on the horizon moving toward them. As Sundal said in his obituary for Jonette, "It was not a time when the family went to pick up their father or husband at the train station. No, the women and small children rather went out to stare out over the deserted prairie and the cold short days of autumn when the snowflakes were beginning to fill the air to see if they could see something on the horizon, a dark dot moving toward them, then they expected that the man would soon come wandering home on foot from somewhere between Minneapolis and Benson. Then they knew their husband and father would soon be home."[85]

CHAPTER 2

# Augsburg Moves to Minneapolis

CONDITIONS FOR THE Norwegians at the Marshall location, despite its many needs, were good during its first year, 1868–1869. The old school building had been commodious enough for classrooms, faculty apartments, and a dormitory for the twenty-one students. Except for a bout of typhoid fever, which required Mrs. Valborg Weenaas to minister like a mother to the young men in her charge, Weenaas reported, things seemed to be going well.[1]

In the first year, they were supported by the Scandinavian Augustana Synod, which funded both the Norwegian and Swedish schools. A separation, however, between the Swedes and Norwegians into different synods seemed preferable as the two traditions appeared to be flourishing separately. At a meeting in Racine, Wisconsin, in the spring of 1870, the Norwegians met to begin planning an organizational separation of the Scandinavian Augustana Synod into two parts: Danes and Norwegians in one group and Swedes in the other. Those discussions went well. They arrived at the annual meeting in Andover, Illinois, that June prepared to amicably separate. The Swedes seemed quite happy to go their own way and build their Zion, Swedish Augustana, on the Mississippi in Rock Island. The Norwegian Danish contingent also looked forward to building its own school and church body in Wisconsin and points west, where the Norwegians were immigrating in large numbers. The Danes from these two groups would leave to establish their own synod and build its school, Dana, in Blair, Nebraska in 1884, forming the United Danish Evangelical Lutheran Church in 1896.

Dissension emerged, however, as the Norwegians began to discuss how to organize a church. It became clear that not all of them could agree on what kind of structure the new church body should adopt. Key pastors, like David Lysnes (1832–1890), Ole Hattlestad (1823–1892), and August Wright (1835–1917), objected to the ideas of Weenaas and Paulson, who wanted a much simpler body than the Scandinavian Augustana Synod had been. As a stopgap, the meeting considered an organization called the Norwegian Danish Augustana Synod, with a structure more like the Swedish Augustana Synod.

A conference to settle the disagreement was held from August 10 to August 16, 1870, at St. Ansgar church in Iowa, Claus Clausen's congregation. Should they create a synod like the Swedish Augustana Synod, with a strong central government, or a looser organization? Clausen and Weenaas preferred the latter;

Weenaas frequently spoke of his ideal church in America as a "free church." So he suggested calling the new organization a *conference of pastors* (*Prestekonferentse*) rather than a *synod*. He favored a plan in which congregations would have a right to meet and belong to the Conference without requiring a formal process to join it. They would remain independent of the Conference but would join together for cooperative projects like schools and missions. This persuasion would survive long into the workings of the LFC. The competing models were cause for long debates. Finally, the idea of the Conference was proposed as an "experiment," an old parliamentary ploy used to get controversial proposals passed.

This attracted a majority, but it was not unanimous. Ole Hattlestad opposed it, saying, "I am too old to be part of a 'churchly experiment.'"[2] He and several others, including Krognæs, David Lysnes, and Andrew Wright (recently ordained), preferred a stronger synod. They also proposed that the new church body adopt the entire *Book of Concord*, something the church in Norway had not done. Hattlestad and the others hoped, according to Magnus Rohne, a well-regarded scholar and the first to treat these issues in a scholarly manner, to "steer the new body into the General Council."[3] This was not acceptable to Clauson and others. The General Council was a group of more confessional Eastern Lutherans led by Charles Porterfield Krauth (1823–1883) who had joined together against the looser General Synod. The latter was led by followers of Samuel Simon Schmucker (1799–1873), who had tried to lessen the confessionalism of Lutherans in America. Not willing to compromise, the dissenters formed their own group, the Norwegian Danish Augustana Synod. It would last until 1890, when it merged with the Conference and the Anti-Missouri Brotherhood (1886–1890) to form the United Norwegian Lutheran Church in America, most often referred to as Forenede/United.

Now the issue was the school building. The two Norwegian Danish church bodies, unfortunately, could no longer support the same school. At a meeting in Jefferson Prairie, Wisconsin, near Clinton, representatives from each side of the matter met. Trinity Congregation in Minneapolis sent a delegation, including Paulson. After much wrangling, it was decided that the Conference would keep the seminary, its students, and its professors, and the Norwegian Danish Augustana Synod would own the building in Marshall and continue the academy with its current teacher. Both groups were woefully short of support and money. The greatest asset was the Marshall school building. It had cost $3,500. Not surprisingly, a battle over the assets of the school soon broke out.

Weenaas had found working with the academy irksome. While he admitted that many American prospective students needed a kind of pre-seminary education in the basics, he was happy to be freed of the responsibility in the new arrangement at Marshall. The new Norwegian Danish Augustana Synod could run the academy, and he could devote himself exclusively to the seminary. The

## Augsburg Moves to Minneapolis

easy amicability they had experienced at first, however, could not be sustained. As conversations within each body continued, the matter of the building caused increasing friction between them. It needed resolution.

On October 17, 1870, two months after what became the Norwegian Danish Augustana Synod left the Conference (*Konferentsen for den norsk-danske evangelisk lutherske Kirke i Amerika*), the principal of the academy, John J. Andersen, came to Weenaas with a letter demanding that he turn over the key to the building and leave it at once. Weenaas meekly complied. Rohne notes that even though the Norwegian Danish Augustana Synod had gotten the property, all but one of the students left with Weenaas.[4] Later, Weenaas wrote that there was no reason to fight the demand.[5]

The Norwegian Danish Augustana Synod opened its school, an American academy, in the Marshall building on January 5, 1871. Weenaas reported, both in his article in the *Luthersk Kirketidende*, published by Gisle Johnson in Norway, and in his memoirs, that the academy might claim to be Lutheran, but "whether it had been so in more than a name, I cannot say."[6] Andersen, the principal, came from a Congregational church background and was a layman of uncertain orthodoxy, and the woman teacher, a Miss Cuckoo, was Reformed.[7]

Christian brotherly love required amicable relations even between those on opposite sides, Weenaas wrote.[8] This, however, made his life more than a little complicated. The order to leave the building meant Weenaas had much more to do to keep the seminary going. Now he had students and a seminary but no building.

Without a building, he had to scramble to find a place where they could immediately house the students, feed, and teach them. They found a farmer willing to rent the second floor in his home to the school. Scholar and pastor Johan Arndt Bergh's (1847–1927) reflections on this time at the fiftieth anniversary of the school vividly pictured the house as

> old and somewhat dilapidated, but it was the only one to be had. It had three rooms, two small ones that were used as lodgings by the students and a larger room, 12x20 feet, in which we placed a long homemade table with benches on each side and reading desk at the end. Here Augsburg Seminary had its classroom, auditorium, etc., from November 1870, until it moved into its new building at Minneapolis, Minn. The students were lodged upstairs in Prof. Weenaas' house and wherever else rooms could be had. Board could be bought at the village restaurant for $1.25 per week. At this rate we could not of course expect many delicacies, but there was enough sustenance.[9]

The privations and struggle of the next one and a half years demanded heroic sacrifices on Weenaas's part, as well as his family and the students. His elderly

1892.

Figure 2.1. Johan Arndt Bergh (1847–1927). Public domain.

mother also lived with them and suffered their deprivations with them.[10] To be sure, these pioneers could manage through scarcity. The immigrants had been poor in Norway and as they were starting out in the United States. Most everyone, well off or poor, was accustomed to living in a time when enough food for the day was a pressing, daily concern. The theological students and their teachers, like the Jacobsons in Chippewa County, knew how to live off the land, both in Norway and the Upper Midwest. Even upper-class people like the Weenaas family in Norway were no strangers to privation. Most of the men, even pastors, would take rifles with them when they traveled in case they came across game suitable for the table.

Once, when their small school had almost run out of food, a farmer in the area from Koshkonong, Jacob Aall Ottensen's (1825–1904) parish, felt burdened to bring half a steer that he had just slaughtered. Weenaas and his students praised God, who had saved them from starving through the good graces of this farmer.[11] Every month, the *Lutheran* (*Lutheraneren*), which Weenaas edited, would print, along with the names of those who gave money to the building fund, professors' salaries, and subscriptions to the paper, the small and large gifts of food and clothing people gave to students in need. These items show that the existence of students and professor was often hand to mouth. For example, one reads that the school received from Engb. Berg, Coon Prairie, thirty pounds of pork or, from the Chicago Sewing Circle, four quilts and two pairs of socks knit for the students. Every gift was gratefully acknowledged.

Paulson, as pastor of Trinity Congregation in Minneapolis, served a growing population of Norwegians who wanted a school in Minneapolis. As he had once called himself a spiritual Viking, he was now looking to provide for a future of the school from which he had just graduated. He was a neighbor of Judge Charles E. Vanderburgh (1829–1898), one of the leaders in the young city.

One day in the summer of 1869, as they had been talking, the judge noted that Minneapolis would soon become a large city and that it would be the "headquarters" of the Scandinavian population flocking into the state. He went on to observe that nothing helped a city grow like a school: "We should get a school of higher education established in the city."[12]

Now, in 1871, after Weenaas and his students had been expelled from the building, the school was operating under terrible duress. Something needed to be done quickly. Paulson went to Vanderburgh again with the possibility of Augsburg Seminary moving to Minneapolis. At a meeting with several of the leading men in town, the decision was made to financially support the move.

Although life continued at the newly constituted seminary, life grew increasingly desperate for the community. At the end of the 1871 school year, on May 25, Weenaas called the students together to discuss their future. A week before the meeting, the seminary had received several gifts to help with housekeeping, but it was still not enough. Things looked dark indeed. "I see no alternative but to quit," Weenaas announced. Bergh described the meeting: "It was a dark night. And grave was the hour. Young, husky men sat with tear filled eyes. Then [Christian Tollefsen] Saugstad (1838–1897), I believe, broke the silence. 'Day is coming,' said he. Others chimed in. All spoke words of cheer. 'No, we cannot quit.' 'Then let us join hands and promise to work faithfully for the cause of the kingdom,' said the president. And as we stood hand in hand, he read a scripture passage and ended with an earnest prayer. Augsburg was saved."[13]

The record does not suggest how they managed to survive and with what resources, but the meeting apparently gave them enough determination to keep going until they moved to Minneapolis the next summer. Saugstad was to prove a fine pastor and leader of what would become the LFC until his untimely death in 1897.

If Weenaas had failed to keep Augsburg Seminary going through this difficult time, many said later, Augsburg simply would have disappeared. Bergh's account gives credence to Carl Chrislock's comment in his book *From Fjord to Freeway* that this time would be remembered by those who had lived through it as one of heroic legend.[14]

The Conference was still struggling to find a polity that would work and be acceptable to a majority of the members. While the idea of a conference of pastors appealed to Weenaas and Paulson, it was too loose an organization for most. Very soon, it was changed. At the 1871 annual meeting in Minneapolis, at the newly built Trinity church, the Norwegian Danish evangelical Lutheran church in America (*Konferentsen for den norsk-danske evangelisk lutherske Kirke i Amerika*) amended its constitution to make it what Weenaas called a more cohesive organization of congregations rather than simply a conference of pastors. Calling one side a *scylla*, with too loose an organization, and the other—a more tightly organized society of congregations—a *charybdis*, Weenaas reported home to the mother church in Norway that they had realized they had to make it more cohesive and less free, and they did.[15] Paulson agreed: "The 'experiment' ended in Minneapolis during the summer of 1871, where it was decided to have a new constitution, a completely new Synodical organization, without changing the name which people had learned to love."[16] He was right. The Conference/ *Konferentsen* remained the preferred name for describing this organization long after it had merged into the United Church.[17]

Augsburg Seminary, the first of the Norwegian American Lutheran seminaries, and something Weenaas repeatedly called "a national" seminary, was still a new idea to the Norwegian immigrants scattered around the upper Midwest.[18] Their experience had been quite different in the old country. There, the state provided for university and seminary education. It was radically different in America. Norwegians had become used to generously supporting independent mission societies, more than most countries at the time, but to support with voluntary gifts everything a church needed to flourish in the new land took some reeducation.

The Conference needed money, always more money. If it was going to build its school in Minneapolis, it needed to gather funds ample enough to support such a school and building. It would need regular contributions from its people, not just once but every year. Even though the contributions were low, their first graduates, now leading Conference pastors, stepped up to the plate. A resolution of the Conference at its summer meeting asked that each congregation, through its pastor, gather up monies to support the school.[19] Although an ambitious goal, it could be achieved, but it would take work. Ole Paulson suggested, in an article in *Lutheraneren,* that the women's organizations, who were beginning to organize in congregations around the church, should make it one of their goals to raise money for Augsburg.[20]

Bergh regretted the support was not as great as it could have been for several reasons: "Denominational interests played in. Furthermore, the school was too Norwegian for a few, too high churchly for others, not orthodox enough for some. It became the object of bitter attacks from many directions. The necessity of meeting these attacks imposed a new burden on the president."[21] In Bergh's comments, one can conclude that Weenaas and the Augsburg community were in the middle, being attacked from both sides.

## The Valor of Valborg Weenaas

The year and a half in Marshall, from the fall of 1870 until the spring of 1872, tested everyone. Since financial contributions were low and not always dependable; Weenaas and his long-suffering wife, Valborg, endured great poverty, often going without a salary. Bergh noted in the fiftieth anniversary speech on the early days,

> In these times of hardship Prof. Weenaas had a splendid helpmeet in his beloved wife. Mrs. Weenaas was beyond doubt one of the noblest Norwegian women who ever set foot on American soil. I would gladly weave a wreath to her memory if I could. As one who often enjoyed their hospitality and had opportunity to observe what a great blessing she was to her husband, I would express, as my personal opinion, that had it not been for the great help God gave Prof. Weenaas in his wife, he could not have endured those trying days—And we should not have been able to celebrate a semi-centennial here tonight.[22]

These testimonials to the grit of both young people, and especially that of Valborg, spoke of an affection that was universally shared. No one doubted that the woman had actually saved Augsburg from extinction. Johan Olsen, president of the Conference, said in his presidential report of 1874 to the Conference, in his farewell to Weenaas, that his departed wife, Valborg, had been an exceptional helpmeet to Weenaas: "Not only was she a strong supporter of our school's dear leader and was for the theological students a true mother. The moment she took over the Housemother's role among us, she was honored and beloved in our church both by those who knew her and those who did not, and Mrs. Valborg Weenaas's name shall be mentioned with thanksgiving and her memory live in fond recollections when these days' battles have been long forgotten and the enemy's arrows long ago shattered."[23]

The Augsburg histories tend to skip over Weenaas in favor of Sverdrup and Oftedal, consequently leaving out the story of Valborg, who had been educated to be the accomplished wife of a pastor the way Linka Preus and Elisabeth Koren had been.

Figure 2.2. Valborg Iversen Weenaas. Public domain.

Weenaas was also a supporter of the burgeoning ladies' aid movement. As a fundraiser in need of constant donations, he had quickly learned what the women's organizations could do. Weenaas had visited the Brønø congregation, where the Jacobsons would be active, with Sven Oftedal soon after it was founded in the summer of 1873. However, Jonette Jacobson and other women in the congregation had begun to organize before 1874, according to Bernt Sundal's eulogy at Jonette's funeral.[24] In an 1871 article, Weenaas began with the observation that anyone who thought about the progress of mission in Norway would have to credit the women's organizations for their major contributions and their work. Noting their help for those widowed and orphaned, Weenaas saw that in being a blessing, they were themselves blessed. Even when he wrote the article, he noted that already several women's organizations in the little congregations of the new Conference had come together to support both their own church and foreign missions. He gave some advice on how to run such groups and ended the brief article with the note that much more could be said but the simpler, the better. "To work in Jesus' Name, that is the main thing," he concluded.[25]

Weenaas was no liberal on the women's question. He had, in fact, applauded the placement of United Seminary, later Luther, in St. Anthony Park because it

Figure 2.3. Hans Paludan Smith Schreuder (1817–1882). Public domain.

was away from the city where Augsburg was and therefore distant from scheming women intent on trapping a pastor so they could become pastors' wives. He early on figured out, however, that the women's groups raised money for churchly causes. He is the first Norwegian American church leader, to my mind, to speak publicly—and approvingly—of this new development in the church. Like many of his followers, and as a fervent supporter of missions, he was aware of campaigns such as the work of Gustava Blom Kielland (1800–1889) in the founding of Women's Missionary Societies in 1844 to support Bishop Hans Schreuder's mission among the KwaZulu.

The various synods chose missions from Norway to support at first, partly because their people knew of them from home and second because they not yet had the resources to establish their own departments of foreign missions. They kept records of how much went to these mission societies in Norway and published them. It is somewhat astonishing to add up the figures. The organizations they supported tended to be connected with their backgrounds in Norway.

Local women were likely meeting together as a ladies' aid from their first year in Chippewa County and before the beginning of the Brønø congregation, founded in 1873.[26] We are not certain exactly when the women's organization in that congregation was started, but we can be sure women like Jonette worked to make the life of the community better from the first. There were women in the neighboring Wegdahl congregation who, at their forty-year anniversary, remembered the women who founded their group in 1873 and especially a Mrs. Holst. She had had a clear connection with the women back home in

Norway who had been instrumental in establishing women's groups in Vefsnes, Nordland. None of them was a stranger to the idea. And they knew their heritage very well.

At the turn of the century, a paper called *Gasseren/Malagsy*, edited by Georg Sverdrup (1848–1907), president of Augsburg, printed a summary of the great work of missions in the nineteenth century. The numbers spoke for themselves. The nineteenth century began with about six mission societies in the world. The century ended with around 250 such organizations. Only a few kroner had been contributed to missions by 1800; in 1900, over seventy million kroner. At the beginning of the century, there were maybe fifty missionaries worldwide; at the end, there were seven thousand ordained missionaries; seven hundred missionary doctors, male and female; and over four thousand unmarried women, including teachers and deaconesses. The article went on to say that if one reckoned missionary wives, the number would rise to over fifteen thousand missionaries worldwide. Further, if one counted the many Indigenous pastors and other workers, there were over eighty thousand workers in missions, including some four to five thousand who were pastors and not a few doctors. The article went on to report how many Christian schools, printing presses, hospitals, and so on had been established over the past one hundred years. It was a thrilling bit of news, especially for those reading the magazine at the time, many of whom were women like Jonette who had gone to women's missionary meetings for the past twenty-five years with a nickel tied into the corner of a handkerchief.[27]

The stories of these gatherings in Chippewa County, like countless other small congregations in the upper Midwest, are fairly well documented but have not made it into history books about Lutherans in this country.[28] They do little to advance the story of mergers on the march, which, until recently, has been the main theme of most Lutheran church histories. There are minutes of these ladies' aids, however, in church archives, and they are a ready source of information, should anyone want to examine them.

In 1872, the Conference sent $208.25 to the Norwegian Mission Society and $59.52 to the Children's Orphanage in Madagascar run by Johanne Borchgrevink (1836–1924). The next year, the sum increased to $525.42. The contact with Madagascar was personal for many of the immigrants. Mission-minded women like Jonette Jacobson knew the story of Johanne Christiane Vang Borchgrevink well. Johanne had left Norway in 1870 for Madagascar to marry Christian Borchgrevink (1841–1919), a pastor and doctor serving there. His leaving, and hers, had been widely publicized in the Norwegian press.

The orphanage that Mrs. Borchgrevink founded became a favorite charity of the Women's Missionary Societies. Her vigorous correspondence with pastors and women's organizations gained her a warm and loyal following. Because the Conference did not yet have the organizational heft or financial surplus to

# Augsburg Moves to Minneapolis

support the founding of a mission anywhere in the world, they gladly watched as ladies' aids sent money to the Norwegian Mission Society for the work in Madagascar. Through the 1870s, there are brief notes of small sums that had been sent to Norway to support the Malagasy mission.

## Building Augsburg Seminary in Minneapolis

At the Annual conference of the Conference in 1871, held this time at the Trinity Congregation's new building, the meeting of thirty pastors and laymen voted unanimously to build the seminary in Minneapolis after Paulson had shown the location on the prairie where the school would be built. The building would cost

Augsburg Seminars Lærere og Studenter 1870.
G. Hoyme. G. Gjertsen. N. L. Kolkin. Ingebrigtsen. J. Tharaldsen.
B. L. Hagbøe. N. E. Boe. A. Weenaas. P. Hendriksen. E. Eriksen.
Nordbo. N. Iversen. C. Borck. P. G. Østby. L. Lund. H. Z. Hvid.
H. Hansen. N. Madsen. J. A. Bergh. J. H. Grøtheim. C. T. Saugstad.

Figure 2.4. Augsburg Seminary professors and students, ca. 1870. Used by permission of Augsburg University Archives.

Figure 2.5. Faculty of Augsburg Seminary ca. 1874. Used by permission of Augsburg University Archives.

four thousand dollars and be ready in the fall of 1872, if all went well. Paulson said that at that time, the school did not have one cent in its treasury. Even so, the foundation had to be lain in the early fall so that school could begin the next autumn. Paulson borrowed fifty dollars from a young woman, Miss Karen Daniels, so that it could be done before winter.[29]

The building was ready for use at the beginning of the 1872 school year. What became the west wing of a larger building, which would be completed by 1875, was ready to be inhabited. This had comfortable rooms for 35–40 students, two good reading rooms, a library, a large tastefully decorated salon, a cellar and a comfortable apartment for one professor. It cost six thousand dollars.

**Figure 2.6.** Text and music of "I Am a Pilgrim Here" / *"Jeg er en vandringsmand."* Courtesy of Gracia Grindal.

Figure 2.7. Milwaukee Road train station, Minneapolis. Public domain.

On October 31, 1872, a large gathering celebrated its dedication. It was a typically brisk late-autumn day in Minneapolis. The temperature ranged between 35° and 42° Fahrenheit, but it did not rain. The city, not large at the time, regarded the event as worthy of citywide celebration. Scandinavians from all around the area attended. At one o'clock that afternoon, Weenaas welcomed the gathering; a large choir under the direction of Ole Paulson sang, probably the song he had written for the occasion, which would become Augsburg Seminary's hymn: "I Am a Pilgrim Here" (*"Jeg er en vandringsmand"*). Mayor Eugene Wilson made a long speech, published in the Minneapolis paper the next day, welcoming the school to Minneapolis and highlighting the importance of good schools and education in the city.[30]

Farmers drove as much as a hundred miles by ox cart to attend the ceremonies. One told of arriving in Minneapolis at night and staying in a rooming house on Washington and Christmas Avenues in Seven Corners, where he rented a room. The next morning, he said, they approached the new building, "a cream colored, three story, building out on the prairie."[31]

A delegation of about three hundred from Eau Claire—five railroad cars full—arrived around 6:00 p.m., some hours late for the opening ceremonies. A large procession of students, pastors, and other friends of the school marched to the Milwaukee Road train station at five thirty with a band and flags to greet the delegation, processing back to the school, where the dedication service was held. The evening celebration at Trinity was postponed for an hour so all could attend.

At eight that evening, the service began in a packed church. The choir sang again, and several pastors newly ordained in the Conference spoke: Pastors Nils Eliason Wikre (1842–1921), an 1869 graduate; Amund Johnson (1838–1897), a graduate of Augustana Seminary in Chicago and now pastor in Eau Claire; and Theodore Halvorson Dahl (1845–1923), pastor in the Litchfield, Minnesota, area, spoke, prayed, and preached. With the church packed to the rafters, many had to stand outside. Festivities were over at 11:00 p.m.

The feeling of accomplishment and surprise at the success of the small school encouraged everyone. It made the young Conference feel proud of its school and new building. There were twenty-four students, which made the cost per student, now supported by gifts from friends of the school, only thirty dollars per year. Things were looking up. Unfortunately, the promised gifts of the leaders of Minneapolis would not be paid in full, as the panic of 1873, which would hit the next fall, began to spread, and farms experienced the terrors of trillions of grasshoppers swarming over every edible green thing in western Minnesota, where the Conference had a growing number of congregations.

What the pastors and professors were doing in Minneapolis had resonance far into the countryside. People were paying attention to the leadership of the church organizations, whom they had come to know through their many visits in search of funding. They knew what each group stood for. The ethnic newspapers and then the church papers helped them understand the differences. Surely at this time, in western Minnesota, the young Jacobson couple, among many others, as busy as they were, paid attention to the different groups and what they believed.

## Ole and Jonette Jacobson

As noted, the Jacobsons' first known contact with a pastor in Minnesota had been with Ole Paulson in Minneapolis. After setting up housekeeping in Rosewood Township in Chippewa County during the winter of 1870, they and their neighbors began working to establish Immanuel congregation, the first Norwegian Lutheran church in their county. Which church body they would associate with had mostly to do with the Norwegian pastor who appeared first.

The minutes of the first meetings of Immanuel congregation of the Norwegian Synod record Ole Jacobson (Bjørge) as taking part in the decisions of the new congregation. The pastor, Lars Johnson Markhus (1842–1885), had graduated from Luther College in 1866 with Hans Gerhard Stub (1849–1931), among others. Markhus had studied at Concordia Seminary in St. Louis, as had Stub. He was called to serve the people around Norway Lake in Chippewa

Paſtor O. Paulſon.

Figure 2.8. Ole Paulson. Public domain.

County, just after his ordination in 1869, a few months before the Jacobsons settled on their homestead. Markhus had been called by the Norwegian Synod Council to minister to the scattered pioneers around the area and establish congregations.[32] Like all the early pastors, he would go from place to place, announce he would have services, weddings, or communion on such and such a day; and wait for the people to come—which they did in great numbers. It served the immigrants as well as anything could during their first years on the frontier.

To the Jacobsons, Markhus resembled most of the state church pastors they knew. His piety with its commitment to Lutheran orthodoxy, influenced somewhat by Missouri's theology, may not have appealed to the Jacobsons. From their experience, however, in the state church of Norway, they were accustomed to needing a pastor's ministerial office even if they did not share his piety. It seems, however, that they were not reluctant members; they were ready to accept Markhus's ministry and joined the Norwegian Synod Immanuel congregation when it was organized.

Markhus was the only Norwegian Lutheran pastor nearby who could baptize their first child, Peder Hegge Norman, born on December 29, 1869. On August 13, 1870, Immanuel Church was founded, and the next day, on August 14, 1870, Ole and Jonette with their baby, along with others with a child to be baptized, arrived in Bellingham, Minnesota, some thirty miles northwest of Montevideo, where Markhus was holding a baptismal service. It was quite an event. Eleven babies were baptized that day. That meant some twenty-two parents and at least that many sponsors, plus families and friends. It was probably a joyful excursion for the families, who were for the most part friends and relations from Norway.

Ole Jacobson was an active supporter of the congregation's work from its first meeting. Over the next year, he contributed $1.50 to the pastor's salary. At the time, pastor's salaries tended to be about $300 a year but could vary from $150 to more comfortable sums of $600. Ole's name appears frequently in the minutes of the congregation as both a contributor and supporter until 1873, when the family left for Brønø Lutheran, the Conference congregation they helped to found.

In 1872, Pastor Ole Edvard Solseth (1844–1908), also a Luther College graduate, was called by the Immanuel congregation, and Trinity church in Swift County, to be their pastor since Markhus did not have a regular call from the congregation. Solseth's health had been weak, especially his eyesight, but he was finally deemed ready for ordination and was ordained by Nils Brandt on May 3, 1872, in Greenfield church, near Harmony, Minnesota, his home congregation, and sent to Chippewa. Solseth shared Markhus's theology but as pastor took an active part in the congregation's life, calling meetings and keeping minutes. As the Conference gained strength, his theological convictions and associations would become an issue.

## Church Discipline

On August 15, 1872, Herman Preus, president of the Norwegian Synod, visited Immanuel congregation on his round of visitations to Norwegian Synod congregations in the Northwest, as they called it. The minutes of the meeting at Immanuel congregation show that Preus stressed home devotions. His listeners were reported to be convicted by his recommendation they read God's word every day and serve their neighbors. In addition, they were to be living in forgiveness with their neighbors. He referred them to what Jesus had recommended for difficult disagreements in Matthew 18:15.[33]

In addition, he talked about church discipline (*kirketugt*) and what to do with open sinners in the congregation, drunkards, dancing, and how to manage those issues. Could one bar such people from the church or the altar? That a congregation could do this was not unheard of; every constitution of these fledgling congregations had some provision for expelling a member who was living in open sin or was no longer a believer as the constitution required.[34]

Most of these organizations thought that public drunkenness was important for the church to discipline, although not all were against drink. There were significant disagreements, however, among the various Norwegian Lutheran church bodies on some other moral issues: card playing, dancing, or other worldly amusements. Frequently discussed were Sabbath rules. The stricter Haugeans thought any kind of work on Sunday was wrong, even to the point of forbidding the use of a needle and thread or scissors on Sunday. Along with the controversies over absolution, lay preaching, slavery, and predestination that roiled Norwegian-American Lutherans, the Sabbatarian controversy also ranked highly. The Norwegian Synod was not Sabbatarian. Members of the Conference tended to be. All my great-grandparents and grandparents were Sabbatarians. My mother remembered her father reprimanding her if she took out a scissor and needle to sew on a necessary button. "Nei, Jonette, not today," he would say. Later, the temperance battle would cause the little Brønø congregation to declare itself in support of Prohibition, but that was not on the table quite yet.

These questions of church discipline caused much consternation and anxiety in the churches. In Norway, the pastors, as employees of the state church and thus the government, had enormous powers of excommunication and discipline, which they were unable to exercise in America, even though congregational constitutions provided for a process for doing so. Even when my father began his ministry in 1942, the question of discipline was alive and well.[35] The main question was what to do with people who lived in open sin, scandalizing the community with their flagrant disregard of God's word.

Thirty years before, there had been a celebrated case that all Norwegian American pastors knew about. Pastor J. W. C. Dietrichson (1815–1873) in Koshkonong had tried to exercise church discipline over a man who had been drunk and disruptive during a church service Dietrichson was leading. Dietrichson, no stranger to conflict, expelled him from the service. The man later sued and won his case. A jury decided against the pastor. It was a cautionary tale to the Norwegian American clergy, who needed to understand the new land and the separation of church and state, and also for American pastors, many of whom were appalled by the ruling.

Preus, as a pastor, was concerned about church discipline for many reasons. He believed it was his duty to keep confession and the Lord's Supper closely linked, so these issues kept coming up. The meeting concluded with plans for a mission festival soon and conversations about how to bear fruit in one's Christian life.[36] I have no doubt the Jacobsons attended these meetings with Preus, as they were devout Christians and this was the only Norwegian Lutheran congregation in their area. The Conference, however, would soon begin its ministry in the neighborhood.

There is a hint of church controversies in Preus's reference to Matthew 18:15. It may have been Preus's way of speaking to what he considered slander from the Conference side. As we have seen, the argument had been fierce from the first appearance of the Conference organization and its school. His response to the students from Augustana Seminary had been sharp enough. The small community knew very well what he was talking about. Through lines of gossip and church publications, his listeners were well aware of the accusations being made by each church body and its pastors. It was by any standard vitriolic. Both replied in kind, and the acrimony continued.

It was at the end of 1872, at a Free Conference of Norwegian Lutherans held in Rock Prairie, Wisconsin. The topic was twelve theses on justification in Traktat No. 4, which had been adopted by the Synodical Conference, led by Missouri in 1872. The group got stuck on a phrase in one of the theses, "justification of the world." This was an argument around which Norwegian Lutherans in America would linger for decades. The Norwegian Synod wanted to make sure God was the source of grace, and the Conference, while agreeing with that, looked at the person being forgiven. Herman Preus became so irritated that at the end of the meeting, he issued an anathema against the Conference, quoting Galatians 1:6–8.[37] This essentially Banebull / bull of excommunication called the Conference members unchristian. It would cause irreparable damages to any efforts at union.

These controversies had begun before 1870, the year the Conference was founded, and reached congregations everywhere. Pastor J. C. Jacobsen reported being "plagued" by a Synod pastor for not being a real pastor because he had not been "regularly" called (*rite vocatus*) per the phrase from the Augsburg Confession, No. 14.[38] The sharp accusations from the Norwegian Synod against the Conference indicated it clearly did not regard the latter as a valid entity able to rightly call a pastor. Its replies gave Preus reason to call for the use of Matthew 18 in such disagreements. Neither side, however, is covered with glory on these matters. Both described the other in the most scathing terms: Most common was to call their opponents false teachers and un-Lutheran.

The roots of this controversy stemmed from the fight between the earliest immigrant pastors, Eielsen and Dietrichson. As mentioned previously, in 1850, Ole Paulson had been repulsed by Stub and the Norwegian Synod as much as he had been by the Eielsen party. His prejudices would have been well known to the Jacobsons before they moved to Montevideo from Minneapolis. Because of his piety and experience as a farmer and pioneer, much like them, they had many reasons to agree with him and accept his position on the conflict. It was in their blood, and they knew the issues from experience and family tradition. Most of the pastors in the Norwegian Synod came from the upper class, the *conditionert*, which the land-holding peasants (*bønder*), especially, had despised for generations as interlopers from Denmark. Norwegian farmers, with a long history of anticlericalism against the Danish clergy and their powers over them, were ready with their epitaphs before even knowing the theological debate, which they quickly mastered.

## The Jacobsons Join the Conference

The Jacobsons could remember stories of their local pastor from a century before, Pastor Ole Hersleb, and his opposition to unconditional absolution. As convinced Haugeans, they would have been quite able on their own to come to these conclusions. As they would argue in their decision much later in 1905 to join the LFC, the Synod was to them, and to many of their compatriots, the Norwegian state church in America. They had seen enough of the high-handedness of pastors in the old country and understood it in those terms. Given their Haugean persuasions and the fact that they knew Paulson well, they would naturally gravitate toward the more pietistic Conference.

They also knew Johan Olsen, the new president of the Conference, from Sømna and felt at home with him and his piety. He had in fact signed the letter against the Norwegian Synod in 1867. In 1872, a new graduate of the Marshall School, Pastor Edvard Martinius Eriksen (1836–1913), arrived in the Chippewa County settlement to establish a congregation of the Conference. Eriksen had come from the same neighborhood as Jonette in Vik i Helgeland. He had been a fisherman in Lofoten and studied at the Tromsø Seminary, where Johan Olsen had also attended. He taught school in Vik, where Jonette would have known him. He emigrated the year after they did, in 1869. On arrival in North America, he attended Augsburg Seminary in Marshall and graduated in the spring of 1872. That summer, he began serving in the Montevideo area, taking the call to Saron and Hawk Creek, near Montevideo. As a representative of the Conference, and well known to the Jacobsons, it did not take long before they joined his church and began a long association with him. He shared the difficult times with them in heroic ways.

A story told by Gerda Mortensen and Luther Seminary professor of New Testament Paul Berge Eriksen's great-grandson gives a vivid picture of the harsh life of the pioneers and their pastors. When Eriksen was called to the Saron congregation, he was promised that even if they could not pay him all the time, he would never starve. Gerda's relatives, the Lars Blixes, were neighbors to the pastor. As Mrs. Isabella Blix was making bread one morning, she said, "Maybe I should make extra bread for the pastor and his family." Then her husband came in from the barn and said, "I have some eggs and have just butchered some meat. I think we should take it to the pastor."

The night before, the Eriksens had no food for supper. There was nothing in the cupboard. The children went to bed hungry and were told to pray for food. When they got up the next morning, they went to the kitchen, and still there was no food. They went to their parents' bedroom and saw through the door that their parents were on their knees praying. As they saw them, they heard a rap on the door. It was their neighbor Blix with the food. The children never forgot the lesson of prayer being answered. The story also tells how marginal life could be on the frontier in the early 1870s.

As the population grew, the need for pastors increased. Weenaas marveled at how the population of Norwegian immigrants had exploded. Each little settlement over time would establish its own congregation and then call a pastor. By 1872, the Conference had ordained ten new pastors, raising their numbers to thirty pastors for 110 congregations. When Conference pastors like Eriksen appeared in Chippewa County, they offered an alternative to the Norwegian Synod pastors, who were the only Norwegian pastors serving them at that time.

Weenaas, in an 1874 article reporting on the travels he had made to western Minnesota and Iowa visiting seminary students who had just graduated, noted that the young pastors' record books told how many services they had conducted in a month, how many services, communions, and so on.[39] In addition, they recorded the long distances they had to travel between sites. Weenaas remarked that Saturday was their day to travel, so one rarely found them home on the weekends. The *preaching places* (*Prekepladser*), as they were called, while not congregations, were places where people could gather for these kinds of services. Weenaas has left us vivid accounts of these trips.

Weenaas knew what the numbers were for Eriksen's neighboring pastors but did not share Eriksen's tally of his work because he had no room left in his article. He marveled that already, four years after his first trip West in 1870, the landscape in Todd, Douglas, Grant, Ottertail, Becker, Clay, Polk, and eastern parts of Dakota looked more established than when he first saw the area. One notices "in so many places beautiful, well cared for farmhouses beside the old, collapsing log houses, or the disintegrating sod huts, which for the meantime had given shelter for the industrious farmer. First something to live off, then something to live in, that is their earthly purpose, and that is clearly the right order."[40]

When one reads the statistics for what pastors had to do, how far they had to travel between congregations and preaching places in bad weather and how many times, one can only be filled with admiration. They traveled by horse, horse and buggy, horses pulling sleds through the snow, skis, and sometimes they had to walk, as Weenaas did on his trip through the western parts of Minnesota and eastern Dakota, which was still a territory and not a state. His description of his approximately fifteen-mile walk from Little Sauk to Osakis gives us a picture of the time: "I traveled by foot through the thick virgin woods in the burning July heat, but was confident that to walk in his service, he who had borne the burdens of the day and the heat for us, made each journey easy. From Little Sauk I walked further to the Danish congregation west of Osakis ... where I stayed overnight with the old Hadersmand Larsk Bjalkerrup."[41]

That same year, Christian Saugstad, now a young, vigorous pastor in the Alexandria area, served as missionary pastor (inner mission) in western Minnesota. He described in the annual report of the Conference the treatment he had suffered at the hands of Pastor Lauritz Annæus Kraft Carlsen (1842–1913) of the Norwegian Synod in Alexandria. Saugstad had made his visits to a site in Douglas County needing a pastor and a congregation wanting to ally itself with the Conference. He minced no words about Carlsen's treatment of him: "When the Lord begins a new work, trials ensue." Saugstad noted that Carlson was a faithful representative of the Synod in his "treachery and false teaching."[42]

After Saugstad left the area to return to his parish, he wrote, Carlson made many home visits to members of Saugstad's congregations to tell them that "he was a false teacher, that he would not stay in the area long, and, finally, that the church I represented also taught false doctrine." Despite that, he reported, the members of the congregation had been faithful to the truth and his ministry.[43]

Just before Eriksen took up the call in Chippewa, Ole and Jonette welcomed their second child, a baby girl named Mathilda Nicoline. Born on March 23, 1871, she was baptized by Pastor Lars J. Markhus as her older brother, Peder, had been. Markhus was still serving congregations in the area like Immanuel, but would leave shortly. On April 23, 1871, the little family again made its way to Bellingham, Minnesota, for the baptismal service, which included at least another eight babies with parents and sponsors, making for a large gathering.

## Breaking Away to Build Brønø Congregation

After the Conference was established in 1870, the Jacobsons, like many of their neighbors were happy to build a congregation connected with it, more in sync with their pieties. When Pastor Eriksen appeared, conversations about founding a congregation connected with the Conference were held by interested potential members before the initial service. Georg Sverdrup visited the congregation in 1874 and wrote in an article in *Folkebladet*, describing an early meeting of the Saron congregation, with Pastor Eriksen, in 1873 in a log house. There may have been men there planning for a new congregation in neighboring Brønø. From Sverdrup's account, the house was packed. As they were ending the meeting, the worst blizzard Minnesota had experienced in living memory, and maybe until the Armistice Day blizzard of 1940, blew out of the west and shut down everything from January 7, 1873, through January 9, 1873.

As far as I know, there is no record of how Ole and Jonette survived this near-apocalypse, except that they did. They now lived in a log house and had three little ones, Peder, Mathilda, and Johan Angel, two months old. This blizzard is also described by Laura Ingalls Wilder in her book *Plum Creek*, which was located not far from the Jacobsons.

The Jacobson's third child, Johan Angel, had been born on October 10, 1872. Jonette had probably been home alone during the blizzard with him and his older brother, Peder, who just turned three, and his older sister, Mathilda, now two. Johan was baptized by Eriksen on March 23, 1873, before the new Conference congregation was officially founded.

The Brønø congregation was constituted in the home of Bendik Hansen on April 21, 1873. The meeting had been called by Pastor Eriksen. Hansen's name was the first on the same membership rolls, followed by Ole Jacobson (Bjørge), then others, including Jonette's brother, Aleksander, who also had homesteaded in the area.[44] The Jacobsons would be steadfast members of the little Conference congregation near their home until 1905. The controversies and debates would continue and become even deeper as the Conference pastors and congregations began to grow in number and take members away "steal sheep" from the Norwegian Synod. Its pastors did not miss this threat to their congregations.

We can see this in the minutes of Immanuel Lutheran Church, the Synod congregation, in 1874. A member of the church, Hans Martin Hanson, had begun to be critical of the pastor and his connection with the Norwegian Synod (often referred to as the Wisconsin Synod).[45] He had not attended church nor paid his dues for the year. The council instructed the secretary to write a letter to him and urge him to return and do his duty, both by receiving the sacrament and paying his dues. If he did not, the congregation, as its constitution stated, would have to expel him. Appealing to the Scriptures that urged people to live in unity, the letter was long and involved. The writer, the secretary of the congregation, appealed to the man's sense of fairness, his biblical understanding, and so on, stating his love and respect for him and hoping the damage could be repaired.[46]

In his answer, Hanson, who had joined Immanuel church with the Jacobsons, noted that the conflict had been too much to bear and blamed it on the Wisconsinism of the pastor, Solseth, and the congregation.[47] Since this happened while the Brønø congregation was being formed, it was clearly the talk of the small community as it worked its way through the controversies among the various church bodies and what they stood for.

From this small item, we can see that Augsburg Seminary and the Conference had begun to make an impact among the pioneers. Weenaas had been an effective leader in both. Now that the seminary was in Minneapolis, there were new realities to consider: first, getting a larger faculty and, second, raising enough money to pay off the debts of the new school and pay its expenses. That was a tall order.

## Building the Faculty of Augsburg

In the fall of 1872, school would begin on the new campus in Minneapolis. Many things had to be done to get the institution up and running. Money needed to be gathered to keep the seminary afloat. First, the school needed to attract more faculty. Weenaas, while gifted, could not do everything. He was overworked in the extreme: running the new school; meeting with the board; trying to raise money and gain support in the congregations; teaching classes; editing the church periodical, *Lutheraneren;* and helping his wife with their growing family.

Another necessary chore Weenaas found onerous was finding room-and-board options for students. To his relief, the students established a boarding club, where they could eat and manage the dormitory. Weenaas approved of this arrangement because it meant the students had complete charge over their daily needs, something he had found tiresome in his work as president: "The seminary was freed from all the issues surrounding housekeeping and the students learned how to manage these tasks for themselves."[48]

The Conference had high hopes of attracting some of Norway's best-known theologians to the seminary, such as Pastor Johan Storjohann (1832–1914), one of the founders of the Norwegian Seamen's Mission, or Lars Dahle (1843–1925), missionary to Madagascar. Both were highly regarded by Norwegians at home and abroad.

Although their hopes were high, negotiations with Storjohann were not successful. Dahle, who had gone to Madagascar in 1870, was never really a likely candidate because of his commitment to the Malagasy. He would remain in Madagascar until 1888, when he took the job of head of the Norwegian Mission Society, a position he held until 1920. Given that Storjohann and Dahle had not accepted the calls to Augsburg, Weenaas felt he should return to Norway to search for potential faculty himself and to refresh connections with the mother church.

The Conference rightly feared that the Norwegian Synod was making closer connections with the mother church back home and winning its approval, something Weenaas could not understand, given Norwegians' strong feelings against the Synod's stand on slavery. The Norwegian Synod, however, had diligently sent its representatives to meetings. In 1867, Herman A. Preus attended with his family; in 1871, Ulrik Vilhelm Koren went with his entire family. In 1873, the Synod sent Peter A. Rasmussen (1829–1898) and Professor Friedrich August Schmidt (1837–1928). Ove J. Hjort of Paint Creek had also attended meetings in Norway that summer. In its own interest, and with some sense of competition with the Synod, the Conference needed to keep the relationships current and warm. These two concerns convinced Weenaas to take the long trip. Given the increasing influence of the Missouri Synod on the Norwegian Synod, some in the Norwegian Mission Society worked to break its connections with the Norwegian Synod and maintain relations only with the Conference.

## Weenaas Goes to Norway to Recruit Faculty

The Conference Annual meeting of June 1873 in Eau Claire voted to pay Weenaas's way to Norway. His traveling companion was the young M. Falk Gjertsen, an 1868 graduate of Paxton and an eloquent pastor of the Conference

## Augsburg Moves to Minneapolis

in Leland, Illinois. Gjertsen and Weenaas would attend the general assembly of the Norwegian Mission Society in Drammen and then a large church meeting in Christiania. They would leave immediately after the annual conference from Eau Claire. It was something of a perk for these pastors to be given the time to travel back to Norway for these meetings of the Norwegian church, to which they still felt close. It meant at least four weeks back and forth aboard ship, where they could rest, relax, and enjoy the company of one or two colleagues who accompanied them. They could renew relationships with schoolmates in the old country, plus visit their relatives and friends. Weenaas needed to rest, but more important, he wrote, he was the only one, really, who could do what needed to be done: find professors.

Weenaas had one misgiving about the trip: His wife was pregnant with their sixth child. It worried him to be gone during the time, but he wrote, "She was among those quiet women who could take whatever came to her in life with wonderful peace, and she sorely wished that I could get a very desirable vacation tour to Norway with some months rest after five years of unbelievably stressful work."[49]

The Weenaas' marriage was a love match. In a book he wrote about her shortly after her death, he lovingly described her as a typical Nordic blue-eyed blonde of remarkable character.[50] Knowing him and caring about the school and church, she urged him to go. She attended the conference with him to bid him goodbye. Little did the Weenaases know that when they said their farewells at the train station, it would be their last time together.

Weenaas and Gjersten sailed on a ship of the Anker Line to Glasgow and then traveled by rail across Britain to Hull. Because of Gjertsen's carelessness about the schedules, they missed their train and had to make other arrangements. They could not take a ship directly to Christiania but had to take one to Gothenborg and then go by train to Christiania. This carelessness on Gjertsen's part did not augur well for Weenaas, who commented, much later, that he had known Gjertsen as a speaker and companion in good times but the closer he got to him and the more time he spent with him, the less he thought of him. While this may be in the memory of an older man who had grown more aware of Gjertsen's failings than previously, one senses that their relationship would not prosper. Gjertsen did not impress Weenaas who had misgivings about Gjertsen's future in the Conference, where Gjertsen did become a major force. Weenaas enjoyed meeting his old colleagues and especially his father-in-law, Niels Iversen (1800–1874), an old-time sea captain who would die shortly after their reunion in Christiania.

The mission society's meeting was held at Strømsø church in Drammen, long devoted to mission work in Norway. There they met Storjohann and delighted in the meeting, especially Storjohann's recommendation that they consider Sven

Figure 2.9. Sven Oftedal (1844–1911). Used by permission of Augsburg University Archives.

Oftedal (1844–1911), a recent graduate, as a professorial candidate. Oftedal soon appeared and made a good impression on both Gjertsen and Weenaas. After some conversation, they agreed to meet again at the annual meeting of the Norwegian church a few days later in Christiania. There they would present the call to Oftedal and get the necessary papers signed.

They knew of Sven Oftedal largely because his well-known brother, Lars Svendson Oftedal (1838–1900), was a leader of the pietistic movement in Stavanger. He would become the pastor of Bethania Prayer House in 1875 but was already famous for his songbook, *Basunens Røst og Harpetoner* (1870). He would become more and more well known in Norway as his ministry in Stavanger grew. In 1875, he would travel to Minneapolis for the dedication of the main building. Sven Oftedal had just graduated from the university and was in some sense an unknown, though people were acquainted with his entire family tree. Like most members of the Norwegian clergy (*presteskap*), which tended to be inhabited by families of long standing, intermarrying and establishing something of a regiment of cousins, they knew each other well. Oftedal's father, Svend, had been a teacher at the Stavanger Cathedral school and was known to many.

Prof. Georg Sverdrup.

**Figure 2.10.** Georg Sverdrup (1848–1907). Used by permission of Augsburg University Archives.

At their meeting in Christiania, after which they decided to offer Oftedal the contract at once, they were especially heartened by the fact that, along with Oftedal, they would also be able to attract two more candidates for the professorships at Augsburg: Sven Rudolf Gunnersen (1844–1907) and Georg Sverdrup (1849–1907). These two men were close friends of Oftedal and fit the bill for more professors as they each had different specialties. Oftedal was an expert in Greek. Sverdrup was a scholar of the Old Testament, while Gunnersen's field was church history. The three of them, combined with Weenaas's grasp of dogmatics and homiletics, gave Augsburg a well-rounded and capable faculty—a stellar faculty for the first Norwegian Lutheran American seminary at the time.

It excited Weenaas and Gjertsen to think they had built such a fine faculty in a matter of days. Oftedal could come immediately and be ready to take up his work in October, with Sverdrup and Gunnersen following in a year. Weenaas wrote that even if the new Conference would be stretched to support three new professors, they trusted that God would send the means to do so.

Happy about their success in hiring Oftedal, Weenaas and Gjertsen traveled to Bergen, Haugesund, and then back to Christiania, where Weenaas lectured about the Norwegian church in America.[51] He gave the lecture in the Missionshus in Akersgate, where, six years before, Herman Preus had given his "Seven Lectures on the American Church."[52] Weenaas was proud to report that the auditorium was filled for his lecture.

Years later, when Weenaas thought about the time he had spent in Norway, he expressed surprise at the impression his Norwegian colleagues had of the church battles in America. He thought that although they agreed with the Conference pastors on most of the issues, for some reason they blamed the conflicts on the Conference rather than the Norwegian Synod, something he could not fathom.[53] To him and his new colleagues, the strife could be blamed entirely on the Norwegian Synod, which had, in the Augsburg professors' views, become extreme on issues of Lutheran doctrine after its leaders had become good friends of Missouri's professors, most of them older, who had become father figures: Walther, Craemer, and others at Concordia Seminary in St. Louis. Their opponents believed that the influence of these men had been too strong on Koren and Preus.

## The Death of Valborg Weenaas

Weenaas and Gjertsen left Norway in high spirits, knowing that Oftedal would follow in their wake. Little did Weenaas know the tragedy that awaited him at home. Weenaas arrived in Chicago on September 19, 1873. Since it was Saturday and the trains did not run on Sunday, he arranged to stay with his wife's brother, Nils Iversen, a pastor in Chicago. On his way there, he met an acquaintance who had just come from Minneapolis. Weenaas could tell from his aspect that he had bad news. Soon he learned that his wife, Valborg, who had just been delivered of a daughter who had died ten days after her birth, had herself died on September 6. She now lay buried in Minneapolis with their daughter. His five other children, from nine to two years old, and his mother now awaited his arrival. It was a crushing blow to him.

On Monday evening, Weenaas came home to his grieving children and the next morning stood over his wife's grave in the Pioneer and Soldiers' Cemetery on Lake and Bloomington in Minneapolis. His grief stunned him. He found comfort in his work as pastor, serving congregations in Duluth and Saint Paul and often preaching in places around Minneapolis. Although these were balms for his wounds, they were not enough.

This was his greatest sorrow, he wrote, and the first of several tragedies he would face in the coming years at Augsburg. He took it as a sign of difficulties to come but also praised the Lord for giving him the strength to continue. The grave of Mrs. Weenaas, which still stands with an angel bearing a cross in the cemetery, is the earliest evidence of Augsburg in Minneapolis.

Oftedal and his wife, Marie, arrived in Minneapolis in October 1873. The recent death of Valborg Weenaas and Weenaas's overwhelming grief, plus his need to find a mother for his five children, took his attentions away from the school. He soldiered on with the help of his mother and others. To assuage his grief, he wrote a beautiful tribute to his wife, Valborg, that he published before the end of the year, "A Christian Woman's Simple Life and Blessed Death" (*En kristenkvindes enfoldige liv og salige død*).⁵⁴ In it, he described her early life—she was his childhood sweetheart—and her parents' resolute opposition to their marriage. She also struggled with her soul, and not until later did she have a conversion experience. Later, his wife's younger sister, Marie, would come to help take care of the children. Soon, he would marry her.

Sven Oftedal quickly began his work, not just of teaching but also helping to lead the young Conference. His good looks, charming personality, and fast wit quickly endeared him to the people as he traveled with Weenaas around the regions where the Conference had founded congregations. The young scholar quickly assessed the situation and would learn before the end of the decade how to raise money from the congregations in the Conference.

## The Public Declaration

Despite the tragedy of Valborg Weenaas's death, things were looking good for the Conference organization. It had a new building in Minneapolis, and another wing was being added; an impressive faculty had been recruited; the student numbers were increasing. Even with bad times on the farms and the financial troubles that were beginning to loom in the panic of 1873, the Augsburg community was hopeful. The west wing of the main building was finished, and they were expecting to complete the entire building in the next two years.

As Oftedal was getting settled in the new land, Norwegian American pastors were holding what they called "free" theological conferences. These were common sorts of meetings among Lutherans for debate and education about contentious theological questions. Because they were free—anyone could attend and participate, there being no decisions made at them—they were popular and helped Norwegian Lutherans think about pressing questions. Oftedal attended these during the fall of 1873 and learned much, along with visiting the Conference congregations wherever he found them, especially in western Minnesota.

In his history of Augsburg, Andreas Helland supposes that Oftedal and Weenaas began to detect a suspicion on the part of Conference pastors as they attended these meetings that Oftedal was secretly an admirer of the Norwegian Synod. For the new church body and school, this was disastrous. Not only did it threaten the new church body but the school as well. When asked what the Conference should do with the Norwegian Synod, Oftedal had answered, without missing a beat, "Do with the Synod? We should pray for it and wish it every good."⁵⁵

While this was a good Christian answer, it was taken very differently by pastors and leaders in the Conference. Fighting to establish their own identity, they could not brook such tolerance and goodwill. For them, the boundaries had to be drawn very sharply. Meetings with pastors and laypeople around the church had focused on the differences between the Norwegian Synod and the Conference. As is natural, the upstart and smaller group felt every slight very deeply. The ferocious attacks on Conference pastors and theologians and the anathema against them by Herman Preus were having their effect. Preus had asked President Johan Olsen to tell the pastors of the Conference "to quit their ungodly and highly disgraceful ways."[56] His anathema against it did not help his cause.

The rumor that Oftedal was a secret friend of the Synod began to weary both Weenaas and Oftedal. After all, it was a long way from the truth. In conversations at the end of 1873, they agreed that something had to be done: some kind of declaration as to what "we are fighting against and why we will fight. It would be signed by both men."[57] Andreas Helland knew Oftedal and had spoken with him about these events. He said that Weenaas wanted such a document and that they agreed both should sign it.

After their conversation, Oftedal agreed to write the piece. As we have seen, the lines between the Conference and Synod were increasingly bitter and sharp. The Conference felt it was being treated like a sect by the Synod rather than an orthodox Lutheran church. On January 20, 1874, Oftedal and Weenaas finished their Public Declaration and sent it to *Skandinaven* in Chicago. Both men signed it with the note that the authors felt compelled to write the document "in order not to stand in a false light with either the Synod or anyone else."[58]

On January 30, 1874, it appeared in *Skandinaven*. One can say without fear of any contradiction that it cleared up all further suspicions that Oftedal was a secret admirer of the Norwegian Synod. It blew up like a bomb among Norwegians on both sides of the ocean. The stunned and angry responses from nearly everyone in the Norwegian churches, whether back home or in America, would fill church and secular newspapers for years to come. Dismayed reactions came not just from the Norwegian Synod. The president of the Conference, Johan Olsen, a mild-mannered, scholarly hymn writer, was, to put it mildly, unhappy about it.

The clergy of the Norwegian Synod were furious. Elisabeth Koren, wife of Vilhelm Koren in Washington Prairie, though rarely openly critical of anyone, could, in an indirect and withering comment, indicate her true feelings to her reader. Regarding Oftedal, however, she was not indirect. She wrote to her best friend, Linka Preus, Herman's wife, that she simply could not bear the sight of Oftedal when he came to visit them in the Washington Prairie parsonage near Decorah. Not even her children could tolerate him and hurried him on his way as he left their place.[59] Herman Preus himself wrote an angry rebuttal defending himself and the Synod against any notion that the Norwegian Synod favored Grundtvigianism.[60] They had, after all, written a new constitution in 1853 to remove the 1843 constitution with its Grundtvigian theology, especially the place of the Apostles' Creed as being prior to and equally as inspired as Scripture plus the notion that one could be saved after death.

Where the Declaration had come from is not hard to say. Fevold and Nelson in their history of Norwegian American Lutheranism say the Preus's anathema "only succeeded in adding fuel to the fires of controversy and in providing an additional source of irritation. The 'bull' of 1872 was the burr in the Conference fur for years to come and effectively ended free conferences for a whole decade."[61]

Those who were members of the Conference and, before, members of the Scandinavian Augustana Synod had been listening to Preus and others since its founding. Preus's *Seven Lectures* had upset Norwegians in 1867 when he raised the issue of slavery yet again. Younger seminary students in Christiania had been bothered by it and were not afraid to say so. The slavery issue had given the Norwegian Synod a bad reputation in Norway in the late 1860s.

Weenaas himself had been harshly critical of the Norwegian Synod from his arrival in 1867, calling it too much affected by its close association with the Missouri Synod. These feelings and opinions continued to grow stronger as the Conference leadership had to face down the criticisms of Norwegian Synod pastors and professors, especially the anathema. The opening sentence of the Declaration stated the cause and set the tone for the rest of the document. It began, "By Norwegian Synod, or Wisconsinism, we mean an anti-Christian emphasis, a dangerous organization, that, borne of papistic principles, works to dissolve Christianity into universalism and hierarchy."[62]

This caveat at the beginning of the document saying this was not about people but ideas did very little to assuage the fury the Declaration aroused. The antipapist rhetoric was occasioned mostly by the extended debate the Norwegians in America had been having, and would continue to have, about absolution and whether the church and its pastors could dispense forgiveness with the same kind of abandon the pietists believed Catholics did. Absolution also raised the issue of the role of ordination and the pastor's powers and relation to the church and/or congregation.

Most everyone agrees the Declaration achieved none of its goals to bring Norwegian Lutherans in America together: it only made things worse, much worse. Now the Conference, which might have been thought of as the genial middle among Norwegian American Lutherans, had taken sides—with a vengeance. As we have seen, however, something like this was almost inevitable, given the increasing conflicts among established Norwegian Synod congregations and the new congregations being founded by the Conference. The young new Conference pastors coming into a community to build a new congregation were seen as sheep stealers and, worse than that, un-Lutheran. The rhetoric from both sides was unremittingly sharp.

Pastors and professors of every ilk delivered themselves of pious and angry retorts that could not have been expected to calm the waters. An anonymous piece in *Luthersk Kirketidende,* Gisle Johnson's journal, accused the two young men of "unending exaggerations, dishonesty, and untruths" without any attempt, according to Helland, to say where the Declaration exaggerated matters. Some suggested that Frederik Wilhelm Klumpp Bugge (1838–1896), a young professor of New Testament at Christiania University and an expert in Luther's works, had written the anonymous letter. This disappointed Helland, who ultimately concluded the accusation was correct.[63]

Adolph Carl Preus (1814–1878), now back in Norway, also wrote complaining about the Declaration. Many others felt like Theodor Halvorson Dahl, a recent graduate who demanded in December 1874 that Weenaas and Oftedal apologize for their words or at least explain them. What both Dahl and Conference president Olsen liked least was the widespread assumption that the two had written it on behalf of the Conference or Augsburg. The storm never ended. It would be brought up endlessly by opponents of Augsburg and the Conference. Many scholars think it marked the beginning of what came to be called the new school (*Ny Retning*) and the old school (*Gammel Retning*). This conflict would simmer for years and become very clear during the fight over Augsburg in 1893 and the subsequent establishment of the Lutheran Free Church in 1897.

Georg Sverdrup, who did not appear on the scene until the fall of 1874, wrote later that though he came to Augsburg after the storm, he was not ignorant of the issues. In his article "Serious Strife, Serious Peace" (*"Alvorlig Strid, Alvorlig Fred"*), published in *Skandinaven* and also printed in the *Luthersk Kirketidende* in Norway, Sverdrup gave his take on the debate.[64] It is, as usual, clear and to the point. Helland describes it as the weightiest of any of Sverdrup's pieces, only ten pages long and easy to remember. Sverdrup's first point was to call attention to the fact that Oftedal and Weenaas had not said the Norwegian Synod was anti-Christian and catholicizing but that there was a part, or emphasis, that was. He had hoped the Norwegian Synod might wonder if this was true and try to address the problem rather than argue that Oftedal had said the entire organization was corrupt.

There could be no rapprochement. The leadership of the Norwegian Synod was livid. It was to their advantage not to make this distinction and rather respond based on the incorrect assumption that Oftedal had said that everyone in the Synod was wrong. When people go to war, nuances are among the first casualties.

As heir to this tradition and one practiced in church fights, I see this battle in a new light. The usual description of this debate is that Oftedal was intemperate, hot-headed, and careless. I cannot deny that and wish he might have tempered his tone, which was his mistake. So was Preus. On reflection, it seems clear to me that the Synod mischaracterized Oftedal's Declaration and its tone to great effect. They won the argument by accusing the other side of ad hominem attacks in the same way that during my debates with others on the Task Force for the Study of Ministry of the ELCA, of which I was a member, my arguments were dismissed as being Haugean and decadent American Protestantism. I did have my own tone problems, but I had been very carefully boxed into a definition from which no amount of nuance could deliver me.

Oftedal had reached out as a Christian brother, Sverdrup said, as one might hope others would reach out to the Conference and seek to correct it. No church was purely anything, he suggested. The writers of the Declaration had been speaking as Christian brothers hoping for a serious peace. Sverdrup's usual clarity was not what Oftedal's opponents might have hoped for. They continued to respond to Oftedal's tone rather than his argument—and effectively so. Oftedal's Declaration could maybe have been more temperate, but I don't think it would have changed the dynamics much. These parties had come to despise each other and were not looking for ways to declare peace.

In 1875, Weenaas wrote a short book, *Wisconsinism Illuminated by Historic Facts* (*Wisconsinismen belyst ved historiske Kjendsgjerninger*), in answer to why he had signed the document and to clarify their argument.[65] In it, Weenaas defended the Declaration in ways that have not been adequately reported in the histories, although Fevold and Nelson imply, correctly, that Weenaas is perhaps even more strident in his pamphlet than Oftedal had been.[66]

Most of what Oftedal and Weenaas wrote on this is dismissed as being unfortunate and not analyzed very carefully. Both Weenaas and Oftedal made the point, however, that Grundtvigianism and Missouri's pure teaching were not as opposite as they seemed; in fact, the Norwegian Synod had in some way "smelted" them together. This is an astonishing claim, but Weenaas argues the case well.

What Weenaas saw in Grundtvigianism was a romantic wish to return to the early church, which was true, and the theology of ministry we know today as the historic episcopate. Where Weenaas espied this most clearly was in the argument about lay preaching or leadership in a meeting, but it ran through all their disagreements with the Synod. The Norwegian Synod, under the influence of Missouri, had come to hold that while a layman could lead devotions in the home and among friends, the minute the gathering approached a public meeting, like a church service, if the layman led in prayer or the liturgy, he was sinning. This was even harsher than the Conventicle Law back home. Weenaas and Oftedal sniffed hierarchicalism behind this theology. They were not wrong. Weenaas makes the point very clearly with reference to many articles in the church papers showing that in fact this was true. Adolph C. Preus and Herman Preus were both guilty of yearning for this kind of a theology of ministry. The historic episcopacy seems

Figure 2.11. C. F. W. Walther (1811–1887). Public domain.

to be something like the cicada that only arrive once every seventeen years, an endemic infection among Lutherans that breaks out every so often.

Weenaas wondered why these leaders in the Norwegian Synod could have been so gullible under the tutelage of Walther. He suggested, in something of a condescending and, frankly, nasty argument, that Peder Laurentius (Laur.) Larsen (1833–1915), whom the Synod called to be its Norwegian teacher at Concordia Seminary in St. Louis in 1858, was only twenty-five; a classics teacher, not a theologian; and something of a tabula rasa in theology when he arrived in St. Louis. Weenaas, who had been the rookie teacher at the Paxton seminary and not of the same national background as his colleagues, understood Larsen's situation rather well. But he made his argument clearly to the point of enraging even further the leadership of the Norwegian Synod. Most damning is Weenaas's listing of the one course that Larsen taught, isagogics, after Professor Gustav Seyffarth (1798–1885) had left. In other words, Larsen, "the Norwegian 'theological' professor," Weenaas averred, "had no theological discipline."[67] This is more of an ad hominem argument than the "Open Declaration" was, and rather mean, yet Weenaas did not suffer so much criticism for his attack as Oftedal did.

Weenaas's book was popular enough for a second printing the next year. Unfortunately, the fury against Oftedal began to grate on Weenaas. His growing antipathy for Oftedal caused him to recall his signature on the Declaration at the end of the second printing of his book in 1876 as he was preparing to leave Augsburg and the United States. Weenaas had made his argument clearly, but personal conflicts in the faculty, growing more and more bitter, made him rethink his stance. Oftedal and Sverdrup were becoming the leaders of the Conference and Augsburg Seminary. Both Weenaas and Gunnersen came to accuse the two of ignoring them in what they thought was their takeover of the school.

In response to Weenaas's calling back his signature on the "Open Declaration," Oftedal later wrote that he had read through the piece again:

> There are a couple of things, formally, that I might wish changed, but other than that I thank God for each word, that is written, especially the words about "the disdain for all revival and spiritual life in the congregations" and that is in respect to that point my unshakeable conviction, that is built on and strengthened each day of the two years since the publication of the Declaration, that if the Norwegian Synod had learned to bear this fruit, disdain for awakening... there would have been neither a Conference or any opposition to the Norwegian Synod. And I declare here officially that the day these marks fall away, I am willing to work in union with the Norwegian Synod.[68]

Oftedal has eluded biographers for many reasons. He seemed to live in the present: Other than his extensive journalistic writing in *Folkebladet*, he never wrote a book with an extended theological argument, although his arguments are cogent and well thought through. He was a gifted and prolific journalist, polemicist, musician, linguist, and public orator; he was more a politician than a theologian; he was the spirit to Sverdrup's mind, which he said in his eulogy to Sverdrup as he stood by his casket at his funeral.

Church historians and biographers tend to gravitate to figures whose theology made a difference and is worth learning, not to outsized figures whose personality is their main contribution to the survival of a movement or an institution. Every movement needs a team at its head: one a strategist and thinker, and another who has charisma and good people skills. Oftedal is a larger-than-life character whose oratorical gifts and ability to raise money from financially strapped farmers struggling with bankruptcy over grasshoppers and low grain prices helped to save Augsburg many times.

If Sverdrup were the hedgehog in this relationship, Oftedal was the fox. Sverdrup was almost monomaniacal about the congregation; Oftedal, even though he agreed with Sverdrup, was not. He learned modern Greek and was something of a hero to the Greek community in Minneapolis; he traveled widely in southern Europe, the Middle East, and the Mediterranean world and kept voluminous notes on his travels. He was a gifted singer and knew the repertoire of the art song well enough to give recitals or be a featured soloist at large concerts in Minneapolis and around the state. Some have thought he probably should have gone to Washington rather than stay in the confines of Augsburg and its little world. But he stayed and, in many ways, gave his life for it, serving reluctantly as its president in his last years. In some ways, he loved it too much and finally died of his love for Augsburg. He is at least owed a closer look.

In the LFC's fiftieth anniversary volume, *Our Fellowship*, Oftedal's "Open Declaration" was remembered as having two points: assuring free and living congregations and keeping the school actively preparing pastors who could lead such congregations.[69] It was, according to the author of the article, the chief preoccupation of Sverdrup and Oftedal throughout their entire careers.

## Augsburg Professors Visit the Congregations

As the small Brønø congregation began its life—with forty-seven members—it appears to have been well regarded by the leadership of the Conference. The summer of 1874 that Pastor Eriksen ended his ministry with the Brønø congregation, Ole Nilsen-Bergh (1842–1922), an 1874 graduate of Augsburg, began serving Brønø, Camp Release, St. Petri, and other small, beginning congregations in the neighborhood. In a later article in *Folkebladet,* Sverdrup reported on the ministry of Bergh and of the work, especially of the ladies' aid, in the congregations. In 1874, he noted there had been two successful mission festivals and an auction sponsored by Pastor Eriksen's congregation that brought in $250, almost a year's salary for a pastor! The Augsburg professors knew these congregations well and the sufferings they had experienced from the 1873 blizzard and later grasshoppers.[70]

In an article in *Lutheraneren* reporting on his travels in the West, Weenaas gives a rich travelogue of the area: the conditions of the farms and congregations as well as accommodations for travelers.[71] They were on a fundraising trip in the late summer of 1874. The new Greek professor, Oftedal, preached and spoke while Weenaas observed the young churches in action. He gives us a hint about what happened to make Brønø congregation join the Conference church and good reasons for Preus's distress over church discipline:

> It was a humid, close sunny, day and I was sweating profusely, weak, and tired as I was after the long journey. But the Lord gave me also this time, his weak servant, new strength to give a little testimony to the Pharisaism of the human heart which alone can be granted a sound conversion and living repentance. We saw in this congregation a living partnership with our church body and our seminary. Hawk Creek congregation [near Renville] gave an especially good example

of how they, seekers of the simple truth, could not be led astray. They seemed to have carefully read our opponent's writings. They had convinced the congregation's leading man of the wild and crazy teachings of the Norwegian Synod. These people over the years have read carefully *Kirkelig Maanedstidende* [the Synod paper] and *Fædreland og Emigranten* [a newspaper partial to the Synod] and these papers have caused them to seek fellowship outside of the Synod. Subscriptions to our journal have now exceeded $325 in Pastor Ericksen's congregations. And there is good reason to believe there will be more as time goes on.[72]

No doubt this is what happened in the Brønø congregation. While Weenaas's accusations of Pharisaism seem overwrought, it is on par with Oftedal's tone in the Declaration, to say nothing of the depredations raining down on them from the Synod. They are all a piece with the polemics of the day. Church publications would reply to each other's polemics in kind. People in the congregations would read these papers with great interest, although today it would be hard to imagine a current readership of a church paper following the old Lutheran arguments on absolution, justification, and ministry.

It was said that when the church debates grew fiercest between Norwegian Lutheran church bodies in the upper Midwest, the people in the congregations were able partisans. Farmers would meet at the fencerows with copies of their church papers, ready to debate the neighboring farmer when he appeared with his church paper's opposing view. A new book on Hauge in Norway argues successfully that the Hauge movement taught its people well and had a solid basis for its teaching since all Norwegians were catechized with the Pontoppidan *Explanation* and many knew their Bible and theology well. This made them able theological polemicists. While it may seem unimaginable today, it was not then. Pontoppidan's *Explanation*, Luther's *Small Catechism*, and Landstad's hymnal were their sources. Many could be rather skilled theologians ready to go to war with another at the drop of an invective—which, truth be told, was frequent.

Rohne concludes his very fine book with the same notion: "All of these religious controversies, which were invariably carried on in dead earnest, gave opportunity for the development of a fine theological sense all along the line, the average layman studying very profound theological questions in order that he might give answer to those who gainsaid him."[73]

The Jacobsons and many others would hear of what the Augsburg and Conference were doing in "Minnaplis" when they gathered for church meetings. Many visiting pastors from the school and city would appear for special meetings, "oppbygelse—edifying" meetings to strengthen the congregation's faith, its connection with the school and church, along with their familial connections.[74]

Weenaas and Oftedal's appearance at Brønø congregation was not unusual. These professors lived close to their people and supporters. Visits like this gathered support and money for both the school and the work of the small denomination. Weenaas reported that at the end of this trip, they had raised over one thousand dollars for the school and church body, close to nineteen thousand in 2019 dollars. Oftedal could raise money.

It is surprising they did so well. Augsburg's building program in the city had suffered from the world economic panic of 1873. People who had pledged money to the school simply could not keep their pledges, so the school was strapped for funds. In addition, farmers in western and southern Minnesota, where Norwegian Lutherans, and especially the Conference, were most populous, were busy building congregations. In the summers of 1873 and 1874, especially, they suffered the ravages of the grasshopper plagues that swept in from the West and decimated the crops. The grasshoppers hit Cottonwood and Swift Counties the hardest in 1873–1874. Chippewa County would be spared until 1876.

CHAPTER 3

# The Early Years

THE YEAR 1874 held many changes for the Conference and Augsburg Seminary. Both the church and the school were growing, almost faster than Weenaas could manage. After two years, when the seminary had added the center wing and second wing to the main building and completed the professors' triplex, it had more than doubled its building capacity. They were also doubling the size of the faculty with Sverdrup and Gunnersen. Much needed to be done simply to keep the seminary in business. The financial needs were far outpacing the ingathering of funds. The Conference pastors and the whole Norwegian American Lutheran church were still reeling from Weenaas and Oftedal's "Public Declaration." Johan Olsen, the president of the Conference, who had been appalled by the Declaration, would address it at that summer's annual meeting. Many other pressing issues needed to be dealt with.

On June 10–18, the Conference met in Green Bay, Wisconsin, for its annual meeting at one of its most well-known congregations. Fort Howard had been founded in 1867 by the Scandinavian Augustana Synod and was now a leading congregation in the Conference. Green Bay had attracted many Norwegian immigrants because of its central role in Lake Michigan travel and industrial shipping. It also had several large paper mills.

The Fort Howard congregation had been served by Pastor Johan Olsen, elected president of the Conference the year before. He had just moved to St. Ansgar in Iowa. Olsen, a talented poet and hymn writer, has not been acknowledged for his poetic gifts and contributions to the Conference and United Church, which he served faithfully. His pacific character, however, got him into trouble with the litigants whose controversies would unfold in the next decade. Trying to affirm both sides, while a typical move for a peaceful man, simply created more controversy. Over time, he attached himself more to what became the "old school" and would oppose Sverdrup and Oftedal in the 1890 fracas yet to come.[1]

Theodor Halvorson Dahl, the host pastor, an early graduate of Paxton Seminary and a leader in the Conference, had taken the Fort Howard call in 1873. Like Olsen, he had also been distressed by Oftedal's "Public Declaration" and called for its withdrawal.

The Conference first had to issue calls to Gunnersen and Sverdrup as professors; secondly, the seminary needed a curriculum that would meet the requirements of future Augsburg students. Weenaas had developed such a plan to be approved at the annual meeting that June. To prepare for it, the congregations meeting in their various judicatories during the spring approved Weenaas's proposal for the growth and development of the seminary, "Proposal for Augsburg Seminary's Growth and an Updated Educational Plan for the School" ("*Forslag til Augsburg Seminariums Udvidelse og forandret Undervisningsplan for Skolen*"). This would include an academy and college for those seminary candidates who needed schooling before seminary and some who wanted an education but were not planning to be pastors.

In addition, the annual meeting had to approve plans to complete the seminary campus. Finishing the main building and other necessary edifices would cost twelve thousand dollars, including provisions for high school and college departments. These funds would be gathered by Weenaas and Oftedal on their journeys west to visit the new congregations springing up, especially in western Minnesota and the Dakotas, as the immigrants moved further west to find available land.

The convention unanimously approved the motions with great enthusiasm, Weenaas reported. It immediately sent a telegram to Norway informing the waiting professors of the decision to call them to the school, setting aside five hundred dollars for their travel expenses. With that, Weenaas and Oftedal planned to spend late July and early August traveling around the Conference congregations, especially in the West.

When the Sverdrups and Gunnersens arrived in New York on August 13, 1874, Weenaas and Oftedal were visiting Conference congregations in the western counties of Minnesota and eastern Dakota, raising money for the school. As they were gathering funds and making contacts with pastors and congregations, they took pains to visit those congregations where their most recent graduates served: in Todd, Becker, Grant, Clay, Polk, Douglas, Chippewa County, and the Brønø congregation, where Ole Nilsen-Bergh (1842–1922) was now serving and which the Jacobsons had joined as charter members in the spring of 1873. Bergh, a recent graduate of Augsburg Seminary, would become an important member of the Augsburg and LFC community. (He would be a pallbearer for Georg Sverdrup at his funeral, and his children would continue his loyalty. Son Luthard, the Jacobson family's doctor in Montevideo, married Sverdrup's daughter Gunhild in 1907. His grandson, George Sverdrup Bergh, served at Deaconess Hospital for many years and was my mother's doctor in the 1960s and 1970s.)

Weenaas knew these visits were fundamental to the growth and survival of the seminary. He was happy to report that not only were the pastors excited about the growing numbers at Augsburg Seminary, but the laypeople in the Conference also shared that enthusiasm. He was correct about that. The congregations cherished the moments when they could meet the leadership and come

The Early Years

Figure 3.1. Old Main lit up at night. Used by permission of Augsburg University Archives.

to know them personally. Weenaas was confident they were on the right track. By then, he had a lot to show in buildings, students, and faculty.

Weenaas also reported to the meeting that the professors' house, a triplex (*professorbolig*), had been finished with "American speed," so the professors' families could move in soon after their arrival. Furthermore, Weenaas boasted, and rightly so, that "Augsburg Seminary was now an impressive building with a length of 108 feet, and two wings on either side of the middle building at 54 feet. The middle part had four floors, the wings three stories. Under the walls was the basement with a dining room for around 80 students. The entire building with the professors' dwelling cost about $18,000. The school had room for 80 to 100 students, including family apartments for the president, a reading room, and an auditorium 54 x 50 feet with a library."[2]

Weenaas had reason to be proud of his accomplishments. Later, from his vantage point in Norway, thinking back on the work he had done, he marveled at all they had accomplished. He also noted that just when they had finished this work, the American economy had cratered. No admirer of Oftedal in his later years, Weenaas did have the grace to admit that without Oftedal's superior sense for financial matters and practical ways of gathering money to fill the treasury, the buildings could not have been built nor the school have endured. The Norwegian Lutheran church in America, he concluded, had been well served by Oftedal.[3]

While there was good reason for hope, the financial panic of the previous autumn still had not run its course. This decade would be marked by depression, crop failures, and bad weather, causing many farmers to either flee the frontier or hunker down, living off the small produce they could garner from their land. Contributing to a building in Minneapolis, even if they had wanted to, was not possible given the exigencies of their lives. In August 1874, the harvest in the western Minnesota countryside was reported to be less than average. Farmers near Elbow Lake in Grant County, Minnesota, north of Chippewa County, reported on their threshing that they were only getting about eighteen bushels of wheat to an acre, when they had gotten up to fifty bushels an acre in a good year. The weather had been unsettled and the grasshoppers virulent in many Conference parishes. Rain made for bad harvest conditions. How things went on the farms always affected institutions like Augsburg, dependent as they were on the gifts of their mostly rural membership.

One week after Sverdrup and Gunnersen arrived, on Tuesday, August 25, 1874, Trinity Congregation held a festive welcome for them. It was a significant moment: all four professors and their families, a building in the process of being expanded and finished, and a warm welcome from the community. It was an evening filled with excitement and hope. Sverdrup spoke to the moment in words that have long been remembered:

> We stand here permeated with the conviction that we are in more than one sense standing in the land of the future, for this land is the land of freedom. We are certain that the Norwegian people here have a great and glorious vocation, that is to carry forward the truth that freedom cannot be without God, but only in God; to witness to freedom and Christianity is not two things, but one. For the Norwegian people to

Figure 3.2. The Sverdrups. Used by permission of Augsburg University Archives.

live out their calling, wherever they find it, out in the world, or at home, that is what we live for. We know that in this effort, we will meet opposition, strife, and hate, but in all of this our strength and power we know is from God, not human beings. He has set us on our way.[4]

Together, these three young men formed what Fevold and Nelson called a "brilliant triumvirate."[5] Weenaas called Sverdrup "the mind of Augsburg, Gunnersen the heart and Oftedal the spirit."[6] Georg Sverdrup, just twenty-six, immediately began to take leadership in the small school and young church. His incisive mind began to take over the triumvirate. Soon he was writing extensively in the church paper, *Lutheraneren*. Barely two weeks after his arrival in August 1874, he was already visiting congregations in the West. This was the year of the worst grasshopper invasion in Minnesota history. One of his first articles was about the congregations most affected by the grasshoppers and that many families in each congregation needed help: "In West Brook congregation [near Lamberton, Minnesota] September 9, we had a meeting to find out what the conditions were. We discovered that 36 families with 170 souls had not been able to harvest anything. And 26 families with 129 souls who had been able to harvest from 15–50, or 70 bushels, but the reports they had gotten were sketchy, meaning that many more had just as bad, if not worse, conditions."[7]

People were in danger of starving to death. It was estimated that over $200 million in crops was lost. While it was possible in those days to manage without cash and live off the farm, it was not possible when every green blade of growing crops had been consumed by the hoppers. Cows and chickens, a good source of food, needed grass and grains to live. Some animals and birds ate the grasshoppers. People were told grasshoppers could be eaten as a delicacy. Some did, but others, horrified by the destruction they brought, could not bring themselves to do so.

Settlers were lucky if they had found a way to cover their wells effectively to keep the water from contamination. Estimates calculated that the hoppers infested over two million square miles that summer. In the fall, when the colder nights made it difficult for the insects to move, they landed on railroad tracks and, because of the cold, could not move off them in the morning. The tracks became a slippery mess that meant trains could not climb even low-grade hills.

## The New School Year with the New Faculty

Augsburg's 1874–1875 school year began on October 1, with good feelings all around. Weenaas remarked that the church supporting them, and the seminary, could be glad that their greatest difficulties now lay behind them. "A good foundation had been laid," he said, really the result of some ten years of work accomplished by the Scandinavian Augustana Synod.[8]

It had not been without personal cost to Weenaas. The loss of his wife and baby daughter the year before had taken a toll on him. Just as the seminary was getting a fresh start with its new faculty, his eight-year-old daughter succumbed to a virulent throat disease, probably diphtheria. After three days of a violent struggle, she died and was buried next to her mother and baby sister in the Minneapolis cemetery. This, understandably, deeply distressed Weenaas and made him long for home, he later reported. As the conflicts among the professors grew, his longings became keener.

At the beginning of 1875, Weenaas wrote a glowing report in *Lutheraneren* on the progress of the new building. School had begun again on January 13 after the Christmas vacation. Happily, the number of students, forty-nine, was so high that they had to rent facilities in a nearby building. With its completion, the Conference owned a facility worth over twenty-five thousand dollars. Weenaas appealed for more support: Augsburg would not have to pay any interest if each congregation and pastor would give generously. This sacrificial giving would bear much fruit, and all would be well, he urged, concluding with a prayer: "The Lord have mercy on our church and bless our little church body so it can be more and

# The Early Years

more of a fruitful branch in our Lord's church tree, who is the sturdy trunk... Dear Brothers and Sisters, do not forget to pray for us."[9]

Very soon, however, Weenaas began to regret the high hopes he had had for the school. His relationship with the new professors began to sour, causing difficulties for both the school and the church body. Many things needed to be decided. The seminary's debt was growing, partly because interest had to be paid on the building and partly due to the new faculty salaries. Several of the faculty members took on other work to survive. Weenaas became something of a traveling pastor, while Oftedal began serving Trinity as assistant pastor and was ordained in February 1874. Shortly after Oftedal's arrival, Paulson left the parish, and Weenaas was called as "temporary pastor" of the congregation. This did not improve relations between the two, leading Weenaas to resign in a rage.[10]

Many years later, Andreas Helland, the historian of early Augsburg, observed in reflecting on Weenaas's temperament that he was capable of great mood swings.[11] This may account for his sudden changes of opinion about his colleagues. Weenaas reluctantly reported that while at first the church had prided itself on its brotherly unity and good feelings, things began to change.

> It was, unfortunately, not long after the new Professors arrived before one could notice that Professors Sverdrup and Oftedal joined together often while Professor Gunnersen stood back and worked by himself. It was obvious, unfortunately, that the harmony between these friends—Oftedal and Gunnersen had from childhood been very good friends—was disrupted and it soon became all too clear that here was a mistake or a misunderstanding that could have easily been cleared up, but there was a deeper disunity in their working methods and their churchly views that was often attended by some uncertainty as to whether it was theological or simply personal animosity.[12]

Weenaas was living in the new main building in the fourth-floor apartment intended for the president, so he did not quite realize the personal animosity that was beginning to develop in the professors' dwelling. He had felt there was something going on that was not quite intellectual or theological and hints at it here. Gunnersen was a good man, decent, and conscientious as a teacher, but he had to work harder than Sverdrup and Oftedal because teaching languages was not nearly as difficult as teaching history. Gunnersen could not wing it, especially during his first year of teaching history, he would say to his wife, Elise.[13]

The young professors immediately began working out the new educational plan for the school: one year of preparatory work followed by four years of college and three years of seminary. The college course was divided into two lines, classical and scientific: one for preseminary students, the other for those preparing for other vocations. Sverdrup called the college the Greek school, rather than the Latin school of the old country, like the cathedral school he had attended in Christiania. Like Grundtvig, he deplored the Latin schools for creating an elite class whose education may have made them feel superior to others. The scientific line of the college was soon discontinued because the faculty and Conference lacked the resources to staff it, and the attention of the faculty was almost exclusively on educating pastors.

The 1875 annual meeting of the Conference was held June 2–10 in the Conference congregation in Shell Rock, Iowa, some miles northwest of Cedar Falls. Sverdrup reported to the convention that the work of the faculty was "first and foremost to the need of helping its students to become fitted for a serious work in harmony with the nature and needs of free congregations and their peculiar position in this country."[14] It was clear that Sverdrup was displacing Weenaas, who presented his resignation to the board in the spring of 1875, to be effective at the end of the school year in 1876. Over the year, things would not improve; however, the young faculty and school could rejoice at the dedication of the new completed main building on June 14, 1875.

The dedication was a sparkling event. The *Star Tribune* reported that over one thousand of the Scandinavian elites in the city attended. The building had been beautifully decorated with flowers and garlands by the women of the church. Sverdrup gave the main address. In an eloquent and detailed way, he put the place of Augsburg into the history of the church in Norway, which was engaged in a struggle between the "freedom or bondage of the Church of Christ" as it battled with rationalism and unbelief. For Sverdrup, Augsburg was heir to that struggle: "Although even Augsburg is a sign of struggle, yet it is a fact that it is a sign of peace. For it cannot be otherwise that the work which is to be carried on here, the quiet search in the Word of the Lord for His Truth, will put a damper on this passion."[15] He even saw ahead a healing that would bring unity to the warring parties among the Norwegian Lutheran bodies in America, "a day of gathering together, not a day of disruption."[16] This was a clarion call that Augsburg's supporters could understand and be moved by.

After a welcome from Conference president Olsen, Pastor Gjertsen spoke in English to the gathered crowd, remembering with gratitude the pioneers in the far West who one day, when the Norwegians had "reached the age of maturity," would "contribute their share to the spiritual and political welfare of this commonwealth."[17] Sven Oftedal spoke "in the most eloquent terms" of the calling of the seminary "to promote the true and pure faith, with its foundation stone in liberty and liberality, and wished that from this, the first Norwegian university in the State," there would be many who would go out and preach the "true spirit of Christ."[18] Between the speeches, a choir sang, along with a trio made up of the Oftedal brothers. Lars Oftedal (1838–1900), Sven's older brother, came with Johan Cordt Harmens Storjohann (1832–1914) for a tour of the new settlements.

Lars Oftedal, also an eloquent speaker and preacher, expressed his good wishes for the school and the Conference. He had recently published a book of spiritual songs, which he now introduced to those gathered. He and his brothers, Gustav and Sven, often traveled as a trio in the Conference congregations, introducing his new book of songs, *Basunrøst og Harpetoner.* The most famous song from the collection endured until the *Lutheran Book of Worship* (1978), "My Heart Is Longing to Praise My Savior" ("*Å at jeg kunne min Jesus prise*").[19]

Weenaas wrote in the *Lutheraneren* that the festival had "all in all given a good impression. Now the friends of the 'National Seminary' in Minneapolis left the festivities with utter sympathy for the cause for which it strives and works. The building looked brilliant in the dark evening. From the 108 windows light streamed all 648 candles and gave a view which one had hardly seen in Minneapolis."[20] Now all they had to do was gather financial support from the congregations to go forward in their mission. That would prove a challenge.

Weenaas had done a good thing without a doubt. The building proved that, and he had recruited a strong faculty. While he himself had been a strong and sturdy character, he did not quite have the personal and intellectual powers of Sverdrup and began to be overwhelmed by him and his program. Furthermore, Sverdrup, a man John Evjen called "the best theologian of the Norwegian American professors" with a "trenchant mind," began taking over the work of Weenaas as a frequent writer in the *Lutheraneren*.[21] By 1877, only three years after arriving, Sverdrup would be its editor and leader of the school.[22] By then, Weenaas had returned to Norway, somewhat broken by the death of his first wife and the conflicts he was beginning to have with the new faculty.

While these events totally engaged the lives of the professors at Augsburg and the work of the pastors in the Conference, an intermural skirmish among the Muhlenberg Lutherans, German American Lutherans in the East, was coming to a head. Simon Samuel Schmucker (1799–1873), president of Gettysburg Lutheran Seminary in Gettysburg, Pennsylvania, had rewritten the Augsburg Confession to fit with the American context. This created a firestorm among Lutherans in America. Schmucker wanted to establish some kind of rapprochement with the Reformed tradition. He held to the Calvinist notion of the Lord's Supper, among other things. As head of the General Synod, he was fiercely attacked by William Sihler of the Missouri Synod, who called him and his supporters apostates. Opposition arose against him in the person of Charles Porterfield Krauth (1823–1883), who, with William Passavant (1821–1894), established the General Council in 1867. Krauth became a champion of the Lutheran Confessions, writing a book on Lutheranism, *The Conservative Reformation and Its Theology*, in 1872. In the early 1870s, while the Augsburg community was founding its school and church and brawling about Oftedal's "Open Declaration," Krauth and his cohorts were brawling about the Lutheran Confessions. Krauth, with others, developed what became the Akron-Galesburg rule, which was, in brief,

"Lutheran pulpits for Lutherans ministers only and Lutheran altars are for Lutheran communicants only." While Missouri was much concerned about this, as was the Norwegian Synod, the Augsburg party did not have time for the debate. These happenings in the East, however, would later impact the LFC and Augsburg. Sverdrup and the leaders of the LFC would not go along with the Galesburg rule. But for now, they were marshalling their resources to pay their professors' salaries and the debt incurred for the new building. Krauth's Galesburg rule would later figure in many of their conversations.

## Ole and Jonette Jacobson

Chippewa County and the Jacobson family seemed to have been spared the worst of the grasshoppers in 1873–1875. They had enough disposable income to give small gifts to Augsburg Seminary. In December 1874, Ole's gift of one dollar to the building fund at Augsburg was recorded, as was a gift of $1.50 in May of 1876, a year that had started out as promising. The area had not yet been attacked by the Rocky Mountain grasshoppers. The worst year for grasshoppers in Chippewa County would be that one. The newspapers told of farmers sweeping their arms around and catching almost one hundred of the creatures at once. The best description of what it was like for the Jacobsons can be found in an early history of Chippewa County:

> I had planted a little garden around my house in Montevideo, and one forenoon about ten o'clock the young grasshoppers that had cleaned up John Kohr's wheat field came hopping down over the bluff. The first vegetables that they encountered were a bed of onions. By noon they had eaten the tops all off and were digging down in the ground for the bulbs. I had a melon patch just below the onions and thought I would save the melons by covering them up. I put newspapers over the melon hills and covered the edges with earth, but the grasshoppers gnawed holes through the newspapers and went into the tent and ate up the plants. There was a patch of tomatoes at the lower end of the garden and the grasshoppers stripped these of the leaves before they finally got their wings and flew away. Along towards fall the stubs of the tomato plants put out new leaves and there were a few green tomatoes on them in October. We fried the green tomatoes and thought they were good, for we had no other vegetables that year. No wheat was harvested in Chippewa County that year except a few acres near the middle of the township of Havelock that the grasshoppers did not find.[23]

Reports in the papers indicated little hope for the next year, 1877. Meetings were held in the areas most affected by the plague to see what could be done.

The Early Years 97

Farmers saw the grasshopper eggs in the soil and despaired for the coming year. Minnesota's governor, John Sargent Pillsbury (1827–1901), hesitated to give farmers relief because he felt it would make the citizens dependent on government handouts, although the state did pass laws giving the farmers some aid. At the same time, he was personally generous to many farmers with his own fortune. Bounties were offered on bushels of dead grasshoppers or the eggs that could be picked out of the soil easily. One farmer estimated there were 30–600 eggs per square foot in the ground.

Some tried to burn them off, while others plowed the land trying to smother the eggs beneath the turned-over soil, but nothing seemed to kill them off except bad weather. A Willmar inventor came up with a machine that helped some—a steel plate covered with tar that the hoppers would leap onto and then be stuck. While it had some effect, nature provided the only way to truly kill the beasts. The grasshoppers tended to like dry conditions and flourished best in heat. When it rained and then froze at just the right time, the eggs would be destroyed. This happened in the spring of 1876 in some places. When it rained just as the eggs were hatching and then froze, the grasshoppers could not survive. That was the only thing that stopped them. But the weather had not cooperated in Montevideo that year.

For some reason, the grasshoppers disappeared for good in 1877. Believers ascribed their disappearance to the day of prayer on April 26, 1877, called for

**Figure 3.3.** Period illustration of the grasshopper menace. Public domain.

by Governor Pillsbury. The insects were decimated about this time and did not return with the ferocity they had during the years of 1874–1877. A snowstorm on that day of prayer had affected many of the grasshopper eggs, freezing them, a mercy for which believers thanked God, though the grasshoppers were still plentiful. Father Leo Winter, a priest of St. James Parish in Stearns County, the oldest incorporated Catholic parish west of the Mississippi, in the Catholic Diocese of St. Cloud, got the idea to build a chapel in honor of Mary to ask her to protect them from the grasshoppers. Assumption Chapel, which is also known as Grasshopper Chapel, was built in 1877 near Cold Spring, Minnesota, to ask God for more help. Laura Ingalls Wilder, whose book *On the Banks of Plum Creek* described her family's surviving the plague, wrote that around that day, August 15, 1877, the locusts disappeared for good. That species of locusts went extinct by the early years of the twentieth century.

Most farmers might survive this kind of devastation, as Laura Ingalls Wilder's father did, by going east to where the grasshoppers had not devastated the land to work on a farm or going to Minneapolis to work in the mills. Since the hoppers tended not to fly farther than the western counties of Minnesota, there was still good farming in the eastern part of the state. Many pioneers simply fled the frontier and returned to relatives in the East or other places where the hoppers had not come.

As the American frontier kept moving west, conditions were ultimately proving inhospitable to many pioneers. If not grasshoppers, then droughts, which were not unusual in this part of the country, increased, exacerbated now by the plowing up of prairie grasslands, which had helped to keep moisture in the soil. The droughts were especially drastic in the Dakotas, which were being settled during the 1870s as land-hungry immigrants went farther and farther west to find free land to homestead. The saying that "the rains followed the plow" had been furthered by scientists like the ethnologist and entomologist Cyrus Thomas (1825–1910) and Ferdinand Vandeveer Hayden (1829–1887), the geographer of the Rocky Mountains in Colorado. While there was indeed a temporary and coincidental increase in rain due to long-term climatic cycles as land was broken west of the one hundredth meridian, the scientists' saying turned out to be false. The weather was as unpredictable as ever, making farming as chancy as always.

If the farmers escaped the hoppers and the droughts, frequently huge prairie fires would devastate their farms and lives. While prairie fires were not unknown before the settlers came, their devastations did not involve western-style settlements when they raged over the land. If the crops flourished and the yields were good, however, prices could fall to levels that made it impossible to get back whatever it had taken to buy the seed and run the farm. Farmers might subsist in those conditions but not make any money. How the farmers did in the western regions of Minnesota and the Dakotas was critical to Augsburg.

# The Early Years

Augsburg had trouble gathering money at this time for obvious reasons. Many of the congregations belonging to the Conference had settled on farms in the western parts of Minnesota, where the grasshoppers had been the worst. By 1877, a debt of sixteen thousand dollars, funds that Augsburg had used to build the second addition to the main building, was crippling the faculty's efforts to run the school. They needed to pay off the debt. Augsburg needed more gifts from its supporters to survive.

Oftedal, a promoter and skilled fundraiser, spent the summer of 1877 working to pay off the debt. To do so, he began publishing *Folkebladet* in August 1877 as a monthly paper. To explain its reason for being, the first sentence begins, "*Folkebladet* is from poor, but worthy parents. Its mother is 'good will', and its father is 'debt,' that is the debt of the Conference. It is sent out into the world in the middle of August as a foundling. Therefore, it is little and lame. It is also in reality, a child of its time, a Mayfly. A campaign paper, whose foster mother is nothing other than 'hard times.'"[24]

The entire issue explains and pushes the relief of the debt and its importance. Here we can also see Oftedal's many gifts as a writer. One column features a sob story about a child wanting to give his few cents so the school could survive. It is almost certainly by Oftedal and worthy of any second-rank Victorian author.

Oftedal frequently wrote, very effectively, as though the paper were a person speaking directly to its readers. It presented itself as a poor thing needing the friendship of everyone—those who were poor, rich, old, and young, men and women, the elderly and children. It was, in fact, a poor little child, a beggar. The message was that the school needed $16,000 by January 1, 1878. The facts are

**Figure 3.4.** Masthead of *Folkebladet* newspaper. Used by permission of Augsburg University Archives.

carefully spelled out: how much money had been spent on the new buildings and how much was still owed. The professors' triplex had cost $3,425, the seminary building $9,884, and the outhouse and fence, among other necessities, $623. Combined, the costs of the buildings had been $13,932. Insurance, interest, and the payment for two additional lots, among other expenses and the old debt of $2,097, raised the total to $18,918. The gifts they had received up to August 1877, when the first issue came out, were $7,500, bringing down the remaining debt to $10,418.

Because *Lutheraneren*, the current journal of the Conference, had a smaller audience—mostly pastors—and was more theological, Oftedal rightly supposed it could not reach the people in the congregations who would be able to help. With ten thousand copies of the first issue sent out to Conference members and friends, *Folkebladet*'s reach would be much greater than *Lutheraneren*. To make it more interesting to its readers, Oftedal promised there would be news from Norway and secular news about the country, such as the grasshopper infestation that had hit at the most inopportune time for the debt relief. Many of the Conference congregations recently founded in the western regions of Minnesota would be interested in that kind of information.

Because of the grasshoppers that invaded Chippewa County in 1876, Ole Jacobson may well have returned to Minneapolis to work, leaving his family on the farm, but we do not know. His family was growing fast. By the summer of 1877, the Jacobsons had six children: Peder Hegge (December 26, 1869), Mathilda Nicolina (March 22, 1871), Johan Angel (October 10, 1872), Emma Jerthina (February 24, 1874), Richard Emerentzen (September 22, 1875), and Octer Jonathan (June 18, 1877). They now lived in a handsome log cabin, sixteen by twenty-four feet. Ole had built it during the winter of 1870–1871 from logs he harvested near the Minnesota River.

A school had been built for Rosewood Township, and by 1876, the Jacobson children began attending it. Conditions were extremely primitive. The school had been organized in 1874, with a public school built on section 30, very near their farm, in 1879, when Peder was ten. The school was a frame building, eighteen by twenty-six feet and nine feet high. The cost for the building had been two hundred dollars. In 1882, a visitor complained that although the teacher, Victoria Thorn, seemed to be competent, it was difficult for her to manage over forty-one students in the small room, which was noisy and crowded. By my count, five or six of those children would have been Jacobsons. Few records exist, but stories are told of the children having to sit in the school and enduring temperatures far below zero without adequate clothing or heat. Chilblains and illness must have stalked the group, although all the Jacobson children survived childhood.

Their lives, however, were not easy. Mathilda Nicolina, the oldest daughter and second child, attended her first school in the attic of L. L. Morton. It had

# The Early Years

been established in 1873. Mrs. Bartlett was her teacher. While she learned reading, writing, and arithmetic there, she was expected to work at home since the farm needed workers. She and her brothers had to begin helping on the farm very early.

Her father needed her help with the hay on a piece of his land, a pasture that was two miles from the farmstead on what they called river bottom land. They had two oxen now. She had to help pitch the hay onto the wagon so they could take it to the barn for feed. Lifting the shocks of hay into the wagon was not impossibly heavy work but was hard for a young girl. As they were getting the wagon loaded one day, a thunderstorm came up with wind and lightning. They started for home, Mathilda sitting on top of the load of hay. Lightning struck, and one of the oxen fell over as if dead, but then he stood up and began walking, so they got home safely.[25]

That piece of land was especially good for pastures, so she herded the cattle for their own farm and for other farmers who paid her to do so. This prepared her for the life she would live after she married Richard Hanson, a neighbor whose family also came from the Sømna area. Richard was an ambitious and hardworking man like her father, but he became ill with pancreatic cancer and died in 1910. Auntie Tildy, as Mathilda was called by her nieces and nephews, lived a hard life, farming with the help of her boys, especially Bernt.

In 1880, Ole filed to make his claim of eighty acres in Rosewood Township permanent. By then, the grasshoppers were gone, and Ole and Jonette were soon ready to build a frame home to take the place of their log cabin. Ole would buy two more eighty-acre tracts of land, one of which was rich bottom land. At the end of his life, he was said to be among the most prosperous farmers in Chippewa County.

## Common School Debate

The Jacobsons, with their growing family, appreciated the common or public school, no matter how primitive, that the county ran in their township. They were happy to use it since their resources were minimal. School took their best workers from them when children were required to be in attendance. Mathilda, as a girl, was not seen as needing much education and did more than her share of work around the house and farm, both inside and outside.

Almost from the arrival of significant numbers of Norwegian immigrants and pastors in the 1850s, there had been a debate among the pastors and educators about the common schools and whether Norwegians should send their children to these schools, where they would not receive an education in the faith. Like the newly arrived Catholic immigrants, Lutherans sensed the public schools were teaching things that contradicted their faith. By law, they knew the schools could not teach the faith to their children, given the separation of church and state enshrined in the First Amendment. Most appreciated that, remembering the tyranny of the state church back home in Norway. Regardless of where their children received a secular education, however, they were bound by their baptismal vows to teach the faith to their children. How best to do that? Herman Preus had once argued for a system like the Missouri Synod, which had begun to establish church schools run by congregations. This became controversial and financially stressful to church members.[26]

Education had always been a high priority for Scandinavian Lutherans. Confirmation in Norway had been required by both state and church. It assured that boys and girls could read. This was considered necessary for passing on the faith to children and came highly recommended by Martin Luther.[27] For this reason, the Scandinavian immigrants tended to be among the most well-educated population of immigrants to settle in this country at the time.

However, this system would not work in the new land with its antiestablishment clause in the First Amendment of the Constitution. They could not expect the public schools to teach confirmation as they had in Norway. People understood this intellectually, but they faced the question of how to assure that their children knew both the skills they needed to succeed in the secular world—reading, writing, and arithmetic—and the basics of the faith they had been baptized into, with their *børnelærdom*, the children's teaching, taught through the *Small Catechism* of Martin Luther with extensive explanations added by Erich Pontoppidan (1698–1764), the Dano-Norwegian bishop who had prepared the explanation in 1737. This had become the fundamental book of the faith for Norwegians. It and the Augsburg Confession were the only parts of the *Book of Concord* that the Norwegian church accepted.[28]

This treasury of faith was dear to the heart of Norwegians. It had been called "reading for the pastor" ("Leser for presten") and involved teaching children how to read. Norwegians had thought of it as the way to pass on both secular and spiritual knowledge to their children. What to do in the new country, where such a combination was not allowed in a public school? The debates about it were lengthy and learned. To be sure, the common schools that first appeared on the scene were woeful, and the pastors did not want their children to receive a bad education in the basic skills of communication and math. Some suggested that congregations try to establish grammar schools so they could do both.

Herman Preus had prepared a document containing one hundred theses on the issue, which was debated extensively in the Synod. It won the day with the Synod members, maybe because it was too much material to debate effectively and Preus was highly regarded.[29] Georg Sverdrup, along with the Conference pastors, watched all these debates closely. While the idea of doing what Missouri or Preus suggested was distasteful to them, they were sympathetic to the idea of parochial schools. They really did not quite know what to do.

# The Early Years

In 1877, the Annual Meeting of the Conference met in Willmar, where Ole Paulson had been pastor for three years since he left Trinity in Minneapolis. The Willmar congregation could become a central one for the Conference and later the LFC, partly because of Paulson and because of its location as a transportation center. In spite of its poverty, the little congregation of 176 members had taken the risk of inviting the convention to meet in its church. The grasshoppers had so decimated the resources of the little group that Paulson noted in his memoirs, "We hardly had anything to eat ourselves, but in spite of this we took courage to receive the annual convention. For two years in succession the grasshoppers had ruined everything in the whole county, so that there was hardly enough left to feed a chicken. But we invited the meeting, and all went well!"[30]

The weather when the annual meeting began was Minnesota June weather at its finest, not too hot and not too cool. The sun shone over Foote Lake, the lake in Willmar, as the delegates began arriving. Those coming to the conference by train enjoyed the scenic ride from parts east and west. From Minneapolis, the trip took all day, but compared to horse-drawn wagons or buggies, it was lightning fast. The new church had been carefully prepared for the event with platforms on the outside of the church and the windows taken out, an old solution to bringing large groups together in small churches.

Given the bad times with the grasshoppers and the 1873 Panic and Depression, funds had simply dried up. There are no records, for example, of the Jacobsons giving anything after 1876 until the 1880s began. This was a typical situation on the farms. Despite that, Augsburg Seminary and the Conference had to raise sixteen thousand dollars by January 31, 1878, to survive. Oftedal would do a yeoman's work raising the money during the next six months.

Other issues demanded their attention as well. Weenaas had resigned and returned to Norway in the spring of 1876, embittered by the struggles he had had with Oftedal and Sverdrup. The acrimony between the Norwegian Synod and the Conference only seemed to be growing. At the same time of these ferocious debates, immigrants could still be seen going west in long lines of oxcarts. These represented for the leadership of the Conference, especially, both responsibilities and opportunities. Not only did they have a larger and larger flock to shepherd, but they also had more people who could support the school, even in these parlous times when one dollar was a big gift.

In 1877, the annual report stated that the Conference included 29,066 baptized members in 227 congregations. Brønø, served by Pastor Ole Nilsen-Bergh (1842–1922), had 105 members, 49 of whom had received the sacrament of the altar that year. Those who had not partaken at the table were very likely not yet confirmed. Gifts to Augsburg from the congregation, given the bad conditions, do not appear as frequently or as generously as they had previously.

Figure 3.5. Botolf Botolfsen Gjeldaker (1837–1885). Public domain.

Whether out of a sense of urgency or not, the meeting had set aside almost a full day to debate the issue of the common school and what they should do to assure their children had good educations in things both secular and spiritual. This had been a pressing matter for the first immigrant pastors two decades before, when the Norwegian Synod found itself in the same situation. It continued in all the churches for the next twenty years, and the Conference meeting reflects all the same concerns reiterated.

The debate is reported on in an almost verbatim record in *Lutheraneren*. The members of the committee were pastors and leaders already well known in the organization: Professors Botolf Botolfsen Gjeldaker (1837–1885), Sverdrup, and Oftedal; pastors Ole Paulson, J. A. Bergh, Christian Saugstad, and Ole N. Bergh; and three laymen, Egeberg, Rustad, and B. Strand.

Beginning with the words of Jesus in Mark 10:14, "Let the little children come unto me," the discussion started with the notion that while it was the clear duty of the congregation to provide education for its children, it also had the mission of bringing the unbaptized in their neighborhood into a relationship with Jesus Christ. While children belonged in the worship service, the pastors realized that it was not enough for a child to listen to sermons and sing the hymns on Sunday; the parents had the first responsibility to raise the child in the faith as they had promised in the baptismal service. The mother's prayers and the father's discipline would strengthen the children in their baptismal promises, many said.

The pastors deplored that some parents thought their duties as teachers of the faith should be taken over by the congregation. What was taught in the bosom of the family—which should include Scripture, Bible history, and the *Small Catechism*—was fundamental to the child's spiritual education. The congregation should support Sunday school, as well as encourage members to teach the faith at home, and the state should see to the secular skills. That was the ideal. But one can read in the record that it made them feel uneasy. Sometimes the public schools were not good enough, and sometimes the congregation did not have the means to provide good Sunday schools.

Sunday school was an Anglo-American invention that many Norwegian Lutheran pietists, especially in the Hauge Synod or Conference, were happy to adopt, arguing that Sunday, the Sabbath, should be devoted to such teaching. Nor did they mind the way the Sunday school movement pressed for conversions. They understood that in a way their more orthodox Lutherans neighbors did not. The language issue also presented some difficulties: Could one teach the Lutheran faith in English? Or did the children have to learn Norwegian to be instructed in the faith? These were difficult questions that all Lutherans wrestled with well into the twentieth century.

The Conference committee on the common school issue put forth five theses that should be discussed:

1. The Congregation has no right or duty to educate students in anything but God's word—spurning the notion that the congregation should meddle in the work of the state by mixing Norwegian and English and religious and worldly things. Both were ruinous to state and church.
2. All things considered, where it is possible, the congregations should establish Sunday schools, and the pastor and congregation should see to it that the instruction was done in the right way.
3. Where the religious school cannot be a Sunday school, it should be run like a regular school with a teacher from the congregation.
4. As long as the language of instruction is Norwegian, the congregation should operate public schools where the children can be instructed in Norwegian.
5. The school should be scheduled at a time when the children are not hindered from receiving good secular instruction in the common school.[31]

The conversation began immediately with a speech by M. Falk Gjertsen on the place of the congregation in the education of its children. For him, the only duty of a congregation in this world was to teach the faith through God's word. The next speaker, Professor Gjeldaker, who had been appointed to take Weenaas's place in the Augsburg faculty and quickly came to oppose Sverdrup and Oftedal,

Figure 3.6. Peter Andreas Torgersen Nykreim (1839–1924). Public domain.

took issue with the notion that a congregation had no right to teach other than God's word. He pointed out, rightly, that Norwegian was not God's word. If this notion was true, then Augsburg Seminary had no vocation. It, by necessity, taught courses other than God's word. Gjeldaker would soon resign from the faculty to serve a congregation in Lyle, Minnesota, and would return to Norway to serve in Hol, where he died.

A biblically learned conversation asking questions about how one could separate the worldly from the spiritual when teaching geography or world history ensued. What about creating good citizens? Would not a religious education do that as much as a common school?

Peter Andreas Torgersen Nykreim (1839–1924), pastor in Audubon, Minnesota, brought up the old problem of there not being good enough schools in the region. In the West, where the common schools were not yet fully organized, should not a congregation teach everything in its religious school? Would a congregation be breaking the first thesis if it did what seemed necessary? This issue had plagued the pastors ever since the 1850s, when they were debating the same question, facing as they did an almost nonexistent public school system in Wisconsin.[32]

Pastor Ole Paulson agreed that the first thesis was too strong, but it was not a law for the congregations to follow. If it had been that, then he would have to oppose it with all his might. He noted that Gjertsen sat at one end of the bench

Figure 3.7. M. Falk Gjertsen. Public domain.

and the Norwegian Synod on the other: "Gjertsen says that the congregation does not have the right to teach anything but God's Word. The Norwegian Synod says that it is sin to send your children to the common school."³³ It was almost impossible for them to think straight without considering what the Synod was doing. In a way, it helped them clarify their position.

Gjertsen delivered a long speech on his having written the first thesis and why. He agreed it was perhaps too strong but also pointed to problems with the arguments he had thus far heard. He concluded his speech by saying, "I support religious schools, congregational schools, or Sunday schools, so that our children can be brought up in the Christian faith, but I also support the secular education our children receive in the common school."³⁴ Most agreed that the first thesis posed problems but wanted it to be clear that the congregation had reason to provide education for the children in all subjects if the common school did not.

Then Sverdrup, who had been on the committee, spoke briefly and with his usual clarity. He thought the conversation good but wished that the first thesis had been better understood. There were two points he wanted to make: The congregation has its goal in heaven; the state has its goal on earth. The family must have both goals before it as it worked to have its children educated both for time and eternity. After he had spoken, not surprisingly, the conversation took a turn.

He listened for a bit and then remarked with astonishment that the position some of the pastors were urging was exactly that of the Norwegian Synod. He then gave a longer speech that explained how they were missing the point. If indeed those speaking believed that a congregational school could do as well as the common school, plus teach the faith, then "let us say it right out: it is each Christian congregation's duty to oppose the common school and instead build a congregational school." He went on to say there are "three elements in the society that need to be understood separately: The family, the congregation, and the Common school or state. These three must not be mixed, although they must work together to prepare children for life." The one thing, he said, that stands over the congregation and the state is the parents.

He was insistent that the family had to be held over the other two. He kept clarifying his point as he spoke, reminding them that when the school teaches religion, it becomes too powerful and teaches the children things that are not appropriate, such as the time when rationalism took over the church in Norway and the schools became places for indoctrination.

He concluded by making the Roman Catholic church the example of what happens if the church takes over secular education. They want to raise the children, teaching them God's word, and they want to educate them in secular subjects:

> And there is nothing that sounds so beautiful, so true, so Christian as exactly this Catholic principle, where the church is all, and the family and state are entirely overwhelmed. But there is nothing more dangerous. For it is not God's kingdom that is over all; it is the power mad clergy. And among us the same thing will happen. If one requires the congregation to teach secular subjects, then it is in a field where it does not feel at home, one gets out on slippery ice, where it can be led by the nose. The clergy get control over the people and uses its power to keep people in darkness. While the Christian church wishes a free people and a true education, the clerical powers always want slavery and darkness . . . America has treated the Christian congregation in its common schools correctly, let the Christian congregation be upright with the American people in its religious school.[35]

This put the nail in the coffin of the idea of congregations opening year-round parochial schools and clarified Sverdrup's position. Although it was

# The Early Years

good rhetoric to say his opponents favored the same position as the Norwegian Synod, a fact that by itself would kill the idea, he was right at the time. People like my great-grandparents were happy not to have to support congregational schools in addition to the seminary and the colleges and academies that would spring up in the next decades. The 1870s had brought great suffering to the farmers, especially, and also the church, which depended on the gifts of the farmers. Building a grammar school for every congregation was not practical, and many were relieved to hear Sverdrup's rather sharp decree on the issue. In addition to being an argument they understood, it was, of necessity, the better solution.

One issue remained, however. Does one have to teach Norwegian so that kids can learn the faith? The answer was yes, at least for the time being. What developed over time was a system of schools to teach the faith: parochial summer schools, not instead of public schools but held during the summer, for six to eight weeks, when the children would receive education in Scripture, hymns, and the catechism with the explanation by Pontoppidan. The solution also made it possible to teach the Norwegian language and the hymns, history, and literature as formal subjects. Congregations began to hire young people to teach parochial school in the summer, after the public schools had closed. This would become a good opportunity for both young men and women to earn extra money in the summer after nine months of teaching in the common school. Even small congregations like Brønø reported they had offered religious school for their students, amounting to twenty-three days in the summer. A system to provide teachers for these parochial schools began to develop as normal schools (now the academies) began producing thousands of educators who could teach in the common schools during the winters but also serve their congregations in the summers. The Conference pastors and congregations would be vigorous promoters of these schools, as were the other Norwegian Lutheran church bodies.

The church papers, among others, kept the people informed about the work of the church and seminary, as did the frequent visits of the professors with whom they formed personal relationships. Very little else could have created the kind of loyalty that the Conference garnered from its people. In every way, the visits were goldmines, even with the poor pickings—both financially and organizationally—available to be mined to keep Augsburg viable. Leaders of all these schools knew this was their work, exhausting as it was, if the schools and church body were to survive. These relationships between the people and their church leadership were especially critical to the survival of small groups like the Conference.

The common school debate, and the gravity with which the pastors and laity in the Conference engaged it, shows how seriously these Norwegian pioneers took education. That they spent a day debating the issue, even in the face of the almost certain demise of debt-ridden Augsburg, indicates its importance. Then, however, they had to address the fate of Augsburg. Helland reports that when the group heard the news of the need to raise money, they wondered whether the school had a future. Paulson called the deacons and trustees in his congregation together in his office: "There they all fell on their knees and prayed to God for wisdom and courage to do the right thing. Then they agreed upon a relatively large sum of money which they would guarantee on behalf of the congregation."[36] Helland reports that this disarmed the opposition, and the convention unanimously passed a vote to liquidate the debt. Paulson reported wryly in his memoirs, "When the members of the annual convention left, the grasshoppers also left for good and have never returned."[37]

Oftedal, however, had the financial and political skills to get the debt paid off. Carl Chrislock's history of Augsburg pays tribute to Oftedal's importance to the school and church by quoting from Isaac Atwater's history of Minneapolis. Atwater is probably quoting Oftedal himself concerning what he achieved in a few short months:

> He went about the work in dead earnest. He first started a paper and printed 10,000 copies. Through this instrumentality, chiefly, and with very little traveling, he organized Committees in every Church, gave them detailed instructions, and wrought up in two or three months an enthusiasm hitherto almost unknown amongst a cool-headed, conservative people like the Norwegians. The results followed. From the beginning of October, most of the Committees were ready to work, and in three months the whole amount, $16,000, and some to spare, was subscribed. In three weeks, from the 1st to the 21st of January 1878, after having given orders to send in the amounts subscribed, Professor Oftedal received cash $18,000, contributed by over 30,000 individuals. The school was saved and more; from now on Augsburg Seminary was not the concern of some ministers or a clique, but—as of right it ought to be—the school of the Churches, of the people. The farmers got the habit of calling it "Our School."[38]

It was a remarkable plan, getting small groups and leaders from local congregations to support the school not only with financial gifts but also constant prayer among the pastors and laity. They did think of it as "our school." It, however, only kept the school going for a year. By the next year, donations had ebbed, maybe in the flush of success, so the 1878 budget once again showed Augsburg Seminary in the red. Getting the people in the habit of contributing regularly was the next task for the leadership.

## Normal Schools for Girls

In the midst of these turbulent times, St. Olaf's school had opened in 1874 in Northfield. It was really a high school when it began. It included both males and females among its students. This was noteworthy. Its main goal was producing lively Lutheran laymen and laywomen who could improve their status through education and be good members of congregations that would support the church. While Pastor Muus, the founder, was a member in good standing of the Norwegian Synod, it was not the Synod's school. The Conference, at the same time, regarded Augsburg as its main school and concern. At the very time that Muus established the school, Herman Preus was talking about a ladies' seminary that should be built by the Norwegian Synod, probably in Red Wing. They never quite regarded St. Olaf as theirs, even though a pastor in their Synod had established it.

The first school associated with the Conference to educate both young men and women was St. Ansgar Seminary in St. Ansgar, Iowa. Begun in 1878, it served many students until it closed in 1910. St. Ansgar had been the congregation Claus Clausen had founded and where Johan Olsen served at this time. He and Professor Gjeldaker encouraged the building of the school, and on October 1, 1878, Professor Halsten S. Houg (1851–1910), an Augsburg graduate, opened a school that occupied two vacant rooms in the local public school. In 1882, the St. Ansgar Circuit of the Conference agreed to support the building of a school. By 1890, it had six teachers. Its mission statement, according to Norlie's *Norwegian People in America*, was to "give to young men and women an opportunity of acquiring a thorough, practical education on a Christian foundation."[39]

While this to some extent answered the Conference pleas for the education of women, they were no girls' schools. *Folkebladet* featured a column, obviously by Sven Oftedal, in its August 1880 issue on "Women/*Kvinder.*" It began with the statistic that at the time among Norwegians in America, there were 50,000 mothers and about 150,000 daughters, all at least as "spiritually gifted as men and hearts that were very likely richer than men."[40] That made 200,000 women who could, if they worked together, "do marvelous things to help advance spiritual gifts and development."[41] Fathers wondered where to educate their daughters, and mothers, "who had borne them under their hearts," wondered what would become of their beloved daughters in this new land, hinting that things were much rougher here than in Norway. Given that, the writer went on to discuss a woman's vocation. He clearly believed that women were the guardians of the hearth and meant to see to the spiritual welfare of their daughters, who, in turn, would raise another generation. They were the ones who planted the "seed corn" of the faith in their children: "Do not our growing daughters need more education than that which the state can officially provide and are they prepared for the storms of life when they are actually cast out into them and put into a mothers' responsible position?"⁴²

The politicians in America and Norway had begun to see this, he argued, and educated women for careers, even in public schools. Should our church stand back and not provide anything for our women, opposing what was developing with women? He expressed disgust that many men, even pastors, had "reduced the idea of women to things, an important and necessary housekeeping machine meant to keep the house comfortable for the man."⁴³

Had we come so far in this country, he asked, to still view women in this old way? Different times need different ideas. We needed to change our ideas, he concluded, and get with the times as they roll along with a Christian understanding of what is happening in the world. We should not be slaves to the world's view of things, Oftedal continued. From there, he began to make the argument that these women, mothers and daughters, could, by changing their ways, make a difference and found a school. Those women who worked as maids or had other vocations, working from morning until night, should stop spending every cent on clothes and save it up for school.

While, today, people might disagree with this argument, Oftedal did see that the need to be like rich Americans was not helpful to young Norwegian American women. Setting aside the cliché about women wanting to look good and wasting their money when they could be saving it for an education, the argument is right out of the American playbook of Benjamin Franklin and others. Save, and you will be rich; spend, and you will be poor.

This proposal seemed sound but, given Oftedal's other responsibilities, was impossible for him to effect. As he rightly argued, it would be a blessing for the daughters of all Norwegian Americans, not just for the Minneapolis girls but all 150,000 Norwegian American girls. This could easily happen, he concluded, if we just had the will and the way. That Oftedal, overburdened with teaching, raising money for Augsburg, editing the paper, and navigating brutal conflicts in the leadership, could think of such a thing is somewhat astonishing. Although it was far too much for him and the Augsburg faculty to do, he could see the issue and how to handle it. He worked hard and had ideas far ahead of his time.

Two months later, in October, a woman wrote in to support Oftedal's proposal and argument. The column was ascribed to a "woman/*kvinde*," so one could be suspicious of the author. The story is heart-rending but edifying, as it was meant to be. As a young woman, she had begun working in the city and made three dollars a week, most of which she spent on clothes, as Oftedal's column had suggested. All she could think about was the silk dress she wanted. After a couple of years, she became engaged and married a young man. Things went well during their first summer, but when winter came, her husband lost his job, and she was now caring for a baby boy. Fortunately, it was 1877, considered the year

**Figure 3.8.** Augsburg Seminary faculty wives, ca. 1874. From left to right: Elise Gunnersen, Katherine Sverdrup, and Marie Oftedal. Used by permission of Augsburg University Archives.

without a winter. Still, it was winter. She movingly described what it was like to live in a cold room with a baby and no income.

The silk dress became an emblem of her vanity and poor management. Although her husband got another summer job, he lost it in the winter. While she had attended church and loved dressing up in the silk dress to go to church, it hadn't meant all that much to her. In the deepest need, however, she confessed her faith and began to rely on God. Finally, they decided to move to the country and begin farming. They needed money to make the move. She sold the dress for five dollars; it made the move possible. Now they were doing well, even though the work was hard. They had two daughters and were thinking of their future. What she wanted for her daughters was what she had not had: a good education. She wanted people to see in her story a good reason for building a school for girls.[44]

This story got the attention it was meant to. Letters kept coming to the paper asking about the idea of a girls' school. In 1881, the next year, a young woman wrote to *Folkebladet* pleading for a girls' school. "Will this idea just go up in talk?" she asked. She had been attracted by Oftedal's dream and wished with all her heart that it could happen. She had the same reasons that Oftedal had about the necessity of women's education.[45]

These pieces appeared at a crucial time for women in the Norwegian American community: the Muus "divorce" case. It was about as sensational a case as can be imagined for the times and even today. B. J. Muus was the founder of the coeducational St. Olaf's School. The issue was a feminist one that in many ways had been the spark for the feminist movement worldwide: whether a woman was her own person, able to inherit money and have a say as to its use. Oline Christine Katherine Muus (1838–1922) had received an inheritance from her father in Norway, and B. J. Muus had claimed it as his, which it was, according to Norwegian law. This was the beginning of the spectacular case, which ended in the separation of the Muus couple but not, ultimately, a divorce.

American law had changed due to pressure from feminists like Elizabeth Cady Stanton, a rich heiress, who argued that the marriage law needed to be changed since it left women civilly dead. Because marriage made the couple one, and the man was the head of the entity, the wife had no say in managing her inheritance. If any issue sparked the beginning of the feminist movement, it was this one. It began a movement of rich women who had found themselves without recourse when a fortune hunter had married them for their money.

*Folkebladet* and the other Norwegian American papers entered the Muus fray fully armed. Divorce for a clergyman and his wife was almost unheard of. It was never really determined who was at fault, but it was an ugly contest followed closely by the Norwegian American press. Oftedal and Sverdrup took the side of Mrs. Muus; the Norwegian Synod pastors, while privately appalled by the case,

## The Early Years

argued that a wife was to be obedient to her husband. The fact that Muus had not spoken to his wife except under the most extreme duress for some years did not make him easy to defend, even for the Norwegian Synod pastors.

Sverdrup and Oftedal, who watched with disgust the way Muus and the Synod were treating Mrs. Muus, took pity on her and welcomed her to the Augsburg neighborhood while the case proceeded in court. She was especially fond of Oftedal, to whom she gave her love letters from Muus for safekeeping.[46] He understood her, apparently enough so she felt she could do this. From the first, Oftedal took the feminist side, as did Sverdrup, whose interests were more focused on his plan for the seminary. This case was on the minds of everyone in the Norwegian American community at the time. Those who were reading *Folkebladet* and this column were thinking about the question of women and their place in society.

There were several answers to this first column. Most were not signed except as *Maid* (*tjenestepige*). This makes me suspicious. The writers were obviously literate and accomplished writers. Why did they remain anonymous? Would it have embarrassed their husbands? Were they too well known? Or were they ghostwritten by Oftedal himself to further the argument? We cannot know, but we do know he sympathized with women's causes and supported women's suffrage from the first.

The column, which I suspect is Oftedal's, inspired several women to write in describing their desire for further education. One of the more specific letters in *Folkebladet*, from April 21, 1881, suggested a curriculum: Norwegian, English, geography, and history, with religion as the foundation. The school should provide room and board and be something of a safe home for young women. The women, like the men at Augsburg Seminary, could run their own boarding club and learn how to manage these things—learn housekeeping, in other words, with some attention to laundry and ironing, with handwork added. In all these comments, one can sense the fear of establishing a school that was too elite; at the same time, this list of courses differed not at all from the normal school curriculum at the Norwegian Synod's Red Wing Lutheran Ladies Seminary, which would be built in the 1890s.

The Norwegian Synod, as the most established and richest of the synods, had built the largest number of these institutions. While such academies had several lines of study, the most popular one was what people called the *normal school* line. Called *normal* because they met certain "norms" for teaching, these schools fulfilled the mandate that common schools be built on the frontier and provided with educated teachers.

Many of these graduates would find communities where they could teach and, when the summer arrived, could very easily qualify as teachers for the parochial schools that were being established in the congregations filling up the frontiers. The one special requirement that the Norwegian congregational school or parochial school had was that the teacher be able to teach Norwegian and Norwegian Lutheran traditions that the people considered vital: Scripture, Luther's *Small Catechism* with Pontoppidan's explanation, the hymns and songs of their tradition, and Norwegian language, literature, and history. These schools served to tie the communities together and keep the Norwegian language and culture alive longer than might have been expected.

The Deaconess Institute in Minneapolis gave young women from the Augsburg fellowship one route into a public vocation. That was, however, a very special calling. It would take another fifteen years before it finally established Oak Grove, a ladies' seminary very much like the one the Norwegian Synod had built in Red Wing, Minnesota.

CHAPTER 4

# Teaching the Faith in a New Land

THE 1880S BEGAN with increasingly bad feelings between synods and within them. Things would become more and more contentious in the Augsburg faculty and the Conference, which was still smarting over Preus's anathema and divided in its response to the "Open Declaration." The bad feelings continued so much so that Peder A. Rasmussen, pastor of the Lisbon, Illinois, congregation, attempted a reconciliation. He had begun his service in the Norwegian American Lutheran Church as a strong follower of Elling Eielsen and had changed over to the Norwegian Synod after some schooling at Fort Wayne Seminary. He now tried to bring peace to the brawling church leaders, asking that they work to heal their wounds and "repent before the Lord both for us and those whom we call our ecclesiastical adversaries."[1] His suggestion was to ask three or four theologians from Norway—C. P. Caspari, Gisle Johnson, Bishop A. Grimelund, and Sven Brun—to come to a meeting in the United States and referee their disagreements. The response to this simply exacerbated the conflict. Preus replied by saying he was not sure the men from Norway agreed with them on the Word of God, and Peder Laurentius (Laur.) Larsen, president of Luther College, wanted nothing to do with the proposal: "We shall avoid even the appearance of placing ourselves side by side with those who oppose the truth and defend falsehood."[2]

Despite this, Rasmussen did get a group of six presidents of the synods, including Johan Olsen of the Conference, to meet and discuss seven theses on "Redemption and Forgiveness of Sin." The theses were debated and agreed on. When they came out, Sverdrup, whose formidable intellect made it impossible for him to suffer fools, was appalled and responded with an article in *Lutheraneren og Missionsbladet*, "As Sheep That Have No Shepherd."[3] Regretting that there was no mention of the work of the Holy Spirit in the theses that supposedly encompassed the Third Article of the Creed, Sverdrup concluded that these "theses are truly a masterpiece of absence of spiritual content. They are a systematic exclusion of the activity of the Spirit in the work of salvation, and the six presidents stand before all our church people as those who consciously or unconsciously have lent their hand to anything so spiritually barren."[4]

Sverdrup especially lamented that even President Olsen had appeared to have been overwhelmed by the Norwegian Synod in the deliberations and for the sake of peace accepted them.[5] This attack caused Olsen to reply in kind. The acrimony threatened the very existence of Augsburg Seminary.

As had been foreshadowed in the school debate in 1878, the battles within the Conference would grow fiercer. They had begun with the reaction to the "Open Declaration": those who favored Weenaas, now represented by Gunnersen and Professor Gjeldaker, and those on Sverdrup's and Oftedal's side. Gjeldaker, briefly a professor at Augsburg from 1876 to 1877, would grow more opposed to the new school and to Sverdrup and Oftedal. As with many of these arguments, it became personal.

During Gjeldaker's time at Augsburg, he and Gunnersen suggested that a student congregation be established, something Weenaas had also espoused so students could be kept from the worldly attractions of the neighborhood.[6] Sverdrup and Oftedal opposed it because it would create what they thought of as an "artificial and unreal" congregation without the burdens of an actual congregation. While this argument could have been civil and respectful, and the question fundamental—I, too, opposed a congregation of the students at Augsburg when I was there in the 1960s for the very same reasons, without knowing what Sverdrup had said—it became fairly nasty and brought an end to Gjeldaker's tenure.[7] At President Olsen's suggestion, he left Augsburg in 1878 and took a call in Silver Lake, Iowa. His opposition, however, was an ember of the old school that simmered in the community.

The 1881 convention of the Conference was filled with acrimony and bad feelings between pastors and professors, the old school and the new school. Gunnersen came to feel increasingly on the outside of the Sverdrup and Oftedal wing. Things exploded during the next year. On December 11, 1882, Gunnersen resigned his professorship. Theodor H. Dahl, the new president of the Conference, suggested that Oftedal do so, as well, which he did on Christmas Eve of 1882. Sverdrup waited until April 11, 1883, to resign. Gunnersen claimed that the new school faction had made it impossible for him to work with them, especially as they were coeditors of *Folkebladet* and the source of his opposition. Sverdrup, protesting that Oftedal had felt it necessary to resign, called him "the man who has done more than any other individual to build it [Augsburg] up and preserve it."[8]

At the 1883 annual meeting, the issues seemed mostly personal, and Augsburg had no professors for the coming year. At the end, the convention voted on whether to retain the three professors or accept their resignations. Sverdrup received 194 votes, Oftedal 175, and Gunnersen 156 out of a total of 258. Gunnersen lost because he had not received the required two-thirds. After more painful and unpleasant actions, the three were reconciled and issued a statement of their friendship.[9] Despite that, Gunnersen left for the newly established Hauge Seminary in Red Wing. Peace was restored on the Augsburg faculty and to a much lesser extent in the Conference, but the embers of division and disagreement smoldered through the decade, despite the peace that seemed to have finally prevailed.

## Establishing Schools for Children

When the Jacobsons arrived in Minneapolis in July 1868 and began associating with Pastor Ole Paulson and members of Trinity congregation, there was already a Sunday school program for children of Norwegian immigrants. Founded by Aron Hendrick Edsten, the movement grew to be an active program that spread throughout the Norwegian immigrant community.

The history of Sunday schools, according to one source, is the history of how nineteenth-century families could raise their economic and social standards through education.[10] Not only did the children themselves learn the Bible and catechism, but when they brought home their books, their parents could also learn along with them, not only the religious content but also the rudimentary skills of reading, writing, and arithmetic. As families moved away from the tight-knit communities of the farms and small towns to larger, less intimate communities, Sunday schools organized people into groups that gave them social connections that would prove valuable in their lives.

The pietists who came to this country from Norway knew about this movement from Scandinavia. In her work at Evangeliska Fosterlandsstiftelsen (EFS) publishing house in Stockholm, Lina Sandell spent considerable time translating English Sunday school materials to be distributed around Sweden and eventually Norway. Edsten, born into a Swedish family that had moved to Norway, would become an important leader in the Norwegian community in Minneapolis. He knew what to do almost the moment he established his furniture business in the Cedar and Riverside area. He settled in Minneapolis on May 15, 1867, the year the city was incorporated. That same month, he began a Sunday school for Norwegian Lutheran children. It met in a public school on Sixth Street and Seventh Avenue. His first class included four children. That was, according to an article in the January 6, 1886, issue of *Folkebladet,* the tiny seed that blossomed into a much larger number.[11] By 1886, the Conference congregations had 59 teachers and 451 students in Minneapolis alone.

By 1885, the Norwegian congregations in the city, including Norwegian Methodists, Baptists, and Unitarians, were educating 859 students under the tutelage of 102 teachers. The article estimated at the time that over four thousand children in Minneapolis were receiving Sunday school training.

The meetings were generally on Sunday afternoon for two hours, but some met on Sunday morning from nine to ten-thirty or on Saturdays. The list included all the teachers who were currently teaching the classes, as well as superintendents. There was an impressive number of women teachers in both teaching and leadership positions. The Scandinavian Augustana congregation's Sunday school had been the first in 1867; the Norwegian Synod, at Our Savior's, began two years later in 1869. Most of the other congregations would not organize Sunday schools until the early 1880s.

The concern to educate their children in the faith in Norwegian was a serious concern, an issue with all immigrants. Their children were often the reason they had come to America, hoping to provide them a better future. They could not do this without educating them well for the new world, but they also wanted them to know their roots in the Norwegian Lutheran faith. We can see how important that was and the place of the church in their thinking from the reports of Conference leaders' visits to the local congregations, including the Brønø congregation of the Jacobsons. The system of parochial schools and normal schools that they came up with to prepare teachers to educate their children remains remarkable.

## Visitation to the Brønø Congregation

On April 30, 1882, some years after the Conference's discussion about how to educate their young during the annual meeting in Willmar, Ole Paulson, now pastor in nearby Eagle Lake, made an official visit (*visitas*) to the Brønø congregation on behalf of the Conference. He preached on the Gospel text for the Sunday and later, during the catechization service, Ephesians 5:15, "Look carefully then how you walk, not as unwise, but wise." Paulson was functioning as the bishops in Norway did when they visited their flock, pastors, and congregations, catechizing confirmands while they also examined the spiritual life of the congregation at the time.[12]

These official reports followed a standardized form, and the answers give a detailed picture of the congregation at that time. One sees clearly in these reports how important the education of the young was. After the morning service, Paulson heard the pastor, Ole Nilson Bergh (1842–1922), catechize a group of the young people and children from the congregation. He concluded that they possessed a good understanding of Christianity.

At five in the afternoon, "after a nap," Paulson wrote, the congregation met with him again for the official visitation meeting. Neighboring pastor Edvard Erikson (the founding pastor of the congregation, who was still serving the nearby Saron congregation) and Pastor John Jørgenson of the Camp Release congregation met with them as well. They were given the right to take part in the meeting partly because some of the questions in the protocol asked about how the neighboring congregations and community viewed the Brønø congregation.

At this time, the congregation claimed 138 members, 69 of these confirmed members. During that year, it had baptized 4, one of them the Jacobson's youngest daughter at the time, Hilda Kornilia; confirmed 4; married 4 couples; and 15 had left, either for another place or departing this life. It was a small but vigorous congregation that the pastors of the Conference knew and valued.

# Teaching the Faith in a New Land

Figure 4.1. The Brønø Church. Public domain.

The first question had to do with how many members of the congregation were regular attendees of the Sunday services. The answer was that most were "very diligent" in their attendance, but a few were less faithful. Church services happened about once every fourth Sunday, with some evening services, led by the pastor.

The second question asked about the frequency of spiritual gatherings, edifying/*oppbyggelse* meeting, led by the deacons: Bible studies or other meetings for the edification of the congregation. These were important small groups, really, where people could learn about their faith, pray, and testify about their Christian lives. People faithfully attended these and other devotional meetings, Paulson reported.

The third question involved how many of the families in the congregation were faithful in their home devotions. The conclusion of the group was that this practice could be greatly improved, although there were some who were quite faithful. The fourth topic was how well the congregation took care of its oldest members. Paulson deemed the answer satisfactory. The fifth question concerned the relationship of the congregation to its neighbors. It was deemed peaceful and good. As to the sixth question, concerning the offerings of the congregation, the conclusion was that the congregation could not particularly praise—*rose sig*—itself and could do much better, but it had contributed to causes both inside and outside the church body, especially children's homes and foreign missions.

The seventh topic involved the teaching of the faith to the young. The congregation had in the previous year offered two months of religious education in its summer parochial school. Sunday school was something they did offer, but at the time, it was not a major effort of the congregation. The next questions dealt with church discipline. Their major concerns showed that this congregation was not a Norwegian Synod congregation but a Conference congregation. The Conference tended to be Sabbatarian, as opposed to the Norwegian Synod, on this question. Did members of the congregation observe the Sabbath? The conclusion was that yes, it did, as did people in the neighborhood, even those outside of the congregation. The ninth question had to do with swearing and cursing, which did not seem to be a problem among their people. The tenth had to do with drunkenness. The answer is typically droll: "Drunkenness is not entirely unknown except in certain places."[13] Brønø would become more and more of a temperance congregation as time went on.

The final questions concerned the relationship of the pastor and the congregation. Paulson concluded it was among the best. There was one problem, not really a split, but the fact that members, up to half, had been attracted to the Conference congregation in town, Trinity. While there was no bad feeling between them, it had diminished the numbers at the country congregation.

The thirteenth topic was the relationship between the congregation and the Conference. This was very good, according to Paulson. Brønø congregation had contributed to the Conference and was now gathering in funds for Augsburg. The next-to-last topic was the economic situation of the people and the congregation, which Paulson judged was rather good. Finally, he noted that the church book had been kept up to date and was in order. With that, he read what he had written to the assembled group, and they unanimously approved it.

This was the basic order of the visitations back in the old country, and the people were accustomed to such meetings. The questions give us a picture of not only how well the congregation was doing but also what the church thought important to ascertain about the work of the congregation, as well as the congregation's assessment of its progress in teaching and keeping the faith. Obviously, the teaching of the faith to the young ranked highly.

The Jacobsons must have enjoyed the time with Paulson, remembering their wedding and the year with him as their pastor at Trinity. The questions he asked in the formal meeting gave them reason to examine their work with their own growing family. While there is nothing specifically about them in this report, that they had eight children under twelve at the time of his visit meant they had to be thinking about their role as parents and teachers of the faith. From the results, one would have to conclude that since most of their children became lay leaders in their respective congregations, the Jacobsons were doing the right thing regarding teaching the faith at home. Although none became pastors, two became pastor's wives.

Georg Sverdrup visited the congregation that summer of 1882 after the annual meeting in Eau Claire. Pastor Bergh, who had served the congregations in that parish for eight years, had just left for a new call to Audubon, Minnesota, some miles north of Fergus Falls, so Sverdrup had preached in Brønø, Camp Release, St. Petri, and the other congregations in the parish. He had taken the opportunity after the annual meeting to go around to the congregations in the Minnesota Valley and noted in his report in *Folkebladet* some of its history, especially its trials over the previous decade, including the 1862 Sioux uprising, or Dakota War of 1862, the 1873 blizzard, the grasshoppers, and then the building of the Milwaukee and St. Paul Railroad company, which had opened the West. It had lain tracks from Minneapolis that went as far as Aberdeen, South Dakota. A railway station had been built in Montevideo, where the Minnesota and Chippewa Rivers met. He praised the "elegant sleeping cars" in which one could ride from Glencoe, Minnesota, to Aberdeen and now farther and farther.[14] After their trials during the last decade, he thought the people in the area were now ready for good times. They were expecting a good harvest, which meant that Augsburg and the Conference would also benefit when the farmers would give of their bounty to both.

He pointed with special admiration to the mission festivals that ladies in the Hawk Creek and Saron congregations had sponsored, with an auction that raised $250, an incredible sum at the time and the yearly salary of many pastors. There would be more, he noted. He also praised the Camp Release congregation for sending Pastor Bergh a beautiful writing table as a departing gift. By then, Sverdrup had come to know many of the people in the area and enjoyed the gathering they had sponsored for him in the city park beside the river. Surely the Jacobsons were there for that. He described the place as one of the most beautiful settings he had seen on his journeys: "A summer evening with the sunset's rich colors over the fields and hills and the Minnesota and Chippewa Rivers by Montevideo is incomparable. Quiet peace and beauty in the natural beauty awakens reminders of paradise in the soul and lays a wonderful, blessed longing for the heavenly city in a person's heart. Finally, only this: our church people in the west are unanimous in their approval of our fellowship: they tell us 'continue as from the beginning and fight for personal Christianity, for the simple children's teaching and free congregations.'"[15]

When I told my father to read this, his eyes filled with tears. Then I told Gracia Christensen, widow of Bernard Christensen, about it; she had known Elise, the second Mrs. Sverdrup, whom she reported had once not washed the walls above his desk, brown with tobacco, to see if Sverdrup noticed (he had not). She sighed and wondered if Sverdrup could not just for once forget his program!

## Church Fights

While it might be possible to think that the Jacobsons and other members of the congregations in the country around Montevideo remained oblivious to the church fights that rumbled around the professors and schools and were fought over in the press, it is very unlikely. They knew Paulson, Sverdrup, Oftedal, and their pastors and read *Folkebladet*. They most likely had read Sverdrup's description of the trip to their congregation and approved. They could read about these theological battles, but they also saw it in person as these conflicts were acted out in their midst. As a predestination debate among the Norwegian Lutherans began to heat up through the 1880s, congregations began to be aware of the battle. Their debates on the issue were noted by the local press. Without a doubt, the most vivid picture of the conflict happened not far from Montevideo in Norway Lake, Minnesota, during the spring and summer of 1885.

Lars Markhus, the pastor who had baptized the Jacobsons' two oldest, Peter and Mathilda, had been the subject of several news stories in the secular press, to say nothing of the church papers. In conversations about the matter of election (*Naadvalg*), his two congregations and he came to loggerheads. According to Ole Paulson's column "*Smuler*/Crumbs" in *Folkebladet*, Markhus, "by an overwhelming majority in both congregations, was dismissed" for defending the position that the leaders of the Norwegian Synod and the Missouri Synod held on predestination, or election, as it was popularly called.[16] This controversy, which would soon tear the Norwegian Synod apart and cause the formation of the new United Church, had to do with how one became a Christian. Crudely put, was it through baptism, God's election of a person, or conversion, when a person came to faith through an experience?

The trustees locked Markhus out of the church building. Some days later, he was found crawling into the building through a side window, breaking the window and creating a mess. He was carried out of the building by the trustees of the congregation. Markhus, an early graduate of Luther College and Concordia Seminary in St. Louis, was a respected member of the Norwegian Synod clergy, a trustee of the Willmar Seminary. When he was arrested, brought to court, and charged with breaking and entering, as well as perjury, the gossip mills exploded. His lawyer was the prominent Norwegian American lawyer Knut Nelson, who would become governor in 1892 and go on to be elected a US senator from Minnesota. Paulson wondered why on earth Nelson had agreed to represent Markhus in a case Paulson thought he would surely lose.[17]

The lawyer for the congregation was the colorful John Arctander (1863–1920), a resident of Willmar, whom Paulson knew well. The courtroom was packed for the trial. During the questioning, it turned out that Markhus had not been issued a regular call from the congregation but rather from the Norwegian Synod's Church Council. As a pioneer pastor, he had established many congregations in the area but not been officially called by any of them; maybe this was an oversight of necessity, but it was a legal loophole that Nelson used to full advantage. This gave Markhus a call for life, he argued, saying the congregation could not legally rescind his call. Paulson could not resist the comparison between the king appointing pastors to congregations in Norway and the way the Norwegian Synod had appointed Markhus. This fracas only continued to besmirch the Norwegian Synod in the eyes of Conference people.

Markhus was given the right to be in the church in the morning but not in the afternoons. This was unsatisfactory to all sides. By this time, Markhus was mortally ill and could not really suffer a trial. He died on December 19, 1885, so the case became moot. One can imagine the talk about this scandalous case on both sides. It made the argument about election all that more concrete and compelling to people as they wondered how Lutherans could believe what Conference pastors successfully called Calvinism. These fights caused great ruptures in nearly all the communities where the Norwegians had settled. The debate would soon cause a serious rupture in the Norwegian Synod, when, in 1886, Professor Schmidt of Luther Seminary in Madison, Wisconsin, left Luther to begin a seminary in Northfield. Along with him, a group of Norwegian Synod pastors left the synod, calling themselves the Anti-Missouri Brotherhood—that is to say, against the Missourian influence they accused the leadership of having. They were, on the whole, younger pastors such as Ludvig Marius Biørn (1835–1905). P. A. Rasmussen, however, was the oldest and most esteemed. Their Nestor, they called him. Bernt Julius Muus of St. Olaf worked with them but never left the Norwegian Synod. Realizing their small numbers, they called for a merger of the Conference and Norwegian Danish Augustana Synod. Together with the second generation of the Conference pastors and Norwegian Danish Augustana Synod pastors, they called for what became the United Church in 1890. The years from 1886 to 1889 were filled with meetings, free conferences, speeches, and resolutions about what they agreed on and what they did not. The scandal of the bitter fights between the Norwegian Lutherans in America at the time was noted by leaders such as Gjermund Høyme, a graduate of Paxton Seminary, who had become a leader in the Conference and then president of the United Church. He marked the need to heal those wounds and act like Christians. This came to be a significant theme in the discussions leading up to the forming of the United Norwegian Lutheran Church in America.[18]

The Hauge Synod participated in early talks but ultimately withdrew from them. Sverdrup was disappointed in that, never really trusting that the Anti-Missourian Brotherhood, with its deep roots in the Norwegian Synod and thus the Missouri Synod, had changed its spots. Despite his original mistrust of merger talks, he finally agreed to participate, adding his intellectual heft to the deliberations. As his thoughts about union ripened, he argued that the Norwegian

Lutherans had agreed on the Augsburg Confession and the *børnelærdom*, which he thought was enough. Having to agree on theses like those put forward by the Norwegian Synod and Missouri only divided them more. This conviction would continue in the Lutheran Free Church through the 1950s.

## Haakon and Torjør Tinseth

The year 1886 was a big one in our family history. That June, my mother's paternal grandparents, Haakon Nicolaus Tolvminius Anderson Tinseth (1860–1944) and his wife, Torbjør Olsdatter Kaali (1855–1930), arrived in New York. They had, at the time, three children, Ole Haakonson (1880–1928), Anton Haakonson (1882–1951), and Kari (Carrie) Haakonsdatter (1884–1969). They stayed for some months with Haakon's oldest brother, Anthon Theodore Anderson (1843–1915), a jeweler on North Avenue in Chicago. He had immigrated in 1865. According to family lore, he had been bitter about his parents' treatment

**Figure 4.2.** Haakon and Torbjør Tinseth, ca. 1899. Used by permission of the Grindal family.

of him. He was born out of wedlock to Maren Dorothea in Kongsberg, Norway, on December 7, 1843. His parents married the following spring on May 6, 1844. They left him with family in Kongsberg when he was three years old so his mother and father could move to Oslo, where she studied midwifery. Maren Dorothea was the daughter of a shoemaker in Oslo with strong ties to Kongsberg, the silver mining capital of the Dano-Norwegian kingdom.

Maren Dorothea Trulsdatter (1817–1877) and Anthon Anderson (1819–1886) came from the emerging middle class of Norway. Anthon, according to records, was the illegitimate child of Anne Erichsdatter (1798–1869) from the Skyberg farm near Tretten in Gudbrandsdalen. She had left her home with Anthon when he was quite young for Vang in Hedemark.

Both were affected by Hauge's revival. In 1822, she married the father of Anthon, Anders Simensen. Anthon would be confirmed by Jacob B. Bull, the pastor of Vang church. Bull, a strong supporter of Hauge, had written a favorable biography of him, not expected among the clergy at the time. He instilled in Anthon a strong faith, which he and his wife taught their children. Anthon had met Maren Dorothea when he worked as a journeyman (apprentice) with her father, Truls, a shoemaker in Oslo. Dorothea, as she came to be called, moved from Kongsberg to Oslo for some time while she pursued her training as a midwife, graduating from the school in 1846.

Anthon bought a small store when they moved to an acreage near Gransherad, Telemark, called Nymoen. In the 1850s, the area was being discovered by tourists from as far away as England who relished the wild nature and hunting and fishing in Telemark's forests and lakes. As time went on, he built a hotel on the west side of Lake Tinn, the lake that would, during World War II, be the scene of the fight against Germany's efforts to produce heavy water.

By the time their youngest son, Haakon, was born in 1860, they were forces for good in their small community of Gransherad. As a midwife, Dorothea brought spiritual succor to her patients spread out in the mountains surrounding Tinn Lake, as well as medical knowledge. When she died, the cantor/*klokker* O. Svensen in Gransherad wrote a hymn to mourn her passing. Even though her grandson Fred (Fritjof Johann) was born twenty years after she died, he could still be brought to tears by the wonderful stories he had heard about her from his father, Haakon.

Anthon, Haakon's father, my great-great-grandfather, emigrated to America shortly after his wife's death in 1877. He had gotten into a few altercations with one of his sons-in-law and decided to leave for America. He came to Manistee, Michigan, where his daughter had settled with her husband, John Fossil. It had, from its beginning, been a significant destination for Scandinavians—Ole Paulson went there to find work. There, Anthon attended the Conference church, the First Scandinavian Lutheran Church of Manistee, which was served

**Figure 4.3.** Tinnosett Hotel in Norway. Used by permission of the Grindal family.

by P. B. Norman (d. 1901) a Conference pastor who was disciplined for unchristian behavior at the 1888 annual meeting of the Conference but continued to serve congregations in Minnesota. (He was buried by Trinity congregation in 1901.) When Anthon went to Chicago during the summer of 1886 to visit his son, Anton Theodor, about whom he was spiritually concerned, he succumbed to a heat stroke on July 17 during a heat wave that swept over the country that summer. He was buried in Chicago in Mt. Olive Cemetery.

In 1886, Haakon (and Torbjør) had followed his father, Anthon, and brother Anthon Theodore, to America. They lived with Anthon Theodore and Haakon's sister, Elevine, during their stay in Chicago. Sometime before November 1886, they came to Redwood County and bought a farm in Ann Township near Lamberton. The property included a large house, but it was not well appointed. The children slept on the floor in the attic on mattresses filled with straw. Before meals, Haakon would lead them in devotions. Theodor, my grandfather, was born there on November 20, 1886. They began farming, although Haakon preferred trading and dealing like his father. His sons would soon be of an age to help on the farm and were able to make it successful.

After getting settled, the family prospered. They were faithful members of the Conference congregation in Westbrook, near Lamberton. Johan Christian Jacobsen (1841–1920), a pastor of the Conference, had served that congregation since 1881 and would remain there until 1911. Jacobson had attended the Stavanger Mission School, which had been a model for Weenaas and others who

# Teaching the Faith in a New Land

**Figure 4.4.** Tinseth homestead near Lamberton. Used by permission of the Grindal family.

were building Augsburg Seminary. Even the Norwegian Synod had realized they needed a model like the Stavanger Mission School for the education of its future pastors able to serve congregations in America. When Pastor Jacobsen arrived in America in 1868, he joined the Scandinavian Augustana Synod, where he became acquainted with Weenaas, Ole Paulson, Sverdrup, and Oftedal, and connected with other leaders of the Conference as it began its life in 1870. He baptized my grandfather Theodor. Pastor Jacobsen would join the United Church in 1890.

Haakon served on the congregation's board of trustees, and Torbjør became an active member of the ladies' aid, hosting it and helping it raise money for local charities and foreign missions. They came to know and revere Sverdrup, Oftedal, and the Augsburg Seminary community as the leaders of the Conference, and Augsburg professors made their way to Lamberton as much as they had to Montevideo.

## Fruitful Progress for Augsburg

Helland calls the years between 1883 and 1890 at Augsburg the "years of fruitful progress."[19] Things settled down enough to make it possible for the faculty and Conference to move forward with its plans for educating and maintaining a church body that was growing and flourishing. Their mission was to provide an education for pastors that was *menighetmæssig*, or appropriate for congregations. Sverdrup and Oftedal wanted the education of the pastoral candidates "to correspond to the needs and nature of the Christian congregations throughout the whole course, from the first preparatory class to the senior class in the theological department."[20] They regarded this as innovative and radical. Their proposal came to mean that the entire course of studies at Augsburg, from preparatory to graduation from seminary, would be aimed at the preparation of pastors in harmony with the goals of Augsburg. Their original plan to have a scientific line (*realskiole*) as they knew from Norway had failed for lack of faculty and students. Given that the school now aimed at educating pastors, they had to have a faculty in the prep school and the college who were also in harmony with the goals of the curriculum. Finding such teachers was something of an issue, which Sverdrup solved by hiring graduates of the college and seminary. He began by hiring John T. Bugge (1851–1891), an 1879 graduate of the college, in 1882. Bugge became the first professor in the college. He taught Norwegian, Greek, and history. Next, Sverdrup hired John H. Blegen (1851–1928) to teach Norwegian, German, and Greek and Theodor S. Reimestad (1851–1920) to teach Norwegian, Latin, and music in 1885. They were Augsburg College graduates of 1880 and continued at Augsburg for many years. In 1885, A. M. Hove (1859–1943), a Luther College graduate, was hired to teach English. He became a loyal and beloved teacher at the college over the years. The strengthening of the offerings of the college would be of a piece with other colleges in the area, which had also begun expanding their offerings.

The Conference was growing through this period and began to benefit from the strife in the Norwegian Synod over predestination, or election, a controversy that would rend the older body and reduce its numbers significantly. Over one-third of their membership left the Norwegian Synod during this argument. This argument would persist among the Norwegians until the Madison Settlement of 1912. It lived on at Luther Seminary through my time there. The settlement included language indicating that while God wanted all to be saved, one could think of it in two ways and still be Lutheran. The first form was that God made the decision, and it was for the church to announce that to people in what might be an unconditional absolution. The second form was that people hearing the word might be so moved by God's action that they would come to a decision, led by the Holy Spirit, and be converted. In either case, God was the actor, but the focus in one was God, in the other, the person. As a Lutheran Free Church pietist, at the seminary I was called a *second-form adherent* because I believed in evangelism and conversion. While most Norwegians would have adhered more to the second form when they arrived on American shores, the close relations between the teachers at Concordia Seminary with the young Herman Preus and Vilhelm Koren moved them further in the direction of what many called predestination, or election. That emphasis lasted at Luther Seminary through the Preus-Aus debates all the way down to the Forde-Burtness struggles. As chair of the George Aus lectureship series for several years, I was clearly branded as being on the second-form side. This explanation is far too rough, in a way, to explain the controversy, but it is the way the people understood it. Debating about it at Luther Seminary gave the students theological chops that were important.

One can see that while the Conference leadership, led by Sverdrup, was deeply concerned with teaching the faith to their young in the children's teaching (*børnelærdom*), they were also devoted to evangelistic meetings and gatherings, which came to be the practice of most Norwegian Lutheran churches in America, even those of the Norwegian Synod.

It would also be in this period that Augsburg and the Conference would send out its first missionaries, John Hogstad in 1887 and Erik Tou in 1889, both to Madagascar to join the Norwegians in mission there. This was an exciting time for the strongly mission-minded ladies' aids and pastors who had been supporting the missionaries by sending money to Norway. Sverdrup was a passionate supporter of missions, especially in Madagascar, and would begin editing a journal, *Gasseren* (*Malagasy*), in 1900 focusing on that mission. Now they had their own missionary and no longer needed to send money to Norway. They were justly proud.

## A Second Visitation at Brønø Congregation

On February 7, 1887, Edvard Eriksen, the founding pastor of Brønø congregation, visited the congregation on behalf of the Conference, as was the general routine of most of the Norwegian American Lutheran churches.[21] The membership at that time was ninety-three baptized members and forty-seven confirmed members. Three Jacobson children had been baptized there, one of them the Jacobsons' youngest child, my grandmother Inanda Regina (1886–1924). Six confirmands had been confirmed that year. Eriksen preached; after the service, he and the pastor, Ole Gulbrandsen (1855–1914), catechized the children. They answered the questions somewhat well, according to Eriksen. After the exam, Eriksen spoke on the Word from 2 John 1:4: "I have no greater joy than this to hear that my children are walking in the truth."

After dinner, the congregation again met with the visitor and the pastor for their conversation. This time, the questions were fewer but got at the same issues. First came the state of the Christian life in the congregation. The answers were similar to those noted before: The worship services were well attended when they were offered, and given the exigencies of travel, the services were rarely more than once a month. The deacons had not been quite so diligent in scheduling edifying (*opbygelige*) meetings, usually Bible studies or the reading of church postils, usually sermons by Luther, Hauge, or Bishop Nils Jacob Jensen Laache (1831–1892) of Trondheim, whose sermons, influenced by Carl Oluf Rosenius (1816–1868) of Sweden, were popular with Norwegian pietists. They liked Luther's postils

Figure 4.5. Ole Gulbrandsen (1855–1914). Public domain.

and those of Laache and were exhorted to continue or start home devotions. Laache's writings, with their Rosenian mildness, softened some of the harshness of Hauge's works, so he became well known among the Norwegian pietists. My grandfather Grindal used Laache for daily morning devotions and Hauge or Luther at night.

Many held home devotions on the Sundays when there was no service. The father or grandfather would lead the service, singing hymns, reading Scripture, reciting the catechism, and reading a postil. Most of the families, according to the report, used prayers before and after the meal, led by the fathers. Attendance at the Lord's table was good from both old and young. They agreed that on matters of church discipline, there were no pressing issues. Relations between the congregation and its neighbors were once again considered to be peaceful and good.

The second concern was the state of the religious school, or congregational school. Eriksen complimented them on their serious concern for the teaching of their children: each child had received eight weeks of religious education in the summer parochial school. They had also begun teaching Sunday school on the Sundays when there were no services and circumstances permitted. When the pastor could be there, he catechized the children after the sermon, a regular and expected occurrence in Norwegian churches. Worship services could not be every Sunday, given the weather, the distances the pastor had to travel, and the number of congregations in a call.[22]

As to the third set of questions, the relationship between the pastor and the congregation, Eriksen deemed the congregation as among the best, as was the congregation's relationship to the proposed United Church. It had voted to join the new church once it was formed. The congregation's financial position was good: it owed nothing, but it did not yet have a cemetery of its own. The church books were examined and found to be up to date and in order. With that, the protocol was read to the group. It was approved. The meeting concluded with the singing of a hymn and prayer.

By this time, all ten of the Jacobson children had been born. Educating their children in the faith was the main concern of the congregation. It was a small congregation, as we have seen, but as those things go, it was flourishing. Guldbrandsen had been their pastor from his ordination in 1887 until 1895, when the conflict concerning the new church would cause a parting of ways.

## The Conference Sends Missionaries to Madagascar

As we've seen, in 1887, the first Norwegian American missionary, Johan Peter Hogstad (1858–1911), an Augsburg Seminary graduate, left for Madagascar to serve the Norwegian mission. He was supported by both the Norwegian Missionary Society and the Conference. He was followed the next year by Erik Hansen Tou (1857–1917), who also had a joint call from both the Norwegian Missionary Society and the Conference. He served first in St. Augustin and then moved to Manasoa. Although Tou did not remain in Madagascar long, he established an orphanage that remained dear to the hearts of many supporters, including Jonette, through their lifetime. After the death of his first wife, Caroline Knudsen, and his son in 1901, he married a deaconess named Sister Alida Olin and left Madagascar to serve a congregation in Puckwana, South Dakota. He served there until 1909, when he took a call to Napoleon, North Dakota. While Tou's health was broken by the difficult life in Madagascar, his presence back in the Dakotas helped publicize the mission. He wrote a book about the mission and frequently spoke about it to the local congregations, so he kept the link fresh. These men rightly made the young Conference proud.

The church presses soon began producing textbooks for these schools. When the children went to parochial school in the summer—daily classes for several weeks—they used the book *Norwegian Textbook for Congregational Schools* (*Norsk Læsebok for Menighed skoler*). Prepared by a committee after the passing of a resolution by the Conference and published by the Conference publisher in 1889, just before the United Church merger, it gives us a good picture of what the congregational summer parochial schools of the Conference taught. They included not only exercises in Norwegian but also Norwegian history, literature, and culture.

The books contained some of Aesop's fables, short stories like "The Turtle and the Hare," stories from the Bible or church history, and a brief recounting of St. Augustine's life. There are hymns, such as Grundtvig's "Deilig er den himmel Blå" ("Bright and Glorious Is the Sky") and "Glade Jul, Hellige Jul" ("Silent Night, Holy Night"). They are printed in the old gothic type, which made it a bit difficult for the students to learn if they had not seen it before, although their parents did not think Norwegian was correct if it was not in gothic print. This book pleased parents and taught the young something of their parents' culture and faith. Several battered and beaten copies of this book were part of our family treasures and show the hard use they received.

With the growing population of immigrants through the 1890s, the need for such teachers increased. Teachers were most often sought among young women because they were much cheaper to employ than young men. The Norwegian Synod would build the Red Wing Lutheran Ladies Seminary, which opened in 1894 to educate young women to be ladies and probably pastors' wives—so it taught music, art, and fine hand work along with its regular course for women teachers of history, literature, geography, and so on. Neither Luther College nor Augsburg Seminary could imagine enrolling women because they were preparing young men for the ministry, a career impossible for women to consider at the time. So the question of educating women for both traditions had to be separate from the schools on which they had spent most of their substance.

## Founding Deaconess Institute in Minneapolis

The education of women had been broached for both Augsburg Seminary and Luther College in their early years but dropped when the leadership in both traditions opted against including women in the student body.[23] However, both traditions knew they had to think of educating women in one of their schools of higher education sooner or later.

One way to address it was by establishing a Deaconess Motherhouse. They knew Elisabeth Fedde (1850–1926) had done so in Brooklyn, and when Pastor Gjertsen in the late summer of 1888 heard Elisabeth Fedde was in the Midwest visiting family in Missouri, he found a way to invite her to Minneapolis. Gjertsen had been eager to build such an institution in Minneapolis and moved with dispatch. It was an opportune time. His congregation had proposed calling a deaconess from Norway to build such an institution in Minneapolis. Now the opportunity seemed to be opening to them. The leaders of the general council were in town for their annual meeting. Dr. Adolph Spaeth (1839–1910), professor at the Mount Airy Lutheran Seminary in Philadelphia, had just delivered a speech on the Deaconess movement as he knew it from Kaiserwerth, Germany, and from the motherhouse in Philadelphia, which he knew well. Along with him was elderly William Passavant (1821–1894), who had been something of the Davy Crockett of Lutherans in America, whom Fedde had come to know while working in Brooklyn. Along with Sven Oftedal and Gjermund Høyme, Georg Sverdrup was there in the living room, but he did not take a leading role. It was Gjertsen and, to a lesser extent, Oftedal who led the charge. To everyone's surprise, even her own, when they asked Fedde to found a Deaconess Hospital and Motherhouse that day in September 1888, she said yes. The group moved forward quickly, with Fedde's full participation. She had been on vacation from her work at the Deaconess Hospital and Motherhouse in Brooklyn, which she had established five years before. Fedde knew the drill. Within six weeks of their meeting in Minneapolis, on November 11, 1888, a dedication service was held at Trinity, and there was a primitive Deaconess Hospital running with young women training to be sisters.

The diaconate offered a career for single women but a hard one. While the Deaconess curriculum resembled the normal school curriculum, with subjects appropriate to nursing added, it was both religious and medical. In some ways a minor religious office, it combined spiritual counsel with nursing and very hard work—cleaning, washing, and doing chores most nurses would consider beneath them today. Florence Nightingale had been attracted to the idea of deaconesses when she first visited the first Deaconess Motherhouse in Kaiserswerth near Düsseldorf, Germany, and based some of her ideas for reform on what she had learned there. Later, she criticized deaconess's training for not being rigorous enough in medical skills, but she approved of the emphasis on cleaning, dressing the wounds of, and feeding those who were poor. Even though Nightingale did not agree with the germ theory for some time, her work to clean up filthy hospitals and homes had the same effect as if she had believed in germs. While this offered an education and career to young women, many did not feel called into the diaconate and preferred being nurses. To meet that need, in 1916, the institute began preparing young women to be nurses without training for the diaconate. Jonette Jacobson raised money from her ladies' aid to send to Deaconess Hospital many times. She would continue to support it through her life. When Inanda was older, she also helped to support the work.

At the time, Augsburg and the Conference were focused on their own work and paying little attention to that of other Lutheran churches in America. Just as the Anti-Missourian Brotherhood, the Norwegian Danish Conference, and the Norwegian Danish Augustana Synod were beginning talks that would culminate in the United Norwegian Lutheran Church in America in 1890, the General Council of Eastern Lutherans at Philadelphia Lutheran Theological Seminary produced a liturgy known as the Common Service. It had been compiled from service books created just after the time of Luther's liturgical revisions. It was

**Figure 4.6.** Sverdrup teaching an Augsburg Seminary class. Used by permission of Augsburg University Archives.

created to return Lutherans in America to the liturgical traditions of which they supposed Luther would have approved.[24] It would be used by more and more churches as they compiled their own hymnals, and the service began to be used around the country, giving Lutherans in America something that unified them. Later, the Norwegian Lutheran Synod, United Church, and Hauge Synod worked together on the *Lutheran Hymnary* of 1912. They included the Common Service alongside a new service created by Gustav Jensen in 1887, no longer using a hymn service, which had been the norm since 1699. Over time, the Common Service became a great force for the union of the various Lutheran churches in the United States.

In October 1887, Georg Sverdrup's wife died of typhus. He suffered this loss just as the greatest burdens of the school and church were beginning to press in on him as president and professor at Augsburg and leader in the Conference. Caring for his family had been daunting for him at the time. The students watched closely as he ministered to his wife and son, Carl, who also died of typhus. Most of the other children had also contracted the disease. The community remarked on his strength and calm demeanor even as he was stretched to the limit, and Gjermund Høyme had commended him for his work: even though he had been "bent down by sorrow and emaciated by many a sleepless night and the care of his suffering wife and children, he took care of his work as teacher and president with his usual faithfulness and without much interruption. The Lord gave him strength to bear it all."[25]

After her death, Sverdrup asked his wife's sister, Elise, who was working at the Deaconess Hospital of Lovisenberg in Christiania, to come and care for the children. Lovisenberg was where Elisabeth Fedde had trained, so Elise knew of her. While Elise was never consecrated as a deaconess, she was considered one and taught at Deaconess in Minneapolis after she arrived.

The hospital had suffered an immediate blow when its first patients died of typhus and the first sisters also became ill with the disease. It had to be closed for fumigation. Fedde left Minneapolis to return to Brooklyn and the motherhouse there. In the spring of 1889, the project in Brooklyn looked to be finished. Fedde, however, had found it impossible to work with Pastor Gjertsen. When it became clear that she had come to despise Gjertsen and, to a lesser extent, Oftedal, regarding them as blowhards, Sverdrup came to the rescue and became chair of the committee.

Fedde had to remain in Brooklyn longer than expected when needed replacements from Norway did not arrive when expected because of a shipwreck. It looked as though the entire project would have to be abandoned. Sverdrup received a letter from Fedde written on May 4, 1889, in which she poured out her heart to him. She had in hand her call and a letter of acceptance or resignation to the Minneapolis organization.

Sverdrup answered her quickly. We do not have that letter, but her answer indicated it was welcome. She thanked him for his heartfelt letter, praising him for being "a safe place to go."[26] Over the summer, Sverdrup sorted things out for the entire group. He wrote Oftedal on July 2, 1889, telling him that things had settled down and he thought that Fedde would return soon. She did and attended the board meeting on July 30, 1889, where the articles of incorporation were settled and ready for signing. This saved the institution. On August 17, 1889, the articles were filed with the state of Minnesota. Sverdrup had named Fedde as a member of the board, something she had wanted, so she was satisfied with his work.

Andreas Helland agreed that it was Sverdrup who saved the work "and brought it to a successful realization."[27] Sverdrup continued through his life time to work with the Deaconess Institute in Minneapolis, especially during a very difficult time when Fedde was essentially fired by the Minneapolis board for inappropriately supporting the founding of a Deaconess Motherhouse in Chicago, an episode that came during the very difficult and enervating struggles over the new United Church. The leader of the Chicago Motherhouse was Nils Brun, a pastor in Chicago who had become a ferocious critic of Sverdrup and a leader in the United Church they were now planning.

Sverdrup became a champion of the Deaconess movement around the world and wrote several articles defending it, especially the work in Minneapolis. He continued to lead it even in the turbulent decade after the founding of the United Church. It was a tribute to his strength of character and sheer capacity for work that he could do so, and the fracas with Fedde gives us an insight into how some people viewed both Gjertsen and Oftedal.

CHAPTER 5

# Mergers, Disputes, and the Founding of the Lutheran Free Church

As the car sped west to the 1951 annual meeting of the Lutheran Free Church (LFC) in Seattle, my father could not explain to my eight-year-old mind, nor did he know the whole story of, all that had transpired in the 1890s during the fracas over Augsburg, but clearly the wound was still raw and open. Being against any kind of merger with the ELC was written in his and my mother's DNA as deeply as anything could be. The stories had been rehearsed by their grandparents and parents over and over again as they sat out on the summer porches drinking lemonade and playing rook or inside, around the woodstove with its isinglass flickering into the darkness.

During my life of two ecclesiastical mergers, I have always joked that the worst one for me was the merger of 1890, which I had not yet gotten over. That is even truer than I thought now that I have had to delve deeply into the story to get a sense of how members of my family, without exception members of Sverdrup's party, were experiencing the debacle. In what follows, I have tried to tell the story as clearly as I can to understand more fully what actually happened. (The resemblances between the merger negotiations and schism of what became the United Church and the merger negotiations and schism of the ELCA are eerie.) To do that, I have relied on contemporary newspaper and church paper reports of the fracases in the 1890s to experience how it must have felt at the time to my great-grandparents and grandparents. Too many histories of this time have, as a matter of necessity, been more in the nature of summaries of what happened. My reports here are unfiltered by time or, I hope, my historical bias.

There are three events that shape the conflict: (1) the place of the Augsburg Seminary educational plan and buildings in the United Church, which was a curricular dispute that became a legal dispute about property; (2) the Augsburg Publishing House conflict; and (3) the refusal of the 1895 annual meeting of the United Church to seat Trinity's delegates, Sverdrup and Oftedal, and, not incidentally, the split at Trinity congregation, which resulted in a sizable number of Trinity members seceding to found Bethlehem Lutheran Church, today on Forty-First and Lyndale Avenues in south Minneapolis.

## The 1890s

The 1890s were a time of unrest and agitation throughout the nation. Populism was raising rebellions on the farms, while labor unions were forming and beginning to strike. Violence broke out during conflicts like the Haymarket strike in Chicago. In 1892, the new Populist Party offered a full slate of candidates headed by James B. Weaver. They won enough of the popular vote to vote in the Electoral College. Minnesota's Ignatius Loyola Donnelly (1831–1901) was a leader in the movement and wrote the platform for the People's Party in 1892. These tremors against the powers that be affected everyone in the country but especially on the farm. A member of the Augsburg Quartet, Theodore Reimestad, ran for lieutenant governor on the Prohibition party ticket.

In 1893, another worldwide financial panic made the gathering of funds for charitable institutions difficult. It had started in Argentina and spread around the world quickly. Unemployment soared. The farms suffered not because of bad crops but because of the markets. Populism was in full swing as the farmers, especially, responded to the arguments of William Jennings Bryan, the great orator who became a candidate for president in 1896, campaigning against William McKinley mostly on the strength of his support for silver rather than the gold standard. His great "Cross of Gold" speech painted a picture that appealed to the rural population, where most Americans still lived: "You can come to us and tell us that the great cities are in favor of the gold standard; we reply that the great cities rest upon our broad and fertile prairies. Burn down your cities and leave our farms, and your cities will spring up again as if by magic; But destroy our farms and the grass will grow in the streets of every city in the country."[1]

Farmers, although cash poor, were not starving. They could raise food and sustenance on their farms. They could scrape together some cash for appeals like the ones Augsburg had to make over time. Whether cause or effect, Augsburg's most intense times happened during financial panics and depressions. Augsburg's conflict to some extent mirrored the national debate about bigwigs having control of the levers of society. A politician with sympathies toward this movement, Henrik Shipstead (1881–1960) from Willmar, who later represented Minnesota as a congressman and US senator, is recorded as attending these first meetings of the Friends of Augsburg and the LFC and giving money to the church.

## The Union of 1890

June 1890 brought three Norwegian American Lutheran church denominations—the Norwegian Danish Conference (1870–1890), the Norwegian Danish Augustana Synod (1870–1890), and the Anti-Missouri Brotherhood (1887–1890)—together into what came to be known as Forenede, or the United Norwegian Lutheran Church of America (UNLCA). The union had

Figure 5.1. Friedrich August Schmidt (1837–1928). Public domain.

been called for by the Anti-Missouri Brotherhood soon after they had separated from the Norwegian Synod. They had been members of the Norwegian Synod who came to disagree with the Norwegian Synod's leadership on predestination, or what they called *election*. Heavily influenced by the Missouri Synod's view of election and predestination, the old leadership—Preus, Ottesen, and Koren—were accused by the dissenters of being too closely allied with the Missouri Synod.

Several key pastors and congregations withdrew from the Norwegian Synod in 1886 and opened a seminary at St. Olaf with the professors Marcus Olaus Bøckmann (1849–1942) and Friedrich August Schmidt (1837–1928), a German Lutheran theologian. Schmidt, a longtime professor at Luther College, had learned Norwegian to teach there. In 1886, these pastors and professors formed the Anti-Missouri Brotherhood. They did not want to be a church body, nor did they have the resources, really, to be one. For these reasons, they called for a merger with the Conference and the Norwegian Danish Augustana Synod. They invited the Hauge Synod to their negotiations as well, something that Sverdrup approved because he felt the Hauge Synod members were closer to the Conference than either Norwegian Augustana or the Anti-Missouri Brotherhood. Sverdrup, according to Fevold, was uneasy about the Anti-Missouri Brotherhood.[2] He had locked horns with these professors on enough occasions to wonder about

P. A. Rasmussen

**Figure 5.2.** Peter Andreas Rasmussen (1829–1898). Public domain.

their acceptance of the Conference's adopting the *Small Catechism* and *Augsburg Confession* as their confessional documents instead of the entire *Book of Concord*, as had the Norwegian Synod and the Norwegian Danish Augustana Synod. The Norwegian church had not adopted more than these two parts of the symbols, but Missouri strongly recommended it to the Norwegian Synod pastors.

The leaders in what would become the UNLCA tended to be younger pastors, especially from the Conference. The Norwegian Synod leadership was growing long in the tooth. Preus would die in 1894; Koren took over for him as president and presided until 1910, when he died at eighty-four. The younger pastors in all three synods would play a big part in the success of the United Church. One exception was Peter Andreas Rasmussen (1829–1898), longtime pastor in Lisbon, Illinois, often called the Nestor of the group. He had joined the Eielsen Synod on his arrival in America in 1850. He became a pastor in that church body and, briefly, a professor at its failed attempt at a college and seminary in Chicago.

After further education at Fort Wayne, Rasmussen left the Haugeans for the Norwegian Synod in 1862. There he became a leader, editing its church paper and serving on the church council. However, as the predestination debates grew more intense, he could not brook the unyielding stance of the Norwegian Synod regarding election. After some struggle, he joined the Brotherhood and became a leader of the group, taking his congregation in New Lisbon, Illinois, with him in each move he made.

Rasmussen, along with Ludvig Marinus Biørn (1835–1908) of Land congregation near Northfield and Bernt Julius Muus of Holden congregation, also

Figure 5.3. Gjermund Høyme. Public domain.

nearby, were part of the movement, although Muus did not leave the Norwegian Synod. He went along with the rebellion and supported it, but his health was in decline, and he would leave for Norway, where he died in 1900.

Some of the leaders of the old school in the Conference were also happy to join together with the Anti-Missourians and the Norwegian Danish Augustana Synod, now centered in Canton, South Dakota, and connected with Augustana College in Sioux Falls. The old scars from Oftedal's Public Declaration had never healed. Johan Olsen would become a strong supporter, and leader, of the United Church, as would T. H. Dahl (1845–1923) and Gjermund Høyme. All were members of the committee negotiating the merger. Høyme went from being president of the Conference to president of the United Church. T. H. Dahl would succeed him on his death in 1902. Their friendship was old and tested. They still remembered Weenaas fondly and had sided with him against Sverdrup and Oftedal. While they were leaders in the Conference, until talks of a new church began, they were also dominated by Sverdrup and Oftedal and had suffered several defeats in some vicious intermural disagreements in the Conference at the beginning of the decade, as noted in the previous chapters.

From the outside, Augsburg Seminary looked to profit the most from the merger. It would become the seminary of these three church bodies. Augsburg would gain an expanded faculty, including two distinguished professors, Bøckmann and Schmidt, with long associations with the Norwegian Synod but who now belonged to the Anti-Missourians, and one from the Norwegian Augustana Synod, David Lysnes (1832–1890), who unfortunately died before the school began, as well as Sverdrup and Oftedal from the Conference. This made for an accomplished seminary faculty. Things looked good for the proposed new church on all counts.

People around the church shared the excitement. Layman H. Bottelsen and Pastor Høyme had traveled to the western parts of Minnesota on the first of May 1890 and held meetings in Montevideo and the small congregations around it. Bottelsen reported on the excitement of people looking forward to the union meeting in Minneapolis the next month. Most encouraging had been the meetings where Høyme had preached to great acclaim. Without a doubt, the Jacobsons heard him preaching. His text was "Is Your Name Written in the Book of Life?" It was a powerful sermon and made people glad for the new church.[3]

Some were still apprehensive. Pastor Ole Paulson admitted in a column from Blanchardville, Wisconsin, where he now served a congregation, that one could view the coming union meeting in Minneapolis with a mixture of hope and fear.[4] Most worrying to him was what kinds of attitudes the Anti-Missouri Brotherhood would bring with them. He hoped that the prophets who were prophesying failure were wrong. He clearly was responding to opinions abroad in the church.

Although Sverdrup had been a leader in the negotiations, he had not been an enthusiastic proponent of the merger, nor did he think that everything had been settled by the time of the merger. He believed that Norwegian Lutherans were already one in faith. The questions of polity and theological education were the issues that he feared would split them. He was right about this.

These events, however, have a way of sweeping everyone along in the pent-up desires for such a union. It is almost standard the way these negotiations go: disagreements seem petty and in the way of progress, especially to the winners of the battles, who often become the leaders of the new church. They use biblical language about peace and harmony to stifle opposition. John 17 and Jesus's high priestly prayer have always been used to make it seem as though Jesus in the garden was praying that Lutherans in the United States would merge.

This is hardly what Jesus meant, but one cannot fight pious logos, fluttering in halls, "that they might be one" without seeming blasphemous. It is possible to be one in faith but not one in a church structure. The enthusiasm of the pro-union group has a way of making dissenters feel guilty for not wanting what Jesus prayed for. However, as veterans of these mergers can attest, unsettled matters will rise up in the new organization and cause, if not schism, troubles that rarely are resolved but simply swept aside by the new establishment.

In the documents presented to the congregations for approval before the merger could be consummated, there were two articles of union that were not sufficiently clear, Articles 10 and 23. Helland quotes a few more to give a better context to the debate (original numbers in parentheses):

1. A training school for pastors shall be founded and operated.
2. This training school for pastors shall be Augsburg Seminary in Minneapolis.
3. (7) The new church body should be incorporated as soon as possible.
4. (8) To this incorporated body shall be transferred all school property—both real estate and endowment fund—to the aforesaid church bodies may be in possession of.
5. (10) The preparatory departments at Augsburg and Red Wing Seminaries, and the Academy in Canton (SD) shall be operated in the same form as heretofore, at least one year after the union has been consummated.
6. (23) The Boards of Trustees of the respective church bodies, as they have heretofore been elected by them, shall continue to function after the union has been consummated, until the new church body has been incorporated after which they shall immediately transfer by deed to the new corporation all the property which they hold as Boards of Trustees.[5]

What it meant for the preparatory departments to operate at least one year after the union was not clear. It seemed to be a place where lack of clarity gave opportunities for Augsburg opponents to close Augsburg's preparatory department. For the Augsburg party, this was a clear threat and nonnegotiable. To close down the preparatory department would, in essence, given the Augsburg plan, close down the seminary and at the very least nullify Sverdrup's curriculum. Further, they discovered that the notion of transferring property was legally much more complicated than the union committee, or the Augsburg party, had foreseen. These became insurmountable issues, conveniently, for the Friends of Augsburg, who used legal warfare when arguments no longer worked. So both sides finally had to resort to the courts.

## Festival Events in 1890

That June, the three organizations came together with much excitement. The Anti-Missouri group gathered at St. Paul's Hauge Lutheran Church in the Seven Corners neighborhood, the Norwegian Augustana group at Augsburg Seminary. All three had to pass the appropriate resolutions ending their organizations and enabling the formation of the new church. The Conference, meeting at Trinity, closed its existence with a hymn by Graumann, "My Soul, Now Bless Your Maker." After a prayer by Oftedal, the group prepared to welcome the

**Figure 5.4.** Main building at Augsburg Seminary. Used by permission of Augsburg University Archives.

representatives from the Anti-Missouri folks and Norwegian Danish Augustana, who had processed from their respective gatherings to Trinity Church. When they arrived, the group, over one thousand, sang lustily "God's Word Is Our Great Heritage" and then the first stanza of the Kingo hymn "Praise and Thanks and Adoration" ("Lov og takk og evig ære"). Together they prayed the Lord's Prayer, confessed the Apostles' Creed, and then left in a parade out the door on their way to Swedish Augustana Lutheran Church on Seventh and Eleventh, which was a much larger building. Pastor M. Falk Gjertsen of Trinity congregation, and the Conference, was the marshal. When they arrived, the group sang "A Mighty Fortress Is Our God." Oftedal was elected temporary chair of the meeting.

The first action of the convention was to elect Høyme president. He won over his competitors by a wide margin. Høyme was an impressive character. His figure loomed in all these debates. The *Saint Paul Globe* in 1895, after most of the strife was over, gave a somewhat lengthy sketch of the man about whom they had been writing extensively during the past three years. A pastor in one of the key parishes of the church in Eau Claire, Wisconsin, he had been born in Valdres, Norway, in 1848. His family had immigrated in 1851. He was the youngest of twelve children. They moved to a place near Decorah. Very soon after they came, his father died, leaving his wife and family in poverty.

Høyme began studying at the Marshall Academy, the University of Wisconsin, and then Augsburg Seminary, from which he graduated in 1873, some months before Oftedal arrived. This had been a key year in the beginnings of Augsburg. Høyme was ordained and called to serve as pastor in Eau Claire that same year. He built his congregation into a very lively and prosperous one and served as secretary of the Conference from 1881 to 1886. During this time, he became a strong and forceful member of the old school that had developed at Augsburg after Oftedal's Public Declaration. He had written down the thirty points that marked the split. Then he was elected president of the Conference in 1886–1890, serving until the merger, when he was elected president of the United Church. He was considered among its most eloquent preachers, with a kind of poetic, even flowery, flair, not surprising since he did write poetry now and then. He was tall and handsome, "straight as a pine; but his magnificent dark hair and whiskers make one think of an ancient Hebrew rather than a modern Norwegian," the paper commented.[6]

He would become the nemesis of Sverdrup, especially, who opposed him when he ran for president of the United Church again in 1893. Although he had worked closely with Sverdrup and Oftedal on projects such as the establishment of Deaconess Hospital in 1888–1893, he seemed to have grown weary of the duo by the time of the new church.

Contrary to Høyme and others, Sverdrup liked conflict. It was a way of cleansing the church, he said. He preferred walking in blizzards against the wind to sitting at home in peaceable retirement. This wearied many of Sverdrup's colleagues. Høyme quickly saw his new allies in the Anti-Missouri Brotherhood and among the Norwegian Augustana leaders as perhaps a way to prevail over the dominance of Sverdrup and Oftedal. He was in the prime of his life at this moment. Although he became ill and wanted to quit earlier, he continued as president until he died in 1902 from his lingering illness.

## First Day of 1890 Meetings

After singing and prayer, the deliberations of the first meeting of the United Church began. Attendees hoped the churches could put aside their strife and gather to do evangelism and mission more effectively than before. The hurrahs, however, had barely died in the throats of the supporters of the union before a serious conflict arose between Augsburg leaders and the leaders of the new church. The issues were almost exclusively about Augsburg: What kind of a seminary was it? What was its role in the new church? And what was its relationship to St. Olaf?

In the founding documents of the United Church, Augsburg had been named the seminary of the church, putting an end to St. Olaf Seminary but not its college. What was the place of St. Olaf College in the church? This began a conflict that could not be resolved. The main issue was Sverdrup's commitment to a school with three departments: preparatory, college, and seminary.

The problem became clear when the annual meeting proposed two resolutions to which Sverdrup objected. One resolution directed the board of Augsburg Seminary to agree on "the necessary regulations with respect to the division of labor among the theological professors at the school."[7] Sverdrup opposed this with all his might. He thought it infringed on the role of the faculty as guardians of the curriculum. He also worried that it directed its attention only to the seminary program and not the preparatory school and college, which Sverdrup had made integral to the others.

This was at the heart of the theological debate. Sverdrup would argue persuasively, and had over the past years to the Augsburg contingent, that the church could not achieve unity if the pastors had gone to different preparatory schools or colleges for their theological education. If there was going to be unity in the church, the pastors needed to be educated according to Augsburg's plan, from the preparatory school through their graduation from seminary. This notion about the curriculum for preparing pastors was at the root of the entire debate. It tragically degenerated into a legal battle about property and ownership.

Supporters of St. Olaf could not agree with Sverdrup. They believed Augsburg should not be the only college of the church. They had prepared a resolution stating that St. Olaf College at Northfield, Minnesota, "shall be the college of the United Norwegian Lutheran Church."[8] Fevold noted that the St. Olaf contingent thought of this resolution as a gift to the United Church, but its substantial debt and uncertain stability made it look less like a gift to the Augsburg party than a gift horse, one that needed the merger to survive. In any case, it was a clear threat to Augsburg's educational plan and even its existence. The Augsburg contingent ferociously opposed the motion. Others thought that Augsburg should not be the only college of the church, disagreeing with Sverdrup's notion about the full Augsburg program.

Sverdrup's program was well understood by Augsburg supporters. When Augsburg had been in trouble, its supporters around the church had given sacrificially to support Augsburg since it promised a radically new education for a new kind of pastor fit for the American context. It was the one nonnegotiable they brought to the table. Disagreeing with Sverdrup's curriculum might be one thing, but making the institution transfer its property and, with it, control of the school—and by doing so, eliminating Sverdrup's plan—seemed like more of a hostile takeover than a compromise to the Augsburg supporters. While the debate at first centered around the program, the Augsburg supporters began to see it as a power play on the side of the St. Olaf supporters—if not a takeover of the whole church, at least an effort to damage Augsburg's place as the church's sole theological enterprise, no matter what the establishment, led by the old-school veterans, said.

These surprise resolutions shocked the Augsburg party. They had known nothing about them, they claimed, until they appeared on the floor of the convention. This had the effect of humiliating them by not keeping them in the conversations. Not surprisingly, the convention broke into open and bitter conflicts that would not bear good fruit.

John A. Bergh (1847–1927), one of the students at Marshall when Weenaas was struggling to keep the school alive, tried to formulate a compromise by suggesting that the convention approve the resolution to make St. Olaf the college of the church with the same good feelings as it had adopted Augsburg as its seminary. His proposal brought the house to call for the question, and before anyone could stop it, the resolution to adopt St. Olaf as the college of the church passed by acclamation.

None of this was quite yet writ in stone since the 1891 convention would be the place where the church would be incorporated. Augsburg and the other preparatory schools were to stay as they were until the next year's convention. The festivities continued despite this surprising development. Ole Paulson described the entire week of meetings in two articles for *Folkebladet*. His description of the final worship service indicates that joy overshadowed the storm cloud the size of a man's hand on the horizon. The meeting adjourned, and "an hour later flocks of men and women, young and old, came together for the meeting on the east side of the river near the University to a place called by the Latin name, Coliseum. The building resembles an immense, great open umbrella, designed so that song and music sounds very good. When all had gathered there were probably about 5000 people in the building which can hold 6000. The program consisted of song and speeches."[9]

Professor John Dale of Luther Seminary led the singing with a choir of some sixty pastors, while the well-known Norwegian American Lutheran organist in the city, Hallvard Askeland, accompanied. Høyme told the crowds to "go home, pastors and lay delegates, and let the church bells ring from all the steeples—ring so loud that they echo among the Norwegian fields and tells the mother church that the emigrants, her separated sons and daughters, have found one another!"[10] There was rejoicing and gladness among the crowd as they made their way home with hope and courage in the future. Paulson found it amusing to see the people scrambling down the hill, "almost crawling like snails up and down the banks over stumps and stones." He wondered why on earth such a building had been built in that location as he watched lines of people walking on the railroad tracks to the depot, running to the side when they heard a train coming.[11] He was very optimistic about the new church, although in hindsight one can see his sense that problems could develop. But *Folkebladet* until the end of 1890 was calm and advocating for the new church.

These feelings of joy permeated the church from Minneapolis to its farthest reaches and smallest congregations. Minutes of the meetings of the new districts were published. All of them pondered the meaning of the new church. The Montevideo district where the Jacobsons lived had a meeting in November, which spent a day on theological talk about the church. The topic was treated with the best of Luther's notions about the congregation. It looked peaceful and edifying. Several local pastors led the meetings. The Jacobsons' pastor, Ole Guldbrandsen (1855–1914), was a leader of the meeting. St. Petri, a church he served in Lac Qui Parle County, would be dedicated during their conference. After a report from the Malagsy mission read by a pastor, the meeting raised over sixty dollars for missions.

At the end of the meeting, a worship service was held in the church that was about to be dedicated, at which there was communion. Eriksen, the first pastor of Brønø, led the confession and absolution portion of the service. Oftedal preached. After the service, an offering to help pay the debt of the church was held, and eighty-four dollars were raised. After the offering, Oftedal sang a Gunnar Wennerberg psalm, as was his wont. The people left satisfied and encouraged by the preaching. To them, it felt like the United Church was much the same as the Conference.

After the festive meetings in June 1890, Ole Paulson wrote that he felt as though he had been at a wedding feast. At the same time, he wished that the Anti-Missouri folks who had "sailed in the same boat as Missouri" would have less strife and more "hugging: like the hugging boxers used before their fights."[12]

*Folkebladet,* which, like all newspapers, loved to report on conflicts, had none to report on. Columns on the history of Leif Erickson or short stories filled up the next issues of the paper. Political news about the latest election and advice on farming continued. The only slight notion of difficulty was contained in Sverdrup's two columns on his wish that the Hauge Synod had joined the United Church. One can hear in his articles that he had been quite disappointed about its withdrawal from the negotiations at the last minute.

*Folkebladet* does report, however, that soon after these United Church merger festivities, Sverdrup remarried in August 1890. It was his second marriage. Like many men in such situations, including Weenaas, he married his first wife's sister, Elise Susanna Heiberg.

## Erickson Letter

While things seemed on an even keel, storm clouds were gathering. January began a series of explosions against Augsburg that baffled its supporters. In the January 21, 1891, issue of *Folkebladet,* Paulson's regular column referred to a letter from a seminarian named A. Erikson. Most infuriating, extraneous, and damaging to the Augsburg side, it had first been published in the January 7, 1891, issue of *Skandinaven,* a Chicago paper. "A. Erickson" turned out to be the nom de plume for Albert Erickson Egge, a professor at St. Olaf. Erikson claimed to have received the letter from an Augsburg student, who said that Augsburg was a nest of anti-intellectuals who opposed rigorous study of anything, allowing students to take whatever they wanted, even permitting Greek and Latin to be optional rather than requirements. The fact that the letter was poorly written, some thought on purpose, only proved the point that Augsburg was not a very good school, unworthy to be the college of the new church. This started accusations that lived on—that Augsburg was a bunch of pious fools and, from the other side, St. Olaf was a bastion of anti-Christian liberal humanism.[13]

Not until January 28, 1891, did *Folkebladet* answer the charges. The paper supposed it was a student from the Anti-Missourians who had written the letter. That other papers, *Norden* and *Amerika*, two influential secular Norwegian American papers, joined the fracas made the writer think it was an organized attack. *Folkebladet* discounted the letter and its supporters, calling *Amerika* Pastor Vilhelm Koren's organ and saying that it had published its piece the same day as *Skandinaven* had printed the Egge letter.[14] Augsburg had weathered many storms before, and it was in the same good hands as it had been and would weather this one as well.[15]

The letter began to turn the debate into ad hominem arguments against the personalities on each side. Augsburg's faculty, which was as stellar as any in the Norwegian American community and maybe even more so, was stung by the accusations. Against all one might expect, the Augsburg professors demanded students sign papers swearing that they had not sent the letter to Erikson.[16] This went against everything Sverdrup and Oftedal said they believed. *Freedom* was their watchword. That they felt pressed enough to do this was a sign of how bad the situation had become. As many a loser in such a debate discovers, trying to prove one is not something is impossible.

Some two weeks later in the February 18, 1891, issue of *Folkebladet*, Friederich August Schmidt published a column attacking his Augsburg Seminary colleagues and the Augsburg party for not holding to the agreement they had signed saying that after one year, the situation of the preparatory schools would be reconsidered. While his argument against the Augsburg party made some sense, it could have been less incendiary. He closed the article by saying that Augsburg's plan that a student study for nine years with the same professors had the effect of making them "uniform, immature and one-sided."[17] Hans Urseth's brother remarked many years later that it was Schmidt who had really caused the schism.[18]

*Folkebladet* exploded, as did the rest of the Norwegian American press. The next years would be a dreary season of accusations back and forth. If the leadership, Sverdrup and Høyme, for example, seemed to be moving toward a settlement, the Augsburg constituency, having read the arguments in the press, began to feel that they had been had deceived by the St. Olaf partisans. They could not brook the idea of a compromise. This made it difficult to achieve any settlement, even if they had wanted to. Naturally, the Norwegian American press, especially *Skandinaven* and *Folkebladet,* covered these debates with great interest. Their readers knew pretty much which side the papers were on.

The Yankee press in the Twin Cities avidly covered the events as well. They knew their readership had many Norwegian readers, so they reported extensively on each step in the conflict, meeting by meeting, fairly sympathetic to Augsburg. The reporters, who obviously understood Norwegian, clearly got a good sense of the debate. Since they knew both Sverdrup and Oftedal well and thought of them as distinguished and accomplished men, they tended at first to see things from Augsburg's point of view.

## The 1891 Annual Convention

The 1891 national convention of the United Church was in Kenyon, Minnesota. Sverdrup's report as president of Augsburg accepted the authority of the United Church over the school while arguing passionately for his notion of what a seminary should be. For him, the Augsburg plan was "the only way to assure the theological department [had] a sufficient number of adequately trained students."[19] In addition, the church could not begin to change an established educational program given its somewhat precarious financial and institutional standing at the time. To many, this sounded conciliatory and gave hope to those who wanted a resolution to the conflict.

While it may have been conciliatory in the eyes of the Augsburg party, Høyme, for his part, appeared to overwhelmingly favor St. Olaf, proposing that the United Church give the college $7,000 and Augsburg $4,500. On the surface, it looked partisan, but things were a bit more complicated. Augsburg had a larger endowment at the time, though how liquid was not clear. The numbers by themselves proved to the Augsburg party, and its supporters reading the papers in the country, that Høyme was hopelessly partial to St. Olaf, especially when the convention enthusiastically approved the amount.

One can see clearly in this battle the old-school/new-school split. Former old-school losers were rising into dominant positions, now able to take their revenge. One can mark it by the names of the antagonists. The most vociferous opponents of Sverdrup and Oftedal in the new church would turn out to be Weenaas's former students, leaders in the old school of the Conference—Johan Olsen, T. H. Dahl (1845–1923), Høyme, and so on. They all had suffered the fury of the response to Oftedal's "Public Declaration." They agreed with Weenaas, who had retracted his support of the Declaration, even as he had published a book that same year against Wisconsinism that was even more virulent than Oftedal's.

Added to this, the Anti-Missourians, who had lost respect for Herman Preus and Ulrik Vilhelm Koren theologically, could not forget they had previously been targets of some of the slings and arrows from the Conference, and especially Sverdrup and Oftedal, in their parries against the Norwegian Synod.

The Augsburg party without a doubt thought it was a conspiracy, whether it was true or not, although given the dramatis personae, it is hard not to think so in retrospect. Even if there was no actual plot, the opinions of these opponents of Sverdrup were suspiciously alike.

Sverdrup would not relent on his commitment to a school that involved several years of preparatory work followed by seminary. He thought that one could prepare better pastors if they had been thinking and working together on their calling from the beginning of their education. The St. Olaf professors, especially Egge, and the president of St. Olaf, Thorbjørn Mohn (1844–1899), argued that a good liberal arts education was foundational to any profession, whether doctors, lawyers, or pastors. Mohn made the mistake of implying that Christianity was, of course, assumed at St. Olaf but not specifically required.[20] While this could have been said much more clearly, it was not. This gave the Augsburg party proof against St. Olaf, which they did not overlook. They ran with the accusation that humanism was the basic starting place for St. Olaf.

As many who come from the Augsburg tradition would claim, this argument had good points on both sides, but the virulence of the conversation simply made rational thought impossible. Augsburg taught the humanities as rigorously as Luther College, or St. Olaf, although it spoke about its priorities differently. Augsburg professors thought of themselves as modern innovators building a school fit for the new environment in which it found itself. Sverdrup's arguments were subtle: he called his program Greek, arguing that Greece was the higher culture than Rome, a widely held belief among classicists; Luther College and St. Olaf, he said, were Latin and humanistic (elitist).[21] Greek was the language of the New Testament; Latin was not a biblical language, though fundamental to studies of things Christian and important to the education of a theologian.

Sverdrup was a gifted professor of Hebrew and knew the language well; he had spent time in Paris and had learned French well enough to teach it, besides being an able writer and speaker of German.[22] All told, he was a gifted theologian and scholar in the traditional sense of the day, as one can see in his many volumes of writings.[23] One of his most learned students, John Oluf Evjen (1874–1942), called him "the greatest Lutheran theologian that America has ever had" at a symposium on Lutheranism in 1930.[24]

The Augsburg Catalogue of 1892–1893 made a full argument for the Augsburg program, describing it as something that had been developed to meet the special needs of the congregations of the Norwegian immigrants in the American West. It argued that the preparatory department, which took two years, favored students who were thinking of becoming pastors. The training—the first year in Norwegian, the second in English—was designed to "awaken spiritual life as much as to impart mere religious information."[25] Students who enrolled in these courses could receive a teacher's certificate and were expected to work in the congregations during the summer vacations. This meant as parochial schoolteachers, no doubt.

The college department was described as a classical four-year course of studies that built on the preparatory department. Greek was most important, followed by Latin and German. Since most of the students were already bilingual speakers of English and Norwegian, it made sense to teach them the literature and history of both cultures. Although this was not carried out, there were in this proposal several ideas from Grundtvig's folk high school, especially its emphasis on Nordic origins rather than Greco-Roman ones. In Grundtvig's proposal, one could get an education in one's Nordic heritage, a living tradition with its own classical background, by studying Old Norse and its great literature and history. Grundtvig's fear—that the classical education given the boys at the old Latin schools in Denmark had created an elite class that would be set against the people—was Sverdrup's persuasion as well.[26]

Those graduating from the college department received bachelor of arts degrees. They were then ready to begin studying at the seminary, where they would receive intensive work in the languages of Scripture, history, theology, and practical courses like homiletics. Saying the Augsburg professors and curriculum were not rigorously intellectual was simply untrue, as was the notion that Luther College or St. Olaf was basically humanistic.

In arguing that Greek was a biblical language important for pastors to know, and suggesting Latin instruction created an elite thinker open to free thinking, Sverdrup had a point, but it came to sound like he was entirely against Latin and education in the classics. In his strong defense of his program over St. Olaf, Sverdrup almost proved the case of those on the other side when he argued that humanism could make it difficult for students out on their own to stay close to their Christian faith. Chrislock commented that Sverdrup, in making these arguments, did give his opponents grist for their mill—and somewhat hamstrung the future of Augsburg College as it tried to both defend Sverdrup and go against his plan for a college, which it needed to do by the next decades simply to survive.[27] Sverdrup did see the danger of the new anti-Christian thought emerging from the intelligentsia of the West and thought it needed to be opposed. This was coming from many of his political allies on the left, where he and his family stood in Norway. Svedrup's family in Norway, and especially the government officials, had also made arguments against the way humanist education had created elites.[28] It is hard to see from this vantage point that Sverdrup and many at Augsburg were on the progressive left much like pietists in the old world, given Augsburg's commitments to Prohibition, women's rights, and the congregation.

In May, before the June 1892 annual meeting, a long article by Sverdrup on the school question appeared in *Folkebladet*. There he once again made his case for the Augsburg plan. Clearly, he equated the Norwegian state church with the Norwegian Synod, which he, not surprisingly, also saw in the St. Olaf Lutheran Divinity School and especially the Anti-Missourian party, which had recently emerged from the Norwegian Synod. His question was how Norwegian Lutherans in America could educate pastors to be devout Christians who "understood the hearts of their people, whose call it is to pour oil and wine in the sores of the human heart." This resonated with his pietistic supporters. The subjects for the young seminarian should be "God's Word and the history of humanity." That also meant knowing the necessary languages. If anyone asked how much that should be, he answered "as much as possible." He then made a point that was too subtle for the opponents (and maybe his supporters) to understand: "Each Christian already has in principle all the knowledge one needs, because he is a Christian; for if he has clung to Christ as a poor sinner, he has grabbed onto Salvation and blessedness, so then he has met the one in whom all wisdom and the treasury of knowledge is hidden."[29]

This point could be interpreted to mean that all one had to know was Jesus and nothing else, but it is more spacious than that. It means that one needs to continue to study more and more to know all that is necessary. Augsburg's motto was "the word became flesh." For Sverdrup, that meant that in Christ, one would meet all worldly and spiritual truth, and in him study many worldly subjects, to be a good pastor.

This sounds shocking to those educated on the notion that one should learn everything and not be bound by a commitment of faith. For the liberal Western mind, there is no forbidden knowledge. Sverdrup and his generation had been raised hearing about the time of dead rationalism in the Norwegian churches during the Enlightenment. Hauge's revival railed against this. To Oftedal and Sverdrup, the new science developed by Darwin, especially, and antichurch positions of the intelligentsia in Norway and America were the same thing as the old rationalism of the Enlightenment but in slightly different and more distressing clothing. Sverdrup rightly worried about it.

This sounds restrictive to the modern ear, but one must ask whether or not the schools we built did not in fact lead to exactly what Sverdrup feared. Could one's learning, in fact, lead one astray? Is this development unavoidable and natural? Are there indeed some things we should not learn? He thought so. The question today is whether that could have been avoided or if secularism is a natural outcome of all liberal education: "Too many young men who had gone to the religionless Latin School and its heathen study of literature have fallen . . . or led into the ice cold night of reason, morality and doubt."[30]

Sverdrup was astonished that now his opponents were arguing for the same system as the state church in Norway, with its Latin schools and a university for its pastors' education. He thought it remarkable that an education thought appropriate for the state church would be thought appropriate, indeed the standard, for a free church.[31] All of his energies had been spent on creating a school that would not resemble the schools of the state church and university in Norway.

This point had been made, oddly, years before, when the founders of the Norwegian Synod realized they had to have a seminary in this country since the Norwegian state church and university simply could not provide an educational plan that could prepare a student for the rigors of the new land. Now that Sverdrup was making the argument for his new plan, the other side had to defend the old ways, the status quo. Nuances are what you lose in a brawl like this, but Sverdrup's argument still should be taken seriously.

Fortunately for Augsburg supporters, the issue of transferring Augsburg property to the United Church was legally problematic. A legal opinion had been issued by the law firm Pattee-Bacon in the spring of 1892. It suggested it would be difficult for Augsburg to transfer its properties to the new church because the original board from 1872 had not made provisions for such an action. They argued that since "neither of the boards of trustees could transfer the respective school properties to the United Church without being guilty of 'breach of trust' both boards (The United Church Board and Augsburg Board) should meet and amend their articles of incorporation" so that the members of the boards would all be members of the United Church. Then the delegates to the United Church could convene as members of the Augsburg Corporation at one time and as St. Olaf's at another.[32]

This had been an issue since the founding of the school. Minnesota did not have appropriate laws for incorporation of religious bodies until after Augsburg had been established in Minneapolis. Only if the group of men who constituted that board could meet again and change the legal requirements of the school for this kind of a dissolution, as the Augsburg representatives thought of it, would the transfer be legal. Remarkably, the members of the original board, Ole Paulson, Andrew Tharaldson (1847–1926), T. H. Dahl, K. Olsen, and Amund Johnson (1838–1897), were still alive.

## United Church Convention in 1892

The annual meeting of the 1892 United Church in Dawson, Minnesota, approved the Pattee-Bacon plan, although the Augsburg party vociferously opposed it. It

# Mergers, Disputes, and the Founding

was obvious to them they would lose control of the school if all the members of the convention were to be voting members of the board. The respective boards were to meet by September 1, 1892, and amend the articles so that the proceedings of the next summer would be legal.

Ole Paulson, as the head of the original board, convened a meeting at Augsburg on August 3, 1892. Every one of the original members was there, except for T. H. Dahl, whose absence probably indicated disagreement and avoidance of the conflict. As a leading member of the old school, he had long been critical of Sverdrup and Oftedal. Before the meeting, Paulson had gotten the opinion of another law firm, Jackson and Atwater, which disputed the Pattee-Bacon plan. They had three reasons:

1. It would cause a confusion of the two boards' affairs.
2. The corporation membership would be too unwieldy and changing to maintain any continuity.
3. Emergency meetings would simply be impossible, given the nature of the boards as convention delegates.

The Augsburg side agreed with this opinion for obvious reasons. Examined under klieg lights, however, these reasons also seem sound. As the lawyers argued, it would be impossible to again call together the entire voting body of a previous annual meeting.

## 1893

The actions of the 1892 convention of the United Church began to threaten the unity of the new church. Storm clouds gathered as the disagreements grew shriller and more desperate.

The convention of 1893, held in Minneapolis, was a watershed for both the United Church and the Augsburg party. At the previous year's convention, the decision was made to have a congregational referendum on the question of whether the church should have power to control the board of the two schools— the preparatory program at Augsburg and St. Olaf College—or, if not both, to decide on which one the church should support.

For Oftedal and the Augsburg board, this was tantamount to nullifying any other prior agreements they had made. Until the results of the referendum were known, it would be impossible to proceed. This meant that over the year 1892–1893, congregations that had been part of the old Conference, the largest part of the new church, held vigorous debates about the place Augsburg and Sverdrup's ideas about schooling had in the new church. They cast their votes with a great deal of knowledge of what was at stake.

In his lecture on the history of Augsburg to the November 1893 meeting of what became the Friends of Augsburg, Christian Saugstad reported that Høyme did not reveal the results of the vote when Oftedal asked for them after December 31, 1892.[33] The numbers were not announced until well into the June business meeting. Since he had known the results for some time, this was regarded by the Augsburg party as treachery. They had been called on to save Augsburg from disasters many times before. Now, the issue for the Augsburg supporters was whether they should support its dissolution.

The June 7–14, 1893, annual meeting of the United Church was at the Swedish Tabernacle (later First Covenant Church in Minneapolis), which could hold the large number of delegates and observers attending the meeting. Several tents had been set up by businesses and congregations for the convenience of the delegates: a concession where a temperance lady gave out temperance drinks, the publishing house's booth selling books and materials, and the St. Luke's congregation's large tent, where attendees could buy fruit and snacks, with a large dining facility in the back.

The delegates numbered about five hundred, with two hundred of them pastors. T. H. Dahl of Stoughton preached the opening sermon on Psalm 50:2, "Out of Zion, the perfection of beauty, God hath shined." The sermon, which a reporter described as "able, scholarly and highly edifying," focused on the beauty of the congregation, something even the reporter found oddly incongruent with the terrible conflicts raging in the group.[34]

President Høyme's report was long. The church was growing and flourishing, and there was a new American version of the Landstad hymnal ready to be presented for approval, including several hymns by Gjertsen, Biørn, and Wright. Mission work was expanding, especially in Madagascar. He could not, however, glide over the Augsburg question.

After some organizing business and a brief debate about secret societies, the convention got to the Augsburg question, the real issue of the meeting. Høyme revealed the results of the referendum. Five hundred and eighty-two congregations had participated in the vote. Five hundred and fifty-seven of them voted to have the church support only one preparatory school. Of those favoring the one preparatory school, 404 favored Augsburg, 138 St. Olaf, and 15 demurred. Other contingencies made reading the results rather like reading a murky crystal ball. Of the congregations favoring Augsburg, a clear majority also agreed that their vote was unenforceable if Augsburg transferred its property to the new church. A minority (165) voted unconditionally for the educational plan that Sverdrup had developed.

Høyme proposed a solution to the conflict with a five-point plan:

1. The United Church would neither recognize nor support any school that was not under its control.

## Mergers, Disputes, and the Founding

2. The United Church should maintain and operate only one college.
3. The United Church should revoke its resolution to adopt St. Olaf as the United Church college.
4. The United Church should continue to support and maintain Augsburg, providing it followed the Pattee-Bacon plan.
5. a. Under no circumstances would the United Church use monies it could find in the Augsburg property to pay its debts;
   b. Augsburg Seminary's college would remain the preparatory institution of the seminary and operate as it had been operating;
   c. The United Church endowment fund would be used exclusively for the payment of Augsburg theological professors' salaries.[35]

Høyme hoped this would calm down the Augsburg party and give the church a chance to put the conflict behind it. He conspicuously failed.

This proposal seemed innocent enough, except for the requirement to follow the Pattee-Bacon plan. The suspicions that had been building meant there was little good faith between the two parties. Whatever there might have been vanished completely when the committee preparing the president's resolutions based on his report added two more points: authorizing the United Church board to make minor concessions to the Augsburg board, but on the other hand, if the Augsburg board did not do so, the United Church should make arrangements to move its divinity school and provide for its support until the next convention. The threat in the last point could not be talked away by the St. Olaf side, which seemed to think that it would not be an issue since the Augsburg party would accept the first resolution.

The reporter for the *Minneapolis Tribune* noted the drama of the meeting as he listened in hushed expectancy for the report of the committee. It had appeared to be conciliatory on the transfer of the property to the United Church and at the same time threatening to build another seminary if it did not. Delegates erupted. Oftedal made a motion that "the United Church hereby authorizes the board of trustees in connection with a committee appointed for that purpose, to negotiate with the board of trustees of Augsburg Seminary, with the view of settling a question transferring Augsburg Seminary in a peaceful and brotherly manner and to the satisfaction of the parties concerned."[36]

The resolution evoked strong expressions of emotions on both sides, which the paper said theologians might call the "old Adam" but that seasoned observers might see as the old "furor teutonicus," something the German races shared since the days of the Roman empire. "The ministers and professors simply proved themselves to be descendants of their Viking forebears."[37]

When Oftedal asked for a roll call vote so the names of voters and their vote would be recorded, he was shouted down. He shouted back to the assembled,

"This is the last injustice done to the Minority by the Majority of the United Church." The presiding officer, Pastor T. H. Dahl, retorted, obviously irritated by Oftedal, "If anyone is bound to the United Church by such slender ties, he was apt to drop out anyway."[38]

After that outburst, a resolution from Committee No. 1 was acted on: "The United Church will not regard as its school, nor appropriate money for any school which it does not own or control." This further enraged the Augsburg party, which now had what it thought clearly documented proof that it had been right to suspect a secret plot against it. When people in the Augsburg party had urged a postponement of the vote until additional negotiations had been completed, Dahl, who was turning more and more against his former school professors, was quoted as saying, "Why should we wait any longer? The Board has had three years and still they have taken no steps to have the seminary transferred."[39]

After further parliamentary wrangling, the convention got to the two resolutions proposed by Høyme: "The United Church shall support and manage only one college. St. Olaf College shall no longer be the college of the United Church but shall be given back to its original owners." They passed unanimously because the minority refused to vote. The majority thought this should appease the Augsburg party, but it was the next resolution that hedged the supposed conciliation so significantly that it turned the Augsburg supporters implacably against the United Church leadership and made them oppose the first resolution: "The United Church shall manage and support the college department of Augsburg Seminary, provided the seminary be transferred to the United Church before June 30."

The vote was not taken then but was expected to pass when it came before the convention the next day. The notion of the church managing any part of the school's work offended the Augsburg party, which by now had no illusions which way the United Church "management" would go.

In a brief column, something like an editorial, the *Minneapolis Tribune* tried to put the conflict in some historical context, giving a short history of Augsburg Seminary and the merger that had brought the school to this pass. It concluded, "The great majority of the United Church, however, know that they have absolute moral rights to the seminary property and they demand it with increasing vehemency. Too many are inclined to look upon the whole difficulty as a creation of the brain of Professor Oftedal. In fact, he has become so obnoxious to a majority of the church that they might bounce him from his chair of theology."[40]

Many at the meeting blamed the controversy and its increasing bitterness on the press, especially *Folkebladet,* and wanted it, especially, according to one delegate, O. Wilson, "to die a decent death, rather than lead such a wretched life." Another, Pastor Svein Olsen Strand (1852–1945), wondered whether after such bitterness and unkind attacks on one another, "we are justified in calling ourselves a Christian church at all."⁴¹ There was also an implied dig at the Yankee press, especially the *Minneapolis Tribune*, suggesting that the conflict would not have been so awful if the press had not been reporting on it with such glee.

*The Tribune* had obvious connections with Oftedal, who had been an active member of the Minneapolis political and journalistic community. One can hear that respect in their columns and articles. It concluded this column with the comment that "Professor Oftedal has been found in the right and the majority wrong in the past. It is possible that the future may prove him to right now, too."⁴²

Given the spirit of the meeting, and Høyme's reelection as president, which Sverdrup opposed, both Oftedal and Sverdrup tendered their resignations as professors of the United Church but not from Augsburg. Both letters of resignation reveal deep hurt and frustration. They realized that their treatment by Høyme and others had made it almost impossible to restore relations amicable enough for them to work together. Sverdrup's letter noted that it would be impossible for him to work with a board that disagreed fundamentally with him and his ideas about a seminary: "Since the annual convention of the United Church has with an overwhelming majority voted down every motion tending to an amicable settlement concerning Augsburg Seminary, and as this irreconcilable attitude according to my conviction points back to a deep-seated disagreement with the principles for the training of pastors and for church work that is represented by Augsburg Seminary, I am forced to resign as theological professor in the service of the United Norwegian Lutheran Church in America. From December 31 of this year."⁴³

One also has to say that Augsburg Seminary at the time had more money in the bank than St. Olaf College. That the money and property would be transferred to a different school made people who had donated to Augsburg feel betrayed. To them, the Høyme party had used false pretenses to get the money and property, to say nothing of the entire operation.

## Augsburg Publishing House

Three days after the 1893 United Church convention had concluded, there was a memorable kerfuffle at the publishing house. Lars Swenson, longtime trustee, treasurer, and financial leader of the Conference and of Augsburg, had his office in the Augsburg Seminary main building, which served as dormitory, classroom space, president's apartment, and boarding club. It also housed the publishing company of the Conference. It was not known then as Augsburg Publishing House, which it would become, but simply as the Conference's Publishers Union Printer (Konterentsens Forlagsforeningens Trykkeri).

As feelings grew more emotional and threats to the seminary and its buildings seemed more likely, Augsburg officials, most notably Sven Oftedal and newly minted treasurer H. Engemoen, came to the seminary library on June 17, 1893, where Swenson's offices were, according to the complaint. Swenson's complaint alleged that the Augsburg delegation, "forcibly thrusting him [Swenson] from the front of the safe, shut its door and altered the combination, and afterwards deposed Swenson." The question that had to be settled, according to Swenson, reported the article in the *Tribune*, "is whether the publishing house belongs to the church or Augsburg seminary. I have telegraphed the Board of Directors of today's occurrance and a meeting will be held in the city Monday. The church will undoubtedly bring suit for possession of the property and we will win in the end. As to my being deposed as treasurer of the seminary, I have nothing to say."[44]

The safe was said to contain sixty-five thousand dollars in notes and mortgages, ten thousand dollars in accounts, fifteen thousand dollars in accounts due from congregations, and one hundred dollars in cash. In addition, the office had books worth twenty thousand dollars and its printing plant worth some ninety-five thousand dollars. The United Church asked the court to issue an injunction to give up this property and ordered parties to move nothing until the court ruled on the case. Whether these assets could be made liquid was not answered at the time; later, they would be described as mostly just so much paper.

The United Church executives asked that a deputy be ordered to stay there to make sure nothing was "molested" until a settlement was reached. The Augsburg leadership asked the court to remove the deputy, but he was there by order of the court. Augsburg Seminary trustees stood outside the building and guarded it, allowing no one to enter. Later in the morning, Seldon Bacon, an attorney for the United Church, and a deputy sheriff arrived and served Engemoen with a restraining order. Since the doors were locked, no one could enter without a key, which the Augsburg party had. Some among the United Church trustees wanted to force the doors open. Since this would have been illegal and, of necessity, involved some measure of violence, it was not done. The United party left for the courthouse to get a writ ordering the ejection of the watchman from the building.

Professor Oftedal arrived at the school with his attorney, Kolliner, wanting to speak with the attorney for the United Church, who had just left for the courthouse. Engemoen, to the amusement of the crowds milling around, began to take down names of those whom he regarded as trespassing on the property.

When the dust settled, briefly, the United Church sued Oftedal and Augsburg. At issue was who owned not only the publishing business but also the money and bank drafts in the safe. The courts had to make the final decision. Since court proceedings take a long time, there was no resolution for almost a year. This meant sensational coverage through the year. Meanwhile, everything in the church was reaching a boiling point from which it could not return.

Mergers, Disputes, and the Founding 163

Not long after that drama, reported breathlessly by the two main papers in the Twin Cities, the conflict ended up in the courts. It would be a typically long and drawn-out process, giving truth to the adage that the mills of justice grind slowly but exceedingly fine. It would not be until the next summer that a decision was made, but while the trial dragged on, it provided many chances for the papers to review and explain the controversy.

The ultimatum issued by the United Church that Augsburg transfer its property by June 30, 1893, created a crisis for Augsburg Seminary, which came to an immediate head when the Augsburg party met. After a brief meeting at which they refused to transfer the property, they planned for a meeting in November. With this refusal to comply with the deadline of June 30, the United Church carried out its threat and began organizing its own seminary a few blocks away in a vacant building on Sixteenth and Franklin Avenues, with Bøckmann and Schmidt as the professors. This made the schism final in all but the documents.

There was bitterness as Professors Bøckmann and Schmidt gathered their things to move down the street to their new school. *Folkebladet* closely followed the progress of the rogue seminary, ridiculing the opening speeches of Bøckmann and Schmidt. Bøckmann thought of the new venture as simply Augsburg Seminary in another place. At the same opening ceremony, Schmidt said it was a new venture.

Both were on record as having contributed to the melee with their words against the Augsburg professors with whom they had briefly been colleagues. Schmidt, as we have seen, had begun ridiculing Augsburg's original faculty for its narrowness and intolerance of diversity a year before, while still on the Augsburg Seminary faculty. This caused an avalanche of articles, letters, explanations, and clarifications that lasted for the next years.

He had to publicly withdraw some of the more caustic remarks he made against Augsburg at the convention. Along with this, Lars Swenson and others were leaving Trinity to found Bethlehem congregation, understandably so. Swenson, an alderman in Minneapolis, member of the Minnesota Senate, and decorated veteran of the Civil War, must have wanted out after being treated as he was by Oftedal and Engemoen in his office on that fateful day. M. Falk Gjertsen had his hands full with all these meetings and conflicts. When the new seminary started, its student numbers cut into the Augsburg numbers, which meant financial problems for Augsburg.

Congregations began meeting to declare their positions on the situation through the fall. A cold front was sweeping out of the Dakotas over Minnesota, with flurries and temperatures well below freezing when the Brønø congregation met on November 17, 1893. It was some days before the meeting of the Friends of Augsburg in Minneapolis, and they wanted their vote to be reported at the meeting. They reported to the December 6 *Folkebladet* that they had passed three resolutions: (1) The congregation would support Augsburg Seminary as far as it was able; it passed 13-3. (2) Furthermore, the congregation felt it had no obligation to support the United Church in its efforts to pay off its debt until things had settled down. That passed by a vote of 10-5. (3) Finally, they voted to send these resolutions to *Folkebladet* and the church.

The conversation in the little church on that cold November day must have been intense. The Jacobsons, and maybe even their three oldest sons and daughter, Peder, Mathilda, Johan, and Richard, who would have been old enough to vote, were there. Certainly, their neighbors attended. Most of them knew Paulson especially well, and to some extent Oftedal and Sverdrup, who had visited their congregation on several occasions.

They were all reading the minutes of these meetings in *Folkebladet* along with the comments of Sverdrup, Oftedal, and others of their leaders. *Folkebladet* bristled with comments from correspondents, editorials, and columns on these events. *The Minneapolis Tribune* and *St. Paul Globe* carried reports, and although the immigrants could not always read English reports, enough of them could read those accounts.

While *Folkebladet* continued to publish news of the world and political news from both the nation and nearby states, the focus was the impending split and the hurtful things that were being said by each side. People in the congregations far away were well aware of what was going on and could feel for their friends, the professors, whom they knew and supported with their prayers and gifts.

The Augsburg professors had cultivated in their supporters the notion that Augsburg was "our school." For some former Conference congregations and individual members who belonged to these congregations, that notion apparently still held firm. The intimate connections the leadership had forged between the idea of the school, its curriculum, and the congregations were difficult to break. Furthermore, the people innately understood Sverdrup's argument about a seminary having to do something different from the Norwegian state church educational practices. Even if they might have decided against Sverdrup's argument that there could not be another proseminary school or college, by this time, they had supported it, suffered for it, and cared about it as their own. Any threat to it was a threat to them.

## Friends of Augsburg Meeting November 1893

The Friends of Augsburg met in Minneapolis on November 21-23, 1893. Seldom had the city suffered such a cold spell so early as it was experiencing during the first official meeting of the Friends of Augsburg. Lake Minnetonka had frozen quickly, so it was as smooth as glass as far as the eye could see, the paper reported. One could see sun dogs shining on the horizon as the Friends,

## Mergers, Disputes, and the Founding

about three hundred strong, emerged from trains and buggies to get to Augsburg. The gathering briefly visited the Augsburg campus and then moved to Trinity Church, where they held their meetings. Pastor M. Falk Gjertsen called the meeting to order. Elias Peter Hansen Harbo (1856–1927), later a professor at the school, was voted secretary.

Christian Saugstad (1838–1897), one of the few new-school men who had not studied with Oftedal or Sverdrup, was voted president of the meeting. Saugstad was a gifted and clear-thinking man, but the conflict grew to be too much for him. By the next spring, his congregation, Bardo Lutheran near Crookston, Minnesota, was so torn up by the conflict led by a follower of B. J. Muus that Saugstad and a number of his members fled to Bella Coola, British Columbia, where they started a colony. Saugstad died an untimely death, probably from overwork on his farm in the new colony, but the tensions caused by the controversy did not help.

Augsburg's grandfather, Ole Paulson, preached the opening sermon on Psalm 122 to the gathering as they began. "Pray for the peace of Jerusalem" was his theme. It made clear that while their opponents needed prayer, so did their own party. Both sides had things to be forgiven for and prayed for.

Oftedal and Sverdrup gave speeches on the unity question, and Johannes Hanson Blegen (1851–1928), a professor at Augsburg, reported on the state of the mission program in Madagascar, something that would become a special sore point in the coming years as Tou and Hogstad, the missionaries the Conference had sent out had been Sverdrup students. Circa 1893, however, both men were active missionaries whose salaries could not be paid until things were ironed out, causing them great suffering. Sverdrup complained about the way the United Church dragged its feet on this support, saying it was easier to find out what was going on in Madagascar than just down the street.

The small group organized committees on foreign and inner missions to deal with the urgent need of these missions for their regular moneys but most significantly an ordination committee for future graduates of the seminary. This was a deal-breaker for the United Church, but the group, looking to the future, felt it was necessary. Students needed to know there was a process for getting them calls to congregations and a procedure for being ordained. This, especially, was an indication the group knew it was going to leave the United Church.

The group wrote a sample resolution for congregations to use to declare their independence from the United Church regarding support of its new seminary. Because the United Church had broken its own rules and was setting up its own seminary, "be it resolved, that this congregation declare itself released from all obligations to support the new theological seminary."[45] Thirteen congregations would pass this resolution, and the United Church ultimately would vote to expel them as of January 1, 1897.

In addition to continuing to have a board for Augsburg, these committees indicated that they were fully prepared to start a new organization as soon as possible. While they were still members of the United Church, this new venture turned them toward a different goal and a different relationship with both the church and especially its new rival just down the street, the United Seminary, as it was called officially, although *Folkebladet* referred to it as the Sakarias's school since the owner of the building was named Sakarias Anderson.[46]

Before they adjourned, the Friends of Augsburg approved a series of propositions that named the conditions they would have to meet before they would make any transfer of property to the United Church. They were essentially demands that the Augsburg board of trustees would continue as theretofore and not be changed—the preparatory program remain, the professors remain, and the property be leased from the United Church for ninety-nine years. Finally, the board wanted to retain control over all the funds and buildings they now owned. A cry of resistance, these propositions would irritate the United Church leadership for the next several years. From Augsburg's point of view, these were simply statements of what they owned and felt was theirs.

Two of the Jacobsons' closest neighbors attended the November Friends of Augsburg meeting: Andreas Herndickson and his son Henrik Norman Hendrickson (1869–1948), a student at Augsburg. Henrik would become a longtime professor at the school. While his son stayed there, Andreas returned to the Brønø congregation with reports of what had transpired at the meeting. Anybody who has been party to these kinds of debates and conversations in the past knows exactly how interested the people in the congregations were in these disputes and, as they discussed and debated, how aware they became of every move and every slight each side received. Each was a wound that could be nursed over the next decades—and was.

Meanwhile, the case involving who owned the publishing house was grinding on in the courts. Lars Swenson, the longtime treasurer for the Augsburg community and the publishing house, had switched sides. One could hardly blame him after the treatment he received at the hands of Oftedal and others in ousting him from the publishing house office. The trial began on December 11, 1893, in the Minneapolis district court. Judge Smith presided. Swenson became a key witness, testifying that he had received no orders from the Augsburg trustees and made his reports to the United Church. This tended to prove that the United Church owned the corporation and the house. The Augsburg side argued that it was their personal property. To keep the peace, the property was replevined (an action taken to recover goods wrongfully taken), and a sheriff had charge over the property. This, said the paper, made things even more exciting.[47]

On December 14, 1893, Sven Oftedal was questioned in court. He translated the documents into English as he was testifying. The paper marveled at his command of the material and noted that his "answers were delivered in a ringing tone that would have sounded to anyone entering the room like an impressive sermon."[48] The defense rested after putting Engemoen, the new treasurer of the publishing house, and Ole Paulson on the stand. In rebuttal, the plaintiff examined T. H. Dahl and Iver Tharaldsen of the United Church. Judge Smith would consider the arguments in January.

Oftedal as the chief witness for the defense argued that the publishing house "was created for the purpose of assisting him in the work, and not for the purpose especially of being the will of the Conference."[49] The reporter did not seem to regard this as a good defense.

That evening, after the trial had adjourned, students held a party to honor and celebrate the work of President Sverdrup, presenting him and his wife with a silver tea service. They wanted to encourage the professors in the face of the bitter attacks coming their way. Part of the entertainment was Oftedal's reading of an anonymous letter from Starbuck, Minnesota, which he read to great merriment. The writer called Oftedal and Sverdrup "thieves, robbers and 'synagogues'" for not transferring the property to the United Church.[50] The case hung until just before the 1894 convention of the United Church.

In late December 1893, an unsigned column in *Folkebladet* titled "Test the Spirits" ("Prøver Aanderne") made the argument that it was the Anti-Missourians, really the Norwegian Synod in sheep's clothing, who had caused the ruckus and had made things worse by joining with the old-school Augsburgians. The writer argued that one could discover who the Anti-Missourians really were by looking at their fruits.

At the trial in Minneapolis concerning the fate of the publishing house, "the old warriors (*stridsmend*)" were all there: Professor Schmidt, Iver Larsen, Professor Bøckman, and some from the old school of the Conference. This courtroom process was, according to *Folkebladet*, whose editors remembered the conflicts of the early 1870s, "something new for the Conference, but the old Synod men were accomplished in these processes as they had gone around the settlements fighting against the Conference."[51]

## 1894

The winter of 1894 began as the previous year had ended, with brisk, cold temperatures as the conflict grew hotter and hotter. It continued to worsen as the courts began their work.

Meanwhile, Octer Jonathan Jacobson (1877–1920) turned seventeen on June 18. He was ready for some kind of further schooling. His older neighbor Henrik Norman Hendrickson, a student at the seminary, would soon be ready to graduate and take a call. The Augsburg Quartet had visited the congregation

**Figure 5.5.** The Jacobson brothers. Right to left: Peder, Octer, Lindor, Richard, and Johan. Used by permission of the Grindal family.

several times, and they knew the men in it. One of them, Bernt L. Sundal, was showing interest in his sister Sylvina. For a young man like Octer, wondering what the future held for him, Augsburg's preparatory program might help him decide what to do with his life. Among other things, he was a good singer, like most of the rest of his family, and would enjoy the required music programs there while taking some formal education.

As he was deciding that summer whether to attend Augsburg, the upheaval among the school's supporters, still known as the Minority and/or Augsburg's Friends, was at full tilt. The annual conference meeting of the United Church made it clear that the refusal of the Augsburg party to transfer its property to the United Church would have dire consequences. Everyone knew it probably meant schism.

Octer Jacobson enrolled at Augsburg in fall 1894 and attended the school for a year, during the most turbulent period in the school's history. He enrolled in the second year of the preparatory school, which was in English, rather than the first year, which was in Norwegian. His course of studies involved what we would today consider quite rigorous: English four times a week, with McGuffey's fifth reader; Norwegian twice a week, with readings, declamations, and compositions; arithmetic three times a week; algebra daily; physiology with a mannequin twice a week; physical geography three times a week; religion three times a week using Belfour's *Epitome of Pontoppidan's Explanation*—in English, this version reduced the original 703 questions to many fewer; US history twice a week, with written work on selected topics; and civil government twice a week. Each student took vocal music one hour a week. This was a typical high school curriculum at the time. Why Octer did not continue his studies is not part of family lore, but he probably had other interests than the ministry. Not long after he returned to Montevideo, he joined his older brother Richard in his construction business.

His oldest brother, Peder, had established a business as blacksmith in Montevideo—his shop is now in the Heritage Village there. Octer's older sister, Mathilde, had married Richard Hanson in 1893. Richard was a close neighbor whose family had also come from Brønnøysund, Norway, in 1873. Richard and Mathilda had bought her grandfather's land when he returned to Norway after the death of his wife, Nicolina, who is buried in the old Brønø cemetery in Montevideo. Richard had begun a business as a carpenter with the help of Octer. Richard would be a mainstay of the LFC congregation, Trinity, in town. When Octer returned from Augsburg in 1895, most of his siblings would still be living on the farm or in the area. They were slow to marry and leave home, many still living together on the farm at the 1900 census. The youngest, Inanda, would complain bitterly that she had to stay home and take care of her parents rather than go to school.

## The 1894 Annual Conference

The annual conference of the United Church in 1894 simply confirmed the deterioration of the relationship and possibilities for compromise. Much of the conflict now gathered around legalities. The new seminary down the block, using the same educational plan as Augsburg, with a preparatory program and college, had made inroads on the number of graduates Augsburg had that year. Only three students graduated that May from Augsburg's college department.

Just before the United Church met in convention, Judge Smith handed down his verdict in favor of the United Church, causing elation on that side and depression on the other. The reporter allowed as how most of the pastors and delegates more familiar with issues of soul and salvation did not quite comprehend the mass of complications in the suit, but nevertheless they waded into it. By now the paper was picking up that the majority party vastly outnumbered the minority. Gjertsen admitted the seminary needed to find a way to build a new publishing house. Sverdrup wondered if the minority could stand the situation.

**Figure 5.6.** M. Falk Gjertsen. Used by permission of Augsburg University Archives.

"If they can, I can't," he commented, causing the reporter to wonder if Sverdrup would be leaving Augsburg for good.[52]

The annual meeting of the United Church was held in St. Paul at First Swedish Lutheran Church in early June. The business of the church involved more than the seminary conflict, but it would be the central issue. Headlines in the Minneapolis papers indicated the major topic of the convention would be what to do about parochial schools, but tensions simmered. M. Falk Gjertsen appeared and asked if he could speak and report on what the minority had to say. He was given permission and spoke briefly about the desires of the Minority to come to some conclusions. Nothing more was done that day after his presentation as the convention turned its attention to the great needs of the parochial schools.

On the morning of June 19, however, the actions of the committee assigned to deal with the Augsburg issue reported that it could not and would not deal with the group that Gjersten claimed to represent, "as this meeting represented only individual members of the United Church and does not consist of delegates from churches belonging to the United Church or any other organized body of churches." It went on to say that it could not recognize the board of trustees at Augsburg because it was "unjustly retaining the possession of property justly belonging to the United Church." Furthermore, it could not recognize this group as a minority of the old Conference; it had no right to say it did represent them because they were only a small group from that now defunct organization:

The union of the three bodies of churches has been completed, as shown by their united work during the past four years, a fact which was also recognized by the civil court in handing the publishing house, once the property of the Conference, over to the United Church. The circumstance that the Augsburg Board is unable to deed the Seminary and property over to the United Church because such action is contrary to the laws of the state, does not relieve that board from transferring the said property to the church in a manner that is not forbidden by the civil law, and as long as the board persists in retaining the property, it is doing a grievous wrong to this church.[53]

It continued in language that made it clear it was now a legal issue:

Augsburg Board of Trustees having no legal or moral right to retain the property in questions, the United Church instructs its board of trustees to demand the transfer of said property in the manner prescribed at the annual convention of 1894 and if the Augsburg Board is unwilling to complete the transfer in the manner indicated, then the church makes the demand that the Augsburg Board obey the resolution passed by the 'Conference' to amend its articles of incorporation in such a manner as to give to the United Church the same control as that exercised by the Conference over said institution, in electing the board of trustees for the same.[54]

The convention balked at the tone of the statement, especially the implication that it was going to go to court again. Several motions were made to tone down the original language. The convention came up with the notion that a completely new committee of nine members, who had not been involved in the previous fracases, be asked to meet with the Augsburg board. As Oftedal and Gjertsen were out of town, this did not augur well for the meeting, although the Augsburg board, for the most part, was available.

The next day, the paper reported that as far as anyone knew, the board and committee had been in meetings late into the night, but very little hope for a solution could be found. One worry of the convention, and especially the Augsburg party, was the situation in Madagascar. The Friends of Augsburg from the Conference had strong connections with the Norwegian mission in Madagascar, begun by the Norwegian Mission Society in 1866, ever since the 1870s and the Borchgrevinks' much publicized beginning efforts there. Both missionaries, Tou and Hogstad, had emphatically taken the side of Sverdrup. Hogstad had sent back his letter of call from the United Church and announced his loyalty to Sverdrup and Augsburg. This meant there was no organization that could support them at the time. This frustrated Sverdrup, who, in 1900, began editing a magazine, *Gasseren* (*Malagsy*), about the mission there.

Although the United Church did not prosecute its position during the summer of 1894, things continued a downward slide. With the United Seminary now functioning, Augsburg could continue as it had. Sverdrup noted that after the other professors left Augsburg, things went well, as there was no dissension in the faculty about fundamental issues like the curriculum. This was the year Octer Jacobson joined the student body. Without a doubt, his parents were curious as to what he would report. Their sympathies were no secret, and Octer probably shared them as he sat around in the dormitory and cafeteria talking with his peers, many of whom came from strong Conference homes that were now Friends of Augsburg homes.

## Twenty-Fifth Anniversary

The year 1894 was the twenty-fifth anniversary of the founding of Augsburg Seminary. The Friends of Augsburg marked the occasion with a festive celebration. The program began on October 10 at Trinity. Pastor Christian Saugstad called the meeting to order, but Sverdrup was elected permanent chair of the meeting. It heard a long report from Gjertsen on the state of the conversations between Augsburg and the United Church. Nothing had come of the deliberations. Gjertsen suggested Augsburg was now on its own. Oftedal presented his report on the legal suit concerning the publishing house and the new United Seminary in its neighborhood.

The credentials committee of the Friends of Augsburg meeting reported that 48 congregations were represented in the group; 50 had come as Friends of Augsburg, 50 more as unaffiliated but interested. Thirty-six clergy were there, as were 30 Augsburg students. That meant about 240 had gathered for the meeting. Oftedal made the motion that everyone in the group, including the students, be named as members with voting rights.

The festival worship service was scheduled for Wednesday October 10, at 10:00 a.m. at Trinity. Gjertsen preached. His sermon, eloquent as usual, summed up the situation. I translate his conclusion to give the flavor of his eloquence and to show the nub of the hurt. Gjertsen is colorful and clear about the issues: The United Church was saying that

> Augsburg was not good enough, now it can be improved and changed. And what was it they said was needed. Not Christian seriousness, piety, fear of God, zeal, that was needed, no, they said that Augsburg did not have enough worldly knowledge to make good pastors and the pastors that it produced were lower class and peasants.

The strife would not go away. Augsburg asked if it could stay the way it was, like it had been, and work in the same spirit as before, and the fight grew, and Augsburg had to fight for its life. And so came the day to decide, for many of us so hurtful, and painful, that we were asked to choose between the old, tried, and beloved school and a new and unknown one, and people called to us from all sides, Leave Augsburg! It is not to be wondered at that we with sadness and tears asked, What wrong has Augsburg done that we should leave it? Augsburg is the same now as before, the same well-known teachers, the same spirit of the school.

When my mother who has borne me and raised me is hit in the face by enemy hands is it honorable and filial of me to hide? Or to lift my hands against her, too? No, that is the time to clasp hands and form a ring around her. And that is, therefore, why we are assembled here today. I see a small flock of old, well-known faces in this gathering. It is not many, but it is very encouraging to see you here today. These are the old guards, the old veterans who from the beginning have held out against the storms and bad weather until this moment. The ice is breaking, now, it is toward evening, and the day is ending, but yet a little time and we will find rest. But I see another and larger host, it is a host of young men whom Augsburg has raised up to work among our people here, and that host grows in number and power and the future belongs to them. Augsburg is not childless yet, there are sons enough to raise up. But I also see another and a much greater, larger host. A great host of witnesses around us. Row on row they are, witnesses and saints, angels from the gathering under this roof here today all the way up to the throne, and the place where our King and God is looking down on us, and the numberless witnesses' eyes are upon us. God bless us and keep us faithful and after our work is done let us find a place among the blessed choir of saints.[55]

Gjertsen's eloquence comes through somewhat in this translation. But it also states the reason for the hurt as clearly as anything.

The next speaker, Andreas Helland, at the time the youngest of Augsburg's pastors and, later, the historian of Augsburg, spoke of Sverdrup's critique of the Latin schools of Norway. They put so much stress on the classical culture, he argued, that they train free thinkers: "Augsburg's aim was to combine secular learning with a true Christian life."[56]

Theodore Reimestad also spoke. He was the singer and teacher in the college and a strong advocate of Prohibition. He had run in 1888 as the Prohibition party's candidate for lieutenant governor of Minnesota and was nominated by the party as congressman of Minnesota's Fifth District. In 1896, he became a passionate supporter of Bryan and ran for a place on the Minneapolis Library board.

Reimestad's speech runs contrary to what we might think today. He stressed that Augsburg was progressive and had taken the lead in progressive issues: against hierarchy, as a pioneer in foreign missions, and in the establishment of the Deaconess Hospital and Home: "Strong schools are so apt to become hot beds of conservatism, but it is a dangerous thing to allow oneself to be carried along on the broad waves of conservatism."[57]

Reimestad's speech clearly says that pietism in Europe and in this context was liberal and progressive. The Norwegian Synod and now the old school, with its mixture of Anti-Missourians, were conservatives who wanted to preserve the status quo. Sverdrup and Oftedal's plan was presented as radical and new. Was this the reason it evoked such hatred from the status quo? Through the mists of time and the prejudices of the past century and a half, it could be a new way to see this movement and its rejection.

Pastor Johannes Hansen Brønø, the son of Bendik Hanson, the Jacobsons' nearby neighbor who had been raised with the Jacobson children, also spoke against the conservatives who opposed them. What did Augsburg want?

> Why, we simply want to go right ahead—go right ahead in church and state. It is hard work to go ahead, though, when so many are tugging and pulling at us, trying to keep us back, but we have a strong will, and we must get ahead, though we have to go through showers of bullets, or even death. We have so many conservative preachers. They tell about what happened centuries ago. But they will not condescend to tell Hans and Ola and Carrie how to live. Well, I am somewhat straightforward, but you must excuse me, for I am an Augsburgian, you see.[58]

Trinity was packed that night for the gala concert and program. Some say over two thousand people were packed into the church. Just before the concert, Oftedal gave a brief talk on the history of the school, noting it had always been "under the opposite sign" and always a storm center. But "every time it seemed like it was going under, it was lifted up out of the deep and saved from disaster; and every time it had won the victory, and over the difficulties, the Lord had pressed down on it again so that it would not sink down in sleep and the temptations of the flesh."[59]

At seven thirty, attendees heard a performance of a cantata written by two brothers, Augsburg professor Wilhelm Mauritz Petterson (1860–1932), a poet in his own right, and his brother, a composer. Gjertsen described it as the finest piece of music written by Scandinavians in America up to that point. (The competition at the time was not particularly stiff.) Reimestad sang the tenor solo and

Oftedal the baritone. The paper thought their solos were "highly meritorious and were artistic and effective."[60] Octer, himself a fine singer, must have been impressed by the numbers of people who attended the celebration, as well as the thrilling choirs and congregational singing.

At the closing service on the afternoon of Friday October 12, the Friends of Augsburg, on the basis of a resolution they had passed, ordained Severin Eilefsen Odland (1862–1934) to serve three congregations in Kittson County: Skjeberg, Oslo, and Two River. Although he had applied to be ordained by the United Church, it would not ordain him since he would not swear he would not take the side of the Augsburg party. Pastor Peter Nielsen read the candidate's vita along with Ephesians 4:7–16. Gjertsen preached the sermon on Ecclesiastes 11:30, and the candidate was ordained with prayer and the laying on of hands, "as is the custom and use in our Lutheran Church."[61]

The evening ended with concluding speeches by several pastors and Sverdrup, who thanked the congregation for its hospitality. After a musical number, the convention sang the hymn by Martha Clausen "And Now We Must Bid One Another Farewell" ("Saa vil vi nu sige hverandre Farvel").[62]

These battles, as pitched as they were, did not dampen, and maybe increased, the enthusiasm of the Jacobsons for Augsburg and what would become the LFC.

**Figure 5.7.** Octer and Hilda (Hendrickson) Jacobson. Used by permission of the Grindal family.

Octer came home to work with his brother's construction company in Montevideo and farm, where his father and mother had homesteaded in 1869. He remained there, farming the homestead and contributing to Augsburg and the many causes of the church and school, until his untimely death in 1920 of tuberculosis of the brain. In June 1904, he married Hilda Hendrickson, a member of Immanuel Lutheran Church, the synod church. When she died in 1908, she was buried, surprisingly, in the Norwegian Synod Church, Immanuel Lutheran, cemetery.

Norlie's book on Norwegian congregations, *Norsk Lutherske Menigheter i Amerika 1843–1916 vol. 1*,[63] lists Octer as a trustee, deacon, and treasurer in 1915 in the recently established Brønø Lutheran Free Church, founded in 1904 after it split with its former congregation in 1903. Octer would also serve as janitor and frequently sang duets with his sister Anda at church meetings in the area. If he had been embittered, this would not have happened. In fact, his parents and the rest of the family were, by all accounts, among those who closely followed the debates and conflicts and always remained loyal to the Augsburg party.

## United Church Convention of 1895

When the United Church convention met in session on its first day, June 14, 1895, in St. Paul at the First Swedish Lutheran Church, it refused to seat Sverdrup and Oftedal as delegates from Trinity congregation. Although they had lost their right to be there as seminary professors after they had resigned as professors in the United Church, they had been duly elected by the congregation to represent it.

Some thought this was the end of the turmoil and were glad of it, hoping the church was "forever rid of these breeders of strife."[64] During the debate about whether the church had a right to reject the elected representatives of one of its congregations, intemperate statements were made against the two professors. One old pastor, according to Helland's biography of Sverdrup, had defended the right of the majority to do this, as "the Church certainly must have a right to deny unworthy delegates a seat in the convention, as for instance drunkards and adulterers."[65] Sverdrup's only response, apparently, was a side comment on his way out of the meeting: "This is their hour, and the power of darkness."[66]

The majority hoped the church could then get on with its business. Others thought the silence of the minority only was the calm before the storm. The reporter said he could find no one in the gathering who regretted the action of the church to refuse credentialing the leaders of the Augsburg party: "All seemed to be contented and well satisfied."[67]

Soon, however, Endre Larsen Jaastad (1846–1937) broke the mood. Pastor in Rushford, Minnesota, a Luther College graduate, and a member of the

Anti-Missourian Brotherhood who strongly supported the majority, Jaastad had come to repent of the actions of the meeting to expel Sverdrup and Oftedal. He offered a resolution asking the church to consider whether "we, the members of this church, have not been guilty of some great sin in permitting our matters to come to such a pass that we are compelled to expel some of our formerly most prominent members. I fear we have sinned before the eyes of God and that this is our punishment. Let us consider and try to ascertain where the fault lies. For the sin must be torn out from the midst of Israel before we can have permanent peace."[68] This caused T. H. Dahl, the temporary chair of the meeting, who apparently did not accept the motion, to retort dryly that he thought those who had sinned had need of repentance, but not those who were "unconscious of any wrong."[69]

By this time, the acrimony was clear between the main characters in the dispute, like a civil war between family and friends that was growing internecine and ugly. T. H. Dahl had been colleagues with all his opponents not long before. Dahl's wife, the formidable Rebekkah, was Pastor M. Falk Gjertsen's sister. She would be a leader in the beginnings of the national organization of women in the United Church and in the founding of Lyngblomsten home for the aged in St. Paul.

With that, the meeting went on to discuss parochial schools. Two speakers later, however, Pastor Rasmus Anderson (1853–1914) of Lacrosse, Wisconsin, responded to Jaastad as Dahl had: "I am rather in favor of giving thanks to the Lord that he has guided us out of these serious difficulties and shown us a way to get rid of our troubles. This church has not sinned and it is not necessary to consider any wrongdoings. Let him who thinks he has sinned make repentance to the Lord."[70]

The bitterness continued. The matter of expelling twelve congregations (a thirteenth had dissolved) who had announced they would support Augsburg regardless of the actions of the United Church promised continued dissension. In addition, there was a perceived threat from Gjertsen to pursue the legality of the church refusing to seat delegates from its own congregations, whether they were at one with every decision of the church in convention. It seemed a bottomless cauldron of bad feelings.

On Sunday, June 16, 1895, regular festive services were held, and the evening would be an ordination service for seven candidates for ministry who had at one time been Augsburg students and were now graduates of the new United Seminary. The next day, Monday, June 17, there would be a service exclusively for pastors at which Bøckman would preach, with the service of Holy Communion for pastors only.

Conversations about the tone of the speakers kept thrumming under the business of the meeting. One scuffle broke out concerning ordination. A group of

**Figure 5.8.** Gustav Oftedal. Used by permission of Augsburg University Archives.

pastors in the Minority had, on the authority of the Friends of Augsburg, assisted in ordinations of candidates who had been refused ordination by the United Church because of their commitment to the Minority.[71] The convention wanted those pastors to repent. Then Sven Oftedal's brother Gustav spoke, arguing that pastors were right to do so because "congregations had a right to have ordained the men they called for ministers."[72] This was seconded by Gjertsen, who asserted that "the deacons of any of these congregations can ordain these men, and they will in that case be as well ordained as if 'selveste' President Høyme had ordained them."[73]

The convention reacted strongly against Gjertsen's slur of Høyme. Pastor Halvard Roalkvam (1845–1926), a dyed-in-the-wool Luther College and Concordia Seminary graduate from the Anti-Missouri Brotherhood, rose up and objected to the term *selveste* and moved that the meeting disapprove of the expression. The insult, while almost impossible to translate, implies that the person is prideful or thinks he is special. The objection was quickly seconded and passed unanimously. Gustav Oftedal would be expelled from the United Church on these grounds in 1896. The conversation about ordination resulted in a lengthy paper by Oftedal on the church in the New Testament, delivered

**Figure 5.9.** The Oftedal brothers, Lars, Ommund, and Sven. Used by permission of Augsburg University Archives.

at the first annual conference of the LFC in 1897. I would say it stands up to any that were written for the Task Force for the Study of Ministry of the ELCA in 1988–1993.[74]

On Wednesday, June 19, the convention voted to seat Pastor Knut Bergesen Birkeland (1857–1925), editor of *Folkebladet*. A tone of regret seemed to be felt by some of the delegates who discussed several resolutions declaring that both parties had sinned in their fight over the future of Augsburg. The speeches against such resolutions continued, however, with increasing acrimony toward the Minority. When one milder resolution suggested the United Church might have sinned, even if no evidence of such a sin could be found, Professor Bøckmann vigorously opposed it. When it was watered down enough to state simply that there was sin on both sides, he accepted it because "all of us sin against each other and it is best to deal with that now." The final resolution was milder yet: "The annual meeting requests the individual members of this church to try themselves in order to ascertain if they have in the controversy with the so-called minority been guilty of sinful actions that they reconciliate [*sic*] themselves with their enemy while he is with them."[75]

One of the main concerns of the meeting now was finding property where the United Church could build its seminary. This also hurt the Augsburg supporters. Several prime pieces of property were discussed, none of them where it would finally be built in St. Anthony Park.

At the end of the meeting, as had been expected because of an opinion by Ueland and Cohen, a new board of trustees for Augsburg Seminary was elected by the United Church. The minutes record that this took some time because of the refusal of some to serve and the uncertainty about the process. As suggested, however, the new board was chosen using the old Conference rules and chosen from old Conference people to represent the same regions as the original board had included: one each from Iowa and Wisconsin and three from Minnesota. Those elected were O. O. Aanestad for one year, Lars Swenson and O. A. Veblen for two years, and Nils Christian Nilsen Brun (1846–1919) and L. F. Clausen for three years. Brun would be elected chair. All these men were Conference men. Brun had been with the founding of the Deaconess Motherhouse in Chicago and had become virulently anti-Sverdrup. A student of Weenaas, he had helped teach at the Paxton Seminary and graduated in 1870, long before Oftedal and Sverdrup arrived. Of the old school, he would become a leader in the United Church, editing its twenty-fifth anniversary book, a handsome piece of work.

Meanwhile, the day before, the Friends of Augsburg had filled up the seminary chapel in Minneapolis to discuss their next moves. Given that the church had refused to seat Sverdrup and Oftedal, there was consensus that they needed to build their own church organization: "The more bitter their assailants the more steadfast would they become."[76] This was hardly an exaggeration.

## Mergers, Disputes, and the Founding 181

The next annual meeting of the Friends of Augsburg would be in Willmar on June 26, 1895. They knew it was urgent that they deal with the missionaries in Madagascar and decide about a new church organization. The paper reported that one of the leaders of the group had confided in him that the Minority "did not propose being kicked out of the church but would go before such action would be taken."[77] There was still a slight hope, but not much, that this would not happen.

The Willmar meeting lived in memory for many years, not only for the actions it took, which were significant, but because of the program, which attracted hundreds from the region. We find it difficult to imagine what this looked like before taxis and automobiles. *Folkebladet* described it thus: "Already by Tuesday a large group of people were gathering in Willmar and were immediately taken to their lodgings around the city and its area. Many farmers drove nine to ten miles to the Willmar station with horses and wagons to pick up their guests."[78]

*Folkebladet* estimated over one thousand people sat hour after hour listening to the presentations and debates with interest, most of all the gripping sermons of Lars Skrefsrud, missionary to the Santal people. He had been distressed by the strife and hoped to end it with a compromise that found no takers, but he did not take sides and was warmly received by all Norwegian American Lutherans.

The meeting began in the Willmar Opera House. They began by singing a hymn by Hans Adolph Brorson, "O Father Let Thy Word Prevail," an appropriate hymn that was a fervent prayer for revival in the church where millions had been baptized but had lost "Faith's pure flame."[79]

The revival the song prayed for did come to the church. It happened that year across the Norwegian American community with the preaching of Skrefsrud, whose year in America sparked a revival that changed many lives for good.[80] According to one source, the meeting included much less business than edification, though attendees did discuss not only the Augsburg situation but also the inner and foreign missions, which had come on hard times now that the Augsburg party was moving away from the United Church. Inner mission congregations and pastors were left in the lurch financially, to say nothing of the Malagasy missionaries.

The convention ordained five candidates for ministry. Skrefsrud preached. Georg Sverdrup, the chairman of the group at the time, admitted that the decision of the Minority to take steps to ensure something of a permanent organization was inevitable. With the obvious split, the Friends of Augsburg were now responsible for continuing the seminary, home mission, and foreign mission simply because the United Church had neglected to do so. He concluded, "Should the United Church illegally and wrongfully expel the minority and thus put the church to shame, we cannot be made responsible for such action. Our work lies clear before us.... Let us be faithful to it."[81]

The Friends of Augsburg would not turn back, nor would the United Church change its decisions. The courts were the last place to go. It was all extremely ugly.

## 1896: Movement Toward a New Church

Before the annual meeting that June, some of the leaders of the United Church tried to find ways to deal with the issues and, hopefully, bring peace. One notable meeting was held on Tuesday, April 21, when Høyme and Dahl appeared at Trinity Congregation. The *Saint Paul Globe* reported on it, with a headline of "Rev. Høyme as Peacemaker," but after reading the article, one has to think the phrase is tongue-in-cheek.

Trinity had been among the first congregations in the United Church to pull its support for the United Church Seminary and continue to support Augsburg. Twelve congregations were going to be expelled by the United Church for that action at their June convention if they did not retract their decisions.

It was a dramatic moment. Høyme and Dahl walked in together. Over one thousand people were in attendance. Pastor M. Falk Gjertsen opened the meeting with devotions. He then told the gathering that both Høyme and Dahl had asked for the floor, and with a unanimous standing vote, they were given the right to speak.

Høyme is reported to have been cordial, admitting he would have much preferred to have been there for a worship service but that, given the emergency nature of the situation, he had to endure the unpleasant conversation they were about to have. He then began to explain why the resolution of the congregation to withdraw its funding, founded on the charge that the United Church had violated the articles of the union, had been "mistaken." The congregation should make amends, he argued, by retracting the resolution: "The address of Rev. Høyme was an earnest and strong effort, and he was ably assisted by Rev. Dahl, who also tried to explain that Trinity was wrong and the United Church right."[82]

Gjertsen as moderator and defender of his congregation thought that the conversation was too late. A retraction would mean "abject humiliation." He also suggested there had been a contradiction between the two in their arguments. Høyme had claimed the "United Church had both 'moral and legal rights to Augsburg seminary,' while Dahl had claimed the church had no legal control of it." Trying to explain, Dahl said even though they had a right to the property, that would not happen without intervention from the courts.[83]

Dahl insisted that the 1896 annual meeting of the United Church would vote to officially expel the congregations favoring Augsburg. With that, the

**Figure 5.10.** Bernt and Sylvina (Jacobson) Sundal. Used by permission of the Grindal family.

conversation ebbed. Sven Oftedal, whom the paper noted was the unnamed object of much of the conversation, made the motion to adjourn, and it was approved.

Events like this were common as the United Church looked toward the 1896 convention, but the meeting at Trinity was the most significant. Trinity was Augsburg's protector. As the largest congregation among the Friends of Augsburg and one of the oldest, it received much scrutiny. Gjertsen was one of the ablest defenders of Sverdrup and Oftedal, and at this meeting, he did not fail. They must have left the meeting knowing the die was cast. Nothing much could be done to save the union.

On May 22, 1896, seventeen-year-old Sylvina Amanda Jacobson married Bernt L. Sundal, newly graduated from Augsburg Seminary, in Watson, Minnesota. He had been the valedictorian of his college class at Augsburg and a member of the Augsburg Quartet, whose main mission at this time was Prohibition. As a good friend of Hendrickson, their neighbor, and an acquaintance of Octer, who had been at Augsburg during Sundal's eight years there, he was welcome in the Jacobson home. Brønø congregation was a strong Prohibition congregation and featured many temperance meetings in its quarters. The quartet had been there for the Fourth of July a year before. It was probably on the frequent tours that he had come to know Sylvina.

The first summer of their marriage, Sundal taught parochial school in the Bardo congregation near Crookston. As noted before, it was common for seminary students to teach such classes in the summer. He also led the choir, which was remembered many years later by choir members. He was praised for his teaching and music but also for his prayer meetings. During his time serving the congregation, there was an awakening, and many young people gave themselves to Christ.[84] Sundal had passed all his exams with high marks and was ready to be ordained at the time of his marriage. In addition to that, he was well known around the church for his membership in the Augsburg Quartet, which traveled extensively around the area and even to Norway.

Georg Sverdrup, president of the Friends of Augsburg, reported in his address to the Fargo meeting in 1896 that the strife among the United Church leadership, pastors, and congregations had resulted in conflicts that were unseemly throughout the Norwegian American community. Several congregations on the majority side had driven out their pastors if they showed any sympathy for the minority. He accused the leadership of the United Church of first splitting Augsburg Seminary, then continuing with the split of Trinity congregation, and "now leading to a split of the entire organization (*samfund*) which will be completed—on New Year 1897—when it breaks its connection with the twelve congregations that were being expelled."[85]

Because of the confusion about who could ordain candidates, and whether the United Church would ordain candidates with clear sympathies for Augsburg, pastoral candidates had to be ordained differently than if they had remained in the United Church. During the year 1895–1896, Sverdrup reported that Oftedal had ordained two men: Ole Larsen Torvik (1863–1925) and Gudbrand Blessum (1859–1937). These ordinations had been performed in the local congregations. Now, at the 1896 meeting, the Friends of Augsburg would ordain seven candidates for ministry during its convention. Sundal might have been expected to be in the group but was not.

## The United Church Convention of 1896

As the United Church prepared to meet in convention in St. Paul, not much was left but to enter legal proceedings. Not seating Sverdrup and Oftedal at the 1895 convention, plus expelling congregations that supported the Augsburg party, had made it clear that the Friends of Augsburg were no friends of the United Church.

# Mergers, Disputes, and the Founding

On June 3, 1896, the United Church convention got underway in Saint Paul, once again at the First Swedish Lutheran Church on John Street. The *Globe* enthused about the good-looking crowd of ministers and laymen gathered there:

> They look exactly what they are—the indomitable pioneers of a country which but yesterday was the home of the bear and the bison and today teems with myriads of happy homes. What a paradox, anyway, that such an assembly of giants hail from such an insignificant country as Norway! And their physiognomies are no less marked than their physiques. Foreheads as rugged as though hewn out of the rock by a Viking's battle-ax. A firmness, nay, a rugged stubbornness in every feature that almost makes one feel uncomfortable upon passing his eyes over those hundreds of heads arranged in rows as if in battle array.[86]

Almost as a prelude to the conflict about to break out in the group, the reporter marveled at the capacity of this group for stubbornness, which would be on full display at the meeting.

The leaders of the Friends of Augsburg had advised their people not to attend the convention. Despite that, the Twin City papers predicted the gathering would be unusually large because of the action on the Augsburg question. The convention had heard with delight the legal opinion of lawyers Andreas Ueland and E. Cohen concluding that the United Church did have the authority to run Augsburg based on the founding documents of the merger. Furthermore, they suggested that the United Church elect members to the Augsburg board: "The United Church has not lost its right to control Augsburg Seminary and its remedy for the deprivation of that right is by electing trustees at the next annual meeting, with the direction to commence proper proceedings to test the claims of the acting board of trustees."[87]

The journalist writing the report supposed that this solution was so acceptable to the delegates that "it now seems highly probable that a majority of the annual meeting will vote in favor of the remedy proposed above."[88] The Friends of Augsburg, who would be meeting two weeks later in Fargo, June 17–21, had let it be known that they would fight this opinion to the last. One told the reporter, "We believe we are right, and we have struggled persistently and conscientiously for our honest conviction."[89] The writer of the article presumed that the Friends of Augsburg would have to relent, given the reluctance of the parties to go to court, as had been threatened.

The headlines that week read that Høyme was announcing his retirement. He was weary of the strife and longed for relief. His presidential state-of-the-church speech was lengthy, clocking in at sixty-five minutes. In it, he covered the main work of the church and its schools, plus other works. He dwelt in some detail on the Augsburg situation. He thought that the offer of the Friends of Augsburg to make one more attempt at reconciliation could proceed "as soon as the [Augsburg] Board of Trustees makes a voluntary transfer of the Augsburg property to the United church."[90] This was not going to happen. The only hope they had of resolution was legal. Høyme concluded his speech by wishing "God would bless all who stood by him in the hour of trouble, and also thanked those who had abused him, and wished their action might be of benefit to him."[91]

Things deteriorated quickly when the Augsburg question came up. Pastor Gjertsen began by arguing that the convention should have heard Sverdrup and Oftedal the year before and not refused to seat them as duly elected delegates from Trinity congregation, nor should it expel the twelve congregations that were aligned with the Friends of Augsburg. His main point was that the assembly refused to hear the two "for fear they would deliver such wholesome truths as would make the congregations of the different churches side with the minority and elect delegates favorable to Augsburg."[92]

At this, the assembly began hissing so loudly that he could not be heard. The paper reported with some admiration that he kept on speaking as though nothing were hindering him. Høyme made every effort to stop them, but the hissing continued. Høyme answered Gjertsen's charge, but as he spoke against the Augsburg party, the loud approval of his points made it impossible for him to be heard.[93] This conspicuously failed to calm the troubled waters.

The next day, as predicted but contrary to his wishes, Høyme was unanimously reelected as president, and T. H. Dahl was named vice president. The members of the newly elected nominating committee showed the strength of the old school in the new church; elected were Johan Olsen of St. Ansgar; Rev. Johannes Müller-Eggen of Lyle, Minnesota; Mr. Christianson of Chicago; and Andreas Øfstedal (1855–1930) of Moorhead, a member of the Anti-Missourian Brotherhood. Olsen had presided over the Conference for some years and ended up opposing Sverdrup and Oftedal. Johannes Müller-Eggen (1841–1913) had been an early graduate of the Paxton Seminary and knew Weenaas. He served as vice president of the Conference in its early years. His biography also shows him to have been a member of the old school and close to Weenaas.

On that same day, June 9, the convention voted by a wide margin to expel the twelve congregations that had announced their support of Augsburg Seminary, rather than the new United Seminary, as of January 1897. Unless they repented, made amends, reconciled with the United Church, and agreed to the transfer of the seminary property to the United Church, they were out. By this time, the Friends of Augsburg, especially Oftedal, came in for ridicule. During one exchange, Rev. Lars Johan Mathiasen Hauge (1860–1936) from Moe, South

Dakota, a member of the Anti-Missourian Brotherhood, scoffed at the idea of taking over the buildings: "They may soon need new roofs and new walls.... Put the property on the shoulders of Oftedal and you will finish him up quicker than any other way."[94] The conversation continued in this vein for a bit, with one speaker calling the Augsburg buildings rotten. It closed by noting that Lars A. Stenholt had sold fifty copies of his lampoon of Professor S. Oftedal. Stenholt, a successful scandalmonger or muckraker, was among the only Norwegian American writers who made money in his trade.[95] His fictional accounts of easily recognized people bordered on libelous but were eagerly bought for their wicked humor.

Ridicule is a potent weapon. That it was now being used against the leaders of the Friends of Augsburg and long-esteemed professors Oftedal and Sverdrup meant that they had lost their place of authority with the majority of United Church pastors and laity gathered in St. Paul for the convention. It hurt.

## Friends of Augsburg 1896

The Fourth Meeting of the Friends of Augsburg (Augsburgs Venner) met in Fargo from June 17 to 21 at the invitation of Pontoppidan Lutheran Church. The opening sermon was by Endre Eriksen Gynild (1859–1928), pastor in Willmar and soon-to-be president of the LFC. His sermon focused on Jesus's saying, "I have come to cast fire upon the earth" (Luke 12:49). At the time, a revival had been sparked that was affecting all Norwegian Americans in the Upper Midwest because of the preaching of both Lars Skrefsrud and Peter Nilson (1852–1926). Gynild marked that and gave thanks. My great-grandfather Ludvig Watne from Minot attended this meeting and must have passed on to his daughter, Anna Grindal, some feelings about events during it.

The report from Sverdrup, president of the Friends of Augsburg, was hopeful and clear as usual. This was the hundredth anniversary of Hauge's experience, and he remarked that it was a good thing to remember for its awakening of Norway. He pointed to the last meeting in Willmar, where Skrefsrud had preached, and the revival that Pastor Peter Nilsen had sparked with his preaching among Friends of Augsburg congregations. Nilsen served as evangelist in what would become the LFC from 1893 to 1902 and is credited by many with helping the fledgling church body survive. After praising both Skrefsrud and Nilsen, Sverdrup gave a bill of particulars on their situation: he was glad for the conversation about the work of laity and of how *Folkebladet*, which had come in for much ridicule at the United Church convention, was a blessing to their movement and needed support. He briefly discussed the cases of the Friends of Augsburg, the seminary, inner mission, and foreign missions. The lack of support for inner mission had meant that several pastors serving newly established congregations were woefully lacking in resources. Worst was the situation that the split had caused for both

Hogstad and Tou in Madagascar. Also vexing was the peace committee's failure to achieve anything: "During the past year the United Church's committee for peace had practiced uncalled for rudeness so our hope for a solution by this meeting was not successful."[96]

He went on to note that the recent annual meeting of the United Church, from first to last, had been filled with a decided and energetic battle against the Minority and the Friends of Augsburg, which ended in a victorious vote to expel the twelve dissenting congregations. For Sverdrup, this meant that the United Church had been the author of the split, not the Friends of Augsburg. Now, with the work to establish the Lutheran Free Church of America, he concluded, Americans will have the chance to have a truly free church. This would also be an example to the church in Norway. Like Paul and Silas praising God in prison, we should sing and wait, knowing "that when the night is darkest and the suffering greatest, God will come in good time to free us."[97]

In his report as chair of the board of trustees, Sven Oftedal, while optimistic, expressed his exhaustion at the slanders and difficulties of the past year. Given his usual optimism and high rhetoric, this weariness is telling. He rejoiced that during the past year, the school had 165 students, 32 in the seminary and 133 in the preparatory schools, a larger number than any before. He credited the revivals with this. It had provided them with a greater majority of "living Christians" than ever before. This caused a happy problem: they had to rent space for classes and take down a wall in one of the classrooms to make it able to accommodate a larger class.

Oftedal also boasted that 200–300 congregations had sent in money over that past year, $500 more than last year. He credited the revivals of Pastor Nilsen for this. He noted that the United Church through its publications and pastors had done all it could to ruin Augsburg supporters' faith in the school and thus lower contributions.

He hoped that the peace committees still could function but had little reason to believe they would now that they had named a completely new board for Augsburg. Since all had roots in the old Conference, he suggested that the United Church was really the Conference in new clothing since neither the Anti-Missourian Brotherhood nor the Norwegian Augustana Synod had much to contribute.

Oftedal concluded with a lengthy personal note. He was leaving the board of trustees. He had been called, he said, to a morally holy work of keeping the seminary true to what it had been incorporated to be and what its supporters had believed in. To transfer it over to another group that did not share that understanding of the seminary was for him a breach of trust and betrayal of the people's most sanctified interests. For good reason, he was suffering the hurt of the ridicule and opposition.

> Friends, it is not difficult to understand what inner battles and suffering I as president of the Board of Trustees during these five years have had to experience. I am only a man, yes, only a wretched and unsteady man. The unremitting bitterness and unfair attacks, the awful invective, the almost unbelievable shameful slander, official and private, the building distrust and misunderstanding which over time has thrown a little shadow over me even with the Friends of Augsburg. The personal humiliation and the unending emotional expense have not been without effect. I would not be honest or even human if I did not say that there has not been a day when I have not sighed to God in my deepest heart, O Lord, set me free! Take me from this work![98]

He went on to say that he had not lost hope, nor had he become downhearted, but he wondered how much longer he had to live. The past twenty-three years had been difficult and long: "I have tried to keep my spirits up as well as possible and smile." A smile sometimes covers a bleeding heart, he noted, but he took comfort in the fact that the young who were going to inherit their work would take it forward. For him, the meeting in Fargo was like a spring bud ready to blossom. It would give all Norwegians a new model for church in a free church.

He concluded by noting that what was now needed from them was to love our enemies as Christ loved us and continue in patience to go forward. His last hope was eloquent: "For suffering will certainly come, and before all [we need] to continue in prayer, so that we in all things and in all times go to God in heaven, innocent and faithful, because he is not only all powerful but 'Our Father.'"[99] The meeting began drafting founding documents for what was to become the LFC.

## Ordinations by Friends of Augsburg

These meetings and resolutions had immediate implications, especially regarding the calling and ordaining of Augsburg Seminary graduates. Gustav Oftedal and P. G. Nelson had been expelled from the United Church for attending meetings of the Friends of Augsburg. Dahl told Oftedal in a letter that he could not belong to two different church organizations at the same time. The letter informing them of this action was reported on in the January issue of *Folkebladet*.

Bernt L. Sundal had received a call to the Bardo/Crookston congregations in August 1896 while he was teaching parochial school there. Christian Saugstad had resigned from the Bardo congregation in 1894 and left for Belle Coola, British Columbia, because of the stridency of the conflict. Sundal had accepted the call, the paper announced, remarking that he would be ordained as "soon as possible."[100] Therein lies a tale.

Figure 5.11. Bernt Sundal as a young man. Used by permission of the Grindal family.

According to Hans Johannessen Villesvik (1864–1944), pastor in nearby Climax, Minnesota, on July 7, 1896, the Bardo Lutheran Church voted at a regularly called meeting of the congregation to sever its ties with the United Church—so, contrary to Høyme's letter, it could not be expelled. It then called Sundal to be its pastor. This meant it had to find a way to have Sundal ordained since it knew the United Church would not ordain him given his sympathies with what became the LFC. At a regularly called meeting on August 30, 1896, the congregation voted that he should be ordained in their congregation as soon as possible.

The church also had built a new church building that was to be dedicated at the same time. In the middle of its celebrations, the congregation invited neighboring pastors to take part in the services of dedication. The ordination that happened at the same time as the dedication may have not been part of the invitation, but the neighboring pastors were invited to participate in the ordination service when they arrived.

Bardo's dedication and Sundal's ordination were held on October 11, 1896. Pastor J. H. Brønø, who grew up in the Rosewood Township near Sylvina Jacobson, ordained Sundal. Other pastors also participated. Ole Knutsen Quamme (1852–1904), pastor in Cooperstown, North Dakota; Søren Emanuel Sørensen (1849–1931), pastor in Maple Bay, Minnesota; Hans Østgulen (1855–1922), pastor in Warren, Minnesota; and Hans Johannessen Villesvik were in attendance. There is still something of a mystery about the proceedings and consequences.

Pastor Johan Hansen Brønø, son of Bendik Hansen, a close neighbor of the Jacobsons—he had changed his last name to Brønø when he reached his majority—had gone along with the Friends of Augsburg but would later return in 1909 to the United Church. The ordination recorded in *Folkebladet* made no reference to the trouble that the rite would occasion in the next few years. Although the lines between the United Church and the Friends of Augsburg had not been officially drawn, they were very clear to those in the United Church and Høyme especially.

In the March 21, 1900, edition of *Folkebladet*, the editors included some of the story, as well as a letter from Høyme to one of the participants. In the March 28, 1900, edition of *Folkebladet*, Villesvik wrote in to further explain what he called "one of the darkest pages in the history of the United Church."[101] Both Villesvik and Quamme had received a letter from Høyme after the report of the ordination was published. In it, he told them that by their actions, they would be removed from the list of United Church pastors.

> Eau Claire, Wisconsin
> March 11, 1897
>
> Hr. Pastor O. K. Quamme:
> According to an official report that you have participated in an ordination of a candidate called to be pastor in a congregation of the United Church, and that the candidate was not approved by said organization nor approved by its Ordination Committee and that this organization's constitution, Chapter 4, Article 1, says that "a candidate's ordination is approved by the organization's annual meeting or of said ordination committee." It is therefore my duty according to the Constitution Chapter 7, article 3 to direct your attention to the following resolution approved by the United Church at its annual meeting in St Paul Minn. 1895, following:
> "The pastor, from now on who goes against the constitution of the church shall after fruitless admonitions for such actions will be considered removed the from church's clergy." (*Aarsberetning*, 1895, Page 166, Point 7, letter b.)
> Therefore, I respectfully and in Christian love on behalf of the church inform you that you have broken the church's constitution and worked against the above resolution, so I hereby respectfully ask for your explanation for this case.
>
> Respectfully,
> G. Høyme, President.[102]

After he had received the letter, Quamme wrote Høyme to say he would prepare a report in his defense and give it to the next convention of the United Church, not just a committee. He did not receive an answer, he wrote. In addition to Quamme and himself, Villesvik noted the others in the group should also have received such a letter, nor had he received official notice from the United Church that he had actually been removed from the roster. This would be announced, however, at the next annual meeting of the United Church. Without so much as a letter explaining why, he said, he had been expelled from the roster of the United Church clergy. All the pastors who had been named in Villesvik's letter were, in fact, expelled or became clergy in the Free Church. Some returned to the United Church later, as Brønø did.

Quamme explained that at the time of the ordination, he was at home with his parents, charter members of Bardo congregation. Michael Mickelsen (1863–1949), a neighboring pastor in Crookston, asked him to help with the dedication service. When Quamme accepted the invitation and came to the service, he discovered that Sundal would also be ordained. Should he have left in the middle of the service? He asked, somewhat plaintively, "Why could I not participate with them in the reading of Scripture, prayer and song?"[103] *Folkebladet* commented that next thing he knew, he had been expelled from the clergy roster without any ceremony or further research. He read this news in the annual report of the 1897 meeting of the United Church. In his report, Høyme made clear that any pastor guilty of such participation would need to give a good explanation. Their explanations appeared in an appendix to the report.

Sundal would come to be one of the sturdy veterans of the battles, with his crusty sense of humor and good sense. He was a respected pastor and leader in the church. He remained good friends with F. Melius Christiansen, with whom he had sung in the Augsburg Quartet. They would visit on Sunday evenings over the years when he lived in the Highview Christiania parsonage above Chubb Lake.

Many years later, one woman remembered how Sundal would smoke his pipe and chew tobacco fifty years back when he began his ministry in Bardo. His ability to spit across the room into the spittoon was known even then. (This talent was something I witnessed when I was about eight years old.) She also remembered him all dressed in heavy fur boots and coats to travel with the horses and sled between Bardo and Crookston on Sundays for church. He was such a good raconteur that she would not go to bed but sat up to hear his stories.[104]

On July 23, 1896, the United Church went before Assistant Attorney General Edgerton in Minnesota and filed to secure writ of quo warranto against the old Augsburg board of trustees led by Oftedal. The writ asked them to "show cause why they should not be removed."[105] The charges, not new, simply stated in legal terms that the question of the "validity of the Augsburg organization, the United church, so-called, claiming to have as good a right in the premises as the Augustana Synod, to which the Augsburg churches remain true."[106]

The case was argued in September. In November, the *Tribune* noted that newly elected Minnesota attorney general Henry Warren Childs (1848–1906) would bring charges against Sven Oftedal and the other trustees, requiring them to show cause why they should not surrender the Augsburg property to the United Church.[107]

## 1897: Founding of the Lutheran Free Church

On April 9, 1897, Judges Belden and Simpson decided that the case of the new United Church Augsburg board led by Pastor Nils Brun against the old Augsburg board led by Sven Oftedal could go forward. It would not be heard until September 1897.

This was the year the LFC would be born. The 1896 meeting of the Friends of Augsburg in Fargo had made provisions for such a break. The writers of the constitution, and especially a founding document called the Twelve Principles (see below), were careful not to create a church that was hierarchical.

In an article anticipating the coming meeting of the Friends of Augsburg to establish the LFC, Sverdrup wrote that the rules and the constitution were written so that the congregation would ascend and the church organization would descend. Therefore, they made the annual meeting a free conference. One could attend and vote at the meeting regardless of whether one was a member of a Free Church congregation. All one had to do to have voting rights was sign a statement that one agreed with the rule or principles. In the old country, Sverdrup argued, the state had power over the congregations. Here, that was not possible, but church organizations like the United Church now had that power and had put the congregations in a kind of Babylonian captivity such as Luther had found in the Roman church!

The first rule, therefore, stated that the congregation, according to Scripture, is the right form of the kingdom of God on Earth. This principle was burned into the memory of everyone who was a member or grew up in the tradition. When I was giving a brief introductory biography of myself to the first meeting of the Task Force on the Study of Ministry in 1987, I noted I was the only person there who had drunk in an ecclesiology with my mother's milk. This was our motto, our confession, and we understood it deep in our bones.

When the first annual meeting of the LFC was held at Trinity congregation in June 1897, there were four women delegates, three of them pastors' wives: Mrs. Jacob (Christine) Mortenson, Mrs. M. Falk (Sarah) Gjertsen, Mrs. Peterson, and

Mrs. Aamodt. This had been a victory of Gjertsen and Oftedal, both pro-women's suffrage. In his closing remarks in the sermon, Sverdrup said "brothers and sisters"! *Folkebladet* described the first meeting in glowing terms.

> At around ten Wednesday morning the 9th of June the large auditorium of Trinity Church on the corner of 9th Street and 20th Avenue south was mostly filled with people who have traveled far and others, in the Free Church's first Annual Meeting. Minneapolis, the ideal place for representative gatherings, prepared itself again this time. This was not only the city and the nearby congregations that were represented. There were pioneer pastors with sunburned healthy faces—from the wild woodlands and flat prairies. There were farmers and city dwellers, men with the battles of their work impressed on their appearance and bearing, but with the fire of life in their eyes. For the most part young and middle-aged people who looked as though they could pick up a roof if necessary. We say that it was a representative gathering of pastors and laity. Even more so it was a simple gathering—one could wonder who was pastor and who was a layman. Pioneer pastors or buggy pastors—mostly young men—who in significant levels have lost their clerical look and the Clerical stiffness as people call it. The long black robes, the collars around the neck or completely around it that never fail to give a distinguished appearance needed to give place to purely worldly cutaways and trolls.[108]

They gathered in the new not-quite-finished Trinity Church. The meeting began with F. Melius Christiansen playing Handel's "Largo" on the new organ.

When the meetings began, the discussion centered mostly around the leading principles. Most at issue was the definition of the congregation, point 2. Originally it had read, "A congregation consists of believers who regularly receive the sacrament and the means of grace and seek the salvation of all unto eternal life." Some wanted more doctrine in the statement. Sverdrup defended it as being biblical, not doctrinal. Doctrine comes a long time after one's awakening, he argued. Some saw a contradiction between point 2 and point 4, which argued that a congregation needs revival and preaching for conversion. If the congregation were made up only of believers, revivals would be unnecessary, argued Ole Paulson.

Then they discussed what it meant that the congregation was the body of Christ. Should one cut off a dead limb? Judas had been a member of the church. This brought them to a discussion of judgment. Gjertsen saw the danger in the notion that all were believers. People could easily begin to judge and wonder if someone was a "living Christian," as the lingo went. Who could say that

**Figure 5.12.** The second Trinity Lutheran Church building in Minneapolis. Used by permission of Augsburg University Archives.

except about themselves? Therefore, words of awakening must be preached in a congregation. The notion of the visible and invisible church began to drive the discussion.

Oftedal made an interesting and, to some, shocking observation. The great secret is, he argued, that a person can at the same time be a Christian and a sinner, as in the same way there is a relationship between the visible and invisible congregation, the organization and the believing people who belong to it: "I stand here to put in a good word for the ungodly in the congregation. It could well be that the limb which we would like to cut off from the congregation because it is dead, it could happen that it could be saved, and healed with our prayers and confession."[109] It was at this first annual conference where Oftedal gave his speech on the congregation referenced above.

After some more discussion, the two points remained: "2. The congregation consists of believers who, by using the means of grace and the spiritual gifts as directed by the Word of God, seek salvation and eternal blessedness for themselves and for their fellow men." Point 4 was made to be more in line with 2: "4. Members of the external organization the congregation are not, in every instance, believers, and such hypocrites often derive false hope from their external connection with the congregation. It is therefore the sacred obligation of the congregation to purify itself by the quickening preaching of the Word of God, by earnest admonition and exhortation by expelling the openly sinful and perverse."

The rules and articles of the LFC were adopted on Saturday afternoon, June 12, 1897. That was the birth of the LFC. About 125 congregations were said to be associated with the new church. Many of them were small; the total number of members was estimated at something over six thousand. This was not the result that Sverdrup and Oftedal had expected, but they took comfort in the promises of God to sustain them and educate pastors who could help congregations produce living faith to living congregations through their preaching and ministry.

## The United Church Annual Meeting in 1897

The eighth annual meeting of the United Church began on June 16, 1897. The papers said it started slowly, given the rain and inclement weather and the conviction of the delegates that not much happened on the first day. But Høyme opened the meeting with praise to God for all his goodness. In his report, he had many new exciting and good things to say about the growth of the church but also had to deal with the Augsburg case once again. He believed that the struggle had almost reached an ending and was confident the courts would decide in their favor. He regretted that the "so-called friends of Augsburg" persisted in keeping property that did not belong to them.

He then felt the need to comment on the new church that had been born the week before, the LFC. He ridiculed the rules of church, which he thought had been correctly criticized for being an "oligarchy... papacy... or tyranny." These things would not have been noticed, he suspected, if it had not "been the settled policy of the 'Free church' to try to crawl into and split up other Lutheran churches where there is the least chance. The audience was visibly delighted when the president made a slight allusion to Henrik Ibsen's 'master builder.' 'Thus they have gone to the extreme; thus they have placed the wreath upon the pinnacle of the tower.'"[110] The audience understood the reference to Ibsen and hooted.

These were not the only such moments. Several derogatory comments directed at Augsburg were recorded, like the remark of Pastor Saterli, a graduate of Augsburg, who supported Bøckmann's proposal to hire another professor because "as a student at Augsburg seminary he had been sorry to see the sad results of devoting too little time to the work."[111]

Nils Brun, chair of the Augsburg board of the United Church, wanted the convention to pass the resolution that "the Board of trustees of Augsburg Seminary be authorized to act according to their best judgment in regard to that institution." The writer editorialized, saying that "there was the faintest trace of a possibility that the old board may conclude to confer with the new board with a view to having the difficulty settled without a trial." Andreas Wright suggested, humorously, that the "best thing the United Church could do was get the property and sell off the whole thing." With that, the resolution passed.

That Wright would be party to those ridiculing Augsburg is also a sign of how bad things were for the Augsburg Minority. As a longtime pastor in the Norwegian Augustana Synod who had been ordained as a layman without

# Mergers, Disputes, and the Founding

**Figure 5.13.** The Tinseth boys ca. 1899. Left to right: Theodor, Ole, Anton, and Fritjof. Used by permission of the Grindal family.

seminary education, he should have been in sympathy with Sverdrup. But clearly he was not and piled on abuse along with the others. I have always admired Wright and his piety, so this to me is surprising behavior.

That fall, after the founding of the LFC, my grandfather Theodor's brother, Ole Haakonson Tinseth of Lamberton, enrolled at Augsburg in the first year of the preparatory department. While the conflict, to some extent, had died down, court proceedings as to who owned Augsburg were ongoing. His parents, active in their Westbrook congregation, were naturally interested in what he would report in his letters or when he came home on vacations, which the *Lamberton Star* reported was frequently.

His mother, Torbjør, was active in the ladies' aid, hosting the meetings in her home. Their pastor before the schism, J. C. Jacobson, had graduated from the Stavanger School of Missions, so the subject of missions was clearly of interest to the aid. The next year, on October 2, 1898, when Missionary Tou was on furlough, he visited Lamberton. One can be sure the Tinseths met him and supported his work, especially through the ladies' aid. Haakon, Ole's father, was working closely with Jacob Mortensen on the orphanage they were building in Lamberton.

On September 16, 1897, the *Globe* reported that at last the suit for possession of the seminary had reached the docket. Ueland spent the entire day reading documents for the court on the issues at hand. The paper thought it would be a protracted fight.[112]

On October 19, 1897, Judge Russell of the district court ruled in favor of Brun and the United Church. In the ruling, the United Church was given the "right to assume possession and control of Augsburg seminary property." Sverdrup said that the case would very likely be appealed. All due speed was required, he noted, since the seminary held notes from supporters worth some twenty thousand dollars from friends, who would not want their moneys used to support Augsburg if it became the United Church school.[113]

When the Augsburg board of the United Church, led by Nils Brun, requested that the state help them by ousting the original Augsburg trustees, the attorney general of Minnesota ruled against the United Church, saying it had no right to elect trustees for Augsburg. Brun and his board immediately brought the case to district court, where Judge Robert D. Russell found in their favor, ruling that the United Church trustees were the right board. The Augsburg party appealed the verdict to the Supreme Court of Minnesota.

On June 9, 1898, the Supreme Court, led by Chief Justice Charles M. Stuart (1839–1919), reversed the lower court's decision regarding the legal identity of the board of Augsburg and not on other issues. Once again, the original five trustees were the only ones who could appoint new trustees to the board. The reasons that the Supreme Court overturned the decision of the district court had to do with arcane problems in Minnesota law. The court did not like to interfere in the spats of religious bodies, but it could rule on this. The United Church was told it could seek redress in a court of equity. The United Church at the time was meeting in convention. The possibility of further legal wrangling lay before both bodies.

As Fevold remarks, "Fortunately this step was made unnecessary by a settlement out of court."[114] The committee chosen to seek this redress decided to seek a settlement and end the conflict. The papers were not confident of this on July 20, noting that it was harder to "reach an agreement out of court, than it is in other matters among business men."[115] Overnight, however, they did reach an agreement, which resulted in the Memorandum of Settlement signed on July 21, 1898. This agreement indicated that the right of both parties could be adjusted without further recourse to the courts. The two sides agreed to divide the property, now in the name of the Seminary Corporation, in such manner as to give each of the parties substantially one-half of it.[116] This meant the United Church got the endowment fund, which consisted of mortgages and real estate, notes, interest due on mortgages, and a small amount of cash. Its paper value was fifty thousand dollars. Also included were some of the books given to Augsburg Library by the Norwegian Augustana Seminary, which were few.

The United Church provided quitclaim deeds. Augsburg would retain the campus and buildings. The value of the property was believed to be slightly higher than what the United Church received. The Memorandum of Settlement concluded, "The difference relative to the Seminary and the Seminary property having thus been settled in a just and equitable manner, the United Church and the Seminary Corporation bind themselves (and so far as is in their power their members and supporters) never to claim that the settlement hereby made is unfair or unrighteous, or that it gives either side any unjust or improper advantages."[117] The agreement was signed by N. C. Brun, O. A. Veblen, and L. F. Clausen for the United Church and by A. M. Hove and Olaf Hoff for Augsburg. *Folkebladet* published the statement in English on its fifth page on July 27, 1898.

The next week, it gave an account of the meetings, as well as noting that Oftedal was on a trip in Europe. After a telegraph from him approving the settlement, the committee agreed to it. The editor of *Folkebladet* thought it good that the issue was finally settled: "It is good that the troubles can come to rest and we can use our strength for the school rather than to spend it in endless trials."[118]

It was finally over. But the wounds were fresh sixty years later as we drove west to vote against any kind of merger.

## "Twelve Principles of the Lutheran Free Church"

1. According to the Word of God, the congregation (local church) is the right form for the kingdom of God on earth.
2. The congregation consists of believers who, by using the means of grace and the gifts of the Spirit (*charismata*) as directed by the Word of God, seek salvation and eternal blessedness for themselves and for their fellow men.
3. According to the New Testament, an external organization of the congregation is necessary, with membership roll, election of officers, stated times and places for its gatherings, etc.

4. Members of the organized congregation are not, in every instance, believers, and such hypocrites often derive a false hope from their external connections with the congregation. It is therefore the sacred obligation of the congregation to purify itself through the quickening preaching of the Word, by earnest admonition and exhortation, and by expelling the openly sinful and perverse.
5. The congregation governs its own affairs, subject to the authority of the Word of God and of the Spirit, and recognizes no other ecclesial authority or government above itself.
6. A free and independent congregation esteems and cherishes all the gifts of the Spirit, which the Lord gives it for its own edification and seeks to stimulate and to encourage their use.
7. A free and independent congregation gladly accepts the mutual assistance, which the congregations can give one another in the work for the furtherance of the kingdom of God.
8. This mutual assistance consists both in the exchange of spiritual gifts between congregations through conferences, exchange of visits, laymen's activities, etc., whereby congregations are mutually edified, and in the voluntary and Spirit-prompted cooperation of congregations for the purpose of accomplishing tasks as would exceed the ability of the individual congregation.
9. Among such tasks may be mentioned specifically a theological seminary, distribution of Bibles and other books and periodicals, home missions, foreign missions, Jewish missions, deaconess institutes, children's homes, and other institutions of charity.
10. Free and independent congregations have no right to demand that other congregations shall submit to their opinions, will judgment, or decisions; therefore all domination of a majority of congregations over a minority shall not be tolerated.
11. Cooperating agencies that may be found desirable for the activities of congregations, such as larger and smaller conferences, committees, and officers, cannot, in an LFC, impose any obligations or restrictions, exert any compulsion, or lay any burden upon the individual congregation, but have the right only of making recommendations to, and requests of, congregations and individuals.
12. Every free and independent congregation, as well as every individual believer, is prompted by the Spirit of God and has the right of love to do good and to work for the salvation of souls and for the quickening of spiritual life as far as its abilities and power permit. In such free spiritual activity, it is limited neither by parish nor by synodical bounds."

CHAPTER 6

# Passing the Torch

IN THE FALL of 1898, after the Augsburg question was finally settled and the Lutheran Free Church founded, Anton Haakonson Tinseth, Ole's younger brother, enrolled at Augsburg in the second (English) prep school year. Up until then, its twenty-ninth year, Augsburg Seminary had graduated 245 students and the college 111. It was still offering three departments of study: the preparatory section, a two-year course of study, the first year in Norwegian, the second in English; the college section, a four-year course offering a bachelor's degree and what we would regard as a liberal arts education; and three years of seminary. In all, a typical Augsburg Seminary graduate would have studied for nine years at Augsburg. Of course, not every student finished the entire course. Many children of Augsburg's supporters studied for only one or two years in the preparatory school or perhaps, like Ole Tinseth, took just another year or two at the college.

As noted above, Octer Jacobson had also taken the second year of preparatory studies in English. He clearly wanted more training in English, as did Anton Tinseth. Tuition in 1898 had gone up to twenty-five dollars a year, with room and board costing forty-five dollars for thirty weeks and books twenty dollars more. Chapel was at 7:45 a.m. except on Saturday, when it began at eight; classes began at eight and study hours at four. Prayer meetings were held every Saturday evening and Sunday morning. Ole was now a freshman in the college, or Greek section, and had to take Greek, English, and Norwegian classes every day; Bible history four days a week; the history of Norway, plus physics. This was the curriculum somewhat in the Nordic classical tradition that Grundtvig and Sverdrup had promoted. Ole had not really expressed any interest in the ministry that I know of, but he was taking the college courses leading to seminary enrollment, which served many students as a liberal arts education preparatory to any further work. Now the brothers were at Augsburg, hearing the gossip and frequently bringing it home to their parents during the year.

In addition to building and maintaining Augsburg, the LFC, now much decimated by the separation from the United Church, was starting to build other institutions of mercy and schools. It continued the work of the Deaconess Institute in Minneapolis and the children's home in Beloit, South Dakota, now belonging to the United Church, which Elisabeth Fedde had pushed for and Sverdrup had helped establish. An orphanage in Lamberton, which would become Bethesda Homes, turned out to be one of the lasting and most important legacies of the LFC.

## The Haakon Tinseth Family

The Haakon Tinseth family had continued farming near Lamberton. Their pastor now was Jacob Mortensen, Gerda Mortensen's father, who was also serving Mankato Lutheran church. He challenged the congregation to found an orphanage in Lamberton. Mortensen had served several congregations in the region, some near Montevideo, so he knew the area well. He was a good fund-raiser and shrewd man with a sense for the mission of the church. Now that the Friends of Augsburg had become the Lutheran Free Church, younger pastors like Mortensen felt the call to expand the small church's ministry. He found good support from many in the Lamberton area, especially the Haakon Tinseths.

Haakon had gone to school in Hamar, then known as Stor Hamar, and could manage businesses as he had learned from his father in Gransherad. The idea of an orphanage appealed to him. As a pietist, he believed he should serve his neighbor. Building institutions like an orphanage or an old people's home were part of the duties of a Christian. So, from the first, he helped Pastor Mortensen with the work.

An orphanage had special resonance through the history of Lutheran pietism. August Franke, in Halle, Germany, founded an orphanage in the late seventeenth century that became the center of a large institution—a publishing house, school, mission center, library, place of scientific research—that had great effects throughout Lutheranism at the time. The orphanage that Johanne Borchgrevink ran in Madagascar was one of the most popular causes of the missionary movement among Norwegian Americans. Since the orphanage in Beloit now belonged to the United Church, there was call for an orphanage run by the LFC.

Those in the Augsburg community had contributed to orphanages around the world. Madagascar came first, and the Borchgrevink children's home appealed especially to Jonette. A favorite charity of hers was the Martha and Maria Children's Home in Poulsbo, Washington, begun in 1891. She frequently gave money to it. Several fundraisers were held by the Conference in the 1880s for the orphanage that Lars Oftedal ran in Stavanger. It attracted support from Midwestern Norwegian Lutherans. So the idea of establishing such a place in their midst was not strange. It was what Christians did.

As the congregation worked on establishing the home, the Lamberton paper followed the progress carefully, noting that a group was meeting to discuss possibilities, then a board; then Pastor M. Falk Gjertsen came to make the case. He gave a stemwinder of a speech, which was well reported on in the Lamberton paper, on why there should be an orphanage near Lamberton: He thought it is a good location since it was in the middle of several large Norwegian communities. As the Norwegians had large families, he argued, they obviously cared for children. Helping the orphan was the first on the list of causes in the prophetic tradition—we were to care for the widow and orphan—so it was a natural thing for Christians to do. He would be a member of the committee to help found the institution.[1]

Among other things, Gjertsen suggested that Pastor Nils Heggernæs (1845–1909) of Mankato could be the leader, as he had begun taking care of three children from a broken home in Mankato. The site should be put in an already existing school building, he said, and given a Lutheran name since the institution would be surrounded by Lutherans. He thought Lutheran Orphans' Asylum would be an appropriate name. With that, Gjertsen said, articles of incorporation should be drawn up very soon.

The paper reporting on his speech noted that the board met shortly afterward to draw up such articles. The first version of them appeared under the report on Gjertsen's speech. They were signed and sealed on September 29, 1897, and soon the institution was ready to open. Workers were needed on the farms, so many children had been adopted into farm families to be workers, sometimes with less than salubrious effects. Orphan trains were said to have brought some 150,000–300,000 kids from Eastern cities to the Midwest.[2]

Gjertsen wrote a column in *Folkebladet* describing his visit there on November 17–19, 1898. Arriving on Friday, he was able to visit with many of the laity in the congregation and remarked on the "lively participation of the laity in prayer, testimony and exhortation."[3] Among those laity, I am sure, were my great-grandparents, Haakon and Torbjør Tinseth. It pleased Gjertsen greatly to realize that the strength of Christianity in this small town was not only with the clergy but also with the laity. Other neighboring pastors appeared on Saturday for the festivities, and on Sunday they held the dedication service in the church. Gjertsen, eloquent in both languages, preached in Norwegian in the morning and then in English during the afternoon dedication service. The church was packed for the morning service, and the offering was $120, a nice sum at the time. After the service, the entire group walked in a procession to the orphanage at the edge of town. As they arrived, Gjertsen led them in singing the doxology, after which the service continued with prayers, speeches, and hymns.

The home occupied eight acres of land for a farm where the children could work to raise their food; it had two stories with a basement, with room for twenty-five children. It would be run by the head deaconesses, Sister Mathilda Swensen, a native of Sweden; Sister Antoinette Slettevold (1873–1955); and Sister Carrie Skeie from the Minneapolis Deaconess Institute. Gjertsen admitted the home needed further support from a larger circle of people in the LFC and appealed for gifts. He was heartened by the participation of the six pastors in the area as well as the laity, including Haakon and Torbjør, and Christian O. Batalden (1844–1923), who, after his first wife died, married Sister Antoinette Slettevold.

On August 20, 1899, a group from the Westbrook church, which had remained with the United Church, met for a picnic in a grove on John Alfson's farm to raise money for the orphanage. Sisters Mathilda and Christine appeared with all nine of the children currently living there. Several laypeople spoke, among them Christian O. Batalden, Johannes Rongstad, Carl Skogen, and Pastor Mortensen. After these speeches, a choir sang, and then the group gathered thirty-eight dollars.

During this time, Haakon changed his name from Anderson to Tinseth because there were so many Andersons in Lamberton, even another Haakon, transcribed as *Hogan* in the English press. Torbjør was a frequent hostess to the Ladies Aide Society of the Scandinavian Lutheran church and was the hostess for the first meeting that Mrs. Jakob Mortenson attended after they moved to Lamberton in the fall of 1899.

An old family story tells of how Gerda Mortensen, born in 1895, was a friend of the young Tinseth children, especially Fritjof Johan (Fred), who was her age. Gerda, who became the woman leader of Augsburg and the Lutheran Free Church, was about four when she had been invited to spend the night in the Tinseth home. She awoke in the middle of the night and began weeping, wanting her father. Apparently, she pitched such a fit that Haakon had to bring her to her parents' home in the middle of the night. This may have been the first, but by no means the last, time Gerda made other people do her bidding. Uncle Freddie, as we called Fritjof Johan, loved to tell the story and would flirt with Gerda about the event whenever they met over the next seventy years. She would take his arm and say, "Remember?" And her musical laugh would fill the room as she enjoyed the memory with him.

The needs of the home always demanded more than they could raise. In April 1899, Haakon gave $15 to help retire the debt. Mortensen wrote a plea in *Folkebladet* saying their debt was unsustainable. They would suffer a blow when the Tinseths decided to briefly move back to Norway. On July 14, 1899, the *Lamberton Star* reported, "Land Agent Anderson sold the Tinseth farm, southwest of town Saturday consisting of 240 acres" for $6,240. The September 22, 1899, edition of the paper announced, "H. Tinseth residing 3 miles southwest of town will have a public sale on October 9. He will spend the coming winter at his old home in Norway and may decide later on to make that country his future home."[4]

Haakon's reasons for moving were not entirely clear, except that he had gotten a quit claim deed on the farm he had sold in Norway. When he found he had title to this rather substantial property in Norway, he put the farm in Lamberton up for sale and sold everything at an auction. The auction sale list shows him to have had a substantial head of cattle and horses, with a goodly number of valuable farm implements and riding gear. Fritjof Johan, or Freddie, who was five, remembered the auction sale quite well and a dispute he and the sons of the new owners of the land had concerning a buggy seat. Torbjør also had a reed organ to sell. When the sale was over, the family prepared to leave for Norway on the *Oceanic* of the White Star Line on November 15, 1899. Before they left, Torbjør donated a sack of flour to the new orphanage in Lamberton. They bid farewell to Ole and Anton, who were now students at Augsburg, and prepared to leave for Norway.

On March 21, 1901, *Folkebladet* noted that the Tinseth brothers had quit their studies at Augsburg to either work in the congregations or go back to farming. What actually happened, according to family lore, is that they became lonesome for their parents and left for Norway. While they could help their father with his farmwork in Norway, he had expected them to be at school. It angered Haakon so much that family lore indicates he really found it difficult to forgive them. They were only in Norway until June 14, 1901, when the entire family boarded the *Thingvalla* to return to America. The manifests said they were destined for Lidgerwood, North Dakota, near Geneseo, where they would buy land.

In 1903, they moved to Cyrus, Minnesota, between Starbuck and Morris, where Haakon would build a farm on the shores of Lake Charlotte and raise his family. Later, Anton would buy a quarter section just north of his father's farm, and Theodore would buy the farm from his father, who moved into town and farmed another quarter section with the help of Fritjof (Freddie), who bought that farm and worked it until 1972.

The Tinseths were central to the support of St. Petri Lutheran Free Church. Haakon served as secretary of the congregation for many years and continued working for Bethesda Homes, now in Willmar. Through the years, *Folkebladet* would report gifts from the Tinseths for Augsburg and for Bethesda Homes. In 1910, for example, Carrie is reported to have collected twenty-five dollars from the family and neighborhood, ten dollars from Anton, fifty cents from Fred, one dollar from Carrie, and five dollars from Haakon. Announcements such as this went on through their lifetimes. The family remained loyal to the home for years. Every summer, my mother said, they would spend a day packing up to drive the fifty miles southeast to the annual meeting of the Homes, have a big picnic on the grounds, and play while their grandfather went to the board meeting. When they got home, dusty and tired, she said, it was like they had traveled to another continent. They went to bed, hot and exhausted.

## Inanda (Anda) Regina Jacobson

Inanda Regina Jacobson was just eight years old in 1893, when the Friends of Augsburg had its first meeting in Minneapolis at Augsburg College. She was born on the Jacobson farm on August 21, 1886. On September 9, 1886, she was baptized by Pastor Ole Guldbrandsen (1855–1914) of the Brønø congregation and confirmed in 1901 by William Bull Dahl (1864–1932), pastor at both the Brønø and Montevideo Trinity congregations.

The Jacobson family followed the news closely in *Folkebladet* and from traveling pastors and professors. When Octer came home from Augsburg, he was filled with stories of the strife. Anda must have heard much about the politics of the coming split and its personalities, many of whom they had met and entertained in their home. In the summer of 1894, the Augsburg Quartet performed for the congregation, and Bernt Sundal became acquainted with the Jacobsons. That fall, her brother went to Augsburg, and the relationship with Sundal continued. Her older sister, Sylvina Amanda, would marry Sundal on May 22, 1896, when Anda was ten. Sundal would be ordained in October after receiving a call to the Bardo parish near Crookston, Minnesota, where Christian Saugstad had been pastor.

Figure 6.1. A young Anda Jacobson's growing musical skill was recognized in the *Minneapolis Daily News*. Used by permission of the Grindal family.

## LFC Annual Meeting in Montevideo

When Anda was fourteen years old, the LFC had its fourth annual meeting in Montevideo. It was held on June 6–13, 1900, in the Montevideo Opera House, which could seat some 1,500 people. There is no doubt the entire Jacobson family was involved in that meeting, hosting members of the convention in their home, helping to feed the masses of people who came, and attending the events, all of which were rousing spiritual meetings with good preaching and singing. Anda's father, Ole, and brother Richard attended as voting members. This annual conference lived in Free Church memory as one of the best, both spiritually and fiscally.

Most exciting was the report that Augsburg was building a new main building for $30,000. Optimism seemed in order. Student numbers were higher than they expected after the slugfest they had just gone through with the United Church. The meeting featured Missionary Christian D. Borchgrevink (1841–1919), who spoke on behalf of the Norwegian Mission Society, still warmly regarded by the members of the LFC. An offering of $74 was collected for the Society's continuing work in Madagascar. This, in addition to the $241 received after the mission sermon of Missionary Erik Tou, showed the strong commitment to missions, especially Madagascar, which the community cherished. Tou was a popular missionary and well known among the congregations of the LFC, who generously supported his mission despite their small numbers and the times.

During the meeting, five men were ordained into the ministry: Olaf Rossing, Andreas Johannes Pederson, Bernhard Iversen Land, George Larson (who officiated at the wedding of my father's parents, Svein Torson Kivle and Helga Marie Jensen, in 1907), and Elias Pedersen. Three of them were born in Norway. All five of them described in their vitas a spiritual conversion that shook them to the core, a necessary part of their calling to be a pastor.

Sverdrup gave a lecture on the ministry during these meetings. It featured a clear description of the congregation's calling to preach the word along with the pastor: "Is the pastor the only organ that the congregation gets to do its work? Certainly not! The New Testament shows us clearly that the congregation does this work as well through its teaching."[5] He spoke about two kinds of preaching: evangelization and edification. Both were necessary in every congregation since there were still unbelievers in their midst, but when revival came, it was usually through the second type of preaching, where there were "edifying meetings, conventicles, prayer meetings, testimony meetings, etc. where believers in the congregation have taken the word into mutual encouragement and admonishment."[6]

Thus, it was the responsibility of the congregation to assure that the proclamation of the word was not lazy, making the hearers of it satisfied with themselves, otherwise referred to as *sleeping themselves into heaven*. Preaching Christ and him crucified was the only way to kindle spiritual life in the congregation, Sverdrup continued. With that, he hoped the meeting would bring a renewal like rain on the dry ground as those who were listening to him proclaimed the word in their congregations.[7]

Sverdrup gave the lecture on the morning of June 11, 1900. Everyone listening to this lecture could understand it and take it to heart, including teenager Anda and her parents and siblings. Sverdrup was known as a careful lecturer who spoke in his rich Bergen dialect that had been enriched by his contact as a young boy with the Sogne farmers around Balestrand, where he grew up. He was not complicated but clear and direct, so everyone could understand him, even Anda. Visitors marveled that during the sessions, one could hear a pin drop. It must have been exciting for the Jacobson family to see up close and personal the leaders of the Free Church: their old friend Ole Paulson, Georg Sverdrup, Sven Oftedal, Missionary Tou, and, probably most exotic, Missionary Borchgrevink. The people at the convention from the small communities all around the area must have been thrilled to see and hear him. Not since Lars Skrefsrud's preaching at the Friends of Augsburg in Willmar in June 1895 had they had the privilege of hearing from someone so famous and highly regarded. People marveled not only at his speech but also at the amount of the offerings received that day for missions.

The neighboring pastor in Willmar, Endres E. Gynild, was reelected president of the young church. The Jacobsons' neighbor, pastor, and professor, Hendrik (Henry) Norman Hendrikson, was elected secretary by acclamation. The elderly Hans Andreas Stub (1822–1907), now serving as pastor emeritus at Sacred Heart, Minnesota, attended as an observer from the Norwegian Synod. Michael Benjamin Ericksen (1868–1950), son of Brønø's first pastor, was the observer from the United Church. He now served the nearby Wegdahl parish and was well known as their first pastor's son.

Something to be noted, although this had been the practice since the first meetings of the Friends of Augsburg, is that there were seven women officially numbered among the attendees. At least one was a single woman, Miss Mathilde Ditman, from Irving, South Dakota, and two were pastors' wives: Mrs. Hans (Christine) Helseth from Brainerd and Mrs. Christopher (Agnes) Ytrehus from Hillsboro, North Dakota. The latter's husband would serve as president of the Free Church from 1903 to 1905. Three other women—Mrs. Martha Johnson from Bethania in Fergus Falls, Minnesota; Anna Martinson of Sarpsborg congregation near Fergus Falls; Mrs. G. Rollefsen from Pierpoint, South Dakota; and Mrs. O. Sveom from Hillsboro, North Dakota—seem to have come with friends or on their own. Anda and her family would have noticed this.

Although it did not happen this year, in the previous years, almost every speaker began his address with "dear brothers and sisters." One who wrote a few weeks later about the meeting marveled at the spirit of the entire gathering but noted especially "the host of intelligent women's faces one saw all around the meeting. It was for me a hallmark of our church. For where women are kept from the work of the congregation, there will be dry rot in our church work. Where would our mission be without women?"[8]

The citizens of Montevideo were stunned by the crowd and their general good behavior. They had expected cranks, given the harsh debates of the previous decade, one merchant said. Another observed that the crowds all went in to listen to the speeches, sermons, and meeting, and one heard barely a cough from the audience. All the speakers were eloquent, another noted.[9] It was unforgettable, and as many said, the spirit of that meeting would last for many years.

While the Jacobsons knew many of the LFC and Augsburg leaders and had entertained them in their home, this showing of a large number in their own town, with sermons, speeches, and singing, would have been thrilling to them as they saw the fruits of their commitments before them. Although the Brønø congregation had not yet chosen to join the LFC, they were pushing for it. This event must have given them more urgency and evidence for the change.

**Figure 6.2.** Anda reading a letter with a friend. Used by permission of the Grindal family.

When Anda's sister Sylvina died on March 12, 1902, Sundal had no one to take the children, and especially the baby, Sylvina, so the children came to live on the home farm, where Sylvina's sisters Hilda and Anda could care for them. Hilda was registered in the 1900 census as living with the Sundals in Crookston, Minnesota, so the children knew her well. Sylvina may have been sick and needed more help, given her three pregnancies from 1897 to 1902. Sundal married Hilda in September 1903. As Anda grew older, she frequently went to help her sister Hilda in Badger. The turmoil in the Brønø congregation regarding whether to leave the United Church reached its peak that year and would end in something of an acrimonious debate within the congregation that radiated out to Sverdrup and Augsburg.

## The Gjertsen Affair

Just as things seemed on the upswing for Augsburg and the new church, a devastating accusation was made by a woman in Norway against the pastor at Trinity, M. Falk Gjertsen, in December 1900. Coming not long after his appearance in Lamberton, the charges ultimately caused him to resign from Trinity. It took the wind out of the sails of the new church and its school. While the accusation of an inappropriate relationship with a woman back in Norway was never quite proven—the chief evidence was a letter, supposedly by him, to the woman containing rather salacious language—it was enough to cause his resignation. Few had been so loyal and worked so hard for the Conference and Augsburg party as Gjertsen. Gjertsen, and Trinity, had been a cornerstone of the work at Augsburg, the Conference, and then the Lutheran Free Church. His fall, considered unfair by some in the Minneapolis community, caused trouble for the school as it was trying to solicit the community's support, especially for the construction of its new main building. He maintained his innocence until the end, but his earlier actions caused trouble; it looked as though he'd left Norway secretly to avoid the law. As with all these cases, it is hard to say. The woman who accused him was something of a groupie and had wanted to travel with him on the boat to America, which he flatly opposed. However, the letter he was said to have written looked to have been done so in his hand.

As a leader in the congregation, Sverdrup was in a bind. Gjertsen had his defenders in the congregation who did not accept the allegations but also powerful opponents. I have looked closely at these documents and cannot decide what I think. These things never end well. While Gjertsen did resign after several attempts to clear himself, in defiance of the accusation, he and four hundred of his followers walked a few blocks down Franklin Avenue from Trinity and established Bethany. F. Melius Christiansen followed them and became the organist there.[10] This was a loss to the institution and to the three friends, Sverdrup,

Oftedal, and Gjertsen, which created bitterness that was never healed. Gjertsen had done yeoman work for the Augsburg, and this was a sad development.

There were other issues, too, that the young organization had to solve. Enrollment at the seminary had declined and been unpredictable through all the turmoil. The 1901 annual meeting, originally scheduled for Trinity, was quickly rescheduled for Willmar, given the turmoil in Trinity Congregation caused by the Gjertsen scandal. This meeting authorized the construction of the main building and agreed to raise some thirty thousand dollars to pay for it.

That summer, the entire faculty at Augsburg went out on the hustings to raise money for the new building. *Folkebladet* reported on the many places they went. Sverdrup traveled to Goose Lake in North Dakota, Oftedal to northern Minnesota, Hendrickson to Montevideo, and so forth. On these trips, they once again renewed their connections with their supporters and friends, gathering resources one dollar at a time. Oftedal loved the effort, talking about the joy of collecting money for the seminary just as the farmers were planting seeds. In the same way, the seminary was a seed that needed to be supported so it, too, would flourish. His closeness to the farm and the supporters of Augsburg is clear in his reporting of his work collecting money. He still enjoyed visiting and talking about Augsburg. On his way through Willmar to Hills in Rock County, Minnesota, he experienced rainy weather, which would bring joy "in thousands of farmer's homes."[11] In his journey, he traveled with Pastor Winther, a longtime supporter of Augsburg. When they got to Willmar, they stopped for dinner. They could not help remembering the significance of the place in the history of Augsburg: 1877, when the grasshoppers threatened the existence of Augsburg; 1895, when Lars Skrefsrud preached and brought revival as the Friends of Augsburg began forming the LFC; and 1901, when the young church voted to fund the new main building for which they were raising money.[12] But his weariness also shows. He was getting older. Ultimately, the seminary did end up raising almost enough money to pay for the building, which was an imposing one for the tiny fellowship.

In 1901, Sverdrup celebrated his twenty-fifth anniversary as president at Augsburg. Things had settled down some, and the new main building was going to be finished and dedicated in January 1902. He was feted by many of his supporters in the LFC with a gift of one thousand dollars. It filled him with gratitude and some satisfaction. Now he could build a summer home in Saga Hill on Lake Minnetonka, where he had bought some land years before. This gave him some respite from the work and worries of his position. In 1903, he was happy to be able to entertain pastors, who were at the Pastors' Institute meeting that summer, in his home by the lake. He thanked the group at the 1901 annual meeting: "I am most keenly appreciative of the forbearance of the brethren, and as I thank many of them for a cooperation that has lasted for twenty-five years, and in many other cases for shorter periods, it is my prayer to God that He will preserve Augsburg Seminary through many generations and soon place the work on younger and stronger shoulders."[13]

The dedication festivities of the main building began on January 1, 1902, and lasted for three days, with lectures and gatherings to celebrate this accomplishment. Things were looking up. The building had been built with funds mostly from Friends of Augsburg and the LFC and was a tribute to the leadership as much as anything. However, on the last day of the festivities, Oftedal tendered his resignation to the board, effective at the end of the 1903 school year. It was a shock to everyone. Oftedal had good reasons. One, he and Sverdrup had thought that it would be good to retire at sixty, an age he would reach in 1904. Second, his health had not been good. Earlier he had received treatment in Carlsbad, Austria, and he wanted to return there for further treatment. The years had begun to wear on him, especially the turmoil of the 1890s, and he was tired. Third, with the dedication of the new building, he felt it was appropriate to turn over the leadership of the school to the next generation.

Sverdrup was somewhat surprised by the announcement and noted in his 1904 report to the annual meeting, "For myself personally I wish to add that it seems like an impossibility to continue the burdensome labor at Augsburg when that help in the work is removed which in all these many and difficult years was to be found in Professor Oftedal."[14] Still, Oftedal's good humor and optimism are clear. In a moving piece he wrote for *Folkebladet* as he was collecting money for the building, he expressed the joy he had one morning when a woman came to him with a small gift of $1.50.

About this time, the young church was working on its version of the Landstad hymnal. They could not accept the 1895 version from the United Church. Their version did not change the hymns in the 1869 Landstad hymnal from Norway, and it could be purchased with or without the supplement, which skewed more toward the LFC writers. One of the issues the new book with its liturgy raised was the question of communion practices. People were abandoning the old custom of registering for communion, which meant a visit to the pastor; this could be a time of spiritual counsel resulting in confession and absolution.[15] The question began to be asked in *Folkebladet* whether confession should be required before communion. That was a radical departure from the notion that one had to be "worthy" of the supper by being properly shriven. This understanding kept many a devout member of the LFC from the table because they began to interpret it as meaning one had to be worthy (i.e., sinless) before receiving the sacrament. It did provide for a brief service just before the reception of the sacrament in which the pastor would go to the altar and read a biblical passage on self-examination and then a brief consideration of it and application to the people. Then they were invited to come to the altar and receive the sacrament.[16]

The liturgical committee advised the usual meeting with the pastor on the Saturday before communion Sunday but seemed to recognize things were changing. It did not change, however, the gravity of the encounter. My uncle Freddie once told me that before communion, he would "go out behind the barn and just holler for his sins." This practice became that the individual person should prepare for the table by confessing one's sins—if not to the pastor, then at least at home.

## Svein and Helga Kivle

That April 18, 1903, my father's father, Svein Torson Kivle, arrived in Detroit from Norway. A younger son with few prospects on the family farm above Seljord, in Telemark, he came to America, the family says, as a crewmember who could entertain the passengers with his dancing. He had a place to go in the new land. An uncle of his, Sven Ole Kivle, lived in Silver Lake, Iowa, near Northwood, a hotbed of Haugeanism. Svein had fallen in love with my grandmother Helga Marie Jensen while working with his brother in Kragerø, but she, a newly converted Methodist, refused to marry him until he was "saved" or "born again," as we said in English. On December 31, 1905, he experienced a spiritual awakening that made it possible for him to marry Helga, who came in September 1906, after she heard of his conversion. By this time, Svein had moved to Washington as Helga had gone directly from Ellis Island to her sister, Martha, who lived in Everett. They were married on May 2, 1907, in the LFC congregation in Sylvana, Washington, by Pastor George Larson.

Helga died of puerperal eclampsia on October 14, 1916, while bringing my father into the world. She was buried on October 18 in Sylvana. Pastor Tobias Johnson Moen (1859–1931) of Bellingham officiated, while Pastor Arne Olsen Kolden (1873–1951) preached the sermon on Joshua, noting that Mrs. Kivley [*sic*] had prepared for her traveling by packing good food. In the weeks before giving birth, she had attended every session of special meetings in nearby Ferndale. It was traditional for women about to give birth to attend to their spiritual condition, as death was a frequent visitor to women giving birth, which it proved to be in my grandmother's case.

In a letter to my father many years later, Svein told him about his mother, Helga: "She was a kind believer; I have never seen her match. The 9 years we were together were like heaven on earth. Not one harsh word was said during the 9 years we were together. She died when you were born, so there are two who have died for you. Your mother so that you could be born into this world, and Jesus died so that you could be saved by faith in him. It was a hard blow when your mother died, I wept every day for 6 months."[17]

## Brønø Congregation Leaves the United Church

Anda was confirmed by W. B. Dahl (1869–1932) in 1901. Two years later, in 1903, when Anda was only seventeen and still in high school, she became the superintendent of Sunday school in the little congregation that had just left the United Church. The reasons for the split were carefully explained in an article in *Folkebladet* on June 3, 1903, included here in its entirety:

> New Congregation
> Montevideo, Minn.
> I thought I would send a few lines into *Folkebladet*. It is very common that when something of importance happens in the neighborhood or in a congregation it is sent to the papers.
>
> What has happened here in the Brønø congregation is not of the happy sort, in that the congregation on December 11 after last fall has been either cleansed or split in which almost all the original members who have been with it over thirty years, found it good to leave. A new congregation is organized under the name of Brønø Lutheran Free Church Congregation. It numbers 36 voting members, 40 confirmed, and 62 souls.
>
> The Free Church's Rules with some small changes were adopted unanimously. Since many have joined, we had as many members as before the split. It is our hope that the new congregation will in the future have some more when we count the enlightened Christian people among us.
>
> The beginning of the uproar, which ended in a split, was that Pastor W. B. Dahl worked against the Free Church's Annual Meeting in Montevideo in 1900. We began to understand what sort of churchly positions he had taken. From that came actions, of which we did not approve, in the congregation, among other things, which had as a consequence that the pastor was sent a letter asking for his resignation. Despite the fact that a majority of the congregation had signed the letter Herr Pastor [Dahl] did not think it was worth an answer.
>
> Brønø congregation was born in the Conference and believes in the principles of the Free Church as the correct ones for all churchly work. Therefore, it has tirelessly supported Augsburg from its founding until now. For that reason, it was impossible to have a pastor from an organization (samfund) that in every way represents the State church. Other things can also be named: that he tried gradually to shut down the work of the Free Church. This we can prove, when the congregation's pastor was invited to announce a meeting with Pastor

> Strand, the Free Church's representative for foreign missions, he refused the request and passed it off as a private matter.
>
> It is sad to have to go through such a split at the same time it cannot be denied that it is easier to work now that we can work with free hands and at the same time open a door for the Free Church; we have long enough sighed in captivity; we have long enough been obliged to the United Church and it could be desirable if the Free Church people in our neighborhood could be manly enough to sweep away all the hindrances in the way of our Free Church principals, which we believe are grounded in God's Word. May the Lord bless us all in this work.[18]

With that, the Brønø Lutheran Free Church Congregation started, without a church building. From then until the congregation closed in 1916, it met in homes and schools around the neighborhood. The pastoral records show the Jacobsons hosted many of those meetings almost weekly, from the ladies' aid to church services, Bible studies, young people's gatherings, and annual meetings. The congregation closed in 1916 and merged with Trinity Lutheran Free Church, which had been built by Richard and Octer Jacobson some years before.

The letter reveals that the behavior of Dahl, a nephew of T. H. Dahl, was like that of several other pastors in the United Church who were also Augsburg graduates. Many had gone with the Friends of Augsburg and even joined the LFC, but as time went on, some fourteen such graduates changed their affiliation to the United Church. While Sverdrup acknowledged that it was possible to do so, several did so with acrimony. The conflict became somewhat troubling when the Augsburg and LFC contingent argued that Augsburg had paid for the education of these young men and thought that at least they owed something to the school and the LFC. Sverdrup believed the ardent opposition that several showed toward Augsburg had endangered their souls. Their failure to recognize their debt and their bitterness against the school would cause their work as pastors to suffer spiritually, he said, and he brought the issue to the board of directors of Augsburg and the faculty. It appointed a committee of two, Sverdrup and Helland, to "address itself to the proper authority in the United Church to ask for information concerning the colloquy which is held in that church body with graduates from Augsburg Seminary."[19]

The two men's approach to the United Church leadership for a meeting was refused. When Helland and Sverdrup tried to meet with the president of the United Church, T. H. Dahl, he said no on the basis that the United Church had not made any arrangements for such moves on the part of its pastors. The organ of the United Church, *Lutheraneren*, which had published a nasty anonymous letter from one of the candidates, refused to print Sverdrup's letter, "The United Church and Augsburg Seminary." The editor, who acknowledged Sverdrup's letter was refreshingly civil, refused it on the basis that it would continue a long series of personal attacks of increasing bitterness.[20] This was the last trial for Sverdrup before his untimely death in 1907. In a brief note, he expressed his concern for these young graduates who "had become bitter in their minds against Augsburg and the Free Church in the transition to the United Church and what is connected therewith."[21]

## Anda's Vocation

Anda's work as Sunday school superintendent at a young age had given her a sense for her vocation—both religious and musical. During this time, her family was giving generously to Augsburg, the Malagasy mission, Deaconess Hospital, and the Poulsbo Children's home, as well as the inner mission. She gathered ten dollars in November 1902 to send to the inner mission of the LFC at a time when the congregation was in turmoil about its pastor and whether to join the LFC.

Working in the small congregation while attending to her parents and the children of her sisters and brothers may have satisfied her vocational urges at the time, but she clearly had ambitions for a career in music. On July 21, 1905, her brother Octer and his wife, Hilda Hendrikson, had a daughter, Inga Mildred. Hilda was sickly and would die of tuberculosis when Mildred was three. By the time Hilda had died, Aunty Anda was caring for the little girl as her own.

Anda's aspirations were clear: She knew that she was musically gifted. In 1906–1907, when she was twenty, she studied piano with the local music teacher, Mr. W. S. Shardlow, and his school of music. He ran a studio in Montevideo. Shardlow had over 115 students that year. While she practiced, she could live on the farm and help her aging parents and siblings who were still at home. As the youngest daughter, Anda was expected to help in the home more than the others.

There are reports that she also taught parochial school in LFC congregations in the area, but it is impossible to ascertain where. Her daughter, Borghild, remembered that her mother taught parochial school in the St. Petri Congregation in Cyrus, where she met her future husband, Theodore Andersen Tinseth.

Windom College in Montevideo did offer normal school training, but there is no evidence Anda attended. We know that she yearned to attend school and cultivate her voice. She would later wish she could have attended Oak Grove Lutheran Ladies' Seminary, but it was founded too late for her.

## Gjertsen

A brief note appeared in the January 18, 1905, *Folkebladet* describing the dedication of the new Bethany Church, where M. Falk Gjertsen now served as pastor.

It dryly noted that the United Church had been "well represented" at the event. Their attendance had to have been painful to the Trinity and Augsburg party. Worst was that Nils. C. Brun had officiated at the dedication service. A strong opponent of Sverdrup, he had led the suit against Augsburg. Mrs. Rebekkah Oline Dahl, Gjertsen's formidable sister but also wife of the president of the United Church, T. H. Dahl, blessed the new ladies' aid organization, among other groups. Pastors Boe and Heggernæs, who had helped found the Lamberton orphanage, were also there from the United Church. F. Melius Christiansen, who also followed Gjertsen from Trinity, would play the organ at Bethany for some years.

Gjertsen had been an important member of Minneapolis society. He served on the school board for ten years, had helped with the labor strike of the mill workers in the 1880s, had published songbooks and written hymns, one of which is still in the Norwegian hymnal of 2013. He had relatives in the city who were in high society and had remained his supporters. A cousin, Henry Gjertsen, was a state senator, and his niece Beatrice, a mezzo-soprano, sang with the Bayreuth Opera Company in Germany run by Wagner's widow, Cosima, and his son. While Gjertsen may have been comforted by the gathering of his former enemies, now friends, it must have disgruntled the Augsburg professors on the other side of Franklin, who had been watching with interest. The bitterness was a tragedy on both sides.

## Oak Grove Lutheran Ladies' Seminary

The LFC was small and poor, and Augsburg was the center of everything the LFC did—in fact, it has been argued that Augsburg was a school that built a church rather than a church that built a school. For years, the LFC had felt the need to educate its young women as the Norwegian Synod had with its Ladies Seminary in Red Wing. The Deaconess Institute in Minneapolis helped some, but it also required students to have some prior education before enrolling and, most important, an interest in nursing. If they did not, they had to make up what they had missed in primary school. In 1905, however, the talk about such an institution began to become serious. A committee was elected by the Lutheran Free Church in convention in Battle Lake in June 1906 and instructed to establish such a school and find the best place for it.

The committee met on October 2–4, 1906, at Pontoppidan Lutheran Church in downtown Fargo. Pontoppidan was a key congregation in the Lutheran Free Church. Austin A. Trovaten (1861–1927), a local businessman and member of Pontoppidan, had gathered three thousand dollars from businessmen in Fargo to help found the school. Trovaten had already located a possible property and begun working the deal with the owners, the Barnes family.

After looking at the site, he thought it had very good prospects, as did the board, which voted to buy it and incorporate the school.

Ole Paulson, who had retired in Fargo, watched these developments closely, writing that the board of Oak Grove had found eight acres of land in an Oak Grove beside the Red River. It was on a rise that made it drier than other places along the river and generally safe from the yearly flooding common there. The brick house they had found was large and spacious—it had a basement under the entire building, steam heat, a laundry room, gaslights, spacious rooms that could be used for the teachers' apartments, and room for thirty students. There was also a well-built barn, which, with some work, could be remodeled into a dormitory.

The house had cost forty thousand dollars to build. Paulson estimated that the real estate value on the open market would be about fifty-five thousand dollars. It had been sold to the Oak Grove corporation for fifteen thousand because the Barnes reduced the price by ten thousand dollars for the sake of the school. The church would owe only fifteen thousand for the entire estate, which seemed to be a good deal. It would be paid for in five-thousand-dollar sums, the first given by the city, the next by the school over the next two years.[22]

At the October meeting, the Oak Grove board agreed on the articles of incorporation and prepared to open the school. The name raised some eyebrows for not being a religious or Lutheran name, such as Wartburg, but Paulson thought it spoke well of its location and was already well known by the name Oak Grove.[23]

After only four weeks of planning and remodeling the house, Oak Grove Lutheran Ladies' Seminary began its existence. It held a festive dedication service on October 31, 1906, and opened for business on November 1, much to the surprise and joy of many in the small church body. Since it was in North Dakota, it appealed to farmers in the far west who had a history of disliking Minnesota, and especially Minneapolis, for its flour mills, which they believed had frequently cheated them. They did need a finishing school for their daughters—and in any case, would have to send them away from home to receive that schooling—so they were happy to send them to a school of their own church in North Dakota rather than Minnesota.

In the same issue of *Folkebladet*, Pastor Ole Larsen Torvik (1863–1925), a member of the board who would later become chairman, wrote to give reasons for the building of the school. The argument gives a picture of the school situation at the time: "Our position as both Free Church and as immigrant people makes it necessary that congregations see to the education of their youth. We have no right to give over this important matter either to secular private schools or to the public schools that cannot be anything but secular."[24]

The need for higher education in the Norwegian Lutheran faith for their youth was met in several ways. Instead of parochial schools competing with the common schools for the primary grades, which Sverdrup had opposed, most Norwegian Americans relied on their summer parochial schools and the academies and colleges to teach the faith at a higher level.

Providing schools for their young was, for the LFC, a matter of survival. Torvik argued that it was the responsibility of congregations to take up this work in order that the "young can be kept in this church close to God and be a blessing to the congregation and its work."[25] He noted that such a school for girls had been something that had been talked about in the group for years, going back to the early 1870s. At the end of his article, Torvik reminded the readers where to send their gifts and hoped that the school would be for the "young women in our congregations what Augsburg Seminary is for our young men: a Christian educational and finishing school for great and lasting blessing for our people."[26]

## The Grindals/Tjons

As noted, North Dakota farmers had reasons to be against Minnesota, especially Minneapolis, where the flour mills were. The mills wielded a great amount of influence over the prices the farmers got for their crops. In addition, even if all roads in the Upper Midwest did, and still do, lead to the Twin Cities, Oak Grove and Fargo seemed a safer place for their daughters than Minneapolis.

Augsburg and the LFC constituency had spread west with the railroads through North Dakota and along Highway No. 2 from Escanaba, Michigan, to Everett, Washington, on the Great Northern railroad with the small junctions every eight miles or so along the way. Congregations of the Lutheran Free Church were clustered in Minnesota, North Dakota, and along the northern tier of North Dakota counties to Williston, with a few across Montana, and then on the West Coast, especially in northwest Washington, with some in Oregon.

An example of this is the story of my father's father and mother, Svein and Helga Kivle, and his adoptive father, Sjur, and Anna Grindal, who all emigrated to Washington from the Midwest after first establishing themselves in America. Sjur's sister, Torbjør Grindal Tjon (1858–1947), came from Norway to marry Hans Tjon in 1888. Sjur had settled on land about eight miles southwest of Rugby, North Dakota, the geographical center of North America, near his sister's farm. Hans, Torbjør, and Sjur had been born in Norway near the Sognefjord in Feios, where they were raised and educated.

In 1885, given the poor outlook for his economic future, Hans emigrated to Douglas County near Alexander, Minnesota. Much of the best land there had been taken. He felt the call of the west and left in 1886 for Fargo, where he stayed briefly. He then went to Tunbridge, in Pierce County, in the middle of the state and some thirty miles south of the Canadian border, where he squatted on some land near Tunbridge, a typical granary and railroad stop. It had been

Figure 6.3. Svein and Helga Kivle. Used by permission of the Grindal family.

named by James Hill after a town in England, as most of the towns on the Great Northern were. Tjon filed a preemption claim in 1889 and farmed the land until his death in 1921, when his sons, Norman, and Herman, who had both studied at the Augsburg Academy, took it over.

When he was a boy, Hans Tjon lived across the fjord from Balestrand, where Georg Sverdrup had grown up and where Georg's father, Harald Ulrik Sverdrup (1813–1891), had served as pastor from 1845 to 1883 while Tjon was being catechized. Pastor Sverdrup had prepared a shortened version of Pontoppidan's *Explanation*, which became the standard version and translated into English, so it was used by most Free Church confirmands over the next seventy-five years. It was even my confirmation catechism through my Sunday school and confirmation years in the 1950s.

When Tjon came to this country, settling in Douglas County, Minnesota, and then Fargo, there is no record of his belonging to a church, although it would have been natural for him to know something about the church situation since the theological debates of the various synods were lively topics of conversation in the secular Norwegian American press. Without a doubt, the fact that Sverdrup, the neighboring pastor's son, was the leader of Augsburg and the Conference made an impression on him.

Carl Sivertsen Vang (1862–1958) had been Tjon's pastor in the Rugby parish. Vang wrote in Tjon's obituary, printed in *Folkebladet*, that it was after the new church in Rugby had been founded in 1887 that Tjon had a powerful conversion experience.[27] This deeply affected his life and that of his family. As Vang wrote, "The entire time since [his conversion he] had a living and warm interest in all that supports God's congregation and his work on earth."[28]

Tjon became a faithful supporter of Augsburg, the LFC's inner mission, and foreign missions. After Oak Grove Lutheran Ladies Seminary began its work, all three of his daughters—Anna, Manda, and Tina—attended. As he was dying, he instructed his wife and children to give a quarter section of a farm they owned near Barton, North Dakota, to Augsburg, Oak Grove, and the Inner Mission Society, as well as the foreign missions board of the LFC.

Anna, his oldest daughter, enrolled in the first class at Oak Grove. Out on the rich Dakota prairie, rather isolated from any city or chance for higher education, she must have longed for such a school. When the decision was made to locate the ladies' seminary in Fargo, North Dakota, Anna and her family, like many other Free Church families, must have been following the process very closely. Such a school could provide what their daughters needed. Given the distance many farming families in the west lived from a town with a high school, a residential school in the state seemed a fine solution to their problem of educating their children, especially their daughters. When Oak Grove opened, there were twenty-four women students ready to enroll. By the end of the year, there would be fifty-five.

The school had as its goal the teaching of young women to be young Christian ladies. It would be, as its catalog said, a "school to which parents can send their daughters and know that they will be under the influence of Christianity. The Seminary aims to give its pupils a practical education on a Christian basis, and as far as possible prepare them to become a power for good and coworkers with Christ, whether it be in the home, school, church, or community. Much emphasis is therefore laid upon the study of the Bible and the tenets of Christianity, and these studies are carried on coordinately with the secular subjects through all the courses."

A look at the courses shows them to be comparable with those offered at Red Wing Lutheran Ladies' Seminary and the Deaconess Institute. While the emphasis was on practical education, the arts were important, partly because the founders believed, along with most people at the time, that women were the ones to pass on the higher things to their children in their homes. Because their spheres were different from that of men, a school for ladies was desirable for the development of the young woman as well as the family she would raise. They could devote their studies and time to the specific development of their vocations as wives and mothers.

There were three lines of study: the normal course, parochial course, and domestic science. Normal schools, named for the French name *École normale*, were early teacher-training schools, which prepared students to teach in the primary grades both with some courses in pedagogy and then the basics of reading, writing, and arithmetic. The normal course at Oak Grove was like most every other normal course with a strong dose of religion. Those preparing for certification in parochial school teaching had to take similar courses but in Norwegian with more courses in religion.

Domestic science was divided into two parts: household sciences and household arts. The sciences were to teach girls some of the scientific knowledge necessary to run a modern home, including cleanliness, theories of preserving food, and cooking. The arts had to do with the girls' ways to express themselves as they made a home for themselves and their families: sewing, fine handiwork, sometimes with painting and drawing. Literature, music, and drawing were all fundamental to the education of women. Opportunities for those studies were offered as well. These courses had been taught to girls of the upper classes for many centuries in western education.

One can see the wide variety of subjects the girls were required to study to receive their teaching certificates for the common schools. One can also notice the strong emphasis on religion. The parochial school curriculum is more so, of course. With both certificates in hand, a young woman, such as Manda Tjon Tweet, could teach all winter in the common school and in the parochial schools in the summer. Her sister Anna, in the first class, graduated in the parochial line.

Learning Norwegian in the parochial schools made it possible for their graduates to teach the Lutheran faith in Norwegian. They learned both Norwegian history and literature and were able to sing the hymns and recite the catechism in the old language. This kept the language alive in these communities much longer than would have been the case among aggressive Americanizers. In 1946, when my father took the call to the Rugby parish, he preached in Norwegian half the time, especially in Tunbridge, where his aunt, Torbjør, and many cousins were members. Manda Tjon Tweet, his first cousin, was the organist until she moved into Rugby in 1963.

When the Tjon girls returned to Tunbridge with their certificates, Anna married Osmund Selland and began raising a family of five. Manda taught for the next fifteen years before she married Anfinn Tweet in 1931. They lived on Sjur Grindal's land and raised two daughters, Agnes and Swanhild, who later graduated from Augsburg. Their homes were lovely and cultured. After the Thanksgiving or Christmas dinners, where they would serve us groaning boards of the best the farm had to offer, we would retire to the parlor, where the girls would favor us with piano solos or duets while the men fell into a heavy sleep.

Oak Grove was a desired destination for many a LFC young woman who had found Christ at these meetings and wished to further her education. Haakon Tinseth's youngest daughter, my great-aunt, Henriette, attended the school for a year, 1915–1916, before she married. It served as a finishing school for her after high school in Cyrus.

## Deaths of Ole Paulson and Georg Sverdrup

The fellowship of Augsburg and the LFC were saddened to hear that on April 20, 1907, Ole Paulson, retired and living in Fargo, where he could observe the proceedings for the building of Oak Grove, had died. He had been suffering from chest pains for a bit, but they did not seem serious. One morning, Mrs. Paulson came downstairs and found him in his rocking chair, seemingly asleep. When she went to wake him, she realized it was his final sleep.

The story of his life, which had been so closely knit to the happenings in the fellowship, gave people a chance to review both his history and their own. Services were held at Fargo and in Willmar. He was buried in the cemetery at Eagle Lake, where he had served years before. Georg Sverdrup could not make the funeral as he was not feeling well enough to travel; he would be dead in two weeks. Sven Oftedal went to the funeral to speak on behalf of Augsburg. A poem by the Augsburg professor Wilhelm Pettersen called him "a faithful old pastor" (*"trofaste gamle Prest"*). Many were the accolades for him, praising him especially for being a trustworthy friend who always spoke the truth.

Pallbearers and friends met at the Paulson home to bear him to Pontoppidan Lutheran Church in Fargo, where the funeral was held. Pastor Ole Nilsen-Bergh led the prayer before they left the Paulson home and served as pallbearer along with Elias L. Aas (1855–1947), pastor in Northwood, North Dakota, and treasurer at Oak Grove; Hans J. Villesvik (1864–1944), pastor in Bagley; Ole L. Torvik, pastor in Morris, Minnesota, who had been chair of the board of trustees for Oak Grove and knew Paulson well; Andreas Jacobson Vartdal (1867–1940), pastor in Churches Ferry, who would leave for the United Church in the next year; and Halvor S. Quanbeck (1862–1923), chair of the board at Oak Grove. The church was packed. The choir sang his hymn, which had become the signature anthem of Augsburg Seminary, *"Jeg er en vandringsmand,"* after which Oftedal preached on Isaiah 41:1–2 and Deuteronomy 5:24. He praised Paulson for "walking with God and being faithful in his call." It was especially gripping, the report had it, when Oftedal laid a wreath on the casket "and with tears falling down his cheeks bade farewell to his old friend and brother."[29] Olai Sletten, who had been a neighbor pastor, reported that his congregation in Blanchardville, Wisconsin, thought of Paulson as a dear father who had cared for their spiritual well-being for twenty years. There were more tributes and hymns, especially one from a Swedish Augustana pastor who had married one of Paulson's sisters and remembered Paulson from the very beginning of his ministry. The group left in a procession behind the hearse, which carried the casket to the railroad station. He was escorted to the train by Civil War veterans with whom he had served.

The casket arrived in Willmar at 5:00 a.m., where it was met by family and friends. The service began at eleven on Friday, April 26. A new group of pallbearers carried the remains of Paulson into Calvary Lutheran Church, where he had served. There, Pastor Elias Peter Harbo preached the sermon on John 17:4–5. Pastor Peterson of the Swedish Augustana church in Willmar spoke on behalf of the Augustana Synod. Michael Britanius Michaelsen (1868–1938), now pastor in Willmar, also spoke and sang a solo. The choir of the congregation also sang some anthems, and a soloist sang Paulson's hymn again. The gathering was large and included Norwegians, Americans, and Swedes. After the service, the procession then made its way to Eagle Lake church outside of Willmar. Paulson had lost two young children, who were buried there, and all his life he had made it clear he wanted his bones to lie next to theirs. As old friends and admirers, the Jacobsons very likely made the trek to Willmar, not too far from Montevideo. They had a car now that they could drive.

The writer of the column describing the funeral ended his report by noting that everyone who had attended had now returned to their home and daily lives, but "over the entire event, his memory shown, as of a faithful brother, faithful in his life, in his call which God had given him who now has called him to his Sabbath rest quietly and peacefully like a child who had slept in."[30]

## The Death of Georg Sverdrup

It had been clear that Sverdrup was ailing when he could not attend Paulson's funeral. Only fifty-seven, he had grown wan and rundown over the months. He wished to retire when he turned sixty and devote himself to writing and enjoying his home on Lake Minnetonka. As he grew older, he was said to have suffered increasingly painful migraine headaches, which he bore without much complaint. While he continued his responsibilities as president of Augsburg as well as professor, the community realized that his condition was serious when he had to leave the chapel on May 2 because he felt poorly. Later that day, the community was relieved to see him sitting on his veranda signing diplomas, but he failed to appear at graduation. His wife reported that in the middle of the night, on May 3, 1907, he tried to stand by the stove since he felt chilled to the bone and suddenly fell over, dead, onto the bed.

Sverdrup's death left the fellowship stunned. *Folkebladet* reviewed his rather stellar lineage in its report, including his great-uncle Georg Sverdrup, who served on the group in Eidsvoll that created the constitution of Norway in 1814; his uncle Johan Sverdrup, the first prime minister of Norway under King Oscar II; his father, Harald U., and his uncle, both members of the Norwegian Parliament;

and Jakob Sverdrup, the minister of Church Affairs, his brother. The article covered his birth in the parsonage of Balestrand, Norway, to his brilliant performance as a student in the Latin School of Aas and Voss, and in Christiania, where he excelled. He studied at the university there and also in Erlangen, Germany. In 1873, he went to Paris to continue his studies in Semitic languages, Old Egyptian, and Assyrian history, along with more studies in the Old Testament. Sven Oftedal was also studying there, and they became fast friends.

The funeral was held on Tuesday, May 7, 1907. Sverdrup's body lay in state in the new main building in the aula, the large space between rooms in the building. It seemed as though the entire school from teacher to student, oldest to youngest, was there as one in their sorrow. The casket, with candles at its head and foot, was covered with expensive bouquets. At two, the gathering sang a hymn, and Professor Johan Blegen offered a prayer, followed by another stanza of the same hymn. The space was packed with many pastors and those who worked closely with him.

From there, the casket was taken to Trinity for the funeral service. The congregation sang Landstad's hymn, "I Know of a Sleep in Jesus' Name," after which Oftedal preached the sermon using the text from Revelation 7:13–14. He rejoiced that now Sverdrup had come out of the great tribulation and was free. After his sermon, the Augsburg Glee Club sang *"Den store hvide flok"* ("Behold a Host Arrayed in White"), for which H. N. Hendricksen sang the solo. Pastor Endre E. Gynild, president of the LFC, spoke on behalf of the church. Again, the Glee Club sang, and then Strand, pastor at Trinity, spoke on behalf of the congregation. After another song and speech, Oftedal spoke, representing the faculty but most of all himself. He laid a wreath on the casket with great emotion, saying Sverdrup had been "spirit of his spirit, thought of his thoughts, and half of my life." Reports were that there was not a dry eye in the sanctuary.

After another stanza of the hymn, the president of Red Wing Seminary, Martin Gustav Hanson (1859–1915), spoke on behalf of the school and laid a wreath on the casket. Professor Bøckman, president of United Lutheran Seminary in St. Paul, did the same, as did President T. H. Dahl. J. J. Skørdalsvold, the founder of the South Minneapolis Temperance Society, gave thanks for Sverdrup's support. Professors H. G. Stub (1849–1931) and Johan Ylvisaker (1845–1917) of Luther Seminary and Pastor J. W. Preus (1861–1925) of Our Savior's Lutheran Church in south Minneapolis were spotted in the audience as well.

After the ceremony, a procession of over sixty cars made its way to Lakewood Cemetery, where the graveside service was led by Pastor Strand. As his casket was covered over by the earth, the onlooker who wrote the report thought of what Sverdrup would say to our people: "Be faithful, be faithful in the call God has given you, use your talents and gifts for the good of your brothers and sisters in order to save souls for the Lord and further God's mission her on earth. Give the Lord your talent back with interest, then you will receive the payment he gives all his faithful servants."[31]

Augsburg and the LFC were bereft at this sudden death. His thoughts and his personality had been at the center of their lives from almost the beginning. He had been, as was frequently said, the mind of Augsburg, while Oftedal had been the spirit and Gunnersen the heart. While in some ways he seems forbidding and unbending, which he was, he was also a humble and kind man whose own needs were of no account to him. He had a droll sense of humor and a witty way of speaking. One can only regret that he became the object of such ridicule and hatred, to be sure, partly because of his unremitting stance on the congregation. In many ways, he was better than Norwegian American Lutherans deserved. Many would accuse the LFC of being a Sverdrup cult, but his thinking was so clear and forceful that people at all levels understood him and would either hate him or love him.

The next annual meeting, at which Haakon and Torbjør were present, felt empty without Sverdrup's presence. The loss was palpable.

## The Young People's Federation

The Young People's Federation, earlier known as *Ungdomsforening*, took some time to be nationally organized. In 1906, the English conference of the LFC sponsored youth rallies in the LFC strongholds of Chippewa Falls and Minneapolis. While sporadic, they began a tradition that culminated in the first official convention of the Young People's Federation in 1920. Its stated goals were as follows:

1. To bring young people to Christ;
2. To promote and foster a true Christian spirit and fellowship, so that those who are Christ's may grow in his grace and knowledge;
3. To help the young people to find their places of service in the kingdom of God;
4. In a general way to work for the spreading of God's kingdom and to support such activities as may from time to time be designated by the Federation.[32]

## Anda Finds Her Way

Although Anda soon began to be well known as a singer, it was as a pianist that she first achieved success. In January 1909, she won a piano-playing contest in Minneapolis sponsored by the *Daily News* in Minneapolis. The prize was a

Guldbrandsen piano that we had in our family until we traded it for a smaller spinet. *Folkebladet* also noted that a Miss Jacobson played the piano at a spring festival that year, at which several Augsburg groups sang and played as well, so she was in Minneapolis for some months at this time.

The organization that gave her an outlet for her gifts was the Young People's Society of the LFC congregations in the Willmar district. When she was twenty, she began to appear as a leader in the meetings, not only singing but also on the committee to choose music for the next meeting, planning, and announcing it in the papers so people could come prepared to sing together in festival choirs. This required meetings together with the others, as well as extensive letter-writing to the church papers that would print the announcement. From her diary and *Folkebladet*, we know that she was frequently elected a member of program and music committees and a leader of music at the conventions.

In the late winter of 1910, Anda traveled by rail and buggy to visit her sister Hilda Sundal in Badger, Minnesota, near Rouseau, where Hilda's husband, Bernt, served Lutheran Free Church congregations. On her way there, she kept a diary describing the railroad depots and hotels where she stayed along the way. Her diary also gives us a picture of a vanished Minnesota, with depots, hotels, and restaurants in little towns now just a bump in the road, with maybe a grain elevator still standing by the railroad. She seems to have been fearless, traveling with every type of person and to every place.

Her language also reflects the lingo of the times, even with her less than easy command of English. We hear it when she describes the hotel she stayed at in Appleton, Minnesota, called the Saint James: "a swell place and I am all right because the Great Northern is two hours late. There are two swell girls in this parlor, so I felt a little lost, but pshaw I don't care."[33]

On her way home from Thief River Falls via Crookston to Fargo, she reflected on her time with her sister and her children. "Sella [a nickname for Hilda] has been just lovely to me. And God has been so good. Hope all goes good hereafter to. (*sic*) And I can say I have had a very pleasant journey." When she got to Fargo she was met by some friends from the Young People's Society, Julia [Nilsen?] and Emma. They took her to the Johnson family home, where Julia and Emma roomed while attending Oak Grove.

The next morning at eight thirty, they went to Oak Grove after a "fine breakfast," where they "attended the geography class and then chapel exercises after we went through the school buildings. It has been a fine mansion. Julia went in for her serving class and I went with her. I got such a headache. I felt real sick. Than (*sic*) we had dinner. Than (*sic*) one class more and we went home. Just fixed up a little and went over to Løbecks. My I had a fine time there . . . We went to have my luggage transferred, came back to Løbecks and had supper there. Sang a song and heard some fine pieces on the piano."[34]

John Engebretsen Løbeck (1862-1937), a distinguished educator and later LFC pastor, was the chair of the board at Oak Grove and very likely knew the Jacobsons from Lutheran Free Church gatherings. While there was no upper limit on age in the Oak Grove catalogues, it may be that by the time Anda visited in March 1910, when she was twenty-four, she felt it was too late. With some resignation, she went home, where she had both her parents to care for, as well as several nieces and nephews. Mildred, for example, was five, and Mathilda's husband, Richard Hanson, had become ill with pancreatic cancer. Mathilda needed help with her children as well. He would die on October 26, 1910, leaving Mathilda on the farm alone, pregnant with Peter Adolph, who was born on December 22, 1910. To help her, Grandma Jonette and Anda took the children, Selma and Rudolf, for a while until their mother was able to do anything but care for the baby. Bernt, only ten, had to help her with the farm as a young boy. She knew well how to do all the work on the farm from her girlhood. This meant that when Anda came home from Badger, she now had at least three and up to eight children to care for with her mother and three sisters.

## The 1910 Young People's Society Convention

On July 3-4, 1910, the Society gathered in the Eidskog woods near Ortonville, Minnesota, in Big Stone County. Anda was there with her music. The reporter Pastor Andreas Jakobsen Vigestad (1862-1912) raved about the weather: "The air was pure and clear, and the sun shone beautifully. The woods and meadows looked like they were dressed like a bride for her bridegroom, everything in nature joined with its beauty and life."[35]

Although there were not so many people at this event as had been at the previous one, the pastors did their best to challenge the youth to prepare for their futures, helping them to become parents, something that was a constant theme of these meetings. Nothing concerned the leaders of these churches as much as assuring a future for their children.

In that spirit, Pastor Gynild focused on the importance of mothers in the raising of a spiritually aware child, going way back to Moses and his mother. Vigestad noted that the message powerfully and seriously laid on the hearts of the young that they needed to choose the right partner and how they were to live. This message to the young has always been a main theme of those working with the young people in the church. In fact, it was the hope of parents and pastors that the time together with other young people of the same faith and culture would spark romances and lead to marriages that would continue the tradition.

At this meeting, Anda was reelected to be on the music committee for the next annual meeting, which would be in Cyrus, Minnesota. At the end of the meeting, a choir led by Nels Brygman Leines (1874–1933) of Dovre, near Benson, sang between the speeches, and an offering was taken for Bethesda Homes, now moved to Eagle Lake and the Willmar area. It amounted to $63.73. Vigestad remarked that the songs and testimonies made their way into the hearts of the young people there. He prayed that the meeting would bear blessed fruit in the harvest of eternity.

As well as Pastor Gynild, Pastor Michaelsen of Calvary in Willmar, whom Anda knew well, was a speaker. She described it in her own words: "Many happy moments have I experienced in Willmar, but perhaps never ever as happy as I am this evening. I believe this meeting was exceptional."[36]

The songs the group sang were a mixture of English and Norwegian hymns and spiritual songs. One of the pastors had recommended that they use both English and Norwegian to give both languages their proper place in the services. The pastors knew full well that English would be, and already was, the language with which the youth would be more comfortable. Anda used both Norwegian and English interchangeably, almost in a mixture, and her command of either language does not seem exceptional. She probably spoke Norwegian, her native tongue, more fluently but found it difficult to write it since her parochial school education, while rigorous, had not been sufficient for her to gain mastery over either the old language or the new.

A favorite song from the *Frydetoner*, the Hauge Synod publisher K. C. Holder's choral anthem book that most of these choirs used, was "*Den Himmelske Lovsang*" ("The Heavenly Praises"), the first anthem in the collection. Miss Stensland and Anda sang it as a duet. They then received communion, which was more common at gatherings like this than I had thought. While receiving the sacrament was extremely serious for this generation, and required deep soul searching, these meetings did not have, as far as I can see, occasions for talks with a pastor about the state of their souls. Gisle Johnson, professor of systematics at the University of Christiania and teacher of most of the Norwegian professors who came to America, including Weenaas, Sverdrup, and Oftedal, had taught, based on 1 Corinthians 11:22–24, that it was dangerous for one's soul if one went to communion unworthily, by which he meant not appropriately shriven of one's sins. People picked up that that they had to be worthy of communion, and very few people, to their credit, thought they were. If someone went up, people would then think the person was a hypocrite and not a sinner in need of assurance! It was a catch-22.

My father told me there were times when hardly any member in the congregation would dare to come to the altar. Once, he heard from the previous pastor in Tunbridge, Luthard Gjerde, that when he had invited people to come forward to receive the sacrament, no one came. He could not believe how a good teaching—that the sacrament was an assurance of the forgiveness of sins—had been skewed to mean one had to be good enough to receive it. They were right to think they were not sinless, but they missed the point.

## The Death of Sven Oftedal

Sven Oftedal had been a reluctant president of Augsburg. He had never been a stay-at-home office type. His travels on behalf of Augsburg to gather money had been effective but exhausting for him. His character fit that work. He would return to Augsburg to teach and work with Sverdrup on their dreams. Every night promptly at nine, he would knock on Sverdrup's door and go in for an hour of conversation, which ended exactly at ten. He knew how to raise money. When he was president, he grew unsatisfied with the work of Jacob Mortensen, who had moved to the city to work as a development man for the school. As the school faced more issues of financial need, he fired Mortensen, a slight for which Gerda Mortensen, Mortensen's daughter, never quite forgave him.

Sverdrup's son, George, had left his promising career as a scholar to serve as vice president of the school while the community found a good successor for Georg Sverdrup. Oftedal was traveling to Europe to treat what was a gall bladder ailment and spend time in Greece. He had become fluent in modern Greek and was well loved by the Greek community in Minneapolis. Being an administrator was not his cup of tea.

In the spring of 1911, Oftedal needed an operation. While he came through it successfully, he did not rally and died in Deaconess Hospital surrounded by his wife, Marie; his three children; and George Sverdrup Jr. Many said he died for love of Augsburg. His funeral was on April 4, 1911. It was much the same ceremony as it had been for Sverdrup. The casket lay in the aula of Main while people came to pay their respects. People from the community who knew him well were among the crowds that passed by his casket. His shining, faithful courage had influenced many of those who walked by his body.[37]

As with Sverdrup, a candle burned at the head and foot of the coffin draped with flowers. The brief service was led by Professor Blegen, who read a psalm and prayed. Then the casket was brought to Trinity Congregation, where a large group, over 1100, packed the church. The congregation sang Landstad's hymn "I Know of a Sleep in Jesus' Name" (*"Jeg ved mig en Søvn I Jesu navn"*). Pastor Strand led the service and spoke on behalf of the congregation. He remembered that Oftedal had preached just four weeks before at Sunday services. Andreas Helland spoke on behalf of Augsburg in the words of Ephesians 2:14, "He is our peace." The Glee Club sang, and Pastor Paul Winther, chair of the inner mission board of the LFC, greeted the gathering on behalf of the LFC.

Pastor Sletten spoke in English about Oftedal's gifts as a leader, working as a member of the Minneapolis school board and its library board, where he had worked to assure that the libraries in immigrant communities had books in their languages, especially the greatest literature from the various ethnic traditions represented in the population of the cities—German, Greek, Norwegian, Swedish, and so on. Over twenty pastors from around the church served as pallbearers. The gathering processed to Lakewood Cemetery in Minneapolis, beside Lake Harriet, where he was buried alongside Sverdrup's grave. The reporter noticed that the masses of flowers that had accompanied him in the spring weather overflowed and covered Sverdrup's grave as well, almost as if to say, "Now he has come after you and has been lain down by your side."[38]

Wilhelm Pettersen, the poet of the LFC at the time, wrote a eulogy for Oftedal, as he had done for Paulson and Sverdrup. He ended it "You were a man, in strife, and the work of peace, the last of the greatest in our church."[39] The editor of *Folkebladet* wondered, "How would it go with Augsburg and the Free Church when even he is gone?" It was a terrible loss, the writer noted: "Let us see that it is the Lord's work that this great man has given us as a heritage, and it is through us that he will have it developed."[40]

Oftedal is more difficult to evaluate for his part in the heritage of Augsburg and the LFC. He left no books behind, although his writings filled *Folkebladet* for years. He was an eloquent preacher and writer. Speeches and sermons do not last long; they die in the breezes that blow around speakers as they speak. If he was the spirit of Augsburg, which I think he was, that spirit has blown where it will, and no one can track it except to point to deeds or monuments. As he grew older, with his long hair blowing in the wind, he appeared to the students as something of a character whose days had passed him by. He was much diminished when Sverdrup died. Whatever Sverdrup accomplished and left behind would not have been possible without Oftedal cheering him on. I have come to admire him more and more over the years.

## Cyrus Youth Society Meeting in 1911

The program for the Cyrus meeting on June 30–July 2, 1911, was published in the June 7, 1911, issue of *Folkebladet* but not the songs. The reporter of the event, Pastor Michaelsen, was a popular speaker and leader of the youth and the Free Church during this period. Anda frequently sang duets with him and enjoyed his preaching.

Cyrus, Minnesota, about six miles east of Morris, in Pope County, Minnesota, was largely Norwegian. The rich farmland is dotted by sloughs and small lakes that make the vistas pleasant and green. This had attracted Haakon Tinseth and his family as good farmland, with Norwegian Lutheran congregations all around. Every little town in Pope County seemed to have two Norwegian Lutheran churches in it, one on either side of the highway. One was usually an old

Conference church and the other a Norwegian Synod Church. The Conference church would have joined either the United Church or the Free Church. In Cyrus, St. Petri was LFC, while St. John's was a United Lutheran church. Eight miles farther east, near Lake Minnewaska, was Starbuck's Innhered church, led by Nils Forde (1849–1917). It was the stalwart Synod congregation in the area, known forever, even to this day, as Forde's church.

Michaelsen noted that the St. Petri congregation had prepared very well for the meeting. It took for granted that the crowd would be bigger than the church could hold, so they had built a platform outside the church and took out the windows so people could hear the proceedings. People could hear rather well if the speaker spoke to that side of the church. This was a common practice that made large gatherings in small church buildings possible.

On Friday morning, June 30, 1911, the small town was overrun by some six hundred young people who were hosted by members of the congregation, as was the custom at these kinds of meetings. When the festivities began, Andrew Olson (1868–1947), the pastor of the congregation, welcomed the crowd to the convention. He announced there would be three large sessions. The first would be from ten to twelve. The first half hour would be a prayer meeting, followed by some singing. The afternoon meeting would be from two to four and the evening meeting from seven thirty to nine.

The theme of the meeting was the rich young ruler, Luke 18:18–27. This text made an impression on the young people there, most of them second-generation immigrants. They were beginning to see the growing prosperity of their parents, who had lived through trying times as they established their farms and towns. They were now harvesting the riches that grew around them. The theme of remembering the Lord when you are young ran like a red thread through the meeting, which pushed toward decisions at every turn.

The instructions to the delegates had been very specific about where to go and at which depot to detrain, depending on their starting points. Anda took the train from Montevideo to Benson. The train was very crowded with young people on the way to the convention, she noted. When they got to Benson, they had to wait for the train to Morris. Their stop was just before Morris since they were to be met there. They were picked up and went to stay at the Otto Stensland farm with three other girls, the Netland sisters.

The meeting included music by both the massed choir and individuals. The choir was led by the director Leines from Benson. The speakers were Frantz Weltzin (1863–1937), Pastor Andreas Jakobsen Vigestad, and Ole Larsen Torvik, head of the Oak Grove Ladies Seminary Board. They all took the opportunity to urge that the young people not walk away from Jesus when he asked that they give up everything to follow him. "Time bears us on its wings toward eternity," Vigestad warned them, "so make your commitment now in your youth." Consistent with the LFC's strong emphasis on conversion and living Christianity, these pastors and the youths all understood that an experience of salvation or at least a recommitment was fundamental to their Christian lives.

During the evening session, Anda and Pastor Michaelsen sang a duet. They both thought all three of the speakers had been pithy and powerful. Anda wrote that the sermons and talks were warm and filled her heart with joy. She sang a solo during the evening session as well. Along with the speeches by the pastors, several women spoke, including Amalia Weltzin and Clara Larson from Scandia congregation near Cyrus, recommending Oak Grove to any of the girls in the group who wanted further education. Later, Anda would remark that this meeting was the best of all she had been to. It may have also been the time she met and maybe even fell in love with Theodore Andersen Tinseth, my mother's father, whom she would marry six years later.

She still had ambitions to cultivate her voice. She continued singing and teaching in the congregation and at these events. On March 27, 1912, a correspondent wrote to *Folkebladet* about how Trinity Lutheran, the Montevideo Lutheran Free congregation, was doing in the interim between pastors. The congregation was waiting for a new pastor, but it was doing well, especially because "of the service of Miss Anda Jacobson, with her lovely voice and deep faith which showed itself in her singing," he commented.[41]

During the following year, she became even more active in the Young People's Society, singing at the annual meeting of the group in Benson on June 5–7, 1912. A month before the meeting, a note appeared in *Folkebladet* announcing the songs that would be sung in the mass choir at the meeting: "Be diligent and practice these songs before you come to the meeting so we will need much less time practicing when we meet together."[42] The same leaders were in charge, including Pastor Michaelsen. This year, their theme was "Will you Live for the Lord?" Among the texts was Ecclesiastes 4 and the story of Jacob as an example. The meeting, as usual, would start with prayer and then a "singspiration," as we might call it, to get the meeting started off on the right foot. From then on, there were speeches and sermons, interspersed with edifying music: usually choirs, especially the Montevideo choir, considered one of the best in the region, as well as several solos by Anda. One of her duets was with Miss Harbo, the aunt of a future president of the LFC. Among the most repeated songs again was "Den Himmelske Lovsang."

On July 19, 1912, Anda wrote her friend Manda with whom she had sung a duet at the convention. She was filled with concern for her friend's spiritual condition but also her own issues. Her friend wanted to go to Oak Grove. She was about twenty, younger than Anda, who was twenty-six at the time. For some reason, her parents resisted her plans:

Montevideo, Minn.
July 17, 1912

My dear Friend,
Your letter was received a week after I came home from the convention. You were so good to write so soon. But me than (*sic*). I'm slow as ever but I have been thinking about you so much and have read your letter many times.

You wrote such a very good letter this time. I thank you so much.

O Manda! How I felt for you when you said you are afraid your dream about school will have to be blasted. So many of your plans look so impossible. I have felt that way so many times. And I have had hard fights too.

So many say that if its Gods will that we shall become any workers in his vineyard. He will make a way for us. Than (*sic*) again we know that many of those that are both ministers and missionaries have not only waited to see an opening or a way to get thru but have worked hard many times thru hard obstacles.

That's what I think of so many times now, perhaps if I had forced my will thru more perhaps, I could have been more than I am. But when one always shall look at what there is to do and obey your parents and stay at home you don't get any further. Sometimes I feel it's hardly right of parents not to offer more for their children when they know it's a good spirit that leads them and they want to do something good. That's the way I fight with myself and then I pray to Jesus to quiet the storm again I see things much different.

God alone knows what was best for me. And I hope I have done His will. My offering myself for my parents and folks. It seems so small and humble. But it's much my own fault too. That I don't work more personally for Jesus. I could do so much for my folks and friends. Perhaps God sees I am so incompetent in the small so why should He put me to something greater. I have tried to humble myself. It's been a hard lesson to learn. But shall learn it at last.

So, what encouragement can I give you dear young friend. I hope and pray God will open a way for you. That it shall not be so hard for you. I know you are very sincere, and you have the ambition too. I'm sure. And you are young yet. Don't get discouraged. If you can't go this year plan for next. But when you have an unmarried sister, I should think it was her duty to change off with you. So, you could go to Oak Grove. Work hard for it.

No, the last Y.P convention was not near as good as the one in Cyrus. I never felt so warmed up as I did then. And still it was so good, so much good to hear. And so grand as it is to meet the dear friends again. God bless them all. It's strange how good one can feel when you meet with Christians. One can just feel the warmth.

I could see that you were feeling bad about something on Saturday. And I just wondered what it could be, but when I shook hands with you, I could see it was no spiritual trouble.

Tomorrow I am going over to Nelsons place (our choir leader) they have a nice new house and a lovely home. They shall entertain the Y.P. Society on Friday evening. And I shall help Mrs. Nelson prepare for it.

I only hope it won't rain so much that we will have a poor crowd.

My sister from Badger [Hilda] was here visiting. She went home a week ago Sunday. She had her two youngest boys with her. We enjoyed her visit so much.

I am going to get up early in the morning and wash clothes. So, mother says I had better go to bed.

Dear Manda, I hope I can do you some real good by our friendship. I feel you are very near to me.

I have not had a chance to talk with Christine L. only over the phone. She is going to Dawson to work now so we will be farther apart yet. And it's so hard to because we are such friends.

Well, I must close my long letter.

Sanna greets you.

Your loving sister,<br>in Jesus<br>Anda J.[43]

## Off to Minneapolis, 1913

By this time, Anda must have become desperate about her own education. Somehow, she persuaded her parents to let her go to Minneapolis. On January 22, 1913, she was finally on her way to the city to take voice lessons. She was filled

Figure 6.4. F. A. Schaffnit. Public domain.

with excitement about the opportunity but also somewhat daunted by being on her own in the big city: "I am now on my way to Minneapolis. It seems like a dream that I should really get my dream fulfilled. This to go away and have my voice cultivated further. I feel so at ease. I'm not in the least worried, but all will be all right. And I am trusting Jesus will take care of me.... I suppose when I come nearer Minneapolis, I will feel more worried and lonely but I have the best of all companions. Jesus is with me. I shan't get lonesome."[44]

When she arrived, she was met by two boys, the sons of Rev. Schaffnit. She had expected to be met by Sister Gina from the Deaconess Motherhouse. The Deaconess community had advertised in *Folkebladet*, "If your daughters are coming to Minneapolis, let the deaconesses meet them at the station."[45] The readership knew young girls who were coming to Minneapolis for school or work would be comforted to know they would be met by friends. From the depot, they would take them to the place they had arranged to stay. Although Sister Gina had in fact been there to meet Anda, they did not connect.

She was taken directly to the Lutheran Home for Young Women (*Herberge*) in Minneapolis, on Sixth Street and Ninth Avenue. It had been established to provide a safe place for poor convalescent girls in the city who could not afford room and board and also for young women working in the city. It was established and run by the Lutheran Inner Mission in Minneapolis. The group was headed by F. A. Schaffnit and assisted by many other pastors such as Carl Knutson Solberg (1878–1954), the longtime pastor at Bethlehem Lutheran and St. Paul's in Minneapolis, along with John N. Kildahl (1857–1920), president of St. Olaf College. The home was run "without regard to religion or nationality" for the many young women flocking to the city from the farm. They would be met at the depots by representatives and taken to the home, where they would be given a place to live and help finding a job.

Founded in 1905, it was part of the inner mission work that especially German Lutherans thought inner mission should be—help for indigent people in the city. For most Norwegians, inner mission meant home missions, the founding of congregations, or working within congregations for spiritual renewal. The Schaffnits had established an inner mission in the city to help poor and disadvantaged girls. They were effective in getting German Lutherans and Scandinavian Lutherans from Swedish Augustana, the Norwegian United Church, and Augsburg to help them, something that was much needed at the time.

A working girl could receive room and board, with a laundry, for $2.50–4.00 a week. In an appeal for funds to pay off their debt, Schaffnit indicated that many Lutheran congregations in Minneapolis (twenty Norwegian, eight Swedish, two Danish, five German, and eleven English) had a mission to help these girls.

One great fear that Schaffnit used was the notion of a young girl from the country falling into the white slave trade, or in with traffickers. At an annual fundraiser, he told the heartrending story of one innocent young girl who came into town and was met by a well-dressed man who asked if she wanted work. Of course, she did. He took her to dinner, got her drunk, and then took her to his establishment. Fortunately, the police caught him and released her to the Schaffnits, where she flourished.[46] Schaffnit and his supporters regarded his work as one of uplifting the moral welfare of the city: "There is hardly a day during which the trains do not bring to our city a number of girls seeking employment. While it would undoubtedly be better in many cases for country girls to remain at home, nevertheless, the attractions of the city are so great that they continue to come, regardless of the fact that they are often told about the dangers and disappointments of city life."[47] He went on to estimate that there were some five thousand such young women in the city working for about three to six dollars a week.

The Jacobsons had read these appeals and reports in the *Folkebladet* and made sure that Anda would be kept safe by both the deaconesses and the Schaffnits when she arrived in the big city. Their yearly statistics indicate the Schaffnits filled a need. By September 1913, the year Anda came, they had registered over 587 girls, with a current roster of some 40–50 roomers. They needed more room and were hoping they could sell the home to the

**Figure 6.5.** Mrs. Schaffnit. Used by permission of the Grindal family.

Milwaukee Railroad station, which was nearby, and build a new home, as well as one for young men who had similar needs. In addition, they realized it was necessary to provide child care for working mothers who could not find anyone to take care of their young children while they were at work; these children were often left alone to fend for themselves, sometimes with drastic results. The Schaffnits felt it part of their mission to build a center for child care near their building.

While there, Anda kept detailed records of her spending. In it, one can see the world of the single girl in the first years of the twentieth century:

> For choisnois and powder—$.20
> For presents—$.27

> For biscuits—$.05
> For ticket—$2.66
> For dinner—$.25
> For card—$.05
> For carfare—$.25
> For Valentines—$.10
> For candy—$.10
> For music—$.75
> $4.21
> For collection $.15
> Offering—$.25
> For ring—$.10
>
> For room—$6.60
> For lessons—$10.00
> For ticket—$4.00
> $20.60[48]

The voice lessons were her highest expense by far.

There is not very much more from her about her time in Minneapolis. Family lore says she took lessons at MacPhail Music School, which would have been possible, but their records do not go that far back. Some even said her teacher wanted her to go to New York to try her hand at opera, but once again, whether that is true is impossible to determine. It was a long-held belief, and the comments on her singing that lasted down through the decades would certainly have supported that story. Over the years, I have come to believe much of that lore. She clearly had a gift and resented not being able to cultivate it further than for Young People's Society meetings in the region.

We do know one of her first appointments was a visit with H. N. Hendrikson (Henry), her old neighbor, now teaching at Augsburg:

> Jan 23, 4 o'clock: I feel both lonely and queer tonight. I just hope I will soon find a good teacher. Alvin Ronning is coming over to get me and go to Prof. Hendrickson. I do hope they will treat me nice. And that I can get some good advice from Henry in regard to a teacher.
>
> It is nice here in a way, but my its strange tho when you see only strangers you can't possibly feel at home. Margaret Schaffnit the older daughter of the owner here has been very good to me today and I think she will be a good friend but then it's not like having those that you know well as Christine or Lizzie or Manda.[49]

Six months later, that summer of 1913, Margaret Schaffnit left Minneapolis for Madagascar, where she would marry a Malagasy pastor named Eugene

Rateaver and take over Johanne Borchgrevink's school for girls that Anda's mother, Jonette, had regularly supported. A native Malagasy, he had been educated in Madagascar in the Norwegian Lutheran schools and come to the United States to study. He received his BA at St. Olaf, then from 1908 to 1911 matriculated at United Seminary in St. Paul, where he received his degree (candidate in theology). He had returned to Ft. Dauphin, Madagascar, as a teacher that same year. Margaret was feted at parties in the city before she left. This connection would make the feelings between the mission in Madagascar and Minnesota even closer.

In the fall of 1913, Fritjof Johan Tinseth, Haakon's youngest boy, enrolled in the first year of the preparatory section at Augsburg. His course of studies was essentially the same as Anton's, except that penmanship, music, and a specific course in US history had been added. The cost had risen to $162 a year, including electric light and steam heat, which was $20. He enjoyed the two years in the city, attending Trinity congregation and singing in the choir. Often, he would walk downtown to hear the singing at the Swedish Tabernacle. In addition, he would go for entertainment to Dania Hall on Cedar. It had been the center of the Scandinavian culture on Snus Boulevard. It had a large auditorium where concerts, lectures, and gatherings were held until it was destroyed in a fire in 2000. It also had a cafeteria where one could get a bowl of soup for a low price. While at Augsburg, he said, he heard Anda singing at Trinity and got to know many of the future leaders of Augsburg and the LFC, especially T. O. Burntvedt, who went by T. Olsen at the time.

## Death of Ole Jacobson

Ole Jacobson, Anda's father, died on December 17, 1913, after suffering several months of gangrene in his feet and legs. His obituary appeared in the February 4, 1914, issue of *Folkebladet* and was written by his pastor, Ludvig Cornelius Christian Pedersen (1874–1938), who noted that Ole, with his quiet faith, would be greatly missed by his family but also his friends and acquaintances in Montevideo. (Pedersen had been born in Madagascar to Norwegian missionaries so brought renewed interest in the Malagasy mission to the congregation.) Pederson described Ole Jacobson as a pioneer in Chippewa County and told the story of his dying, as was common for pastors to do, to witness that the person died in the faith. "Like a child giving himself over to the care of his parents, Ole went to his rest without fear and glad in his heavenly Father's graceful arms and rejoiced that soon he would be freed from his captivity to suffering, and he went peacefully into the sleep of death."[50]

Nor did Pedersen miss the chance to give Jacobson's Free Church credentials, noting that Ole Paulson had married the Jacobsons in Minneapolis and they had been founders of the Brønø congregation in 1873. From the beginning, he said, Jacobson had been a Friend of Augsburg Seminary and was among the leaders who supported the Brønø congregation since he had been among the first supporters of the Free Church, helping to establish the congregation.

Pederson also noted that "faithful and filled with love, [Ole's] loving wife and children cared for him and did what they could to relieve his hard suffering which he patiently bore to the last."[51] The funeral was held at Trinity Lutheran Free Church in Montevideo, which his sons Richard and Octer had built.

Anda returned from Minneapolis that summer to help her mother and siblings care for Ole in his last days. After living in town and helping Richard with his construction business for some years, Octer was also now living on the farm so he could farm the homestead and be with his daughter Mildred. Anda was needed at home to care for her nieces and nephews, especially Mildred.

In August 1916, Anda would be thirty. After her father's death, she could leave some of the work on the farm and in the home to her mother, Jonette, but her mother's health was failing. She had fallen and broken her hip and had been unable to walk much on her own since. Anda still continued as a leader in the Young People's Society meetings, bringing her music and deep faith to those in attendance, but she was getting older now.

At the spring meeting at the Eidskog congregation in Ortonville, held March 21–23, Anda sang several solos and performed with a mixed quartet from her home congregation. Among the speakers were the usual: M. B. Michaelsen, Andrew Olson, and several laymen. A constant topic was how to make Bethesda Homes in Willmar more beloved by the people so they would give money to it, always a concern—and a strong concern of the Tinseth family that Anda was to marry into.

Andrew Olson, the pastor at St. Petri in Cyrus, the secretary of the district, and a reporter on the gathering, wrote that Anda's singing had brought its blessings to the group and made "the meeting evocative and warm. Let those gifts of grace be used to the edification of the congregation."[52] Given the quality of her voice and the conviction with which she sang, she was able to evangelize through her music. Whether her future husband, Theodore Tinseth, was there, we do not know, but Olson, his pastor, commended Anda with kind words in his reports of the meetings during their courtship. Olson was known for his sermons that always ended with "Do you know where you are going? What if you should die on the way home?" This frightened my mother, who, as a young motherless girl, wanted to go to be with her mother in heaven but hardly dared to go home, she would say later. Her uncle Freddie would laugh and say, "The trouble was he never really told us what to do about that!"

In the summer of 1916, the Young People's Society met in New London, near Willmar, from Thursday evening to Sunday afternoon, June 29–July 2.

"Fight the Good Fight," from 1 Timothy, was the theme of the conference. As young people, they were especially aware of the war in Europe. The next year, many of the young men in their midst would be called into the military. Still, as Pastor Torvik noted, it was far away at the time. Woodrow Wilson was campaigning on the slogan "He kept us out of war." The war Torvik spoke of, however, was the war between spirit and flesh. Most important was that the young people in the group were not simply moral but that they belonged to Jesus. He called to those who may have fallen. "Confess your sin, grasp onto eternal life today," he urged.⁵³

At this meeting, the group also heard from George Sverdrup Jr., who had taken his father's place as president of Augsburg Seminary. He spoke movingly on the calling of the disciples Andrew and Peter by Jesus. They were moved by the Holy Spirit to follow him, Sverdrup said, and answered Jesus's simple question, "What do you want?" with "Where do you live?" All of us, he said, long for more talk with Jesus. We want to be with him forever, so therefore we advise seekers to seek after God: "It can be a sore, heavy, and painful matter to be awakened; but it is absolutely necessary. Do not delay, you that are seeking, until you find Jesus."⁵⁴ After his speech, Anda sang a solo.

## George Sverdrup Jr., 1879–1937

When George Sverdrup Jr. took over after his father, he represented quite another generation, like those who were now in the Lutheran Free Church Young People's Societies. Although he understood and could speak Norwegian, he wrote to his father in English and was more at home with English than Norwegian. Like his father, he was not ordained. It had been his intention to be a scholar of Near Eastern Languages. The son of the first Mrs. Sverdrup, Katharine Elisabeth Heiberg, he had graduated from Augsburg in 1898 and attended the University of Minnesota immediately after that. In 1901, he attended Yale to get his master's degree. From there, he studied at the American School of Archeology in Jerusalem and then taught in the Syrian Protestant College in Beirut, a well-known school for Americans. He hoped to be studying for his doctorate at Leipzig and Berlin Universities in 1908–1909. His goal was to teach and be a scholar. He had already translated documents from Arabic to English, for example, "Letter from Mahdi Muhamed Ahmad to General Gorden," which appeared in the *Journal of American Oriental Society*.⁵⁵

At his father's death, however, in 1907, he returned to Augsburg. While the constituency trusted the name Sverdrup and knew him, they were somewhat suspicious of his schooling. Yale was outside Augsburg's sphere. Nevertheless, he was elected vice president of the school. In that capacity, he served in a kind of triumvirate with Andreas Helland and Hans Andreas Urseth (1866–1909). In

**Figure 6.6.** George Sverdrup Jr. (1879–1937), the second generation of Sverdrups to serve Augsburg. Used by permission of Augsburg University Archives.

the meantime, he taught Hebrew and Old Testament exegesis at the seminary. After Sven Oftedal, a reluctant president of Augsburg, died in 1911, Sverdrup was called to become president. There he stayed until his untimely death in 1937, struck down like his father of a heart attack at fifty-eight. They both may have died of exhaustion and love for the small school that never flourished during their time the way they would have liked it to.

While he had large shoes to fill, George was capable, devoted to his father's idea of the congregation and of Augsburg. Probably to his surprise, he spent the rest of his life traveling around to small towns and congregations like this one in New London, speaking to the young and challenging them to live for Christ. Augsburg, always Augsburg. His main problem was to figure out how to bring the preparatory department into the twentieth century and make a college out of it without betraying his father's commitment to a three-level seminary program. Along with the change in offerings, he would have to move the school and its supporters to accept coeducation.

As thirty-year-old Anda sat there taking notes on his speech and warming to his talk of Augsburg, however, she knew it was not open to her yet. Anda carefully noted his lecture on the congregation and the Lutheran Free Church principles. She wrote in English, showing that he spoke in English and that she understood the principles—first, "The Congregation is the starting point for all our ideas." From there, he went on to explain why Augsburg Seminary needed to continue to educate young men "who come from Free church congregations. And they can teach the seminary again what we need in our congregations." Because this was so significant, he noted that "when the congregations demand the best from us, it is their duty, when they call a man to be their leader, [to realize] they must also give their best to the school. Even though we do our best, it is but little. We must wait on God's blessings to increase our effect. For that reason, the young people who work in our congregations ought to go to our schools and learn what we really have to do. The common schools also need Christian teachers."[56]

He urged the young to read again the Free Church principles as "they are the only basis upon which we can ever get together which is the desire of so many Christian hearts." Here, he is echoing his father's notion about Christian unity or even Lutheran merger: Our unity is not in theological agreements but in Christ. It sank deep into my grandmother's heart and came straight down to me.

Speaking after Sverdrup, Pastor Torvik, the Oak Grove board chairman, noted, in Norwegian, "that we need to learn a little about our motto that we have heard so much about these past days." After that, Anda had written, "Back to the Farm." Whether that was her own comment or a record of what someone had said is not clear, but it was what she would do. Torvik continued, "Back to the congregation, back to the church, and its work." He concluded with a promotion of Oak Grove again: "The work that is done there will be a great blessing for our congregations."[57] From there, Anda went home.

Mildred was now ten years old and badly needing a mother. Her father had remarried that summer, and her stepmother, Mina, was cruel to her. Mildred said that Mina had even tried to scratch out her mother's face on pictures. As Mildred's godmother, Anda took seriously the pledge such an office entailed: That if the parents died, you were to look out for the child and raise them.

The last notice we have of Anda's singing before she got married was on July 25, 1917, at the wedding of Peder Konsterlie and his wife, Pauline Pederson, in Benson, Minnesota, before the couple left for their work as missionaries in China. She sang "A Perfect Day" and "Behold a Host Arrayed in White." The wedding was in the home of the bride, near Willmar, as was common in that day. Guests included Andreas Helland, the E. E. Gynilds, and several other leaders of the Lutheran Free Church. Konsterlie would go on to become the director of Foreign Missions in the LFC.

Sometime during this year, Anda went to Tacoma, Washington, to live with her brother Lindor Jacobson and seek her fortune there. (Lindor was an active member of the LFC congregation in Tacoma and was mourned in a *Folkebladet* obituary when he died in 1936.) She was closest to him of her siblings, and his moving to the West was a blow. Now that her father had died, she was no longer needed at home, and her mother's health did not require her to be there, so she could leave for a time.

Anda is listed in the Tacoma city directory as living with her brother, but while her time in the city was long enough for her to be included in the directory, it was not very long. Family lore says that her brother had a recording made of her singing, but that cannot be proven. Everybody knew her voice was special. She did, too, as her letters and diary clearly stated. While there, she must have decided to return and marry Theodore Tinseth of Cyrus, Minnesota. She had been with him at many of the Young People's Society meetings and certainly knew of the Tinseth family from the small world of the LFC district congregations she inhabited. Both had been raised by parents with strong personal faith in Jesus. They were both over thirty and ready to establish a family as soon as possible.

As they were planning their wedding, the St. Petri congregation in Cyrus was planning a "surprise" party for Andrew Olson, their longtime pastor, on February 14, 1918, Valentines' Day, to celebrate his fiftieth birthday. He had just spoken to the boys in Beardsley, Minnesota, who were leaving for the army. Because of bad weather, he decided not to go to the ladies' aid meeting in Cyrus, but Haakon Tinseth and his son came by and offered him a ride there. He decided to go, and when they arrived, the choir was singing, the church was filled, and C. E. Nordberg, a friend of Olson's, was there. He gave him six valentines, speaking on behalf of Scandia and St. Petri congregations. C. K. Weltzin spoke for the Kongsvinger congregation, all part of the Morris parish that Olson served. When he arrived at the parsonage in Morris, another group from the congregation there was waiting to surprise him again. All told, he received nearly two hundred dollars, over half of his yearly salary at the time.

Anda and Theodore would marry on March 20, 1918, at the Trinity Lutheran Free Church in Montevideo. When Theodore married her, he got three women in the bargain, including grandmother Jonette, who, because of her bad hip, had to be carried to the bathroom and to bed; and Mildred, whose father, Octer, told Anda as he was dying of tuberculosis of the brain, "You have to take her [Mildred], Anda. Minnie is so mean." Anda did.

On July 22, 1918, Uncle Fred Tinseth left Hill County in Montana, where he had gone to homestead in the Sweet Grass Mountains near Joplin, to Fort Dodge, Iowa, where he would enter the army. This was probably the worst time to be with thousands of young men, given the Spanish flu that would ravage the population in October through December, but he survived and, to my knowledge, did not catch the flu. He soon became a sergeant and remembered the army with pleasure, even the making of a living flag in the blistering heat of an Iowa August. The Cyrus paper noted when he came home to visit his parents

**Figure 6.7.** Theodore and Anda (Jacobson) Tinseth. Used by permission of the Grindal family.

for the holidays that "apparently army life agrees with him."[58] He remembered that after the armistice, they were going to be sent to Russia to fight on the side of the White Army against the Bolsheviks, but as they were being shipped to Detroit to be sent to Russia, the idea died.

A year before, Fred had made a homestead entry for the quarter of land he'd been farming, which he could do after three years. He claimed the land on November 10, 1920, in Chester, Montana, after he was demobbed from the service.[59] For him, this was the glory of America—he described life on the frontier as thrilling. Every kind of person was there and treated equally. He had been employed at a café while working his claim. He gave vivid descriptions of taking the land, lying in a tent on the ground with a thick rope around him to prevent rattlers from striking him. He described building up a shack there so he could make his claim, even driving through a raging snowstorm with a neighbor to vote in the 1920 election for president. When they finally got back, they realized

**Figure 6.8.** Fred Tinseth during his time in the US Army. Used by permission of the Grindal family.

they had voted exactly opposite on every candidate and measure. Fred's vote was without a doubt a straight ticket for Republicans.

## The Chicago and Minneapolis Theses

During the worst part of the influenza pandemic, the Norwegian Lutheran Church of America, the Augustana Synod, the Joint Synod of Ohio, the Iowa Synod, the Danish Lutheran Church, and what would become the United Lutheran Church in America (1918) joined with the LFC to form the National Lutheran Council (NLC). Dr. H. G. Stub (1849–1931) was the first president of the NLC. Part of its mission was to help those suffering in Europe after World War I and those Lutherans who had moved from rural areas to industrial centers. It would not be an organization on the way to merger but was rather focused on the question of home mission boards and how to manage the home mission efforts of Lutherans so they would not unnecessarily compete with each other by founding congregations in the same neighborhood. Stub, president of both the NLCA and the NLC, feared he would be accused of unionism. Consequently, during these negotiations, he wanted a resolution clearly stating that a "Joint Committee [was] to confer on questions of doctrine and practice, with a view to the coordination of their home mission and other work."[60] Unionism meant wanting to be united without proper agreements on doctrine. Stub faced growing opposition to union from his church and began to draw back.

At a meeting in Chicago on January 27–28, 1920, the group worked on a statement that came to be called the Chicago Theses, authored mainly by H. G. Stub. As the scion of the Norwegian Synod who attended Concordia Seminary for his theological training, he tended to side with Missouri on doctrinal questions. The group was reported to have approved of his theses, which mostly had to do with doctrine. Controversy broke out, especially on the lodge question and unionism.[61] Stub preferred his short and succinct Chicago Theses to the longer document, "The Essentials of a Catholic Spirit," proposed by the more liberal members of the council. Dearest to Stub's heart was the declaration that the Bible was "inerrant" in matters of faith and doctrine, something he needed to appease his constituency.

On hearing the word *inerrant*, many heard the language of fundamentalism, but Stub had very shrewdly left out any language saying Scripture was inerrant in history or in text. It was in matters of faith and doctrine that Scripture was inerrant, not in history. Thus, he avoided accusations of fundamentalism to some extent, although the charges were made by those who only heard the word *inerrant* and not the careful proscribing of history from the list.[62]

These documents were intended to declare what was necessary for church fellowship, not merger. They reaffirmed the Galesburg Rule of Lutheran pulpits for Lutheran pastors only and Lutheran altars for Lutheran communicants only. This was to their minds a rejection of "unionism and syncretism," necessary for "sound and conservative Lutheranism."[63]

Meanwhile, family life on the Tinseth farm revolved around the heavy labor necessary to get the farmwork done. Theodore's father, Haakon, was the church secretary for many years at St. Petri, and his mother, Torbjør, worked tirelessly for the work of the ladies' aid. Anda's voice brought her many invitations to sing at congregations in the area, and Theodore would drive her to those engagements despite his weariness from his daily work on the farm.

On February 16, 1919, my mother, Jonette Torbjor, was born, named for her two grandmothers, as was the Norwegian tradition for naming children. On March 9, 1921, her sister, Borghild Theodora, came into the world. The young girls were well cared for by their parents, grandparents, and flocks of cousins.

In Cyrus, Anda contributed to the spiritual life of St. Petri, the Lutheran Free Church there. She and Theodore bought his father's farm on Lake Charlotte, and Haakon and his wife moved into a new house at the western edge of Cyrus looking west over the Tinseth farms. Anton, Theodore's brother, had bought a quarter section next to the home farm. As far as you could see, looking on the northwest side of the road from Cyrus, were Tinseth farms. As much as she

Passing the Torch

could, Anda sang for church events in the area. Theodore would drive her to her engagements in their Model A Ford.

Anda and Theodore had married just before the great influenza epidemic broke out, and Anda was pregnant with my mother during the worst of the epidemic. Later, scholars noticed that many of the children in utero during the late 1918s would have a variety of nervous difficulties such as anxiety and other disorders. That would certainly cover my mother. In any case, she was well loved by her parents, grandmothers and grandfather, and her cousin Mildred.

Jonette Adrianna Martinusdatter Jacobson died on November 1, 1922. The obituary written by her son-in-law Bernt Sundal described her last days in Cyrus with her son-in-law Theodore; daughter Anda; and granddaughters Mildred, Jonette, and Borghild around her. The last twenty-five years, he said, she had suffered much from rheumatism and had broken a hip, so she had difficulty walking. This meant Theodore had to lift her onto the chamber pot and otherwise move

**Figure 6.9.** Jonette Jacobson with granddaughters Borghild (left) and Jonette (right). Used by permission of the Grindal family.

her around the house. In 1917, she suffered a stroke, which had affected her memory and speech, although she could sit up and had no pain after that.

A month before she died, Sundal said, "she suffered a heart attack and knew that it was the last call for her last journey, glad to give herself over to God's will and looking forward to the hour of salvation. On November 1, she slept away peacefully in her last sleep, firmly believing in the blessed resurrection when Christ will call to her."[64] She was buried in Montevideo beside her husband, Ole. In her will, one can read her devotion to the LFC, Augsburg, and her granddaughter, Mildred, to whom family lore says she left over ten thousand dollars.

CHAPTER 7

# Coeducation at Augsburg

SHE WAS A beautiful young woman. The family and photographers seemed to know this and featured Mildred in pictures that show her at her best—although we cannot see her red hair and hazel eyes in the black-and-white pictures. My favorite is below, in front of the Jacobson farm. She must have been about fourteen, just before she moved with Anda and her grandmother to Cyrus.

Mildred's obituary says she came to Cyrus in 1918 to live with her aunt, my grandmother, Anda Tinseth. The census records her as living in the Tinseth home on January 23, 1920. She likely came with Anda and her grandmother Jonette Jacobson after Anda and Theodore's wedding and honeymoon in March 1918.

Whenever it was, she entered the life of Cyrus, the school, and the church with her natural enthusiasm. She played on the women's basketball team and sang in the choir. On October 31, 1920, when she was fifteen, she was confirmed by Andrew Olson, pastor at St. Petri. He graded her work as "especially good"

**Figure 7.1.** Mildred Jacobson on the family farm. Used by permission of the Grindal family.

("*Særdeles gode*"). He did not record that she "read" in English, which means she most likely learned the catechism in Norwegian and spoke the rich Norlanding dialect of her grandparents who had raised her.

Her life had been sad. Her mother died when she was three, her stepmother was cruel, and her father passed away from tubercular meningitis in 1920 when she was fifteen. She did not like to speak of her childhood for good reason. On the other hand, she was fortunate to have a close family of grandparents, aunts, and uncles who cared for her with love and affection. Augsburg and the LFC were central to her family's life, and she knew it. She received a generous inheritance, some ten thousand dollars, from her grandmother Jonette when she reached the age of eighteen in 1923. Although some women students enrolled in 1922, 1923 should be counted as the year coeducation at Augsburg officially began. This was the year Gerda Mortensen was engaged by Sverdrup to be the dean of women. That was the beginning of Miss Mortensen's lifelong career at Augsburg. Mildred was there when Gerda began her work at Augsburg, but she knew her well before then.

George Sverdrup wanted to make Augsburg coeducational for financial reasons as well as conviction. The LFC had built Bethany College in Everett,

**Figure 7.2.** Mildred Jacobson as a young woman. Used by permission of the Grindal family.

## Coeducation at Augsburg

Washington, as a coeducational college in 1904, but it closed in 1917, so there was no opportunity for women to attend college in the LFC system. Jonette had included Bethany in an earlier will, maybe thinking of her daughters, so it had some reputation in the Midwest.

In considering how to provide a college for its young women, the LFC and Sverdrup had several options: make Augsburg coed, upgrade Oak Grove into a coed college, or turn the Willmar Bible School into a coed college. These ideas received considerable attention from the church as it was discussing the need for doing something.

The conversation had to be delicately handled by Sverdrup since many in the constituency had fought almost to the death for the notion of a school that was exclusively a seminary (*Presteskolen*). By then, however, the Augsburg Academy and Augsburg College were attracting a significant number of male students, like my great-uncle Fritjof (Fred) Tinseth (1893–1983), who had no intention of becoming a pastor but wanted some education at their church school.

World War I did not help enrollment. In 1918–1919, only twenty-three students were enrolled in the college department, as the number of males not participating in the conflict was small. Although the war ended on November 11, 1918, simply getting the soldiers home and demobbed took time. Something needed to be done to assure the future of the school—and soon.

The college's lack of credentials did not help either. Neighboring institutions like Hamline had been fully accredited for some time, but Augsburg's meager library and endowment, plus its poor space for chemistry labs, among other deficiencies, had prevented the accreditation board from giving Augsburg College full accreditation. The University of Minnesota, however, did let Augsburg students in classics, English, and Norwegian enroll in its graduate school. This was not enough, however, to increase enrollment. The decreasing number of students gave Sverdrup an opportunity to make a virtue out of necessity and work for coeducation.

As many men-only colleges were discovering, especially during the war, coeducation could be a solution to enrollment problems. The issue at Augsburg began to appear in the papers and especially the *Echo*, the college paper. For the students writing in the paper, the solution seemed indisputably clear. For the constituency, it was a bit more complicated, given Augsburg's history. Augsburg Seminary had built its base of support on the notion that it was a seminary to educate pastors both schooled in Free Church principles and fit for the American context. Furthermore, the idea had been cause célèbre in the conflict that resulted in the formation of the LFC when the United Church made every effort to take over the college department and shape it into a typical American college. Twenty years later, the debate was still fresh in the minds of those in the constituency. However, enrollment desperately needed to be increased in all the departments of the school, and many solutions for how to do this began to appear.

A letter to *Folkebladet* from a former student praised the school but complained that it was not growing. It could accommodate four times as many students as were currently enrolled, he argued. For the writer, the main issue was that the curriculum needed to be changed so it was more in keeping with a college that educated men who were not planning to be pastors. "Every student who has left Augsburg, has left because of the curriculum," he noted.[1] He went on to regret the fact that Augsburg was not paying its professors a living wage, which was true. Their supporters, farmers and businessmen, all had homes and cars of their own but not the professors. The writer, however, said nothing about coeducation. Still, as was the case at Luther College, also a pastor prep school, the pretheological curriculum was understood to be an impediment to more students—men or women—enrolling. The curriculum, with its emphasis on ancient languages and theology, was not deemed appropriate for women.

## The Golden Anniversary of Augsburg: 1919

The golden anniversary of Augsburg was celebrated with great festivities during the fall of 1919. One senses in reading the reports that the participants were almost surprised they had made it that far. The event attracted Minnesota's Governor Joseph Alfred Burnquist (1879–1961) and J. Edward Meyers (1862–1944), mayor of Minneapolis, both of whom spoke. The glee club sang, as did Professor Hendrickson, who had been pivotal in getting music into the curriculum.

The focus of the celebrations naturally tended to be on Augsburg's history. Pastor Johan A. Bergh, an 1869 graduate and scholar who had written on the beginning of the Norwegian American Lutherans, gave a moving speech on Augsburg during its time in Marshall, when the school almost had to close.[2] President Sverdrup lectured on the principles of Augsburg. Both Professor John H. Blegen and Pastor Peter Nilson, the evangelist who had traveled around the Friends of Augsburg congregations during its bitterest times, spoke of the history of the school in the later decades of the century.

Bishop Bernt Støylen (1858–1937) of Norway, well beloved by the Augsburg community, preached at the anniversary worship service held in Trinity. Støylen had visited the Conference, and the Brønø Congregation, years before. He ended the festivities by warning they should not forget the work of those who had gone before, quoting Rudyard Kipling: "Lest we forget—lest we forget."

One can feel the thrumming of anxiety about the school, as always, in much of the talk. The country and people had just survived a brutal war and the Spanish flu pandemic. The war had taken over two thousand lives. The flu had been much worse. Scholars estimate it caused over twelve thousand deaths in Minnesota alone.[3] Scholars are beginning to mark it for its widespread effect on the state and nation. I suspect Octer Jacobson's death in August 1920 of meningitis of the brain was very likely complications caused by influenza. One reads in the *Echo* at this time of a couple of deaths of students from the epidemic. Each death had been a private tragedy, one scholar argued, so the extent of the devastation was individual in a way the casualties of the war were not. At the golden anniversary festivities, influenza had lost its grip on the population but was still present.

The Alumni Association met during the celebrations. After what Chrislock called a "lively" meeting, a committee of seven members was named to "investigate and recommend new departures in education policy for both Augsburg and the Lutheran Free Church."[4] It was to be led by John Asbjørn Houkom (1890–1950), chair of the board.

One of the first things the committee did was conduct a survey of its alumni about many outstanding concerns: 149 people were surveyed, and of that number, 102 favored coeducation in the college. Forty did not. Reasons for the opposition had to do, as one might suspect, with the idea that Augsburg was a school to prepare pastors. Women simply could not be admitted at the time while maintaining Augsburg exclusively as a theological seminary.

Many also agreed that Augsburg should be moved from its current location. Ideas as madcap as relocating it in Glacier Park, the national park in Montana, emerged, but the logical place most agreed on was in Richfield, a suburb south of the Twin Cities. Another question asked whether Augsburg was a divinity school. Forty-six said yes, forty-four no, and thirty-eight made qualified answers. Houkom concluded from the survey that the school should emphasize "that henceforth there is conducted, in close harmony with a school in theology, a first class and standard college department, where young people may acquire a splendid education under Christian leadership."[5]

While this seems self-evident—the faculty could teach more students, and there was ample space in the facilities, although they were hardly glamorous—the issue was how to change the idea of the school in the minds of its constituents without changing the kind of commitments it had to educating pastors. Two decades before, that is what the congregations had fought for.

The Nineteenth Amendment to the US Constitution, which made women's suffrage legal, had been passed by Congress on June 4, 1919. It would be ratified on August 18, 1920. The idea of women's rights was in the air, and Sverdrup, along with others, knew something had to be done.

To add to Sverdrup's leadership problems, in 1919, the same year as the golden anniversary, Professor John Evjen, one of Augsburg's most brilliant graduates, began criticizing the LFC, and ultimately Sverdrup, in articles he wrote in *Folkebladet*. Evjen, an accomplished scholar, had gone on to earn his PhD in Leipzig. When he came back to Augsburg, one might have thought he was quite

Figure 7.3. John Evjen. Used by permission of Augsburg University Archives.

a catch. His credentials outshone every other member of the current faculty. That alone brought credit to the institution.

Evjen, however, was a typical product of his culture and difficult to deal with. Imprudently, he attacked the main Free Church principles and especially the first principle that the "congregation was, according to the Word of God, the right form of the kingdom of God on earth." He whipped out his credentials from Leipzig to prove his point that Luther would not have gone along with Sverdrup. While that is true—I, too, believe that Luther would not have agreed with it—it was foolhardy to go to the lists for this. Luther believed that any form of church organization could be evangelical, even the papacy, if it were not required. However, one could argue that a church really cannot exist without vital and living congregations, making it descriptive rather than prescriptive. The elder Sverdrup might have agreed, although he was a Johnny-one-note on Principle One.

Evjen prosecuted his case so vigorously that the younger Sverdrup submitted his resignation to the board. He was convinced by the board to reconsider. It also made clear to Evjen his services as professor would no longer be required. He became president at Mayville College in North Dakota, where he later had to leave because he wanted to forbid dancing, a ruling against which the students rebelled. From there, he went to Wittenberg College in Ohio, ending his career at Carthage College, at the time in Illinois.

Alongside the conversation about coeducation and the Evjen affair, the new Augsburg board chair, Pastor Knute B. Birkeland (1857–1925), pressed the college community to approve moving the Augsburg campus to the nearby Minneapolis suburb of Richfield, on the shores of Wood Lake. Birkeland, a wheeler-dealer who died in mysterious circumstances that did not redound to his credit, convinced the leaders of Augsburg that they could buy this land.[6] They could pay for the land with the profits made by breaking up a major portion into small lots that members of the Lutheran Free Church would find desirable as they looked to move out to the suburbs from their homes around the current Augsburg campus.

All these questions pressed on the younger Sverdrup as he worked to assure that Augsburg had a future. As always, things were never easy, but by the celebration in 1919, Birkeland had raised enough money to pay off the debt of some twenty-nine thousand dollars from 1915. The future looked promising, for once. Still, the future was not secure, and there were important leaders pushing every which way. Sverdrup's job was hardly easy. That almost everyone who got to know him well deeply respected and admired him was to his great benefit in these delicate discussions.

The March 1920 issue of *The Augsburg Echo* featured an editorial by Oscar M. Mehus (1894–1983), from the class of 1916, titled "Augsburg's Three Needs."[7] He argued that Augsburg was stronger than ever before: it had paid off its debts, proving that the congregations were fully behind the school; it had a dedicated and hardworking faculty led by a fine president in Sverdrup; and third, the state had approved Augsburg graduates for teaching certificates, and the university had voted to admit Augsburg graduates to its graduate programs. These were all positive developments that should be noted. What he wanted was to plan for the future of Augsburg.

The three things holding it back at the time could be easily remedied, Mehus argued. One, Augsburg needed to escape to the suburbs, where it would have more room and space for contemplation, rather than remain amid the hurly burly of the city, especially the neighborhood it was in. Two, it needed to introduce coeducation. He admitted that, historically, the idea of admitting women to almost any kind of school of higher education was something the founders could not have thought of as they were building a school and especially a seminary. Few schools enrolled women when Augsburg was founded, although in the next decade, women began to expect to enroll at many schools of higher education. There was a good number of schools already on the scene exclusively for women, but now it was time for Augsburg to go coed, as many colleges in the country were doing.

Mehus spoke for many in the constituency when he said that the times dictated the introduction of coeducation at Augsburg. He feared, however, that among the leadership of the school there were "fossilized standpatters to domineer our Annual Meetings and allowed [sic] them to squelch all sentiment in favor of coeducation."[8] He urged the next annual meeting of the LFC to discuss this question. Those procoeducation should make a special effort to come to the annual meeting so it would pass. In making this remark, he was pointing to something built into the principles of the LFC and a signature value of the

Free Church: Everyone who attended the conference could vote, regardless of their congregational affiliation, if they could in principle support the Twelve Rules. This meant the "standpatters" could pack the meeting and vote against coeducation—or, on the other hand, it could be packed with those who wanted coeducation at Augsburg. To that end, he urged all those in favor of coeducation at Augsburg and who had its "welfare . . . at heart to come out squarely for coeducation. The world had moved, and Augsburg must move with it."[9] In addition, he concluded, the school needed more loyalty from its alumni. His sister, Belle Mehus (1896–1988), would be one of the first women on the Augsburg faculty. She later made an international name for herself as a pianist, becoming the youngest American pianist to solo with the Berlin Philharmonic orchestra.

The 1920 annual meeting at Zion Lutheran, the LFC congregation in Thief River Falls, dealt calmly with three proposal options from the alumni council on how to educate its young women. One was to establish a Bible school on the West Coast, the second proposed coeducation at Oak Grove, and the third asked Augsburg College to adopt coeducation. Further, the group asked that the board of trustees make inquiries into the idea of moving the school to a better location, with the academy moving there first, to be followed by the college and seminary. This was a fundamental change in the traditional definition of the school.

Of these proposals, coeducation was the easiest to effect. A school dedicated only to educating pastors, no matter how good or necessary, simply could not be supported by most American seminaries or colleges, especially the LFC, whose congregations were not numerous enough to require great influxes of pastors every year. The seminary would need to produce enough graduates to remain viable as a school. Everyone sort of knew this.

The standpatters, as they were called, mounted some strong opposition, led by Pastor Christian Ytrehus, whose own wife had been one of the first women delegates to an annual conference. His opposition was not against the education of women but against coeducation at Augsburg Seminary. He argued, to some effect, that the entire fight about Augsburg as a nine-year school for pastors, which had caused the Friends of Augsburg to split from the United Church, would be rendered moot by the admission of women to the academy.[10]

The proposal to admit women and move the campus to Richfield seemed to Ytrehus a complete breach of trust against the founders of the school. The Augsburg community had fought tooth and nail, he said, against the proposal to make St. Olaf College the college of the church and destroy Sverdrup's dream of a nine-year program. Now he noted that one could make the same argument—that to change the nature of the two departments was a breach of trust against the founding principles of the school. Or was the argument simply that the United Church did not have the right to change Augsburg, but the LFC did? In effect, that was what the proponents of coeducation were saying.

## Coeducation at Augsburg

His logic was impeccable but out of step with the needs of the school. It is exactly the issue George Sverdrup had to deal with. It was necessary to have coeducation so the school would survive. The younger Sverdrup knew well this went against everything in his father's plan. Ytrehus thought that the membership of the LFC should fully understand the gravity of the decision to depart from the practices of the first fifty years of the school, over which much blood and treasure had been spent. He thought it would be better to create a college for women in Fargo, at Oak Grove, than to "send girls to our seminary."[11]

Ytrehus was not the only formidable opponent of coeducation at Augsburg. Gynild, president of the LFC, strongly opposed coeducation as well, as did other leaders of the church. The discussion was of necessity complicated because it involved several moving parts. One could be for coeducation at Oak Grove but not Augsburg or for it at Augsburg and not at Oak Grove. The Willmar Bible School, in the city where Gynild lived, also made for complications. Reading the list of voting members at the convention is interesting. There were many women in among the voting members, often wives of members but single women as well. My great-uncle Ed Kivley and his wife, Mary, were there, as were Anna Tjon Selland and her husband, Osmund. Gerda Mortensen and her mother were also voting members. These discussions on coeducation at Augsburg and/or Oak Grove must have been of great interest to all of them.

For one who grew up knowing the LFC intimately, the Willmar Bible School is a blank space in my understanding. I cannot ever remember hearing of it, although the Lutheran Bible Institute in Minneapolis was an important part of my growing up. My mother had attended there for a semester before her wedding. The Bible school in Willmar, however, while a gathering place for meetings and conventions, never took hold. It would serve the constituency until its resources were sent to Oak Grove in the later part of the 1920s when debt once again threatened the existence of Augsburg and Oak Grove.

The 1921 Convention of the LFC was held in Minneapolis. It dealt with some of the proposals but delayed approving coeducation at Augsburg until the next annual meeting. When the convention met in Fargo in June 1922, it voted for coeducation at Augsburg. The *Messenger Press* editor, Pastor Claus Christian Morgan (1879–1959), noted that resolution was approved "after a lively, but sane discussion. Seldom have we witnessed a discussion on an important issue, which to some involved a matter of principle, which was more thorough and freer from personalities than this one. Discussions of this kind afford the proper kind of a tonic for us all. Naturally *The Messenger* is pleased with the result."[12]

Little could be done to prepare the school for women by September 1922, but some women did enroll. The next year, Sverdrup called Gerda Mortensen to be dean of women, a post she would hold until 1964.

## Mildred Jacobson

Mildred Jacobson enrolled for the 1923-1924 school year, the first official year of coeducation. She took part in the life of the college with her usual energy, singing in the glee club and playing on the girls' basketball team. She did not, however, live on campus. The housing there was too grim for her, and she had enough money from her grandmother's estate to live better than that. She first lived with a family at 4312 Linden Hills Boulevard in Minneapolis, a place where several Augsburg students lived and worked. It was a fancy home, and she learned about how rich people lived and ate, for example, covering the asparagus in the garden so it was white. Transportation was also readily available.

When Mildred enrolled at the school, the curriculum provided essentially what it had for the nontheological students in the college. There were courses that appealed to her interests in music, athletics, and business. All women were required to take two hours a week of physical education, which involved tactics, calisthenics, and light apparatus, with an hour per week of outdoor recreation. School days began at 8:00 a.m. and ended at 4:00 p.m., six days a week. Students were required to attend daily chapel. If they did not, they had to have a legitimate excuse. There were several societies they could belong to. Students could write for the *Echo* or the *Augsburgian*.

The costs of a year were estimated to be $282. Tuition plus room and board were $60 a quarter. Students were required to bring their own bedding and laundry bag. Books were estimated to cost about $25 a year. The students had to pay for their electric light and steam heat. The price was $22 for a double room and $25 for a single room. One could rent furniture, probably a bed and desk. Included in the estimate were the required fees for insurance, gymnasium, the library, and medical aid.

To be admitted, one needed sixteen units required for graduation from most high schools or academies: These included four units of English, including English and American literature; two units each of history and mathematics; and one of science. If one were lacking in English skills, there was a remedial course in the preparatory department.

The coursework was simple but rigorous by our standards. To graduate from the college, every student had to take twelve credits of Christianity and fifteen in English and rhetoric, with foreign language requirements of some twenty credits if one had received no such instruction in high school. Those who had studied languages in high school received credit for those courses. One needed twelve credits of social science, fifteen of natural science, and fifteen in mathematics.

The catalog indicated courses a student preparing to go into law or business should take. Business was Mildred's main interest. During her freshman year, she would have to take four credits of history, five of English and mathematics, and two of Christianity. The history courses were taught by their family

Figure 7.4. Mildred (third from right) as a member of the Augsburg women's basketball team. Used by permission of Augsburg University Archives.

friend and relative H. N. Hendrickson. She would have taken Hendrickson's freshman course in medieval history, which lasted two quarters, followed by Renaissance and Reformation in the last quarter. The required religion courses for the freshman year were the Life of Christ, the Founding of the Church, and Church History.

Evidence in the *Annual* and the *Echo* indicates Mildred had a lot of fun. She fell in love and became engaged to a young man named Arne Gynild, the son of the president of the Free Church. The *Annual* noted that she had received a special delivery package from someone. "Was it Arne?" it asked. The couple seemed to be serious. He visited the farm in the summer, apparently. My grandfather, however, was not in favor of the liaison and told Mildred once to get that "sport off the farm."

The relationship did not survive. Mildred left school and went home to the farm before she began working at Dunwoody School and later Investors' Diversified Services (IDS) as a stenographer. In the fall, she returned to Minneapolis to work. She lived at several places in the Twin Cities, first with her uncle Richard, now a contractor in Minneapolis. She faced similar problems to those her aunt Anda had to deal with when she came to Minneapolis fifteen years before. Where was a safe place for young women to live in the city? Many places sought to meet that need as young people came flooding into the cities in the Roaring Twenties. On November 23, 1924, just as Mildred was getting settled into her work, Anda, her aunt and mother figure, died in childbirth of preeclampsia after giving birth to a little boy, Herbert Orlando, who died two days later. His grandfather Haakon Tinseth baptized him at home before he died. They were buried together in the St. Petri graveyard.

For some time, Mildred stayed with Anda's girls, my mother and her sister, Borghild, aged five and two. The next year, she went back to Minneapolis and worked at Dunwoody as a secretary. She took care of the girls when she would come home from Minneapolis on weekends and holidays. She would always bring them treats and clothes that would delight them in their difficult times; Anda had been a good model of how an aunt took care of her nieces and nephews. Frequently, Mildred was driven back and forth from the city to the farm by Fred Tinseth, Theodore's brother, who had gone to live with them on the farm to take care of "them little girls" after the death of their mother. In addition to farming, he had a business of shipping cattle from the farm to the stockyards in South Saint Paul. He would leave every Sunday evening, bring the cattle to the yards in South Saint Paul, and then return as soon as he could.

The death of Anda, for all intents and purposes Mildred's mother, was the signal event in my own mother's life. She was the five-year-old and remembered coming down into the room where her mother's lifeless body lay with a baby nearby. He would die shortly. Her father sat in the rocking chair, holding her little sister in his arms and weeping. It was a cold November day. My mother never forgot that some days before her death, her mother had had looked at her and began singing "God Will Take Care of You." Her preeclampsia may have given her the sense she would die giving birth. She even told someone she had heard a bird calling outside and thought it was calling her name.

Andrew Olson, her pastor, wrote an unusually emotional obituary for her in *Folkebladet*. Given how small the LFC was, pastors of well-known laymen and women frequently wrote obituaries for them in the paper. Olson noted that her death was caused by a hard period of labor in giving birth. He was saddened that now the widower "sat alone in the house with two little girls grieving the loss of a beloved wife and a loving mother." The funeral was on Thanksgiving Day. An unusually large crowd followed after Anda—as the saying goes in Norwegian, people marked how beloved or important the person was by how many people followed the body to the church or cemetery. Family from Montevideo and Cyrus, and even her brother Lindor from Tacoma, walked behind the coffin from the home to the church and then to the graveyard, which lay a couple of blocks from the church, adjacent to the Tinseth farm. At the funeral, a wreath with seventy-five dollars for mission was laid on her coffin.

Pastor Andrew Olson wrote a heartfelt notice of her death in *Folkebladet*:

**Figure 7.5.** Mildred with nieces Jonette and Borghild. Used by permission of the Grindal family.

A heavy sorrow has fallen over the entire neighborhood; for we all feel the heavy loss. For her entire life Anda had great interest in the work of the church; she was a teacher in the parochial schools, president of the ladies' aid, she was always part of the choir, was always helpful wherever she found herself, not least with her beautiful voice at various church festivals. Long will her memory be cherished in the Willmar District Youth Society where she always participated, giving joy to both old and young with her beautiful singing. To the young people in the Willmar District: she will no longer sing for us here but let us meet with her in God's eternal mansions where she will sing for eternity. Something she said before her death was, "Now I am going home to Jesus." Yes, of him she sang. I cannot remember when she sang a song that wasn't about Jesus. She lived for Jesus; therefore, she sang of him. I believe there were some that were brought to Jesus through her song. A song I heard her singing and marked the seriousness which overtook the gathering when she sang it, "Skal du møte din mor paa opstandelsens morgen/Will you meet your mother on resurrection morning?" Thank God for all you were for those whom you met here below. You made life lighter for us all. Blessed be your memory![13]

My grandfather never married again, saying if he could not have Anda, he did not want to marry anyone else. He and his brother Fred raised the little girls with help from other aunts: One of Anda's sisters, Mathilda Hanson, who had been a widow for fourteen years, moved in to help raise the girls as the Depression hit. One of my mother's best memories was how Tildy, as she was called, remembered how much Mother liked pink. For her birthday one year, she tinted the cake's frosting with beet juice, making it pink. Mother never forgot that kindness.

Mother also told the story of how they went to visit the Sundals near Lakeville. Hilda Sundal, Anda's sister, may have agreed to take my mother and her sister, Borghild. Hilda's husband, Bernt, was serving the Highview Christiania Lutheran Free Church, where he would be until his retirement. Mother feared their father had brought them to the Sundals to leave them with that family. She says that when she realized this, she got her sister up early in the morning when her father had said he was leaving and hid in the car until her father came out to depart. When he saw them there, he threw his arms around them and wept, saying they could stay with him.

One of Theodore's sisters, Ella Tinseth Hanse, also helped take care of them. Their grandmother Torbjør, who lived a mile from the old farm, assisted when she could. In those days, family stepped in to help—aunts and uncles, grandmothers, cousins, and older siblings knew it was their responsibility to help raise the next generation.

When Mother started first grade in 1925, the year after her mother's death, she could not speak English. She had to learn it quickly, which she did. She did well in school and Sunday school and even skipped third grade but suffered for it when she had an emergency appendectomy. Her second- and third-grade teacher, Eva Folin Pederson, became a mother figure for her as well. She taught Mother piano and Sunday school, directed the choirs in St. Petri, led Bible studies, and brought the St. Petri choir to a high pitch, having them sing Mendelssohn's oratorio "Elijah" with the help of the community singers.

While a young grade school girl, Jonette participated in the typical activities of a congregation at the time like box lunch socials, in which girls would prepare box lunches the boys and men would bid on. The first time she tried this, Grandma Torbjør helped her make lovely sandwiches and cakes for her to sell. She was so excited, she could not sleep the night before. The next day at the auction, the highest bidder for her lunch was an old man with only two teeth with whom she had to eat the lunch. She cried all the way home, she told me.

## Gerda Mortensen

The year Mildred started school in the fall of 1923, Gerda Mortensen (1895–1974) was also new to Augsburg. She had been recruited by George Sverdrup to serve as dean of women. She was no stranger to anyone from Montevideo, as her father served the Wegdahl congregation close by. The Jacobsons, especially Anda and Mildred, knew her, as did Fred Tinseth from Lamberton. One could say that everyone in the LFC had an experience like this of knowing Gerda from her childhood forward. It seemed like she had been destined for this work from her birth.

While she was a very young child in Mankato, Henrik N. Hendrickson spent the summer in their parish teaching parochial school as an Augsburg seminarian. He stayed with them in the parsonage. She remembered that at night he would sing her lullabies from Norway and Gospel songs from the American Sunday school movement, which she also learned. A dapper young man of small stature, he had a remarkably lovely tenor voice, she remembered. Later, when she arrived at Augsburg in 1923, he was a senior professor in what would be her Department of History.

When Mortensen was about ten years old, in 1905, her father was asked to be a financial officer for the seminary. They moved from Lamberton to Minneapolis and lived in the Seward neighborhood for the next three years. Her family attended Trinity Congregation, of course. In the church, she would see the professors preaching or leading friends' meetings (*vennermøter*), which were a lively part of the congregation. These meetings forged long and abiding ties among congregants. When I talked to her in the late 1960s, it was remarkable to think that she had known both Sverdrup and Oftedal, among others. She probably attended Sverdrup's funeral in May 1907.

Mortensen went to public school in the Seward neighborhood, where she got to know the children of many Augsburg professors, including the Sverdrups, Oftedals, and Hellands. She forged alliances that would last her entire life. The older Sverdrup had spoken to her when she was a young girl at Trinity one

Sunday, giving her a kind of benediction, telling her and her parents he hoped she would grow up to be a good person.

When Miss Mortensen was about thirteen, in 1908, there was a financial panic that naturally affected the finances of Augsburg. Oftedal, who was president and had spent his life raising money for the seminary, disagreed with Mortensen's father about his methods of raising money. According to Gerda, her father, whom she adored, had made connections with every congregation in the LFC and tried to know the names and faces of all those whom he had visited on his journeys. He would watch for the names of those who had given money to the school, always published in *Folkebladet*. When he would see them at annual conferences, he made a point of remembering them and speaking with them. Although Gerda did not speak against Oftedal for this, her private feelings come through as she spoke. By this time, Oftedal had wearied of the role he had to take for the school and had perhaps grown much more set in his ways, besides being grief-stricken by the loss of his lifetime colleague, Sverdrup.[14]

Meanwhile, Miss Mortensen studied piano and voice so that she could accompany church meetings, like most pastors' daughters, and sing. At the fortieth anniversary of Wegdahl ladies' aid in 1913, she played the piano for the last service of the celebration. During that event, she learned much of the history of the early years of Montevideo, an area already familiar to her from her youth.

## Women's Missionary Federation

On a typically beautiful June day in 1916, during the annual conference of the LFC in Willmar at the Willmar Bible School, a group of 150 women gathered to discuss whether to form a national organization. On June 19, 1916, Gerda's mother joined with several other women of the Lutheran Free Church to form the Women's Missionary Federation (WMF) of the LFC. The president was Mrs. C. M. Roan, the wife of Carl Martin Roan (1878–1946), a medical doctor who served on the Augsburg board. The vice president was Mrs. William Hagen, pastor's wife and mother of Dr. Kristofer Hagen; Gerda's mother, Mrs. Christine Mortensen, was recording secretary; Mrs. Johan Mattson was corresponding secretary; and Miss Ragna Sverdrup, sister of George Sverdrup, was the treasurer.

Their first project was to buy a cottage for $1,709.52 near Augsburg where missionaries could spend their furloughs. In addition to supporting the church extension fund, they began taking very seriously a program of building houses in Madagascar and China for their missionaries. By 1936, during the heart of the Depression, they took on the sole support of Sister Milla Pederson in Madagascar. When they celebrated their twentieth anniversary, they reported that they had gathered almost $50,000 for missions in that time.

**Figure 7.6.** The Women's Missionary Federation Board ca. 1916. Used by permission of Augsburg University Archives.

**Figure 7.7.** Sister Milla Pederson, missionary in Madagascar. Used by permission of Augsburg Fortress Publishers.

While Mortensen was a little too young to be a leading member of the WMF at the time it was founded, she accompanied her mother to many of these meetings. Her mother was emerging as a leader in the new WMF society. Mortensen appears in the church papers as having both played and sung for meetings around the LFC during her late teens and early twenties. After her graduation from high school in Montevideo, Gerda had to choose a college for further schooling. For some reason, she had not chosen to go to Oak Grove for her high school training. Since Augsburg was not coed at the time, she chose to attend Mankato State, from which she graduated in 1917. She went to teach junior high school in Ashby, Minnesota, and then moved to Thief River Falls, where she taught from 1918 to 1923.

This put her near her parents in Fosston, Minnesota, where her father was serving the Kingo LFC congregation. In the meantime, she began academic work at the University of Minnesota in American history. Her term paper for her class in Topics in Minnesota History, "Extent of Settlement in Minnesota about 1850," was a bibliography of sources. While it is not today's graduate work material, she did have a command of these sources. In her oral history, she makes a great deal of the fact that her mother's family members were very early settlers in Bostwick Valley in Wisconsin, where the Conference was strong, and came early to Minnesota. Her father came to Camp Release near Montevideo for his first year in the United States, so she had a natural interest in the earlier history of the state.

## The Roaring Twenties

Although enrollment improved with the admittance of women, Augsburg did not roar with the new age. The Depression started in the 1920s on farms, which affected Augsburg, especially given its agricultural support base. The optimism evidenced by Birkeland and his swashbuckling ability to raise money to pay off the debt and propose buying Augsburg Park matched the times but not the bank balances.

The debate about what the character of Augsburg should be in the future grew more heated in 1923. Dr. Carl M. Roan, a member of the board of trustees and an aggressive Americanizer, wrote several articles for *Folkebladet* on the future of Augsburg, beginning on April 2, 1924. He argued that the issue of accreditation, both with the University of Minnesota and with the North Central Association, needed immediate attention. He wanted Augsburg College to become like other American colleges. Roan was formidable. A graduate of the academy and the college in 1904, he went on to become an MD. He studied at Tulane University, New York University, and the University in Copenhagen.

A member of the surgical staff at Deaconess, Roan also taught at the Deaconess Institute for thirty-two years. His wife, Marie O. Sletten, had been a nurse at Swedish Hospital in downtown Minneapolis. A sister of the powerful Olai Sletten, pastor at St. Olaf congregation in North Minneapolis, Mrs. Sletten herself was an important presence in Minneapolis. In 1911; she was elected the first president of the Deaconess Auxiliary. In 1915, she served as president of the first WMF board in the LFC. Her name and picture appeared frequently in the society pages of the local papers. In some ways, they were like the power couples of today. Roan had become a Fellow of the American College of Surgeons in 1922 and was a deputy coroner of Hennepin County from 1908 to 1918. He had been cofounder of Ebenezer Home for the aged and a director of the Lutheran Brotherhood Life Insurance Company. His memberships on the boards of key service organizations, such as Sons of Norway and the Commonwealth Club, were many and impressive. For him to oppose Sverdrup was no small thing. He was, in addition to his place in society, a graduate of Augsburg and knew it well from the inside. He and his wife were faithful supporters of Augsburg and the LFC at the time. Opposing Roan and his powerful wife was a bit ticklish for the school.

Sverdrup had a problem with Roan's argument and tone and wanted to reply in the pages of *Folkebladet*. The editor, Hans Carl Caspersen (1869–1955), did not want to let the paper be used by one party over another, so he refused Sverdrup's request to stop printing the Roan pieces. This was not surprising from Caspersen, a fanatic about free speech, but many have wondered about it.[15] Caspersen asked John Evjen for an opinion on the issue and received one that warned against the "excessive standardization inherent in any effort to meet accreditation requirements."[16] Evjen argued that Augsburg should maintain its unique character and remain true to its founding principles. He would further assert that if Augsburg changed, it would be like all the other American schools and become secular in the long run.[17] While Sverdrup agreed somewhat with Evjen, he responded in a statement in *Folkebladet* that the latter had gone "as far in one direction as Dr. Roan in the other."[18]

Sverdrup agreed that some kind of conformity to the standards of the North Central Association (NCA) was necessary for the success of Augsburg, at the same time admitting that the NCA had nothing to say about the seminary's calling to train "other laborers for the Lord's vineyard."[19] This question of Americanization and the ability to teach one's tradition haunted all immigrant communities that established schools and wanted to keep their identity while also being American.

The conflict continued through 1925, when the Augsburg board, finding the conflict threatening, established a committee to "investigate the relationship between the school's president and one member of the board of trustees."[20] Birkeland, also a strong presence with progressive ideas about Augsburg, disagreed with Roan, making work on the board difficult. It became a clash of titans. At the 1925 annual meeting, the entire board of trustees resigned. Only two came back: Åsmund Oftedal (Sven Oftedal's son) and Michael B. Michaelsen (Sverdrup's brother-in-law).

Miss Mortensen had spent two years (1921–1923) at the University of Minnesota, so she was in the city for those years and active at Trinity. Sverdrup saw her at least every Sunday. When she got her degree, she gave her parents an engraved letter of thanks saying, "To my dear Mother and Father by the help of whose self-sacrificing love this has been possible."[21]

After graduating from the University of Minnesota in 1923 with a BS at the age of twenty-six, she began as the dean of women at Augsburg in 1923. While there had been a few young women who attended the year before, women did not have much provided for them at the time. When Miss Mortensen arrived, things changed.

I had a conversation about Miss Mortensen with Inez Olson Schwarzkopf, Professor Iver Olson's daughter, who grew up in the Augsburg community and commented that she had always wondered what Mortensen's job description was. Mortensen was a force of nature. George Sverdrup, who had grown up with her, was no dummy. He understood who she was and knew that she could do well at whatever he asked her to do when he hired her. The thought of a job description is almost funny. She would make any job what she saw it needed to be and what she wanted it to be. In her oral history, one can pick up that in some ways, she was the one both Sverdrup and Christensen relied on for advice and could do the things they assigned her to do, whatever they were.

Fully aware of her need for credentials, she looked for a graduate school to attend. Gertrude Hilleboe at St. Olaf, her mentor in many of these questions, advised her to go to Columbia. In the summer of 1924, she went to Columbia Teacher's College to work on a degree in what became student services but at the time was really training in being a dean of women.

This summer gave her a rich experience in the big city, with its cultural offerings. As a typical extrovert, she thoroughly enjoyed attending concerts, operas, and art exhibitions, determined to squeeze into her busy course work all the extra activities she could. She had convinced Dean Sarah M. Sturtevant (1881–1942) at Columbia to let her take two courses rather than one during the summer and spoke of having to sit up until morning doing her work for class.

When she started teaching at Augsburg, she taught American history, as she had majored in that subject at the university. Mostly, however, she worked as dean with the women students. This vocation had been developing ever since coeducation had been introduced in many formerly all-male colleges. The profession strove to adopt the highest professional standards and academic research in its work, using the latest pedagogies and social science of the day, especially those of John Dewey, the professor of education at Columbia.

If Columbia was the premier place to study the work of being a dean of women, one of the university's most important teachers was Sarah Sturtevant. Her position and influence made Teacher's College, Columbia University, a leader in this field over the first part of the twentieth century.

While Columbia led the educational field, the emerging field of deans of women had strong roots in Minnesota. One of the first women to serve in such a position, Ada Louis Comstock (1876–1973), had been born in Moorhead,

Figure 7.8. Gerda Mortensen ca. 1933. Used by permission of Augsburg University Archives.

Minnesota, into a very wealthy family. Her father, Solomon Gilman Comstock, a fabulously rich lawyer for that time, doted on Ada and saw to it she had a fine education. She went to high school in Moorhead and then went to the University of Minnesota in Minneapolis in 1892. The university had been coeducational from its beginning, although no woman graduated until 1875. In 1890, just before she enrolled, there were 160 women students among the 781 students in the school. They were, however, not treated well. Jana Nidiffer says in her book on deans of women that they were simply ignored.[22] Ada Comstock came to be a good friend of Cyrus Northrup, the university president, and he hired her after her graduation to be a dean of women there.

This was around the turn of the century, and these first women began to take on their vocations as members of the university. At first, they were hired to be deans, but they also wanted to be on the faculty. Many had degrees that would have qualified them for such a role, but it was not easy to persuade presidents and boards of this.

Miss Mortensen began her career in the middle of this growth and lived through its flowering and subsequent decline. When she began, the position was developing into a profession with a strong national organization. These women would meet at yearly national conferences, with regional meetings in between. They forged a strong network that reached across color and ethnic lines. As a twenty-six-year-old at her first meeting, she was the youngest. By the end of her nearly forty-year career, she was the dean of the deans of women. Shortly after her retirement, however, with the rise of the second wave of feminism, the office, like that of the Protestant deaconess vocation (something similar to nurses) developed in Germany and furthered by Sister Elisabeth Fedde, disappeared to be replaced later by an office in the threefold ministry of the Roman Church.

The younger Sverdrup regarded Mortensen as a leading light in the faculty. In her oral history, she speaks of him as asking her to do things far beyond what most presidents would ask of the youngest member of the faculty. He wanted her to be on the lookout for designs for dormitories or other such buildings they would need to build. In addition, he appointed her to be the official hostess for the college and seminary. That was right down her alley. No one loved to plan social events like she did. She used these occasions to teach the students and others how to conduct themselves in social situations that required what the medieval world would call *politesse*. Teaching boys from the farm how to serve food on the right of the diner and remove it from the left, and teaching girls how to keep conversation going pleasantly at the table by keeping a diary of interesting comments or experiences of the day that they could bring up during the meal, raised the social graces of the students, something that she took as a mission.

It worked, one must say. American young people coming off the farm into the world of professions were eager to learn these skills. My father, from a less than fancy home, lived by her rules and became a gentlemen's gentleman. My mother, who had been raised without a mother, learned from her how to serve feasts to people of all kinds and make them feel good about their time at the parsonage. These were not insignificant skills, and they were grateful to her as they hosted thousands of people over their lifetimes in the parsonage.

In the summer of 1928, Gerda returned to Columbia on a nine-month leave to complete her MA. Her minor was American history, so she could teach that subject as well as function as dean of women. Once again, she thoroughly enjoyed the city and the school. This was her time to grow and have experiences she could not have in western Minnesota or even Minneapolis.

She describes the thrill of going to church in New York to hear great preachers in massively huge churches like St. John the Divine or even going to mass at St. Patrick's. She had never been to a Catholic mass before. Then she would go to be with friends at Trinity Church in Brooklyn, served by S. O. Sigmond (1872–1972), an old friend of hers and maybe a potential beau. As far as she could afford it, she went to concerts at Carnegie Hall, giving careful attention to the clothes she wore, proud that she had gotten a coat made of squirrel fur for fifty dollars that looked smart enough to wear when she was invited to a concert by a friend and sat in an important box she could never have afforded on her own.

She heard Kirsten Flagstad singing *Carmen* at the Metropolitan Opera house. She remarked, with her musical laugh, that although Flagstad was not quite the right-looking kind of person to play Carmen, the sound of her voice was enrapturing. She eagerly visited the art museum, other concerts, lectures, and generally soaked up as much of the culture of the city as she could do in the nine months she had.

As she had done before, she made good friends of all kinds, from every part of the country. She had learned from her father how to meet and connect with people. She remembered her father's motto as hers too: When I wake up in the morning, I wonder what I can do to make someone happy.

Miss Mortensen's most difficult job at the beginning was finding adequate housing for the girls that was safe and their parents would approve. At the time they arrived on the campuses, boarding clubs for the boys were the rule. Run by the men, they included rooms and board. They left much to be desired for women, especially in terms of cleanliness and convenience. Before steam heat, the dorms had individual wood stoves in each room. Water was pumped from the campus well outside, not far from the dorm. The privies were also on the college grounds, of course. Some seven years before the girls arrived at Augsburg, Ralph Mortensen, Gerda's brother, and his roommate spent the summer traveling around the Lutheran Free Church raising money to install steam heat (*varme apparat*) in the dormitories.

When deans of women began having regular regional and national meetings, the question of adequate housing for the women, where they could live in clean, well-designed, and well-furnished buildings, was pressing. George Sverdrup assigned Miss Mortensen the task of gathering plans and discussions about dormitories while she was on her travels because he knew she would be involved in the building of a dormitory during her time at Augsburg.

When the first class of girls came to Augsburg in 1922, there was really no place for them. When Mortensen arrived a year later, however, Morton Hall, the old professors' triplex, became the dormitory for the girls. Miss Mortensen would live with the girls too. At twenty-six she was nearly the same age as some of her charges and not very much older than most of them. Mildred was eighteen. She remembered Morton Hall much later in life as barely habitable.

The most important part of this *networking*, which was not a word Miss Mortensen would have used, was that she had colleagues who could support her efforts and give her advice on how to introduce reluctant administrators, usually male college presidents, to the new idea of student services. Most crucial to her in that effort were the annual national meetings of the deans of women, where she got to know many memorable people. One could tell as she talked that her memories always associated appearance and dress with the person so she could remember them more easily. She was a leader in desegregating the association. She never forgot her meeting with the dean of women at Howard University. One story she told with relish was the time she noticed a young Black dean dressed in a lovely dusky-pink gown with a matching rose in her hair. She met her thirty years later and remembered her, asking if she had been the Howard dean. When the woman affirmed her question, she was pleased she had been remembered for so long.

When Gerda returned with her degree, she continued her work both in the school and in the church, which were indivisible. One of her activities was writing a kind of locals column in the *Lutheran Messenger* called "Altar, Hearth and Campus: Glimpses of Church, Home and School." It is like reading the locals in a small-town newspaper. Among other things, it indicates where she traveled. She returned as frequently as possible to the West Coast, where her parents had lived for two years and she had family.

Nevertheless, Augsburg's future, always in question given its small base of support, seemed threatened again in 1926 when Professor Lars P. Qualben, an Augsburg graduate, began teaching New Testament at the seminary and headed the education department of the college. His credentials were superb: a PhD from Hartford Theological Seminary in 1923 and an MA from the Columbia Teachers College in 1924. Qualben began agitating for the LFC and Augsburg to begin merger talks with the Norwegian Lutheran Church in America (NLCA). His argument was like Ytrehus and Gynild's: Since Augsburg now had begun coeducation and the academy's future was in question, the reason to remain separated from the NLCA had disappeared. The LFC was no longer a movement but now functioning as a church body (*kirkesamfund*) with its corporations such as Augsburg Seminary, Oak Grove High School, and Martha and Maria (now anglicized to Martha and Mary) Orphanage. Augsburg was becoming what the United Church had first proposed, and thus the LFC could and should join with the NLCA for no other reason than that given its small population of twenty-seven thousand members, it desperately needed more funding to flourish as a college. He looked forward to a lively discussion at the annual meeting in a few days![23]

As Chrislock points out, these arguments were persuasive. However, Sverdrup and the esteemed professor of religion John Sigurd "Silas" Melby (1887–1944) violently opposed them, Melby thinking of Augsburg's financial situation—a fight now would imperil efforts to increase support from the constituency—and Sverdrup opposing a merger for personal reasons.[24] He bitterly

# Coeducation at Augsburg

opposed it because he feared that what he had done in changing the course of the college would be seen as a betrayal of his father's ideas; he denied any break with his father's notion of Augsburg.[25] Qualben's proposal, and its supporters, caused a ferocious debate that threatened the LFC at its core. Letters poured into the magazines, and people talked about it with passion, so much so that *Folkebladet* concluded the proposal was "unbearable" (*"uutholdelig"*).[26]

Olai Sletten of St. Olaf LFC congregation in North Minneapolis, a longtime supporter of Oak Grove High School, and Claus Morgan (1879–1959), longtime pastor at St. Luke's in South Minneapolis, also pushed for merger. Qualben and Morgan wrote a small pamphlet on church union (*Norsk luthersk Kirkelig Forening*).[27] The 1928 annual meeting debated Qualben's proposals and took a stand against them, vindicating Sverdrup's position and setting the college on a direction in line with his notions, but the future of the college and its support did not benefit from these altercations. Sletten's connection with Roan's previous argument is not clear, but his support of Qualben's proposal is consistent with Roan's opinion. After the dustup, Qualben left Augsburg for St. Olaf, and the Roans became active members of Central Lutheran in downtown Minneapolis. With those departures, the question died down to some extent, but the debate had been costly to the community.

## The Depression Takes Hold

The Depression began to sink its teeth into Augsburg in 1930. Fortunately, the deficit had been reduced to $4,000 by 1929, $10,000 less than the year before. While this was the reason for optimism, there was a sense that trouble was looming. The board had prepared in 1928 for the school to raise $200,000 in 1930 in commemoration of the 1530 signing of the Augsburg Confession. The money was to be divided between Augsburg and Oak Grove. Maybe this could have been achieved in the ebullient twenties, but now the goal seemed impossible—although, to its credit, the church raised $104,396 in a drive led by Professor Hendrickson. Considering the small constituency, these numbers are phenomenal. Augsburg received almost $64,000. Without this money, the school would have collapsed. This made it possible for the school to end the fiscal year of 1930 with a surplus—a miracle, something rarely achieved even in good years.

On May 7, 1930, my great-grandmother Torbjør died. Andrew Olson, her pastor, praised her in his *Folkebladet* obituary as a "faithful worker in many activities of the congregation and rejoiced when the work went well, both at home and abroad." He then noted that her greatest concern as she was facing her last days was that she was saved and her family as well: "Then there would be a sure hope of meeting in heaven where they would never part." During her last days, he reported, she sighed and said, "Now all I have is Jesus." This was a typical prayer of many of the saints in her day, and I like to think her prayers have been answered.[28]

The next year, however, was dire. Instead of receiving the usual fifty thousand dollars the school needed in order to scrape by, it only received thirty thousand. This left it with a deficit of sixteen thousand dollars. Consequently, teachers could not be paid in May 1931. They were also notified they could not be paid anything during the summer. Whether the school could even open in the fall of 1931 was not yet clear. To their credit, however, the faculty and staff agreed to a 10 percent cut in their salaries. The LFC and its pastors remained devoted to supporting Augsburg as their highest priority, despite the debt. As Chrislock says, "A combination of austerity, faculty privation, faith, improvisation, Hammer's credit rating, and the generosity of supporters still having financial resource kept the school open through 1931–1932."[29]

The next year brought even worse conditions. In April, the coffers were nearly bare. The indebtedness of the school rose to seventy-four thousand, with the annual moneys available only twenty thousand dollars. Once again, the board was forced to approach the faculty. It saw two ways out: reducing the number of faculty members or having the faculty take salary cuts. The faculty took the second option and made a proposal that they not be given any salaries for the year but only a share of the school's income. This gave the school some room to manage its situation. They permanently closed the academy out of sheer necessity and made it through the year 1933–1934 with untold sacrifices from the faculty. It should be noted, however, that this kind of choice faced faculties dependent on private donations throughout the country. Many sacrificial acts like this made it possible for many schools to survive. Many others did not.

This also sets the story of Miss Mortensen into its context. She never talked much about money during accounts of her life and work at this time. One could read about her life and maybe wonder why she was doing certain things but not understand until these facts are placed as the context for her work during great economic privation.

Meanwhile, by 1930, Mortensen had found her teaching style. Living as she did in Morton Hall, she made it uniquely her own. She took a parlor room on the first floor and refurbished it. The room had "a fireplace, curtains and was comfy. But there were small tables with chairs grouped around them, and a large bookcase near one window."[30] She also made it into a classroom for US history. There were no lectures, only supervised study. The students could read the books in the bookcases that pertained to the era they were studying, and they would discuss issues together, which made the class highly successful, the *Lutheran Messenger* reported.[31] This kind of innovation in instruction methods was typical of her. It also meant she did not have to prepare lectures. Given her

**Figure 7.9.** Morton Hall at Augsburg Seminary. Used by permission of Augsburg University Archives.

busy schedule and her character, it would be hard to imagine her doing well at detailed lectures, although she was a fine speaker. Even now I can remember much of what she said when she spoke in chapel.

Miss Mortensen made connections, found old friends, and soaked up the historical places everywhere she was visiting. This is what anyone who knew her would expect. Sverdrup also gave her the job of organizing the faculty wives and women not only for fellowship but to prepare for the annual reception they put on for the students. As she told in her oral history about the work this involved, she described the wives and their health or social situations. Many were invalid, like Henry N. Hendrickson's (1869–1953) wife, Gina Marie, or Karl Ermisch's (1878–1954) wife, Annie, remembered as a beauty like a fragile China doll. Mortensen spoke highly of Mariane Lindeman, the French teacher, with whom she had a long friendship. Belle Mehus (1896–1988), the first music teacher along with the voice teacher Jennie Skurdalsvold (1897–1986), was well qualified for her work but also socially ambitious. She demanded a lot of her students and of Miss Mortensen, if one can glean what she was saying beneath her evaluations.

Listening carefully to her conversation about her entry into the cultural center of New York, you can hear her also saying it was her job to introduce the young students from the farm to the wider world as well. She was not critical of her own background, very like that of the farm or of small-town girls who enrolled at Augsburg, but she did describe it as narrow.

That she was not married made the young women in her charge curious and a little scornful of her lack of experience in the domestic side of things, even if she did teach marriage and family for thirty years. Once my mother noted that she was escorted to a banquet by a male faculty member. Dressed to the nines—she did like fine clothes—she walked out of Morton Hall, where she lived with the girls, with great dignity as he sat in his car honking his horn for her to come out. However, these chuckles seem cruel as one reads more deeply into her story.

When her brother Harold's (1899–1965) wife, Nora Gynild, died, Gerda took over the care of this daughters, Hildegaard and Elizabeth. Later, she kept her parents in her home with her. The idea that she knew nothing about marriage and family is unfair. She did what many a single aunt and sister has done forever: She became mother for her nieces and caretaker for her mother and father. Furthermore, every Augsburg student thought they could stay with her free of charge when they came back to Minneapolis. Even my dad and mother stayed with her while my mother was convalescing after a serious operation at St. Mary's Hospital in Minneapolis in 1949. Once in her oral history, Mortensen alluded to the work she had to do at home as well as for the school, and it was crushing.

She continued as a leader in the Lutheran Free Church and especially of the women. Naturally, she worked closely with her mother and her friends as a leader in the WMF. At the annual meeting in 1930, she performed a vocal solo as part of the meeting, something she did quite frequently, along with accompanying others on the piano. She was elected president of the literature committee. At this meeting of the church, people rejoiced to hear that Augsburg had received a kind of accreditation from the University of Minnesota so that its students could attend graduate school in several of its departments.[32] Getting the school accreditation from the North Central Association (NCA) became a serious duty that Mortensen took on after World War II.

As secretary of the Foreign Missions Committee No. 3 of the 1930 convention, Mortensen led a long discussion on the seventeen points the committee was presenting to the group. One can tell that in their deliberations, they knew things were difficult, but there was no expectation the panic would last as long as it did. She visited the West Coast with her parents after the convention and enjoyed visits with both church friends and relatives.

The next summer, she celebrated her parents' fortieth wedding anniversary and the fortieth anniversary of her father's ordination in Fosston. It was a typically gracious occasion, the kind she was already known for planning. President T. O. Burntvedt preached in Norwegian and brought greetings from the LFC. Several others spoke, including Pastor Christian Olson of Lamberton. Miss Mortensen spoke on behalf of her siblings and read a letter from her brother

Ralph in China. One can see in these reports that she both spoke at women's events and also took central leadership roles in mixed meetings.

When the Augsburg students built a radio station, WHRM, she was a frequent contributor as vocal soloist, accompanist, or speaker. On March 19, 1932, she spoke at a banquet for the women students, reminiscing on the first days of coeducation at the college. Some who had been students in the beginning, very likely including Mildred, who now lived in Minneapolis and worked for IDS, were also there to speak about their experiences in the first classes of girls. The occasion was enhanced by the girls' chorus, which sang several songs, accompanied by a couple of piano solos, a serious speech by George Sverdrup, and a closing presentation of thanks to Miss Mortensen for her "important and faithful work" during those ten years. T. O. Burntvedt, president of the Lutheran Free Church, gave a stirring prayer and led the group in the Augsburg song.[33]

As the Depression deepened, the troubles at Augsburg became almost insurmountable. Although faculty members were ill paid, they remained loyal, going without pay to keep the school afloat. As did many schools, Augsburg faced disaster as finances dried up, and the country turned to President Franklin Delano Roosevelt and his promises of relieving the problems caused by the crash. If Augsburg had not had coeducation by the 1930s, it most certainly would have had to close for lack of students.

Mortensen continued writing her column in the *Lutheran Messenger*, presenting notes on cheery news and items that gave people a stronger sense of what was going on in the church community. The June 8, 1932, *Folkebladet* announced she was leaving for Europe on June 18 with Hilda Gynild, daughter of the late president of the LFC and her brother's sister-in-law. They traveled for ten weeks, beginning in England and then spending two weeks in Norway with her relatives on Karmøy. From there, they traveled to Stockholm and Copenhagen and then continental Europe: Germany, Switzerland, and France.

On her way home from the East Coast, she planned to visit colleges in the East and then return home by September, when school would begin. She said the entire trip cost her about seven hundred dollars. The two were in Norway when Hitler won his first election, and they were fearful of going to Berlin, but they did. Later she reflected that although they felt safe, they ultimately were there at a very dangerous time.

On September 11, 1932, she reported on her trip in Fosston, her father's parish. In the morning, she gave the lecture in Norwegian and in English in the afternoon. The reporter commented on her capacities in both languages. Although she had been born in this country, she knew enough about Norway to have heard about its beautiful scenery and people. Grateful she had learned Norwegian and English as a child, she urged the young people in the group to learn the language from their parents. The reporter, Ole N. Hem (1858–1943), recommended that organizations like the Sons of Norway and others would profit from hearing her lectures. Those who did would reap a good harvest, he concluded.[34]

At the beginning of the 1932 school year, Mortensen started her work with her usual élan. The Depression was taking its toll. Although anxiety isn't recorded in the stories of faculty and others, it was expressed very clearly in the moneys taken in by the church. Things were going very badly. The annual conference in Willmar the next summer began discussions about limits to giving and its effects on the institutions of the Lutheran Free Church. Miss Mortensen led devotions at the Women's Missionary Federation meeting that Saturday. She focused on John 11:15. She and Kristofer Hagen were responsible for seeing to the music for the event. This was the year that the WMF took on the full support of Sister Milla Pederson, the deaconess who had grown up in Nordland congregation near Paynesville, Minnesota, a key LFC congregation in the region. She had gone to Madagascar some years before and had developed a following among the women's groups in the LFC.

## *Concordia Hymnal* II

Surprisingly and almost of out nowhere, the *Concordia Hymnal: A Hymnal for Church, School and Home* appeared in 1932. Edited by Andreas Bersagel, V. E. Boe, T. O. Burntvedt, Oscar Overby, and S. O. Sigmond, it was published by Augsburg Publishing House. The reviewer H. N. Hendrickson noted it was much more than a revision of the former book. It was "a new book, superior both in character and content and more than twice as large."[35] Its genius was that for the first time, English hymns, German chorales, Norwegian spiritual songs, and some American gospel songs were together in one book. It worked for both Sunday morning and Sunday evening. The compilers had also worked to include Scandinavian folk tunes for English texts so even if people did not know Norwegian, they would know some of its musical sounds. F. Melius harmonized the hymns so they could be sung as anthems by the small choirs around the upper Midwest, where it became the preferred Norwegian American hymnal and remained cherished through the century.

It also provided two liturgies for Sunday morning. One was the liturgy developed by Gustav Jensen that the Norwegian church was using, and the second was a shorter version with the same music for the Kyrie and Gloria, which most congregations used. The longer version, including communion, also had an absolution that would be called the *conditional* one—meaning it included the condition that the forgiveness of sins was to those who "truly believed." This argument, as I have noted, goes way back. However, for my family, I would say what bothered them about it was not the condition so much as the fact that it was pronounced to an entire congregation by the pastor as though he were the one with the power to forgive sins and not simply to announce it. It reminded many of the powers of a Catholic priest. This is a slightly different take from the classic Lutheran argument. Nonetheless, that the little fellowship had the capacity to prepare such a volume as the Depression began to grind down on the group is surprising but also a testimony to their faithful service, no matter what.

## Life Goes On Despite the Depression

On June 6, 1933, Mildred Jacobson and Fred Tinseth were married at Highview Christiania parsonage by her uncle, Pastor Bernt Sundal. The wedding party was hosted by her aunt Hilda, Sundal's wife. After their wedding, they honeymooned by going to the Chicago Exhibition. Historians consider this year the darkest and most dire of the Depression. Only after President Franklin Delana Roosevelt (FDR) closed the banks and instituted the Federal Deposit Insurance Corporation (FDIC) program to assure that depositors would get some of their money back did things seem to improve. Life went on, however, despite the deep inroads of the Depression into every part of life.

The next year, 1934, the college and seminary kept going but were more and more pressed for resources. This was the silver anniversary of George Sverdrup's presidency. A celebration on May 22, 1934, planned by Professors H. N. Hendrickson, Mortensen, and Andreas Helland featured a surprising cast: Professor Friedrich A. Schmidt and Carl Weswig from Luther Seminary were there, and both spoke kindly of George Sverdrup. This was noted by everyone who could remember Schmidt's sharp and ad hominem attack of Sverdrup and Oftedal in 1891. Helland gave the main lecture. The seminary choir sang, as did Jennie Skurdalsvold. The event sparkled with Mortensen's usual spirit.

If Augsburg and the Free Church were at the nadir of their Depression troubles in 1934, so were many other private schools around the country. In fact, the Norwegian Lutheran Church in America, the body that became the ELC, discussed drastic plans for trimming its educational expenses. Proposals were made to combine Luther College and St. Olaf and move Luther Seminary to Decorah, as well as closing many academies. That had the effect of concentrating the minds of attendees at the church's conventions from 1933 to 1936, when Luther College alums rose to the occasion, partly to avoid a merger with St. Olaf, and paid off the staggering debt it had accumulated. Luther opened its doors to women, whose numbers helped save it then and particularly when World War II broke out.

That year, Miss Mortensen received an invitation to teach at an English mission school in Hankow where her brother Ralph Mortensen (1894–1986) and his family lived. He was working for the Bible Society there with interests in translating Lutheran literature for China.

The idea intrigued Miss Mortensen. Her term would be for a year. She asked Augsburg for a year of unpaid leave, which they were happy to give since they were not paying their faculty in any case. The mission school would help her with her finances, and she could live with her brother and his family.

On August 18, 1934, Miss Mortensen sailed from Vancouver, British Columbia, for China on the steamer *President Jackson* of the American President Line. She had spent a somewhat leisurely time traveling among relatives and friends on the West Coast before embarking on the journey. She thoroughly enjoyed her time on the long trip and maybe even got some rest, which she richly deserved. However, as an extrovert, she got energy from people rather than resting, so she may very well have organized soirees on the boat.

When she got to Hankow, she began teaching at the school. Peder Konsterlie, the mission secretary in China, reported the joy she had given them by her presence, although he noted she was not teaching in an LFC school. The time in China gave Mortensen a chance to be with the LFC missionaries there, for which she was as thankful as they were. Konsterlie later expressed his thanks to her for spending her Easter vacation traveling to meet the LFC missionaries in China.[36] In Kweiteh, now Shangqiu, she gave several lectures to the missionaries and the native leaders at their spring meeting. He thought they were very edifying and helped the native pastors and teachers feel much closer to the mother church in America.[37]

Miss Mortensen returned to Minnesota in time for the 1935–1936 school year. Her experience in China would inform much of her teaching from then on. As adviser to the Mission Society, she arranged a banquet with Professor Anne Pederson (1910–1995) and Fritjof Monseth, during which Augsburg students could contribute to a mission fund.

In early February 1936, she participated in a youth gathering that included all the Lutheran young people's societies of the American Lutheran Conference churches and run by them. Thaddeus Francke Gullixsen of Luther Seminary was the leader, along with many dignitaries of the other churches, who led discussions. Miss Mortensen was the only woman among the leaders.

At the June 1936 annual meeting of the LFC at Pontoppidan in Fargo, North Dakota, she was elected president of the WMF. On her return, she met with the LFC missions committee and brought her enhanced mission interests from her year in China. Andreas Helland, the secretary of the group, took personal privilege to compliment Miss Mortensen on her very effective efforts encouraging the work of missions. Several students had been challenged to become missionaries through her enthusiastic support of the China mission and missions in general. At the WMF convention, she gave the main address, "I Have Set Thee to Be a Light." In the report of the convention was a picture of the first unit of Oak Grove congregation in Richfield, at the edge of Augsburg Park, a new start of the LFC.

When Mrs. John Mattson left the office of president of the WMF, she wrote a farewell letter to the group published in *Folkebladet*. She was pleased that Miss Mortensen was taking up the work: "She loves missions and is well trained for the position to drive the cause forward during her service.[38]

Mortensen noted in her first official letter to the group that its mission was to "awaken interest in and love for the work of the kingdom both here and abroad." She went on to say that this was a great and blessed enterprise. Because God had forgiven her many sins, she could with courage and zeal work for the saving of souls both here and abroad. She asked the members to come along in that work and noted that now it was the turn of the young to take over from the older generation: "It is needful that we are all together in this work, both with prayers and intercessions, as well as in the work and with our gifts. May the Lord lead us deeper into the truth, in our spiritual lives, and in our understanding of the eternal worth of our work for God's kingdom on earth."[39]

To that end, she and a group of her helpers had written a book, *Hitherto...*, about the mission of the church women over the past twenty years—a mission she knew intimately. A review by Andreas Helland reported that its eighty pages contained rich pictures of the work, not just in foreign lands but also in the inner missions. He thought it worthy of being in every home in the LFC.[40]

Mortensen took to her presidency with her expected vim and vigor. One can sense in her reports to the *Folkebladet* her pleasure in being able to write as well in Norwegian as English. The evangelical appeals for money to bring the gospel to the unsaved are clear and something one would hardly read in Lutheran appeals today. She estimated that some 17,000,000 young people in the country were unreached. If they were not confronted with the gospel, she estimated that the "young rising irreligious population would someday cause wreck and ruin to our land."[41] I remember her last Mission Society banquet in the spring of 1964. I helped put it on. She gave a very funny and serious speech. One of her remarks was to Melvin Helland, the son of Andreas Helland (1870–1951). Three of his children had been missionaries around the world: Ben in India, Melvin in Madagascar, and Petra (Mrs. Ralph Mortensen) in China. Like the British Empire, the sun never set on them, Gerda said. Melvin Jr. noted dryly, "Father said that was because he couldn't trust us in the dark!"

## Harald Daniel Kivley Grindal Enrolls at Augsburg

On September 25, 1936, my father arrived on the Augsburg campus, a young man from a small LFC congregation in Ferndale, Washington. His foster parents, Anne Kathinka Watne (1892–1959) and Sjur M. Grindal (1877–1946), had deep roots in the LFC. As somewhat prosperous farmers for the time, the Grindals were able to contribute money to the school and its mission and send

**Figure 7.10.** Harald Grindal at ten. Used by permission of the Grindal family.

their adopted son to the school. He grew up knowing his real father, Svein, and treating him as such. When Svein married his second wife, Ethel, the families remained close to each other: his real brother, Josef; sister, Ruth; his four half sisters, Marion, Mabel, Mathilda, and Myrtle; and half brother, Sam. At the age of ten, Dad was officially adopted by the Grindals. He remained well acquainted with his father and family throughout his life.

As noted before, Sjur and Anna had strong Free Church roots. My father drank deeply of the tradition both from them personally and through his reading of *Folkebladet*, where he practiced his Norwegian, a language he learned to speak well with his foster father.

My father's early diary and letters home to his mother, Anna, show his concern for her and her interests, especially the work of the ladies' aid. Anna was a generous hostess and frequently would invite friends to their home for grand repasts, the table groaning with good things. On being thanked, she would remark, *"Det var bare skam"* ("It was only a shame, or nothing"), a typical saying at the time.

Anna, who taught him to play the piano, was a great storyteller with a wry sense of humor. She also suffered mental instability and was committed several times to the Sedro-Woolley "insane asylum," as it was called then. Dad reported she even had to wear a straitjacket to keep from harming herself. He would go with his foster father to visit Anna and see her sitting and laughing uncontrollably in the corner of her cell. Grindal would look at her and say to him, "That is the devil."

Father saw her mental problems early on and knew she did not like housework, preferring to be out in the barn milking or doing other outside work. When he was old enough to help, he told her to go outside and work, and he would keep the house clean and cook. He would be embarrassed when company would come and see how truly messy she was, almost to the point of revulsion. Doing those chores for her and working with his father on the farm, helped him when he became a husband and father. There was almost nothing in the house or outside that he could not do as well as my mother. He greatly admired her Christian faith and love of doing good for others; frequently, my father remembered, they would have an indigent person over for dinner to entertain what Scripture called an *angel unawares*, a tradition my mother later flatly refused to observe, as we lived on the Great Northern Railway in Rugby, and hobos would knock on our door and want food.

A devout Christian, when she was institutionalized for a deep depression once while my father was small, she heard a meadowlark singing and heard it to be saying, in Norwegian, "Say you are happy" (*"Si du er lykkerlig"*). It gave her the strength to get well. We have thought for years it was a bipolar malady, but when we talk about it with trained psychologists, they are not so sure. All we can say is that she had periods of instability that apparently were bad enough to have Sjur send her to the asylum. These mood swings imprinted themselves on my father, but having his real father nearby gave him a sense for another part of his heritage. Sjur Grindal, a dour, serious Christian, was no picnic, either. Most everything in the world, he thought, was of the devil. He forbade my father to read the funny papers on Sunday until after church and refused to buy any kind of insurance until my father began driving a car. Whenever he drove anywhere, Anna would sit in the back seat "to balance the load," something my mother found to be hilarious. Whenever she sat in the back seat of our car, she would repeat the phrase, to our merriment.

During his high school years, Dad ran with a group of Luther Leaguers of the Free Church in the Puget Sound area and came to know many of them well. Those ties remained close for a lifetime. As an active member of the Young

**Figure 7.11.** Jonette Tinseth's first-grade class in Cyrus, Minnesota. Jonette is third from right. Used by permission of the Grindal family.

People's Society, he learned both leadership skills and things about congregations that stood him in good stead for the rest of his life.

Dad spent the year after high school working in Ferndale, helping his parents with the farm. He had been raised to speak both Norwegian and English fluently; his father would not speak to him in English, but his mother, who could speak and write both, taught him good English. Like Miss Mortensen and many of his contemporaries, he read both *Folkebladet* and the *Lutheran Messenger* in Norwegian and English. During his time at Augsburg, he would serve as president of the Norse club and frequently, when he needed special favors, would write his papers in Norwegian to impress his teachers. He even spoke in Norwegian at Mindekirken in Minneapolis during this time.

Meanwhile, 1936 brought extreme weather that was bad for my mother on the farm in Minnesota. The heat during the summer made records that still have not been surpassed, and the lack of rain on the farm in Cyrus was so bad, Mother said, that her father did not ever take out the binder. Despite that, the year was considerably better for Augsburg, and many schools around the country, than the previous ones had been, alongside general improvements in the country. Abner Batalden, born in Lamberton to Christian O. Batalden and his second wife, Deaconess Atonette Sletten, and for several generations the businessman of Augsburg, had begun a vigorous student recruitment program that raised

Figure 7.12. Gerda Mortensen in her Augsburg office. Used by permission of Augsburg University Archives.

the freshman class from 83 to 147, five of them from the Ferndale area. It was also the year that Gerda Mortensen returned from China. She would continue as dean of women and in her job teaching American history, a class my father took that coming year. He and his friends would later remember it, laughing, as a course that stressed the Chinese contributions to American history. The increased numbers made for a much more sustainable economy at the school, though it was not rolling in money.

The young Norwegian theologian Sverre Norborg (1902–1983) also began teaching at Augsburg that year. He attracted a lot of attention with his scholarship and teaching. An attractive man, and learned, he strongly identified with the LFC, Augsburg, and its tradition of Haugean lay activity. He wrote about it and lectured on its peculiar gifts many times in these first years. He came highly recommended to Sverdrup by the young Bernard Christensen. In the fall issues of the *Folkebladet*, Norborg was described as an exciting new teacher. He taught at the Augsburg Summer School for pastors, which had become an important event for the school and the pastors of the LFC. It always featured important speakers from around the Lutheran churches, even including faculty of Luther Seminary. Over the next couple years, he traveled around the LFC with the Augsburg Choir and other Augsburg groups and spoke to young people's groups to great acclaim. My mother, still home on the farm, noted several times in her diary that she had heard Norborg at some Augsburg event or another and thought he was a very good speaker.

The sports teams were more energized by the new spirit, new musical groups were formed, and the attention of the community turned to building a new dormitory, which was desperately needed. As these things go, it was a more exciting time at Augsburg than it had been for years and perhaps since the construction of the new main building in 1902.

## The Death of Sverdrup and the Election of a President for Augsburg

My mother enrolled at Augsburg in the fall of 1937. She had spent a year at home after high school with her father and sister, helping them on the farm. It had been a tough year on the farm. This year, as she was thinking of Augsburg, she knew her chances of attendance depended on the rains and weather. She described, with prayerful anxiety, what was happening on the farm with the crops, how the threshing went, and when they could fill the silos.

It is difficult for us to understand what it must have been like to spend the summer on the farm, watching every cloud in the sky to see whether rain was coming. Without a good crop, Mother could not go to Augsburg. After the awful summer of 1936, they were rightly fearful of a repeat of the drought, but the harvest had been much better this year. Mother and Borghild put up enough food for the year before Mother left for school.

After farewell parties at home, shopping trips to get the right clothes, and long sewing hours with her aunt and sister, she was ready to go. Three nights before she left, she prayed, "Please dear Lord, may all my dreams of school be fulfilled and may I not be disappointed but find it more to my liking than I expect."[42] Her cousin Ernest Tinseth, living on the neighboring farm and an Augsburg student as well, was never quite clear when they would leave but suddenly announced that they would depart on September 20 about noon. It was about a three-hour trip from Cyrus. By that evening, Jonette was in Minneapolis.

She immediately settled in and found her roommate. She said the room was different from what they had expected. They had a double bed that they would share. Today, people find that very strange, but people rarely had their own beds until after the 1950s. There was neither room nor money for such luxury.

The next day, Jonette found Richard Jacobson Jr., her cousin on her mother's side, who was also a freshman, and they had a good talk. On Wednesday, they attended chapel. President George Sverdrup preached on wrestling with God, a subject she found interesting. Dr. Norborg spoke at a special service that evening. She thought the service was inspiring and prayed that her "life could be given in a fuller measure to the Lord's Service."[43]

Figure 7.13. Jonette Tinseth in high school. Used by permission of the Grindal family.

That evening, she, her roommate, and friends walked to downtown Minneapolis and then met others for an evening of fun at the Augsburg Inn—probably a little coffee bar. The next day, she tried out for choir and hoped that she would make it, which she did. She had also had a literature class with Miss Anne Pederson, whom she decided she was going to like.

Each day she began with a "morning watch" of prayer at about quarter after six, something she would never miss if she could help it. All the professors would speak in chapel. One of her favorites was Professor Karl Ermisch. She would come to love him and what he taught her about the book of James, which she memorized for him. One evening, after he spoke, she heard a recital by some in the music faculty, including Jennie Skurdalsvold, who impressed her. Mother prayed she could learn to sing like her someday. It was very soon that she came to be known for her voice and sang solos at many meetings and services in the community.

One evening, her boyfriend, Conrad, a seminary student, appeared, and they had some time together that evening. Because of him, she felt like she knew the territory a bit better and bragged that other girls were jealous of her. She knew many of the LFC students from youth conventions and the faculty from their visits to the congregations. Being the extrovert she was, she started enjoying the

Figure 7.14. Borghild and Jonette Tinseth. Used by permission of the Grindal family.

time at once. She also had an aunt and an uncle—her mother's brother, Richard, and her father's sister, Henriette—living in the cities, and with two first cousins in the same class, she felt at home. Not only was she eager to study, something she loved, but she was also eager to enjoy a deeper spiritual relationship with her peers and especially her new roommate, Ruthie Gudim Wold.

In one of their first times of prayer, she told me, they decided to ask God whether they should be deaconesses, a vocation still open to them at the time. As they knelt by their bed, fervently asking God to guide them in this decision, Ruthie looked up at her and said, "Jonette, I can't be a deaconess. I look terrible in black!" They laughed and laughed.

On September 30, she heard that she had gotten a job in the dining hall that would begin after Christmas. Although she did not know it yet, this would be a life-changing event, as it was where she met my father, the head waiter.[44]

While the students studied and worked, they could feel that the world was heading toward war. *The Echo* noted it now and then, as did *Folkebladet*. My mother mentioned it several times in her diaries, which are mostly devoted to her friends, her prayer life, and her studies. As has been noted in many sources, the Norwegian American community tended to be pacifists before World War II until Germany invaded Norway, and then feelings changed dramatically.

The freshman class in 1937 was 162, with the total enrollment just under 400, the number the college had been working toward. The *Echo* featured a regular column by faculty with spiritual advice. The first one that year was by Professor Christensen on keeping Christ in one's schedule—the one thing essential, he noted, was a quiet spirit, like that of Mary of Bethany sitting at Jesus's feet. While these could be regarded as good words but impossible to keep, there were many like my mother who did follow that advice with her daily morning watch. Her devotions were much affected by what the chapel speakers said.

The campus and Augsburg community had a challenging goal to meet that year. At its annual meeting in June 1937, the LFC had voted to raise $125,000 to build a dormitory for men. To their great joy, it appeared they would be able to raise it from pastors, alums, and friends of the school. Batalden was key to organizing the fund drive and had arranged for dinners around the districts of the LFC as a fundraising strategy. Like all good fund drives, they began with a private campaign to raise enough so that when they went to the public, it did not look impossible. Sverdrup, whose father had died at fifty-eight of a bad heart, was now fifty-eight and suffering the same illness. Few but his family knew about his condition. His selfless giving of his time to raising the money and running the college must have been stressful in ways difficult to understand.

Sverdrup had given up much to lead Augsburg. One might think of it as a gift of loyalty to his father, whom he admired. When he was called to Augsburg in 1907 on the death of his father, he had to leave a promising career in foreign service for the US government. Working for Augsburg and carrying on the legacy of his father was a sacrifice for him, although one never heard him grumble about it.

He was not a charismatic man, but from what one reads, he had a character that impressed everyone with its spiritual authenticity, a true charisma, as they got to know him. He was not flashy, but everything he said could be banked on, and people came to revere him for that quality as his time in office progressed. He did have a hard job. If the college was to grow and survive, he had to change the character of Augsburg's lifelong commitment to being a seminary (*presteskol*) and make it a college independent of the seminary, in essence abandoning the original and strongly shared mission of Augsburg Seminary and its founders. To make it a college to educate students who were not going to be pastors had been a profound change for the supporters of Augsburg. It had to be done to keep the school alive, and most everyone knew it. Keeping Augsburg true to its mission while making it possible for it to grow so it could be a viable American college was

Figure 7.15. George Sverdrup ca. 1937. Used by permission of Augsburg University Archives.

difficult, but Sverdrup did so, and his reputation for quiet integrity and Christian faith with the Augsburg constituency continued to grow throughout his life.

Things were looking up for Augsburg. Optimism about the school seemed to be rising. Then on a dark and gray November 11, 1937, Sverdrup died. The death of Sverdrup at such a relatively young age hit the college hard. My mother's diary notes the death with shock: "Dr. Sverdrup died this A.M. about 1 o'clock. It hardly seems possible and yet it is the truth. Oh, how we shall miss him! It doesn't seem half as real now as it was this morning and how touching and striking it was then. Chapel exercises this morning are something I shall never forget. Dr. Norborg broke down and could hardly keep on speaking. He said Sverdrup was his best friend. It brought death so close to us."[45]

Mother knew that Sverdrup had known her mother from their frequent appearances at Young People's Society meetings in his first decade as president. She also knew Hendrickson, who would become interim president, from her mother's family, so she was confident in his leadership. As things settled down, the school and church began to focus on the next president. The struggle to find a new president occupied both the LFC and the school over the next eight months. While some thought Hendrickson should be kept on longer, there were only two likely candidates who emerged during the year: one was Bernhard Christensen, who had been something like the heir apparent almost from the first when he began appearing at LFC Young People's Society meetings in his teen years. His pastor, Michael B. Michaelsen, Sverdrup's brother-in-law, who had served as a pastor in the district in Wisconsin where Christensen lived, saw almost from the beginning that the young man was a worthy candidate for leadership at the college. The arrival of Norborg, however, someone Christensen had highly recommended to Sverdrup in the '20s, created something of a rivalry. He was attractive, brilliant (as was Christensen), and more conservative. He seemed a likely candidate as well.

Norborg could not quite decide where he belonged—Norway or America. He had worked for the Sunday school movement in Norway and had been taken up with the Oxford Group as well, although he later criticized it. Norborg was a writer and lecturer as well as a pastor and potential professor. His thesis on Josiah Royce, an American philosopher, a strange choice for a Norwegian theologian, gave him entry into the American university world. After his arrival on the Augsburg campus, he could be found lecturing on a variety of topics around the state. At the pastor's convocation in late August 1936, he gave three lectures on "Luther's Message for our Times."

In the fall of 1937, Norborg could be found holding special meetings and events with students as frequently as Christensen. Jonette went to Norborg's lectures on spiritual life in October that year and remarked on how challenging they were to her. His talk had made her realize how much more she could be doing to spread the good news to others who had not heard. She had heard him speaking several times before in Cyrus with the Augsburg Choir when it was on tour. Now she was able to hear him more frequently, and she admired him. His politics and piety in many ways matched hers more than Christensen's did.

Norborg also made quite a splash in the press—both English and Norwegian. *Folkebladet* wrote about him frequently, and he wrote many articles in the paper arguing for the LFC in ways that surprised many. Nothing is more flattering to a small and struggling group that has spent three-quarters of a century living and dying for its principles, and just barely succeeding, than praise from an outsider of distinction. I have no doubt that he was sincere, but it clearly put him in contention for a leadership position at Augsburg or in the Free Church, if he was thinking of such a thing.

In her frequent letters to my father during this period, my grandmother Anna Grindal asked several times if Norborg had yet married. When I first read those letters, it seemed like I needed the other part of the conversation. Once when we were out having dinner, I asked my mother what the story was with Norborg. She looked at me with her brown eyes sparkling. "*Kvinnerne* (women)," she said.

Then she told her story. There had been a movement by some of the students, led by Abner Batalden, to nominate and elect Norborg as president of Augsburg. There was a feeling that Christensen, while a fine man, would not be a good administrator. A pastor from Seattle wrote Dr. Burntvedt just before the election that while Christensen would be okay in things theoretical, when it came to "practical things he was a big baby."[46] That was a feeling widely shared by the Batalden faction.

In that same letter, the pastor surmised that Norborg would not be happy if Christensen became president. It is not clear from the context if he meant that Norborg would lose face because he lost the race or that he did not approve of Christensen. The pastor on the West Coast may well have confirmed my grandmother Grindal in her opinion. She may have known the pastor—they all knew each other in that tight-knit community. She continually asked my father about Norborg, whom he was obviously impressed by and worked with at Mindekirken. From Grandma's letters, one can see how intimately the Augsburg and LFC community paid attention. In October 1938, she wrote my dad, "We read a great piece about N. [Norman] Myrvik's wedding in the *Tribune*. J. Stensvåg was present. Have you heard if Dr. Norborg is really married yet or not?"[47]

One can see something of Norborg and how he viewed himself in a long, heartfelt letter written from Norway to Burntvedt and Christensen on the last day of 1934. In it, Sverre Norborg discusses his future. He saw no future for himself in Norway, given the financial straits of the time and his interests. He was longing to come back to the United States. He asked rather obliquely if there would be an opportunity for him in Minnesota, reminding Burntvedt that he had said once that in his long life, he had never seen more promising young theologians than Bernard Marius Christensen and himself: "What would my two friends say about possibilities for me if I come to America for good?"[48]

In the same letter, Norborg spoke of the Oxford Group and its powerful effect on the Norwegian leadership through the work of Pastor Frank Buchman. He was grateful that the "*overklasse*" ("upper class") had been affected by it. He thought Buchman had found the way into the Norwegian soul. He concluded that observation with the comment that "it looks like I will never be anything but a Haugean in my Norwegian sense of the church."[49] My father told me once about Norborg's approving of the Oxford Group and its four absolute laws. He had been affected by it, along with other Augsburg students at the time. Given the revival at Augsburg during this time, which influenced my parents, I have a suspicion that the building of Mt. Carmel Bible Camp, Bethany Fellowship, and World Mission Prayer League all emerged from this revival and the challenges of Buchman to the church.

One senses that by the time of the president's election, Norborg had abandoned the idea of the presidency, if he ever had it, or even the possibility of staying as a professor. He was a man of large ego, many said, and there is also a possibility that after Sverdrup died, he had lost his best friend and now was left with his rival, Christensen. And he was alone in the world without a wife or family.

Norborg, in his autobiography, says very little about his professorship at Augsburg or the possibility of a call to be president.[50] A woman who grew up in Mindekirken said that she remembered Norborg as a handsome and attractive man, but there was something not quite reputable about him in the talk of the adults she knew.

What mother told me then was that Burntvedt got on the phone to all the people he knew he could count on to go to the annual meeting that year in Thief River Falls, not an easy jaunt, and vote for Christensen. Apparently, the rumors about Norborg's relationships with women had attracted attention and disapproval, gossip that had made it all the way out to Ferndale—and Cyrus. When I asked my late colleague at Luther Seminary, Roy Harrisville, about him, he said, without pausing, what mother had said: women. Those were the rumors that caused his candidacy to fail, but there is no proof of them, as far as I know.

My mother noted several times in her diary that Norborg continued to impress her as a speaker at Young People's Society meetings. She less often mentions Christensen. I could take this to mean either that he wasn't on the road as much for Augsburg at the time or that Norborg was more eager to enhance his reputation in the field. There was significant opposition to Christensen in the ranks, partly because of his liberalism, especially as it had to do with interchurch cooperation. He was broadly ecumenical, something that irritated many conservatives among the LFC membership.

Norborg was not of that ilk and seemed to understand some key things about the LFC that rang true with its membership: Its lay emphasis out of the Hauge movement and its stressing of conversion and awakening. While Christensen did not disagree with those convictions, his ecumenism shocked people, especially his love of Catholics. (One of the more shocking apocryphal pieces of gossip that spread widely in the LFC was that a daughter of a stanch LFC member came to Augsburg and, attracted by the nuns at St. Mary's across the street, took holy orders, which Christensen approved!) He had in fact seen a play about some Spanish nuns with a character named Gracia, which so impressed him that he insisted his wife, Lily, adopt the name Gracia. It is complicated for me to consider, given my name, and not surprising that she changed her name back to Lily immediately on his death. Obviously, one could assume she did not like his rechristening her.

Figure 7.16. Breaking ground for a new dormitory at Augsburg. Used by permission of the Grindal family.

Things at the time were progressing at Augsburg, including its necessary building program. On May 23, 1938, just before the election of the president, longtime pastor Claus Morgan of St. Luke's in South Minneapolis, the president of the board at Augsburg, broke ground for a new Sverdrup-Oftedal dormitory that would be finished for the winter term.

Mother told me a rather vivid story then about how, when her grandfather and uncles returned from the annual meeting and the victory of Christensen as president of Augsburg, they all sat on the summer porch telling the story of the election. What they said about it, however, she did not quite relay.

By all reports, the meeting had been a wild one. Batalden and his cohorts had made the election debate seem more like a basketball game than a somber church meeting, according to Burntvedt, who had to work mightily to keep order. He admonished the students several times to act with more decorum.

The election went as Burntvedt had hoped but was not a clear victory from Christensen's point of view. Of the 300 votes, 214 were for him, and 70 opposed him. Thirteen were abstentions, and three were for Norborg. Christensen did not like the number of votes against him. Perhaps he was somewhat shocked by

Figure 7.17. Bernard Christensen as a young professor. Used by permission of Augsburg University Archives.

the opposition. Without doubt, he was a liberal, and he was bitterly opposed also by the son of Sven Oftedal, Åsmund Oftedal (1878–1950), who knew Christensen from his time in New York as a student and member of his congregation. Christensen and Gracia had met at Trinity Lutheran Church in Brooklyn, where Gerda had attended. Oftedal, the pastor at the LFC church in Brooklyn, had sniffed out Christensen's liberal views on biblical criticism.

Furthermore, Christensen had an odd mystical piety, even for the LFC. Neither of the Sverdrups had been ordained—for good Lutheran reasons—and neither one had been a pastor of a congregation. Christensen shared the same reason—he was not a pastor of a congregation, the only reason to be ordained. He had not been ordained, nor had he served a congregation. While that might not have bothered most of the people, his expectation that he should have received more than so many votes before he would take the position kept him from wholeheartedly affirming his answer to the call. His description of his call and ordination process—something of a mystical encounter in a wooded glen—struck many more sober church people as rather suspicious. He regarded this as a sufficient ordination and never was ordained since he, like the Sverdrups, never served a congregation as pastor. I had not heard the story until I began studying his life and must admit it appeared to me to be strange. While pietists are touchy-feely, they are not often charismatic nor mystical.

Mother's diary tells a slightly different story from what she told me much later. On June 11, 1938, she and her sister were working at home on the farm when Grandpa Haakon called to say that the Sundals—Mother's aunt and uncle—had come to visit Mildred and Freddie. After they found Mildred, she invited everyone to dinner that night. Sundal told them about the meeting: "Is it ever fun to listen to Uncle Sundal talk. We found out all about the convention. Christensen is our new president." While this does not negate the story above and could well have involved them all sitting on the porch into the evening, Mother was not very interested in recording their talk—as a teenager, such things didn't interest her as much as they would later. She knew Christensen well and respected him, but she spoke much more warmly of Norborg in her diary than Christensen.

After the vote, Christensen wrote that the lack of unanimity felt like a bad sign. He wrote Burntvedt, "We need to be one in the Lutheran Free Church if we are to be able to carry on the work as it should be done."[51] Still, the board of trustees voted to name him president. He accepted and took over as president in the summer of 1938.

CHAPTER 8

# A New Augsburg President and War on the Horizon

THE SCHOOL YEAR 1938–1939 at Augsburg began with a welcome increase of students from 367 to 413. Sverdrup-Oftedal Hall would be dedicated and ready for occupancy in the middle of the fall term. It was an exciting time. Included in those festivities was the installation of President Christensen on Friday morning, October 27, at Trinity Congregation. This was the first formal installation service at Augsburg, which had not previously evidenced much interest in such pomp. Christensen gave his inaugural address on Augsburg's motto, "The Word Became Flesh." He argued that nothing could save the world but love. Justice could not fix what was wrong—only love. With that, he affirmed the unity of Augsburg and the LFC, saying that Augsburg was "one protagonist for the Truth and Light which the darkness can never overcome."[1]

That night, there was a large homecoming banquet at Dayton's Tea Room in downtown Minneapolis. At the event were a great many friends and colleagues, many of whom made remarks in honor of the day and the new president. Christensen spoke on "Dienst und Dank" ("Service and Gratitude"), which he believed to be the essence of Christian life. Among the usual LFC dignitaries were, of course, LFC President Burntvedt and Thor H. Quanbeck, the president of Oak Grove Lutheran High School. Others from like institutions in the cities were there as well: Thaddeus Franke Gullixson, president of Luther Seminary; Dr. Paul H. Roth, president of Northwestern Seminary; and Dr. Lars W. Boe, president of St. Olaf College. The MacPhail music school string trio performed, and the Augsburg Quartet sang. Mother thought it was a beautiful event, with all the presidents of the colleges there to give toasts, even though what she noticed was that she did not have a date. It was an evening of high ceremony and good fun. During the homecoming festivities, Jonette went with her girlfriends on a tour of the new dorm, which she thought exciting, but she said nothing about its design, just that it was new.[2]

Now Christensen had to begin leading the school. At the inaugural banquet, he stressed the history of the college and seminary, but it was not until his report to the LFC annual meeting the next June that he laid out some of his goals for his leadership of the school. He also had the difficult task of redefining Augsburg's identity and role in the world—which had to be changed if it were to survive. As

**Figure 8.1.** The inauguration of Bernard Christensen as president of Augsburg. From left to right: T. O. Burntvedt, Kristofer Hagen, Bernard Christensen, and H. N. Hendrikson. Used by permission of Augsburg University Archives.

early as 1933, he had stated his position that Augsburg was a school for training lay leaders in the "congregation." This was the correct rhetoric, but he was using it to significantly change the self-understanding of the college. The *congregation* had been the focus of all of Augsburg's work from 1874, so people resonated with that word. But then Christensen denounced the idea of the school as being simply a *presteskol* (pastors' school or seminary), which he defined being like the "elitist" seminary the Norwegian Synod had run. This was a brilliant rhetorical ploy that would have been astonishing to the founders and longtime supporters of the school. They had always valued it for being "our *presteskol*," entirely congregational in its focus and dedicated to producing pastors who would be different from other seminary graduates. One could say that Christensen took the spirit and rhetoric of the founders and rebranded it for a college of the liberal arts, in a way the humanism, which had been the very thing Sverdrup had opposed. From that time, Christensen would work to shift the identity of Augsburg College from being a prep school and college for the seminary to being a place where students could be challenged to be lively lay leaders in congregations—while claiming that had been at the heart of the school from the beginning.[3]

This was a necessary move to keep the school flourishing, but I have never before quite understood how drastic this move was. He effectively redefined the mission of the school in a way that countless graduates and its supporters could understand and agree with, believing it was consonant with Sverdrup's mission. He urged a strong liberal arts curriculum with service as the focus. Sverdrup might have agreed with this rhetoric, but the idea of such a curriculum had not been something he would have approved of—given his passion for creating a ministry that was not elitist. Christensen's new vision would be set into the documents of the school at the 1942 annual meeting.

The excitement of having the new dormitory ready to be occupied after the Christmas vacation dominated the campus community. My father, the head waiter in the new boarding club, was the first to wash the floor of the new dining hall, something he counted as a privilege. The odd architecture of the building won praise at first—it seemed luxurious after the privations of the old dorm and boarding club—but later generations would wonder about its strange design, which had something like suites that included several dorm rooms, that began to seem like rabbit warrens. Later remodeling tried to reconfigure it, with little success. The *Echo* said its model was the City Hall in Stockholm, but its charms eluded many students, and it grew less charming as time went on.

## International Cooperation and Forebodings of War

The year 1939 would be filled with increased forebodings of war. British Prime Minister Arthur Neville Chamberlain (1869–1940) had pronounced on September 30, 1938, after his meeting with Herr Hitler, that he held in his hand a document that meant "peace in our time." By September 1, 1939, when Germany invaded Poland, the world would see that was an empty promise. One can feel the anxiety, even in my mother's diary, as she faces the new year with unease: "Dear Lord, wilt thou alone guide and lead us into this New Year."[4]

*Folkebladet*'s editor, Hans C. Caspersen, took stock of the past year in a column for the January 3, 1939, issue and noted that while that last year had been approached with "deep misgivings" ("*Bange anelser*"), they greeted this year "with fear and trembling." He noted the undeclared wars and barbarisms of the day: Italy's attack on Ethiopia, Franco in Spain, the reputed complicity of the pope, Mussolini and Hitler supporting Franco, and the Japanese brutally attacking China. In sum, he agreed with Carl Hambro, prime minister of Norway, who said the Munich agreement was a "fiasco."[5]

He also wrote about international church meetings, like the Conference on Life and Work in Oxford in July 1937 and the Conference on Faith and Order in Edinburgh in August 1937 that began a movement toward founding the World Council of Churches (WCC). Because of the war, this process was not concluded until 1946 in Uppsala, Sweden. Caspersen wondered what that movement had to do with Lutherans and particularly the Lutheran Free Church. He feared that the stronger, more high-churchly denominations would find it possible to rule over the less high-churchly ones, for example, the Episcopalians lording it over the Presbyterians. However, he supposed that among the Lutheran churches, it would be the most theologically rigid who would force themselves on the less so, especially what he called the "Calvinistic" Missouri Synod, with its strong stand on election. He saw that the Baptists and Methodists were coming together with other churches of their own confessions, while the Lutherans were still separated. However, he noted, conversations about merger were beginning, led by the American Lutheran Conference, which the Lutheran Free Church, under the leadership of President Thorvald Burntvedt, had helped create in 1930. Burntvedt became a beloved member of the presidents forming the group and, in his later role as president of the Conference, would help lead the LFC toward

**Figure 8.2.** LFC President Thorvald Burntvedt preaching. Used by permission of Augsburg Fortress Publishers.

merger, a notion it had soundly defeated in 1928 when a reunion with the NLCA was proposed.[6]

The mergers of the various American Lutheran Church bodies had been a gleam in the eyes of Lutherans since the patriarch Henry Melchior Muhlenberg, in 1787, on publishing his hymnal, had hoped for one book and one church a century and a half before. Very few Lutherans in the pews knew of this or how much their leadership was looking for such a union between at least some, if not all, American Lutherans. So it is surprising to read Caspersen, who saw this from the beginning. It puts my struggles later in the century into a context I did not understand at first.

Caspersen, with his prescience, feared, rightly, that the LFC would be overrun by its counterparts: Missouri with its strict doctrines, the ALC with its legalism, and the ULCA with its worldly associations that permitted lodge membership, to say nothing of what he saw as its ritualism. He was suspicious of the idea of merger, thinking it would involve giving in to the larger churches for the sake of church unity, which to him clearly meant merger. He then gave what he considered should be the LFC's approach: In Christian friendship, the LFC should reach out its hands to the other churches but not lose its identity in an organizational merger. This had been the position of Sverdrup and most of the LFC from the beginning.

What he proposed is what many, such as ALC's Bishop David Preus, weary of endless church merger negotiations, also suggested when the ELCA was proposed almost fifty years later: a unity in spirit but not of organization. "Spiritual emphases cannot be squeezed into formal directions and regulations," Caspersen noted. LFC pastors were free to welcome any Lutheran pastor to preach and administer communion without any further permissions, à la the Galesburg rule, he said, "but were they free to do the same in other churches?" In other words, would other Lutherans treat LFC pastors with the generosity the LFC treated them? That was another matter, occasioned by the refusal of other Lutherans to approve the LFC's theology or understanding of the ministry. Our unity was spiritual, not organizational, nor could it be otherwise.[7]

He then proposed a series of ifs: *If* it meant there would be one organization that could rule over the teaching and worship of the congregations, then he thought it would be a long time before that happened. *If* it meant creating one Lutheran Church built on the pattern of the earlier Lutheran churches in American, then the largest organization, the ULCA, would dominate with its progressive emphases. *If* that happened, he concluded, such "a union would then meet its Munich."[8]

This had been pretty much the stance of the LFC in its documents and its clergy at this time and one that Professor Norborg supported, opposing what he considered the all-too-generous approach of his rival, Christensen. Many still remembered the ugly organizational clash that had ended up in the Friends of Augsburg leaving the United Church to found the LFC. But that was not Caspersen's point here: He was articulating Sverdrup's and others' very clear stance that we were one with other Christians of all sorts and greeted them and worked with them in Christian love, but merging into one denomination with others was an entirely different matter.[9]

Lutherans across America and in Europe were having similar difficulties regarding some of these ecumenical questions. While Burntvedt and other leaders were not a part of the meetings of the Lutheran World Council, which would become the Lutheran World Federation (LWF), other American Lutherans were also struggling to understand each other's situations. While the Swedes, after the death of Archbishop Nathan Söderblom (1816–1931), were trying to continue his ecumenical work, they found their counterparts in America dealing with different issues, among them a rather strong opposition to anything like what would become the WCC.

The LFC had the kind of ecumenism that began from the bottom, the kind urged by Count Nicholas von Zinzendorf (1700–1760) in the eighteenth century, that was its way of being. It looked for other Christians, not just Lutherans, many of whom could be unchristian and unwilling to share the spirit. As its founding documents made clear, the LFC did not expel nonbelievers from its midst but, through evangelical preaching, sought to bring them into fellowship. Thus, a pastor's duty as a preacher was to evangelize the congregation constantly, something my father and his classmates were devoted to. Sven Oftedal had shocked many when he argued that nonbelievers could be included in the congregation because hearing lively evangelical preaching might cause some to be converted.[10] It was the kind of ecumenism that Christensen espoused, finding our unity in our shared relationship with Christ, although people like Caspersen may well have disagreed with Christensen's broader approach to the issue.

This ecumenism was in the air the students at Augsburg were breathing at the time my parents were there—and which I grew up with—but it was not based on the writing of documents, the kind that involved the smoothing over of theological differences by church bodies, one with another, to achieve unity. It was personal. Sverdrup had opposed that from the beginning of his work in America. On Sunday evenings, my parents would go to churches around the city to hear powerful preaching and good singing. They looked for free and living Christians and shared that spirit, not their confessional positions. Mother tells her diary every Sunday where she went on a date, and it was usually the Swedish Tabernacle or Broadway Temple, where Henry Opseth, the Augsburg Choir conductor, whom Mother adored, directed the choir. Once, she went there with Leland Sateren and Eldora, a good friend, whom Sateren would later marry. There they heard the Wheaton College Glee Club and had coffee together afterward.

## A New Augsburg President and War on the Horizon

One of the places they frequented, after such an outing, was Brodahl's Café on Cedar.

That year, Jonette also began working in the dining hall in the basement of the Sverdrup-Oftedal Memorial Hall. She found it "strange to work in the new kitchen" when she had returned from Christmas vacation, but she enjoyed it. Her diary tells of her activities and the people she was with. At the time, she was dating several young men who would become pastors in the LFC and was beginning to mention Harald Grindal as a frequent escort. As head waiter in the dining room, he had come to know her and was falling in love with her. They were active members of the Mission Society and gladly prayed for and worked for revival at the school, especially during the Religious Emphasis week, when a powerful speaker would be asked to hold meetings for a week. It was during these meetings, especially one led by Sverre Norborg in 1938, when Mother had wondered if she had been called to Madagascar as a missionary. One of her beaux was planning to go to Africa, and it interested her, an interest my father did not share, to her disappointment.

On June 1, 1939, Mother came home from Augsburg to work on the farm for the summer. On her way home, she noted that she had been seated on the train with Nils Nilsen Rønning (1870–1962), with whom she had a good talk. N. N., as he was known, bought her a fish dinner as they spoke of what it meant to be from Telemark, as her father was. He had written a book, *The Boy from Telemark* (*Gutten fra Telemark*, 1933), in which he told the story of his growing up very near Bø i Telemark. He described to my mother the soul of people from Telemark—they were like valleys of sorrow through which a river of joy flowed. She never forgot that and would tell it to me many times. Little did she know then her future husband's family was the subject of the opening chapter of this book, which told of the *Kivle Møyane*, the three girls on the Kivle farm, in Kivledalen, where her future father-in-law, Svein Torson Kivle, had been born. They had been dancing around the maypole, playing music in a pagan celebration, when the pastor, a strict Lutheran, came out of the church beside where they were playing and cursed them. They turned to stone, but as they died, the most beautiful music that had ever been heard died in the valley. You can still hear it, they say, if you stand beside those stones and listen carefully.[11]

As the summer began, Jonette and her younger sister, Borghild, started teaching parochial school in St. Petri, their congregation. This instruction was no longer in Norwegian but in English. They taught Bible and hymns like the parochial schools had done. Now it was called vacation Bible school, with the crafts long associated with that venture. Her mother, Anda, had done the same in the St. Petri, where Borghild said she had met my grandfather Theodore Tinseth. Mother confessed to her diary after a few days, "I haven't told a soul but I'm getting actually to dislike teaching. I don't know why and I hate to say it even to

Figure 8.3. Harald Grindal's uncle and aunt Ed and Mary Kivley—the former a descendant of the Kivles portrayed in *The Boy from Telemark*. Used by permission of the Grindal family.

myself. But I did feel rotten today perhaps that's the reason. I don't want anyone to know—that's for sure."[12]

## A Crown Prince in Minneapolis

The annual meeting that year, 1939, was held at Trinity in Minneapolis. It was the seventieth anniversary of the founding of Augsburg, and things seemed to be going rather well, all things considered. In preparing for the meeting, *Folkebladet* featured articles on the church and what a church was, reprinting the old articles by Evjen on the LFC, of all things. Norwegian Crown Prince Olav and Crown Princess Märtha were touring the United States, visiting President Roosevelt as well as the large diaspora of Norwegian Americans. A picture of the royal couple and their children graced the cover of *Folkebladet* on June 7, 1939.[13] They would appear at the annual meeting in the Augsburg Chapel in the main building for a service on the morning of June 13 at ten o'clock. Burntvedt's announcement in the *Folkebladet* made clear that it was an honor to receive the royal family given the rich heritage the LFC had received from its Norwegian forebears. The royal family's itinerary included the Norwegian settlements all across the upper Midwest and Pacific Northwest. Although their visit was brief, Burntvedt's greeting in Norwegian expressed for all present the thrill it was to have them there. Christensen, whose greeting was in English, welcomed them, connecting Norway, Augsburg, and the faith in his typically eloquent way: "Augsburg prizes the heritage of the Kingdom of Christ. And we bid His Royal Highness, welcome among us today most of all because He represents a nation where the Christian Gospel has in a notable way been permitted to permeate and inform the life of the whole people."[14]

It was no secret that the Norwegian palace was making every effort to solidify its relations with America given the menace they saw growing in Nazi Germany. Barely three months later, Germany would declare war on Poland, followed by Great Britain's declaring war on Germany, and World War II would break out.

Grandma Anna Watne Grindal followed this closely. She wrote my father that they had listened to both Olav and his cousin George VI of England on the radio. Olav had visited White Horn, Washington, and spoken to immigrants there. She noted that Olav was a better speaker than King George, something I didn't understand until I saw the movie *The King's Speech*.

The 1939 annual meeting of the LFC began with its usual worship services, sermons, and singing. *Folkebladet* published the speeches that Burntvedt and Christensen had given in honor of the crown prince. From the reports, one can tell that no matter how brief, the visit gave the meeting a special aura, which shone throughout the week. The school was flush with good news at the time. Fifty students had graduated, six from the seminary, and now the college had sixteen full-time professors. The commencement speaker had been Petrus Olaf Bersell (1882–1967), longtime president of Augustana Synod. The school had gathered $121,000 and needed some more to fully furnish Memorial Hall. Still, the event had the glow of success.

Christensen's speech at the convention was his first report as president. There he laid out his seven-point plan for Augsburg College and Seminary. The goals had mostly to do with the spiritual vocation of the school:

1. To give full opportunity to the Spirit of God to do his creative and quickening work among the members of the student body.
2. To maintain and deepen our devotion to the expressed ideals and program of Augsburg. The heart of that ideal and program is given in the words we have long loved: "The free and living congregation."
3. To raise and strengthen the standards of academic work in both College and Seminary.
4. To choose very carefully the students who are admitted to the Theological Seminary.
5. To cultivate more intimate relations with the congregations and people of our Church.
6. To build ever greater efficiency and deeper confidence in the business management of the institution and its resources.

7. To lay emphasis on Christian service as a definite part of Augsburg's program, on the part of both students and graduates.[15]

The speech was admired by the constituency and fit well with its piety and concern for Augsburg, especially its service to the congregation. *Folkebladet* thought it rich and enlightening. Later it would remark that Christensen's report helped his standing in the church. The gathering voted unanimously to approve Christensen's call to president of the school, aware that the division of the convention the year before had left a bad taste in everyone's mouth. The unanimous vote included approval of Christensen's seven objectives. The goals are not surprising to someone who knew Christensen or the history and commitments of Augsburg and the LFC. The school was to work so that the Spirit of God could quicken the student body with revival, and the devotion to "free and living congregations" would deepen. As to his third point, he already knew he needed help with the business management of the school and that it needed to be streamlined and made efficient. To that end, Pastor Olaf Rogne (1895–1954) of Duluth was called to be business manager. Finally, Christensen urged that Augsburg stress the notion of Christian service as its creative center. These goals were entirely consistent with the history of Augsburg and sounded good to the constituency. In fact, this became his theme throughout his presidency and affected most of its graduates in one way or another. He concluded with a rousing description of the school: "A Christian school is more than an educational institution. It is a creative center of life and activity."[16]

Also a pressing issue, and one Christensen realized needed to be faced immediately, was that the student body was no longer mostly LFC. Lutheran students from the city were attracted to Augsburg for its low tuition rates and its location. They could live at home and take courses at the school. While these students may well have been faithful Lutherans, the peculiar piety and culture of the LFC may not have appealed to many of them. The question of Augsburg's identity and mission had to be addressed again and again. To survive, the school had to change how it thought about itself; it had to ask the question of how a school keeps and passes on its traditions when a majority of the students are not interested in them. Christensen realized this, and he expressed his views on how to address the issue to the annual convention in 1939: "We need, however, if we are to serve the highest interests of our Church, to put forth a more definite effort to secure a larger representation of young people from the congregation throughout our own Lutheran Free Church."[17]

To assure that happened, Augsburg students toured in the summer, a common practice of most religious schools. The Augsburg Quartet visited six states in the Northwest. My father and Waldemar Anderson—Mutt and Jeff, they were called—formed a gospel duo that traveled through northern

Minnesota, singing and connecting with the congregations there. These were student recruiting trips as well as occasions to raise money for the school. It gave people a good feeling about Augsburg as they listened to attractive and faithful youths both singing and speaking. It also brought in money from LFC congregations, something that had waned from 55 percent of income in 1935 to just under 30 percent in 1940.[18]

One of Mother's best times that summer was welcoming the gospel duo Waldemar and Harald, who closed out their summer tour in Cyrus. Mother noted that during the meeting, "they brought Augsburg so close to me again."[19] They stopped at the Tinseth farm, where Mother cooked dinner and lunch for them: "I do so hope the dinner and lunch tasted all right—one thing I surely got them to eat pretty good."[20]

The next week, on September 18, her father and uncle Freddie drove her back to Augsburg, along with Mildred and her sister, Borghild. This was home for them all, and they enjoyed each other and the community as they moved Jonette into West Hall, the old professors' triplex from 1874, where Mildred had briefly lived during her days there. "It's fun to be down there again," Jonette reported, "but didn't dream that it would be this bad." Everybody knew that the women's dorms were nearly uninhabitable, and this building was long past its prime.

Amid the festivities of the new school year and homecoming, Jonette noted she had gotten a call from Harald G. while at home in Cyrus, just before coming to school for the fall semester. He would be her constant companion that fall. Their common commitment to Jesus, their reading of the Bible together, and their enjoyment of the cultural riches of the Twin Cities drew them together. Jonette felt comfortable with him as they walked to the First Covenant Church for Sunday evening services, with singing and good preaching by Pastor Paul Rees. And they enjoyed the music of the Minneapolis Symphony at Northrup Hall, led by Dimitry Metropolis.

On September 1, Jonette noted that war had broken out in Europe but said almost nothing about it. She was occupied with other things: her studies, the choir, and singing. She was frequently asked to sing at meetings around the city, which she enjoyed very much. Occasionally, she mentions teachers like Peder Andreas Sveeggen (1881–1959), her English teacher, whom she could hilariously imitate reciting Edgar Allen Poe's *The Raven*, and Henry Peter Opseth (1890–1950), plus speakers in chapel, but her concentration is on her classes, work, and friends—a typical sophomore in college.

By now, she and Harald were dating more frequently. She noticed when he was with someone else. The girls often walked downtown together to shop, and Jonette dutifully noted her purchases. On October 7, she got a "wintergreen dress, brown purse and gloves, a rain cap, and oh! We ate in the Forum." Anyone from the upper Midwest who knew Minneapolis well would try to eat at the

Forum Cafeteria on 7th Street in Minneapolis. The food was reasonable and typical of a buffet at the time but presented in an opulently art deco room. It was open even when I was in college.

On October 13, Jonette planned a surprise party for Harald's twenty-third birthday with a cake made by the Augsburg Boarding club cook, Miss Wyman, who carried it in to him with all the candles lighted while singing "Happy Birthday." My mother wrote, "He never realized once I had anything to do with it and tonight I cried and felt like God was laughing at me. Oh, I felt so terrible—so did Ruthie (Gudim) until Palmer (Wold) called. Forgive me, Lord!"[21]

The next day, she recovered some and sang a solo of a new song by Leland Sateren, which she thought especially beautiful.[22] On October 15, while Harald played the piano, she sang hymns: "Oh, how beautifully he plays! I sang until 3 o'clock while he played. I finally had to run out because I was so affected."[23] For the rest of the year, they would be steadies. Harald was not only falling in love with her but also caring for her, and she was glad for that, given her many anxieties that would continue through their marriage.

In November 1939, H. C. Caspersen wrote an editorial on bishops and Lutherans, and especially the LFC, in its incipient merger conversation. His main argument was that it was entirely possible to imagine that in fifty or one hundred years, even the LFC, if it were still around, could adopt the Historic Episcopate. He wrote, "I have a feeling, amounting to a conviction, that if this movement is not nipped in the bud it may become a formidable obstacle to a democratic and free church conception of the church in American Lutheranism."[24] He urged that pastors and leaders acquaint themselves with this issue so they could oppose it successfully. Nothing could have been further from my father's thoughts at the time, nor any of his compatriots, but Caspersen's prophesy would occupy his daughter during the last two decades of the twentieth century. And I would lose, as he predicted.

A response in *Folkebladet* on January 31, 1940, agreed with Caspersen. The writer noted that even in the Hauge Synod, more and more of the pastors had become high church. The words used innocently for districts (*stifter*) could very easily become bispedømmen (dioceses/sees) with an erkebiskop (archbishop). He noted it was common to call Burntvedt the bishop of the LFC. He then explained to the readers the nature of the Historic Episcopate and how it required real bishops to ordain other bishops and pastors. Would we have to send our bishops over to Norway or Sweden to be ordained by a real bishop, or would they come over here and ordain them all at once?

To those who thought it ridiculous to posit this, he noted that a sentence that was often used in his day was "times change and we along with it" (Tiden forandrer sig og vi med). A church could change its mind on such an important issue very easily, he noted. If the Hauge Synod could change its mind about merger in thirty years, the LFC could also change on episcopacy. Only God was unchangeable, the writer noted. He also feared the notion of one Lutheran Church in America, scoffing at the idea that Christ was praying for merger in his high priestly prayer in John 17: 20–23 that they may be one, as we are. He ended by warning the church to remain awake.

The author of this piece is only named Chr. Who that might be is hidden in the past, but the prescience of it seems remarkable today. His prophecy came true exactly as he feared, except for the Association of Free Lutheran Congregations (AFLC). The LFC congregations that merged with the ALC and then ELCA now have the Historic Episcopate and have organized themselves into exactly what Chr. said would happen.

## 1940

Jonette spent the Christmas holidays at home, working with her sister and making clothes. Every day she looked for a letter from Harald and usually got one, always exclaiming about how beautifully he had written. She arrived back at Augsburg on January 3 and went to talk with Miss Mortenson about work but noted that she simply let Mortensen tell her all her troubles, during which they both wept and then prayed. She went to meet Harald's train from Ferndale, where he'd had spent the holiday, on January 9. He brought with him a gift from Anna (his foster mother) and a rose. This deeply affected Jonette.

The semester began with a record number of 460 students at the college. The war in Europe was being watched closely. Articles appeared in the *Echo* on various topics, including one on February 9, 1940, about the courageous pastor Martin Niemöller and his resistance to the Nazis. He was clearly a hero. Many students and faculty, however, began to work at least for American neutrality, if not against war of any kind. Toward the end of February, a poll was taken about the most pressing social problems of the day. Keeping the United States out of the war was the most important problem by a wide margin. Around 47 percent thought that war in Europe was the most serious question of the day. The American presidential campaign was beginning to heat up, and Roosevelt's popularity remained high. Each issue of the *Echo* had one or more columns on the war, and speakers were invited to talk on it, such as Paul Shinkman, who had been in Germany in 1938 and observed some of the massive rallies by Hitler in Berlin.[25]

Campus life proceeded as before. *Gone with the Wind* was the big movie sensation of the day, and despite the semi-official stance that movies were not good, many students, including my parents, went to see it and many others. Jonette was involved with the writers' club and the publication of the *Dial*, the literary magazine. Until then, life continued as usual, her relationship with Harald becoming deeper. She began writing to his mother and was challenging him to think of being a missionary, which he had apparently not been eager to do at first. He was preaching in chapel now and leading meetings, to her pleasure. Their talks were most often devotional and spiritual. She was beginning to experience some of his down times as well, something she might have understood, but for her, the semester was filled with joy. He was getting ready for an internship experience in Newman Grove, Nebraska, which he would serve concurrently with his studies, something that would stretch his energies greatly, but he became a beloved intern—every time the congregation needed to call a pastor after that, they called him and asked if he was interested.

On April 9, the Nazis invaded Norway, and the day "was filled with a kind of despair" for students like my mother, who briefly reported on this. Harald comforted her with the verse "Let not your hearts be troubled," from Philippians 4, a verse they would repeat to each other for the next sixty years, and then they went on with life as they were living it. *Folkebladet* printed a cry for prayer by Burntvedt on its first page. With great sorrow, he reported on the occupation of Denmark and Norway. He advised the readers to pray for Norway and proclaimed that on April 28, LFC congregations should observe a day of repentance and prayer. As a native Norwegian, he spoke for most of the people in the LFC in asking for these prayers "for our forefathers dear homeland in its needs."[26]

At the end of April, Jonette traveled with the choir on their longest tour thus far—1,800 miles from Minneapolis to Tioga in the far northwest of North Dakota and back. She had no idea she would be living there soon. In fact, on April 27, the day before the prayer and repentance day called by Burntvedt, she wrote, "And as I lay waiting to fall asleep after our devotions, the wind howled around the corners of the house and it was cold. That always makes me feel blue and lonesome. I, of course, couldn't help but think I hope we never have to live in this God-forsaken country. North Dakota is a strange place. I like it in a kind of a sort of a way, but honestly, I've never known you could see such a long way in one stretch before. The people are great. Last night we stayed in the parsonage at Tioga, North Dakota."

The choir returned to great acclaim on Monday morning. A small item in the *Echo* noted that a gospel trio from Augsburg had held meetings in Cyrus. The trio consisted of Harald Grindal, Donald Ronning, and Les Dahlen. In her diary, Jonette thought that was a strange combination of singers. Although they were good friends and fellow students, singing was not Don Ronning's or Les Dahlen's forte. This marked the introduction of Don and mother's sister, Borghild, who would end up marrying him rather than going to Augsburg.

That same issue of the *Echo* had a short column on what had just happened in Norway on April 9. The author concluded by saying the students of Augsburg, with their largely Norwegian backgrounds, needed to do something to help their kinsmen in their hour of need. By the end of the month, student opinion had changed slightly, and one-third of the students were very pro-Allies, though they thought the United States should only fight if the war came to its shores. Even so, a group of students organized a peace drive to support peace and freedom without military action.[27]

Just before the annual meeting at Bethel congregation in north LaCrosse that year, an article by G. O. Oudal appeared in *Folkebladet* on bishops' names and work. He was responding to the previous article by Caspersen and Chr., as several had previously done. His argument was that *bishop* was the biblical name and should be kept, as the other names like *president* or *foreman* were not. I am sure he did not know that early Protestants like Tyndale and Wycliffe had translated *episkopos* as *overseer*, not *bishop*, and were martyred for it. However, he did make the point that some of the district presidents or church presidents wielded more power than many a bishop. In my view, though, he was naive about what the name brought with it. It was no longer a word from the early church but now gave people who read it the picture of a typical Catholic bishop in his medieval regalia.[28]

That summer, Sivertsen Hall, a former clinic building, had been given to Augsburg by Dr. Ivar Sivertsen if Augsburg would pay off the mortgage of twelve thousand dollars (which they gladly did). It was renovated to house women students, a great need. It also had a heated garage for nine cars, a good addition to the facilities. The annual report also informed the church that Augsburg had received a gift of twenty-five thousand and Oak Grove ten thousand dollars from the will of Hans Hansen of Finley, North Dakota, an almost unimaginable gift at the time. While this was much appreciated, the debt of the school still stood at fifty-four thousand dollars, while gifts from the church had fallen somewhat. The meeting heard a report on how much congregations enjoyed meeting the teachers from Augsburg and reported that several, including Si (John Sigurd) Melby (1887–1944) and Kristofer Hagen (1909–1987), had spent the summer teaching the Bible at Bible camps around the fellowship.

At the time, the LFC comprised 112 congregations served by 43 pastors. Forrest Monson had just been called to start a congregation in Richmond Beach, Washington, near Seattle. The LFC had taken in somewhat less than the year before, down $4,000 from the $22,000 that had been its goal. The annual conference also heard about conditions in the various mission fields. Missionaries studying French in Paris, like the Molviks, came home, while the Melvin Hellands could not return from Madagascar, given the uncertainty of the ships' schedules. The Arthur Olsons, Ina Heggem, and Lenorah Erickson had bought tickets home from China, but it was not quite clear whether the ships could sail and how dangerous the trip would be. Marcy Ditmanson, newly graduated from Augsburg, was on his way back to Beijing, China, to study medicine.

Bernhard Helland and his wife were expected back from the Santal Mission in India, where they were serving, at the end of August. He would continue working for the Santal Mission from the United States. Norwegian mission efforts had halted with the invasion by the Nazis, so now King Haakon had asked Dr. Johan Arnd Aasgaard (1876–1966) of the NLCA to handle payments to Norway's missionaries. Taxes from Norwegian shipping companies and other Norwegians working outside of Norway would help defray these expenses, he said.

Bethesda Homes had closed its orphanage and now housed some sixty-eight elderly people, among them Sjur Watne, Anna's brother. At its annual meeting several days later, the Bethesda board discussed a proposal to use the now-empty orphanage as a home for retired LFC pastors and their widows. Even as the first Social Security retirement benefits came into existence, retired pastors often faced poverty, so this was a good idea; unfortunately, nothing came of it. Many wanted to address the issue of pensions for the pastors, given how dire their circumstances could be after years of very low salaries, wrote Sverre Torgerson in his account of the meeting.

The Conference also heard a report from Pastor Krumbholtz, the head of the National Lutheran Council (NLC), who reported that two-thirds of American Lutherans now belonged to the Council. The meeting elected eight members to represent it at American Lutheran Conference meetings. In addition, Clarence Carlsen was elected the ordinator of the fellowship, a position created to avoid any connection between the presidency and the power to ordain. The same meeting saw the retirements of Henrik N. Hendrikson and Andreas Helland, who had served Augsburg for decades.

Talk of the National Council and of bishops began to appear in the papers through the rest of the year, along with talk of the war, Augsburg, missions, and the projects of the church. Caspersen wrote a long article on the difference between a congregation (menigheten) and church (kirken). He was responding to a letter sent to all pastors in the NLC by Conrad Bergendoff concerning the NLC and what church was. "Should a Solution Be Possible" was the title of the column. Bergendoff, president of Augustana College and Seminary, and highly respected by LFC pastors, had wondered how it was possible to have ecumenical discussions among a variety of Christian communions when there was no shared definition of what the word *church* meant. Without that, he said, "a discussion between individuals of various communions [was] hardly more effective than shadow-boxing."[29]

That quote was the occasion for Caspersen to think about the definitions of congregation and church, which he did for several columns in that issue. He continued a learned discussion of the question from the beginning of the church after the giving of the Holy Spirit, through the Middle Ages, and to the current day. He even opined that the current mess in Europe was a consequence of five hundred years of false proclamation of the God that Jesus came to reveal. A congregation was divinely created by the Holy Spirit; the church was a collection of congregations joined by their desire to do larger things than a single congregation could do. For Caspersen, the "totalitarian meaning of church stood in absolute opposition to the democratic characteristic of Christendom."[30]

With that, he concluded by noting that the editor of *Lutheraneren*, Herman Emil Jørgensen (1885–1962), had written an article different from his and that Pastor E. M. Hanson of the LFC had written in favor of the term *bishop*, which was different from both points of view. The discussion should continue, he said, to explore the issue from different sides.[31]

Jonette spent the summer writing letters to Harald, who was enjoying his work at Newman Grove. At the time, the LFC required of its students three summer internships rather than a full year, so candidates could earn their degree, candidate of theology (CT), in three instead of four years. Harald had tried to cram his college years into three as well and found himself running around the track as a senior in seminary to fulfill all righteousness regarding his college requirements.

He shared many of his firsts with Jonette—the first funeral, wedding, and so on. She recorded that he had had his tonsils out but did not really remark on how narrowly he escaped death. She probably did not know at the time. The operation consisted of his going to a doctor's office and having his tonsils pulled out of his throat. He was something of a bleeder and told me he almost bled to death after the procedure.

While Harald was beginning his internship, *Folkebladet* authors continued to discuss the definitions of congregation and church. As he and Jonette had learned from their parents, the congregation, according to Scripture, was the right form of the kingdom of God on earth, Principle 1 of the Twelve Principles of the LFC. Caspersen made efforts to define that and teach it to make it clearer to the readers and to followers of the LFC. For Caspersen, there were two congregations—the local and the universal. For him, the local was divinely inspired in a place with people called together by the word. While it could be seen in the preaching and sacraments, not everyone in the congregation was a believer. Only God knew who those were. On the other hand, there was a universal congregation, invisible but made up exclusively of believers, whom God knew as well. This was not the same as a worldwide church. That was a secular organization. This concept of a universal congregation was spiritual in the sense that it could never gather in one place, but it was also pure. It was different from the Catholic church, which thought of all its members as believers and part of the universal church.[32] Caspersen performed a very helpful task in clarifying these ideas for his readers and the pastors of the church, who probably did not realize how much these discussions would ultimately impinge on their lives and their work in the kingdom.

Harald came to the farm in Cyrus for a visit and helped with the farmwork, something he knew well from his own upbringing on a farm. The family liked him very much, but Grandpa Theodore had told Borghild that he didn't think it would last—they were too taken with each other. Jonette thought that strange, but when she returned to Augsburg, she began dating other men again, especially one with whom she had had something of a romance on the choir tour. This sent Harald into a tizzy. Leland Sateren, who spent some time with Jonette, reported on how crazy my father had been when it looked like Jonette wasn't going to be with him. He laughed at what it had been like. From Mother's diary, I can well imagine that.

That September 11, *Folkebladet* printed a letter from King Haakon to Norwegian Americans in which he described his sorrow at having to flee the country. Although it was a stunning loss, he remained confident that the Allies would ultimately prevail. It was a grave concern for many Norwegian Americans. Haakon knew that it was important to keep them informed and on the good side of his regime. In the same issue was an article wondering how Christians should act in the face of tyrants like Hitler. Was Hitler the anti-Christ? The author thought not, but Hitler was still evil. He concluded with a quote from the Oxford Meeting in August 1937 that war was unchristian and a demonstration of the power of sin in this world.[33] It would be attacked vigorously by many in the next issues. They argued that it was necessary to fight evil, too, deploring the pacifism of the writer as well as his socialist leanings.

While in the Twin Cities, Jonette could also visit her family, her mother's brother, Richard, and several Jacobson cousins who lived there. On September 15, she celebrated her uncle Richard's birthday at his home and also met with Mildred and Freddie, who had come from Cyrus for the party. While they were together, they went downtown to shop and bought a hat, purse, and shoes. Both loved nice clothes, so it was a pleasure to be together for the excursion.

On September 19, Jonette and her friends were thrilled to move into Sivertsen Hall. She had gotten a job working there as something of a janitor and found it to be fine—having grown up as she did, she did not think any work too low and thanked God for the opportunity.[34] One day, Anne Pederson, her English teacher, asked her where she was working. When Jonette told her she was cleaning toilets in the dorm, Miss Pederson had said, "My dear, how unfortunate! You must work for me." So, much to Jonette's delight, she became Pederson's assistant.[35]

When school started on September 25, 1940, the student numbers stood at 421, of which 182 were freshmen. With the addition of the new girls' dorm, it felt like the college was growing successfully. Meanwhile, Jonette was trying to decide which of her boyfriends would be the one. She was praying diligently for guidance, and both Vern Blikstad and Harald were courting her. She knew

God was guiding her, praying even as she was cleaning the bathrooms in the dorm. Her girlfriends were getting engaged now and discussing and praying for insight in these momentous decisions. While Jonette was in this turmoil of deciding on a life partner, the churches were also in a turmoil on the questions of union and merger.

Caspersen kept the issue before the fellowship. For him, the question turned on the argument between Sverdrup and Evjen and the theologian Sohm. The September 25, 1940, issue of *Folkebladet* contained many articles on the question of what a congregation was, referring to Evjen's recent articles on Sverdrup and his ecclesiology. Chr. again appeared, this time irritated that Evjen could not find a better way to express his thoughts on the "visible congregation" (synlig menigheten) than "worldly union" (verdslig forening).[36] He recommended that all the readers of the journal go back and read Caspersen's fine articles on these issues, "Shall We Have Bishops" from the *Lutheran Messenger* and especially his column "Skulde en løsning være mulig?" ("Is a Solution Possible?"). He claimed, and I would agree with him, that it was one of the wisest and most thorough articles on the congregation that had appeared in *Folkebladet* in a long time.[37] What most impressed Chr. was Caspersen's argument that when Christians leave behind the notion that the local congregation is the highest authority, they are on thin ice and will little by little glide closer to the Catholic church's orders: "Church historians show us that this is rather clear."[38]

In that same issue, Caspersen wrote a long piece on the congregation and ordination. He was thankful that the Oxford and Edinburgh meetings had put the question before all the world. This did not reveal uniformity but great varieties of practices. Only Protestants were having the discussion, he believed, because for the Orthodox and Catholics, the question was moot. Their ecclesiology was who they were.

He also noted that about every five hundred years, the church changed some practices or rules drastically, citing the establishment of the historic episcopacy around 500 CE and then the great change caused by the Lateran Council, followed by the Reformation around 1500. He expected that a similar break would occur in 2000. Leaders needed to find some connecting links among the various churches. He did not think ordination would be a fruitful discussion to have because it was not central to every communion. The solution, he thought, was a powerful evangelistic movement and not lesson plans and conferences.[39]

These papers and columns continued at high volume through this season with some of the same fury of the Ministry Study of the ELCA in 1988–1993, as well as the same topics and learned polemical approaches. I am sure neither of my parents paid much attention to it as they were making their plans for the future, but one day my mother would be on her knees, praying that I would be successful in arguing the same principles at the 1993 ELCA Assembly in Kansas City.

One question that cannot quite be answered is why Caspersen was so alarmed. Why were his prophesies so dire and accurate? I cannot tell, but I can see and hear my formidable aunt Borghild, a good friend of Mark Hanson's parents, who frequently called Mark to upbraid him, now upbraiding me with her own take on things: "You think it would have been better not to have merged into the ELCA or even the ALC. No matter what, Mark Hanson would have been president, and all of his convictions would have won the day here too." Her conviction remained strong and undimished into her old age.

For the moment, Jonette was trusting that God would guide her in her choice of a husband. Harald was always in the mix but not around so much because of his internship at Newman Grove. On November 4, he called her to say his mother, Anna, had just been committed to Sedro-Woolley, the mental hospital near Ferndale. She had suffered such episodes several times before. Jonette was sympathetic but probably knew very little about what he was suffering. Mental illness, or insanity, as it was called at the time, was thought to run in families, people said, often supposing that insanity and diabetes came together. Arthur, Anna and Sjur's son, who came very late in their marriage, had contracted juvenile diabetes and would later die of it at the age of ten. Because Dad had been adopted, I don't think it bothered my mother too much when thinking of marrying him and having children with him.

Almost nothing about the presidential election between FDR and Wendell Wilkie was noted in the *Echo* or even *Folkebladet*. Early on, some had said that voting for FDR because he "kept us out of war" reminded them too much of the slogan Woodrow Wilson had campaigned on in 1916 but reneged on barely three months after his second inauguration. It felt like the war was inevitable, though there were still strong voices against it. There were more and more letters from Norway to families in the Midwest printed in newspapers, bearing terrifying news of conditions in Norway with the imprisoning of pastors and officials most Norwegian Americans knew of. The heroic resistance of the Norwegian pastors led by Eyvind Berggrav, the bishop of Oslo, became a frequently reported topic.

Throughout this time, Jonette started almost every entry in her diary by saying how grand the day had been and how happy she was, despite her turmoil about boyfriends. Through the Christmas festivities at Augsburg, she went with several others to the events, always noting whom Harald was with. When she got home to the farm that Christmas, she thoroughly enjoyed the festivities with family and friends but disclosed to her diary every night how much she missed Harald. On December 28, she mused in her diary whether her increasing and persistent desire to see Harald "is becoming true love or maybe selfishness? Dear Lord, I don't know, and I want to know!"[40]

Figure 8.4. Crown Prince Olav of Norway and his family. Used by permission of Augsburg University Archives.

## 1941

The New Year 1941 began with increasing forebodings of war. The Battle of Britain, when Britain stood alone, caused many to think that America would eventually have to declare war. They all listened for news from King Haakon VII and his government in exile in London. Most knew that Crown Princess Märtha with her children had come to live in Washington at President Roosevelt's invitation. The crown prince and princess had become good friends with the Roosevelts during their 1939 tour of America, and the friendship deepened as the war progressed. Olav spent most of his time in London but would return to Washington, when possible, to be with his family and very likely update Roosevelt on the war from the Norwegian and English points of view.

More and more information from Norway, now suffering under the dictatorship of Quisling, was being published in the Norwegian American Lutheran Church magazines. The letter the Norwegian bishops wrote against the Norwegian Nazis under the leadership of Berggrav was published in the January 1, 1941 issue of *Folkebladet*. It received a great amount of attention and made Berggrav one of the ecclesiastical heroes of the day. While the students were aware of these things, they did not make much of an impact on Jonette. She was praying for guidance in her relationship with Harald. He had been riding the train every weekend back and forth from Newman Grove and was weary. In the meantime, the semester was ending, and after her tests, she briefly went home. When she returned for the second semester, she came to realize, on February 7, that "Harald was God's will for me. I just shouted Hallelujah! I couldn't sleep and sang 'The Lost Chord' in bed—especially the phrase—'It quieted pain and sorrow like love.'"[41] Later she would tell me that she had spoken with Miss Mortenson and Miss Pederson, and both had warmly recommended her marrying Harald. She does record that just after she had come to understand God's will in the matter, she met with Miss Mortenson on February 10, after which they prayed together for some time.

At the same time, her sister, Borghild, was now engaged to Donald Ronning. They would be married on October 4, 1941. Her father, Theodore, ailing from his diabetes and arthritis, was getting ready to rent the farm to his nephew Ernest and his wife, Vivian, something that was a bit traumatic for both the girls.[42] Soon, Jonette had to do her required practice teaching to be certified as a teacher. She went to Frost, Minnesota, where she enjoyed herself in the community. She approached the end of the school year with dread, hating to leave Augsburg and the community there but at the same time looking forward to married life with Harald, who was spending the summer as an intern at the Faith congregation in South Dakota.

On Sunday, June 2, they celebrated cap and gown day with an excursion to Taylor's Falls. That evening, she got her engagement ring and praised God in

# A New Augsburg President and War on the Horizon

Figure 8.5. Harald Grindal and Jonette Tinseth. Used by permission of the Grindal family.

Jesus's name for it. The next day, she left for home, where the congregations near Morris were preparing for the annual meeting of the LFC. The Morris West Central Agricultural College, six miles from the farm, was where the meeting would be held from June 10 to 13. Her uncle Freddie was on the committee planning the event, so they were aware of all that was happening in Morris. It also meant that the students and teachers from Augsburg would be around for a while. Most important to Jonette at that convention was the ordination of her future brother-in-law, Donald M. Ronning. She went with her aunt Ella Tinseth Hanse to one of the services and sang a solo in Norwegian at the WMF meeting. A good part of most of the services were in Norwegian, as it was still the native language of a great number of the people gathered there.

The convention did not have many pressing issues before it. Among the plans it made were for the 1943 celebration of the centennial of the Norwegian American Lutheran churches. The LFC voted to publish a book, *Our Fellowship*, edited by Clarence Carlsen. It would tell the story of Augsburg, the Conference, and the LFC with pictures of all the churches, pastors, institutions, and boards of the church. The convention heard from President Burntvedt that there were now 380 congregations in the church, with 444 pastors. Over 16,000 children were in Sunday school with 2,000 teachers. The number of members in the church body was around 53,000. Bernhard Christensen announced that Augsburg was flourishing. During the year of 1940–1941, there had been 495 students, 18 of them seminary students. Missionary Melvin Helland, now returned from Madagascar with his wife, Emily, was called as professor at Augsburg. John Stensvaag was given a scholarship to pursue further studies in the Old Testament.

While talk of mergers and the like was not consuming the church the way it would after the war, Caspersen, who had an eagle eye for any talk of merger, reported on discussions the American Lutheran Conference was having with the Missouri Synod. In an article of several pages in *Folkebladet*, he reported on the meetings and papers coming out of those discussions. He thought it was impossible that the LFC could in any way participate in a merger with Missouri without utterly betraying Sverdrup and the past convictions and principles of the LFC. His allergy to Missouri was one shared by many of the more pietistic Norwegian Lutherans, especially those with Haugean backgrounds. The Little Synod, at Mankato, which had broken off from the Norwegian synod in the merger of the NLCA, would, of course, be interested, since its leadership had long ties with Missouri, as had several from the old Norwegian Synod centered at Luther College.

These reports made little impression on Jonette, who did not refer to them. As a seminary student, Harald had probably thought about these issues some. Conrad Bergendoff, president of Augustana College and Seminary, Rock Island, spoke at the annual Fall Pastors' Conference at Augsburg. The relationship between him and Christensen was a fond one. Both were intellectuals and spiritual leaders whose voices were much respected among the LFC pastors and professors. His topic was the "Unfinished Reformation," which Caspersen found to be completely in line with Georg Sverdrup's thinking. Sverdrup had, in fact, thought the Reformation could be finished by Lutherans in the United States, where there was freedom of religion. Bergendoff considered several unfinished questions among Lutherans, especially justification and sanctification, as well as church and state. There was little talk of merger at this meeting; it seemed not to be on anyone's mind. One could also feel some sense of the inevitability of the war coming, but few spoke of it in the papers.

For the LFC to avoid any likeness to the Historic Episcopate, the group traditionally named one of its pastors as ordainer. *Folkebladet* had a small note that P. A. Strommen, newly named to that position, had ordained Hamar Benson of Benson on August 31, 1941. The question of the episcopate was pushed when Nathan Söderblom, the Swedish archbishop, appeared in America trying to sell it. Although there were some Swedish Augustana pastors who hankered after an episcopate, the idea was put down by the president of the Augustana church, Oscar Benson. Usually, the LFC ordained its young seminary graduates at the annual meeting. At this time, Strommen was the official ordainer, so when candidates needed ordaining out of that sequence, he was called to do so.

At about this time, on August 12, 1941, Franklin Roosevelt and Winston Churchill met on board a ship near Placentia Bay, Newfoundland, for a conference. During their time together, they developed the Atlantic Charter, eight principles for the alliance "to ensure life, liberty, independence, and religious freedom, and to preserve the rights of man and justice." As the writers noted, this war was not simply one for more land or other grievances. It was to thwart Hitler's notion of world domination for his evil regime and its ideas. Their declaration, which stressed Western values of freedom, religion, speech, and other mainstays of liberal democracies of the West, was ratified by twenty-six nations in January 1942. This document would become the founding document of the United Nations after the war.

Jonette had spent the summer helping on the farm and with her father's declining health. On July 9, she received a call from the Swanville, Minnesota, school asking her to apply for a teaching job in English composition and electives in Latin, drama, and music. She accepted the offer. On September 2, she had her first day of classes. While she threw herself into the work and enjoyed the home where she had a room, she did not thrive as a teacher. The kids were mean to her, and she could not make them behave. She became increasingly frustrated and began thinking of other possibilities such as parish worker. Her time was busy, however, with her sister's wedding in Cyrus on October 4, classes, directing the school play, and working with the music, which she enjoyed. Her freshmen English class continued to defeat her. One day, she found out the boys called her Miss Paleface. Her family must have been noticing her difficulties and came often to take her home to the farm. Harald was a constant presence. Although they had not yet set a date for their wedding, they were thinking about it. On November 15, Jonette wrote that Harald had gotten a call to Tioga, North Dakota, where she had been so dismayed with the landscape and the parsonage.

Meanwhile, *Folkebladet* was watching the churchly scene and plans for ecumenical progress. Months before America entered World War II, on August 27, 1941, Caspersen wrote a column in *Folkebladet* on the two movements in the world working for international unity: the WCC, still unrealized but well on its way, and the League of Nations and whatever might replace it. He argued that it was the responsibility of the church to care for the world, and being united might help that: "If it did not it was not worth its salt."[43]

Jonette's sister, Borghild, now lived as a pastor's wife in the Hawley Minnesota Lutheran Free Church parsonage, somewhat closer to Swanville than Cyrus, so they began meeting there with her father, aunt, uncles, and cousins. On November 22, Jonette and Harald decided to get married on June 6, 1942, before his ordination in Fargo at Pontoppidan Lutheran Church at the end of the LFC convention. As they began preparing, Jonette spent time in Minneapolis with Harald, shopping for things they would need during their married life as well as preparing for the wedding. On November 29, they attended a symphony concert where Marian Anderson sang. Jonette thought it was the most thrilling concert she had ever attended.

## The United States Enters the War

When Pearl Harbor was attacked by the Japanese on December 7, 1941, Jonette noted the attack and worried about what would happen. Next to her difficulties teaching, "now this war makes my job seem so little a problem. May thy will be done," she concluded. Still, she felt more and more that she needed to leave Swanville. When she resigned is not clear, but by December 16, the kids in her class knew she was not returning after Christmas. Her students gave her presents, which surprised her. She returned to the farm, her home, and her father, praying and wondering what to do before their wedding.

On January 14, 1942, *Folkebladet* announced the sudden death of John Olof Evjen on January 4 of a heart ailment in Chicago, Illinois. He had been teaching at Carthage College and serving as dean. During the previous decade, he had contributed several pieces on the first principle of the LFC's Twelve Principles. Caspersen, who disagreed with him on his use of the word *verdslig* (*worldly*) held a high opinion of Evjen's scholarship and devotion to the work of Sverdrup and the tradition of the LFC. His accomplishments included being one of two Americans who were members of the Society for Church History in Germany and the German Philosophical Society in Berlin. Notice of his death appeared in newspapers from Connecticut to California. Without doubt, he was the most well-known Augsburg graduate at the time. He was lauded for his many scholarly accomplishments and the regard his fellow scholars held for him.

*Folkebladet* continued to report on the war and especially the work of the underground in Norway. Reports indicated a great deal of suffering on the part of Norwegians. Food was scarce, meat impossible to find. Word leaked out about how Norwegians such as Professor Ole Hallesby were being imprisoned and tortured. Grini prison near Oslo was filled with church leaders and underground leaders. Few events were as closely followed as the protest at Trondheim Cathedral on January 26, 1942. The Nazis had planned a service to install Quisling as the minister president of Norway. Bishop Fjellbu of Trondheim refused to participate and announced a prayer service at two that afternoon. The police locked the church after some had made it in. People started gathering outside the cathedral and began singing hymns, most notably "A Mighty Fortress Is Our God." The police could do nothing to stop it.

People all around Norway asked whether they had any freedom left in the church. Bishop Berggrav and the other seven Norwegian bishops resigned their positions in the state church but remained as pastors. This action was highly regarded by Norwegian Americans, and papers like *Folkebladet* made it their business to report on such goings on. Fjellbu and others attributed the courage of the people to the Oxford Group led by Frank Buchman, the Pennsylvania Lutheran pastor who had founded it.

# A New Augsburg President and War on the Horizon

The college was also making progress as a liberal arts college. Until Christensen's tenure began, there had not really been a dean of the college. Martin Quanbeck was appointed in 1942, but his other responsibilities kept him from being able to effectively hold the position. Several new teachers had been appointed in the past years: Leland Sateren, Joel Torstenson, K. Berner Dahlen as dean of men, and Philip Kildahl in philosophy and history. Their tenure would be interrupted by the war.

On January 8, 1942, Jonette registered to take classes at Lutheran Bible Institute (LBI) in Minneapolis. At the time, she was staying at Sivertsen Hall with her friends. The school was now reeling from the demands of the war—especially the male students and younger faculty who were either enlisting or being drafted. The war meant a drastic reduction of students at the school, which in turn meant more financial issues. The college was thinking of offering summer classes to speed up the time it took to graduate, especially for the men. The *Echo*, edited by Gerald Thorson, who would be my English professor, studied many of these issues. One column noted the effect of the war on the athletic programs of all the schools in America. Jonette would soon room at the Hildebrand home nearby so she could remain close to Augsburg and attend classes, which she enjoyed, plus take voice lessons from Hendrickson, whom she knew through her family in Montevideo, while Harald was finishing his seminary classes.

As part of her rent, she cooked and cleaned in the home and minded the little boy, Dicky; she was able to entertain friends, especially Harald. She also

**Figure 8.6.** Augsburg Seminary's 1942 graduating class and their wives. From left to right: Helen and Luther Strommen, Olive and Alfred Sevig, Jonette and Harald Grindal, Marian and Lester Dahlen, and Fern and Larry Gudmestad. Used by permission of the Grindal family.

continued to be in demand as a soloist. "Jesus Only," the Mount Carmel hymn by Samuel Miller, was her most frequent offering. As Harald would graduate that June, there were festivities she could attend with him at the seminary as his intended, "Pastor Grindal's wife!" On February 5, they went downtown and bought a maple bedroom set, mattress, and the oak dining room table, buffet, and chairs that were at the center of her life as pastor's wife and which I now own. Harald bought her a cedar chest as well, which she regarded as a grand thing for her "honey" to do, she exclaimed. Later, her father, Theodore, gave them a car, as her dowry, she would joke, something they would need in Tioga, where there were six little congregations to serve over a wide area in the parish. She concluded her studies at LBI on March 20 and sang "Jesus Only" at the graduation ceremony.

She and Harald drove back to Cyrus, where he helped with the chores, milking and the like, in overalls and a farm hat, which she thought made him look cute. For the rest of the time until their wedding, he would be with her there on weekends while working on the arrangements for his new call in Tioga, taking the train to Minot to settle some issues about the call and otherwise finishing up his work at school. The war is hardly mentioned in her diary, but there are hints. On May 6, they had to appear at the local school to sign up for their ration of

**Figure 8.7.** Newlyweds Harald and Jonette (Tinseth) Grindal. Used by permission of the Grindal family.

sugar. On May 14, they went to the courthouse in Morris to get their marriage license, which really impressed her.

After some time at Augsburg for Harald's graduation from seminary, Jonette spent the rest of May preparing for the wedding and packing things for the new house in Tioga, which they shipped on the train. Freddie helped pack the music cabinet and the rocker. Then there were showers, the rehearsal, and dinner with all the relatives. Her grandfather Haakon and his second wife, Johanna, had a dinner for the young couple as well.

The wedding day, she recorded, was filled with thrills that she could not express. The ceremony had gone well. Her aunt Mildred picked fifty white peonies for the wedding. They became the flower most beloved by her. After the ceremony, when the newlyweds finally got going, they stayed in a Fergus Falls hotel. It had been a hilarious check-in. Uncle Freddie had asked Harald for the keys to the car, which Freddie claimed was in the way in the granary, and Harald naively gave them to him. When they arrived in Fergus, they found that the luggage had been bound and tied with oily rags and twine. It took considerable efforts on Harald's part to free the luggage, which sent Jonette into gales of laughter at his frustration. A perfect beginning and an emblem of the rest of their lives: Mom laughing at Dad when he got frustrated—pure joy. Now they were one, she wrote.

CHAPTER 9

# A World at War

HARALD ACCEPTED THE call to Tioga in December 1941, just after the attack on Pearl Harbor. He wrote in his acceptance letter, "In assuming the great responsibility and requirements which a call demands, I do so, looking to God for wisdom, strength, and love, with the prayer that I may be wholly yielded to Him so that I might be a useful servant in His vineyard."[1]

The call had come in November 1941, after he had preached a trial sermon in the Tioga churches. He would finish school in June, be married in Cyrus on June 6, and then, after a brief honeymoon in Battle Lake, return to Cyrus to pack, attend the annual meeting, be ordained, and travel to the West Coast so Jonette could meet his family.

The annual meeting that year began on June 9, 1942, in Fargo, North Dakota, at Pontoppidan Lutheran. Dad's home pastor from Ferndale, John Hjelmeland (1881–1968), preached what Torgerson called a powerful and soul-searching message, which set the tone for the rest of the annual meeting.

Pontoppidan had been the location of what might be called the first annual meeting of the LFC in 1896, where the leading principles of the LFC were first presented. It was thus an appropriate place for Harald to be ordained. Harald's grandfather Ludvig Olsen Watne (1854–1944) had attended that meeting in 1896 and participated in the adoption of the leading principles that shaped the character of the LFC—and my family—through its years.

The past year had gone well for the fellowship; money had come in, although the war was beginning to affect enrollment at Augsburg, to say nothing of its effects on the mission fields. In China, the growing hostilities had forced the Peder Konsterlies to flee. Home missions had progressed, establishing and maintaining new congregations. They had taken in twenty-two thousand dollars, the same as the year before. Although that was promising, it was not enough to increase its work into the future, John T. Quanbeck, leader of the board, reported.

The LFC was using the occasion of the centennial of the Norwegian Lutheran Church in America in 1943 to raise money to pay off its debt. It had already gathered $120,000 of the $140,000 it was hoping for. The report from the schools was good, although Christensen was too ill at the time to give the report. Most pressing was the ramping up of the war. The Board of Organization,

Committee No. 1, expressed its support and loyalty to the country: "In the present world crisis, which so unexpectedly plunged our country into war, we pledge our loyal support to the government of the United States and pray that God in His wisdom may guide them so that justice, righteousness, and freedom may prevail."[2]

The board also approved a resolution the National Lutheran Council (NLC) had adopted on May 14, 1942, expressing sympathy and support for Norwegians in their "bitter time of trial." It hailed Bishop Eivind Berggrav and his colleagues for their courageous opposition to the Nazi regime. In addition, it presented a resolution stating its strong opposition to the liquor traffic, support for which had been dwindling since the repeal of Prohibition.

In that same issue, *Folkebladet* reported on the work at Camp Little Norway in Toronto. The camp had been established to train Norwegian pilots so they could take part in the war as Norwegians. The Norwegian government in exile in London paid close attention. Later in the year, the crown prince and princess would visit Minneapolis on their way to Camp Little Norway. The press would continue to report on the workings at the camp, which had gained much support from Norwegians and even Swedes in North America. Carl Sandburg appeared at several gatherings to support the project.

Thursday, June 11, was the day of the annual meeting devoted to the Women's Missionary Federation, which heard from Peder Konsterlie after his flight from China. Jonette and Harald arrived in time for that meeting, where Mrs. Gracia Christensen spoke. The next day, while the fellows—the seminary students—were being colloquized, Jonette and Marian Dahlen, wife of Lester Dahlen, also in the class, went to get their hair done.

During the meetings on Friday, June 12, the conference heard from Ralph Long, the director of the NLC, who urged the group to support the Lutheran World Action (LWA) funds to help the European "motherlands" suffering from the war. Long expressed his dismay that the Missouri Synod would not work together with other Lutherans in this effort. This was a common theme among other American Lutherans. The failure of German American Lutherans to apologize for the Nazi invasion of Denmark and Norway grated on many Norwegian American Lutherans. It continued to be an irritation all through the war and after. On Saturday, June 13, after the colloquies with the seminary students, the annual meeting approved the recommendations of the ordination committee that all five candidates be accepted for ordination.

On Sunday morning, June 14, 1942, the young couples attended the morning service where Melvin Olson, pastor from Trinity in Minneapolis, preached to a packed church. That afternoon, Harald and his seminary class—Lester Dahlen, Harald Grindal, Lawrence Gudmestad, Alfred Sevig, Luther Strommen—were ordained by P. A. Strommen, the ordinator of the LFC that year. Pastor J. M.

# A World at War

Halvorson read the *intimitationstale* (introductory materials) and statements of faith written by the ordinands before the rite of ordination. At the closing service of the LFC convention, led by Kristofer Hagen, Jonette sang "Jesus Only," her most popular solo.

## Meeting Dad's Family

After returning to Hawley to finish packing, Jonette and Harald left for Tunbridge, eight miles west of Rugby, for her to meet his family, the Hans Tjons. Hans's widow, Torbjør, was still living with her children in Tunbridge. Jonette would meet all of Han's children—Norman, Arthur, Herman, Anna, married to Osmund Selland, and Manda, married to Anfinn Tweet. The couple had bought Sjur's farm, and their regular payments to Sjur and Anna had made it possible for them to send Harald to Augsburg.

Jonette was charmed by the ride across the Central Plains, where she had traveled with the Augsburg Choir two years before. The next day, they drove into the Great Plains and reached Minot, where Aletta "Lettie" Watne, Anna Grindal's sister, showed them the Watne Estates, which Anna's father, Ludvig Watne, a lawyer and realtor, had owned and developed. Although he was still

**Figure 9.1.** Ludvig Watne. Used by permission of the Grindal family.

alive, he was quite infirm, and they did not visit him. The next morning, they were driven to the train for their trip out West.

Three days later, on June 18, they arrived in Seattle and had breakfast with Forrest and Thelma Monson. When they got to Ferndale, Jonette met her father-in-law, Sjur Grindal, and his ten-year old son, Arthur, who was suffering from childhood onset diabetes. Anna was at Sedro-Woolley mental hospital after suffering another breakdown. They began cleaning the house, just as Harald had done many times before, given his mother's condition. The next day, they met Papa Svein Kivley, Harald's father; his four sisters—Mable, Marion, Mathilda, and Myrtle; and brother, Selmer. She loved them at once, she wrote. They had a picnic birthday party for Marion and enjoyed ice cream. On Sunday, June 21, Harald preached in his home congregation, Ferndale Lutheran Free Church. Jonette thought his sermon on the rich young ruler was wonderful, as did the congregation.

After the service, the congregation hosted a reception in their honor, and then they visited other friends in the congregation. The next day, they had a chicken dinner with the woman who took in Harald when he was a newborn. She had kept him until the Grindals could fulfill their vows as sponsors at his baptism. They also went to Stanwood to meet Ed Kivley, Dad's uncle, and his wife, Mary.

Jonette and Harald then went to Bellingham to speak with the draft board the next day, and Harald got his 4-D classification. Pastors tended to receive this deferment, but it was not assured. Jonette confided to her diary that she had been more worried about that than she should have been. That evening, they had dinner with Harald's full sister Ruth and his full brother Joseph and his wife. Jonette was amazed at how much the brothers resembled each other. While they were staying at the Grindals, Harald kept cleaning and washing all the floors, fixing supper for Arthur and his dad. They had dinner with the Kivleys again. There is no record of them visiting Anna, Harald's foster mother at Sedro-Woolley. When they left Washington by train, Jonette was filled with thanksgiving for the time with the family and the beauties of Puget Sound. They would arrive in Minot three days later and drive to Tioga, eager to set up housekeeping in the parsonage two doors from Zion Lutheran. Their excitement at the prospect of this house kept them busy for some time, probably not thinking much about the annual meeting except for memories of his ordination and her solo.

In retrospect, looking back at the 1942 annual meeting, Caspersen and Torgerson both commended it as a pleasant and edifying time. Caspersen, who had been at the 1896 meeting in Fargo, however, worried some about the new rules that had been approved but would not be introduced until the 1943 meeting. He felt other issues such as the centennial would make it difficult to discuss those particular changes.[3] Some feared that even though the new rules were intended to shorten the meetings and deliberations, it was also possible that the deliberations would be more politicized. It might even cause "underground" movements to develop, which Caspersen was not sure was a good thing.

Alongside watching developments in the church, Norwegian Americans were paying close attention to the situation in Norway. Many commended the Norwegian teachers who had fought the Nazi takeover of the schools, when thousands of teachers opposed the new regime and suffered jail. Fifteen hundred were arrested and five hundred condemned to a deadly sentence of labor in Kirkenes. Many would say later that the courage of the teachers and what they had taught gave young Norwegian students the courage to resist as well.[4]

## Installation and Beginning Ministry in Tioga

On July 19, 1942, Harald was installed in the Tioga parish as pastor. Tioga was a small town of about 450 people in 1942, situated between Minot and Williston, North Dakota, in rolling Great Plains country. The Tioga Lutheran Free Church parish consisted of six churches: Zion, in town; Norman, ten miles to the northeast; St. Olaf, ten miles to the northwest; Lindahl, ten miles straight north; Temple, five miles west; and Beaver Creek, twenty-five miles south of Tioga in the Nessen Valley across the Missouri River.

Jonette wrote about the dinner before the installation service, which involved both the president of the district, Clarence Carlsen, and Burntvedt: "Pastor Clarence Carlsen from Minot, North Dakota, and Dr. T. O. Burntvedt from Minneapolis, our LFC president, were guests in our home to be there for Harald's installation services the next day. At the supper table I told them I was a niece of Uncle Sundal and they immediately began to laugh heartily with all sorts of stories of his quaint and deliciously wry sense of humor."[5] This was something of a surprise to Jonette, who feared Sundal when she was little. They told several stories relished by Sundal over the years. Burntvedt thought him such a fine preacher that he would drive down to Christiania to hear him preach if he happened to be free on a summer Sunday.

Western North Dakota was an entirely new landscape for the young couple from western Minnesota's lake country and the Cascade Mountains abutting Puget Sound. Mother asked the mother of a friend, Mrs. Stenberg, "Is there anything of beauty out there?" Mrs. Sternberg thought for a moment, then a smile spread over her beautiful, wrinkled face, and with delight in her voice, she said, "Oh yes, Jonette, there is lots of sky."

At the time they arrived, western North Dakota was only beginning to emerge from the devastating drought and Depression of the '30s. After the rains returned, the crops were bountiful, and the price of wheat was high. Still, the churches and the parishioners' homes were small and simple, in need of paint and repair after fifteen years of drought and the Depression.

**Figure 9.2.** The backyard of the Tioga, North Dakota, parsonage after a frost. Used by permission of the Grindal family.

After getting the key for the parsonage, they stepped into their first home: a Spanish villa that the trustees had recently remodeled. They came in the front door into the living room. It was square, as was the dining room, which was the same size. The kitchen was another square room with only a pump by a sink with a drain that ran outside the kitchen window into a bed of hollyhocks. The bedroom was square also, which made the floor plan a square divided into four squares. Between the living room and bedroom was a huge doorway with a wide stairway going upstairs. The house had been built with a flat-roof Spanish-villa style, a rather inappropriate design for that region. The roof had leaked so badly that the walls and ceilings were water damaged. The trustees of the parish had voted to build a gabled roof over the whole house, creating a huge porch upstairs with twelve windows. There was no bathroom or running water; only a huge cistern under the kitchen, which filled with rainwater. When it was empty, they had it filled with soft water hauled in from a slough in the country. Their drinking water was "running" water, they said, because Harald "ran" to get it from across the street at the schoolhouse well, where most residents of the village got their water.

The young couple heated the soft water in the cistern for washing clothes in a copper boiler on the stove. Jonette was used to this, having grown up on a farm with no conveniences. It was more difficult for Harald to take a bath in a metal wash tub beside the small round kitchen sink because he had never had to live in such primitive fashion. In the home where he grew up, they had an indoor bathroom and electricity. Fortunately, the Tioga parsonage had electricity and phone service.

They described the house as eight rooms and a "path." The path led to an outhouse built in the '30s by Works Progress Administration (WPA).[6] It had been scientifically designed by the government, and most homes in the region sported one of these new inventions. When I asked my grandpa where he was going when he was taking the path, he would say, "Chicago!" In the winter, they used a chemical toilet installed in the basement, which was really only a large pail with a comfortable seat, creosote added to take care of the odor. They immediately began making plans to fix up the house.

The salary was nine hundred dollars, a free house, and the free will offerings on festival Sundays. This is forgotten today, but it was a custom from Norway that on the festival Sundays, the congregation would stand up and process around the altar, leaving gifts for the pastor, the janitor, and sometimes the organist. It made getting to the churches on those days an economic necessity. So my father would drive through snow, sleet, blizzards, everything to make those Sundays. He never missed, if at all possible. They were necessary for our survival. Once, a treasurer in Lindahl congregation, where Dad had only appeared on Christmas, Easter, and Pentecost, gave an oral annual report noting that they had had a good year: "The Lord, he been wid us, and the preacher, he been wid us... most of the time!"[7]

Dad traveled through terrible weather because they desperately needed every penny to help them with the debts they had incurred in establishing a home. They had bought a blue davenport and chair, an oak dining room set and two red area rugs, a maple bedroom set, a refrigerator, and a bottled gas stove in Minneapolis on credit and had it all shipped out. Those were the days when credit buying was not common. Their monthly bill from New England Furniture Store in Minneapolis was fifty-two dollars, and their total salary was only eighty-three dollars a month. One of their pastor friends in Williston, Gudmund B. Rundstrom, my godfather, said to Dad when he came to Tioga for Easter services, "Ah, buy anything you need. God wants you to have it good and He will pwovide."[8]

In spite of the interest of the people in the congregation, who were eager to meet the new pastor and his wife and tour the parsonage, no salary appeared. The couple decided to take a trip to Williston forty-five miles away and try to borrow money. How could they borrow money with no references in that city? Jonette sat and waited in the car. Then she saw Harald coming down the street with a grin—not walking but virtually running. "Joey," he said, "Rasmussen just handed me $75.00 and gave me a year in which to pay it back." Mother wrote, "We felt like millionaires."

They bought a secondhand table and four chairs for the kitchen with fifteen dollars. They now had all the furniture they needed. Their experience of moving into a parsonage and learning the unpredictability of salary payments and strange houses that were not theirs taught them many lessons young pastors needed to learn at the time.

That fall, *Folkebladet* reprinted an article by Fredrik Wisløff, who had spent 1930 in the United States, teaching at Augsburg and observing the school and the LFC. His article had come at a special moment given the occupation of Norway at the time. He prayed that Augsburg could continue to graduate talented pastors who had a deep acquaintance with their Bibles and Lutheran doctrine. In addition, he wished Augsburg could become a power center in America for the saving of souls, first and last. To do that, the school needed to create "warm hearts" burning with love for the Gospel to bring an awakening to its people.[9] If there was any creed that my parents held about Augsburg and its preparing them for such work in the far reaches of North Dakota, this would be it. And it would be among the many reasons they would name me Gracia, for Mrs. Christensen. When I was born, they immediately took out a college scholarship policy from Lutheran Brotherhood. Alt for Augsburg!

It was typical to send new young pastors out to small parishes in the fellowship to test them. Most of these parishes had several congregations, but Tioga parish, with six small congregations, had among the most in the LFC. Most often the Zion Church had the eleven o'clock service; Temple, closest by, had morning service at eight thirty. Every other or every third Sunday, Lindahl had services at one thirty, and St. Olaf had a service at three o'clock. Norman would then have an evening service. If Beaver Creek had an afternoon service, the folks would most likely be invited someplace for dinner—the noon meal on the farm at the time—so it was hard to hurry back for another service that evening. Dad became ambitious and wanted to schedule services every other Sunday, but they objected. "Don't bother, Reverend, every three weeks is plenty often. We don't want you to kill yourself," they would say.[10]

Jonette always went along, probably because she thought they expected her to, all the time enjoying company with Harald. In four of the churches, she served as organist or pianist and often would sing a solo. If Jonette didn't go, Harald could play the organ or piano.

Beaver Creek Church was a meeting place for the people of the Nessen Valley, which ran seventy miles along the Missouri River. It was a place people came together once every three weeks to relax, talk, and enjoy each other's company. The men would sit on the steps or on wooden planks alongside the church in the shade, smoking their pipes or chewing their tobacco until the preacher would drive up into the churchyard from the county road. Then everyone was all smiles. "Howdy, Revener, ya made it right on the minute."

The church bell would ring across the quiet countryside, and the men would file into their side of the church. The women were already there with their babies

A World at War 337

and younger children on the left-hand side of the aisle. Then the children would come in from their games of tag in the cemetery, which was usually in the back of the church: The altar railing was built as a semicircle, with the idea that the other half encircled those in the graveyard together with those at the altar. They would sit quietly with their mothers, sometimes running back and forth between parents.

The hymnal was *Hymns of Praise*, the service accompanied by Mrs. Harold Lund. Jonette described it vividly: "After a short altar service Harald would preach with all the fire that he could muster, and they would sit reverently (or spellbound?) for those thirty minutes. This was the only entertainment they had. There were no TV's, no magazines, not many radios or newspapers in those days. During those hell fire sermons, I wondered if anyone ever quaked with fear? Or were they just amused at how serious Harald seemed to take the stuff he found in 'that Book?'"[11]

As the days went by, Harald became more and more occupied with parish duties. Six confirmation classes had to be organized. He wanted to get young people's work going. The ladies' aids insisted that he had to do the Scripture reading, praying, and often lead the meetings. When he objected and suggested that the women do their own devotions, one woman's husband said, "But that's what we hired you for, Reverend." The men came to these country ladies' aids meetings, too, because very few women could drive, and they liked the lunches. There were sick people to visit, funerals to conduct, weddings at which to officiate, babies to baptize, and church business to administer. They started a Bible study and prayer meeting in Zion Church in town. Very few came, but my parents felt the need themselves. The confirmation classes met in the one-room schoolhouses close to the churches after school was dismissed, to save heating up the church for those two hours.

## Centennial of Norwegian American Lutherans

As they began their ministry on the prairies, the war came to be more and more the focus of the country. The August 12, 1942, issue of *Folkebladet* was filled with stories of Haakon VII becoming king of Norway and how he had led the country against the invasion. If he had not yet been highly regarded by Norwegian Americans, his near-sanctification was beginning. Accounts like these told of his courage as he led parliament and then fled the country, ruling with his government in exile from London. Nearly every issue would tell one or another story of the resistance in Norway. Also, in preparation for the coming centennial of the Norwegian Lutheran Churches in America, every issue featured a historical account by Andreas Helland of the founding of Norwegian

Lutheranism in this country: *Arven Vi Fikk: et kirkelig tilbakeblik* ("The Heritage We Received: A Churchly Look Back"). These had the effect of making the history seem relevant and contemporary to readers as the articles took them back to the very beginning of Augsburg and the LFC.

The August 26, 1942, issue carried an account of the ordination in the Northwood, North Dakota, congregation of John Stensvaag, who was serving Oak Grove Lutheran in Richfield, where Harald would be called twenty years later. Stensvaag had just received his doctorate in the Old Testament from Hartford Theological Seminary and had returned that summer to Minneapolis from a year at John Hopkins University, where he had studied Semitic languages. The ordination service was attended by Burntvedt; Sverre Torgerson; Pastor Ingvald Norum of Grand Forks, North Dakota; and Northwood pastor Johannes Ringstad. Ringstad, who wrote the account, explained that the service had been at Northwood because Stensvaag had just married Hannah Ovidia Mehus (1916–2010), a young woman from that congregation, from an important family in the LFC. The Mehus name had figured for some time in the LFC—Oscar M. Mehus, and Belle Mehus (1896–1988) had taught music at Augsburg from 1922 until 1935, when Gerda began teaching there. Ringstad remarked that Stensvaag was a promising young man who had distinguished himself in scholarship, but more to the point, he had had a strong LFC education. He understood sin and grace and had become a great admirer of Georg Sverdrup through reading his *Collected Works* (*Samlede Skrifter*). This made him a "gift from God to our church. We thank God for the gift but let us also remember that with each gift there is a responsibility or work that is just as important. We should pray for him. God bless Dr. Stensvaag's beginning and his work among us!"[11]

Pastor Ringstad's report appropriately marked the beginning career of Stensvaag. His comment that Stensvaag had read Sverdrup closely meant he also understood Norwegian and had gone to the deepest source of the LFC. That he had done so convinced pastors, like Ringstad, of Stensvaag's devotion to the principles of the Free Church.

About this time, Caspersen visited congregations in the northwest quarter of North Dakota to drum up subscriptions for *Folkebladet*, which had a circulation of about 3,500 at the time. He enjoyed the hospitality of the pastors in the region: Johan Dahlen in Palermo; G. B. Rundstrom in Williston; Fritjof Monseth, who had just moved from New York to serve four congregations north of Williston, Zahl, and Bonetrail; L. H. Luthard in Fortuna, with four congregations; J. P. Leeland in Wildrose, east of Fortuna; and Haukness, serving the Westby, Montana, congregation. Farther west in Medicine Lake, Montana, Oliver Sidney served five or six congregations, and then there were the Harald Grindals, the newlywed couple in Tioga, with five congregations. The purpose of Caspersen's trip, besides gathering subscriptions, was evaluating the state of the congregations in that part of the LFC.

In addition, he was able to attend a district meeting of the pastors in Minot. Given the rationing of rubber and thus tires, some pastors had arranged to drive together to Minot, and Tioga was where several would meet to "change horses," he wrote. While he was there, he was able to visit the Tioga parsonage. He had been there twice before, when A. T. Moen served the congregation and then when E. M. Hanson was the pastor. He noted that the parsonage had been much improved from the previous visits and was now "really a beautiful and cozy parsonage."[13] He concluded his report by noting that things had finally gotten better for the farmers, the future looked brighter, and people had more means in their hands to support the magazines. All the work of the LFC would benefit from the Centennial Fund—as always, the concern about its schools and missions was central.[14]

That same number of the magazine carried the obituary notice of Mrs. Georg (Elise) Sverdrup on September 10, 1942. Widowed in 1907, she had lived in the Augsburg community ever since Sverdrup's death, attending Augsburg events and Trinity Congregation. She was buried next to her husband in Lakeview Cemetery beside Lake Harriet in Minneapolis. Gracia Christensen had befriended her in her old age and told me of Mrs. Sverdrup's report on how devoted he was to his work. Gracia always thought Sverdrup's fanatic devotion to the idea of the congregation too much.

Helland's columns on the history of Augsburg continued through the next year. They reveal many nuggets about the founding of Augsburg. Helland had been there at Augsburg from the 1880s and had lived through the stressful days of the 1890s. While Helland was thoroughly committed to Sverdrup and his ideas about the school and church, there were insights he may have missed in his *Augsburg gjennem Femti Aar* (*Augsburg Through Fifty Years*). In discussing the strife among Weenaas, Sverdrup and Oftedal, Helland mused on Weenaas's temperament as being what we might call almost bipolar, going quickly "from light to darkness, from spirited courage to the deepest depression."[15] He did allow as how Weenaas's time at Augsburg would have been crushing to almost anyone. He even gave credit to the generosity of Pastor Jacob Aall Ottesen (1825–1904) in Koshkonong, a keen Norwegian Synod pastor and polemicist, for helping the starving students by urging his members to contribute to the struggling school. Ottesen's initials appear in the names of several sons of the Synod, including J. A. O. Stub Jr., Ottesen's grandson, and J. A. O. Preus, later governor of Minnesota.

## More Merger Talk

Although it was far from the notice of most members of the fellowship, there were also further stirrings toward church union. *Folkebladet's* editor was a member of the National Lutheran Association (NLA), a group of editors of Lutheran magazines. He came to know representatives of all the Lutheran groups in America and faithfully reported on their conversations, most often on Lutheran union. Always wary of Missouri's requirement for dogmatic agreement before there could be unity, he praised the NLA for its awareness of its shared concerns and issues, complimenting it on its comradeship and harmonic gatherings.

As these leaders were discussing unity, my parents were experiencing ecumenism at the parish level in surprising ways. It was Thanksgiving time in the new parish for my parents. They had been invited to the Beaver Creek Thanksgiving dinner. Jonette never forgot it:

> Overnight an ice storm had transformed the whole world into a winter fairyland. The sun was shining on the snow and the prairies looked like a sea of diamonds. Even the Russian thistles caught in the rundown fences along the road were dazzling. I remarked while we were driving, If God can make even the thistles dazzle for Him, I guess he can make even the most ordinary creature a beautiful creation by His touch.
>
> The old schoolhouse was full to overflowing with all the residents in the valley. The smell of turkey and dressing, mince and pumpkin pie greeted us as we stepped in the door. This was one of the finest examples of community caring we have seen in our thirty-six years of ministry. Every bachelor cowboy and every lonely person in the valley was brought into the Beaver Creek family to feast together that one day each year.[16]

Even as my parents were getting accustomed to the rhythms of the parish and war was raging, church life on the denominational level did not cease, nor did their work in the congregation. That fall, they had to put up thirty-eight storm windows, many on the new porch on the second floor. That meant naming each window since there were no standard sizes—each window had its own measurements. They finished by October 13, Harald's twenty-seventh birthday, and then the storms came. Jonette wrote, "The snow piled higher and higher until it was as high as the houses and the church windows. People were dying for lack of care out in the stranded farm homes. Neighbors would meet Harald's car with horses and sleigh to take him across the fields to the churches for the funerals."[17]

The American Lutheran Conference met that November in Rock Island, at Augustana Seminary and College. Dr. Bergendoff, president of Augustana, and Dr. Emmanuel Frederick Poppen, president of the American Lutheran Church, spoke on Lutheran Unity. They both took positions that were very like what could be called the "free church position" on agreements, which meant unity, not union.[18]

In the next issue, Pastor Olai H. Sletten (1878–1946) gave an extended report on the meeting in Rock Island. He wanted to write it in Norwegian so the older people could understand what was going on in the church concerning union. Sletten, longtime pastor at St. Olaf in North Minneapolis and seasoned observer of the LFC, had an interesting take on the participants. He evaluated representatives of each group and concluded that despite the ALC's being anti-Missourian—and the rancor against Missouri is palpable in these reports—the Germans were still Germans, as the Swedes were still Swedes. He saw in Johan Arnd Aasgaard (1876–1966), president of the NLCA, a man who had unusual leadership skills and would be important in later negotiations: "He has a deeply Christian sense, free-spirited in his attitude, exceedingly fraternal in his attitude toward others."[19] Aasgaard had no need to create disciples and had been the perfect man after H. G. Stub to keep the new NLCA together. Sletten considered Aasgaard to be the most democratic of all the leaders in the group. With a leader like that, Sletten was somewhat optimistic about the future of the Conference.

In his column, however, Caspersen wrote an English report on the meeting, which really turned out to be a screed against Missouri. He was not happy that the question of altar and pulpit fellowship had come up again, this time with the ULCA and Missouri. For him, any talk of this—which involved the Galesburg rule of Lutheran altars for Lutherans, Lutheran pulpits for Lutherans again—seemed unnecessary. For Caspersen, adherence to the Augsburg Confession was enough for Lutheran Unity. That was the stance of the LFC and had been since the beginning. He deplored the fact that the American Lutheran Conference continued to want to confer with Missouri so that such a union might be possible: "We hope that the American Lutheran Conference will never agree to the Missourian position on unionism. That position is unbrotherly, unBiblical, unChristian, and therefore in the truest sense un-Lutheran."[20]

He praised both Dr. Poppen and Bergendoff for their views on the future of Lutheran Church unity, especially Bergendoff for his suggesting closer proximity to the Federal Council of Churches and approval of the World Council of Churches.[21] Fevold and Nelson note that in these years, it became apparent that there were two opposing groups in the American Lutheran Conference—one that wanted to "enlarge the Conference to include the ULCA," something supported by Augustana, and another that wanted "to withhold fellowship until the ULCA demonstrated doctrinal soundness."[22] The Norwegian Lutherans, on the whole, were on the side of withholding fellowship.

## Parsonage Life During the War

Life in the Tioga parsonage was far from these conversations, but one can be sure the pastors spoke about such topics as they gathered for their meetings.

Meanwhile, life was primitive and the winter weather harsh. Jonette described it vividly:

> The parsonage was cold. Lignite coal cost twenty-five dollars for a big truckload. Lignite was a soft coal mined right in the area and burned by most families in their stoves or furnaces. It burned fast and produced a lot of ashes. The house was warm in the basement and by the radiators but only 32° by the thermometer on the wall. Insulation was not heard of in those days. We burned so much lignite to keep warm that it was a merry chase to keep the fire going and the ashes carried out. Harald chided me by saying that he met himself in the door carrying out the ashes. Papa was living with us and graciously paid a couple of the coal bills. By the end of the winter, we had burned forty tons of lignite.[23]

In the same way that Norwegians had been used to paying a tithe of fish or food to the pastor, the people in Tioga understood they needed to help the young pastor and his wife survive and were generous with their farm produce. Jonette especially, but also Harald, having grown up on farms, knew how to receive the food, slaughter it if necessary, and preserve it. They got meat, cream, eggs, and chickens. One day, a confirmand came to the door with a live rooster in a box and gave it to Jonette with the comment "My ma wants the preacher to have fresh meat!" That meant Harald had to kill it. As a farm boy, he knew how to do that but was not practiced. Jonette watched as he chopped off the chicken's head with a dull axe and then looked on in merriment as it ran around the garage, with Harald shouting, "Whoa, whoa."

They were grateful for everything they received. Once they had sixteen jars of cream in the icebox—the old kind filled with a block of ice that an iceman would drop off every so often. They bought a churn and made butter from the cream. From this, the old Sunday evening supper of sweet, thick cream on freshly baked brown bread with brown sugar became a lavish treat.

The winter in Tioga, where chinook winds were common, could suddenly be warmer by fifty degrees in the space of a few minutes. When they subsided, the temperature could plunge again below zero and turn the muddy roads into frozen ruts dangerous for the small Ford with bad tires. Dad would be driving through mud, and suddenly it would freeze, and he would be stuck and have to walk to the nearest farm for help chopping the car out of the ice.

## 1943: The Centennial and My Birth

The new year, 1943, began with the newspapers declaring that it would be tougher than 1942, as the nation "strained for a total wartime status amid official prophecies that each of its 365 days will be a grim, tortuous struggle toward victory."[24] This strain can be seen in the church papers as well. More and more of their copy had to do with stories about the war, its leaders, its costs, and how the church should respond. B. M. Christensen had warned in a special article some weeks before that Augsburg's enrollment had fallen precipitously now that young men were being conscripted. He wanted to reassure the readership that although things were going to be rough, he had every confidence that, with the support of the fellowship, which was his great comfort, Augsburg would survive.[25]

In the first issue of 1943, the centennial year, Andreas Helland meditated on the commitments of Sverdrup and Oftedal. He noted that the one word that marked Sverdrup's program was *freedom* (*friheten*). For Sverdrup, true freedom meant being in full agreement with God's will, not doing what one wanted to do. The opposite of freedom, Helland said, for Sverdrup, was ignorance (*uvidenheden*). To be free was to serve, not to live and let live but to live so that others could live. For Sverdrup, Helland said, the new commandment of Jesus, "You shall love one another as I have loved you," was at the center of his arguments for the congregation.

Sverdrup believed that was the reason for congregations. In the congregation, awakened Christians could help each other and together do works of love for others in their midst as well as support projects that brought love to the whole world.[26] This took education and deep knowledge of the Bible and church history. Helland thought, however, that this was not all. A Christian school needed more. The way to do this was for "the school to create a spiritual atmosphere, a spiritual environment the students which could answer to the Christian congregation's uniqueness."[27] Almost anyone who thinks about this will agree, but making it happen takes a lot of work. It is clear, however, from the way Mother wrote about her experiences at Augsburg—her involvement with Mission Society, chapel, the choir, and her friends—that she found the spiritual atmosphere she was looking for, and she loved and valued it.

In a report on the Centennial Fund, Bernhard Helland, son of Andreas, wrote on the progress of the drive. He noted that of the 379 congregations who had taken part in it, 219 had sent in a report about their ingathering, and 130 had not. All told, they had raised almost $100,000, money that was to pay off debts and increase the support of the schools and missions of the LFC. The new committee on educational policies created by the church body praised Augsburg for "having adjusted its plans and expanded its work to meet the demand and need of young people for college education." In addition, it acknowledged that the increasing number of non-LFC students meant that the college should build its reputation as a "fully recognized Lutheran institution."[28] This was an occasion for praise for the growth of Augsburg, the leaders thought, not something to fear.

Even as these weighty matters were being reported in the press, my parents were discovering that living in the parsonage was rather different from what they had known in their own homes. Congregations thought the pastor, his family, and the parsonage belonged to them. As the cold winter bore down on them, Harald was mortified to hear from Jonette that "three women approached me and said they wanted to talk with me. They pushed me into a corner and the thought flashed through my mind—now what have I done wrong? They asked me in a whisper, 'What kind of underwear does the Reverend wear?' I was so embarrassed I didn't know what to say. They quickly came to my rescue. 'Get him some good, heavy, long underwear or he'll get pneumonia.' I finally talked him into it. He was too proud and incensed with their interference to get the point immediately."[29]

By then, they knew I was on the way. Given that the nearest hospital in Powers Lake, North Dakota, was 26 miles from Tioga, they began reading about how to deliver a baby at home.

*Folkebladet* continued publishing news about the war, especially as it concerned Norway. C. J. Hambro, president of the Norwegian Parliament, had written a book, *How to Win the Peace*. As he looked to the end of the war, which commentators were doing with greater frequency, Hambro described the German situation as inevitable, given that Germans had been taught from childhood that they were God's chosen people, supermen like those Nietzsche had described. Hitler, he saw, spoke to that longing with his thousand-year Reich. The editor predicted that Hambro's vision of peace would be viewed as increasingly helpful as the war ended and proposals for peace would be needed. Because Hambro, president of the Norwegian Parliament, was one of Europe's most well-regarded men, serving on the League of Nations and other such international bodies, his voice was significant.

Andreas Helland, having produced three articles on Sverdrup's convictions, summed them up in a new piece in his series "The Heritage We Received" (*Arven vi Fik*). He named five points he regarded as the key to Sverdrup's theology:

1. A personal relationship with God was the basis for all sound human life.
2. That relationship is mirrored in the spiritual brotherhood (*aandelig søskenforhold*) which is the Christian congregation, revealed visibly to the world.
3. The means by which the individual is kept in a living relationship with God are Word and sacrament.
4. God has in critical times raised up those who through a recognition of their sin and an experience of salvation by the Holy Spirit's leading and created to be a voice of awakening and leader in the congregation.

The greatest help for such edification and true Godliness was the *børnelærdom/children's teaching.*
5. Therefore, the congregation's edification and growth into maturity in Christ is the goal of God's will and must therefore be the goal of all Christian reality, especially for proclamation. Therefore, a correct understanding of a congregationally focused seminary education was necessary for the congregation's growth and flourishing.[30]

As faithful readers of *Folkebladet*, my parents' generation was hearing again the old arguments that had stirred their grandparents, parents, and many before them in Norway, all the way back to Pastor Ole Hersleb (1692–1760) in Brønnøysund and now in America, as the Jacobsons had experienced with Pastor Markhus. As my parents read these articles, the old debates became present to them again, as they had been to the previous generations. These were not lessons in the past but lessons to live by. In refreshing the arguments, they came alive again in the minds of the readers.

In addition to thinking about their traditions in the LFC, as the young couple was adjusting to the parsonage, they were facing privations caused by the war. Rationing of gas, tires, meat, butter, coffee, cheese, and sugar had been inaugurated in January 1942. Harald helped the community project of rationing-book registration. People accepted it as their patriotic duty. Harald and Jonette did not suffer from meat and butter rationing, living as they did in a rural community. Nor did sugar shortages bother them. They used syrup and honey as sugar substitutes in their recipes. Jonette, especially, was used to living close to the bone and came to enjoy showing how thrifty she could be. The worst was the situation of the tires. Given the shortage of rubber, it was difficult to keep tires from going flat. With six congregations spread out across the region, it became vital for them to have tires. The folks finally spoke about the situation with Iver Solberg, a state senator from Ray, North Dakota. He got the flamboyant North Dakota Nonpartisan League US senator William "Wild Bill" Langer (1896–1959) to assure him he could have tires, which lightened the difficulties considerably.

T. Ostby of Fargo, a layman well known in the fellowship, had written a thoughtful article in the December 16, *Folkebladet*, "*Vil vi ha menighet?*" ("Do We Want the Congregation?"). It was a response to Sverdrup's article from 1896, "*Vil I ha menighet*" ("Do You Want a Congregation?").[31] The original was a fierce answer to F. A. Schmidt, Sverdrup's erstwhile colleague at Augsburg Seminary, who had accused the minority party of pride and judgmentalism for its overemphasis on the congregations, especially as he understood it.

Ostby remembered from the 1890s how the movement of the laity flourished, resulting in many blessings. He reviewed the past, complimenting the pastors Augsburg had trained as wanting to serve, not rule. They had worked for revival; at testimony meetings, they encouraged the laity to lead regular worship services and give witness to their faith. Such occasions caused them to study the Bible and pray more. This made the relationship between laity and clergy better, with much less criticism. He had noticed that this had faded over time, and now proceedings seemed to keep the laity from witnessing, even if they might have had something to say that supported the sermon.

The preacher should, for the most part, preach, and the laity give testimony to their faith. Unfortunately, that had changed: "The lay people who should keep watch over the freedom of the congregation and its independence are little by little falling asleep." Even at the annual meeting, the laypeople sat silently in their pews, listening to committees dominated by pastors give reports. All this had the effect of silencing the layperson. Ostby referred to Burntvedt's report to the annual meeting in 1940 on the "Spiritual Condition in our Church." He heard Burntvedt agree with him. Ultimately, he hoped that "the congregations can wake up and take their rightful place, form and shape in God's kingdom here on earth."[32]

The beginning of 1943 had been quiet in Tioga. Many meetings were canceled on account of cold and snow. Harald made it out to the Lindahl ladies' aid annual meeting, but the weather was so bad that no one was there. On January 15, blizzard conditions swept over the state. On the eighteenth, Williston reported a high of twenty degrees below and a low of thirty-three below. Most citizens knew to stay home in such weather unless there was an emergency. There were two funerals, one at Lindahl and the other at Norman, which Harald made it to by horse and buggy. The weather continued to be fiercely cold and kept people at home until the end of February, so the couple enjoyed the cozy time together in their parsonage as Harald ran in and out with lignite coal and ashes, Jonette doing puzzles. If they were able to receive their papers, they would be reading about the bombing of Berlin and the advancing Russian troops in Germany.

## Congregations

On February 2, 1943, Pastor Christian Ytrehus, an old salt close to one hundred, who had briefly presided over the LFC, responded to the article by Ostby. He found it echoed Sverdrup's article *"Vil I ha menighet?"* ("Do You Want a Congregation?"). He thought it applied to the Lutheran Free Church's identity and its mission to conserve the heritage that Sverdrup and Oftedal left us to care for—the congregation!

Ytrehus agreed with Ostby that laymen's activity in the LFC was as good as dead. He also remembered back to the 1890s when there was a great revival led by evangelist Peder Nilson and the laity had been lively. He observed that

Figure 9.3. Christian Ytrehus. Used by permission of Augsburg Fortress Publishers.

it was probably true that the work of the laity always stood in relationship to awakenings and spiritual life: "When that life is dulled and dies, it goes badly with us ourselves and our work."[33] He then went on to consider possible reasons for the death of the lay movement, attributing much of it to the materialism that broke out after World War I, when the automobile and prosperity, rather than spiritual life, became the focus of life.[34]

Caspersen had a clear political stance, especially on the rich—a thread running through much of this conversation even as it had to do with the deadening of the spiritual lives of the laity. On February 24, he mocked the new congressional representative from Connecticut, Clare Booth Luce, for her maiden speech in Congress, in which she called Vice President Henry Wallace's speech "The Century of the Common Man" *globalony*.[35] Caspersen scorned her youth and her riches and clearly favored Vice President Henry Agard Wallace (1888–1965), whom FDR was about to ditch as his vice presidential candidate in the 1944 election for his opposition to the rich. Wallace received plaudits in *Folkebladet* several times leading up to the 1944 political conventions.

About this time, the American Lutheran Conference changed the name of its newsletter to the *Lutheran Outlook*. The publication was now edited by Ernest Edwin Ryden (1886–1981), who would change the emphasis of the paper to be more "newsy" than theological, all to the good.[36]

Ytrehus continued his reflections on the LFC in following issues, focusing not just on its history but also its current state. He despaired over the economic situation—prosperity tempting the young from the faith—but then moved to a couple of issues that he felt had caused or at least contributed to the lack of lay participation in the meetings and especially the annual meeting. He noted that at the Morris meeting in 1939, only six lay delegates had spoken publicly. More serious was the change in rules that all the committees of the church should consist of three pastors and two lay delegates. Furthermore, there were "boards" that consisted only of pastors. Those rules he remembered had innocently come into the LFC from the Conference. This was neither "free church nor democratic."[37] He thought this rule could easily be changed. Finally, he noted that all had sinned against these principles, both pastors and laity. What was really needed was an awakening, but that was not something that could be intended by the church. Only God could send revival. For that reason, we must confess our sins, knowing God, who is faithful and just, would forgive us our sins. God help us, he concluded.[38]

Helland continued his reflections on Sverdrup and his thoughts on church unity. He ended it with Sverdrup's answer—there is unity in baptism in one Spirit, unity in one faith, unity in the same hope, briefly, in Christ's life: "Where Christ's life is found, there is his body and no place else."[39] There is one head but many limbs, all one and yet diverse. Helland continued his reflections in the next issue, as did Ytrehus, whose third column argued for preachers who could preach so that even children could understand, without using a written manuscript or even one memorized word for word. Such preaching by both pastors and laymen could stir an awakening in the LFC and thus stir up a "congregation."[40]

Only by April had the weather settled enough to allow normal services in the Tioga parish. Harald tried to have Lenten services. He also held "special meetings/evangelistic meetings" with Gudmund B. Rundstrom, pastor in Williston, who would shortly become my godfather. On Easter Sunday, April 25, Harald had four services, one at eleven, another at one thirty, another at three, and the last at eight.

On April 7, 1943, Johan Rødvik of Prescott, Iowa, wrote an article on church union that occupied the readership for several months. He thought the centennial of Norwegian American Lutheran churches was a perfect time for them to give each other a brotherly right hand and unite. He concluded by wishing that all the Lutheran churches in America would merge, to say nothing of all Protestants.[41]

As the war progressed and churches looked at society and what it would be like after the war, the American Lutheran Conference began to address questions of poverty and the plight of the worker. Caspersen approved of the move.[42] In addition, the paper featured a column by S. O. Sigmond, of Trinity Lutheran in Brooklyn, New York, on the virtues of Henry Wallace, the vice president. No American vice president of such caliber had directed the US Senate since Thomas

Jefferson, Sigmond said.⁴³ If he could become president, Sigmond hoped, things would improve for those who were poor. While some readers agreed, others most certainly did not.

Various articles in the paper continued to discuss church union. Most of the writers by far preferred *federation* as the word for unity, not *union*. One of the major drawbacks to any kind of unity for most Scandinavian Lutherans at the time was the failure of German American Lutherans to apologize for or regret what Hitler and his armies had been doing in Norway and Denmark. They reasoned that the Germans here were almost as difficult as the Germans in Germany, and they, especially Norwegians, could not brook the idea of a church merger with any of them, especially Missouri.⁴⁴

A letter to the editor from a frequent correspondent, Mrs. Karl Kleppe in Kintyre, North Dakota, took great exception to Rødvik's proposal. Holding out one's hand in brotherly love did not mean one had to live under the same roof as the other. If he really wanted one church, he had the Catholic church to join; there, he could find the "solid front" he seemed to be wanting.⁴⁵

## My Birth and the Birth of a Congregation

The day before this issue of *Folkebladet* appeared, I was born. Mother describes how I came into the world. Dad had just returned from Williston, and Grandpa was a wreck waiting for him to return. In the middle of the night, Mother realized it was time. Dad ran out to the car and discovered, not surprisingly after the trip to Williston and back, that one of the tires was flat. He arranged to borrow a car from the neighbor and had to run down the street in the small town to pick it up. He could run fast and get things done quickly, but he was also very excited. He got the car and picked up Mother, and they left for Powers Lake:

> We took the road past Norman church. It was a shortcut, but the roads were good in spite of the spring rains. When we were within fifteen miles of Powers Lake the horn on the borrowed car we were driving began to blare. The noise burst into the quiet night on the prairie. There was no way to stop it. This added to Harald's nervous state, and he became utterly distraught. In spite of my discomfort, I laughed until I hurt even more. I wondered what the coyotes thought. I'm sure they had never heard an ambulance siren in that part of the country. Let me impress this fact on the world—we really came into town with fanfare! It was as if the trumpets were announcing Gracia's coming, May 4, 1943.
> At twenty minutes to three that afternoon Gracia Marie was born.

**Figure 9.4.** Jonette Grindal and baby Gracia. Used by permission of the Grindal family.

The work of the ministry, however, didn't stop, even while I was being born. While Jonette was in labor, one of the nurses she had come to know during her pregnancy asked her if Harald would help them found a congregation in Powers Lake. They wanted a Lutheran congregation and had none. As Mother rested from her contractions, she said, "Sure!" This was almost a quote from "*Vil I ha menighet*"—awakened laity wanting to call a pastor. It worked out almost like a script from Sverdrup.

The controversy about Rødvik's article caused Caspersen to ask him to write a longer piece defending his idea, which he did. He began by noting that perhaps he needed to go back into the history again to make his point. Rødvik thought of the LFC as the genuine continuation of the Conference. The Conference, however, was not a unified group, theologically or ecclesiastically. The old and the new schools were very different. The old represented the Norwegian Synod's way of thinking, he said, and the new, Sverdrup and Oftedal's thinking. Sverdrup said, "Augsburg and the LFC had been built so that the revival in Norway should have a way and reality in the new land."

Ultimately, Rødvik wrote, the LFC had nothing to feel guilty about over its existence, but it should join with others in fellowship to fight for the truth.

But this fight must be done in freedom. That would come from the Spirit, "for where the Spirit of the Lord, there is freedom."[46]

Just before the annual meeting that year, in which the centennial of the Norwegian Lutheran churches would be celebrated rather modestly because of the war, Helland wrote his last column on the heritage of the LFC. In it, he described the constituting of the LFC and its Twelve Principles. He quoted Sverdrup's statement on the LFC in 1907, on the tenth anniversary of the LFC and days before his death, on the significance of the founding of the church: "The awareness that the LFC is still in its infancy and lives in hope for the future, is the reason it has not assumed a firmer organization . . . It does not wish that an organization's faster boundaries and stiff forms should be in the way for what is sought by the vigorous movement which goes under the name of the Lutheran Free Church."[47]

Helland ended his series with a prayer that if the articles had been a blessing to the readers, it was to the glory of God. While there was a hint that they might deserve publishing in a book form, he pointed to Clarence Carlsen's new book *The Years of Our Church*, which he thought should be in the home of every member of the Lutheran Free Church.[48]

Because Dad was regarded as a good speaker, he was asked to speak at several commencements in the area. On June 2, 1943, he spoke at the Hamlet, North Dakota, commencement, where Lloyd Svendsbye, later president of Luther Northwestern, was a student. Lloyd never forgot his speech, and much of the rest of my life I benefited from that meeting. Lloyd called me to teach at Luther Seminary much later, always regarding with affection what Dad had meant to him.

One layman, J. O. Hoyum, wrote in to *Folkebladet* to note that there now was more talk of union again, something he wearied of, especially Rødvik's assertion that union would come whether we wanted it or not. It bothered him that they had fought so hard for Augsburg and supported it with everything they had. And now to give it up? Even with few resources, they had succeeded with the help of the awakening and prayer. Now, as a much stronger organization, it felt to him as though the organization had lost its spiritual power.[49]

As the national election loomed for 1944, Caspersen would not give up on the Wallace case. He reported favorably on Wallace and condemned those who had called him, along with Eleanor Roosevelt, communists. He added another column from Dannevirket, a Danish American journal, reporting on Wallace's strong Methodist faith. He had spoken at a conference at Ohio Wesleyan on "A World Order Based on Christianity." Wallace had pointed out in this speech that in the last century, Germany had started five wars. Without a cleansing of their culture, they could well start a third world war. The article also feared that Germany and Russia could become allies against democracy and freedom.[50]

## 1943 Annual Meeting

The annual meeting that year was at Trinity in Minneapolis on June 4–7. Dad left by himself on the train for the annual meeting on June 4 and returned on June 7. *Folkebladet* gave a lengthy account of the meeting in its next issues. It began with a sermon by Olai H. Sletten, "*Tilbak til de gamle stier*" ("Back to the Old Paths"). To celebrate the centennial, it had invited Aasgaard of the NLCA to bring a greeting, something that impressed many: Aasgaard was highly regarded by members of the LFC and had been warmly greeted by many who wanted to thank him for his speech. The meeting included the typical events of such a gathering: president's report, schools and missions, anniversaries of churches and ordinations. The centennial drive still needed $10,000 to reach its $140,000 goal to pay off debts. Augsburg had suffered a 26 percent loss in students because of the war and was struggling to manage. There were only 367 students in the college and 22 in the seminary. John Stensvaag had just been called as professor of the Old Testament and Bernard Kleven as professor in sociology.[51] At the time, professors were still voted on by the annual convention.

Several resolutions were of interest, including one that congregations should vote for delegates from their congregation to attend the annual meeting without that affecting the vote of those who came of their own accord, a significant change for the fellowship and one that lasted. Others called for cooperation with the American Lutheran Conference and NLC. The missions in China and Madagascar continued, although several missionaries were interned in the Philippines by the Japanese. The WMF met, three seminary candidates were ordained, and other reports were made.

The next year's meeting would operate by new rules that the previous conference had passed, including a shortening of the sessions by two days. This worried some because it would cut back on the time people had to talk together and learn from each other about the work of the congregations. The committees would meet a couple of days before the entire group gathered. That would begin on Thursday, preceded by an opening service with communion. Proponents hoped it would increase the number of people attending the meeting. At this meeting, 117 pastors had attended, with 375 registered delegates. The numbers grew to 600–700 for the evening services. The next annual meeting would be in Willmar at Calvary congregation.[52]

In addition to coverage of the annual meeting, the paper ran yet another article on union by Christian Ytrehus, sounding a warning very familiar to those in the LFC: People naturally want to be with bigger, more successful organizations and churches. He knew several families in Minneapolis and other places who had left small Lutheran Free congregations for larger, more successful ones. He argued, using Theodore Blegen's report, that because the Norwegian

American Lutherans had so many small church bodies, they had twice as many members as Swedish Lutherans did with their one church body.[53] The many controversies of the Norwegian American Lutherans caused them to build several more colleges than the Swedes did, and most of them turned out to be highly regarded in the twentieth century.

He scoffed at the constant use of Jesus's words, "That they may be one," as a reason for mergers. That was a Roman Catholic idea, he noted, and not what Jesus was praying for in John 17. The arguments for merger always ended up with Jesus's high priestly prayer, and almost always they were shot down by learned biblical scholars or pastors who thought it was close to blasphemy to misuse those words.

On June 18, 1943, I was baptized in the Williston Lutheran Free Church parsonage. The Gudmund B. Rundstroms were my godparents. Home baptisms were common enough at the time, and the folks frequently went to Williston to shop and relax there, usually meeting with the Rundstroms for dinner. Rundstrom, a Dane, had a pronounced Danish accent, which amused the folks, who remembered his very common sermon invitation—"My Fwends, upon the cwoss the wobber pwayed"—with affectionate delight.

In a subsequent piece, Ytrehus continued his argument, returning to the fear of large congregations and societies. He quoted Sverdrup in one of his theological lectures at Augsburg to the effect that as long as congregations were small and poor and few joined with them, the danger was not so great, but when the congregation began to grow large and strong so they could build large beautiful churches, with large, gifted choirs and several societies with parties so that rich and prominent folks began to join the congregation, then the danger began.[54]

While that is very likely true, smallness could become a mark of pride. When I was a teenager playing the hymn "How Blessed Is the Little Flock That Jesus Calls His Own," my mother came storming into the living room and exclaimed, "That's the theme song of the Free Church. They want to be little and think they are better if they are!" She had come to hate the grinding poverty we had to live in because we were smaller but better and found it spiritually proud to glory in our poverty and smallness. While she understood the dangers Sverdrup was warning against, it sometimes became a sinful thing for her: *to be proud of one's humility*, she called it once.

Meanwhile, the summer schedule of vacation Bible school in the parish, with the regular meetings of ladies' aids, ladies' chorus (which Mother directed), and Bible study, kept the folks busy. Sometimes the ladies' chorus opposed Mother's directions, and she would come home weeping. Clarence Carlsen advised her to act as though she didn't even know "Yankee Doodle" and listen to them. She thought it good advice. Bible study was not something the congregations were used to either. Many times, only Jonette and Harald appeared at Bible study. This was not unusual, but the folks benefited from it for their own sake.

In his third article on union, Ytrehus discussed Rødvik's prediction that one day the LFC would have to merge. Rødvik had argued it would be a lovely day. Ytrehus protested, saying it could only happen if the other churches adopted many of the principles of the Free Church, not before. It could happen, he agreed, that just as the Hauge Synod had become more high church, so it could happen that our church would no longer have the call to be what it had been and lose its right to exist. That would be the ending of Augsburg and the Free Church's work and calling. "We must pray to God that this does not happen," he concluded, hoping that Helland's articles on "The Heritage We Received" (*Arven vi fik*) would "absolutely be published in book form in both Norwegian and English so it could be preserved for those who came after us. They needed to read the book as a memorial of the 100 years of church work among the Norwegian Americans."[55]

These articles represented both a repetition of the old histories for the second and third generation and a reassessment of the movement by the writers who were going forward into the postwar world knowing that merger would be a strong force. They needed to be armed with their history to think about the tradition into the future. Furthermore, it is not surprising that a small remnant needs to rehearse these events and refresh them and their hurts over and over again. And those articles did their work. Most of the pastors and their wives, plus active laity, could cogently argue in their gatherings about what had happened and why.

In the August issues, attention turned to the war, with glowing reports of the Norwegian royals, especially King Haakon VII and his reign, with ample pictures of him, his family, and the crown prince and princess. More reports were coming out from the war theater; there was some good news now and then, especially for the LFC missionaries: The Arthur Olsons and Fred Ditmansons were coming home after being interned in China. Thoughts about the postwar period were beginning to arise, especially by Carl Hambro, and people were beginning to feel there was hope of victory.

The summer theological conference for pastors that year, always held just before the school year began, featured Ernest Edwin Ryden of Augustana, who spoke on several issues, most importantly on hymnody for pastors and congregations. John Stensvaag gave a lecture on Sverdrup's thoughts on the work of the laity. Stensvaag's close reading of Sverdrup and his able presentation of Sverdrup's theology made him something of a hero in the eyes of many pastors. A professor of Old Testament like Sverdrup, Stensvaag had read Sverdrup closely enough to agree with him and teach his ideas to others.[56]

On August 10, 1943, we left for Cyrus, where we spent a long vacation. At the time, Mother's father, Theodore Tinseth, was living with us. The family had arranged for him to spend one-third of the year with them, another third with

# A World at War

Don and Borghild Ronning, and another third at the farm with his brother Fred Tinseth. He would be with Mom and Dad until October that year.

After something of a summer hiatus, *Folkebladet* took up the question of church union again, this time the meeting of NLC meeting in the fall. Caspersen had favored both the American Lutheran Conference and NLC, but this time he slammed the NLC for wanting to "swallow up all that could be swallowed." He accused it of wanting to establish a "churchly totalitarianism among us."[57] To that, he said, "We must say stop!" Although nothing had yet happened, he saw behind the doings of the NLC the nefarious workings of the ULCA. He feared, as always, the domination of the Germans over the Norwegians and Danes, who had suffered most from Germans in Europe. In Europe, the Swedes had their front door toward Germany and Eastern Europe and, in this country, would merge with the German Lutherans, he surmised—rightly, it turned out. Even if it had been said that time healed all wounds, he thought it would be a long time before Norway, or Norwegian Americans, could forgive Germany. It would be imprudent to simply cover over the sores without healing them. The right-thinking position of a Norwegian American, he thought, was to be prudent. Talking church union with Germans now was imprudent: "A Christian has no right to make an ass of himself. We should not do that as a church either."[58]

A report on the National Lutheran Editors' Association meeting in Blair, Nebraska, on September 22–23, 1943, recorded many speeches, ranging from "The Ministry to Migrant Communities" by Olaf Gabriel Malmin (1899–1973) to "Federal Relations to Church Colleges," by L. Siersbeck. The question of church union after the war weighed heavily on the meeting, especially given the enthusiasm of the Germans and Swedes for such unions. A resolution asking all Lutherans in America to pray for church union and set aside a Sunday to pray for church union was passed by the group, to the surprise of some.[59]

Given the intensity of the war now in Asia, LFC members were surprised to hear that Ralph Mortensen, who had been interned in Hankow for two years, had received a call to work in Chungking, still part of free China, with the American Bible Society. He returned to China in October 1943. Mortensen had gone in 1918 to study in Beijing for his work in Kweiteh. Since 1930, he had led the Lutheran Book Concern in China and served as secretary of the Lutheran Board of Publication in Hankow. In 1937, he and his wife had furloughed in the United States and returned to Hankow on October 5, 1938, the day before the Japanese took the city. He and his family were interned there for two years. He returned in August 1942 on the ship *Gripsholm*. Originally a Swedish ship, *MS Gripsholm* was chartered by the US Department of State as a repatriation ship bringing Japanese and German nationals to be exchanged with US and Canadian citizens. His wife, Petra, Andreas Helland's daughter, had left China in 1941 because of her health and died on November 4, 1942.

**Figure 9.5.** Donald Ronning and Harald Grindal with babies Donald and Gracia. Used by permission of the Grindal family.

Mortensen felt the call to continue his work in China since the need for Bibles there was overwhelming.[60]

A Youth Convention in Fergus Falls on the weekend of September 30–October 2 brought many LFC youths to the city, along with pastors like Dad. Pastor Johannes Ringstad gave a good report on it in *Folkebladet*. The main speaker was Fredrick Schiotz, now serving as youth leader for the NLCA. He would later become president of the ELC and then the ALC. Ringstad rejoiced that these young people were receiving the heritage they would be able to pass on.[61]

Borghild, mother's sister, and her husband, Donald Ronning, came for the evangelistic meetings in Tioga that year. Ronning was a powerful evangelistic preacher throughout his ministry. Given that it was traditional for congregations in the LFC and ELC to sponsor such evangelistic meetings at least twice a year, it made sense for him to be the preacher in Tioga. It also gave the families time together. Their first son, Donald David, had been born in June, so the families could show off their babies to each other. After the meetings in Tioga, Don would preach at Zion in Minot for a week, while Borghild stayed with us, and then return for a final service at Zion in Tioga.

## More Meetings on Merger

There was a large meeting of Lutheran college professors and Lutheran journalists at Valparaiso University on October 8–9, 1943. This was an opportunity for Lutherans to gather without churchly control. Caspersen was especially interested in what the German American professors and leaders would say. Understanding the independence of the university from the powers of the Missouri leadership, he praised Dr. Kretzmann for his spirit, which he said was other than that of the Missouri theologians: "The hearer realizes one is in a different atmosphere from a theological conference. The way of speaking is different, and the lofty philosophical speech took a while to get used to. Another difference was that there was no talk of church unity. Here we were unified. Our gathering and our common work unified us. It is theology which creates disunity."[62] New Testament professor Dr. Otto A. Piper, a refugee from Germany, now on the faculty of Princeton University, asserted that there could be no leadership in ecumenical work from the Germans, predicting it would be "a long, long time" before other communions would trust them.[63]

When the American Lutheran Conference met for its fall meeting, its Commission on Social Relations had several topics on its docket with lectures by church speakers: race relations, the rural church, reaching the unchurched by Olai H. Sletten; the liquor problem, the movie question, "Church Membership as It Relates to Social Stratification" by N. Astrup Larson; and "The Church and the Changing Social Order" by H. C. Caspersen, who opined, "So far as we can see, the American Lutheran Conference is a more democratic organization than the National Council which is taking the form more of a church council."[64]

On December 2, 1943, Arthur Grindal, my father's ten-year-old foster brother, died in Ferndale of juvenile onset diabetes. Dad left for the funeral in Ferndale the same day, returning on the ninth. At the funeral, Pastors C. J. Nestvold, Christian Mohn, Lawrence Gudmestad, and my father each spoke. While Dad was gone, most Tioga parish congregations canceled services and other regular gatherings except for ladies' aid. *Folkebladet* printed a tribute to Arthur, "A Little Wreath" ("*En liten Krans*"), with a sweet poem in his memory, "*En knopp, som ei helt utsprungen var*" ("A Little Bud That Has Not Wholly Blossomed"), for his funeral. It was written by his Sunday school teacher,

Mrs. Ebertina Nordtvedt, mother-in-law of Matilda Kivley, my dad's half sister. Father and Mother had talked about raising Arthur, but neither his father nor his mother could bear the idea of losing him, despite their inability to properly care for him and his disease. My father vividly remembered, when he was seventeen and Arthur was born, walking around the house and listening to his mother's birth pangs. For some time, he cared for the baby with his mother, helping her when her mental state declined so much that she had to be returned to the state hospital in Sedro-Woolley, Washington. Both Anna and Sjur were devastated by Arthur's death.

As the war became more consuming, *Folkebladet* continued its reporting on the war effort, with a series of twelve articles by Sverre Norborg on the way Norway, especially the royals, and the Norwegian government in exile were working to defeat the Nazis.[65] It began in the last issue of 1943 and went forward through the next year. Norborg had entered service in the Office of Strategic Services (OSS), in charge of espionage activities for the United States behind the enemy line. In that job, he was more aware than many of what was going on with the war.

## 1944 and the Coming End of World War II

Another series, on the congregation as Christ's body, continued through the first months of the year in *Folkebladet*. It was a fairly learned set of articles going back to the seven letters to the congregations in the Book of Revelation. Its main question, however, was whether the congregation was visible or invisible. How could one tell who was a Christian or not? This brought up the pure church notion of the Lutheran Brethren Church and especially the words of Lundeberg, the first president of LB, who had left after coming to reject the LB's pure church theology. At the time, no one could be a member of a LB congregation without being a confessing Christian.[66]

The question of visible or invisible thrummed at the bottom of most of the talk about the congregation in this period. There continued to be more articles on the history of the LFC, but the issue of church unity was somewhat less urgent as the church prepared for its annual meeting in Willmar that June. *Folkebladet* remembered that the meeting of the Friends of Augsburg in 1895 in Willmar had been remarkable. It had occurred after the United Norwegian Lutheran Church convention had refused to seat Sverdrup and Oftedal as delegates from Trinity Congregation. The speaker had been Lars Olsen Skrefsrud (1840–1910), and his preaching had sparked a revival that lasted the rest of the decade. His preaching brought many people to Christ and roused the missionary spirit in many young people. Charlotte Martinson Gronseth said that her grandparents had heard Skrefsrud's preaching and been saved. Afterward they were called to China, where her parents also served, as did she and her brother, Professor Paul

Martinson of Luther Seminary, when they came of age. Skrefsrud and the Santal mission remained important to many Norwegian American Lutherans.

That meeting had also been the beginning of the parting of ways, as the Friends of Augsburg began to realize there was no way to resolve the differences. Caspersen, who had just marked his seventh-fifth birthday, had been there as a student in Willmar fifty years before, so he could give an eyewitness report on what had happened. Having been at these most significant meetings gave him the ability to refresh the memories of those who had heard of, but not witnessed, these events. In addition, these stories kept the wounds fresh, so to speak. They seemed living and present to the readers because not only could he report the stories vividly, but the stories also rehashed the reasons for the LFC's existence again and again.

The Northwest Pastors' Fellowship of Western North Dakota, led by Pastor Clarence Carlsen, gathered on February 22–23, 1944, at Zion in Minot for two days of lectures and conversations about pressing issues. The first lecture was "Our Times in the Light of the Scriptures," given by Rev. J. A. Petersen of Williston. The second topic was "What Will This Area Face in the Immediate Post-War Period?" Six pastors spoke on topics such as "The Returning Soldier." The third lecture, by my father, was on "Should a Pastor Study?" and the fourth was on "God's World of Tomorrow." It was a rigorous group: Each pastor was required to write an essay of 1,500–2,000 words on the subject assigned to him. Pastors Carlsen, Helland, and Monseth had designed the program. These gatherings were edifying and intellectually stimulating.[67]

By this time, the war effort had affected most of the families in the Tioga parish, small in numbers but covering lots of territory. My father began sending the Tioga Zion newsletter to soldiers from the Tioga parish involved in the armed forces around the world. He would always begin with spiritual advice and concern for them as they faced suffering and even death. He would include in the letter quotes from many of them as to their situations, where they were, and what they were doing. Their letters home contained interesting details about their situations. They were filled with thanksgiving for the newsletter. Some in Australia and New Guinea were enduring terrible heat but still found it important to go to church. Others were in France, and one in Italy, who noted the fine weather and beautiful country. One had married a girl in England, and others were stationed in America at bases like Fort Dix. For them, it was surprising to discover there were not very many Lutherans in the South and the need for teachers for illiterate people in Arkansas. Many responded to Dad's message by noting their own spiritual state, their attending church, either on the base with the chaplain or on a congregation in the area. One wrote that he enjoyed going to these services on his base and the "wonderful player there," suggesting that at some future Luther League, they put on a service of favorite songs like he had just heard.[68] He also wrote that his relatives thought that "Rev. Grindal is getting better to preach at every service."[69] These exchanges continued until the end of the war, and the correspondence poignantly evokes the time.

As June 1944 came around, my parents began preparing for the journey to Cyrus, where they would bring Grandpa Theodore and me so they could attend the meetings in Willmar and Mother could spend time at the farm with her aunt and uncle. My mother describes the time well:

> Preparations began early in May for the trip we were going to take to the Annual Meeting of the Lutheran Free Church which took place the second week of June in Willmar, Minnesota, that year of 1944. We studied train schedules as gas and tire rationing made it not only impossible but also unpatriotic to take a 600-mile trip by car. My arthritic father, who was a semi-invalid, had lived with us that winter. He had farmed at Cyrus, Minnesota, for thirty years and was anxious to spend the summer at Cyrus with his brother, Fred. Nana [Mildred] and Freddie meant home for us too. They planned to meet us at Morris, Minnesota, where we would spend the weekend with them before going to the conference at Willmar.[70]

When they got to the depot, they discovered that the train was nine hours late, so they decided to take a local, one that stopped at every station. It was a long night. They got a berth for Grandpa, and they slept fitfully, waking with the clanking of milk cans and boarding of passengers every eight miles or so. We arrived in Cyrus at five thirty the next morning, utterly exhausted and ready to go home to "the farm," where Mother's aunt and uncle awaited them. After a brief sleep, they went to St. Petri Lutheran Free Church, Mother's home congregation. She sang a solo, "Weary, Oh, Lord, I Come at Last to Thee for Rest!" One of the old saints who had known her since she was a baby thanked her and said she really looked the part, weary and worn.

They rested that Sunday and Monday. The invasion of Normandy and France by the Allies must have occupied some of their attention on Tuesday, but there is very little concerning the offensive in *Folkebladet*, although the secular papers were filled with almost nothing else. Two boys from the Tioga parish, Oscar L. Skistad and Annil Bratvold, were killed in that invasion and one wounded, Dad reported to the soldiers.

The annual meeting began on June 7, an evening worship service with communion, led by Pastor Christian G. Olson of Calvary Lutheran in Willmar. Many more were in attendance. Some wondered if that was because of the new rules being introduced at this meeting. Over two hundred delegates had registered by that evening. The next morning, the gathering heard reports from the church president and on the schools. Bernhard Christensen rejoiced that Augsburg had had a very good year, ending with a surplus of almost twenty

**Figure 9.6.** P. A. Strommen. Used by permission of Augsburg Fortress Publishers.

thousand dollars, something that had never happened before. Oak Grove could report the same. They were glad to hear from missionaries like Fred Ditmanson, home from China. That year, there were eight candidates for ordination: Erling Tungseth, Orville Kleppe, John Strand, Karl Stendal, Albert S. Olson, Lawrence Rasmussen, Merton Strommen, and Silas Erickson. Once again, P. A. Strommen was the ordinator. Caspersen remarked that this year, all the candidates wore simple black robes instead of the Prince Alberts LFC pastors had worn for some time. My father was still wearing his "tails" and would until a trustee in the Rugby parish said he thought he looked like a grasshopper in them. As might be expected, the announcement that the seminary class of 1944 only wore gowns rather than Prince Alberts received some response. Mrs. Ebertina Nordtvedt of Ferndale wrote a substantial column on the subject. She remembered her parents discussing their pastor E. E. Gynild's decision not to wear a robe or collar anymore. As a young girl who had never seen the pastor without a collar or gown, she wondered what that meant.[71] She had liked gowns on the pastor because it covered shortcomings such as a bad suit.[72] It would be the reason my mother suggested my dad wear his gown in Salem when we arrived there and were so poor we could not afford nice clothes. She was embarrassed to see pictures of him with bridal couples wearing a tattered suit.

The folks enjoyed the meetings, connecting with old friends and colleagues. The preaching, worship, and edifying speeches encouraged them in their ministries. They were also able to rest at the farm. After a year of hard work, they felt refreshed and reconnected to their church. They left Cyrus for Valley City, North Dakota, where my uncle Don had begun serving First Lutheran congregation. They would be there for his installation on June 18. They left after that for Bible camp at Lake Metigoshe on June 19. Dad was one the main speakers—he taught from Tuesday to Saturday, "The Way of Salvation."

Reports on the annual meeting were good. Even the decision to shorten the meeting seemed wise, given the amount of money that was saved. Almost nothing at the convention had dealt with union, although Ralph Long, the head of LWA at the NLC, gave a report on all the needs in Europe. Since this happened after D-Day and the victory over the Nazis in France, one can sense a spirit of optimism that the Allies were winning. One could feel it on the farms as well—times were good, as were the prices, which filled the coffers of both congregations and the LFC, its missions and schools.

## Overture for Lutheran Unity

In January 1944, an "Overture for Lutheran Unity" had been passed by the executive committee of the American Lutheran Conference. It, along with the Minneapolis Theses, had been sent to all Lutheran bodies in the United States. The document suggested that pulpit and altar fellowship could be established among Lutherans on the basis of the Minneapolis Theses, the Brief Statement by Missouri, and the Pittsburgh Agreement of the ULCA-ALC. It was not well received by either the ULCA or Missouri. It was regarded as too conservative and doctrinal or not enough so. On July 12, 1944, Caspersen discussed the "Overture" and various other possibilities. Most LFC people who commented on it disliked the notion of having to concur on doctrinal agreement outside of the Augsburg Confession for there to be unity. *Folkebladet* diagnosed that hairsplitting on these issues would only cause division among Christians.[73]

President Aasgaard had made a proposal, passed by the Norwegian Lutheran Church in America at its 1944 convention, that he should call the LFC, Lutheran Brethren, and the Elling Eielsen's group to see if they could come together in a larger Norwegian Lutheran Church. These Norwegian churches agreed on many things and, many thought, could easily unite.[74]

In August, the executive committee of the American Lutheran Conference issued an explanation of a resolution the group had made in November 1942 saying that the communions not included in the American Lutheran Conference should all find a way to have "pulpit and altar fellowship." These communions included the ULCA, the Danish Lutheran (AELC), the Missouri Synod, Lutheran Brethren, Elling Eielsen Synod, and the Finnish Lutheran and Finnish Apostolic Church, as well as the Wisconsin Synod, the Little Norwegian Synod, and the Slovak Synod.[75] The executive committee had reported they could see nothing preventing this from happening since all of these groups were good Lutherans and shared the same Lutheran confessions, but they were wrong about that.

The "Overture for Lutheran Unity" proposal brought almost "glowing rejoicing that streamed out of the editors of *The Lutheran Herald* and *The Lutheran Standard*."[76] Caspersen did not see it as so thrilling. Reading more deeply, he saw that the key word was not *unity* but "selective fellowship." What that meant was not clear. There was always an *"aber/but"* in such discussions with Germans, he concluded.

The LFC had always maintained that any of its pastors of good reputation could reach out as a Christian to another pastor with a good reputation, no matter what their synod. But they could not have fellowship with pastors of any of these synods who belonged to a lodge or were unionistic. Unity was not achieved between churches by agreement on theses or confessions but when Christ was Lord of any of these. Christ, not theses, gave them unity. Caspersen was wondering what the executive committee would do at its next meeting in November.

On September 7, Dad went to Minot for a meeting of the Victory Building Fund, a new building fund for LFC schools, with the pastors in the Minot District, most of them young like him and eager to help Augsburg as much as they could. Two weeks later, on September 21–24, 1944, Shell Creek Lutheran Church in Newman Grove, Nebraska, celebrated its seventieth anniversary. Newman Grove was in a verdant valley about eighty miles southwest of Sioux City. Dad had interned there over a summer and through his senior year. He was much beloved by the congregation. My folks, along with other former pastors, were invited to the celebration. Mother and I went along by train to Minneapolis, then Newman Grove on September 20, an overnight trip. Dad spoke at the morning service and was toastmaster for the banquet. Mother met many of Dad's admirers there, and the time was a special one for them.

We returned on the twenty-fifth to Minneapolis, leaving for Cyrus to be at the farm while attending the Luther League Federation meeting in Morris. Soon, Merton Strommen, the newly ordained pastor in Mora, Minnesota, would become the charismatic leader of the youth department of the LFC and began to plan larger and larger youth conventions, most of which would be held at Medicine Lake camp near Minneapolis. After the convention, the folks returned by rail, stopping over at Valley City to visit the Ronnings.

The controversy about gowns murmured along in the paper for some time. A man wrote in from the West Coast, marking the use of robes as one mark of decline. "Has the awakening among Lutherans been spent," he asked. "We are soon finished with the Norwegian language, and layman's work." He quoted Mrs. Nordtvedt's piece on E. E. Gynild's wearing of a robe while he was in the Willmar congregation. He had worn one, she said, until it was worn out, and he was not permitted to get a new one. That caused a discussion at the annual meeting. Some even said that if the pastor did not wear a robe, the people got nothing out of the sermons; some said the opposite. Gynild had reportedly said he would rather give up his call than use a robe. The writer finished by noting that pastors naturally like to see the future in their work and build a big, fine church before traveling to another call. It would stand as a monument to their work. The best monument a pastor can have, however, is how many souls his work had brought to Christ. That is a monument that will stand forever.[77]

At a meeting of the Lutheran editors in New York, Caspersen was overwhelmed by the new digs of the NLC—the Pierpoint Morgan mansion. He described its rich appointments and wondered if he was dreaming. The most surprising thing, however, was that Missouri had sent the editor of the *Lutheran Witness*, Dr. Sommer, who had impressed Caspersen with his sharp mind even at his advanced age, somewhere between seventy and eighty. What shocked Caspersen was that Sommer had participated in their devotions and prayed the Lord's Prayer with them. To top it off, they had invited the meeting to St. Louis the next year. What did all that mean? To Caspersen, it meant that Missouri had moved "a crumb."[78]

Homecoming at Augsburg that year would observe the anniversary with speeches, banquets, worship, games, and concerts. The major guest was Dr. Conrad Bergendoff, president of Augustana Seminary and College, a good friend of Christensen and the Lutheran Free Church. He gave the anniversary address, "A Free Church in a Free Nation," in the Augsburg Chapel on Friday evening, October 27. The Augsburg Choir sang at the event. Burntvedt would preach on "The Word Became Flesh" at the service held in Trinity that Sunday.

A new book by two Missouri leaders, Graebner and Kretzmann, titled *Toward Lutheran Union*, had just been published and was creating something of a stir. President Yochum of the American Lutheran Conference had reviewed it and decided any move toward a union with Missouri was in vain. Another reviewer, Emmer Engberg, had concluded, "The simple truth seems to be that 'Union Now' with Missouri is utterly out of the question. We are fundamentally 'miles apart.' Missouri believes in the dogma of verbal inspiration. We do not! And until we can have 'agreement' on this question, any further talk of union is both unnecessary and nonsense."[79]

At a meeting of the American Lutheran Conference in Milwaukee, controversy broke out once again between those who agreed with the Galesburg rule and those who did not. Bergendoff announced that if it were to be enforced for church unity, he would have to join the Lutheran Free Church.[80] Bergendoff was always finding ways to agree with the LFC and Christensen.

Meanwhile, the LFC's Victory Building Fund sought to raise a quarter of a million dollars to support schools. Olaf Rogne, the general director of the fund and the business manager at Augsburg, reported that the clever young pastors in the northwestern quarter of North Dakota had decided to gather enough to inspire the rest of the church to do so as well. To the surprise of everyone, by November 29, 1944, they had raised $22,379 and were expecting more from several congregations that had not yet reported. The Tioga parish, with Dad's leadership, had raised the most by several hundred dollars—$3,500![81]

On December 8, 1944, my great-grandfather Haakon Nicolai Tolvminius Anderson Tinseth died at the age of eighty-four. His pastor, Sverre Torgerson,

**Figure 9.7.** Four generations of Tinseths and Grindals, pictured: Jonette, Gracia, Theodore, and Haakon. Used by permission of the Grindal family.

editor of the *Lutheran Messenger*, wrote a tribute to him in the magazine. Torgerson noted the help Tinseth had been to him in the congregation, always offering hospitality in his home. He read God's word, church papers, and other edifying literature that made it a blessing for the pastor to talk with him. Torgerson had received a letter from Tinseth not long before he died, telling him what hymns he wanted sung and which Scriptures read at his funeral, among them Brorson's "Thy Little Ones Dear Lord Are We." He had been a pious layman ever since his conversion in his early adulthood. He was an awakened Christian of the kind Sverdrup had said was necessary for free and living congregations.

## 1945 World War II Ends and More Union Talks

The year 1945 began with hope that the war would soon be over, although the Battle of the Bulge had been a costly one that the Allies almost lost except for General Patton's arrival with his army. Norwegians, usually resisters, who spoke in Minneapolis to Norwegian Americans supposed they would be back in Norway soon. Already the Nazis had abandoned sites in northern Norway. Meetings of church officials discussed how the peace would be won and what needed to be done to help Europe out of its ruins.

Talk of unity among nations, and the move toward what would become the United Nations, certainly affected churches as well. The church union issue, while it had not been suppressed, was not the main one for the churches at this time. The work of the church had suffered a great deal during the war.[82] Caspersen's column on the "Overture to Unity" had caused others to oppose him. Bernard Christensen deplored the impression Caspersen had given his readers about the resolution: "One of its main points is a statement that in the opinion of the Executive Committee no further doctrinal statements or theses, other than those that have already been adopted, should be necessary as a basis for full fellowship among the various Lutheran groups in America."[83] Christensen went on to explain further that the conference had "gone on record 'severally and collectively' as unequivocally affirming its allegiance to the Galesburg Rule against which Editor Caspersen has so many unkind things to say."[84]

While Christensen was thought to be irenic in spirit, he could become irate with people who were difficult and against his positions on things like church unity. Those who knew him well could marvel at his rage when he saw beer cans

Figure 9.8. Bernard Christensen. Used by permission of Augsburg University Archives.

on the Augsburg campus or colleagues unable to get along with each other. His temper was not something he is remembered for today, but it was something to remark on by those who knew him well and worked with him. My father never forgot how he had gone to him to ask for help with a difficult colleague in the boarding club. Christensen had blown up at him and shouted, "Young man, as a Christian you are to get along!" Even my father, who revered Christensen, thought this was unhelpful.

Caspersen replied with a long article in the same issue, also in English. He regretted that his article had not been as well written as it might have been, and it did fail to make some things clear. However, he did have some comments that contradicted Christensen's, including the notion of how unanimous the vote had been. There had been considerable opposition to the resolution for two reasons: many thought they had already approved the resolution; and those who resisted approving the Galesburg rule again, like Bergendoff, strongly opposed it.[85]

As they prepared for the end of the war and the opportunities it held for them, the LFC held a Home Mission Institute at Augsburg the first week of February 1945. In some sense, it was a reconnoitering of the home mission pastors as they thought of the near future. The West Coast fields weighed on their minds. Pastor Charles Crouch of Kirkland, Washington, gave a lecture on breaking new ground. He talked about home mission pastors having to take on the "hardships" of the people they worked among: "Such a pastor in a new place should be a man of the people, who could help them with their work if it was necessary, live among them, visit them often, get the laity to do work in the congregation."[86] One of the promising young men there was Robert Krueger, still a student at Augsburg, who was called to be a pioneer pastor on the West Coast when he had graduated. He would be the founding pastor of Central Lutheran in Salem.

As the war was coming to an end, a month before Norway and Denmark were freed, Franklin Delano Roosevelt died. The front page of *Folkebladet* for April 18, 1945, was devoted to his memory. The rest of the issue carried news of conditions in Norway. Berggrav had been set free, and Bishop Fjellbu had become the bishop of the north and was in London with the government in exile. The editor was watching the moves of the Roman Catholic Church as the war approached its end. There were strong reactions to the idea of the United States sending a diplomat to the Vatican, along with deep suspicions about their intentions in the postwar world.

On April 9, the Home Mission Board of the LFC met to plan for more congregations. One of its highest priorities was establishing a congregation in Salem, Oregon, and another in a suburb of Portland.[87] The West Coast figured highly in their calculations about where to build congregations. One might wonder how a home mission office fit in with Sverdrup's notion of *"Vil I ha menighet"*

("Do You Want a Congregation?"). It well may be that believers in these areas were asking for a pastor, but it seems from these reports that the administration of the home mission department oversaw the effort.

Only on page four of the issue was there any mention of the fall of the regime in Norway: "*Norge er frit!*" ("Norway is free!"). It may well be that the paper had been set up before the news came across the wire, and there was no space or time to report fully on the good news from Europe. There would be much to write about. There was a huge rally in Central Lutheran Church in Minneapolis on May 13, 1945. President Burntvedt, one of the preachers, preached on *"Den signede dag,*/O Day Full of Grace" using the great Grundtvig hymn "O Day Full of Grace" to frame his sermon. It was filled with references to many Norwegian poems and hymns that celebrated Norway, from Bjørnson's *"Ja, vi elsker dette landet"* to Grieg's *"Landkjenning."* He drew grateful attention to the place the church had played in opposing the Nazis, even to the point of the bishops being imprisoned. One can read his learning and eloquence in the sermon when he closes, noting it is the end of a freezing-cold time in the country: "Today [in Norway] the spring sun shines and leaves are budding, the brooks are gurgling, the blue birds nod and the thrush sings. Teeming life and sprouting buds forecast a lovely summer. Therefore, in the same freedom and thanksgiving, we join our voices with the redeemed Israel from the old times and join in singing, 'This is the day that the Lord has made. Let us rejoice and be glad.'"[88]

Many greetings and news notes about the situation in Norway appeared in the paper. Other good news was that, contrary to what had been announced earlier, the annual meeting of the LFC would be held in June as always. The government, before the defeat of the Axis powers, had been advising against such meetings because of their cost, but now, to the joy of the people, the government had allowed the meeting to take place. It would be held at Augsburg that year. For that, Caspersen was grateful but worried that now with the streamlined rules, there would not be time for good and open conversations with lay and clergy. Most of the ones who gave the speeches were those who spoke in the meetings as well, something he did not think all that helpful.[89]

On April 18, 1945, the Augsburg Choir gave a concert in Tioga. Henry P. Opseth, one of Mother's heroes, had served as an assistant to F. Melius Christiansen, inheriting his repertoire and techniques. Opseth had also studied with Eugene Ormandy and had brought the choir to a fine finish, according to critics, having "fully proved its ability to take rank with leading choirs of its kind."[90] A student reporter said that recent graduates in Tioga, Harald and Jonette Grindal and Florence Borstad, had given them an enthusiastic welcome.[91]

Mother started being asked to speak at events in the Minot District. On May 2, 1945, she spoke at the Zion Lutheran Ladies Aid in Minot. She could give interesting talks on the Bible, but her most attractive feature was how funny she

# A World at War

Figure 9.9. Fritjof Monseth. Used by permission of Augsburg Fortress Publishers.

could be. She could make people laugh, and people needed that just then. May was filled with confirmations, vacation Bible schools, and baccalaureates of the various high schools in the area, where Dad was often called to be speaker or give the opening and closing prayers. On Memorial Day, May 31, he came down with yellow jaundice, and everything had to be canceled. Fritjof Monseth in nearby Zahl took his place at the McGregor commencement ceremonies.

## NLC and the Assigning of Home Mission Regions

As NLC did its work, it became more powerful in the various communions. In 1945, it passed a resolution concerning the establishing of home missions by the various Lutheran churches in America, "ascertaining areas and fields in which the participating bodies may carry on home missionary work comparatively, or, if separately, without competition or overlapping."[92] This interest in not building competitive congregations become a widely held rule that even the LFC followed in its work for the most part but not always.

That spring, Dad began working with the people from Powers Lake who had asked Mother if he would help them build a congregation there. He wrote to the Home Mission Board of Directors of the LFC about the conditions and responsibilities for work in Powers Lake, and they considered his request in the June 9, 1945, meeting prior to the annual meeting.[93] Laverne Nelson was suggested as pastor, and the board voted to guarantee paying him seventy-five dollars a month, "with the understanding the field will contribute its part." How much work it had taken to get to that point is not clear to me. I do know that Dad was visited by Pastor Casper Nervig of Williston, the representative of the NLCA district in the area. Using the language of the NLC that had been agreed to in February 1945, he asked him, "Young man, what right do you have to build a congregation here? It is NLCA territory." This enraged my father and mother. Dad said to Mother, "Well, we not only have the devil, the world, and our own flesh to fight but the Catholics and NLCA as well." None of this, however, appears in the records of the board's deliberations, only that the regional committee of the LFC Home Missions Board addressed the issue and agreed to the proposal to form a congregation in Powers Lake.

To Dad, it was not an issue of territory but of answering the Macedonian call to come and help us. The nurse at my birth had asked Mom if Dad could help them establish a congregation; it was a call, and he, as a Lutheran pastor, was answering it. It also figured in the establishment of Central Lutheran in Salem, Oregon, where we would move in 1954. Central had been established just after the war and had horned in on the work of Grace Lutheran, an ELC congregation in Salem. The feeling was never great between them during Dad's tenure there.

The "yellow jaundice" Dad had come down with on Memorial Day was what we'd call *hepatitis* today. Mother described the time in her book:

> But during the night I was awakened from a deep sleep aware that Harald was trembling with chills and fever. I was frightened! He was very sick and there was no doctor available to help except at Powers Lake twenty-five miles away.
> "Oh Joey, do something!" All I could do was pile blankets on him for warmth, comfort him and then fall on my knees beside him to pray.
> Somehow we got through the night. In the morning Iola at the telephone office asked all about how Harald felt. We had jokingly said during our years in the parsonage that she was one of the three sources of Tioga's communication—telegram, telephone and tell-Iola. She asked, "What color is his urine? Is it deep brown? Is he nauseated? Does he have a high fever? Yes? Then I know he has yellow jaundice."[94]

He had found the strength to preach at the first service of the congregation in Powers Lake on June 3, 1945. His topic was "Underneath Are the Everlasting Arms." By his account, he was ill for two months. Mother remarked on the enthusiasm of the newly formed group: "The ELC (NLCA) had tried to begin work at Powers Lake but had failed. Now after a number of years the Lutherans in that community came to Harald and pleaded with him to begin work there. These people could not feel at home in the large Baptist church in town. We borrowed an old Methodist church for that first service. Every seat was filled and the enthusiasm was contagious for our kind of LFC ministry."[95]

## 1945 Annual Meeting

My folks gathered the strength to attend the annual meeting hosted this year by Augsburg and Trinity in Minneapolis. Because the government had discouraged meetings like this during the war, when they got permission, the meeting had to be planned very quickly, something Augsburg, under the leadership of Gerda Mortensen, could do. It featured the usual agenda. Burntvedt's presidential address was filled with good humor and relief. He pointed especially to the San Francisco Conference, which was the beginning of the United Nations. *Folkebladet* noted that the churches had begun to understand they could no longer live in isolation. They had to strive for more than personal piety and address the economic and political situations in which they found themselves.

In his report, Burntvedt noted significant anniversaries, among them the seventy-fifth anniversary of St. Petri in Cyrus, my mother's home church, and Newman Grove, Nebraska, where my dad had served as intern and we had just celebrated. The victory drive begun in western North Dakota had now gathered $120,000 and had extended the goal to $250,000 for the Augsburg library and science building.

In addition, Burntvedt praised the American Lutheran Conference for its work and growing influence, as well as that of NLC, the organization leading the relief work in Europe through its Lutheran World Action (LWA) organization, to which the LFC was to contribute thirty thousand dollars. Ralph Long, the longtime director of LWA, had made an appeal to the Lutheran Churches in America to extend their support to LWA, describing the suffering many Lutherans there had experienced for their faith. Most everyone was eager to support LWA, no matter their feelings about the NLC, especially to help the mother church in Norway.

The meeting had some good news for the long-suffering Augsburg faculty. The Board of Organization had recommended that their salaries should be raised to $2,400 a year. The Board of Home Missions had set the salaries of home mission pastors at $1,400. However, the meeting was mostly routine and had no big issues to debate. People were just glad to be together and celebrate the end of hostilities in Europe, knowing full well that there were brutal battles still in store for those fighting against the Japanese in the Pacific.[96]

As to the new rules, the meeting voted to wait another year before making them permanent. They needed some time to evaluate their appropriateness. One of the new rules was more major than anyone might have thought: President Burntvedt had been named ordinator of the LFC, a big change that seemed not to raise much controversy. It would be one step toward making the church consistent with the NLCA (ELC) and other Lutherans and, in hindsight, one move toward the Historic Episcopate. Previously, the ordinator had been appointed to assure that ordination did not require a bishop.

Figure 9.10. Gracia Grindal's debut appearance at an LFC annual meeting. Used by permission of the Grindal family.

The meeting had also, at Burntvedt's urging, begun to think how it would welcome home the many youth who had served in the military. The numbers were high: 8,248 young LFC people had served, 14 were chaplains, and 202 had made the ultimate sacrifice. The veterans could not be welcomed back as children but as grown men and women who had undergone the greatest trials and tests life had to offer. "They are a gift from the Lord," concluded A. H. in his report on the meeting.[97]

From Minneapolis, we traveled to Cyrus, where Dad rested for two months as he recovered from the jaundice. On their way home, they stopped in Valley City to see the Ronnings and then Rugby to visit the Tjons. They arrived in Tioga on July 25 for a funeral of an old patriarch, Mr. Borstad. The work began again with a visit from Laverne Nelson on August 10, 1945. He was courting Grace Carlsen, the oldest daughter of Clarence Carlsen, and had been linked with Powers Lake when he graduated the next summer from the seminary. He preached in Zion while Dad preached in Powers Lake on Sunday August 12. It was also the day for the farewell of Clarence Carlsen, who had accepted the call to St. Olaf Lutheran Church in north Minneapolis. That Wednesday, the little town of Tioga celebrated Victory over Japan day in the high school auditorium, with Dad speaking. Over three hundred people attended, more than the population of Tioga.

During the last week of August, Laverne "Red" Nelson appeared several times in Powers Lake, where people got to know him. On September 2, 1945, the Powers Lake congregation voted to organize officially. Missionary Arthur Olson was the preacher. The next Sunday, Red Nelson left for Augsburg after attending all the festivities surrounding the event. He would be called back to serve the Powers Lake congregation as its pastor the next summer. It would be officially founded on September 28, 1945.

## The World and Church Look Ahead After the War

As the summer went on, the conference in San Francisco that set up the United Nations was held. Many viewed it as a necessity for peace in the world and felt it was the duty of churches to support it.[98] The pages of *Folkebladet* during this time were severely restricted because of a paper shortage, so some issues were no longer than four pages, while others were eight, still much shorter than the usual sixteen.

At the end of August, the pastors' Summer Conference at Augsburg featured a wide selection of speakers from almost all of the various synods: Professor E. H. Wahlstrom of Augustana Theological Seminary in Rock Island; Iver Iverson of Luther Seminary; Theodore Anderson, president of the Evangelical Mission Covenant Church; James Raum, professor of systematic theology at Northwestern Theological (ULCA) Seminary in Minneapolis; and W. E. Klawitter of the Lutheran Bible Institute in Minneapolis.

In September, the editors of Lutheran papers met in St. Louis for the first time at the behest of the Missouri Synod editor. Caspersen found it to be helpful to his understanding of Missouri and was surprised at some of the talk but still disagreed with their literalist take on Scripture. He contrasted it with Sverdrup's phrase that the Bible was a document of revelation and not to be defended with a hairsplitting definition of biblical inspiration and the inerrant Scripture. He quoted Dr. Chr. Ihlen, a theological professor in Norway: "There is nothing in Jesus' preaching which can be used to argue that one needs to have an inerrant teaching about him in order to come into relationship with him."[99]

Leaders of Lutherans in the United States were closely watching the postwar happenings in Germany. Caspersen reported on the new emerging theology of Barth and even Bonhoeffer as being entirely different from the German Christians, calling it a new school (*Nye Retning*), using the same words as had been used by the Sverdrup-Oftedal party in describing their position vis-à-vis the old school (*gamle retning*) of the others.

On October 10, John T. Quanbeck, head of the Home Missions Board, visited Powers Lake and the newly established congregation, as well as the Couteau and Canton areas, where there were also prospects. At a meeting of the Home Missions Board of the LFC, Quanbeck had proposed that the board loan up to 50 percent of the fund to build churches. If the LFC did not build congregations, the LFC would have no future: "If we fail now the opportunity will never come again." The annual conference had voted to set aside thirty-five thousand dollars for such buildings. One pastor had written in response to the goal by the Home Mission department that "our greatest need is for a group of men and women who will carry us before God in prayer."[100]

On November 13–16, 1945, Dad was the featured speaker for the Spiritual Emphasis week at Augsburg. His theme was "The Master Is Here and He Calleth Thee." Every morning, students would meet in the dorm lounges for devotions. After the meetings, he returned via Valley City, where he had left his car. From there, he drove home. That Thanksgiving, we once again celebrated with the Beaver Creek congregation with its usual potluck Thanksgiving meal. This year, however, Bernard Christensen was there to speak at the dinner. This kind of exchange between the leaders of the LFC and Augsburg from the beginning had kept the congregations well acquainted with the leadership, their ideas, and their dreams for the future.

After the harvest, November was also the month for the annual meetings of the Tioga congregations. Norman, Zion, St. Olaf, Beaver Creek, Temple, and Lindahl all met for these meetings in November. All this time, except in bad weather, Dad drove to Powers Lake for services. He grew to love the people in that congregation. On Christmas Day, there were services in five of the churches and a couple the next day. On the twenty-eighth, the exhausted couple went to Williston for a Christmas party with the new pastor there, Pastor Clarence Framstad, and his wife, Goodie, with whom they had become close friends.

Olai H. Sletten wrote a report on his trip to the West Coast and stopped in Hawley, Minnesota, where he met with Søren Gabrielsen Hauge (1875–1964), the well-known and longtime ELC pastor in Hawley. Sletten, a progressive who thought like a bureaucrat wanting efficiency, wondered why there needed to be an LFC congregation in Hawley. It seemed to be small and struggling in the shadow of Hauge's congregation. This, naturally, brought a quick riposte from my uncle Don, who had served the Hawley congregation and was now in Valley City, saying that evangelism was always appropriate and he could assure Sletten that even if the LFC congregation in Hawley seemed insignificant, "we need, as never before, congregations that believe in evangelism, laymen's work, and pastors with a clear-cut message of sin and grace."[101] Among the many things Uncle Don had cherished from the Sverdrup legacy is that congregations be evangelistic at all times.

# A World at War

The year closed with a flurry of Christmas services. Powers Lake was most active of the congregation in Dad's schedule, but driving to all seven of the little churches was wearing. He was starting to get restless for a smaller parish. Calls from other congregations had begun coming, and he was prayerfully considering them. At this time, given his yellow jaundice (which my grandpa with his Norwegian brogue called *jeller yonders*) and the sense that the parish was too large and exhausting for him, he usually answered the many inquiries about his willingness to entertain a call from another congregation by noting that the call was not suitable because it had too many little congregations and his health demanded he take one with less travel and fewer congregations.

With Tioga's large contribution to the Victory Building Fund, Father had quickly become known as a pastor who could raise money, so he was appointed to the stewardship committee of the LFC. They met every February, so for the next ten years, he would leave on the *Empire Builder* from our future parsonage in Rugby, waving from the train as he left and returned.

## Resigning from the Tioga Parish

The weather was typically bad that January 1946. Temperatures plunged to twenty-three below on January 25, and highways were blocked, so meetings were canceled. On February 4, 1946, however, Dad drove to Minot through a terrible snowstorm, what the *Bismark Tribune* called a "raging blizzard, the worst in five years," to catch the train for Minneapolis, where he would attend the stewardship board meeting. When he returned, he resigned to take the call to Rugby. Mother described the response of the trustees in Tioga: "A meeting of the Tioga parish trustees was held in the parsonage in March of 1946 to talk about his resignation. They refused to accept it and made a motion to go on record as never having accepted 'Revener' Grindal's resignation. 'Why are you leaving us after only four years? Is it because they have a bathtub in that house there? Did you get your orders from Minappliss? They just use us for a horse-trading post! Headquarters in Minappliss! Baloney to them!'"[102]

Meanwhile, the activities of the parish went on, weather permitting. The district pastors were also busy planning Metigoshe Bible Camp activities at the pastoral fellowship meetings in Williston. When Dad was in Minneapolis on February 6, 1946, *Folkebladet* commented on a surprising declaration of some forty-four Missouri pastors and professors at a meeting on September 20, 1945, regretting the position some of their tribe had taken on church unity. The editorial would surely have been a topic of conversation at the meeting. The authors of the statement were well-known leaders of Missouri: Theodore Graebner, C. A. Bencke, Richard R. Caemmerer, Adalbert Raphael Karl Kretzmann, Otto Paul Kretzmann, Fred H. Kretzmann, and Herbert Lindemann. Caspersen concluded they had in effect adopted the LFC stand on unionism. There had been several articles written by Missouri pastors and theologians who had attacked *Folkebladet* for its criticism on Missouri's stance on union, to say nothing of its refusal to apologize for the German invasion of Norway. *Folkebladet* warmly thanked the forty-four for their new position but worried about how widely accepted the new declaration would be among Missouri pastors and members.[103] Caspersen was not hopeful.

As usual, parish activities during Lent were many, and now, after Dad's resignation, would involve finishing things up—catechizations, confirmations, concerts by the ladies' chorus—and saying farewell to the congregations they had grown to love. The Ronnings came to Tioga on April 1 so Don could hold another series of evangelistic meetings in Zion congregation. They remained for ten days as Don preached at Powers Lake and other congregations in the parish. On May 17, the Oak Grove High School Choir sang, and on May 27, the Augsburg Choir appeared at the Powers Lake church. The amount of work required is not really noted, but finding hosts for the choir members, assuring an audience with enough receipts to pay their expenses, was taxing.

That June, we went to the annual meeting in Fargo. One of the more important actions of the conference was the vote to establish a social relations committee to address social issues that the church should be interested in. *Folkebladet* thought it was about time Lutherans took the same interest in these questions as the Reformed had done for years.[104]

The convention also heard that Kristofer Hagen would go to the Santal Mission as a medical doctor, as would Bernard Helland, son of Andreas Helland. The most important issue during the Friday session was hearing a report from the Augsburg Board of Trustees on the financial situation at Augsburg. The Victory Fund Campaign had raised $10,234.36 more than its goal of $250,000, which was a minor miracle. However, inflation had made it necessary to raise the goal to $300,000. That would go to build the Science and Library Building at Augsburg, which was crucial to the accreditation of the school. As late as this meeting, the proposal to move the campus to Augsburg Park still had some life, but this finally ended: It was deemed impossible. On July 18, 1946, the Augsburg board voted unanimously to commit to a "campus expansion in [the] present vicinity."[105]

Augsburg was doing well: There were 464 students, 269 men and 195 women. They were looking for the numbers to increase by 100 in the next year, which meant the school desperately needed dormitory space. Space for women was made in the main building, hardly a suitable place for living.

In the west, the weather was better for crops, and people were feeling better about their financial situations. Notice was made by the convention that the call in Powers Lake had been established, along with the congregation in Coteau.

One gets the sense that success and more resources were cause for optimism in both school and church but also an uneasy feeling that the directions of both were uncertain. The dreams of the founders were being adapted to the change, but the new circumstances of the postwar period also brought about changes that the founders' dreams could not quite fathom. The corporate structures of the postwar years would radically change both organizations as they struggled to keep an even keel in what seemed to be placid years but would work changes on the two that would change them forever.

After a week of Bible camp at Metigoshe and finishing up farewells in the Tioga parish, the folks and I left in our new 1946 Chevy on July 30 for the West Coast to visit relatives and rest. On August 23, the van would come to take the furniture from Tioga to Rugby. On August 27, we left for Rugby. A few years later, on April 4, 1951, oil would be discovered on the Clarence Iverson farm in the Bakken oil field near Tioga, and many members who had lived hardscrabble lives through the Depression became unimaginably wealthy.

CHAPTER 10

# Postwar Ecumenism and Its Problems

WE ARRIVED IN Rugby from Tioga, on August 27, 1946, in a drenching rainstorm, driving east on Highway 2, the thoroughfare of our lives. The rain halted the harvest until things had dried out. Dad would preach at Bethany in Rugby and Berwick in the country on Sunday, August 31. A few weeks later, on September 22, he was formally installed at the three parish churches, Bethany at eleven, Tunbridge at three, and Berwick at eight, by Reverend G. J. Bretheim of Bisbee, president of the Rugby district.

Just as we were settling in on August 30, Dad's foster father, Sjur Monsen Grindal (1878–1946), died. The funeral was held on September 5 in Ferndale Lutheran Free Church. Dad and his cousin, Arthur Tjon, took the train to Ferndale for the service. Mother drove with me to Minot to pick them up on Monday, September 9. It interrupted the process of moving in, but Mom and Dad were young and excited to move into the much more adequate parsonage.

The small city of Rugby, with a population of around 2,700, boasted that it was the geographical center of North America. It was the Pierce County seat, with an imposing courthouse and jail across the street from the parsonage. Rugby also had a large population of German Russians who had fled conditions in Russia long after having been invited to settle there by Empress Catherine in the late eighteenth century. In 1898, they first came to Balta, fifteen miles south of Rugby, which continued to attract their people through the first part of the century. They were skilled in farming land like the wide stretching plains around Rugby. While a number of these immigrants were German Lutheran, many were Mennonites or Catholic. Most of the German Russians around Rugby were devout Roman Catholics. They had built a school and church on the other side of town, St. Theresa's parish, with its school, Little Flower. The rectory where Father Cloos and his housekeeper lived was across the parking lot from the courthouse. We regarded them as almost a different kind of people with a strange religion and superstitions. Both my father and Father Cloos told their charges in confirmation or school never to marry a Catholic or Lutheran. So we kept apart.

**Figure 10.1.** The parsonage at Rugby, North Dakota. Used by permission of the Grindal family.

## The World Council of Churches and LWF Debates

As the rebuilding of Europe and the rest of the world commenced after the war, church leadership saw an opportunity, if not a necessity, for world churches to come together like the countries of the world in the United Nations. The February 20, 1946, *Folkebladet* noted with approval that churches in over thirty-five countries had joined the World Council of Churches (WCC). Norway would soon join, as would the ULCA and the Augustana Synod. Some churches in the American Lutheran Conference had not yet decided. The issue with the Norwegian Lutheran Church in America (NLCA), which would change its name at its 1946 summer convention to the Evangelical Lutheran Church (ELC), was that those from the old Norwegian Synod were following the "German influence from Missouri." This was deplored by Caspersen, always ready to sniff out its influence in any church negotiations. He especially disliked Missouri's need to force agreement on theological theses before proceeding with any merger talk with any Lutheran church. The council did not appeal to most of the Free Church membership if it was to be an organized world church. Its position was against mergers but for federations of churches. Otherwise, by its own principles, the LFC could not consider being part of such an organization.[1] This was

Caspersen's constant refrain. Ecumenism yes, corporate mergers no. The LFC would lose everything if it merged with other Lutheran churches but not if it joined in a federation.[2]

These issues, while a constant conversation among pastors and leaders in their pastoral gatherings and informal connections, did not affect the daily lives of LFC congregations until much later. Life went on, improving yearly as recovery after the war made life better for almost everyone.

As we were saying our goodbyes in Tioga, the LWF Executive Committee met in Uppsala, Sweden, on July 24–26, 1946, attended by the leaders of the state churches in Europe, as well as the American churches: J. A. Aasgaard (ELC), Franklin Clark Fry (ULCA), and Dr. Abdel Ross Wentz (ALC). It was the first meeting of this group since 1939. They had much repair work to do given their distrust of the German delegation. They wondered who among the Germans would join them. Would they be members of the resistance, the Confessing Church as it was known, which was associated with the martyr Dietrich Bonhoeffer? Or the German Christians who supported Hitler?

In reorganizing, the executive committee renamed the organization, choosing Lutheran World Federation (LWF) rather than Lutheran World Council. They also planned an assembly in Lund, Sweden, for June 1947. It would be its first full meeting since 1935 in Paris. Participants would be determined by their confessional agreements with other Lutherans. This caused some to fear the dominance of the strongly confessional Lutherans over other churches. The executive committee of the newly renamed LWF voted to join the WCC. This would have repercussions in the churches back home in America, where the conversation became passionate. The question of the WCC, and whether the ELC or LFC, for example, should join it, ignited a flame of resistance. It was a heated conversation that I remember being discussed passionately when the pastors would get together for informal gatherings. Was it about a world church and world domination? Perhaps it seemed something like communism, an increasing threat at the time.

Al Rogness (1906–1992), president of Luther Seminary, and Pastor Rudolph "Rudy" Anders Ofstedal (1897–1959) of First Lutheran in Decorah traveled around their church, arguing the pros and cons, Rogness for and Ofstedal against. They had a good time, doing so without rancor. After the debate, they would enjoy the hospitality of the local pastor together and drink blackberry brandy "for their throats," Paul Ofstedal, Rudy's son, told me once. Similar debates broke out in the Lutheran Free Church as well.

My uncle Donald Ronning and my father were dead against the WCC. A magazine put out by the Innermission Society, called *Morning Glory*, appeared in our homes regularly and kept the controversy stoked every time it came. I can see my dad and Richard Torgerson, the new pastor in Barton, North Dakota, and son of Sverre, editor of the *Lutheran Messenger* and *Folkebladet*, in our Rugby living room amicably preaching at each other in fervent arguments, Richard for, Dad against.

The Lutheran World Relief (LWR) arm of the LWF, however, was highly regarded among American Lutherans. It had met the needs of Europe after the war, sending relief to Europe, especially to Lutherans in northern Europe, and was cheerfully supported by most American Lutherans. German Lutherans looking around the ruins began to rethink their quietism in the political realm. This appealed to Caspersen. He was happy to report that Protestant churches around the world had become more socially conscious, especially in Germany. Pastor Niemöller and Hans Lilje were changing attitudes among Lutherans. Harking back to Archbishop Nathan Söderblom of Sweden, a passionate ecumenical advocate, Caspersen remarked on the stance of Bishop Berggrav and others, rejoicing in this awakening. He was especially happy that Dr. Alvin David Mattson (1895–1970), of Augustana Seminary in Rock Island, was "pioneering" in this breakthrough and leading seminarians to take "an active part in disseminating social knowledge" as the Reformed churches had traditionally done: "The hermit existence of the church must end ... the Lutheran Church is not psychologically prepared to do its best here. It has not yet learned to speak a distinct social language."[3]

Being for the ecumenical movement and being on the left were not necessarily the same thing, but it is not surprising that much of the support for the ecumenical movement tended to be with those on the same side of the political spectrum. Mattson was well known for espousing the social gospel of Walter Rauschenbusch and Reinhold Niebuhr.[4] Because National Socialism had given nationalism such a bad reputation, progressives were quick to move away from nationalism toward international organizations. Many in the leadership of the LFC, especially Christensen, Burntvedt, and Caspersen, were liberals, on the opposite side of most of their membership, who tended to be Republicans. While many knew this about them, they accepted that as the free choice of both men, admiring them for their Christian piety.

About that time, the International Missionary Council (IMC) established two groups that would work for the establishment of the World Council: the Commission of the Churches on International Affairs (CCIA) and the Ecumenical Institute in Bossey, Switzerland. While these efforts may have seemed remote to the young family speeding toward a new call, they would soon have a profound impact on their lives. Even though the WCC had not yet been officially established, it was a reality in the minds of many.

## The Rugby Parish of the LFC

The Rugby parish dated from 1888, when a congregation at Rugby Junction, later Tunbridge, began with Hans Tjon and Pastors J. U. Pederson and Bertle

Figure 10.2. The Tunbridge church. Used by permission of the Grindal family.

Hagboe, the latter something of a pioneer hero of the North Dakota Norwegian Lutherans. A group from Tunbridge left to establish a congregation in Rugby, Bethania/Bethany, in 1906, served by Carl Sivertsen Vang (1862–1958). Berwick Lutheran Congregation, in McHenry County, was also founded by J. U. Pederson and served by pioneer pastor Hagboe, then Carl Vang. Tunbridge was eight miles west of Rugby on Highway 2, and Berwick, sixteen miles west of Rugby, was also on Highway 2. Bethany was a lively LFC congregation that throughout its life always had active Bible studies and prayer meetings, along with ladies' aids and circles that raised money for the congregation and missions, both home and foreign.

The Tunbridge congregation consisted of immigrants from around Balestrand, Norway, on the Sognefjord, most of them were my dad's cousins. My father loved the rich Sogne dialect he had learned from his foster father and would enjoy telling jokes in the dialect whenever he was with them. Their land, at the end of the Central Plains, had feet of rich topsoil.

The Tunbridge congregation could be difficult. They gave Dad no quarter, even if he *was* the nephew of their matriarch, Torbjør Tjon. Once, when he asked for a raise because they were expecting a third child (a common request since, at the time, the husband's pay was partially based on his family situation), his cousin Manda told him that he should have thought ahead. This enraged my normally quiet, nonconfrontational father. He walked out of the meeting in a fury. As he did, another of his cousins muttered, *Prestene skulle ikke bli sint* "Pastors should not get mad." It made him even madder.

Berwick was just over the line between the Central and Great Plains. Their land was much more difficult to cultivate, less fertile, sandy, and rocky. My parents grew to love them for their kindness and deep Christian faith. As the winter blizzards swept across the plains and the hardscrabble life on the farm made people seek relief, many farmers succumbed to the ravages of liquor. Even today I am finding out about men we knew well who were confirmed alcoholics and made life miserable for their wives and children, who never spoke about it to anyone.

I remember many a Second Day Christmas on our relatives' farms when we were invited to a Christmas dinner with tables groaning with good food, delicious turkey, potatoes, gravy, and pies. After sleeping off the big meal in the den, one of the men would say, "Let's go see the machinery." They would ask my father if he wanted to come, and he, knowing their purpose, would politely demur. They would go out into the cold, with the wind beating against them from the west, for a snort.

As mentioned earlier, the town of Rugby was divided right down the middle between Norwegian Lutherans and German Russian Catholics. A widow, Mrs. Bachmeier, lived in a house with a large garden north of us, behind our white picket fence. She was one of the few Catholics on that side of town, very near the Great Northern railroad tracks, where trains rumbled by almost hourly, shaking the houses so badly that the pictures would have to be straightened daily. The Catholic graveyard on the east end of Rugby had headstones with given names of Catholic popes such as Leo, Boniface, Gregory, and so on, followed by German patronyms. We kids would hike out there along the railroad tracks, where we gathered the large railroad rail spikes, and marvel at the crucifix in the middle of the cemetery, which some teenaged boys had used as a target with their BB guns. At the time, although we were too young to know it, Protestants would speak against crucifixes by arguing that our cross was empty. Jesus had been raised. Despite misunderstandings of this kind, my mother tried to keep good relations between our neighbors and us. She got a recipe for dill pickles from Mrs. Bachmeier that became a yearly pleasure for her to preserve.

The Norwegian Lutherans in Rugby were also divided, between the ELC and the LFC. After the war, the two congregations worked together more and more. The week my father returned from his father's funeral, he and Olaf Brandt, the pastor at First Lutheran and grandson of the influential couple, Diderikke Ottesen and Nils Brandt of Luther College, put on a joint Sunday school teacher training program that lasted ten weeks. Dad lectured, and Olaf led the discussions. At the end of the class, those who had attended faithfully were given certificates. These church-wide programs raised the level of Sunday school instruction in the two churches.

## Bethany Burns Down

We were soon well settled into the new parsonage with three large pine trees beside it. We enjoyed its bathtub and the cistern in the basement to collect soft rainwater to wash clothes instead of the rusty Rugby water that left an orange ring in the sink, toilet, and bathtub. The white-frame church in Rugby had just been remodeled and painted to be ready for its sixtieth anniversary and the fiftieth anniversary of the LFC. On January 20, 1947, a fire broke out, burning it to the ground. It was a fiercely cold North Dakota day, winds whipping the flames up to the steeple. I was sitting in my Grandpa Theodore's lap, looking east and watching as the steeple crashed to the ground. I feared that my father had been on the steeple and was inconsolable until I saw him. I can still feel Grandpa's woolen pants scratching my skin and smell the old man odor from him and the pink wintergreen mints he always had at the ready, a bit linty from his pockets, as we watched the fire raging half a block away. All they saved was some old silverware and an old piano.

This meant that the next two years, the parsonage served as a meeting place for the church. It began the very night of the fire when the trustees met there, as well as the Bible study group. Cigarette smoke would curl up the stairway, and a blue haze settled over everything, which mother would try to air out after they left. Mother had to be ready with coffee and treats several nights a week. This was a part of being a pastor's wife she really loved. She had gotten enough money from the Tioga Ladies Aid to buy Syracuse China, with a sterling setting, the Stradivarius pattern, for ten. With the crystal goblets from her family, she set an elegant table. When I was just under four, I remember sitting in the upstairs hallway with my legs hanging out beneath the banisters listening to the conversations. I loved church talk from the first.

On February 11, Mom and Dad and the building committee drove to Fargo in the middle of a snowstorm to meet with an architect, S. M. Houkom, and plan the new church, which was built on the same space as the old one. It was a huge task—cleaning up the old lot, digging a larger basement, getting an architect to plan and design the new church and contractors to build it. It took time and money. Typically, the men, most of them farmers or familiar with farming, wanted to help defray costs. One farmer brought a team of horses to drag the ruins away, and I got to ride one of them for a brief time as they worked. This fully occupied my father and mother for the next two years. They had to schedule church services in buildings around town—other churches, the high school auditorium, the town gymnasium. This necessitated joint Lenten services with First Lutheran. But as the former pastor Luthard Gjerde, still much beloved in Rugby, had predicted, soon "out of the ashes of the old will rise a bigger and more beautiful Bethany."[5] By September, the basement was near completion

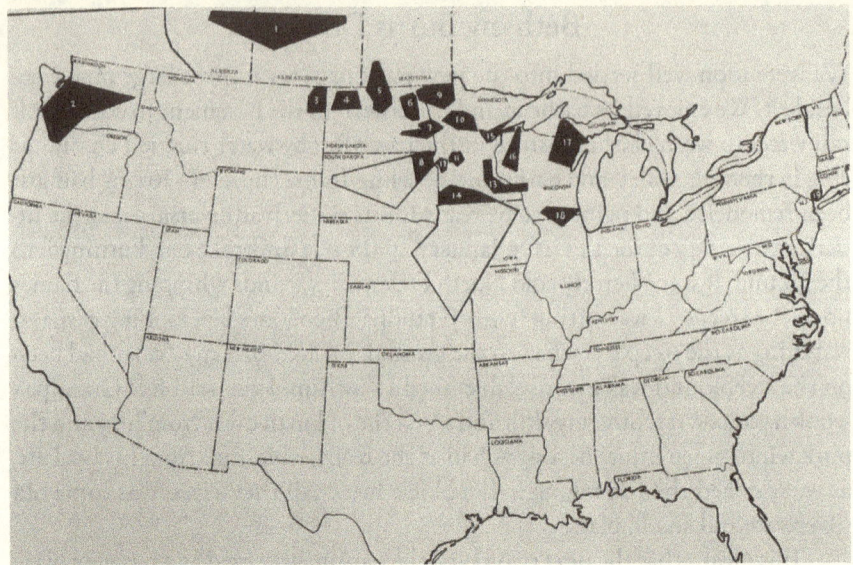

**Figure 10.3.** A map of Lutheran Free Church congregations published in *Our Fellowship*. Used by permission of Augsburg Fortress Publishers.

and would be used for services until the upper sanctuary was finished. Until then, the congregation met at the Presbyterian church close to the schoolgrounds.

This was the year also that the LFC celebrated its fiftieth anniversary. To mark the anniversary, the book *Our Fellowship*, written by Clarence Carlsen and edited by A. B. Batalden, was printed. It featured the congregations and pastors of the LFC with pictures of congregations and pastors, and essays on the history of various organizations such as Deaconess Institute, Augsburg, Oak Grove, and the mission fields. In it, the church was frequently called a *fellowship*.

Every time they went to Fargo in that first year, my parents would visit Dad's foster mother, Anna Grindal, who, after her husband's death, moved there into a home for the aged. It was closer than the West Coast and convenient for the folks to have her nearby, but she was not happy there. She wanted to return to Ferndale and live out her days on the farm, which, given her mental issues, was not possible. They had to sell the farm in Ferndale where she had lived for decades and Dad had grown up. As 1946 went on, the efforts to sell the farm became an issue of frequent letters and calls with the attorney in Ferndale, which also meant trips to Fargo to get his mother to sign the sales documents. She did not want to sign them at all but especially if a Catholic were to offer to buy it. When the lawyer informed her that was illegal, it made things a bit more difficult for my father, although, to be frank, he shared her opposition to a Catholic buying it.

When the lawyer realized from Dad's reports that Grandma had mental health issues, he was alarmed and worried about whether she needed some kind

**Figure 10.4.** Anna Grindal and nurse. Used by permission of the Grindal family.

of legal intervention. Dad finally got it settled, and with the money she received for the farm, she was able to move back to Everett, Washington, and take up residence in the Bethany Old People's Home, run by the LFC, where she flourished until her death in 1958.

## Golden Anniversary of the LFC

On June 9, 1947, we drove down to Minneapolis for the annual meeting of the LFC at Trinity Congregation. In his annual presidential address, President Burntvedt noted that things had changed in how the LFC thought of itself. Although it cherished the notion of each congregation's autonomy and freedom, he said, "circumstances beyond our control compelled us for all practical purposes to function as a church body and none outside of the Lutheran Free church think of us any longer as a movement only."[6] Burntvedt was now redefining the LFC from a movement to a church body. Although the term *fellowship* does not appear much in his discourse, it appears in the Carlsen book many times. Burntvedt would call it *Our Fellowship* on occasion when asking for support, for example, of LWF in helping refugees in Europe after the war, but he saw things had to change as the times changed.

For the LFC to be part of the American Lutheran Conference or to participate in merger talks, the leadership, out of necessity, had to guide the LFC "fellowship" into becoming a church body. Augsburg's founders would likely have disagreed with that move. They had called it a *movement*, a *fellowship*. Considering that Burntvedt was beginning to promote a merger of the fellowship with other churches, however, it was a necessity to change its self-definition. In addition, it was clear that the younger generation raised in the "fellowship" without an immediate experience of the hurts of the 1890s, or the presence of Sverdrup to argue the case, naturally defined the LFC as a church like the ELC or any number of other Lutheran churches. It was not, as Burntvedt admitted, what the founders had had in mind.

In 1898, when the LFC was being founded and getting its sea legs, it established the Board of Organization, which included two laymen and a pastor. It served as a kind of church council over which the LFC president had no authority. His job was essentially to lead the annual meeting and serve as a kind of figurehead for the church. "The Rules for Work" remained the rule of the LFC until 1954, when they were revised, but they were less and less adhered to over time.

Fevold credits Burntvedt with marking that the LFC had, in fact, become a church body. As early as 1937 at the annual convention, he noted that the LFC, although differently organized than other Lutheran bodies in the country, was still a church body. He continued to push for that: "Little by little, pressed by changing conditions and in order to meet new situation, our work has gradually been more strongly organized within our original frame of polity. This, in my opinion, is as it should be."[7]

In July 1947, the LWF met in Lund. Anders Nygren of Lund University in Sweden was elected president. That November, Bernard Christensen wrote something of an SOS on the failure of Augsburg and the LFC to have enough young men entering the seminary. Only two had enrolled that fall. He wondered why and blamed the war, low salaries for pastors, and the lack of a spiritual awakening in the church for the decline. It was imperative that the LFC raise up young men and women by prayer and personal contact to serve the word. He saw hopeful signs in the Luther League Conventions and Bible camps and urged readers to pray to the Lord of the harvest for more young people to give their lives to service.[8]

Questions of Lutheran Unity continued to stir the church, even as it celebrated its fiftieth anniversary. John Asbjørn Houkom (1890–1950), a longtime leader in the LFC, wrote a considerable piece on "Lutheran Unity" for the *Lutheran Messenger*. He noted how the push toward organic union had been strong after World War I, but now the word for the LWF was *unity*, basing its work on Article VII of the Augsburg Confession: "It is enough to agree concerning the doctrine of the Gospel and the administration of the Sacraments. Nor is it necessary that human traditions, rites, or ceremonies, instituted by men, should be everywhere alike."

## Overture to Lutheran Unity

Houkom then recalled the negotiations prior to the adopting of the Minneapolis Theses in 1930. As the American Lutheran Conference was formed in 1930, the Chicago Theses and Minneapolis Theses were prominent in the discussion but not mentioned in the American Lutheran Conference Constitution. Following its traditional stance, the LFC had maintained that agreement in the symbols of the church was sufficient for unity, not agreement on more theses. What Houkom objected to was that the delegates to the conference had agreed to bring to the annual conference of the LFC a proposal that the LFC enter pulpit and altar fellowship (the Galesburg rule) with the five churches in the American Lutheran Conference. Houkom noted the tension therein. When the Commission on Lutheran Church Unity prepared the "Overture on Lutheran Church Unity" proposal in 1944, it had not been presented to the LFC, partly because the members of the church, by constitutional law and general opinion, did not approve of church unity based on theses that added to the symbols of the church. They objected especially to the language: "We, the constituent synods of the American Lutheran Conference, generally and collectively reaffirm our sincere and wholehearted adherence to our mutual pledge as to doctrine and practice in the Minneapolis Theses. We as earnestly expect of those with whom we seek complete fellowship that their doctrine and practice shall confirm to their respective declarations."[9]

When the proposal did come up, Bernard Christensen took a strong and principled exception to the resolution. He could not "in good conscience" agree with the Galesburg rule as it was found in the Minneapolis Theses. As he was for union, he hoped that his failure to vote for the motion in 1944 would not cause his withdrawal from the American Lutheran Conference.[10] T. O. Burntvedt tried to put that to rest by saying, "The Conference would not feel called upon to suggest that any individual or constituent body unwilling to vote for the reaffirmation of the Minneapolis Theses should withdraw from the Conference, but would leave it to the individual or constituent body to decide."[11] Burntvedt did make clear that those opposed to the overture should make their objection known by abstaining or having their "no" vote recorded. Houkom concluded that he could accept the committee members' "tacit approval as sufficient, worth as much to us as formal action on the Theses and the Overture."[12]

After a brief history of the founding of the National Lutheran Council in 1918, which included the ULCA but not the American Lutheran Conference, Houkom's article disparaged the refusal of Missouri to be a part of any group that would not agree on various theses. Houkom suggested that the LFC's reluctance to participate in a search for union, but to work rather to establish "fellowship," was entirely consistent with LFC principles:

1. Not to be drawn into further learned disputations and hairsplitting dialectics about fine points of doctrine as a basis for union.
2. Not to engage in further theses making as a way to reunion.
3. To cooperate cordially with other Lutherans in practical and spiritual objectives where we may for the preservation of the Lutheran heritage and the building up of the kingdom of God among men.
4. Cherish the ideal of Lutheran unity but be wary of union at any price.[13]

Torgerson, looking at the argument, concluded that "unity could be achieved based on Freedom under the authority of the Word of God and his Spirit for the Christian individual and local congregation, and Christian love and tolerance... It is possible along the same road to look forward to and even pray for eventual union."[14]

Although congregations and pastors in most church bodies kept clear demarcations between denominational lines, the national climate of ecumenism was beginning to have local consequences even in towns like Rugby. Things had begun to thaw with the ELC's First Lutheran. Olaf Brandt had worked with Dad, and now its new pastor, Ernest Nelson, and my father got to know each other well and enjoyed each other's Christian fellowship.

Even as this was happening, proponents of the WCC began making plans to reestablish their organization. They traced their development back to the Edinburgh World Missionary Conference in 1910 and an encyclical from the Orthodox Synod of Constantinople that had proposed a "fellowship of churches." It would be an organization of churches like the League of Nations, something Woodrow Wilson had pushed as a solution to nationalistic wars after World War I. Its proponents had almost finalized such plans when the leaders of one hundred churches around the world voted to establish such an organization in 1938. As World War II was threatening to break out, these plans had been put on hold. But the dream did not die during the war; it seemed more and more prudent to establish such an organization as the world peered across the ruins of World War II.

## Ministry in Rugby

Rugby was one of those "focal" LFC parishes that young pastors would serve on their way up the ladder. It was small enough to manage but central enough to bring the work of the pastor into the view of the larger church and its leaders. They could tell if you were succeeding or failing. Pastors and their families from the other small congregations around the area would come to Rugby on Friday afternoons to shop and frequently stopped by to visit. This provided lots of entertainment and fun for Mom and Dad and sometimes for us if the pastor had a family. Gilbert J. Bretheim and his wife, Hilda, from Bisbee frequently came by—four of their boys all grown and either at Augsburg or serving a parish. He was the president of the Rugby district, and Mrs. Bretheim functioned as *bispinden*—bishop's wife. She would offer a dollop of help with a hot dish of criticism to the younger pastors' wives. John Dahlen at Church's Ferry some miles east of Rugby would frequently stop by for dinner. A confirmed bachelor, he would have to deal with Mother's attempts to fix him up with old maid teachers in the high school—a vain hope. The Richard Torgersons, son of Pastor Sverre Torgerson, Mother's confirmation pastor, moved to serve the LFC congregation in Barton one year later, and their visits were lots of fun. Dad and Dick read books of theology together and discussed them. One I remember best was the series of seven books by Kenneth Scott Latourette providing a history of the church, *A History of the Expansion of Christianity*.[15] My dad became a serious reader of church history and theology over his lifetime.

Mother's gift of mimicry gave her many funny stories to relate about parish life, some of which helped dispel the hurts that could accrue there. She learned quickly that living in a parsonage was different from owning your own home. She had to persuade the trustees if she wanted any improvements. She saw this especially clearly after the church in Rugby burned down. For over a year, she had to host trustee and deacons meetings in the parsonage. One of her most persuasive desserts was creampuffs. After serving them, she could manage to get most of the trustees to approve almost any needed home repairs.

To relax that summer, the family went to Ottertail Lake, near Fergus Falls, for a week's vacation, stopping by Mount Carmel Bible Camp to hear William Ernest Klawitter (1905–1989) and others speak. We then went to the farm in Cyrus, returning on August 29, ready for more meetings on the building and all that involved.

That fall, on November 23, 1947, we had a visit from Malvin Rossing, missionary to Madagascar, whose sister Martha was the librarian in the local high school, and his widowed sister, Anna, lived with her children. Members of the Lutheran Free Church and many others over the years had acquired an intimate knowledge of the mission, knowing both missionaries and the names of native leaders in the church. Missionaries like Rossing would return with glass slides, as they were called, and spend an evening telling about the work. Any Junior Mission Band kid could point out the island to the east of southern Africa with the red thread running from Rugby to there. The members of Berwick gathered to hear him speak and show his colored slides and even a film of the work there.

Always, news about Augsburg kept our interest. On February 11, 1948, the Augsburg Choral Club, directed by Leland B. Sateren, gave a concert. He had brought his wife, Eldora, along, so Mother enjoyed visiting with her, an old friend from Augsburg. As they grew acquainted in Rugby, both Mom and Dad enjoyed the new situation, Mother singing and playing the old classics of the day, "Because," "I Love you Truly," for weddings and *"Den Store hvide flok"* at funerals. If there were no pianist, Dad would accompany her. Their musical gifts were not unique in Rugby—the organist Josephine Bale Egeland, a Tunbridge native, had gone to Augsburg with them, and Barbara Blessum, a soprano, frequently favored the people with a solo, as did others. The piano in the parlor was still featured after dinners when the guests, stuffed to the gills, would sit half-dozing, while the girls in the family favored them with their pieces. Later that month, Arthur Tjon came from Ferndale in the middle of a howling blizzard and stayed overnight with us. Mother wrote in her diary for February 28, "We're never alone here, company even during storms."

Another feature of their life in the LFC was board meetings in Minneapolis. Dad would leave for his early spring LFC Stewardship Board meetings on the train, which went right by our backyard, and wave to us as he came and went. Every time, he would bring back clothes for us—shopping at Dayton's for the latest Easter outfits. Both liked fine clothes and cared how we all looked and dressed. That Easter, Mother reported with some satisfaction that they had received $250 in the offering that day, which was a big help. While waiting for the church to be built, we had services in the local civic auditorium. I don't remember much of that building except that my little sister, LaRhae Anne, was born on May 5, 1948, and baptized there on June 6. Luthard Gjerde, the previous pastor in Rugby, and his wife, Sofia, were her godparents, along with Mildred Jacobson Tinseth, a grandmother figure since both our grandmothers had died in childbirth. Immediately after that, the family left for Minnesota and the annual meeting.

## LFC Annual Meeting 1948

At the LFC annual meeting in Willmar in June 1948, the conversation concerning membership in the WCC began to become a matter of real contention. We drove down for the event so Dad could attend the meeting, while Mother stayed in Cyrus with us since LaRhae was only six weeks old. *Folkebladet* had recommended the LFC join the WCC, supporting J. A. Aasgaard's recommendation for the ELC. Caspersen admitted there were a few reasons to oppose the proposal, but in all, they were insignificant next to the reasons to join. "There are always people who imagine dangers wherever progress is concerned," he wrote.[16] Dad was there and heard the arguments for the resolution supporting the LFC joining the WCC. It had to pass by a two-thirds majority. Although most thought the majority was for it, as observers speculated, it could not be voted on right away because of another pressing event. It was postponed until the next day. At that meeting, also pressed for time, the opposition gathered strength. When the vote was held, the numbers were 101 for and 246 against.

This surprised and disappointed many in the leadership. Caspersen regretted the tone of the conversation. It was even more embarrassing because the guest speaker was Bishop Hanns Lilje (1899–1977) from Germany, a strong supporter of the WCC.

On Saturday afternoon, Dad preached to the convention. From the first, he opposed joining the WCC and listened to the arguments that began to grow more urgent as time went on. John K. Rimmereid (1891–1953), a layman from New Rockford, North Dakota, wrote in to *Folkebladet* reflecting on the vote against joining the WCC. On listening to the debate, he observed that not all the Viking (*jomsvikinger*, an especially fierce band of Vikings) spirit was dead: "Both zeal and the knowledge of God were united."[17] When they left the church, an elderly man who had heard the older Sverdrup speak many times commented that John Stensvaag's speech had something of Sverdrup's spirit, "Yes, it did, but he [Sverdrup] was hard," which caused Rimmereid to recall what one historian had said about Sverdrup: "He followed the bloody path. Therefore, his speech contained not those sweet loving words." That pleased Rimmereid, who quoted Ezekiel 3:8–9 with approval. "Yes, we are a stubborn (*gjenstridig*) people," he concluded, counting it a privilege to be part of a group working for living congregations and freedom.[18]

Almost as if to refute Rimmereid, the same issue included a note from the *Decorah Posten* with a clarification of the WCC's work from General Secretary Willem Visser t'Hooft (1900–1985). The general secretary argued that the WCC was not seeking to dominate local churches but to create a fellowship that sought to strengthen churches' freedom both now and in the future.[19]

In retrospect, *Folkebladet* rated the convention as one of the best in history. The reports from the schools were good: Augsburg now had 907 students and Oak Grove 246, a record for both schools. A new building had been finished at Oak Grove, and collections to build the library at Augsburg were gaining speed. The mission in China reported growing difficulties as the Red Army under Mao made progress against the Nationalists, led by Chiang Kai Shek, the hope of Christians in China. Burntvedt lauded the LFC's Women's Missionary Federation for its great support of missions and prayers. What was needed was a new awakening in the church and country, he noted.[20] A short paragraph dealt with congregations in the fellowship that were giving to free will mission organizations not supported by the LFC. This very likely was the World Mission Prayer League, which had recently been founded by Lutheran college students, some from Augsburg, after the revivals of the late 1930s. While Caspersen did not want to say the leadership could not in good conscience hinder other congregations from supporting such efforts, they should not do so at the expense of our own mission efforts. "It says in God's word that one would take care of one's own first," he concluded.[21]

The Innermission Committee, which was responsible for building new home mission congregations, was ramping up its work, especially in the Pacific Northwest. This year, they sent Chester Hoversten to Russellville, Oregon, a suburb of Portland. Fields on the West Coast would become a higher and higher priority to all Midwestern Lutherans as they watched their flocks moving west. That migration would soon involve us.

## Local Ecumenism

While the WCC bothered my parents, so did the Catholics, a strong presence in our little town. In the middle of our time in Rugby, another Catholic family bought the Bachmeier house and moved in. They had to walk through our yard and the neighbors' to get to mass on the other side of town. Our neighbor, Elise Andersen, a feisty photographer from Bergen, put up a picket fence to prevent their walking through her yard and ours on the way to church. It enraged the wife and mother now living there. My folks would watch in wonder—and much amusement—as she took off running toward the fence in her Sunday clothes and dress shoes, leaping over the fence, skirts and slip flying as she cleared the pickets on her way to mass. In an ecumenical gesture, my mother paid the son to wash

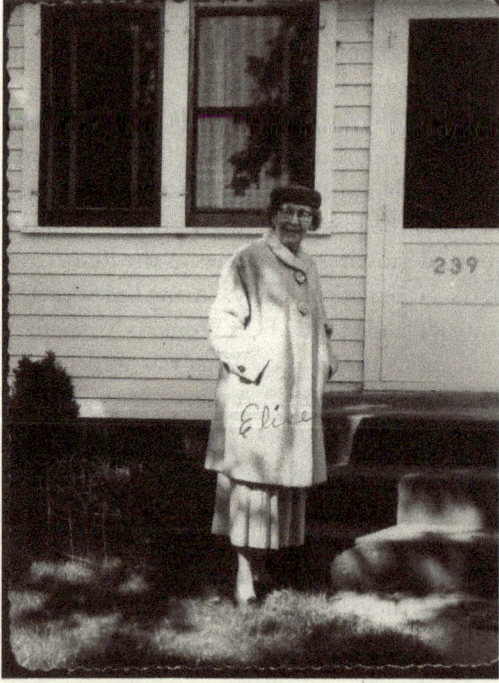

**Figure 10.5.** Elise Andersen. Used by permission of the Grindal family.

off the parsonage siding and clean off the ever-present dust from the prairies stretching out far and wide around the little town. While a nice gesture, many thought she was slightly daft to think one could successfully wash off dust from the parsonage siding.

In the summer of 1948, both the WCC and the LWF met for their first meetings. The World Council met in Amsterdam, August 22–September 4, with the theme "Man's Disorder and God's Design." This was completely in line with the spirit of the age. Exhausted with war and a sick nationalism that had nearly destroyed the world, people began to think international organizations were the way to peace. The United Nations was the model. War-weary, people longed to assure peace.

## Illness

Life was pleasant and exciting during those years. Mother was enjoying her time as pastor's wife, and Father was busy fulfilling his vocation as a pastor in the parish. As part of their civic duties, he recommended that people in the congregation should get their chest X-rays. At the time, TB was still active, and there had been no cure for it other than long rests in the sunshine at sanatoriums. To have an X-ray was helpful in that it would get early treatment for those who had contracted the disease, as well as get them into a quarantine situation where they could not spread it.

In August 1948, Mother was at the beauty parlor and, as she was leaving, debated about whether to have a chest X-ray. She knew Dad was with baby LaRhae, who could be getting fussy without being nursed. As she walked out of the beauty parlor, she saw the truck there and decided to get an X-ray as part of the community effort. Six weeks later, she got a letter from the state saying there was a suspicious shadow on the X-ray and she should talk with her doctor immediately. After several months of watching what turned out to be a tumor, Dr. C. G. Johnson, our doctor, suggested she consult with Dr. Thomas J. Kinsella (1895–1969), a pioneer in thoracic surgery for nontubercular conditions. A professor of surgery at the University of Minnesota, he was also a consultant at St. Mary's Hospital in Minneapolis, on Riverside Avenue, kitty corner from Augsburg.

As my parents were dealing with this stress, Mrs. Torbjør Grindal Tjon, Dad's aunt, died on September 21, 1948. Dad had loved that Mom's middle name was Torbjør because it was also his aunt's name. She had been a charter member of the Tunbridge LFC. At the funeral, Dad preached and Mother sang Torbjør's favorite songs. It was announced that her many memorials were going to schools and missions of the LFC, as her husband had done when he died in 1921. Our little fellowship mattered deeply to these people out on the prairie.

In the fall of 1948, LWR was asking farmers to contribute one hundred carloads of wheat for people starving overseas. My father, along with other Lutheran pastors in the area, Ernest Nelson and George Amundsen of Barton, organized for Pierce County and contributed to the hundred carloads in another demonstration of joint action between the ELC and LFC even in a divided town like Rugby.

### World Politics Impinge Locally

In November 1948, Harry S. Truman (1884–1972) was elected president in a cliffhanger of a vote against Thomas Dewey. Despite the editor of *Folkebladet*'s devotion to the liberal side of politics, nothing appeared in the paper about the election. As the year ended and 1949 began, the situation in China occupied much of the mission news. Fred Ditmanson, veteran missionary to China, reported on the flights of the missionaries from inland China to either Formosa or Hong Kong on the planes of the LWF, *St. Peter* and *St. Paul*. *St. Paul* received a lethal blow while Arthur Olson, head of the LFC mission in China, was on board. It landed safely but afterward could only be used for parts that *St. Peter* needed. My second cousin Per Eivind Kivle, a young missionary to China from Norway's Lutheran Free Church, managed the flights and got the missionaries safely out of China as Chiang Kai Shek and his armies were routed by Mao's Red Army. The LFC missionaries, Arthur and Minnie Olson, the Ditmansons, and Lenorah Erickson, found refuge in the Lutheran Federation Home in Shanghai. Ditmanson reported that the news from the war was not promising. The few missionaries left in the inland might not escape, he feared.[22]

While the reports from China were dire, the mission in Madagascar was flourishing, and the reports from home were encouraging. Morris G. Vaagenes Sr. and his wife wrote a report on the successes of the mission there. They were pleased to state that in 1948, twice as many—seventy-five—native people had been baptized as the year before. However, given the war and the disruption of farming and shipping, they expected a major famine in their field that year.[23] They were hoping their supporters in America could help. It had long been the Norwegians' most beloved mission field. The family had continued its passionate support for the Malagasy mission, following Grandma Jonette's example.

The China mission was much newer for Norwegians, although several from the Hauge Synod had established a mission there in the 1890s that was supported by Norwegian Americans even if they were not Hauge Synod members. The LFC had joined them in 1916, when Peder Konsterlie went to China. By March 1949, the Reds were in control of the Honan province. No one could travel without their approval. This made the missionaries anxious for the native Chinese who were teaching and pastoring their flocks there. Arthur Olson reported on Ditmanson's attempt to return to see how things were going.

Only those who promised they would return and had food and clothing to give to the people in the area they were visiting would receive a pass. Olson concluded that the Chinese had really no option but to obey the new regime and send their sons into military service. Terror was Mao's main weapon.[24] These reports made it possible for readers of the magazine to be intimately acquainted with the goings on in China. While they could read in the papers what was going on in the leadership and in global politics, these inside reports from people they knew and their Chinese sisters and brothers in Christ, about whom they knew much and prayed for, gave many in the churches, compared with most Americans, a deeper feeling for the global forces that affected real people.[25]

## Mother's Operation

After consultations with Mother's doctor in Rugby, in early February 1949, the family left by train for Cyrus, where LaRhae and I would stay with our great-aunt Mildred and uncle Freddie, while the folks were in Minneapolis. Uncle Fred brought us to the farm. We were not used to the farm in winter. As usual, they had closed off the front porch and upstairs to save heat, and I had to sleep on a couch in the dining room. Then the folks left for Minneapolis, taking the bus through a stormy landscape. There had been a terrible blizzard in the Midwest with temperatures below zero. It was blasting its way toward Minnesota as the folks rode to Minneapolis. After some consultation, Kinsella suggested exploratory surgery. On Monday, February 7, Mother was in surgery for nine hours. They had found a ganglia neuroma, a floating tumor the size of a saucer with its roots in her spine. They removed all of it, glad it had not been in her lungs. The anesthesia bothered her for months.

My mother had been nursing LaRhae and weaned her to a cup, not a bottle, in a couple of days. She cried and cried. Mildred could not comfort her. I lay awake in the dining room, listening to her weeping, watching the car lights going east on Highway 29 and casting eerie and strange shadows through the leaded glass windows above the shelves. I can still see them dancing on the walls as the cars whistled by. At five, I knew something was wrong and developed canker sores all through my mouth, so all I wanted to eat was my aunt's rice pudding. For the rest of my life, the virus would flare up whenever I was nervous.

During the consultations and while Mother was recovering, they stayed with Gerda Mortensen, whose apartment was near the hospital. Miss Mortensen often had to do this for students, who made good use of her hospitality when they had emergencies like this. After a few days, Mother was released to go home and have C. G. Johnson take care of her. My father was a good nurse for her, having helped his mother in the house when he was young, so she did not get too tired, but she remained weak for many months.

In a way, St. Mary's and Dr. Kinsella were an ecumenical encounter, as were the nuns who took care of my mother. One night she had what we would call a near-death experience in which she was going down a long hall, turning a corner into the light, when she heard me and my sister calling her back. The nuns understood this. Mother treasured their spiritual succor and thanked God for the fine care of Kinsella and the entire hospital. He became something of a saint in our conversation, as he was to many. He was highly regarded in the upper Midwest and an active member of the Roman Catholic community.

When Dad got back from Minnesota on March 5, midweek Lenten services were in full swing. Given the fact that the church building was still not finished, they held joint Lenten services with First Lutheran, Dad preaching one week and Ernie Nelson the next. This helped Dad a lot. The church was packed for the services throughout Lent. I can still see and smell the damp wool on the coats of the people who had braved the snow outside for the services, which were doleful and sad. In the days without deodorant, people had their own individual smells, and as I remember, these were not offensive. It was part of who they were.

Another emblem of how divided the churches were at the time was a local controversy in Rugby between the Masons and the Knights of Columbus. For some reason, the Knights of Columbus had criticized my father for being married the way Catholic priests were not. This was not surprising, given the divisions. However, things did not improve when the Masonic Lodge offered to defend Dad. While it was serious, it was like the Scylla and Charybdis of ecumenical controversies for him. At the time, the lodge question was still a hot one for Lutherans. That the ULCA allowed members, even pastors, to belong to the Masons was a bridge too far for many Norwegian American Lutherans and one of the main reasons they opposed any merger talks with the ULCA. The lodge question dominated merger questions through the 1950s. So this was a rather strange place for my father, but he stuck to his guns, as I remember, and resisted the support of the Masons, even as he was appalled at the Knights of Columbus's accusations.[26]

## More Unity Talks

Meanwhile, Lutheran Unity continued to occupy the minds of the leaders of Lutheran Churches in America. At its thirty-first annual meeting in New York, the council heard the report that it had been working on establishing home mission congregations in 106 fields. Led by Dr. Philip S. Dybvig, whose foresight as director of Home Missions in the ELC helped it to grow substantially over the next decade, the NLC was working to assign the various Lutheran churches belonging to it places for their work.[27] At this same meeting, Burntvedt, a beloved member of the group, announced along with others, including Dr. J. A. Aasgaard of the ELC and Petrus O. Bersell of the Augustana Synod, that he favored a closer unity of the Lutheran churches in the National Lutheran Council. He demurred, however, on organic union, which he thought improbable for the eight bodies, preferring instead some kind of affiliation—possibly a federation.[28]

Pierce County suffered blizzards and massive snowfall throughout the entire winter and into the spring of 1949. The snow was not the worst; rather, it was the temperatures that plummeted below thirty and made life dangerous on the farms and roads back and forth. Farmers ran out of hay and could not get out of their farms to buy more; the roads, even after being plowed, would fill up again after fierce ground blizzards, which blew blinding snow into hard drifts across the highway, even as the sky was blue and the red light of sundown began to gather over the western horizon as we drove to either Tunbridge or Berwick. The trains barely kept their schedules and commerce almost ground to a halt.

That March 6, 1949, dignitaries at Augsburg, including Burntvedt, who gave the sermon, laid the cornerstone for the new Science and Administration building, which would contain a complete laboratory, classrooms, a home economics department, prayer chapel, and administration offices. This was another step in the years of trying to get the college accredited. The most crucial building was waiting: a new library. This never escaped the work of the administration, especially Gerda Mortensen, who spent half a lifetime working to make it happen.

The last week of March 1949, Dad had evangelistic meetings in Valley City, North Dakota, while Mom, LaRhae, and I stayed in Cyrus on the farm, returning to Rugby on March 26. These weeks of meetings gave pastors time with each other; they stayed in the parsonage, which was almost always a large house with a spare bedroom exactly for this purpose. They got to know each other better and exchange gossip. One can be sure that while Dad was in Valley City, he and my uncle Don, the pastor there, had some conversations about the union talks.

## Annual Meeting in Morris, Minnesota, 1949

The 1949 annual meeting in Morris, six miles from the farm in Cyrus, gave us another chance to come to the farm and rest. Dad could attend the convention, and Mother could be taken care of by her aunt and uncle while we played with our Ronning cousins on the farm. These weeks were like paradise. We kids could play all over the farm but also help bring coffee out to our uncle cultivating the fields on his Minneapolis Moline tractor. Our aunt would pack a nice morning lunch with coffee and brownies, which we would eat with him sitting in the shade of the huge tractor wheel on the newly cultivated field.

The Morris annual meeting would be a marker for the leadership of the LFC. A proposal to "explore the possibility of creating a federation made up of the eight bodies now belonging to the National Lutheran Council" was the major issue of the convention, along with appointing three delegates to the committee of thirty-four charged with exploring the possibility of such a federation. The Conference voted to agree with the language of the Board of Organization on the central issue: "The Conference is not in favor of organic union and instructs its delegates accordingly."[29] Dr. T. O. Burntvedt, Dr. John Stensvaag, and Pastor C. J. Olson were voted as the three representatives.[30] It was clear that a federation rather than a union was preferred by the LFC. In fact, the leadership interpreted the vote as a defeat for any thoughts of organic union.

The meeting made one significant organizational change—renaming the Board of Organization to the Board of Administration. Although its duties were not terribly different from the Board of Organization, the change fit more closely with its changing responsibilities as more of a church council acting on matters between annual meetings.

These changes were described as inevitable by many, especially Burntvedt. The LFC had evolved and needed to face the reality of the day, he said. The congregation was still central, he insisted, as did others. While I can believe this, I am not so sure. Would such a fellowship, or federation, as Sverdrup had described as an organization be impossible? And what were my grandfather, great-aunts, and uncles sitting in the audience at the university building in Morris thinking as they listened to Burntvedt, Sverdrup's convictions running through their minds?

That late summer at their summer institute, the LFC pastors heard Dr. Harold A. Yochum, president of Capital University, in Columbus, Ohio, lecture on Lutheran Unity. He had been an object of some suspicion among the pastors. Consequently, I am sure his being there was an effort by Burntvedt and others to keep the issue of union before the pastors and the church by acquainting them with some of the main proponents of Lutheran merger. Meeting Yochum might assure the pastors of his goodwill. It was easier to convince people to vote for union if they had had some personal experience with those whom they might have feared or thought of in the abstract as representing ideas they might deem alien.

On September 4, 1949, the first service would be in the new Rugby church nave. It still needed furnishings and other appointments to make it ready, but for the time being, we could worship in it.

On October 23, 1949, the Lutheran Deaconess Institute and Hospital dedicated two new floors to its campus. Sister Anna Bergeland (1891–1979), who had come to Deaconess as a young woman in 1911 to study for the diaconate, was now superintendent of the hospital and director of the Deaconess Home and Institute. Fifteen deaconesses were still serving there and in the church around the world. The hospital had 367 workers, 195 nurses and nursing students, 52 doctors, and 120 others. Over the year, they had cared for nearly 8,000 patients with a revenue of $66,705, a pittance compared to what hospitals' cost today, but this was a mark of success along with the new buildings at Augsburg. Augsburg and the LFC were ready to enter the new decade with confidence and vigor.

CHAPTER 11

# A Decade of Merger Talk

THE NEW DECADE, thought of today as a quiet and stable one, began with growing concern for China and the communist takeover there. It also affected the China missions of all Christian churches, even the LFC. Lenorah Erickson (1906–1988) and Arthur Olson wrote compelling reports back home to give people a sense of what was happening there. They were establishing stations in Formosa and Hong Kong now, where they could continue to use their Chinese with the Chinese refugees who had fled mainland China. The mission in Madagascar was going well. Amos and Ovidia Dyrud and Helen Arnseth were in Paris learning French. Members of the LFC were shaken in February 1950 by news that their beloved President Burntvedt had suffered a heart attack and was recovering at Deaconess Hospital in Minneapolis. While it was said he made a full recovery, enough to lead the annual meeting in June, he was weakened by it.

That March, the headquarters of the Lutheran Free Church on 2122 Riverside were remodeled to accommodate the staff's increased work load. Their numbers, like those of every other church at the time, were increasing. They needed more space for the Board of Administration, the Board of Missions, Home Missions, Women's Missionary Federation, and the Minister's Aid Society, plus a retail store for the Messenger Press, another exciting proof of the progress and growth of the LFC.

The 1950 annual meeting, which even those with little Norwegian referred to as *Aarsmøte*, was held in Minneapolis at Trinity from June 14 to 18. Looking toward the meeting, Sverre Torgerson, the editor of *Folkebladet*, noted that the question of "our church's relationship to the proposed union of Lutherans would be discussed." One question before the convention was whether "the Lutheran Free Church would vote to rename the National Lutheran Council the National Lutheran Federation."[1]

There were 478 registered delegates: 131 pastors and 347 laity, who attended the meetings. Torgerson regretted that not more of the people in the Minneapolis area had come—they would have been edified by the quality of the speakers and the people there. All told, it was a peaceful meeting. Burntvedt addressed the question of union by admitting there was little reason to bring it up again "since last year's conference said, 'no' and there seems to have been little change of opinion."[2]

The conference did, however, approve one move toward unity by approving a motion from the National Lutheran Council to change its structure into a federation of eight Lutheran bodies.[3] Two other significant resolutions passed—one to establish a mission in Japan and the other to increase the support of inner mission and foreign missions. Lutherans were taking cognizance of the flight of many from the Midwestern farms and small towns to the West Coast, where there were better jobs. To that end, they had begun founding congregations, usually in the cities not far from the small towns where there were strong Norwegian communities and churches. The community in Silverton, Oregon, for example, helped found Central Lutheran in Salem, where my family and I would be in a few short years.

The most exciting part of the annual meeting that year occurred on Sunday, June 17, when the George Sverdrup Science building was dedicated. It had cost $575,000 and helped the process for the accreditation of Augsburg, which had been a long struggle for the school over the decades. They had to raise a final $100,000 to pay it off, which the community did with some effort.

As the delegates returned home that June, the threat of war once again began to overshadow the world when North Korea attacked South Korea on June 25, 1950. This meant a new draft and military rearmament. China and the Russians supported the North; the United States and other Western nations supported South Korea in brutal battles over the next three years. Several young men from Rugby answered their country's call. Mother taught us to pray for them in spondaic rhythm, a phrase that we still can repeat without thought—"God bless Hank and Raymond, Ted and Howard, Jerry and Ronny and Glen." I think most of them have now gone on to their eternal reward, but their names dance into our minds whenever we do our childhood prayers. Oddly enough, this war received almost no comment in *Folkebladet*.

Any Lutheran Free Church kid who paid attention to the mission in Madagascar would have known of Sister Milla Pederson (1888–1974), who retired in August 1950 with a great celebration in Nordland congregation near Paynesville, Minnesota, where she had grown up. She was an emblem of several projects of the Lutheran Free Church. She had emigrated with her parents to Nordland, which became a strong LFC congregation, in 1890 when she was two. She felt called to be a deaconess and studied at the Deaconess Institute in Minneapolis. After her consecration, she went to Madagascar, where she worked for more than thirty years. She kept the office of deaconess before the LFC for as long as she lived, even if no one was now being consecrated.

## Dedication of Bethany Church in Rugby

On October 22, 1950, a chilly but sunny day, the dedication of Bethany's new church was finally celebrated at three in the afternoon. It had been used for

# A Decade of Merger Talk

**Figure 11.1.** The newly rebuilt Bethany Church in Rugby, North Dakota. Used by permission of the Grindal family.

almost half a year before all the furniture and appointments were in place. T. O. Burntvedt came from Minneapolis for the service to dedicate the building. Carl Sivertsen Vang (1862–1958) and Rasmus Hermanson Hofstad (1881–1963), former pastors, were present. Luthard Gjerde preached the Sunday morning service. The choir sang "Built on a Rock the Church Doth Stand," and other special speeches and numbers were presented. On Saturday night, a festive banquet in the church basement was served by the Tunbridge Ladies Aid. On Sunday, a festive lunch was prepared by the Berwick Ladies Aid.

The church, built in the neo-Gothic style, was beautiful and packed for the dedication. My parents enjoyed the fact that the member most opposed to the size of the church had to sit on a chair in the back because there was no more room in the pews.

One of the issues that distressed my father before the service was that a wealthy member of the church had bought him a handsome Presbyterian-style doctoral robe, and he wondered if he could wear it. He worried what his foster father, Sjur Grindal, would have thought and whether he could in good conscience put it on. As he was fussing, Burntvedt, who was staying with us, overheard him and boomed, "Just wear it!" He did. He wore it for the rest of his ministry. After the ceremony, Burntvedt congratulated him but added, "If you are going to wear it, wear black pants, shoes, and socks!" Ever afterward, he did. Burntvedt enjoyed staying with us and was especially kind to me. His letter of thanks to my folks was warm and fatherly, advising them to find time for a brief vacation or to take a long trip out West to see the family.[4]

The day after the festivities, on Monday, October 23, the district WMF held its annual meeting in the new church. Sister Milla, a favorite of the women, spoke. That afternoon, the congregation hosted the stewardship secretaries of the district, including an address by Burntvedt. He was well known by the laity throughout the church and was an eloquent preacher in both English and Norwegian, so people came out to hear him.

Grandpa Theodore Tinseth died on October 13 in Valley City, just before the dedication. The funeral was held on November 2 in Cyrus. Burntvedt knew Grandpa and sent a lovely letter to the family remembering him and his dedication to the Lord and the church. Torgerson, who had been his pastor for twelve years, noted in his obituary in the *Lutheran Messenger* that he was "an Israelite indeed in whom there was no guile," a loving father, a faithful friend, and a loyal member of his congregation.[5] One of the pleasures and possibilities in a small church was that the leadership knew many laity in the congregations and kept in touch with them.

## The LFC'S Peculiar Organization and Merger

In November, Torgerson reported on the state of Lutherans in the United States and their cooperation. For those who did not know or had forgotten, he explained the forming of the American Lutheran Conference in 1930. It involved five American Lutheran churches—the Augustana Lutheran Church with Swedish roots; the American Lutheran Church of German origin, centered in Ohio, Iowa, and Texas; the United Evangelical Lutheran Church, with a background from the "sad" or pietistic Danes centered in Blair, Nebraska; the Evangelical Lutheran Church with Norwegian roots; and the LFC. Before the National Lutheran Council, he opined, each church had lived more for itself than for others and not come to know each other well. The American Lutheran Conference, however, had given the participants much more contact with each other as they became familiar with the other traditions.[6] In fact, he believed that their joint work helped make possible the goal of organic union among these five. It had been its main goal all through its existence.[7]

Now, three of the churches had voted to merge: the ALC, ELC, and UELC. Augustana and the LFC had not come to the same conclusion. Augustana, although it fit with the Danes and Norwegians in some respects, finally found a relationship with the "happy", or *Grundtvigian*, Danes (AELC), Germans (ULCA), and Finns (Suomi Synod) in what would become the LCA. The

# A Decade of Merger Talk 407

Conference met again on November 8–10 in Sioux Falls, and Torgerson attended. There he heard Dr. Christensen give an eloquent and powerful lecture on American Lutherans seen in the context of the ongoing revival in America. Lawrence Melvin Stavig (1899–1982), sainted president of Augustana College in Sioux Falls, spoke, as did Fredrick Axel Schiotz (1901–1989), who gave a "gripping lecture" on "the hour of destiny (*skjæbnetime*)" that had arrived for Lutheran missionary work.[8]

Torgerson was especially interested in what Burntvedt had to say about the position of the LFC concerning the proposed merger since it had been the only Lutheran Church to vote against an organic merger at the previous LFC annual meeting. In a way, Burntvedt was explaining the peculiar characteristics of the LFC to the others. He argued that the LFC had always participated with other Lutheran churches in their work. If others thought we wanted to live isolated from the other Lutherans, it was our own fault, he feared. We had thought more of ourselves than perhaps we should have and not given a satisfactory explanation to others, he confessed. He then named several reasons the LFC was especially suspicious of a union: (1) that the preaching and practices of some only emphasized getting people to join the church without leading them to a saving faith in Christ; (2) we were afraid that the work of laymen, as we understood it, would be hindered; (3) we preferred a simple ritual during regular worship. Because we believed that there was enough agreement in our synods that had adopted the unaltered Augsburg Confession and the *Small Catechism*, we were not interested in disputations on lesser issues.[9]

Burntvedt then went on to explain the political situation in the LFC: some did not believe that one Lutheran Church was the pearl of great price that we must give our all to buy. He believed there were three groups in the LFC with different positions on the merger: a small group in favor of merger, another small group "absolutely" against the merger, and between these two, a larger group that was more undecided. Burntvedt thought that now more were in favor than had been at the previous conference in Morris but said "organic union is not a burning question in our church."[10] Torgerson then proposed that the LFC nominate a committee to negotiate with the three churches that had voted to merge. This was not, he quickly added, to pursue merger but so that we were not isolated from the rushing stream toward merger in the Lutheran churches in America.[11]

This move is one that many those wary of merger or any other controversial question understood. Those in power kept assuring their followers that these were just discussions, and nothing could be done until the group voted on the question before them. But by then, with all the time and expense of these talks, the change at hand seems inevitable. I wonder sometimes if these talks were a desperate attempt on the part of the leaders to make sure something of Augsburg or the LFC survived into the future. Merton Strommen once told my folks that we needed to merge because we had lived in sin with the ELC so long that we needed to marry to make honest persons of ourselves and, especially, to save Augsburg. That argument made sense to us, on the one hand, but was it true? Hindsight might agree that it was true, but there are arguments made by some, like historian Mark Granquist, that there could have been many other ways to unify the various Lutheran churches without organic mergers.[12]

## Luther League Conventions

Life went on in the congregation as the LFC began to flourish, along with most other Christian churches, after the war. For LFC youths, the most exciting event of the year was the Annual Youth Convention sponsored by the Luther League and led by Merton Peter Strommen (1919–2019), one of the more charismatic LFC leaders. The group usually met at Mission Farms in Medicine Lake Bible Camp at the western edge of Minneapolis. Once again, the accommodations were primitive and the mosquitos unbearable, but at the time, people did not demand the kind of luxury we expect today. As I recall, there would be about 700–1,000 Luther Leaguers gathered there, and they would be challenged to live for Jesus during the nightly services. In addition, they made a choir of 700, which my father sometimes directed. He loved especially "Praise to the Lord, the Almighty the King of Creation." When they got to the last line, "Let the

Figure 11.2. Merton Strommen (1919–2019). Used by permission of Augsburg Fortress Publishers.

**Figure 11.3.** Rugby youth at a Luther League Convention. Used by permission of the Grindal family.

Amen!" He would have them hold that for a bit longer than written. Another favorite was "living for Jesus, a life that is true, striving to please him all that I do." The bracing challenge to live for Jesus and "striving to please him" made the Christian life an exciting adventure that young people responded to.

In Rugby that summer, my parents brought many kids from the Luther League and the family Luther Leagues (*Ungdomsforeningen*) in the country churches. They managed to win the prize for the most delegates from a congregation. I remember the cramped blue DeSoto coupe in which we rode down to the Twin Cities. Three teenagers were crammed into the back seat, LaRhae and I exchanging places on their laps.

Strommen, who had a PhD in sociology and learned about the looming generation gap from people like Margaret Mead, taught the kids that they needed to be apart from their parents in the family Luther Leagues and learn by themselves to be modern. This irritated my mother, especially who saw immediately what it would do to the wonderful Sunday evenings we gathered for in Berwick and Tunbridge when there would be a program centered on evangelizing the young, after which everyone retired to the basement for egg coffee, chocolate cake, and dill pickles while the teenagers found each other.

She was right, and years later, Merton talked about how damaging the notion of the generation gap had been to families in the church. He also noted that it was done based on Mead's faulty scholarship, something he later tried, vainly, to expose. It would be followed in the merged church with *Called to Be Human*, a new book for adolescents during their discovery of sex and their own bodies. Mother found that to be insufferable as well, telling a joke about a woman from the parish calling headquarters to complain: "Hello! Is dis de yout department? I'm calling to complain about *Called to Be Human*. If Yesus knew about vat you were doing, he would turn over in his grave!"[13]

## The Church Builds New Buildings and Talks Merger

As the years turned, the church papers were filled with news of new churches being built, replacing the old wooden frames with more substantial brick edifices; new congregations being started, especially in the West; and anniversaries, plus obituaries, of pioneer pastors and laypeople. To its credit, *Folkebladet* included obituaries of prominent laypeople in the fellowship, proving that its commitment to the laity was true.

As the 1951 annual meeting in Seattle grew nearer, church publications were preparing their readers for the event. Since it was so far away, people were fearful that not so many would attend the meeting, either because of the distance or because of the increasing age of many of the usual delegates and their illnesses. *Folkebladet* urged people to pray for the meeting, that it would do God's will. The April 17, 1951, *Lutheran Messenger* noted several issues that would be dealt with in Seattle: pensions for pastors, church union, united missions advance, and finances, especially at Augsburg, which was once again facing a financial crisis. The union issue was the main reason we packed up to go to the meeting, although it was time to visit Dad's father, Svein Kivley, on his farm in Ferndale, and his foster mother, Anna Grindal, now living in the LFC Bethany Homes in Everett. That made the trip a family tour as well.

After the ALC, ELC, and UELC voted to merge with each other, they had asked Swedish Augustana and the LFC to come along with them. The LFC delegation to the committee of 34—the joint committee of the merging churches—consisted of President Dr. T. O. Burntvedt, Vice President Dr. John Stensvaag, and Pastor Christian G. Olson, who were chosen by the 1949 annual convention. Now they had met as observers at the April 17 meeting in Chicago. On their return, they issued a report from that meeting, recommending that the annual meeting choose a committee of nine members to negotiate on behalf of the LFC with the four other churches on the question. Torgerson was clear that choosing these members did not mean the LFC had decided to merge with these four churches: "It meant only that we are willing to negotiate a plan for merger. If they were unanimous on the idea of merger, they would form a plan for their respective churches which would have the freedom to accept or refuse the plan."[14]

Torgerson hoped that the members of the church would "think, talk and write" about this question. He trusted that the members of the LFC would try to bring forward the principles of the church and defend them: "Here we need faith, patience, foresight and wisdom from God to find the right way for our future work."[15] Burntvedt, however, had told the *Lutheran Messenger* in May that it would "be an unhappy day for me should I live to see ... the four bodies in the American Lutheran Conference ... united without the Lutheran Free Church. I would also regret if the three-way merger was consummated with my church left outside of it."[16]

I cannot remember if anyone talked about this as a typical strategy to wear down resistance to an idea, arguing that the work of the nine would not be to approve merger but only to make a proposal that could be turned down later. Once again, it was coming up, despite the very strong vote at Morris in 1949, and just as it would for the next few years. Every time it lost, the losers would reconnoiter and bring it back, even changing the voting rules of the LFC to get it passed.

## The Annual Meeting in Seattle, 1951

We left on June 4 for Belle Fourche and points southwest. We would take the southern route through Colorado and up to Seattle. Thus, we could see more of the United States, something that, even before the interstate highway system proposed by Dwight Eisenhower, was a common ritual in the early '50s. As we saw the marvels of Colorado, the Mormon Tabernacle in Salt Lake, the mountains in Idaho and Washington, I soaked up talk from my parents on the issues at hand. I thought of them as heroes for standing up for what they had been taught to believe. When we got to Ferndale, they left us with my father's half sisters, who were preparing for the wedding of the youngest, Myrtle. We enjoyed our grandfather's garden and his goats—they scared us a bit—but it was fun meeting our many cousins and playing on Grandpa's farm in the unusually sunny weather for western Washington.

Meanwhile, my parents were in Seattle at Bethany Lutheran, the host church. The pastor was Lester Dahlen (1917–2012), one of my father's classmates in seminary. His wife, Marion, was also a good friend of my mother. While they were busy, the reunion aspect of the convention made it what it always had been: a joyful celebration of our common faith, heritage, and fellowship.

At the opening meeting of the church, Burntvedt was reelected president for his tenth term along with Clarence J. Carlsen as vice president. On the agenda was approving money for the National Lutheran Council and the Lutheran World Action committee resolutions, plus hearing reports from other committees such as the schools and missions. The main issue, voting to appoint a committee to "explore the possibilities of union with the other member bodies of the American Lutheran Conference," passed. The vote passed into my memory as though I were there. In my mind, I saw my father standing alone in the balcony to vote for all the family, dead and alive, with the elderly Carl Vang. My family legend had it they were the two opponents. History, however, records a different number—some 80 opposed it, with 238 in favor. But in my childish mind, I remember the silhouette of my father in his clergy tails standing up for what our family had believed and fought for over the past seventy-five years. I may not even have been there, but that is the image I will have until my dying day.

While we played together with our cousins on the farm and attended my aunt Myrtle's wedding to Morris Larsen, the business of the annual meeting continued. The Committee on Relations (COR) with Other Lutheran Bodies was elected as well, including President T. O. Burntvedt, President of Augsburg B. M. Christensen, Vice President John Stensvaag, Pastor Clarence Carlsen; Pastor Christian Olson of Willmar; Oak Grove president Clarence Larson; and laymen George Michaelsen of Minneapolis, Ole O. Aune (1890-1965) of Underwood, Minnesota, and Gil Berg of Seattle. Stensvaag was the most openly suspicious of the merger; Michaelsen, a nephew of Sverdrup, was thought by the constituency to oppose merger, given his heritage, although he became a strong proponent. The title of the committee became, in common parlance, the COR and would play a key role in negotiations until the merger.

As we drove home from Seattle, things felt uncertain. We knew each one of the representatives personally and what they were for or against. Given both Burntvedt's and Christensen's strong stand for the union, our only hopes were Clarence J. Carlsen and John Stensvaag, both of whom had misgivings about the idea of union, especially Carlsen.

When the group of forty-five from the merging churches met, they decided to break up into two committees, which would have three representatives from each church body. The first would be the Committee on Doctrine (COD), to which Burntvedt appointed Christensen, Carlsen, and Christian G. Olson. The second, on Church Life, Worship and Practices, was where Stensvaag, Michaelsen, and Burntvedt served. They would write one document known as "The United Testimony on Faith and Life." After some revision, they presented it to the Joint Union Committee in February 1952.

While the participants, and especially the LFC, had insisted that the five churches were essentially in agreement on doctrine, the first part of the document, "Concerning Faith," lined out the agreement of all the participating churches on God, the atonement, the means of grace, justification, sanctification, and the church. The second, "Concerning Life and Practice," dealt with (1) liturgical trends, (2) lay activities in the church, (3) the elements in the Lord's Supper, (4) Christian liberty, (5) evangelism, and (6) spiritual fellowship.[17] The Joint Union Committee acknowledged that because of various ethnic differences and traditions, each body had developed "certain distinctive forms of church life and practice."[18] The LFC representatives were especially concerned about the statements on lay activity, which had some restrictions with which they did not feel comfortable, and on evangelism.

Free Church pastors were concerned about the place of evangelism in a new church. It did not seem to be as high on the list of their fellow Lutherans as it was for them. A week of evangelistic meetings in both fall and early spring seemed to have been the rule for these meetings in most Norwegian American congregations, both ELC and LFC, at the time. Dad appeared at a week of meetings in Brockton, Montana, on the week of July 13, 1952, and at the regional Luther League Convention in Minot. On November 3, he braved a blinding blizzard with the family and another couple so he could preach at special meetings in Hoffman, Minnesota, for a week. Merging with churches that did not share our fundamental belief in evangelism as the center of the congregation did not appeal to many LFC pastors and laity for that reason alone.

Despite these criticisms, the COR forwarded the Testimony to the annual meeting to approve without committing the church to organic union. The cautionary language indicates that the COR well knew that the church body was still not ready to commit to the goal of organic union. For one, the future of Augsburg had not yet been negotiated, and its future was one of, if not the main, concerns of those proposing the union as well of those opposing it. Repeatedly, the importance of merger to save Augsburg had been used by those pushing for merger. They foresaw a time when the small church body could not support the school and wanted a merger so that Augsburg could benefit from its connection to the large number of Lutheran students unaffiliated with the LFC living in the cities. They believed it could be saved from constant financial emergencies under the aegis of the larger church body. To be fair, it had always met the need with heroic efforts but just barely. That reason alone became a cry that even my parents could not resist. Augsburg must be saved. In a way, it would also lift the burden of Free Church people and congregation always having to rescue Augsburg from extinction.

We came home from the West Coast ready for Bible Camp at Metigoshe again, on June 25, after a time in Cyrus. Just after we got there, Mrs. Lewis Hagen, a sainted member of the congregation in Rugby, had died, and Dad returned for funeral, coming back the next day, something we understood even though it took him from us for a day. This was what a good pastor did.

## Lake Metigoshe Bible Camp

The Rugby district sponsored a Bible camp at Lake Metigoshe for LFC kids in the northern parishes in North Dakota. Bible camps were flourishing at this time in the upper Midwest. The leadership of the LFC agreed that a good system of Bible camps helped in the recruitment of future pastors and church workers, so they gladly appeared at the camps to speak and help recruitment of students for their schools and the ministry.

Metigoshe was an old army camp with barracks: a long room with bunk beds to house the girls, with the pastors' wives serving as chaperones, and a similar long room for the boys, with the pastors chaperoning them. The boys took special pleasure in keeping the pastors awake. The accommodations were barely habitable, but every summer, the pastors would pack kids into their cars or even the bed of a truck and drive over the dusty roads through the Turtle Mountains to Lake Metigoshe. For true North Dakota kids, the hills and curves in the mountains were enough to make them car sick. They would hang out the back of the truck and throw up onto the dusty gravel roads as the truck rumbled over the highway to Metigoshe camp.

The food also left something to be desired. District President Bretheim, in charge of the camp and the kitchen, kept things close to the bone. One of the less appetizing entrées was a cabbage and macaroni hotdish. As the kids were gagging it down, Mrs. Hilda Bretheim would announce that it was a way to save money: "He does it for the district!" What it did do was make the kids eager to spend their small allowances at the canteen—Babe Ruth, Mars, Snickers, and Butterfinger candy bars became their caloric salvation.

One year I remember that B. M. Christensen was the main speaker for a week. On his way to the camp, he stopped in Rugby for dinner with us. The hierarchy had marked my mother as a good cook and would happily eat there, telling her she was among the best, something they must have said to many LFC pastor's wives because I have heard it from other pastors' kids. At dinner, he looked at me (named for his wife), put two fingers under his elbow, and said, "Gracia, what is this?" I didn't know. "Two crooks holding up a joint," he said to our great merriment.

The sanitary conditions at the camp also left much to be desired. It was clear in our world that the LFC congregations and facilities were always poorer than those of the ELC. Mother was convinced that Dad had gotten yellow jaundice from the poorly washed dishes there. The lack of resources caused by the Depression and war also was evident in the accommodations. The older pastors, many of whom had barely survived the Depression, at who knows what cost, watched closely over any excesses. A favorite story: one night at the campfire, as a preacher was closing the deal, as they called it, he suggested that each camper who wanted to signify their commitment to Jesus put a log on the campfire. A conflagration began to develop, and from the back, the voice of Pastor Ingvald Norum boomed, "Yust a minute, ve can't vaste all that vood! It has to last until Friday!"

Life in the parsonage flourished. Despite the war in Korea, things were better and better on the farm and in the congregations. Farmers left us gifts of meat in our locker downtown, and we got milk and cream enough to make butter with the churn we bought. As one farmer's wife, who would bring a pickup truck loaded with food and newly embroidered aprons and towels to us, would say, "If you don't take it, the pigs will!"

## More Merger Talks

On January 23–27, 1952, all eight of the Lutheran bodies in the National Lutheran Council met in the Twin Cities for a meeting to discuss evangelism. The theme was "Share Christ Today." Torgerson praised the meetings for their spiritual power and the strong spiritual sword that "cleft soul and spirit, bone and marrow, judging the hearts thoughts and council."[19] He had heard only one critical voice, while the others seemed interested "in winning souls for Christ, in the home, congregation, at work, and influence to reach out to everyone with the gospel."[20] This report spoke to many anxieties of Free Church people about the merger, and Torgerson tried to allay their fears.

## Annual Meeting of 1952

In preparation for the annual meeting of 1952, Torgerson wrote an editorial in *Folkebladet* commending the United Testimony of the Joint Committee to the LFC. He thought it was deeply influenced by Scandinavian Lutheran pietism and that it should make the LFC happy. But the questions about schools and missions, publishing houses, institutions of mercy, and the like would be more difficult to manage, he supposed. The sticking point for the LFC, however, was whether it should continue in the conversations. If we were not interested, we should withdraw; it would be unfair to continue working on the new church organization if we had no interest in being part of it. He had been somewhat surprised by the lack of arguments in the papers. He thought that was too bad since believers should be active in prayer both before and during the annual meeting. For either side, it would be difficult if the vote went against their deepest feelings.[21]

The annual meeting that year was in Fargo at Pontoppidan and Oak Grove. We were staying in the dormitory there, and I followed along a little. I had a little money and walked downtown to Fargo's business district and made it back to the church. I told my father, who had been frantic to find me, that I had simply followed the cross on the steeple of the church to keep my bearings, becoming an illustration for many a sermon later!

The convention was to consider a recommendation from its representatives to the JUC to continue talks. In its report, it noted, "Our studies and conversations thus far ... have not brought to light anything which has clearly convinced us that union of the American Lutheran Conference bodies is undesirable or impracticable."[22]

The vote on the United Testimony of Faith and Life was approved at the conference by a huge margin, 383 for and 12 against. The conversation had been lengthy and thoughtful, Torgerson wrote. Although many were very much in favor, there were others who feared that the LFC would lose the principles it had fought for over the years. The decision to go on, once again, was not a decision to merge, he noted, which may account for the low vote opposing it. The LFC could with a good conscience still vote against the proposal. In fact, the representatives felt that the LFC "is not ready to commit itself as definitely to union as the adoption of the suggested motions would involve."[23] Other than that conversation, the meeting was remarkably good, Torgerson thought. The schools and missions' funds were up—the convention even voted to significantly increase the money for home missions from fifty-five thousand dollars to seventy thousand, and the congregations had contributed thirty-eight thousand dollars more than they had the year before.[24]

For me, the phrase *schools and missions* evokes memories of driving with my father and mother across the prairies, following the two tracks of a road to a farm far away from highways. It was always after harvest, so I can see the golden fields of stubble stretching out across the prairie under an endless blue sky, with the wind, as usual, howling around us. The folks would argue about which road to take when we approached a fork in the road. Mother would usually be right. We would then take off at her recommendation, and soon, over a small hill, a farmhouse with the laundry blowing on the clotheslines would appear—since we usually went on Mondays, laundry day—with the farm wife running out of the house, drying her hands on her apron. We would then be invited in for coffee, which meant at least cookies. Usually this would be our third or fourth coffee of the day, and Mother would say, "Gracia, if they ask if you would like some food, say no. If you don't, I will spank you. I can't eat another thing!" It was futile, however. We all had to go into the parlor of the home and wait to be served. My father always said he got more money when the family came along, so we obliged. There was suspicion, as I have said, of supporting schools and missions in Minnesota and not North Dakota, so Oak Grove did better than Augsburg. This was a yearly pilgrimage and necessity for the church—to have its pastors gather money from small donors in their congregations to keep the schools and missions going. Always Augsburg and Oak Grove, and always Madagascar, with which the people were well acquainted because they had met Sister Milla, the Caleb Quanbecks, or Melvin Rossings. The leaders all knew, as did the pastors, that it was these small gifts that kept things going.

The ladies' aids always had the most money. Although they had, by constitution and tradition, always supported the local congregation and its local needs, they would also, by tradition, gather money for the schools and missions of the wider fellowship. Every pastor knew that, as did the leaders of the churches. Dad would always push on the theme of sharing with the wider church. Most of the time, they had enough money to give to the larger mission of the LFC. One ladies' aid treasurer told him, when he asked for money from the aid's treasury, that she would give him fifty dollars, but she was "sitting on the rest."

## Folkebladet Ends Its Work

One sad, but inevitable, announcement in 1952 was that the Norwegian-language *Folkebladet*, which had been central to the work of the LFC over seventy-four years, would end its work in the next issue. It was not surprising, given the ebbing of Norwegian among Norwegian Americans, but interesting to note that it had had enough readers until then to support its publication. Caspersen, in a final column, wrote that it had begun as a monthly in 1877 and became a weekly in 1880, which remained until 1945. At first, it had been a typical, large four-page newspaper, but in about 1915, it had taken the smaller form of regular-sized pages, which it had until its ending, each issue about thirty-two pages. The last fifteen years, it changed to sixteen pages published every other week. It had had 5,000 subscribers for some time but went down to 4,000 when the Depression hit. During that decade, it stabilized at 3,500 and remained there almost until its end. It was the oldest remaining Norwegian American newspaper except for *Decorah Posten*. Its first editor, Sven Oftedal, started it to pay off the crushing Augsburg debt. Caspersen had edited it for twenty-five years, from 1922 to 1947. He noted that the main theme of the paper throughout its history had been the freedom of the congregation, with temperance coming next. He had more to say about its importance in the conversation.[25] People like Gerda Mortensen and my father said they learned their Norwegian reading it and were glad for that.

The last issue contained letters from Bernard Christensen and Abner Batalden in Norwegian. Christensen marked the close-knit relationship between Augsburg and *Folkebladet*. The way the paper watched over, criticized, and championed the school had been the reason for its existence over the seventy-five years it was printed. It was the appropriate thing to say.

**Figure 11.4.** A Luther League Convention at Medicine Lake. Used by permission of Augsburg Fortress Publishers.

## Life in the Rugby Parish

Life in the Rugby parsonage continued as usual with the round of festivities during the Christmas season, Lenten midweek services, and Good Friday services in Norwegian at Bethany—its only Norwegian service, unlike the country churches, and especially Tunbridge, where Norwegian was used at least half of the time. We would see the old women in black coats with canes walking slowly toward the services as we played outside in the barely snow-free yards, knowing that more blizzards could blow out of the west and bring us back to January.

That summer, in July 1952, Dr. Kristofer Hagen, missionary to the Santal, spoke at Tunbridge, showing his slides and other Indian artifacts. My folks, who had gone to school with him, admired his brilliance as a medical doctor, professor of psychology, and pastor. Mother made a delicious dinner for the family, which I remember still. The Santal Mission was dear to the heart of many in our family. My grandmother Anna supported it, as did my aunt Borghild, befriending until her death a Santal native who lived in Fargo. Lars Olsen Skrefsrud's story of being jailed for a crime, his learning of many languages, had made a huge impact on Norwegian Americans. Hagen would also speak at the regular Pastors' Institute at Augsburg on August 26–29. When my grandmother died, her Grindal's Bible had a recent issue of *Santalmissionæren*, the Santal missionary paper, in it. She had marked a story about a woman who had borne a child, like Sarah had, in her old age. Knowing how much she had wanted to have children, and couldn't, brought tears to my eyes.

At the end of August, soon after the Hagens' visit, the Luther League Convention met again at Mission Farms, Medicine Lake, as it had traditionally done over the years. T. O. Burntvedt gave the key address. He, his wife, and Merton Strommen were just back from the LWF meeting in Hannover, Germany, July 25–August 3, along with several Luther Leaguers who had also attended. They gave their reports. The convention featured food from "the Orient" to stress world missions. Leland Sateren led the convention choir and

Bill Robbins the convention band. Paul G. Sonnack preached, marking a new voice in these events.

## International Ecumenical Meetings

The World Council of Churches' Faith and Order Conference had met in Lund, Sweden, during August. The *Minneapolis Star* featured an article by the venerable Willmar Thorkelson on the progress of the ecumenical age. Winfred E. Garrison, an editor of the *Christian Century* and professor of church history at the University of Houston, had cabled his excitement that the Christian church "has advanced another stage on the road to unity."[26] While none of the dividing lines between communions had been broken down, he said, "the mood and temper in which discussions are carried on and which even disagreements are stated" had changed.[27] He repeated the growing conviction of many stalwarts in the ecumenical movement that there was "a conviction of the sin of division." This argument became a shibboleth that made opposing merger for any reason a sin. Our divisions revealed the "scandal" of the Christian church rather than its rich diversity. To its credit, the weight of opinion in the LFC was to the effect that we are already one in faith, although institutional unity was quite another issue involving lots of real estate and traditions.

## National and Church Politics

The Korean War became a drain on life in America. In 1952, Dwight David Eisenhower (1890–1969) ran for president as a Republican against Adlai Stevenson. Eisenhower's military career made him seem more attractive to those who were war-weary, and he was elected as president with the promise that he would deal with the issue. I remember washing our car with my father, listening to the car radio crackling with news of the Republican convention in Chicago and the fight between Robert Taft (1889–1953) and Eisenhower's supporters. Eisenhower barely won the nomination. My parents, raised to be stanch Republicans, were on the side of Taft but gladly supported Ike and his pledge to end the war in Korea. Adlai was attractive to intellectuals, already on the left, but appealed little to the people in our sphere, most of them conservative Republicans—small businessmen and farmers. Stevenson's divorce was also a major issue with them: How could a man who was unable to handle small issues like his marriage effectively run the federal government? To everyone's surprise, Eisenhower won by a landslide, 442 electoral votes from 39 states with 6 million more votes than Adlai. His plan to build an interstate highway system would not go into effect until the Federal Highway Act of 1956. It had consequences for the entire country, and, significantly, the little world of the LFC.

LFC pastors were watching the next moves of the COR carefully as the LFC leadership gradually moved toward good relations with the larger group. On November 19, 1952, the Joint Union Committee met in Minneapolis. It invited the LFC to participate "in order to be fully informed and thus prepared to lead their church body in arriving at an ultimate, and, we hope, favorable decision."[28] During this meeting, the Augustana Lutheran Church withdrew from the negotiations. Ultimately, this was not a surprise. The ALC, ELC, and UELC had passed a resolution in each of their bodies to some extent forcing this. It said that they were "without authority to include in their negotiations Lutheran bodies outside the American Lutheran Conference."[29] Augustana had passed a resolution at its 1951 synodical convention, saying it was not open to efforts to "continue unity discussion that were not open to all Lutheran church bodies, and which did not include considerations of the problem of ecumenical relations."[30] I presume suspicion of the ULCA's liberal policies on the lodge and other opinions were behind this.

When the Joint Union Committee met in March of 1953 in Chicago, it focused on polity and organizational schemes for the new church. A memorandum on making the LFC a nongeographical synod or district intrigued them. Offered by the LFC contingent, it argued, "There is need for a variety of patterns of organization if the varying needs of today's Lutheran church are to be adequately met and the roots of the past not completely severed."[31] It was a creative solution, maybe, to a political reality but not one the leaders ultimately could support. The corporate world was now pursuing mergers for efficiency and progress. Most members of the churches could not imagine such a clumsy or an illogical organization. Even though the idea was seriously entertained at all levels, it would not win the day.

## The 1953 Annual Meeting of the LFC

When the 1953 annual meeting was convened on June 10 at Trinity Lutheran in Minneapolis, Dr. Paul Empie of the National Lutheran Council was there to report on its work. By then the LFC numbered sixty thousand in three hundred congregations. Burntvedt expected the count would continue to increase. In his opening address, he noted that the cry for justice throughout the world should be listened to. Burntvedt admonished them to remember that "the idea of freedom, justice and equality responsible for the current unrest in the world were sown by the preaching of the Gospel and its moral and social implications."[32] Ultimately, he concluded, it was the only way to defeat the red tide of communism. He praised the Eisenhower administration for its "wholesome signs of respect for God, His revealed moral law and His operations in human history."[33]

## A Decade of Merger Talk

The LFC members of the Joint Union Committee presented the memorandum to the gathering, proposing the LFC become a nongeographical conference or district in the merged church. It required no action by the convention. Its reason for being was to make the members of the church body aware that the committee was continuing "to safeguard the fundamental principle of our church in the ongoing discussion."[34] The hope was that the proposal would be studied throughout the fellowship at local and district meetings over the next year. The proposal would allow LFC congregations to still identify as LFC and support Augsburg and Oak Grove but in all other ways participate in the merger. Fevold noted that this was a way the LFC could "combine the concepts of federation, which the LFC already favored, and organic union."[35] To some extent, this was like the English district of the Missouri Synod but more complicated in that it would leave jurisdiction over the two schools to the old LFC members. This would have been unaffordable to the smaller constituency and probably unattractive to Augsburg's faculty and students not from the LFC.

At its October 1953 meeting in Chicago, the Joint Union Committee of the merging churches discussed this idea at some length. They remained eager to find some way to have the LFC merge with the larger body in the same kind of agreement as the others but also realized that they might have to consider other ways to appease some of the LFC's fears. They knew representatives from the LFC might be willing to make a deal, but the issue was having the agreement approved at the annual convention of each church body. The LFC annual meeting was different from most others, and leaders knew a determined faction could organize a large group to come to the convention and vote down any proposal it did not like. This made the negotiations at this time rather ticklish.

On December 7–8, the Joint Union Committee adopted the Committee on Polity and Organization Committee's plan for an organization of the new church, often called the "Blueprint." The LFC Committee on Relations studied the document thoroughly and abandoned the idea of a nongeographical synod. They felt assured that LFC principles having to do with the freedom of the congregation and its rights were sufficient, so they, with the dissenting vote of Clarence J. Carlsen, voted to send the Blueprint on to the next annual meeting. They added several stipulations called "Modifying Agreements" that dealt with the place of Augsburg College and Seminary and other LFC institutions. In place of a nongeographic synod, they proposed an Augsburg Association consisting of LFC congregations that would have the authority to name the Board of Regents as they always had.

On December 16, 1953, my brother, Harald Theodore Grindal, was born in the Rugby hospital. It was a joyful day and Christmas season. Mother took the usual week in the hospital that was expected, a luxury afforded all new mothers then. When she came home on Little Christmas Eve, on December 23, she was greeted by a dining room table stacked with good wishes for the new baby and his family, piles of cookies, and shower gifts for the baby. Weak from the birth, she burst into tears. Having to sort and put it all away was too much for her at the time. Regardless, she summoned up the strength, which she always did, to cook the traditional Christmas Eve dinner from her own childhood: roast spareribs, lutefisk, *lefse*, mashed potatoes and rutabagas, sweet soup, *julekake* (Christmas bread), and mincemeat pie, the only concession to the American menu. With the new baby, we had a real crèche in the house and thoroughly enjoyed it.

## The Plan of the Joint Union Committee

Meanwhile, on December 22, 1953, the *Lutheran Messenger* published the plan of the Joint Union Committee for a merged church. This raised the eyebrows of many. Clemmence E. Dyrud, pastor in Silvana, Washington, wrote a letter to the editor with a response. He noted two issues. First, there was the question of membership in the World Council of Churches. Since two of the merging churches belonged to the WCC, he feared that discussion of the WCC would be damped down and kept on the back burner until after the merger, at which point membership would happen without question. Second, he responded to John Stensvaag's report on the schools, noting that the seminary would be owned and under the control of the new church, while the colleges would be owned by either the church or their own corporations. He mused that this was a strange turn of events: to give freedom to the colleges but not the theological seminaries. "We need a great deal of frank discussion before the next Annual Conference," he concluded.[36]

Conversations on these ideas and proposals were swirling around the church body. Torgerson, as editor of the *Lutheran Messenger*, felt emboldened to publish an editorial from the *Lutheran Herald*, the paper of the ELC, concerning the congregation, lauding it for pretty much agreeing with the LFC. First, it believed in the "supremacy" of the congregation, or its divine origin. This was in line with the LFC's first principle that according to Scripture, the congregation is the right form of the kingdom of God on earth. Torgerson thought that was rather stunning and hoped it would quell many voices against the merger.

P. A. Strommen, a crusty old LFC pastor, submitted an article by Alvin Rogness, ELC pastor in Mason City, Iowa, to the *Lutheran Messenger* titled "Lutherans Are United." In it, Rogness argued that there was a great difference between unity and union. Lutherans were one in faith and had been since the beginning. Appealing to the liberty of the Christian as found in Scripture, he developed his argument that diversity is not disunity. He got at the problem of the thesis, that having unity meant we must unite in one organization. Just because two "hardware dealers are agreed in their business principles, if they like to golf and fish together, if they belong to the same church and the same political party, does their unitedness mean that they ought to sell out their two stores and form one."[37] This question takes apart the idea that Jesus in John 17 was praying for the merger of the ELC and LFC in 1960 when he prayed that we might be one, always the theme at merger conventions!

By December 8, 1953, the Joint Union Committee had its proposal ready to be sent to the various church conventions in the summer of 1954. To prepare the congregations for the LFC annual meeting, John Stensvaag, vice president of the LFC and someone who had been somewhat tentative about the idea, wrote a "Preface to the Union Report." In it, he outlined the issues before the church. He reported that the larger group had asked for the LFC contingent to gather on January 4–5 to discuss the whole process as it applied to the LFC. They listed four options they could recommend:

1. Acceptance of the report without qualifications.
2. Acceptance of the report with some important stipulations.
3. Union with the other bodies as a nongeographical district.
4. Withdraw from the negotiations.[38]

The LFC contingent had decided on option 2. After exploring the idea of a non-geographical district, the problems with it seemed insurmountable and would "result in the slow death to the LFC and her institutions."[39] Stensvaag had come to the conviction that the real question was "How may the LFC fulfill its God given mission?" He and the members of the committee, he reported, had concluded that the LFC might contribute its beliefs about living congregations to the larger body. He and others had decided that in the long run, the merger would, ultimately, be a real blessing to all the congregations in the LFC. With that, the committee recommended the 1954 convention not vote on the proposal but rather suggest to the congregations a year of prayerful study.[40]

## Mission Conferences and Church Life

Epiphany was the regular time for Lutherans to focus on mission work around the world. Every January that I remember in the 1950s, we hosted missionaries, who stayed with us and kept us and the congregation intimately aware of the work they were doing, their lives, and the native people who had become Christians. That January, we had our usual mission conference, with Lenorah Erickson and my uncle Morris Werdal speaking. He was the husband of Dad's half sister Marion. Morris had been born in China to Lutheran Brethren missionaries. His intrepid mother had lost a foot in a mowing accident on the farm as a young girl—but despite a refusal from the Lutheran Brethren Mission committee to support her, she found funding and went on her own to China, where she met and married Werdal. They showed great heroism in their fight against Mao and the Reds. When they could no longer minister in China, many missionaries, like Morris and Marion, moved to Japan and served there for the rest of their lives. Lenorah, on furlough that year, went to Hong Kong and Taiwan to continue her work among the Chinese. She was a compelling teacher and, as she lived with us, taught me several Chinese characters.

That year, we had a lot of time to be with them at home since the temperature was below zero the entire week. On Tuesday it was −36, but we still trudged to school, and the principal, Mr. Pennington, checked to make sure that the girls were not wearing snow pants during school, as skirts were required. I can still hear the snow crunching beneath my feet as we walked the three blocks to the school in the middle of town.

On January 31, the Augsburg Choir, directed by Leland Sateren, gave a concert in the Rugby High School auditorium, a thrill for the folks, as Mother had been a four-year member of the choir under Henry P. Opseth and knew Sateren well. That entailed the usual amount of work. Hosting the choir meant finding lodging in congregational homes for some sixty students, providing dinner for them at the church, and selling enough tickets to pay for the expenses of the event. They gladly did the work, however, knowing it promoted the work and success of Augsburg. It also introduced the choirs and choir directors in the Rugby area to the new music Sateren was writing and singing.

At the beginning of February, Dad went to Minneapolis again for the Stewardship Meeting; while there, he picked up the latest gossip and bags of clothes he had bought at Dayton's for the family. We enjoyed the winter evenings with hot cocoa and puzzles, something to which my mother was addicted. Since the LFC closed its yearly books on April 30, the Stewardship Board received something of a progress report when it met in February. Forrest Monson, head of the Stewardship Office, reported that things were progressing normally for the fiscal year ending in April 1954. Today, the ingathering looks like a large congregational budget: $92,000 for missions, of which they had received 63 percent; $70,000 for home missions, of which they had received 55.9 percent; and $100,000 for Augsburg, 40.5 percent of which they had received by February and the meeting—this from a church of just over sixty thousand people![41]

The *Lutheran Messenger* continued to push merger by publishing articles in support of it by known worthies and ELC leaders that revealed the similarity between the ELC and LFC in its work. Since evangelism was a neuralgic issue between the LFC and others, Torgerson asked his son Richard Torgerson, our neighbor pastor in Barton, to report on his experience of a

Preaching-Teaching-Reaching (PTR) event April 4–8 at Park River, North Dakota, hosted by the ELC congregation there in cooperation with the LFC congregation. Forty pastors came to the event to see how such a program could be hosted in their localities. He found it to be a "thrilling Evangelism Experience."[42] He suggested at the end of the article that the LFC would be poorer if it did not "seek to join hands with our fellow Lutherans and promote such God-inspired movements."[43]

Life went on with the usual events of the year—the festivals, father and son banquets, midweek Lenten services, the catechization of confirmands. As a strong pietist pastor, Dad regarded confirmation as a time to press for conversion. His counseling of his students, a precious time for both, brought many to a personal conviction of their sin and the grace of our Lord Jesus. I remember one conscientious student who feared he could not make the promise. He sat in the parsonage hallway with my father discussing his issue for a long time and finally decided to go through with the ceremony. My father's public examination of his confirmands, a tradition going back to 1737 in Denmark and Norway, was kind and gentle. He gave the students hints as to which questions he would ask which student, so the fear was not quite as great as it might have been.

While he was preparing the kids for catechization on March 28, the church was also engaged in the busy season of Lent, climaxing in Holy Week and Easter. At 7:15 p.m. on March 25, a great fire broke out in the Jacobson Store. The general store, built in 1902, and three other businesses in it burned to the ground, a loss of a million dollars, back when that was a lot of money. It seemed like hell had descended on the little town. As we were settling in for the night, the phone rang. It was to tell Dad that Aaron Gronvold, co-owner of the Chevrolet dealership with his brother Joel, had dropped dead in all the terror of the evening. The Gronvolds had been important members of Bethany. Their mother, Sarah Gronvold, a widow, and her boys had been central to the building of the Bethany church. It seemed like everything was falling apart.

At the ladies' aid meeting in Tunbidge the next day, everyone had something to say. The farmers, who always came for the lunch, had much to report on. I remember grabbing some green olives from the table groaning with sandwiches, salads, desserts, dill pickles, and other condiments and listening to Osmund Selland, in his overalls, saying that the fire had been so great it had filled the skies as far away as Winnipeg, Manitoba, northeast of us.

As we went through the funeral for Aaron Gronvold, we were looking toward Easter and the summertime of the annual conference, Bible camp, and the Youth Convention. The *Lutheran Messenger* appeared every two weeks with information on the merger process, including articles and proposals by the officials in charge. Its reports would be fodder for the pastors and their wives as they gathered for these events.

## Merger Again

Our merger committee sent out an appendix to the annual meeting booklet with a description of what they had done on behalf of the LFC in their negotiations. It was an answer to the request from the Joint Union Committee that they describe in more detail what the LFC needed to have before the merger. In describing the situation of Augsburg, especially, they held out for a way Augsburg could be owned and managed by a corporation that would be specifically related to the LFC constituency.

Augsburg remained the nub of the whole debate. After presenting the case for its proposal, the LFC contingent recommended two votes on two resolutions by the annual conference in June. The first resolution was to "recommend to the congregations the approval of the Report of the Joint Union Committee without any modification."[44] The second focused, "in the event that (1) it is not carried, on a resolution to recommend the approval of the Report of the Joint Union Committee with the stipulations set forth in the Proposal of the Lutheran Free Church Committee."[45]

The report went on to stipulate that if the Conference voted by a majority to adopt either resolution, the question should be referred to the president and secretary of the LFC to manage a process by which congregations could vote on the question. That should be concluded by December 15, 1955. If the vote of the congregations was three-fourths pro the affirmative, "the question shall be considered carried, and the union negotiations shall be continued."[46]

## The 1954 Annual Meeting in Thief River Falls

The annual meeting in 1954 was held at Zion Lutheran Church in Thief River Falls, Minnesota. My parents attended that meeting. My mother's sister and her husband, the Donald Ronnings, were serving Kingo Lutheran in Fosston, Minnesota, an hour or so away from Thief River, so we stayed with them while our parents went to the meeting, knowing it would be significant on the merger question. H. C. Caspersen anticipated the conference with an article in the June 8, 1954, *Lutheran Messenger* on Church Union. He was troubled that during the past year, the congregations had not dealt with the issue of union very thoroughly. He was especially concerned that John Stensvaag's report had not been sent to the congregations before the annual conference.

Since the LFC committee had recommended a "complete integration into the new church body," it really was too late to discuss the previous document; now the question would be whether to join the new church body, not the issues presented in the Testimony. Since this question was the most serious question that the LFC had ever faced, "it would be a heartrending experience to give them

# A Decade of Merger Talk

**Figure 11.5.** The Grindal and Ronning cousins: Gracia, Donny, Merrill, LaRhae, Ruth Ann at Fosston, Minnesota, in 1954. Used by permission of the Grindal family.

[the issues in the Testimony] up and to merge into new church environments."[47] For Caspersen, evangelism, lay activity, and the place of Augsburg remained unclear in the proposal.

Another writer, Oscar J. Johnson, submitted a piece criticizing the constant use of Scripture to approve the merger, especially Jesus's high priestly prayer in John 17. He did not necessarily oppose the merger but rejected the "false exegesis of the Scripture put forth as the 'Light of Scripture.' The verses have been taken out of their context and made to apply to Lutheran merger."[48] He then summed up a set of problems that were marked at a recent pastoral conference. First came items categorized as keeping things in the dark until "we" (the various churches) are married: the WCC; dancing, drinking, and other adiaphora; and premerger debts. Second were a set of challenges: clergy activity in the Lutheran Evangelical Movement (LEM), LBI, etc.; who would appear at the conventions; connection to the grass roots; the make up of the church council; and top-heavy organization. In addition, the conversations had not really described the benefits that a merger could provide that were not already there in the National Lutheran Council.[49]

These two columns sum up what many people were worried about as they gathered for the convention in Thief River Falls. Fevold noted that these discussions, both at the annual meeting and at the district and congregational meetings, and in the *Lutheran Messenger*, were "actually a more intensive continuation of a discussion that had been going on for several years."[50]

The annual conference heard the newly reelected President Burntvedt's message on Thursday, June 10, in which he addressed many of the issues facing the church, among them a shortage of pastors, rejoicing in the recent accreditation of Augsburg College, and the fine work of the WMF. The lengthiest section was the section on union. Burntvedt gave more background on the resolution the convention would be voting on and emphasized that it was not a proposal "to vote for or against union, nor does it commit our church either to favor or oppose union. It simply provides a way spelled out in resolution number two whereby discussion of the Report and the Proposal might be carried on over a period of one year on local and district levels."[51]

To his credit, Burntvedt explained to the gathering that the founders of the LFC had thought of "it as a movement and not a church body," but prevailing attitudes and the need to enter negotiations with the other church bodies necessitated our *functioning* as a church body. Our reason for being was "our commitment to the Fundamental Principles, ideals, emphases and practices."[52] He believed that the people of the LFC could effectively witness to these values in a merged church. With that, he informed the readers that the reason for the American Lutheran Conference's existence, which had been the closer unity of the churches, had been fulfilled, so it was no longer necessary and would dissolve at its final meeting in the Twin Cities on November 11–12, 1954. In addition, he reported on the work of the National Lutheran Council and the Lutheran World Federation. In closing, he informed his listeners that the work of the Commission on a Common Hymnal and Commission on Liturgy had completed its work on what became the *Service Book and Hymnal*. He commended its work and described, briefly, the contents, assuring the group that there were some Scandinavian hymns in it as well as an entire psalter.

In responding to Burntvedt's message, the conference voted to receive "for consideration the report on Polity and Organization of the Joint Union Committee." As it did, it affirmed a procedure for the congregations to deal with the question of merger. The plan was that the Blueprint would be studied in districts and congregations through the year so that the 1955 Conference would be able to vote to recommend it to the congregations for a vote. If that Conference approved such a recommendation, the congregations would then participate in a referendum on the question. The process would finish by December 1955. This procedure would be used throughout the three votes taken by the church in the next five years. In his report on the convention, Torgerson reported several pleas from the proceedings that the LFC be united as it went forward. Although there were differences, he pleaded that "nothing be said that tends to cause division or might create distrust in one another."[53]

In the meantime, the Women's Missionary Federation was flourishing and supporting more and more mission projects, while the Luther League Federation's yearly convention under the charismatic leadership of Merton Strommen had completely outgrown the facilities at the Mission Farms in Medicine Lake. It would now be held in locations around the country including Green Lake in Wisconsin and Pacific Lutheran College in Parkland, Washington. Both accomplishments can be credited to the extraordinary leadership skills of both groups.

That summer, we had Bible camp, vacation Bible school, and the Youth Convention on September 4, the last LFC convention at Medicine Lake. Groundbreaking for the Georg Sverdrup Library would be July 13, 1954, during a meeting of the Augsburg Board of Trustees. The community was thrilled to see this happen after such a long time. The cost had escalated beyond what the college had estimated, so a drive for $170,000 more had to be made. The inside of the September 28, 1954, *Lutheran Messenger* contained four pages with the appeal, with pictures featuring messages from George Michaelsen and many others stressing the importance of gathering that much money. The accreditation of the college depended on it. The seminary would have one classroom dedicated just to seminary education, so it was especially important to the LFC as it educated its pastors, John Stensvaag noted in the appeal bulletin. Librarian Agnes Tangjerd also wrote an appeal in which she described the dreadful situation of the library in the bottom floor of the main building, where things had been tucked away out of reach awaiting the new building. She supposed they would discover many priceless objects that would tell the story of Augsburg. They needed a better place.[54]

That same issue of the magazine contained a message from the World Council of Churches after its historic meeting in Evanston, Illinois. While the editor admitted the LFC was not a member, he thought it vital members of the LFC know what was going on. This meeting did deserve publicity as it was one of the most eventful and important of all its meetings. Torgerson knew that and thought it was essential people in the LFC learn of its strong evangelical witness to which Lutherans had contributed significant positions.[55]

The WCC meeting brought several worthies to Minneapolis to speak at Augsburg, Bishop Eivind Berggrav (1884–1959) among them. He had become a war hero to many who knew of his work during the war to counter the Nazification of the Norwegian church. As one of the six presidents of the WCC, he gave weight to the argument that the LFC should join.

## My Father Is Called to Central Lutheran in Salem

One can tell from my father's appointment book that he was getting restless. He always said that eight years in a congregation was enough and was looking around. On September 26, 1954, he resigned from the Rugby parish to accept the call to Central Lutheran in Salem, Oregon. A home mission congregation started by the LFC in 1946, just after the war, it needed a pastor after Pastor G. B. Rundstrom, my godfather, resigned to serve the Ballard LFC congregation in Seattle. It was an exciting venture for my dad—on the West Coast, not far from where he had grown up.

Dad knew the LFC West Coast district well. As a Luther Leaguer in the 1930s, he had visited most of the small-town congregations where there were LFC congregations. Salem was new, however, and had real opportunities for mission and growth, especially with all the new immigrants from the Midwest who had strong Norwegian Lutheran ties. But as a West Coaster, he was not interested in reestablishing a Midwestern enclave in Salem: he wanted to evangelize the entire city with the good news of Jesus Christ. Members of Bethany were saddened by the resignation, but the family looked forward to the move with high expectations.

Still, the daily life of the parish continued. That year, Dad baptized over thirty babies, more than one every other Sunday. The Sunday School Institute proceeded as usual, this time with a visit from Miss Oletta Wald, who would demonstrate how to teach an unruly Sunday school class—mine—before the whole group! In addition, meetings to discuss the union proposals were held in Bethany on September 28. Clarence J. Carlsen and Clarence Larson of Oak

Figure 11.6. The Christmas program at Berwick in 1954. Used by permission of the Grindal family.

# A Decade of Merger Talk 431

Grove High School, members of the COR and friendly opponents, hosted the meeting.

The merger discussion became livelier. In the October 12, 1954, issue of the *Lutheran Messenger*, O. O. Aune, lay member of the COR, wrote a long article dealing with his take on the Blueprint. He detailed seven reasons people opposed the merger but discounted them as being somewhat trivial, like a child not wanting to change. There were four main reasons: (1) fundamental differences in faith and doctrine, (2) irreconcilable forms of polity and practice, (3) ethnic and linguistic barriers, and (4) a likely division of the LFC. He dismissed these, saying they would not be taken away in the merger and it was time now to say yes to "the American Evangelical United Lutheran Free Church."[56]

As the holiday season ramped up, we were attending not only festival services in every congregation in the parish but also farewell services. On December 15, 1954, we met in the Berwick church for a farewell Christmas tree program. At the end, we sang "God Be with You till We Meet Again," sobbing as the church bell rang, shaking the whole little church with its sound. In addition, we were being entertained for dinner by many in the congregations who were good friends as well as members.

We left for Salem on December 30, 1954, facing blizzards and snowstorms across Montana and Idaho, especially in the mountains, but the highway department assured my dad that as veterans of North Dakota driving, we would be just fine. So we sailed across the Great Plains and through the mountains easily and then dipped down into the Willamette Valley, where the lawns were green and verdant in the winter. A camelia bush alive with red blooms by the new parsonage entry waited to greet us.

## Central Lutheran Church in Salem, Oregon, 1955–1962

As we stepped out onto the lawn beside the new parsonage at 1190 North Winter Street in Salem, just a block from the street that led to the Oregon Capitol building, we felt the soft, rain-soaked grass of winter in the Willamette Valley. We were led into the parsonage by the president of the trustees, Norman Rue, and shown the place where we would live for the next eight years. As we entered it, the fresh smell of pine sawdust wafted around us, as the home was heated by a sawdust furnace. Every fall, a truck would arrive and blow sawdust into the bin for the year. That was new to us, but Dad understood it well. Grant Grade School, where LaRhae and I would attend, was across the street and the church three blocks away on Capitol and Gaines Streets.

The installation service for Dad was on January 22, 1955. L. Warren Hanson, the LFC Oregon District president, installed him. His wife, Nettie, was the daughter of the Hagens in Rugby, so we had a close connection already

**Figure 11.7.** Central Lutheran Church in Salem ca. 1955. Used by permission of the Grindal family.

with them. We not only knew many of those who had come from the Midwest, but Dad was also well acquainted with the Free Church in the West. Still, we began speaking easily of those "back east."

At its founding, Central had attracted members from the newly established Grace Lutheran Church, a new ELC congregation served by Lowell Holte, brother of Carleton Holte, professor at St. Olaf. Although Dad was friendly with Holte, the competition was fierce, and Dad and Holte sometimes would meet at the doorways of new arrivals from the Midwest trying to win members. At the time, Central had about 250 members. Even in Salem, Dad continued preaching in Norwegian on Sunday afternoons now and then. As the migration continued, Lutheran Church bodies were building more home missions churches in the city, and the organizations were flourishing. Missouri's St. John's in Salem doubled the membership in its Lutheran Laymen's League that year.

Salem, however, was not a Lutheran town. Willamette University was a Methodist school established by Jason Lee and the early pioneers from the early 1800s. Saint Paul's Episcopal Church had just finished its new building and had a fine pipe organ newly installed, one of the best in the area. I would soon be playing it for the Youth Choir every Saturday morning and learned the liturgy and Anglican chants from Father John, the vicar there. Salem was much older than Rugby. However, there were many fewer church members per capita than Rugby, and the large majority of those were evangelicals, Baptists, Nazarenes, and every variety of Pentecostal or Assemblies of God congregations. We were a rare species. Lutherans were thought to be like Catholics, if people knew anything about them. Because of our evangelical leanings, we were accepted as Christians, at least by the evangelicals.

The church building, built in 1949, was a cheaply built first unit. We joked that it could be taken down with a ball-peen hammer. Since the locks had failed and the church could only be entered with the use of a knife to jimmy them, my father began carrying a kitchen paring knife in his pocket so he could get into the building. (He was horrified to find he had it in his pocket as the Salem Ministerium toured the state penitentiary. He had been welcomed as their special guest. They were told they would not be searched for weapons since they were pastors. Sometime into that tour, he put his hand in his coat pocket and felt the knife, which he had forgotten, was there. He was terrified he would be arrested for bringing a weapon into the prison but made it through fine, coming home to announce the church was getting new locks ASAP.)

It was obvious from the first that the job of this pastor was to grow the congregation so it could afford the next unit. The parsonage, which had been newly purchased, was dedicated on Sunday, February 13, 1955. A service of dedication was held there after services. I can still see and hear Ray Dahlen, the choir director and treasurer of the church, singing "Bless This House" on the front porch of the house. Later that afternoon, congregants were invited for an open house. By then, we had completely moved in and were ready to show it off.

Paying for the parsonage was the first priority, but Dad's salary desperately needed raising. That first year was difficult. His salary was three thousand dollars—one thousand lower than it had been in Rugby. Furthermore, we didn't have farmers there who would bring us meat and produce. We were as poor as church mice that first year. Mother couldn't buy us new clothes. I was a growing teenager and needed them. We had to take hand-me-downs from the members of the congregation; they tended to be cannery workers or construction workers from Iowa or North Dakota who worked seasonally or would go back to work on the farms to make enough money.

While Dad cheerfully accepted this poverty, it drove Mom crazy. She loved the Willamette Valley and its produce, but we had to go berry and bean picking in the summer to help the family budget. I would be awakened at four-thirty in the morning to climb into a truck of teenagers sent out to pick strawberries and beans all summer. Some would make a thousand dollars, but I wasn't quite up to that, upsetting my mother. She needed every penny simply to feed us. She was good at that, but she kept us aware of our poverty as she scrambled to find enough nutritious food. We would have roast beef on Sunday, tomato and hamburger casseroles on Monday, hamburger and gravy on Tuesday, pork chops on Wednesday, baked beans on Thursday, tuna hotdish on Friday, and fish balls on

Saturday. This was a fairly regular menu. At the time, the fast-food franchises just getting started sold hamburgers for nineteen cents. Very quickly, Mother embraced the lush variety of fruits and vegetables in the valley and would can or preserve up to eight hundred jars of whatever she could find in the fields where we would go to pick the produce.

Except for the salary, parsonage living was no problem for my parents. They were used to sparse living and managed fairly well, all things considered. When we were moving in, the men in the congregation came to remodel some of it—there were five new contractors in the congregation, and all donated a day to work on the house, fix the kitchen, sand the attic floors that made our bedroom, and so on. Much of their work involved tearing out the work of the previous contractor. My sister, who was six, told one, "I don't know why you are doing that. After you leave, my mother will cry, and Daddy will fix it." That sort of summed up the first awful weeks of what would become a wonderful relationship with the congregation.

Services and programs continued as usual at Central. Dad preached a series of midweek Lenten services, and Sunday evening services were regular during the winter. These were often special speakers or films on missions or other Christian topics. Sometimes films from the television program the Lutheran Hour, produced by the Missouri Synod, would be shown. The racket of the 16 mm projector, which often baffled the technical skills of the deacons, and the dark room with traffic hissing by in the rain on Highway 99, Capitol Street, in front of the church are the stuff of my memories of Salem. Missionaries from the LFC also appeared often. On March 16, LFC missionary and deaconess Sister Margaret Dahlen from Madagascar spoke at midweek services, which tended to be Bible studies, at which the entire family always made an appearance. The mother/daughter banquet that May attracted over one hundred, a record attendance.

Dad began to associate with the other five Lutheran pastors in town. He would become close to T. M. Gebhard, pastor of Christ Lutheran Church, an ALC congregation. Now the conversation about merger had to be had at Central. There were a good many in the congregation whose roots in the Midwest made them aware of the different synods, including the demarcations among the Hauge Synod, Norwegian Synod, and LFC. Silverton, our small neighboring town, had three Norwegian Lutheran churches; their members were well schooled in the different synods and brought those experiences to the congregational meetings.

## The Blueprint for Merger from the Leadership

One of the worries of the LFC leadership, and many others, was that the fellowship would split. Repeatedly, they called for unity. "We must stay together" was the cry. It appeared in many Messenger Press publications and especially the *Lutheran Messenger*. The chief issue was, I think, fear that if the merger was defeated, many would defect for the new church, leaving the small group decimated and unable to support what was left: Augsburg, Oak Grove High School, and the missions of the LFC.[57]

As the chatter reached a crescendo among the pastors, leaders, and congregations, we were now far away from the "Holy City," as we laughingly called Minneapolis. When luminaries came west for some official duties, we would sit up late with them, eager to hear the latest gossip and talk. We would not be able to attend the 1955 annual meeting in Minneapolis. We did not have enough money for the long trek back, so we huddled together with the pastors and their families of the LFC's Oregon Circuit: L. Warren Hanson, Oliver Bergs, and others. We read the *Lutheran Messenger* faithfully and the *Morning Glory* with great eagerness for salacious gossip about the WCC and other groups involved in merger talks.

On April 26, 1955, the *Lutheran Messenger* featured a letter from Dr. Burntvedt, "Facing Up to the Merger Question I," his first in a series of three before the convention. In it, he outlined both the process as it was to be carried out and the informational meetings held throughout the fellowship, from large to small groups. He thought the larger groups had been more deliberative, while the smaller ones tended to be dominated by those with pronounced personal opinions.[58]

From there, he went through a history of what had happened thus far, even referring to the deliberations in 1923 and 1928, when the question of reuniting with the ELC had come before the church. He went on to argue what was at stake in the process of the deliberations. He had made sure the secretary of the committee had sent the Blueprint to every pastor and secretary of the congregations along with a reprint of the report with the proposal and procedures, which had been available for all district meetings as well as appearing in the *Lutheran Messenger*.

## Preparing for the Annual Meeting of 1955

The merger would be debated at the annual conference session on Thursday, June 9, 1955; discussion would begin at 4:00 p.m. and continue into the next afternoon if necessary. The first vote would be on the Blueprint. If that failed by a simple majority, the next vote would be on the Blueprint as modified in the proposal. Should that fail, the vote on the memorandum proposing a nongeographical district would be put before the group. Whichever received a majority vote would be sent to the congregations for a referendum to be held between June 15 and December 15.

Meanwhile, Augsburg was launching a campaign to build a girls' dormitory using federal funds. The Gerda Mortensen Hall, as it would be named, began construction very soon after the building of the library. Lest it should seem like too much building, Christensen assured the supporters of Augsburg in another spreadsheet in the *Messenger* that the funding from the government had made it possible, and this was absolutely necessary. About that he was right, although he had worried about the influence these government loans would have on the teaching of the school. There was a fold-in printed in that *Lutheran Messenger* that featured pictures of the former women's dormitory buildings, beginning with what had been the triplex where the first three professors' families—the Sverdrups, Oftedals, and Gunnersens—had been housed in the mid-1870s. My mother had lived there in what were wretched conditions and then moved to Sivertsen Hall for the end of her time at Augsburg. Gerda Mortensen Hall, across from St. Mary's and Fairview, would be ready in January 1956 if all went well.

At the April 13 groundbreaking ceremony, Miss Mortensen addressed the event with one of her typical speeches. What she wanted inscribed above the doors were the words "Worship the Lord in the Beauty of Holiness." This was her theme; she loved what was beautiful: "Only thus can inner peace, poise and true beauty of living be ours."[59] For her, still of the old school in many ways, culture and beauty were marks of the Christian, especially Christian women. No matter what one might think of that today, an ugly and decadent time, she stood for the best and most cultured things, which she found in Scripture and the Christian tradition.

Burntvedt continued his series of articles on the question of merger in the May 10, 1955, *Lutheran Messenger*. In this, he explained the difficulties he saw in the nongeographical district. He thought the Blueprint and proposal would be better for everyone. Augsburg would be directed by a board nominated by the former members of the LFC, but other former members of the other churches could be nominated as well. The safeguard was who was doing the nominating. The school would be supported by the whole church. Furthermore, the proposal assured that the five special concerns of the LFC would be held before all in the new church:

1. The Living Congregation
2. Evangelism
3. Freedom and Simplicity in Worship
4. Informal Christian Worship
5. Christian Conduct[60]

He thought many pastors in the other merging churches would be happy to support these principles, something the LFC should want to share with everyone in the new church.

In the next issue, Burntvedt came clean and explained why he had become a supporter of the merger agreement. Here, he appealed to the witness that church unity helped the mission churches, especially in Madagascar, when the various Lutheran churches had merged, making the group much stronger in its ability to witness. This had also happened in China and Japan. He was convinced that the JUC had been prayerfully seeking the will of God. He could see no reason not to merge. His final paragraph was a plea that whichever way the vote went, the church would not split.[61] Just before the annual meeting, Pastor Christian G. Olson, a member of the Committee for Relations, wrote an editorial saying he had changed his mind about the merger as he had continued in the discussions, especially with the ALC leadership, about which he had been most worried. He believed that although many in the ALC condoned drinking and dancing, many others did not, and they would find new friends among members of the ALC in a new church. He had only one caveat: that the new constitution assure the autonomy of the local congregation. Then he would be ready to support the merger.[62]

## The Annual Meeting 1955: Voting on Merger

The annual conference of 1955 was held at historic Trinity in Minneapolis. Burntvedt stressed in his presidential address that as he had already made his position on the vote clear, he would not discuss it in this address, noting that "the saddest thing would be that in our explorations to unite with others, we ourselves become divided."[63] The gathering discussed the question vigorously until four o'clock Friday afternoon. Forty-three people at the meeting spoke for and against the resolution to an overflowing church.

Torgerson was thankful that the spirit was calm and the prayers were constant. The debate was essentially between a more centralized organization and one that was less so, with a stress on lay activity and evangelism. Those who were pro-merger made it clear they felt this was a God-appointed hour that the Free Church should meet with a positive vote. Motion number one failed with a vote of 426 against and 222 for. The second motion was approved by 450 to 202. This was taken as a very positive vote for merger and a continuation of the process. It recommended to the congregations of the LFC that they approve the Report of the Joint Union Committee with the Proposal of the Lutheran Free Church Committee and the authorization of continued participation in the merger discussions.

Because of that vote by the annual meeting, the congregations were now supposed to vote and have it recorded by the secretary of the LFC by December 15, 1955. The editor of the Lutheran Messenger, Sverre Torgerson, suggested a process for the discussion and presentation of the resolution to the congregations.

He recommended the pastor of every congregation would bring the resolution to his congregation and should hold several meetings where the question could be amiably discussed. Then, after much prayer, the pastor and secretary of each congregation should send a letter to every member urging them to deliberate prayerfully on the questions. Finally, they should meet to vote on the issue, after which the results and actual number of votes should be sent back to the secretary of the LFC. The editor wanted the exact numbers so the church would have an idea of how strong votes on either side were.[64]

At the end of the 1955 annual meeting, in a great celebration, the Georg Sverdrup Library was dedicated as it was being made ready for opening in the fall. Nothing made the leadership as excited as this. Having an adequate library had been the goal for many years. The woeful situation had prevented accreditation by the North Central College Association, which had been a detriment to the college for its entire existence. Augsburg had been denied accreditation on several occasions before, but finally, on March 26, 1954, the NCAA ratified the decision of its committee, and Augsburg gained accreditation. This was a major barrier now broken, and no one was more excited than Gerda, who never took her eye off the ball. The dedication of the library was a time to review with satisfaction how far it had brought the college.

As the congregations discussed the Blueprint, many people, lay and clergy, wrote in to the *Lutheran Messenger* with their opinions. Fred Ditmanson, the revered veteran missionary to China, wrote an editorial urging cooperation, not merger. He used as a model the Lutheran Church in China (LCC), which was made up of sixteen synods whose mother churches were in America and Europe. He thought the federation idea was better than a merger. The LCC supported a seminary, publishing house and store, Bible schools, and charity. Otherwise, each separate synod carried on as it had, from the call and ordination of pastors to other typical mission efforts. Ditmanson thought the LFC principles were enough. They had already been translated into Chinese and accepted by the LFC churches in Honan and were working, to the point of allowing lay members to take over the services. That, for Ditmanson, was "an argument for cooperation rather than merger." The new church would only give the congregations "delegated freedom."[65] Ditmanson's opinion carried a lot of weight in the church. His take on the question from the mission field was also different from most who argued that in Madagascar, for example, the various missions had already merged and that augured well for the merger of the LFC into the ALC.

Two nieces of George Sverdrup Jr., Elsie Michaelsen and Katherine Michaelsen, also wrote a letter to the editor concerning the question. Referring to the debate, they noted that apparently many of the participants seemed not to know much about the LFC's founding and leading principles, especially those

# A Decade of Merger Talk

having to do with the freedom of the congregation and its fear of top-down officials dictating to the congregations. They wondered why members of the LFC would vote to relinquish their rights to join the merged church, where members would have a voice but no vote on critical questions like which professors would serve the seminary. They deplored that the voice of the laity would be limited. Was that what the majority of LFC members wanted?[66] They also wondered about the voice of women in the new church. It would not be as it had been, they feared.

Their voices as granddaughters of Georg Sverdrup, nieces of George Sverdrup Jr., and sisters of George Michaelsen were not insignificant, even if their brother, a lay leader of Augsburg and the LFC, had come to favor merger. The family discussions must have been vigorous!

As the vote by the congregations grew closer, Torgerson wrote, "Now it is up to the Congregations to act." He advised much prayer as congregations began voting.[67] The next week, Leslie F. Brandt, a pastor and former missionary to Formosa, wrote that the Lutheran Church needed to be a United Church to stand against the power of darkness: "Communism, Romanism, Socialism, Secularism, and many others, that we can ONLY as a united Church, and, as far as we are concerned, as a united Lutheran Church. It is just like the devil to get our eyes all cluttered up with slivers so we can't see the logs."[68]

Pastor Fritjof Monseth of Valley City, who would become a leader in the split that would become the Association of Free Lutheran Congregations, wrote that he appreciated Ditmanson's point of view on the merger. He also worried that the congregations, unaware of all that was at stake, would "vote away their freedoms." He thought the structure of the proposed church looked unwieldy. It would not safeguard the issues that the LFC held dearest. He agreed with Iver Olson, an Augsburg professor, who had noted that "if the church voted in favor of the 'Blueprint' with the LFC 'Proposal' attached we vote for trouble."[69]

## The Vote Is Taken

That fall, Central Lutheran in Salem celebrated its tenth anniversary on November 20, 1955, with a membership of 370. Almost 70 had joined the church since our arrival in January.[70] As meeting conversations were reported and votes were made in the congregations, the leadership began to sense the proposal would be defeated. Torgerson wrote an editorial arguing that the congregations, however much people praised the idea, had not really shown themselves to be participating meaningfully in the existential question before their church. Only 156 laypeople of the 554 delegates at the conference represented the 358 congregations of the LFC. Few laypeople spoke at the meeting, deferring to the pastors and professors. Most laypeople came to the meetings uninstructed, he observed, and voted as themselves, not as representatives of their congregations.[71]

In that same issue, Professor John Stensvaag entered the fray, hoping that the people voting against the proposal knew the gravity of their vote, somewhat along the line of Torgerson. He was fairly certain the vote would be negative and complained about the voting process in which a congregation of twenty had the same force as one with two thousand. That was not fair, he thought, but he had not wanted to change the system to avoid being called *political*. Still, outsiders who looked at it would agree it seemed rather unfair if one considered the numbers. The vote still did not mean the church had voted for merger but "simply that we have decided to continue on in serious merger resolutions." The second referendum would vote on the merger after all the documents had been completed. Stensvaag believed the merger was of God and urged those opposing it to be sure that "the victory will be a victory for Christ and His cause."[72]

The letters and articles continued in greater number as the deadline approached. The views usually fell along these two lines—the pro voices urged that the LFC be allowed to take its principles into the new church, while those on the opposing side argued they would not survive in the merged church. Pastors were on both sides, as was the laity. Enoch Thorsgaard, a layman, entered the debate by criticizing those who were against the merger as "refusing others the opportunity to serve in the manner they thought best."[73]

Mrs. Karl Kleppe, a laywoman from Kintyre, North Dakota, summed up the arguments as she had read them and found Pastor Leslie Brandt's argument less than satisfactory. The church would not be united until all Christians were "one huge army to fight 'in this global conflict of the hour.' If that is true why foist on us the necessity of a merger with three Lutheran bodies only, while all the others retain their status quo."[74]

Professor Iver Olson wrote something of a final piece on the question. He had not been known as a strong supporter of the merger, but he had concluded that the situation was now such that failing to merge would drastically reduce the effectiveness of the church. Many congregations would depart for the new church and leave the smaller group to support Augsburg, Oak Grove, missions, and other ministries of the LFC. He feared that enough had already changed to make him, reluctantly, favor union. There is in his piece a sense that while merger would offer more opportunities, there would at the same time be grave losses: "Our time has come in the LFC; the miseries are upon us. We shall simply increase our problems by voting down the merger proposal. Our Church will never be the same again; we shall not be able to go about our work peacefully as in the halcyon days of the American Lutheran Conference."[75]

Ultimately, he thought it would be like 1890 again, and even by "prodigious efforts we could still eke out an ecclesiastical existence, the fruits will be meager in the light of what they might be in terms of spiritual life if we spend our efforts in cooperation with likeminded Christians with the framework of a larger Lutheran fellowship."[76]

As the vote was about to be tallied on December 15, 1955, the *Minneapolis Star* interviewed Burntvedt on his estimate of the vote. Given that three-fourths of the congregations needed to approve it, he said he would "be greatly surprised if this happens."[77] When the vote was finally tallied, 210 congregations (64.3 percent) voted yes, and 117 voted no. While a majority, it did not make the 75 percent required for victory. Still, Fevold counted this as remarkable. Only six years before, the conference had gone on record as being almost unanimously opposed to an organic merger. This marked something of a change.

Burntvedt was quoted saying that since the vote for the union was so large, he did not think the LFC would "be kept out of the union permanently." He had two goals after the vote. First, he wanted to keep the congregations of the LFC together. The church could not afford to lose any congregations to continue its programs. Second, he hoped to maintain good relations with the other three churches in the merger negotiations.[78]

Because of the vote, the LFC delegation decided it would not gather with the other churches until the church took further action at its annual meeting in 1956. However, Burntvedt was asked to meet with the JUC in March 1956 if for nothing else than to "express our hope that the present development will not in any way impair the cordial relations which prevail among our churches."[79] The sense that it was not over is hinted at in several news stories about the future. Most agreed it would be up to the next annual conference.[80]

Meanwhile, from February 3 to 14, evangelist Donald Fladland from Spicer, Minnesota, one of the Free Church's lay evangelists, appeared at Central in Salem along with his wife, a cornetist, for a week of meetings. His preaching was effective, and God used him to bring several important members in the church to Christ. These men, especially, became pillars of the congregation as they read the Scriptures and gathered for prayers. By the end of our time in Salem, I was fascinated by their speech at Bible study. It was almost Elizabethan as they spoke of gainsaying and vouchsafing in the language of the KJV.

On February 5, 1956, the Augsburg College band, under the direction of Mayo Savold, played a concert in Parrish Junior High, a few blocks from the church on Capitol Street. These performances helped give Augsburg some publicity in the area since the choirs and bands of the Lutheran Colleges were well regarded. The musical culture of Salem in general at the time was not on par even with Rugby, given the strong influence of the Lutheran colleges in the Midwest.

At the meeting of the JUC in Minneapolis that March, Burntvedt said that further developments would depend on the next annual meeting in Fargo the coming June. After his report, the committee passed a resolution stating its strong desire that the LFC rejoin the group and its negotiations.[81] Burntvedt would find reasons for hope in the narrow defeat of the referendum. In a report to the Joint Union Committee on March 12-13, in Chicago, he told his colleagues that although he was disappointed in the vote, "I am, nevertheless, greatly encouraged by the result of the referendum. It is a long way we have traveled from our position in 1949, when we went on record as not favoring organic union with anybody."[82]

That summer, we were too poor to attend the annual meeting, a long, expensive, three-day trip back east. Dad filled in at Grace Lutheran for Pastor Holte, who was attending the ELC's annual meeting in Minneapolis that summer, making a little extra money on the side. During that summer, a group of Augsburg students known as canvassers came for a week to Salem to canvas the area the first week of August. Among the students was Andrew Hsiao, who would go on to become president of the Chinese Seminary in Hong Kong. He became fast friends with us, especially my sister, LaRhae. He was a student Gerda had been most proud of in her effort to get international students to Augsburg.

## A Question of Tongues

That fall, there was a push by several members at Central for my father and mother to speak in tongues. In late November, two pastors who thought of themselves as Lutheran Pentecostals came to Salem to encourage the folks to examine the practice and maybe pray to be given the gift. We had a member, a farmer outside the city, who had been healed by Oral Roberts some years before. He was always hankering after the second blessing, which the Pentecostals around him had recommended. During the fall, several healers came to Salem, and he went to the meetings with an ardent interest in their work.

Meanwhile, we were invited to the home of a couple who was enthusiastic about speaking in tongues—enthusiastic in the spiritual sense, one might say, as well as personally. He was a wealthy car salesman, and they lived much, much higher on the hog than we had even imagined. We were invited to their home for dinner with the two evangelists. I was thirteen, my sister eight, and my little brother three. One of them prayed an endless prayer, and then we began to eat. Everything was "pass the potatoes, praise the Lord." There was something hysterical about this time. One of the pastors seemed to be trying to speak in tongues, babbling and crying out.

We finally left. On the way home, we were all upset. The next day, we were sick. It felt like we had encountered an evil spirit rather than the Holy Spirit. While my parents both had been looking for a deeper spiritual life and had been interested, this was the end of that. As we were sitting around the kitchen table, the phone rang. It was for Dad. The farmer had died while or after receiving the second blessing. His heart had not been strong in any case. I had gone with Dad to visit him a couple of times.

# A Decade of Merger Talk

Dad left in a hurry. When he got there, the two evangelists, perhaps feeling guilty for giving the man an experience that stopped his heart, were prancing around the bed, trying to raise him from the dead. They asked Dad to join them: "Just think, Grindal, the witness this will be, if he is raised from the dead!"

My father was repelled by this exhibition and said, "The Lord has taken him home. He is much better off there." They finally relented and crept off while Dad ministered to the family. It was the end of any attempt at tongues or Pentecostal excitement in our house. My parents felt the Lord had spoken very clearly to them to warn them of the excesses that were possible at the edges of the organized church. While they always understood the speaking of tongues to be a gift, it never appealed to them again.

The first Sunday of Advent, the confirmation class was catechized, and communion was celebrated in the evening, as was traditional. First Methodist Church in Salem always presented the *Messiah*, and my folks had become avid supporters of that event, hungering as they were for the kind of music they had known in the Midwest. This was new for them since the Methodist churches in their experience in North Dakota and Minnesota were small and unable to do that. In Salem, Lutherans had the small churches, and the Methodists and the evangelicals like First Baptist were the large ones.

As 1957 began, Central announced it would now have a double service schedule since one service had been filled to overflowing. With two services, the paper noted, over four hundred people would be able to attend comfortably.[83] Once again, Don Fladland appeared for a week of evangelistic services on the first week of March. He had been much appreciated the year before, and his coming was eagerly anticipated, especially by the young men. Fladland's appeal as a sportsman ran deep with them. Most of his sermons used sports illustrations, and eternity was always one minute away from the final bell of a basketball game. Corny or not, it brought many people into the kingdom.

About this time, in March 1957, the Joint Union Committee decided that the constituting convention of the American Lutheran Church would not be held until 1960. This was necessitated by timetables dictated by the 1956 conventions of each group. Each communion had passed amendments to the constitution at their conventions, which had to be submitted and approved by their 1958 conventions. This prevented the ratification of the new constitution from being considered in time. This delay also gave the LFC a bit more time for its deliberations.

## The Annual Meeting of 1957

As the annual meeting of 1957 neared, people in the LFC were discussing Lutheran merger once more. The Minneapolis district of the LFC met at Oak Grove Lutheran Church in Richfield, and its main topic was merger. Dr. John Stensvaag and Dr. Christensen led the discussions. Burnvedt's health prevented

**Figure 11.8.** Forrest Monson. Used by permission of Augsburg Fortress Publishers.

him from attending these meetings and leading them in June, as he was suffering a lingering bout of pneumonia. John Stensvaag began taking his place more and more in the conversation. Despite his illness, however, Burntvedt was reelected president of the LFC in absentia for another three-year term.

In his address to the church, read by Forrest T. Monson, secretary of the church, Burntvedt warned that the unprecedented building of new churches "unequalled in the annals of church history" was not focused on spiritual growth: "Why cannot we harness this enthusiasm and interest, this willingness to work and sacrifice more definitely to a spiritual building program, centered on the spiritual temple not built with human hands?" He even went so far as to suspect Satan as busying people with religious activities that were not genuinely Christian.[84] At the end of the address, he returned to the merger question. A resolution was on the table to reengage in the negotiations with the merging parties: "The decision must be decisive and accepted as such whatever the result of the ballot might prove to be."[85]

## The Annual Convention 1957

The next day, on Thursday, June 14, 1957, the meeting at Trinity Congregation voted to approve the recommended procedure for reentering the talks. Because a basic agreement had already been worked out between the merging parties, what remained were procedural matters. Among them was the voting method in the LFC and the question of how to count the votes of congregations large and small, a sticking point with both sides. If it approved the resolution, it also had to make provisions for another congregational referendum on the question.

On June 15, the annual conference voted 279-185 to send the vote back to the congregations. The vote this time would be weighted so that each congregation had a vote of one to ten, depending on the size of the congregation. The *Minneapolis Star* noted that this debate "was marked by sharp argument and deep differences of opinion over the merits of the proposed united church."[86] The same issues came up: evangelism, the WCC, and the latter's suspected communism. Rudolfs Krafts, a Latvian pastor displaced by the Russian takeover of his home country and now a pastor in the LFC, fiercely objected to the WCC. Although Christensen argued that it was simply trying to serve behind the Iron Curtain, this argument was not persuasive to those already against it. By now, the LFC counted over seventy-five thousand among its members, showing the steady growth almost all churches experienced during this decade.

## The Lutheran World Federation Meeting in Minnesota

In July, the Minneapolis papers printed articles describing Lutherans in the United States and their march toward union. These articles were also preparing the state of Minnesota for a huge influx of Lutherans in August for the Lutheran World Federation Assembly. Burntvedt was quoted as saying there "is no group of Protestants in America that has so few differences as the Lutherans. There also is no group where those differences are so magnified."[87]

That August, all of Lutheranism was focused on the Twin Cities. There had rarely been such a massed number of Lutherans together in this country. The ELC and others had devoted their staffs to planning this event for more than a year, and the LFC worked alongside them, as did Augustana, all three centered in Minneapolis. The logistics of finding space for them to stay, eat, and gather were monumental, but things went off well. It gave Lutherans in the Midwest a thrilling picture of the church to which they belonged and the many different kinds of Lutherans there were around the world. It also gave the various church bodies in Minneapolis a chance to work closely with each other.

Out west, these events were only briefly on the news, though we knew from the church papers that it was happening. The massive service on the ground of the Minnesota State Capitol earned a picture and several inches in the *Capitol Journal* on August 20. After describing the service, which began with a fanfare of trumpets, the paper reported that a voice challenged the church "to explain its faith in the assembly theme, 'Christ Frees and Unites.'" The article concluded with a summary of the major themes of the assembly—a call for closer cooperation among Lutheran churches and among Christian churches in general and a recognition of human rights, asking Lutherans to "boldly face the massive revolutionary facts of our time."[88]

One cannot read these accounts without seeing the beginning of a movement that would change everything. The LWF was aware of the great struggle for civil rights that was growing around the world and in the United States at the time. A few weeks later, in Little Rock, Arkansas, the fight against the Supreme Court's decision on *Brown vs. Board of Education* in 1954 was personally signified by Governor Orval Faubus, resisting the federal government and Dwight Eisenhower on the issue of segregation. The churches were responding in a variety of ways, and racial issues were becoming more insistent priorities, appearing on the agendas of many of the pastoral gatherings and mainline church deliberation.

Lutherans were still *rara avis* in Salem. St. Mark's, an ULCA congregation and the largest Lutheran Church in town, had just built an impressive neo-Gothic church, which attracted attention on the local scene. Several well-known personalities from the ULCA appeared on the occasion, such as Dr. Edwin Moll, former director of the LWF's Near East Branch, who had directed Palestine orphanages, schools, and a school for the blind there and received note for his appearance at a ULCA layman's retreat at Camp Menucha in the Columbia River Gorge. Arthur Olson, the sainted LFC missionary to China and now director of the work of the LWF in Hong Kong, had attended the 1957 LFC Assembly. On his way home, he stopped at Central in September to show films on the work in Hong Kong and Formosa. These opportunities were always cherished by my parents as a way to keep the connections with home base in Minneapolis and the wider church, which seemed very distant.

That summer, in August 1957, eight Luther Leaguers went with the family to Lutherland Bible Camp near Tacoma, Washington. The trip also gave us a chance to visit Dad's foster mother, Anna Grindal, at Bethany Homes in Everett and Grandpa Svein Kivley in Ferndale. While we were at Lutherland, Bernhard Christensen appeared as a teacher. Always on the prowl for students, he engaged with us in thoughtful and respectful conversations. I remember a long conversation with him on the hostilities in the Middle East and what could be done. It was then I sensed he was a Democrat and was astounded to know that a revered leader of the church would be a liberal.

After all the hoopla of the assembly, things quieted down, and the move toward a second vote on the merger began. This time, just two-thirds of the vote would be needed to pass the resolution. T. O. Burntvedt, who had been too ill to give the presidential address at the annual meeting, also had to miss several appearances at the LWF Assembly, although he did attend three meetings there. Almost immediately after, he suffered another heart attack, something his daughter Gloria thought had been caused by that exertion.

## The Service Book and Hymnal and the Merger

At the same time, the long-awaited *Service Book and Hymnal* was being promoted and printed—in the hundreds of thousands—though it was not yet available. It had been in the works for over a decade and expanded in 1946 to include all the churches that would merge into the ALC and LCA in the '60s. Among the agenda for the book was the urge toward unity. As Ernst Edwin Ryden noted at the time, the hymnal would be "the greatest single factor in promoting Lutheran unity in the history of the Lutheran church in America."[89] The LFC had sent Burntvedt and Leland Sateren to represent its tradition in the deliberations, although they did not send anyone to the liturgical committee meetings because, as Sateren would rail, "we aren't very liturgical. We should have been there to make that point."

Hymnals were known to promote unity and were often part of the strategy of those who were pushing for mergers. One could go back in Lutheran history in America to hear Henry Melchior Muhlenberg (1711–1787) saying after his first hymnal, *Erbauliche Liedersammlung (Devotional Hymn Collection)*, came out in 1786 that he looked for the day in which there would be "one book, one church." These words sparked a low-grade fever that infected almost every hymn book committee. It surely was behind the *Lutheran Book of Worship*; Missouri participated in the making of that resource but withdrew when LCMS President J. A. O. Preus saw what would happen if Missouri used the LBW—people would call for merger: We have the same hymnals; what's the difference?

## The Merger Vote Fails Again

About this time, the four groups that would make up the LCA were reported to be very near merger, the talks for which had gone smoothly and without incident. In November, the time plans for various constituting conventions were announced: the ALC would have its constituting convention in 1960 and begin work in 1961, while the LCA would have its constituting convention in 1961 and begin work in 1962. As the fall proceeded, the leaders of the LFC watched the votes from the congregation as they came in. They were hopeful, but on December 6, 1957, they counted them and found that the merger question had been defeated by 16 votes. Of 1,155 votes, 65.37 percent were yes, and 34.63 percent were no. This devastated the leadership.

Forrest Monson, the secretary of the church, told the *Star Tribune* that the main issue raised in the district debates had been the membership of the future ALC in the WCC and the fear of a large, centrally dominated headquarters.[90]

Monson was quoted as saying, "However... the LFC has no intention of withdrawing co-operation from the three other bodies." He doubted there would be another merger proposal sent to the LFC congregations before the ALC began in January 1961. Fredrik Schiotz, president of the ELC and then the ALC, praising the contributions of the LFC members, regretted the vote as well: "Despite the decision rejecting union, we look forward to continuing our fraternal co-operation with the LFC now and when the ELC become part of TALC."[91]

Once again, the leaders, although deeply disappointed that the LFC would not be there at the beginning, all foresaw that it would one day join the ALC. There were still people among the Lutheran leadership disappointed that not all the Lutheran Churches in America were merging in the next few years. Willmar Thorkelson (1918–2002), religion editor of the *Minneapolis Star*, wrote of a surprising report from Dr. Eppling Reinartz, president of the National Lutheran Council, advising that all the Lutheran churches that had voted to merge drop their earlier negotiations and begin "an all-out effort to unite in a single church." A six-member committee led by John Stensvaag considered Reinartz's proposal and presented its response to the council. It stated that the plea by Reinartz was outside the competence of the NLC. Hereafter, it became the Stensvaag Resolution. Schiotz was unhappy with Reinartz's proposal, as the council's constitution did not permit discussing Lutheran union. A true union of Lutherans, Schiotz argued, would have to include more than two-thirds of American Lutherans. Missouri would have to be part of it, he affirmed. Oscar Benson of Augustana, who agreed with Reinartz, however, wished that the resolution had said something about "sharing Dr. Reinartz' 'agonized hope' for achieving Lutheran union," rather than simply opposing it.[92] The Stensvaag Resolution passed with only two or three negative votes, most likely from those who agreed with Reinartz. The idea of the unity of all American Lutherans could not easily be quelled, but the council did stop it.

About that same time, Stensvaag, now acting as president of the LFC given Burntvedt's health, continued to counsel cooperation with the merging churches in the ALC. He did raise the notion that after five years, the LFC could vote again on merger. It needed to work closely with the ALC on mission and education, something it was not able to do well with such small numbers. Urging the LFC members "to take their eyes off the merger and fix them on Christ and the fields white unto harvest," he still held out the hope for merger. The vote did "not mean we have closed the door on eventual merger with the new body."[93]

The March 11 *Lutheran Messenger* mostly contained thoughts from the leadership about how the church could go forward, unmerged but desperately in need of reorganization and support for its projects. Burntvedt had a long article on the need for the LFC to restructure itself so the congregations did indeed have a say in the work of the church. He pointed out some of its greatest needs: the

# A Decade of Merger Talk

boards needed new membership requirements with longer terms and members more knowledgeable about their roles so they could be more effective at their work; the church needed to figure out what to do about a press since Messenger Press had sold its press and was printing its publications through one nearby. Since the press was struggling with a large debt, it was handicapped in what it could do. He and others at 2122 Riverside must have looked with envy at the new church being created—Augsburg Publishing House would be one of the largest presses in the country, highly profitable and well run. The year before, it had done four million dollars' of business and was the second largest user of the Minneapolis Post Office.[94]

John Stensvaag's address was a sober analysis of the LFC's situation now that it had voted against the merger. While he was glad for the cooperation the LFC had with the American Bible Society and the NLC, his concern was how it was going to manage alone: "As a small body we need the help that others can give us. But only as we work closely with these brethren in Christ can we hope to share in their great resources."[95] There was no question that the LFC needed help. He noted the gracious expressions of hope from the Joint Union Committee that the relationship not be diminished. In response to that, the LFC Committee on Relations expressed "its desire to investigate, through conversations with representatives of the JUC possible means or avenues of maintaining and cultivating... close cooperation with the negotiating Churches."[96] He then outlined areas for cooperation: parish education, evangelism, realignment of parishes, and foreign missions. These were urgent, he thought. But Stensvaag would not dismiss the idea of merger, which was, for him, a real possibility after some five years or so. He admitted that the defeat had been bitter for him, but he did note that sometimes God used defeats to move forward: "But accepting defeat in the right spirit need not mean that we give up the hope of one day becoming a part of the new Church."[97] To his credit, he said the church for the time being should forget about merger and fix its eyes on Christ and the fields white unto harvest. He ended with confidence in the Lord to unite them in one purpose "so that the power of God would be released in our lives."[98]

## Open Forum on the Loss

Having heard this speech, a group of leaders from the LFC met and were asked to discuss the future of the LFC in a free-wheeling open Forum at Augsburg on February 12. Walter Lyngdal of Duluth gave a meditation on Romans 12, and several prayed. Dr. Burntvedt, Dr. Christensen, Dr. Stensvaag, Philip Quanbeck, Iver Olson, Melvin Helland, P. K. L. Bueide, and many others took part. Luthard Gjerde gave an address at the beginning of the afternoon session on "The Contemporary Dilemma of the Lutheran Free Church."

**Figure 11.9.** Luthard Gjerde. Used by permission of Augsburg Fortress Publishers.

Gjerde's speech was printed in the next issue of the *Lutheran Messenger*. For those who knew and remember Gjerde and his temperament, this is a remarkable document. A gifted speaker, preacher, and pastor, as well as administrator, and now the executive director of the Lutheran Welfare Society of Minnesota, which would soon become Lutheran Social Services, Gjerde was thought to be irenic and not known for having a critical spirit. This piece, while temperate, is very critical, though deeply imbued with his love for and his own personal experience and knowledge of the LFC. He described the LFC as a "free association of congregations whose adherence is based upon enunciated Christian idealism." He then went on to describe the organization more colorfully as "an aggregation of monoliths interspersed with a miscellany of 'lean-to's' and smaller 'sheds' all tied together with the fresh air of freedom."[99]

He described Augsburg as a structure or entity with its own corporation, board, and administration that needed a cluster of congregations around to support it. The congregations had then found it necessary to create other monolithic structures like the Board of Organization, Oak Grove Lutheran Ladies' Seminary, Deaconess Hospital, and Bethesda Homes as their mission in the world. These were surrounded with sheds like the Luther League Federation, the Pension Society, and the WMF and lean-tos like the Board of Parish Education, the Board of Social Relations, Committee on Recruitment, the Committee on Evangelism, and a stewardship program. The only thing that had prevented utter chaos were the presidents, who had no job descriptions. Burntvedt, Gjerde noted, by sheer force of his "strong and consecrated Christian personality... had held the aggregation of separate structures together, taking to himself authority as the situation dictated."[100]

Bewildered congregations—not a church but a free association—were asking, "Where do we go from here?" Gjerde then outlined the critical issues facing the church. Money problems were inexorable, he concluded. He was right about that—the raising and lack of money never seemed to end. After a list of critical issues, he summed up the problem as a "lack of integration. Each operation is a law unto itself."[101] He found it ironic that the cry of freedom had maybe become bondage to the heirs of the LFC. He even dared to critique the guiding principles of the LFC, especially the first, most precious one that the congregation is the right form of the kingdom of God on earth. Somewhat in line with Evjen thirty years before, he thought it too exclusive. The kingdom of God could be found in many places. He also criticized Principle 10 that the "congregations had no right to demand that other congregations submit to their opinion, will, judgment or decision."[102]

Gjerde concluded his remarks by pleading that the LFC acknowledge its own sins of the past—the "Open Declaration" by Oftedal, the tragic controversy between the Augsburg Board of Trustees and the "United Church," the ill-advised appropriation of the Augsburg Publishing House property, and the rebuff our fathers gave to honest invitations to consider union with the ELC. He felt that although "the battle cry was around the freedom of the congregation, the actual battles were around personalities and properties."[103] He advised the LFC to adopt a humble attitude as it dealt with other Lutherans: "This is the best we can do, because the sins of our fathers, can scarcely be confessed by us, nor can they be forgiven by people long dead. Our attitude to others today, however, should testify to the fact that we walk as those whom God has forgiven!"[104]

This is a document I had not seen before. While Gjerde is arguing for merger here, the tone is very masterfully controlled and descriptive, but it is a scathing rebuke of the LFC and its history and very pro-merger. What he says in describing the condition of the LFC can hardly be viewed as untrue. It clearly affected the conversation after it was given. While he might have been correct on the current state of the organization, his call to repent for the "sinful" history of the organization bothered many. Those who knew him, but not this speech, were shocked and not a little irritated when they read it, especially his criticism of the LFC's "sins." Those "sins" were the DNA of the fellowship.

In response, Forrest Monson, Stewardship Secretary gave something of a similar analysis agreeing with Gjerde, complaining that it was hard for him to even think of a budget when he had never met with several boards that were central to the mission of the church, such as the Board of Foreign Missions or Home Missions. He spoke of how hard it was to be a leader in stewardship when he was not informed of new budget needs and new drives that had been announced without any input from him or his office, at the same time that he was expected to help them raise money after the fact. Christensen also had a list of crises that needed addressing at the college. Most of them had to do with finding a wider base of support to pay for the school. His question stated the main question of most of the leaders: "Is the LFC too small to support Augsburg?"[105]

Fundamentally, that was the worry of everybody and the hope of these leaders for the merger. That whine of anxiety about Augsburg and its future was, at root, the main issue that drove the conversations, whether for or against. The high-minded rhetoric about Jesus's prayer for unity sounded good or the notion that disunity was sin, another abstract reason that could be used to argue for the merger. That was not the reason, ultimately, that these leaders wanted it. The church they were building to look like other churches simply could not do the kind of work they thought necessary to be a successful organization without more resources. Their hope was to join forces with the larger groups to save Augsburg. It was the only reason my parents could imagine being for it.

Subsequent issues of the *Lutheran Messenger* continued the discussion of what we should do now. My uncle Donald Ronning wrote that he thought the church most needed revival and rededication to the cause of Christ.[106] Christian G. Olson pleaded with the congregations and pastors to stay together at all costs, advising that a merger would most likely come, and that would save the colleges and schools.[107] Such columns appeared frequently from pastors and leaders of the church. Merton Strommen weighed in with advice on how to assure a living congregation.[108]

Mrs. Karl Kleppe of Napoleon, North Dakota, reacted to Gjerde's speech with a point-by-point rebuttal of his comments, disparaging them as disloyal. How could one praise the Constitution of the United States and then tear it apart, she wondered, looking to Gjerde's regret at Oftedal's "Open Declaration" or the "12 Principles" as insufficient.[109]

## Burntvedt Resigns

At the end of May, Dr. Burntvedt informed the pastors of the LFC that he would be resigning as president as of October 1, 1958. While he had thought he would recover enough to preside when he was reelected the year before, he now realized it was time he retire. He was Mr. Free Church to Lutherans in America and highly regarded for his clear thinking, eloquence, and steady leadership.[110] While it was not a surprise to the church body, the loss was a body blow. While

Figure 11.10. T. O. Burntvedt and John M. Stensvaag on the cover of the *Lutheran Messenger*. Used by permission of Augsburg Fortress Publishers.

Stensvaag was well regarded, his character was different, something of a partisan. You never wondered what he thought.

## The Annual Meeting 1958

The annual convention would not be so fiery this year. Its main business was electing a new president, given Burntvedt's resignation. John Stensvaag and Luthard Gjerde were the final contenders; the vote was somewhat close, 263 for Stensvaag to 197 for Gjerde. Gjerde moved that the vote be unanimous for Stensvaag, and so it was. The convention was filled with tributes to Burntvedt and the new presidency of John Stensvaag.

Forrest Monson had an optimistic and encouraging report on the state of the finances of the church. Altogether the members of the LFC had contributed $3,327,914 to the church, averaging $63.65 a member. The number of members was up by 4 percent to 77,304. These were positive numbers, astonishing and encouraging even if they were not enough to pay the huge costs of the college and seminary. Once again, the meeting members voted by voice, with few negative votes, to hold another referendum on merger in 1961 rather than wait until 1965. Action was taken to allow the church to work closely with the new ALC on the five issues Stensvaag had noted in his speech. The COR expressed its conviction that merger was the destiny of the LFC, and that seemed to be shared by a good majority of the delegates at this convention.

At the meeting, the LFC honored its veteran missionary couple to Madagascar, the Caleb Quanbecks, and worked to increase funding for both home and foreign missions. In addition, this June marked the twentieth anniversary of Christensen's presidency of Augsburg. The Minneapolis papers featured this event with long and glowing articles celebrating his life and work. Christensen looked to the future with some worry: he saw the dangers in secularism, noting that "we need religious faith and character as much as we need freedom, and the function of the Christian liberal arts college is to bring young people into touch with this fusion."[111]

As he watched the growing power of secularism, he feared "that a society divorced from church and religious convictions" could not "withstand what he termed 'the iron of communism.'"[112] Here he, along with many like Hubert Humphrey in the Democratic Party, saw communism as a danger and fought against it. Christensen saw the future, especially in his fears of the government funding of Christian education. He was most anxious about the failure of the merger votes because Augsburg needed one million dollars immediately to complete its gymnasium, a crying need at the time.

For the rest of the year, the church paper focused on the astonishing growth of the LFC and its very successful programs—the missions, the WMF, and especially the very successful youth program, which had held its most well-attended convention at Green Lake in Wisconsin. Merton Strommen's charismatic leadership and his thoughtful application of his studies in psychology and sociology bore fruit in the evangelism of the youth program.

That fall at the Pastor's Institute at Augsburg, the community gathered to fete Dr. Burntvedt and his wife as he stepped down from his nearly thirty years at the helm of the LFC. The Institute had heard grave warnings from Dr. Kantonen from Hamma Divinity School in Springfield, Ohio, about the growing secularism of the world and church, noting that too many preachers were not preaching the gospel "but a sentimental moralism which consists in trying to practice the golden rule and being kind."[113]

At his retirement banquet, Burntvedt was praised for his leadership through the decades, from keeping the LFC together in the beginning days of his presidency to his concern for the saving of souls. "He never lost sight of this goal as the main objective of his ministry," remarked John Stensvaag. In addition, he never lost his common touch nor his "irrepressible sense of humor."[114] In these comments, one notes little about the politics of Burntvedt or Christensen, even though they were clear to most. Soon, politics seemed to become the main work of the church leaders, something both Burntvedt and Christensen were careful to avoid—and to counsel against. There is an irony here. In hindsight, they saw the dangers of increasing secularism, even as many of the programs they fought for ushered it in as the politics of the day, and then the works of Bonhoeffer and the death-of-God theologians were gearing up to dominate the '60s. This was modernism, pure and simple, and may be the real culprit in the demise of the LFC, as it was for many such institutions.

## Founding the ALC

In November, when the merging churches met to choose the name for the new church—United Evangelical Lutheran Church vied with the American Lutheran Church, or TALC—there was a strong movement not to use *American* in the name because it was too nationalistic. Schiotz made a strong plea for UELC for reasons of mission work and the association of the name with the colonial period.[115] The group, however, voted to retain American Lutheran Church, ALC.

At this same meeting, Stensvaag appeared now in his official capacity as president of the LFC. He advised the committee that the LFC would not be able to join the new church until 1963 after its vote in 1961. Stensvaag then left for a tour of the mission fields of the LFC and other places where it was in mission with other groups. He was the official representative to the Santal Mission, and the Ebenezer Lutheran Church there would become fully autonomous on December 30, 1958. This was a harbinger of many other such events in the 1960s as Western churches sought to decolonize their missions and give the various groups their independence.

In the fall of 1958, while other Lutheran churches were introducing the *Service Book and Hymnal*, Central in Salem held a teaching training school for Sunday school teachers. The Luther Leaguers of most of the Lutheran churches in Salem met together to hear about the new hymnal. I remember reading part of the liturgy from the lectern and looked out at my fellow Luther Leaguers, especially the pastor's son in Silverton, making a face at the new book. This was way too much liturgy by his lights, and I had to smile. But this was what was happening. Our little tradition and its cherished *Concordia Hymnal* were on their way out. This involved all the Lutherans in Salem, except the Missouri Synod. These things that came from the east had some authority but seemed to be from another world.

In November 1958, the idea once again emerged that the two large merging churches should stop everything and find a way to merge all of those involved into one church. It was said to have come from the three merging churches in the future ALC and addressed to the presidents of the AELC, Augustana, the Finnish Evangelical, and the ULCA. It was motivated by the belief that "there is a mutual desire not to let present union negotiations become a roadblock to future Lutheran unity."[116] The presidents of the three merging churches declined this invitation, believing it to be impossible at that time to stop the process toward the new church.[117]

After the convention in June 1958, the *Lutheran Messenger* had stopped writing articles about the merger and focused on the work of the LFC, which was thriving. Churches were being built, old sanctuaries being replaced by larger ones, missionaries, youth work, Sunday school instruction, all the things that one would expect a church to be concerned with. There were increasing stories and news items on racial issues around the world. On the whole, the leadership had clearly taken the hint to stop talking about merger and get on with the mission of the church.

Things were also quiet in 1959. In January 1959, the Willamette Lutheran Home for those who were infirm and aged began organizing with a twelve-man board from the various Lutheran churches in town, except the Missouri Synod. Enough Lutherans had migrated to the Willamette Valley to make such a home viable. It would be located near the Willamette River.

The old customs still held for my father. That winter, the Sons of Norway commended him for holding a Norwegian Christmas service at Central at the end of the year, something that still attracted enough to fill the little church at the time. As my father said, he would do anything to get some of these Norwegians out to hear the Gospel, and preaching Norwegian at Christmas was a good opportunity.

## The Annual Meeting 1959

The annual meeting in 1959 would be held in Minot, North Dakota, hosted by Zion Lutheran at First Lutheran, where John Kildal was a pastor. The most important work of that convention would be the "Report of the Committee on Polity and Organization." Established at the last convention, the committee met during the previous year and dealt with several mandates from the prior convention: parish education and redefining the evangelism program. In addition, it considered new procedures for the stewardship office in its relationship with the other boards and programs, and the nature and function of the annual conference, especially regarding voting rights. These in essence addressed the lingering problems noted by the leadership after the defeat of merger in 1957 and, to no one's surprise, reorganizing once again the way the vote worked in the annual meeting and the congregations for when the next merger vote would come.[118] This report was to be received and discussed in June at the annual meeting. While there were several resolutions to be presented, the most significant one was number 7, "The assignment of voting delegates to the congregations shall be on the following schedule: Congregations with 1–100 baptized members, one delegate. Congregations with 101–250 baptized members, two delegates. Congregations with 251–500 baptized members, three delegates. Congregations with 500 or more members, four delegates."[119] These had already been presented or ordered by the 1958 convention, so they were no surprise to the membership of the congregations, but looked at somewhat realistically, it was an attempt to make it possible for the merger vote to pass. Not surprisingly, some wrote in the paper to oppose it as a fundamental betrayal of the principles of the LFC.

Pastor Ole Johan Haukeness (1888–1984) wrote to address the question "Shall We Adopt the Representative System?" He argued that with the representative system proposed by the committee, people who were not delegates would lose interest in coming to the meeting because they would not have the right to vote. Why would they come to the meeting if they could not vote? If we wanted people to pray and support the church, why would "we deprive them of the vote and [the ability] to make decisions" for the church?[120]

Our family was particularly excited because Dad had been asked to preach the opening sermon, and Mother was going to sing the solo at the opening meeting of the WMF. It was an exciting time as we readied to make the long trip east again. As we sped along Highway 2 toward Minot, Dad rehearsed his sermon, "Lambs that go away from the shepherd to where there are green pastures and get lost. Away from their shepherd." Mother was going to sing "Great Is Thy Faithfulness." She would wear her dark navy-blue dress with pink pop beads. I can still see her singing in front of the church, her sweet voice dramatic now with conviction, like her mother, who sang at many a convention. A woman who had heard my grandmother Anda singing told me how much she had meant to her at conventions like this one and thought my mother's voice was beautiful.

The presidential address by John Stensvaag was long and detailed. While he took cognizance of the international situation with the threat of nuclear war hanging over the world and the culture's growing decadence, he had good news about the church. It had grown from forty-five thousand baptized members in 1930 to eighty thousand now in 1959. He also addressed the shortage of pastors and attributed it mainly to the low salaries they were receiving. He reported that some had estimated that a pastor needed minimum $4,600–$4,800 to live well. Many LFC parishes were not meeting that minimum in their congregations, which was not good.

Parishes needed to be realigned, even if it meant joining an ELC and LFC congregation together. He also complimented the Committee on Polity and Organization for its proposal for reforming the voting process and recommended it pass. In addition, he commended its resolution for streamlining the stewardship process in the LFC. This was much needed and would "make for a more effective, unified approach to the congregations, and should, in the long run, make for a more stable, predictable income for our common endeavors."[121]

Meanwhile, the *Lutheran Messenger* reported on the progress the three churches were making on their way toward the merger so that people would be informed. Burntvedt wrote frequent articles about things that concerned him. In September, he wrote an article commending the work of Lutheran World Action and the struggles in the world that needed the attention of Christians everywhere: the militant atheism of the Soviet Union, the suffering of Palestinian refugees, and the suffering of Christians under the communist rule in China.[122] In October, the *Lutheran Messenger* included an article by Burntvedt on evangelism, part of a series he would write in his last years. He had been asked if he approved of Billy Graham, who was now making his mark on the world. Yes, he did, as well as many other methods, especially for him, the evangelism program Preaching, Teaching, Reaching (PTR), begun in the ELC and joined by the LFC in many areas. He also commended the work of Donald Fladland, whom he thought had been especially successful with youth, as we had seen in Salem. He concluded that the LFC should face the future, whether merged or going it alone, with the scriptural injunction, "Cast not away therefore your boldness, which hath great recompense of reward."[123]

Over the next years, I would be thinking of colleges, and of course there was no other school than Augsburg. Mother started writing letters to her teachers, including Gerda and Anne Pederson. Gerda visited in the summer of 1959 to check me out and be there for Mom and Dad, after they had confided in her about my thinking, even slightly, of another school. Gerda had relatives in Silverton, so she made the trip to see them, stopping by in August, just when the peaches were at their juiciest and ripest. Mother made peach pie, and as they talked and grilled Gerda on Augsburg, she would laugh her trilling laugh and say, "Oh, Jonette, that pie is delicious. Could I have another piece?" Anne Pederson answered Mother's plea as to whether Augsburg was good enough for Gracia with her typical rhetorical sentence structure: "Dear Jonette, the question, really, is whether Gracia is good enough for Augsburg!" The premise at the root of that, really, is: Have you raised a child who will help Augsburg? Everything you did, even how you raised your children, was to sustain and increase the life of the school in our midst.

But I was growing slightly resentful of the idea that there was no other place. When I suggested I might try other schools, I found my dad in the downstairs Sunday school room weeping. When my secular teachers heard about this school in the Midwest, a small Lutheran college that had just been accredited, they turned up their noses with scorn and alarm.

On August 20, 1959, Grandma Anna Grindal died in Everett, Washington, at Bethany Home. I was working at the Blue Lake Cannery and could not attend the funeral, where my father spoke beautifully of what she had done for him and her great love for the missions of the church, especially the Martha and Maria Orphanage. She loved to put on her best clothes, take a basket, and go through the neighborhood collecting money for the orphanage. She also loved the hymns of the church, especially *"Den Himmelske Lovsong"* ("The Heavenly Praises"), which he imagined her now singing in heaven with the angels. He did not say it, but I imagine he thought that now she was healed of her mental anguish and free.

The last year of the quiet decade ended with the *Lutheran Messenger* featuring an article by Robert Paul Roth, a leader in the Northwestern Seminary faculty, which would merge with Luther Seminary in the 1970s. His job was to elaborate on the five theses adopted by the LWF in its Minneapolis Assembly—the unity of the church in Christ is a gift and an obligation. The thrust of his argument was the tragedy of division in the Christian church. His piece was a harbinger of the next decade and the ecumenical movement. Nationalism is "a product of this faithless divisiveness in the body of Christ," Roth argued, saying the reformation was a "tragic necessity." The job of the next decade would be, he suggested in the words of Oscar Cullman, that we "begin our faithful journey back to union in Christ."[124] This journey, he thought, should begin with works of love toward all. He saw this happening in the activities of Lutheran World Action. But his comments sounded a new note for the churches, and they set the table for the next decade.

CHAPTER 12

# Merger

As the 1960s began, talks of merger, corporate and otherwise, appeared frequently in the press. Railroads, corporations, political parties—in Minnesota, the Democrats with the Farmer Labor Party—school boards, schools, and churches (Unitarians and Universalists) were all talking merger. The Somali republic merged with Togo. Even Kennedy's choice of Lyndon Johnson at the Democratic convention was described as a merger. Efficiency was usually the driving force. For churches, that was a partial reason—our combined resources would allow us to do more missions—but there was also a growing sense that denominations were a scandal. Christian unity began to mean not unity in purpose and oneness in Christ but also now a movement toward corporate unity and ultimately one church. It would not be long before the ecumenical dialogues after Vatican II in 1962 began. One can see all this in the growing talk in favor of organic unity among churches and especially church bodies like Lutherans, who had a common confession.

The year 1960 began at Central Lutheran in Salem, Oregon, with evangelistic services from January 13 to 17 led by Don Fladland, an old friend of the church. At North Salem High School, the *Salem Statesman* journal announced that John Holte (the ELC pastor Lowell Holte's son), three others, and I had received straight As. Like our fathers, we were competitors! Good grades were important to our generation. The Russians had launched Sputnik in March 1957, dramatically changing American education for the better. We called ourselves the Sputnik generation. This meant a stress on education, especially in the sciences, but it spilled over into emphases on languages and the liberal arts. Members of what is known as the silent generation (1935-1945), we were born before and during World War II. We were something of the leading edge of the baby boomers. In every class I had from first grade on, schools had to enlarge their facilities to accommodate our numbers. My first grade in Rugby had two classes for the first time. Fortunately, I got Miss Vivien Almquist for two years. A kind woman who treated me with respect, she died of breast cancer when I was in third grade, something that devastated me. I remember standing by her casket outside Bethany, bewildered and terrified by death, as the pallbearers were lifting it into the hearse.

My third-grade teacher, Miss Medalin, understood me well enough to allow me to read library books under my desk and pray for me, she told me years later. My fourth- and fifth-grade teacher, Miss Lear, and I did not get along. I made her life as miserable as she made mine. I could never forgive her for yelling at me when I sought sanctuary in the school during recess from a big Labrador dog who would attack me. It terrified me. Discipline in the Rugby school system was harsh. This was not allowed.

When we moved to Salem, my teachers in both junior high and senior high school encouraged me and taught me the skills necessary to do well in college. The orchestra teacher, Mr. McClintock, introduced me and my flute-playing best friend to the great classical music of the West, especially Handel and Bach. My homeroom teacher, a Catholic Democrat, Miss Lorraine Meusy, influenced me greatly as I began thinking about history and social studies. In 1959, in my junior class of American history, my teacher George Strozut guided me through the business of writing a term paper. I wrote on Lutheran merger. In it, I laid out some of the issues that still plague me—what do the churches bring to merger, and what is lost when they merge?

## The LCA Is Formed

That February, future members of the LCA, the American Evangelical Lutheran Church (AELC), the Augustana Lutheran Church, the Finnish (Suomi), and the United Lutheran Church (ULCA) announced that its representatives had voted by a wide majority to use the name Lutheran Church in America (LCA) after a "storm of protest" arose when the first name, Lutheran Evangelical Church of America, was announced.[1] People thought it was clumsy and too much like other names, with the added problem of the way most Americans took the word *evangelical*. Later that month, when it became clear to the members of the future LCA that there would be a merger of its seminaries—Augustana, Chicago Lutheran, Grand View, and Suomi—to be built in Chicago, another storm arose. Northwestern Lutheran Seminary in Minneapolis would not agree to such a merger, nor would Hamma Divinity School in Springfield. The president of Northwestern, Dr. Clemens Zeidler, thought a realignment with Luther Seminary in St. Paul was far more likely and salutary.[2]

## A Catholic President?

Central Lutheran in Salem was doing well. The 1960 parochial reports indicate that Central was the largest LFC congregation in the West Coast district, with 520 baptized members and money raised over $16,000. It was no secret that the congregation was now large enough to need a bigger facility and especially a larger worship space.

Now the question of John F. Kennedy, a Roman Catholic and frontrunner for the presidential nomination of the Democratic Party, began receiving the attention of the press. The Minneapolis papers noted that the question of Kennedy's Catholicism was greatest in western Wisconsin, close to the Minnesota border and home to some LFC congregations. Kennedy had been annoyed by the questions that were being asked there. He retorted to one questioner, "It is wholly obnoxious for anyone to tell anyone else how to vote."[3]

Oregon had both strong Democrats like Senator Wayne Morse and Republicans like Governor Mark Hatfield, who had become a friend of my folks. A Baptist layman, he had spoken at Central Lutheran several times. The political parties there were said to be more liberal than they were back east. As the Eisenhower era was ending, Morse, Hubert Humphrey, and John Kennedy began to duke it out in the Democratic primaries. Oregon became part of the national theater with its May primary. Always fascinated by news and politics, whether church or national, and coming from a Republican household, I loved the campaigns, especially when Kennedy appeared in Salem.

On May 17, Kennedy visited the Capitol building and then held a rally in the parking lot of the Capitol Mall some five blocks from our house. I walked over to it on my way home from school. Some four hundred people were crammed into the parking lot and spilling out on to the sidewalks. I could not get very close. The papers said he answered questions of those gathered around him while standing on a car's bumper to adequately see and be seen by the crowd.[4] They noted that the crowd flowed out into the street as people jostled to see him. I can remember that and also his charisma. I had never experienced anything like it. I stood probably a block from him, but his charismatic presence swept over me.

This was a movement of youth, many said. Kennedy appealed to them with his good looks, incandescent smile, and heroic military experience. One thing, however, that held me, and many others, back was his Catholicism. Would he bow to the edicts of the pope? It was widely believed that the Roman Catholic Church opposed democracy. That was the argument being made by many throughout the country, and it was a lively debate. One of the chief debaters in the upper Midwest, surprisingly to us, was Mario Colacci (1910–1968), the Augsburg professor of New Testament, Greek, and Latin. When he arrived at Augsburg, he became a pastor in the LFC, but he was also a distinguished scholar with a doctorate in sacred theology from the Pontifical Roman Major Seminary at the Lateran in Rome, as well as a degree in the Bible from the Pontifical Biblical Institute de Urbe in Rome. He was an impressive catch. He ended up at Augsburg in 1952 after leaving Rome and the Catholic Church. While he was at Augsburg, he wrote books on Catholic-Lutheran issues such as *Christian Marriage Today* (1958), which treated interfaith marriages, and *The Doctrinal Conflict Between Roman Catholic and Protestant Christianity* (1962). Discovered by Bernhard

Figure 12.1. Mario Colacci (1910–1968). Used by permission of Augsburg University Archives.

Christensen, who invited him to Augsburg, he became a much loved professor, a brilliant but controversial addition to the Augsburg faculty.[5]

Colacci advised the LFC and other Lutherans with great passion that Kennedy would not be subject to Rome in the way they feared. In the Easter 1960 version of *Concord*, the seminary's bulletin, he wrote a long article on ecclesiology and where the authority lay in Protestant and Catholic doctrine. He concluded that because the older confessions of faith—Apostles, Nicene, and Athanasian—were accepted by most churches, Christian believers who showed their acceptance of these creeds, whether Catholic or Protestant, were followers of Christ and, thus, brothers.[6]

As a high school junior, I was interested in my studies, church politics, and national politics and was an avid reader of the news, with interest in arts and letters. At the time, I was also considering colleges, knowing I had little choice. When my teachers saw that Augsburg had only recently been accredited, they turned up their noses and advised me against it, urging me to try anywhere else. My friends were applying to the University of Oregon, Harvard, Stanford, and the University of Southern California. They urged me to do the same. It was flattering.

Meanwhile, in Minneapolis, Sister Anna Bergeland was stepping down as directing sister of Deaconess Hospital. She had been there for forty-nine years, from her enrollment as a diaconate student until April 1960. It was a clear end of an era. She was something of a symbol of the rise and change in the deaconess movement from a minor clerical office with nursing to a profession with nursing as its main work. She had run the hospital for thirty-two years as an administrator and then thirteen years as a directing sister. Burntvedt, in one of his last public speeches, commended Bergeland for her faithful service. He also remembered some of the history of the institute over seventy years of work in Minneapolis. He marveled at that. From its very small and rickety beginnings, it had succeeded beyond anyone's expectations.

## The ALC Is Formed

On April 22 in Minneapolis, at Central Lutheran Church and then in the Minneapolis Auditorium, the three participating church bodies that would form the ALC met together for a "Ceremony of Joining Hands." Henry F. Schuh (1890–1965) of the ALC, Dr. Fredrik A. Schiotz of the ELC, and Dr. William Larsen (1909–1971) of the UELC solemnly joined hands as the chaplain said, "Now unto him that is able to do exceedingly abundantly above all that we ask or think, according to the power that worketh in us, unto him be glory in the Church by Christ Jesus throughout all ages, world without end. Amen."[7]

John Stensvaag brought a greeting from the LFC that was congratulatory and not a little sad. He spoke of his regret to the group, saying that in 1961, the question would once again come before the LFC, and it was his hope, as much as that of Burntvedt, he noted, that it would be a positive vote. He concluded with a resolution commending the merging churches, which the LFC in convention had drafted at its last annual meeting.[8]

The *Messenger* included excerpts from Schiotz's address as well. He named several things that had cheered him as their work began: one congregation had given $100,000 to launch a Bible study project, another group of laymen had initiated a fund to support missions in Africa and Asia. Deploring the cultural decline of the theater in America, he challenged the new church with its nine "splendid senior colleges" to "produce writers that will pour living water into the reservoirs of American cultural life." He also noted the need for housing reform in Minneapolis to help give Black people access to affordable housing, something he hoped the many Lutheran congregations in Minneapolis would support with all their hearts.[9]

## T. O. Burntvedt Dies

On May 12, 1960, people were shocked to hear that T. O. Burntvedt had died while driving home from downtown Minneapolis. His picture appeared on the cover of the May 31, 1960, *Lutheran Messenger*. The issue was filled with tributes. Sverre Torgerson reviewed his life, from his birth in Kragerø, Norway, in 1888 to his emigration to Brooklyn when he was fifteen. There, he had attended night school while working as a grocery clerk and stone cutter. He graduated from Augsburg College in 1912 and the Seminary in 1915. While there, he had come to know my uncle Fred Tinseth well. He was not only a pastor but also a scholar and musician, a member of one of the Augsburg Quartets. He attended the Northwestern Conservatory of Music and the Biblical Seminary in New York, plus the University of Minnesota. His first parish was Olivet Lutheran congregation in Tacoma. From there, he moved to Brooklyn, where he served as associate pastor at Trinity Lutheran with S. O. Sigmond until he was called to Trinity Congregation in Minneapolis. While there, he lectured in practical theology at Augsburg Seminary (1942–1957) while also teaching church history and Bible at LBI in Minneapolis. He was elected president of the LFC in 1930, where he served until 1958. These appointments gave him a comprehensive knowledge of the LFC and the Norwegian Lutheran Church in America. He also had an experience of the worldwide church movements. In 1927, he attended the World Conference on Faith and Order in Lausanne, Switzerland, and the Lutheran World Federation meetings in Lund, Sweden, in 1947 and Hannover, Germany, in 1952. He frequently traveled to his home country to visit friends and family.

Leaders from other Lutheran churches, here and in Norway, remembered him and spoke at his funeral: Per Lønning, at the time a member of Parliament in Norway, remembered the "high regard" Burntvedt received in Norway; Paul Empie, executive director of the National Lutheran Council, commended his ability to speak with conviction without arrogance; Dr. Olaf G. Malmin (1899–1973), speaking for President Schiotz of the ALC, praised him for his profound influence on the negotiations that resulted in the ALC.

Dr. Christensen gave a long and eloquent description of his friendship with T.O., whom he had known at Augsburg and Brooklyn's Trinity Church. He praised Burntvedt as a counselor and leader. He also noted his deep spiritual convictions and submission to the Gospel, especially his powerful preaching, as well as his efficient administrative skills and intellectual interests. Ultimately, Christensen said he was "a man of a broken heart" (one who knew he was a sinner), despite being something of a natural aristocrat. His pastor at Trinity Congregation in Minneapolis, Martin J. Olson (1898–1991), praised Burntvedt as being for him "in the true sense my 'Bishop.'" That word again.

Irene Huglen Strommen wrote about coming to know Burntvedt while a young girl when he visited her family in Saskatchewan, where her father was pastor. She described how kind he was to her and her sisters, buying them ice cream cones. When her father died suddenly while she was still at home, Burntvedt remembered her and ultimately asked if he could give her away at her wedding in place of her father. His fatherly temperament was obvious to everybody.

Burntvedt had stayed at our house several times during his travels, and we always enjoyed his company. I remember once, when I was not much over six, running to him at a convention as he was enjoying coffee with other pastors. He hugged me and remembered my name and who I was. One doesn't forget that kind of thing. I marvel that I thought nothing of it and was sure he would know me and greet me.

In reading his thoughts and prayers for the merger, one does not get a sense that Burntvedt had contempt for the people he was serving or wanted to change them. He understood the piety of the LFC, I think, and shared it. He never let up on evangelism and spiritual things, from what I can see. I was privileged to know him. And that was one of the benefits of our small fellowship. One knew everybody, including the leaders. They sacrificed much to keep the fellowship going. Burntvedt, Christensen, and Miss Mortensen were, along with other star teachers at Augsburg, essentially the admissions office for the school. They spent every waking moment trying to recruit students and good faculty and to keep the fellowship connected. I shudder when I think of all that work now.

## The Annual Meeting 1960

The annual convention that year was at Pontoppidan Lutheran in Fargo, where my uncle Donald Ronning was pastor. People were still grieving the death of Burntvedt, who had been president throughout the living memory of most LFCers. The theme of the convention was "A Deeper Life for a Stronger Church." Missions, especially, were front and center at both the annual meeting and the LWF convention, which featured several missionaries in their programs—Marcy Ditmanson, who was raising money for a hospital in Taiwan; Mrs. Robert Andersen; Marion Dahlen; Arthur Robert; Emily Helland; C. Arthur Schultz; Miss Mariam Ahlness; and Miss Lenorah Erikson. The convention also heard from Peng Fu, president of the Evangelical Lutheran Church in Hong Kong, who had come to faith after contact with Pastor Stokke in the Norwegian Mission in Honan. He had visited America on several occasions and was well known to the church. He and his wife had come to the States from Hong Kong to celebrate the centennial of the Augustana Lutheran Church in Rock Island. From there, he spent time with Pastor Ingvald Daehlen in Fergus Falls studying literature. Well regarded by all who knew him, he was especially close to missionaries from the Norwegian American mission.

The convention noted the careers of many veteran missionaries as the decade's shift brought the endings of several longtime careers in ministry and missions. Pastor and Mrs. Morris Vaagenes Sr. sent their last greeting from

Madagascar, announcing their retirement after nearly fifty years in the field, even as new missionaries like Sheldon Torgerson were being sent out. Veteran missionaries to China, like the Fred Ditmansons, had also retired and were being replaced by younger people such as Lester and Marion Dahlen.

Peder Konsterlie, executive secretary of the Board of Missions, celebrated the merger of the two Norwegian American Lutheran churches in Madagascar, which had begun on February 1, 1960. He enumerated the successes in the Malagasy church: there were now 7,221 baptized members, 3,031 pupils in Sunday school, 127 organization congregations served by 15 pastors, and 116 catechists. Most exciting was the presence of a native pastor, Seth Pierre Andrianarivo. The Malagasy mission, as we have noted, was dear to the hearts of most Norwegian American Lutherans because of the earliest missionaries from Norway and American who went there. These missionaries forged vigorous connections with the people through letters and appearances in churches while they were on furlough.

Konsterlie also noted the work in Hong Kong and Taiwan, where the Marcy Ditmansons and Albert Olsons had just found property on which they could build a hospital. In cooperation with the ELC, the new field in Japan had just called Rosalyn Holte, who would become an important LFC addition to the work. Konsterlie announced with joy that the next year the LFC had budgeted $178,000 for missions.

Figure 12.2. Seth Pierre Andrianarivo. Used by permission of Augsburg Fortress Publishers.

Figure 12.3. Rosalyn Holte. Used by permission of Augsburg Fortress Publishers.

This annual convention worked by the new rules where congregations elected delegates to represent them. Torgerson found it to have worked since seventy more congregations than before had sent delegates. The Credentials Committee announced that 156 pastors and 326 voting delegates had registered with 90 advisory members, so the total was 664, with many others in attendance. This was good news and showed the seriousness with which the congregations and delegates took their responsibilities to represent their congregations, Torgerson thought.

Stensvaag, in his presidential address, noted the need for stronger emphasis on evangelistic preaching as well as social ministry, deploring racism and its denial of human dignity. He commended the work of Lutheran World Action for its work among refugees. He also urged the restoration of evening services in LFC congregations, noting their demise in favor of small groups meeting in informal settings at home. He did not note it was television as much as anything that was making inroads on the Sunday evening service. Still, Central Lutheran continued to have such services during the winter months.

In a somewhat oblique reference to the presidential campaign being waged, the conference adopted a resolution recognizing "that religion is increasingly becoming an issue in the political struggle to be duly considered by the voter, and therefore urges a complete appraisal of a candidate's views in this area also."[10] My father had raised some issue about this in one of his sermons, and a beloved member told him he should not preach politics from the pulpit. He took the rebuke seriously and almost never did after that.

Since the 1958 annual conference had voted that the issue of merger would be brought before the LFC for decision in 1961, the subject was still hanging in the air. Arnold Hermunslie made a motion to rescind that resolution; Iver Solberg, a state senator from Ray, North Dakota, and a good friend of my folks, was to speak for the motion to rescind and Luthard Gjerde against it. They requested a paper ballot, which took some time, but deliberations continued as the count was made. It was defeated 70 to 361. Clearly, the delegates were ready to move forward on the vote the next year. Pastor Harry T. Sorensen moved that "no articles incumbent with the issues of the merger referendum be carried in the Lutheran Messenger during the time of the congregational voting."[11] The motion was tabled and not reconsidered, apparently, as the *Messenger* was filled with letters and articles on the debate through the entire next year and during the voting period.

As was traditional, Augsburg and Oak Grove dominated the conversations. Clifford M. Johnson, pastor of Oak Grove congregation in Richfield and chair of the board of trustees of Augsburg, announced the initiation of a new drive to support such projects as the building of the new Si Melby Hall, for which they needed to raise $750,000.

Stensvaag also rejoiced that the church had raised almost 10 percent more than it had the year before and had contributed fully to its goal for Lutheran World Action, which was the most popular and well-known program of the Lutheran World Federation. At the time, it had a new refugee problem: There were now, worldwide, over fifteen million people needing resettling.

In his report to the convention, Christensen stated good news, noting Augsburg's calling to continue "providing higher education built on Christian foundations."[12] He called attention to the soaring costs of such an institution: it needed to adequately pay its faculty, speak to the increasing secularization of the culture, manage its increasing enrollment, and thus overcome the difficulty of attending to individual students. Therefore, it coveted the prayers of all.

At Augsburg's commencement a few weeks before, Dr. Theodore C. Blegen (1891–1969), a 1910 graduate, retiring dean of the University of Minnesota Graduate School, and son of John Blegen, an early professor, had been the featured speaker. He praised Augsburg for its modernization over the past fifty years. He noted eight marks of its progress: (1) the rising enrollment from 160 to 1,294 students, (2) the liberalizing of its curriculum, (3) beginning coeducation, (4) discontinuing the academy, (5) the new buildings, (6) widening cooperation with state and private colleges, (7) its recent accreditation, and (8) its presidents and strengthened faculty.[13]

That many church leaders were warning against the growing forces of secularization shows they were keenly aware of the harbingers of a movement sweeping through most institutions of higher learning in the country. It was a mark of their attentiveness to the work of Christ in the world, even as they were, ironically, building schools where secularization would be almost guaranteed because of their efforts to become typical American colleges.

Dad was on the colloquy committee that year to interview the seminary grads before they could be ordained. He had flown to Fargo, the first time for him in an airplane. The convention concluded with an ordination service for six men: Carl Jensen, James Armstrong, Neal Snider, James Glasoe, Daniel Faust, and Kenneth Rhoe. The fact that the LFC ordained men at its national convention and not in their home parish or congregation became an issue in the Task Force for the Study of Ministry. Several accused the LFC of practicing a kind of bishop's ordination like the historic Episcopate, despite its early attempt to avoid this by having an ordinator, which it had abandoned. Now the church president officiated, making the accusation seem not all that outlandish. I would have to defend our practice as not being in any way like the Historic Episcopate, but the way something looks becomes how people explain it even if the theology of the LFC did not square with what they saw.

## Appendix No. 1: Procedures for Merger

The most significant report of the convention was Appendix No. 1, from the Committee on Relations with Other Lutherans Bodies. It recommended adopting the following procedures for the vote on merger, which the 1958 convention had authorized: (1) The 1961 annual conference would vote on the merger negotiations with the ALC. If that was approved, (2) a motion to enter negotiations would be sent to the congregations of the LFC. If the vote was positive, another resolution empowering the annual conference in 1962 to act on all subsequent matters would also need to be voted on. An election committee of the president and secretary of the LFC would comprise that committee. If the referendum was authorized, the voting would be determined "in accordance with the allocated number of votes depending on their membership." A two-thirds majority of votes would be required to pass the resolution.

The voting was to take place between September 15 and November 15, 1961. The meetings had to be legally called and the ballots secret. The final vote would occur in 1962 at the annual conference. This set the stage for a year and a half of fierce merger talk.

| Confirmed Members of Congregation | Votes per Congregation |
|---|---|
| 1–50 | 1 |
| 51–75 | 2 |
| 76–100 | 3 |
| 101–150 | 4 |
| 151–200 | 5 |
| 201–250 | 6 |
| 251–500 | 7 |
| 501–750 | 8 |
| 751–1,000 | 9 |
| 1,000 + | 10 |

Because of the death of Pastor Clarence Carlsen that year, a new member had to be elected to his position on the COR. My uncle Donald Ronning was elected to fill the one-year term. Most people knew that he would argue much as Carlsen had, so his majority was rather comfortable.

Throughout this time, reports by various youth leaders in the ELC and LFC featured articles about the findings of the new work of Lutheran Youth Research, founded by Merton Strommen. These reports were helping to instruct congregations in what the research had found. Either Strommen or his associates would report on one or another finding with recommendations of how to implement such ideas, such as Gordon Smedsrud's article on how the laity in a congregation should form a board on youth ministries. He said the study contradicted the notion that would become the generation gap, noting with a bit of surprise that their research had shown that most youth "were not nearly as critical of their elders as the elders believe they are."[14]

## The Montevideo Congregation

In that same issue of the *Lutheran Messenger,* there was a large spread on the new church plant of Trinity Lutheran Free Church in Montevideo, a daughter of the Brønø congregation the Jacobsons had helped found in 1873. It would cost $180,000 and have room for up to 500 in the sanctuary, with 14 classrooms, a youth room, a scout room, chapel, offices, and a fellowship hall. The little Brønø church would have fit into it several times. It testified to the growth of the congregation and the town, something of an emblem of the way the churches were prospering at the time.[15]

Its pastor, Arthur L. Bervig, wrote a brief article in the next *Messenger* about the congregation's experience in Sunday school. It had enlarged the classes and increased the number of teachers in each class to three: one responsible for teaching the Bible story, another for asking questions, and another for visiting absentee students during the week. This made it easier to recruit teachers, of which they now had thirty-eight, and reduced issues of discipline, Bervig said. He thought it engaged many more people from the congregation in the important task of teaching the faith to the young.[16]

One thinks back to the visitation of Ole Paulson to the Brønø congregation some eighty years before and the concern of the congregation to educate its youth. Now few Jacobson descendants lived in Montevideo, although two sons of Mathilda Nicoline Jacobson Hanson still lived with their families on the same land their grandparents had homesteaded in Rosewood Township. Many in the Trinity Congregation were descendants of the early pioneers who had founded Brønø and Trinity.

## The New Service Book and Hymnal

By this time, the *Service Book and Hymnal* (SBH), 1958, was becoming attractive to many LFC congregations, while others were reluctant to part with the *Concordia* (1932). Because Leland Sateren and Burntvedt had served on the SBH committee, the LFC could take some comfort that its tradition had been faithfully represented, although rather unsuccessfully, when one counted the number of Norwegian hymns that made it into the book. Both were urging LFC congregations to buy the hymnal, although some had misgivings about the lack of Norwegian hymns in it.

The late T. O. Burntvedt's review of E. E. Ryden's *The Story of Christian Hymnody* expressed some of that discontent. Despite his high praise of Ryden's work, Burntvedt brought up a sore point: Ryden's poor treatment of Magnus Brostrup Landstad. Landstad, the beloved hymnwriter and hymn book editor of Norway, had been ridiculed by the eastern Lutherans. Burntvedt was both upset and amused at Ryden's errors regarding Landstad, from misspelling his name to thinking Seljord Lake was a fjord, and then his dismissal of so many Norwegian hymn writers with an overemphasis on Wilhelm Wexels, the Danish pastor in Oslo. Burntvedt thought it "unthinkable" to write about Norwegian hymnody without treating the works of Petter Dass, Elias Blix, and many others.[17] The reproof was well deserved. Later, the *Messenger* would print a posthumous column by Burntvedt recommending that the congregations adopt the SBH. To my disappointment, he repeated with approval Luther D. Reed's preface to the hymnal, that these hymns were Godward and devotional, not manward, and to be preferred. That explains why so many old Lutheran classics were omitted from the canon: they were, by tradition, teaching hymns and even preaching hymns, like "A Mighty Fortress," which, as a sermon, addressed the congregants, manward, not Godward.

Reports from the mission fields were given large spaces in the succeeding pages of the *Messenger,* almost as if to assure people that there were other things besides mergers going on. A long report by Amos and Ovidia Dyrud was included from the Manasoa-Benenitra district in Madagascar on the growing independence of congregations there and the need for our prayer and support.[18] The August 9 issue also featured a similar report from the Morris Vaagenes family, with many additional reports from the work in Madagascar and the other fields.[19] These gave readers renewed connections with their missionaries and their work.

## The WCC Again

Torgerson, ever watchful on issues of merger and large church organizations like the World Council of Churches, which he knew were opposed by many members, wrote a friendly report on the latest gathering of the WCC. Torgerson acknowledged that there were those who wanted the WCC to become a "super church" but then printed a column from the Religious News Service with comments Dr. W. A. Visser 't Hooft, general secretary, had made to the First European Youth Assembly sponsored by the council. Visser 't Hooft criticized those who wanted one super church: "The Biblical idea was that the local congregation must be a place where the One, Holy Church exists and does its work." He added that what the church needed was not information but preaching that resulted in conversion. At the same time, he stressed that unity consisted in "greater communion in the sacraments, consensus in faith, and full fellowship in an organized life."[20]

Torgerson knew his audience would approve of some of what Visser 't Hooft had said but not all. He did share their worry and wondered if there was "a definite planned effort to call these young people together (many of whom may become future leaders in their respective denominations) to try to convert them to the idea of One World Church?"[21]

He concluded his editorial noting that Jesus had not been praying for a world church in John 17. He hoped that if Lutheran leaders saw the council moving toward a super church, they would oppose it with all their might, and "if they do not succeed, get out of the Council."[22] Torgerson had, like Caspersen, been fearing a super church, at the same time urging unity, which did not mean uniformity. His suspicion that the youths were being used brought a sharp retort from LFC students who had attended the assembly.

On October 18, 1960, the LFC youth delegation to the Lausanne Ecumenical Youth Assembly, Carol Nelson, Paul Batalden, Clayton Paulson,

**Figure 12.4.** Augsburg Seminary graduates in 1960. Used by permission of Augsburg University Archives.

and Byron Schmidt, disagreed with what Torgerson had suspected in an article in the *Lutheran Messenger*. Visser 't Hooft and the Central Committee of the World Council of Churches had said that "no church at any time is to be forced to participate in any action, in any common utterance which it considers to be in conflict with the truth and the will of God."[23] They felt Torgerson had been a bit too brusque in his dismissal of the denials by WCC members that they were looking to build a super church. They heard him saying that his attempt was to "seek unity as the outcome of the common effort to express the integrity and the wholeness of the Church of Christ."[24] At the same time, with the gift of hindsight, these young people would indeed become leaders and supporters of the ecumenical urge toward union. Vatican II had not yet been imagined, but stirrings throughout the Christian world were moving in those directions. Giving youths an exciting trip to Europe to attend such a conference would, without doubt, change their minds on many issues.

That summer, the Ronnings came to visit Salem for a week in July on a trip to visit the West Coast. Don preached at the Sunday service, and otherwise we enjoyed ourselves, visiting Silver Creek Falls Park and the ocean near Seaside, Oregon. That was probably the hottest week in our time in Salem, several days of almost ninety degrees Fahrenheit. Mother had raved about the climate in Salem and received a great deal of ribbing from our guests on the tropical heat of their time with us. Among other things, it damaged the blossoms on the bean harvest, something that affected us and many people in the congregation who had moved to the Willamette Valley to work in the fields and canneries. Kids made lots of money picking beans and strawberries. That year, I worked in the Blue Lake Cannery as well and had to join the Teamsters Union to be employed.

### Politics: Racism and the Presidential Election

The August 9 edition of the *Messenger* featured a news report on Billy Graham's statement on race. He thought racial discrimination was "a blatant denial" of the Christian Gospel. Deploring the segregation of America's churches, he commended many who were working to change that and then noted that although he had at first had segregated evangelistic meetings, in 1952, he refused to allow them, holding integrated campaigns North and South without "a single incident."[25] Everyone agrees that Graham was a leader on this score, although few remember it today.

The question of a Catholic in the White House was raising many questions for Protestants. On August 23, 1960, the *Lutheran Messenger* reprinted a column by James A. Bergquist from the ELC paper, the *Lutheran Church Herald*, reporting on the Democratic National Convention in Los Angeles in August. He had attended it as a reporter and came away somewhat disillusioned by the fact that "religion played nothing but an insignificant and sometimes dishonorable role in the convention."[26] He followed that conclusion with his report. Mostly he thought that the issue was deliberately downplayed by both Catholics and Democrats. Few Catholic priests could be spotted at the convention, and the politicians did not mention it. He feared what he viewed as the secularism at the root of the modern American mind: "Religion is not a real issue for the majority of Americans because we have forgotten what it means to believe in the Lordship of Jesus Christ in the light of the First Article and the First Commandment."[27]

Bergquist went on to regard the disdain for the invocations by the press, delegates, and others as disgraceful. The one truly religious expression he saw was a group of Black and white students in prayer led by Dr. Martin Luther King outside the convention. This moved him. He noted it was a Lutheran governor of Minnesota, Orville Freeman, who nominated Kennedy and a Catholic senator from Minnesota who nominated Adlai Stevenson, still a contender. Ultimately, he was alarmed by the "frivolity with which the Christian faith is treated."[28] He called for a restoration of an understanding that God "is the hidden Ruler and Guide in all governing institutions, who both calls us into judgment and blesses us with his providential care."[29]

The presidential campaign was in full swing as school began that September. Mario Colacci had been speaking and writing on the Roman Catholic question.

Augsburg was receiving attention because of Colacci's comments. LFC Pastor Norman C. Anderson protested against what he thought was "the use of the good name of our Church and our Seminary to further the cause of the Roman Catholic thrust for power in this political campaign."[30] He took issue especially with an article in the *Minneapolis Star* quoting an unnamed professor (very likely Colacci) who had said, "A majority of today's Catholic leaders favors separation of church and state and religious freedom for other faiths."[31] He spoke for many. Anderson noted, correctly, that even if individual Roman Catholic leaders had said this, it was not necessarily approved by Rome. He thought that the refusal of many Lutheran leaders to say anything about the issue was a sign that the Lutheran Church "liturgically and doctrinally, is surely on the road back to Rome."[32] This fear was palpable in my circles at the time. The ecumenical movement was just beginning, but the lines between Catholics and Protestants still constituted a deep gulf.

That fall, my father started a preaching series on Nehemiah, which would end with the call, "Let us arise and build!" The congregation was outgrowing the first unit and needed a sanctuary. The home mission department had bought a lot large enough for a second unit, and the membership was now ready to build.

Just before the election, on October 29–30, the Oregon Circuit of the LFC Luther League held a convention at Central Lutheran. It featured the Seattle LBI teacher C. Walden Hedman, who had graduated from Augsburg and then attended Augustana Seminary in Rock Island. He had also served in the Augustana mission field in what was then called Tanganyika, now Tanzania. Most of the teachers at LBI Seattle had come to Central to preach at special meetings, and the connection with it gave us a community of like-minded people on the West Coast.

Clemmence Dyrud, a pastor in Silverton, and his family appeared at those meetings. He was distressed about the national elections. He would later suggest that Mario Colacci had made the difference in the election when he persuaded voters in Wisconsin, where Kennedy's victory was razor-thin, that a Catholic president would not be beholden to Rome. This was a common thought among many LFC pastors who were still solidly Republican.

As last-minute election campaigning grew more frantic, the question of Kennedy's Catholicism became more urgent. Dr. Martin E. Marty, associate editor of *Christian Century*, noted that politics would decide the election, not religion. He had found Kennedy a "son of his time," although a faithful Catholic, "spiritually rootless and politically almost disturbingly secular."[33] Most serious religious commentators found Kennedy's statement on the place of his faith to be rather vacuous, in some ways denying it meant anything to him. They criticized him for it.

Kennedy won the election in the country, but Oregon voted for Nixon. The Electoral College win was significant, but the actual vote was narrow. This proved to many that prejudice against Catholics had bit the dust in America. The roles of Colacci and many other Lutheran Church officials, seminary professors, and pastors have not been evaluated, but in hindsight, one can see that the switch from the Republicanism of their Norwegian American emigrant parents began in this election. It would accelerate as the Vietnam War and the impeachment of Richard Nixon changed their allegiances.

In November, Byron Schmid, one of the youth delegates to the Lausanne Youth Conference, wrote a full report in the *Messenger*. Its theme was "Christ the Light of the World." In his report, he mentioned the new ecumenical directions of many in a post-Christian world, naming the "pain and guilt of our disunity, not only between denominations, but in all areas of life." The scandal of the separation of the churches was taking hold. As he reflected on the experience, he thought of it as an event with "historic importance." It had forced him to ponder both the unity in Christ and the "disunity of the churches and the world itself."[34]

That January, retired LFC pastor James Tofte and his wife moved to Salem, where he became visitation pastor at Central. They became good colleagues and friends of my folks. This was the year that Central would break ground for the new sanctuary and I would leave for college.

On January 20, 1961, I watched the inauguration with my mother on our seventeen-inch black-and-white TV in the downstairs family room. There had been a terrible blizzard in Washington, DC, which made it difficult for the celebrants to get to events. Even the Kennedys and Johnsons were late for concerts in their honor. While the family had supported Nixon, it was thrilling to hear the young and charismatic new president's inaugural address with its rhetorical surges. Knowing full well the importance of the sound of his speech as well as its content, he and his writer, Ted Sorensen, had crafted several rhetorical sentences that would be burned into the memories of all those who heard it that day and would be repeated, both over the weeks following and after his assassination.

Meanwhile, the Luther League Federation of the LFC had a Leadership Conference in Minneapolis to which David Dyrud, vice president of the Oregon Circuit Luther League, and I, the president, went. That meant a three-day trip back and forth on the train. One of my most vivid memories of that conference was Paul Batalden giving a speech in which he explained the Greek word *oikumenes* and what it meant for the Christian church to be ecumenical, really in its very nature. It was a new thought but would become the driving word of the next fifty years.

## Graduating and Leaving for College

When I returned from Minneapolis, talent shows, concerts, and graduation festivities took over. My father had been asked to give the invocation and benediction at the graduation ceremonies. I had been asked to pray at the senior banquet but not to use the name of Jesus. I am afraid I punted on that even after a conversation with my father, who was alarmed. "They can't ask you to do that," he said firmly. "It is a free country." I was playing in the orchestra for the event in the North High School Auditorium. I had given Mother a corsage and father a boutonniere in thanks for their help getting me through school. I was sitting right beneath him in the orchestra. When he ended the prayer in the name of Jesus, I felt the red blood of Jesus pouring down over me from the flower. One of my devout friends, a trumpeter and a strong Baptist, thanked him very much for his Christ-centered message as I felt rebuked and craven.

I had been accepted at Augsburg with a scholarship for half of my tuition. My high school teachers were disappointed, but I had given up my slight attempts to go elsewhere and readied for this new time in my life. Over the summer, I worked at a margarine factory run by a Danish member of the congregation. I was to pick up the packages of margarine as they came off the belt, put them into boxes that I had to build, and close them. As any work on such a line, it was incredibly boring, so I began memorizing poetry as the day went by.

## The 1961 Annual Meeting

Very soon after my graduation, my parents and siblings left for the 1961 annual meeting at Trinity Congregation in Minneapolis while I stayed in Salem with a member of the congregation. Stensvaag's presidential address, as usual, covered the work and issues involved in the church over the past year, with special focus on the merger process that had been approved at the 1960 convention in Fargo. He did, however, note the past election and the critical debate about church and state. Included in that was his concern about federal aid to parochial schools, which, if it were approved, would obviously benefit one faith tradition far more than any other. He was, of course, talking about Catholic schools, and his fear of the possibility of government aid revealed much about his sense that the Roman Catholic Church was still an alien power to him. He urged vigilance on that issue even as he exhorted people to pray for the country as well as the new president.

Stensvaag expressed concern over racism in the South with its school segregation and in the North with housing discrimination. He also held up the number of aging citizens who would need support from the church, as well as the increasing consumption of alcohol among the citizenry. He commended the Bethel Bible Series, which had exploded on the churches with great results. He hoped that the following year would be a time in which Bible study would increase throughout the growing church, which now numbered 87,250.

As to the union question, he warned that even if the congregations approved the union, several more steps needed to be completed before a vote. First, the vote would authorize the Committee on Relations to enter union negotiations with the ALC and authorize the annual conference to "act for the congregations in voting on the article of union when they are ready."[35]

He noted that it was no secret he had come to favor the union after "a great deal of agonizing soul-searching and weighing of the issues, seeking to find the best way for the cause of the Kingdom."[36] Those who knew Stensvaag well believed him because they knew his deep commitment to the theology and work of Georg Sverdrup and had watched his change of mind. Others who had not seen this began to disparage his commitment, which became fiercer and fiercer during the next year.

Stensvaag remarked that there were two kinds of opposition to merger. On one hand, there were those on the outside "constantly seeking to undermine confidence in the church and its pastors, to create confusion and discord, and rake down the American Lutheran Church and the proposed union."[37] Chief among these entities, I suspect, was the *Morning Glory* (1933 to current year) paper published by the Hauge Lutheran Innermission Federation. Published monthly, it provided those of us on the West Coast, far from the center of activities, with much gossip that occupied us whenever the pastors got together. This monthly missive kept us in the mix, so to speak. In a *Messenger* editorial that year, Torgerson had complained about the negativity of the *Morning Glory*, but that proved to be part of its attraction. I can see my father standing by our dining room table exclaiming with Mother over one or another comment. Its whiff of conspiracies and gossip was thrilling. However, my dad was not amused when he discovered the local Innermission Society, supporters of the *Morning Glory*, announcing a meeting at Central on Sunday afternoons without so much as asking his leave. He knew the anticlerical bent of the group from his childhood and understood it.

On the other hand, Stensvaag graciously admitted there were those who were "faithful and staunch supporters of the church, who have honest doubts as to the wisdom of the proposed merger." He respected them and advised the group that they be listened to carefully, which he was sincere about.

## Another Vote on Merger

My parents were at the convention as delegates and stayed in the Gerda Mortensen Dormitory, where I would be living in a few months. The convention voted on the resolution Thursday, June 15, in the afternoon session. After the reading of the resolution by the chair of the committee, Clarence A. Larson, the floor was opened for debate. Stensvaag noted that the issue was basically to authorize the referendum, and given the press of other issues, delegates should limit the debate to ten or twelve speeches no longer than five minutes.

I can see my parents sitting in Trinity, looking up at the Grønvold painting of Jesus praying in the desert, remembering their Jacobson grandparents who

Figure 12.5. Clarence Larson. Used by permission of Augsburg Fortress Publishers.

had attended Trinity in 1868–1869—Mother's mother, Anda, singing briefly in the choir; Father's grandfather Watne at the first Friends of Augsburg meeting; her uncle Fred's attendance while he was at Augsburg—listening intently to the speakers, and thinking of all the prayers of their grandparents and parents. George Michaelsen, whose father had sung duets with Mother's mother, Anda; Merton Strommen, their classmate; and others spoke for the motion. Fritjof Monseth, Arvid Hokonson, E. P. Dreyer, and Ernst Dahle spoke against it. After the speeches, the motion was read again. Paper ballots were distributed. As the ballots were being counted, the gathering sang two hymns from *The Lutheran Hymnary* (1912), "Beautiful Savior" and "Lord of Our Life and God of Our Salvation." Trinity used *The Lutheran Hymnary*, the hymnal common to the ELC, not the *Concordia*. After the vote was announced, with 406 in favor and 163 opposed, the conference voted by voice to adopt both point 2, to authorize the referendum, and point 3, an especially nagging question to all concerned: "The Annual Conference of the Lutheran Free Church respectfully and earnestly requests every congregation to continue faithfully to serve in the fellowship of the Lutheran Free Church regardless of the outcome of the voting on the union, either in the Annual Conference or in the referendum of the congregation."[38]

After those resolutions passed, the group sang "God's Word Is Our Great Heritage." The die was cast.

Consequently, during the fall, Central Lutheran in Salem would have to vote on these questions. While the LFC headquarters in the Twin Cities were back east and far away, a number of members from the Midwest or Silverton were aware of the different church bodies and their emphases, so the vote, while hardly earth-shattering to most, would be close. My parents' opinions were very mixed. Given their background, as this tale has made clear many times, they were not inclined to support merger; indeed, we had traveled from North Dakota to Seattle to oppose it. On our 1959 trip to the annual conference, we had stopped by Tioga, where Dad preached. When asked what he thought now, he said they would come back to Tioga and celebrate when it was defeated. John Strand, who would become the new president of the Association of Free Lutheran Congregations, heard my father's statement. During our time in Minneapolis that summer of 1959, during a visit to Augsburg, I was reading at a table in the new library when I heard my dad and uncle Don exclaiming loudly against the merger. Dad's only caveat was Augsburg. What would become of it? Could a small minority of a minority support it? Uncle Don, who was even more negative on the merger, and chair of the Oak Grove board, was less concerned about Augsburg. He would say, however, he could not leave for what became the association because he didn't see anyone in the leadership who, like Sverdrup, had the qualities of leadership needed.[39] It was back and forth.

My grandfather Svein Torson Kivley died on July 16, 1961. Because of my job, I did not attend the funeral, but the rest of the family did. Grandpa Svein had been a wonderful influence on my father. He had wept when he had to give him up for adoption to the Grindals, but he was always near him and helped raise him in some regards. He had kept contact with the relatives in Norway, so when I went over to live for a year in Oslo, I could contact his family, especially his nephews, who had known or heard of him and admired him as a wonderful man. That encounter made us good friends of the relatives in Norway over the past sixty years.

During that summer, the phone would ring, and on the other end of the line was that strong voice with the peculiar Stensvaag accent asking, "Is Grindal there?" We began saying to Dad, as we called him to the phone on its yellow metal shelf in the hallway, "Dad, it's Big Bad John!" Stensvaag was frantic that the vote pass and knew Central was crucial. It had seven votes and could make the difference. Dad, who knew John from school, would listen carefully and say, as he always did, "Yes, surely, surely." I don't know how much effect those calls had, really, but they were clearly urgent.

For me, much of the summer was spent preparing to leave for school on the *Empire Builder*. Mother was a wreck about losing me but also anxious that I do well. On September 6, I left Portland. My dad, I learned only recently, had called the porter to ask if I would be safe on the train and if there would be anyone I could become friends with. The porter reported that there was another young woman from Lake Oswego, Oregon, traveling to Minneapolis, Karen Paulsen, who was studying at Luther College. She was sitting near me.

When they put me on the train to oceans of tears, I was somewhat ticked. I still was not 100 percent convinced and felt a bit forced. Mother had made me a huge bag of ham sandwiches, fruit, and brownies to eat on the train—the two nights and three days were somewhat daunting and expensive. Dad had experienced the same long trip several times as a student at Augsburg, so he knew something of what to expect. By the time we got to Spokane, I was talking with Karen Paulson and enjoying her wry humor. She was on her way to Luther College in Decorah, Iowa, about which I had heard little, except that it was the "other" school. She was a classics major and engaged to a pre-sem student, Ron Fretheim. As the days passed and our boredom increased, Karen taught me how to play poker. While most people cannot believe I wouldn't know how to play it, face cards were forbidden in my family's long tradition. As we passed over the mountains toward Cut Bank, students on their way to Concordia began packing the car. I knew rook, without face cards but only colors and numbers. I felt quite wicked as we stood around the Minot depot playing poker during a small break in the trip. I tease her even to this day about that. And I still can't tell the difference between clubs and spades.

When I got off the train in Minneapolis, my great-aunt Mildred and great-uncle Fred Tinseth were waiting by the train, ready to pick me up. Both alums of Augsburg, they knew the cities and the school. They took me immediately to the home of Fred's youngest sister, Henriette (Etty), in south Minneapolis, where she fed us a bountiful lunch. We then went to Augsburg to move me into the Gerda Mortensen Hall. I announced that I was not happy about the development, but in the hot, humid summer air of Minneapolis, we moved to my third-floor room, where I had two other roommates. By then, the student body had grown so much that even the new facility was not big enough. There were 1,106 students enrolled, the most ever. The class of '65 was the largest yet.

Mother sent a special delivery letter filled with wholesome instructions and telling me to wear my Pendleton wool suit, which Mildred laughed about merrily. She hated heat and humidity and thought that was the worst idea ever. After I was settled and orientation began, I was still a bit grumpy. At the welcoming banquet at University Lutheran Church on Sunday evening, September 10, I saw many of the PKs I had grown up with, including the Gjerde twins, Mark and Marie; Julie Gudmestad, my oldest friend; Dan Anderson, soon to be the basketball star and son of my dad's compatriot in the gospel duo group; and many others. What blew me away, however, was Bill Strom, the basso profundo of the choir, singing "Jerusalem, My Happy Home." I was transfixed. After that, Paul Sonnack preached at the worship service. I was almost won over.

As I was walking out of the event, Gerda came up to me all smiles, bubbling with excitement: "Is Augsburg living up to your hopes and dreams, Gracia?" It was a bit too soon to tell, so I mumbled something and went off to the hazing that freshmen were still getting, disgusted by the things we were forced to do, like walking barefoot through some pea soup or something. A letter in the first *Echo* of the year complained about the barbaric ritual of the week. Then came the lectures on Plato by William Halvorson, preparing us for our studies. Bernard Christensen also spoke a bit on the death of Socrates. I had never heard anything like it. He preached it. We attended teas at the homes of our faculty advisers. The life of the mind, the freedom of the individual, and life boomed out over the new Si Melby Hall auditorium, which had just been dedicated. I began to relent. I was sure my other friends were getting boring orientations and endless announcements, but here a professor at the school was teaching us Plato. It wasn't a complete conversion, but it was a beginning.

I had Anne Pederson for freshman English and sat in an alphabetical row with the Gjerdes, John Gundale, Julie Gudmestad, and others, all LFC pastors' kids, whose parents she had taught. We sat in the old seminary lecture room in Old Main that was filled with the hints and echoes of my parents and a long line of revered teachers. Miss Pederson could not quite get over how different I was

**Figure 12.6.** Gerda Mortensen pouring tea ca. 1967. Used by permission of the Grindal family.

from my mother. I don't think she ever quite approved of me and did not favor me with high grades. Then I had Carl Chrislock, a classmate of my father's, for history. I was accepted into the Cantorians, a girls' chorus directed by Mayo Savold, and into the band, where I played the flute. In addition to flute lessons, I took organ lessons and would soon be playing for chapel.

The daily chapel exercises led by Philip Quanbeck, who had been my dad's intern and knew me when I was three, were exciting and powerful. The speakers were eloquent and the singing of the packed bleachers thrilling. The activities of the school were beginning to get to me, as we were reading the great classics of the Western world and learning its history and music. I loved that.

All Augsburg students had to take fourteen credits of religion. My first teacher was Terrence Fretheim. His brother Mark was in my class as well, and he became a fast friend. Fretheim had just earned his degree from Princeton in Old Testament. He was young and handsome. When he sauntered into the room, the girls all fluttered and wondered if he was wearing a wedding ring. He was. Faith, his funny and rebellious wife, and he were about as married as anyone I have ever known. He would figure in my life later when he was dean at Luther Seminary and instrumental as they called me to teach there.

Fretheim was a strong advocate of the historical-critical method of interpreting the Bible. The first thing I had to do with my Bible, a Revised Standard Version, was to mark out in red pencil the Yahwist, Elohist, Deuteronomic, and priestly sources of Genesis and study their sources. This was source criticism at its purest. Instead of reading the Bible, I thought, we were reading what came before, what was behind the text. This was, of course, controversial to the constituency. During fall break when I told Borghild, my mother's sister, who my Bible teacher was, she cried out, "He is the worst!"

Although I had some awareness of the changes in theology and biblical scholarship when I got to Augsburg, these ideas were quite new. Neoorthodoxy, the theological movement that the young Turks like Robert Jenson, Carl Braaten, Roy Harrisville, and Gerhard Forde were promulgating, would push the method. At Augsburg, the most fervent proponent was William Halvorson, from whom I took contemporary theology. Still, the intellectual ferment around the interpretation of Scripture was telling. It served as a kind of emblem for the entire religion department and to some extent the whole school. These were exciting new times—there was a new regime in Washington, things were loosening up, and it was a great age to be young and restless.

Christensen had taught historical criticism to my father's class, so it was not new to him; in fact, Dad told me that in his Hebrew class, taught by Warren Quanbeck, Augsburg's greatest talent of that generation, Quanbeck had asked what he had when he had the source P32, and a wiseacre friend of dad's had called out, "Bingo!"

Christensen had been able to teach these ideas to my father's class because his piety was so clear. Thus, he was supportive of the young faculty introducing these ideas to the children of the faithful supporters of Augsburg. On the other hand, the mix of faculty from my parents' generation and teachers they went to school with like Gerald Thorson, Carl Chrislock, Leland Sateren, and even Phil Quanbeck gave the time an exciting sense of the new mixing in with the old in a rather comfortable way. The entire curriculum and outside activities were intended to induct me into the tradition I knew in my bones. When I came back that Christmas, armed to the teeth with ideas about which I was not quite gung-ho, my father asked me what I was learning in Bible, and I told him. He said, "Yes, Christensen taught us that when I was in school. But the real questions, my dear, is what do you think of Jesus?" That was the question.

In the second edition of the *Echo* that year, Victor Svanoe, religious life commissioner, wrote a column comforting students about what they may have been learning in their religion classes—topics like the age of the world and so on. For him, Christianity was about faith, not reason. He concluded by quoting Scripture, "We walk by faith not sight."[40] This question became the topic of many a nightly session in the Mortensen Grill involving french fries and ketchup.

The merger vote was also beginning to impinge on our awareness. The voting began on September 15. The current issues of the *Lutheran Messenger* published letters and articles at full capacity through the summer and into the fall. John Stensvaag had an article in the September 17, 1961, issue on the World Council of Churches, which was a stumbling block for many along the way. He felt the attacks were unfair and intended to derail the merger. He disabused his opponents, whether successfully or not, with quotes from the documents of the council, hoping to clear up the charges that the council denied the authority of God's word and that it had reduced the faith of the participating churches to the lowest common denominator. While he did admit that there was some problem with the language in the council's statements, he showed that the council was in fact amending its documents to strengthen them in precisely those regards. The Central Committee had recommended that the language be changed from "a fellowship of churches which accept our Lord Jesus Christ" to "a fellowship of churches, which, according to the Holy Scriptures, confess Jesus Christ as God and Savior." He felt that changed much and would "help us toward a more just and objective evaluation of the Council."[41]

That same issue had an article, a reprint of his speech at the recent annual conference, by Carl J. Carlsen, son of the powerful Clarence Carlsen, the most prominent, but now deceased, opponent of the merger. Carl's support of the merger was seen by many as a betrayal of his father but also, to those who agreed with him, as a wonderful instance of a rational change by a significant force in the church. Carlsen argued that while he had opposed the merger before, he was now changing his mind. While there were still good reasons to be against it, there were more to favor the merger. He did acknowledge that the merger would mean that the LFC had abandoned its allegiance to the Twelve Principles of the LFC, but he argued it had already done so years before. What he wanted was to observe the spirit of the principles, not the letter. Fully acknowledging the dangers of merger, he also sounded a common warning that many promerger voices had given: spiritual pride and negative defensiveness were not good things either, and too many of those wanting to keep the LFC were often guilty of these sins. He found the opportunities of the new church "thrilling" and urged the congregations to support it.[42]

Milo Bryn from the Berwick congregation, now a professor at the University of North Dakota in Fargo, wrote a long letter to the editor on the issue of dancing. He had heard they were dancing at St. Olaf now.[43] He did not think that was as bad as drinking. He had not been convinced that dancing of itself was a sin, but, as many said, the issue was what dancing led to. He knew that dancing was coming, maybe even to Concordia, although President Joseph Knutson was not going to approve it, I was sure! He then made a twist that is surprising—we should join the ALC so we would have a voice in those discussions and improve the situation.[44]

Pastor Ingvald Norum feared that the freedom of the congregation would be compromised in the ALC. According to the ALC constitution, a congregation could not leave the church without a lot of interference from the bureaucracy. Furthermore, he did not think it was not free to interpret Scripture in the light of the Holy Spirit. The district president, according to the ALC constitution, had the duty "to keep congregation in line on this score."[45]

On September 19, 1961, Dr. Martin Marty spoke at the convocation of the school year on "Can a Christian Culture Prevail?" A young mover and shaker, now the associate editor of *Christian Century*, Marty was beginning to find his voice and become a national force among Lutherans and the American church. Lutherans, the story would go, were now stepping out of their ethnic ghettos to get to know each other and the American church as they had not before. Progress was in the air.

As the vote proceeded, pastors and laypeople wrote letters or articles on one side or the other, and the editor, Torgerson, tried to allot equal space for both sides. Pastor Oliver Sidney, a classmate of Dad's, wrote for merger, saying it was an open door to many good things through which the church should go.

As the voting period came to an end, Merton Strommen wrote an article in which he accounted for most positions on merger as coming from our personal experiences. If we had had good experiences with people from the ALC, we would tend to be for merger; if we had not or had no experience, we would not be for merger. This was a slight criticism of the parochialism of those opposed.

He concluded by arguing that the merger was necessary for the development of a successful youth program: "We can accomplish more for the Kingdom when united into a national church than we can remaining as a separate and regional Church body."⁴⁶ The word *regional* also betrays a fear of parochialism.

The November 8, 1961, *Echo* featured an editorial that the students at Augsburg favored merger: "The old Augsburg, a vocational institute for the training of Norwegian-speaking LFC preachers, is dead." Since two-thirds of the students were not LFC, and the LFC was far too small to support a college with a bright future, Augsburg needed to be released from the limits imposed on it by the LFC: "The Old Augsburg is dead. May the new Augsburg be allowed to work toward its potential through the merger of the LFC and the ALC."⁴⁷

In that same issue, Bill Svanoe argued in a long article that things would be best if "we let the Lutheran Free Church live."⁴⁸ Viggo Dahle, another LFC pastor in good standing, believed the larger body would help us face our problems in supporting Augsburg and Oak Grove and our missions. We would have more opportunities to do more.⁴⁹ John Skurdalsvold, from a family of LFC lay leaders, argued that we should not merge because we had been blessed through the years and could expect blessings in the future as well: "Why should we leave our path?" Another letter from Mrs. Una Kruse supported Strommen. Although she had moved from Salem and Central, an LFC bastion and a good friend of Mother, she had found in her ELC church in Coos Bay that the people from

**Figure 12.7.** The Grindal family at Christmas, 1964. Used by permission of the Grindal family.

the LFC would bring into the "larger sphere a deep and vital ingredient which shall not be unnoticed."⁵⁰

Sometime during these weeks, Central Lutheran in Salem voted on the issue. The congregation had seven votes. The discussion had been long and agonized, Mother said when they telephoned me. The vote had passed 23-21. My parents' two votes had given the pro side a majority. They wept when they got into the car and headed for home. They had been crucial to the vote, maybe in the whole LFC. They had voted for it to save Augsburg. That was their only reason. In the end, it turned out the vote was 645-373 from the congregations, or 10,758-6,827 actual votes, not terribly different from the previous failed referenda. Although the congregations were allotted votes according to their size, the numbers were still about the same as they had been, but now with the new way of counting, it meant victory for the pro side.

The vote would not be tallied until November 16. The leaders of the little fellowship gathered in suspense for the count in the headquarters. It had passed by the narrowest of numbers. Rejoicing burst out among the leadership. God had finally done what they wanted.

Sometime that day, after the counting concluded, I got a telephone call. In the Gerda Mortensen Hall, there was one phone in each hallway for maybe fifty girls. Someone would answer the phone and then holler down the hall for whomever had gotten the call to come and answer. When I heard my name, I went to the phone. It was Julie Gudmestad, my oldest friend. "It passed," she said.

We talked for a bit. Then I stepped out into the hall, where the florescent lights were buzzing and flickering. The window at the end of the hall was dark.

# EPILOGUE

What to make of this all? I needed to tell the story to understand it better. I rediscovered how richly my family experienced it. As I think back on the whole story, I am grateful for my heritage and troubled by its ending. History is almost always sad. The Sun King dies, no matter how glorious his reign. This does not diminish the glories. Nothing in this world can remain as it always was. Change and decay lie around us. I am at the end of something, not its beginning, but I can recount its history through the story of my family from the beginning until its end and maybe see something new being born. Naturally, there are questions about history and the arc of events in the time I have lived. I have lost most every battle I have fought in the church. Has it been the natural ebb and flow of history? Or something else? Unlike the triumphalistic histories of Lutheran churches ending in inevitable mergers, my story is mixed, grateful yet wistful. Could it have gone any other way? I still wish it had.

## The Great Engines of Change

While I have recounted the story of my little fellowship, the LFC, and my family, and their movement through the century, and noted how the leadership slaved to keep the college and seminary going and still faithful to its founding hopes and dreams, I have not dealt with the major force that opened before me when I stepped off the Great Northern train from Oregon into the grand, cathedral-like train station in downtown Minneapolis. As I ascended the escalator with my great-aunt and uncle, Mildred and Fred Tinseth, into that spacious room bustling with activity, its walls covered with paintings of the founding of the upper Midwest, the future looked bright. Then, as we got into the car and drove to my great-aunt Ettie's home near Lake Street in south Minneapolis, our typical route was blocked by great engines of change that had devastated the Gateway Area downtown and cleared it to make way for the new national highway system. It looked like Berlin in 1945. The vagrants had scattered, but so had the old, largely Scandinavian residents of the Seward and Cedar Riverside neighborhood. The excavated ravine ran a block north along Franklin Avenue. It had already devastated the African-American Rondo neighborhood in St. Paul and was now doing the same to neighborhoods in Minneapolis. No one could call it beautiful. As we made our way past the leveled neighborhoods, we might have thought it progress, but even then I remember it as ugly and dispiriting. Worst was when we finally made our way to Augsburg and Mortensen Hall on Riverside; we had to avoid Franklin Avenue, which had always been the front door of Augsburg Seminary.

What we were seeing was the devastations wreaked by modernism, well described in Marshall Berman's famous book, *All That Is Solid Melts into Air*. His book was a *cri de cœur* about the destruction of his neighborhood in the Bronx, among other things, led by urban planner Robert Moses (1888–1981) and his monsters of industry, the cranes and digging machines that hacked through old established and beautiful neighborhoods with "a meat ax." What we were looking at was what the French poet Charles Baudelaire called the "mire of the macadam" ("*la fange du macadam*"). The poet used the expression to speak of the way modernity paved over everything with "mire, filth, corruption and degradation."[1]

No better emblem of this existed in my memory than to see the ravine ending right at the edge of Trinity Congregation. I imagined the WMF ladies standing outside the church about which I later wrote a poem, something like my version of Allen Ginsberg's "Howl":

> though caterpillars furrow the ground
> and engines whine at their open toes
> keep them, Jesus, when their children
> dangle from needles in dark rooms
> to feel the god rush in their veins.[2]

The church would stand there for the rest of my time at Augsburg before the freeway plowed through it in 1966. I say *emblem*, but it was more than that. It was the very physical being of modernity. No matter what Sverdrup, Oftedal, Burntvedt, Christensen, or Stensvaag would do, this modernity, which excited many, would devour us, even as we used it to move forward, thinking we were saving the institutions we loved. As Berman has it, "Our past, whatever it was, was a past in the process of disintegration; we yearn to grasp it; but it is baseless and elusive; we look back for something solid to lean on, only to find ourselves embracing ghosts."[3]

Eisenhower's great dream of an interstate highway system hastened the end of little unique cornices and cultures as his freeways ran like rivers of concrete from East to West. It homogenized the country and to some degree made it ugly. Instead of little neighborhoods with stable residents and distinctive nooks and crannies, Howard Johnsons, all dispiritingly the same, popped up at predictable distances along the way. My train ride across the country through landscapes I had known since my birth was one of the last years the Great Northern served the area, with conductors bellowing down the aisle, Williston, Stanley, Minot, Rugby,

Epilogue

Fargo, Willmar, Minneapolis on the Red River Express, places we all knew, railroads our grandparents and parents had traveled over the years and knew down to every stop. What was at work, according to Ginsburg's "Howl," was Moloch.

It is too much to expect that against such inexorable forces, a small fellowship stretched to capacity could survive or its leaders do anything much different from what they did. On further reflection, the painful thing to see is exactly this. Everything any of these leaders did to preserve our past also helped bring it to an end.

As my years at Augsburg went on, and I studied with teachers who could teach me the great classical tradition as well as Norwegian American history, literature, and music, I got a fine education. Carl Chrislock, Gerald Thorson, Paul Sonnack, Phil Quanbeck, and Leland Sateren were superb teachers. I learned much from them but would come to take a different opinion on the merger.

## Merger Effected

On November 1, 1962, the merger agreements were finished, and President Stensvaag signed the official certification of congregations, pastors, and institutions. Twenty-four congregations and nine pastors had requested separation from the Lutheran Free Church or at least not to be certified by the ALC. The merger of the corporations of the LFC, the Lutheran Board of Missions, the Board of Home Missions, and the Messenger Press had been certified and effected by the secretary of state. On February 1, 1963, the work of the LFC ended.

The final issue of the *Lutheran Messenger* was published on January 22, 1963, with its cover featuring the standard verse, "That they may all be one." The publication printed the last words of the church's leadership. Christensen did not see the merger as the death of the LFC but a new venue: "There will always be a need for an educated Christian leadership where the ideals of Sverdrup were still being met, to study 'the whole Gospel . . . in the setting of the whole of human knowledge.'"[4] He also noted that the present world was filled with new thinking that the church needed to face. Since the values and ideals of the LFC were rooted in the New Testament and were the essence of Christianity, he concluded that "the fires of the future are nearly always lighted from the lamps of the past."[5]

President Stensvaag spoke of the merger with the joy of one going to a wedding. It was in essence a homily with little mention of the church processes, except to thank God for our goodly heritage. He regarded it as the healing of an old wound, a thing of joy. He urged LFC members "to join hands with our brothers and go joyfully and confidently into the future."[6]

Director of Missions Lester Dahlen also wrote a thank-you, remembering that the first Mission Committee of the LFC had been organized on

**Figure E.1.** The final issue of the *Lutheran Messenger*. Used by permission of Augsburg Fortress Publishers.

October 12, 1897, and incorporated on June 19, 1899, at the Dalton Annual Conference. He was grateful for the new and larger mission fellowship team for our missionaries.[7]

The editor of the *Lutheran Messenger*, Sverre Torgerson, expressed his thanks to the church for the privilege of being editor. He directed his remarks especially to the wise counsel and good friendship of Burntvedt. He said nothing about the new church, only describing the difficulties of being fair to each side as the merger discussion had raged.

Leif Sverre Harbo (1897–1991), who for a year served as an interim president of Augsburg, gave the faculty a sense of relief after great worries about who would replace Christensen. His long tenure as a school administrator calmed both the faculty and the student body. I heard later that his steady dispatch with faculty meetings brought questions to a head much sooner than Christensen would have.

Christensen would not move until everyone in the room agreed, even suspending the meeting so people could take a dinner break. Harbo's parliamentary procedure brought several of the faculty to tears, unused as they were to such, but it was a welcome relief to others.[8]

Harbo's thanks included the newly adopted restatement of Augsburg's aims and objectives, which concluded "where there is an atmosphere of free and honest inquiry, truth has the overwhelming advantage; the Christian college, therefore, pursues its purposed not by indoctrination or coercion, but by inviting teachers and students to join in a common search for truth and in a common attempt to see all truth in relation to ultimate Truth."[9]

Paul Sonnack, college and seminary professor of church history, who would soon move to take up a professorate at Luther Seminary after the merger arrangements for the seminaries, expressed his thanks as a member of the board of directors to the Messenger Press. He remembered with thanksgiving, especially the work of Abner B. Batalden for his management of the press along with Ruby Peterson, the secretary.[10] (Sonnack would be joined on the Luther Seminary faculty by Stensvaag and Christensen.) The expressions of gratitude were well deserved, especially to Batalden, who it seemed to me kept the whole organization afloat with his business acumen, rare among the other leaders. Martha, his capable wife, wrote in her column as president of the Women's Missionary Federation that she also looked forward to joining the ALCW, the women's organization of the ALC.

Augsburg held Merger Festival Days the last week of January and early days of February. The Augsburg Choir left on its tour on January 24, so I was not there. We would return for our homecoming concert on February 3, which would end the festival. A special convocation on January 31 featured popular professor William Halvorson, who spoke on "The Spirit of Augsburg." On February 1, 1963, Dr. Fredrik A. Schiotz, president of the ALC, spoke in chapel to observe the day.

I have no memory of that concert but some of the tour. The only thing I do remember of merger activities at Augsburg over the next years was that I was asked to play the organ at the last graduation ceremony of the final Augsburg Seminary class. It was held on May 24, 1963, at Trinity church. The class of nine included Richard Husfloen, one of my teachers. It was a sad occasion. We were sitting there celebrating an ending of something we loved, in the crosshairs of the bulldozers of modernity sitting right outside the church, waiting in the ravine. It was like Moloch in Ginsburg's "Howl," "with its human-devouring sphinx of modernity"

## Adjusting to the New Church

A few of us who were children of the LFC got together and rebelled, as was the fad at the time, against the obvious movement of Augsburg toward something undreamed of by the founders. In a way, Berman argued, many of the protests of the '60s were about this very thing, protesting the machine in favor of the old ways that were natural. We established an alternate college paper called *A Voice, Not an Echo*, in which we muckraked the administration of Augsburg for a variety of things. We thought it kind of recherché to rebel, as many students at the time were doing, but in our case in favor of a lost past.

Perhaps one of the more difficult things caused by the merger was the nomination of Pastor Oscar Anderson (1916–2005) as president of Augsburg. A successful pastor at Trinity in Moorhead, Minnesota, he was, unlike Christensen, not known for his scholarly achievements and represented the ELC more than the LFC, although he had attended Augsburg in his first two years of college before transferring to St. Olaf. He was not an unknown, but there was talk that Oscar had been proposed as president of Augsburg to bring it into the ALC. I came to appreciate Oscar, but at the time, it seemed a sellout of our tradition. His oratorical gifts were impressive, and I still remember his inaugural address in which he pondered, somewhat wryly, whether the current Augsburg could find some way to get the support of the original Fuggers of Augsburg, Germany. When he later served as temporary chaplain at Luther Seminary, I learned about more of his gifts as a crafty old Norwegian American pastor who knew where all the bodies were buried—and if he didn't, he would find out.

Most disastrous was his choice of Joseph Knutson of Concordia to speak at my graduation in 1965. Joe, as he was known, was as crusty as any of the college presidents of the day, maybe except for Seth Eastvold at Pacific Lutheran. This infuriated many of the LFC scions in my class. Worst of all was his opening remark that the only thing the founders of Augsburg had done right was locating it in the Twin Cities. That started a slow burn among us, and the faculty, I am told, had roast Knutson and Anderson for dinner at their final gathering.

I remember with some pain watching my parents dressing up to the nines on a freezing-cold January day in 1963 to go with some LFC pastors and their wives to their first convocation at Luther Seminary after the merger. They were trying to be positive. By then, they had moved from Salem, Oregon. Central Lutheran congregation had just finished building its new unit, and Dad had been there eight years. He had been getting itchy to move again, before the merger, when "no one knew Joseph," referring back to the beginning of Exodus describing the situation of the Israeli slaves under the Pharaoh when "no one knew Joseph." He correctly surmised that the leadership of the new church would not know him and might think of him as Free Church and not very gifted. Their new congregation was Oak Grove Lutheran Congregation in Augsburg Park, the land the college had purchased in the 1920s as a potential relocation site. The parsonage was at 7037 Augsburg Avenue. He was excited to come back to Minnesota to an LFC congregation, the second largest congregation in the LFC. I also remember they came back from the event hurt and upset that they had not been welcomed the way they had expected to be.

Epilogue

## After Graduation

After graduation, I went with the Augsburg Choir on a tour of Norway, Denmark, and Germany—six weeks for six hundred dollars. I had told my parents I was going to stay in Norway and work so I could learn the language, which I did. The choir bid me farewell in Wiesbaden, Germany, giving me all their leftover kroner. I hitched a ride with the bus to Bremen and waited for a train to Oslo. I had almost no money and couldn't leave my suitcases anywhere to roam around or even get very much food. When I got to Oslo, with my last kroner, I got in touch with Solrun Hoaas, daughter of a Norwegian missionary to Japan, who had been at Augsburg with me. Just in the nick of time, she answered the phone. After a few weeks, her mother, weary of me, I am sure, found me a job in an old people's home in downtown Oslo run by the Little Innermission Society (*Oslo Lille Indremisjons Gamlehjem*). There I would work washing floors in the home, helping the aged, and learning Norwegian from women who were living in the workers' quarters with me. They had had German boyfriends during the war and been excluded from their society in north Norway. I learned a lot from them.

## Destruction of Trinity

On Sunday, May 29, 1966, Trinity Congregation closed so it could be torn down. The membership at the time was 700. Many were there to mark the closing. They

**Figure E.2.** Gracia leaving for Norway with the Augsburg choir. Used by permission of the Grindal family.

marched with its pastor, Sheldon Torgerson, to Riverside Presbyterian Church on 2000 S. 5th street, where they were guests. They expected that a new church would be built on Riverside and 20th. The congregation received $296,000 after the condemnation process was finished. Hopes were high that the new church would serve the growing population of university students and faculty who would want to live in the neighborhood. The *Minneapolis Star* reported on February 2, 1967, that some 30–50 churches had been torn down in the oldest sections of the cities to make way for the freeway. "Broad Is That Way That Leadeth to Destruction—Matthew 7:13" was the headline of the story, which featured five old churches that had just been destroyed, among them Trinity and St. Paul's Hauge Lutheran Church in the same neighborhood.[11] As members prepared to abandon the old Trinity building, cleaning out its treasures and, in a way, dealing with their own ghosts, they got to the altar painting of Jesus ascending, which had stood in the basement from the turn of the century. It was painted in 1893, the year the Friends of Augsburg began. A friend said, "Save that for Gracia." They rolled it up with its altar frame to give me when I got home. The painting was done by Andreas Pederson, a painter who had advertised in *Folkebladet* as a *troende maler* (a believing painter). His comment about being a believer was something of a swipe at Herbjørn Gausta (1854–1924), the painter of the Norwegian Synod, who reluctantly painted altar paintings to support his habit, producing a fine collection of portraits and scenes from Norwegian American life.[12]

Another major item that was saved was the large altar painting of Jesus praying in the desert, a copy of an altar painting in Bergen, which the pastor M. Falk Gjertsen had seen while on a trip there and asked that Trinity acquire a copy of it.[13] The stained glass was given to a company that would conserve it for another church. Reports that came to me about the destruction of the building seemed to sound something like glee, almost as if the past was a burden of which they were now free: first the merger, then the closing of Augsburg Seminary, then the tearing down of the church, which had been there since 1902.

When I returned just after that, I had a scholarship to the University of Arkansas English department, where I went, somewhat reluctantly. There I found a teacher who taught me my craft as a poet, for which I have been grateful my whole life, even if he was a difficult man. Both my teachers were what I called "evangelical atheists." They had been saved as teenagers but rejected their Baptist upbringing and faith when they went to university. When Luther College advertised for a teacher of creative writing in 1968, I called John Bale, head of the English department, and he asked me to submit my application. My fiction teacher wrote that I was a fine student and an intellectual, even if I was a Christian. This made me exactly what Bale wanted!

## Learning to Love the "Other" Schools

In August 1968, after finishing my studies for an MFA in Fayetteville, I came to Decorah, Iowa. I joked with President Elwin D. Farwell (1919–2017) when he interviewed me that my ancestors would not have been happy about my accepting a call to teach there. It had been the "other" school and church all their lives—and mine, to some extent. Luther's religion department had just gone through a terrible conflict over the historical-critical method of biblical scholarship, evolution, and neoorthodoxy. The conservatives, led by Gerhard Belgum, a fine teacher and leader, lost to the forces of modernity, represented by Robert Jenson. Later, my colleagues would say that it was the worst time they had ever experienced. Friendships and collegiality were broken and never restored.

The new professors in the religion department at the school, like Augsburg, were devoted to the critical method, and the English department took issue with them. Although the struggle over the method at Augsburg had not been so dire, I knew how distressing this new method could be, as I myself had grown unhappier about it. I wrote an editorial, "The Verge of Jordan," published in *dialog*, the journal established by the young Turks, neoorthodox scholars Robert Jenson, Carl Braaten, and Roy Harrisville.[14] In it, I took on the method from my own experience of it. We had a gathering in the home of my good friends and colleagues Mary Lou and Martin Mohr, which ended in a shouting match. Unfortunate. Ironically, it was not the old Luther College I was battling. It was rebels against the old school itself. They were, in fact, all products of the school and had issues with it. I, naturally, defended their old tradition, which had once been anathema to my side. Sven Oftedal's "Open Declaration" had, in its first sentence, railed against the Synod and Luther College for being papist and Catholic, ultimately deist. As it turns out, using the scientific method on things of the spirit has not yielded much for the church. In my lifetime, it has lost its appeal. It did not feed the people, and so they have found succor elsewhere, something Christian leaders today, like Bishop Robert Barron of Winona, are beginning to realize and, hopefully, remedy.

Then, of all things, I fell in love with the Synod tradition, especially the stories of the wives of the leaders, Elisabeth Koren (1832–1918) and Linka Preus (1829–1880), when I discovered their letters to each other in the archives. By that time, I had forgotten the Norwegian I had learned and had to relearn it to read these missives describing life on the prairie in the 1850s and 1860s. It was a labor of love. I spent every summer in the cool basement archives, learning their language and reading their lives. Then I discovered Linka's sketches in a box somewhat forgotten by the family. This was a true scholarly discovery, which I have spent my life researching.

Luther College was good to me, and I loved it. While there, I was nominated to be on the Hymn Text Committee of the *Lutheran Book of Worship*. So, for three years, I would pack up my orange backpack with edited hymn texts, get on the Braniff plane for St. Louis, and enter the Missouri Athletic Club as the personal guest of J. A. O. Preus! This meant working again with my college teachers Leland Sateren and Gerald Thorson, who were on the committees.

Surprisingly, in the spring of 1979, Seminex, the seminary of the newly established Association of Evangelical Lutheran Church (AELC), awarded me an honorary doctorate of letters. While I had known some of the actors in this movement, some of whom began teaching with me and otherwise working on various projects, I was surprised by the award. My parents, who had resisted honorary degrees at Augsburg, were a bit surprised that I accepted it. At the receptions afterward, around cocktails and fine dinners, I recognized the feelings the Seminex leaders had as very like my own. Their logo, a sprig growing out of an old large stump, could have been mine years before. The pain was palpable. This had been an exit of a sophisticated leadership class that had walked off the seminary campus thinking their people would follow. They did not. And President J. A. O. Preus, whom they despised, was now the leader of the church and institutions they had left behind. As an admirer and friend of the ALC Preus family, and in some ways the historian of the family, the ironies for me abound.[15]

To my surprise, Lloyd Svendsbye (1930–2014) at Luther Seminary, who had briefly been my boss at Augsburg Publishing House when I worked there for a summer, remembered fondly how my father had impressed him when he spoke at his high school graduation. He called and asked me to apply for the homiletics position in pastoral theology. I agreed to accept the appointment but only if I could study theology and history before I taught much. Students would not respect me if I didn't. He generously agreed, and I spent two wonderful years (1981–1983) learning history and theology while teaching part time.

Terence Fretheim, my Basic Bible teacher from Augsburg, who was now dean of the seminary, also worked for my appointment. Even though I had disagreed with him, and came to more and more, we had always been cordial. His brother Mark, a classmate of mine at Augsburg, had been a good friend of mine, and Faith and Terry were very kind to me. I was always grateful to them and especially him. Here, I was in the belly of the beast, so to speak, and feeling at home and loving it. My parents were proud but always a little mystified.

## The Ecumenical Questions Grow More Pressing

Just as I was about to move to St. Paul to begin my work at Luther Seminary, I got a call from the ALC asking me to become a member of its Committee on Ecumenical Affairs. I accepted. I remembered the LBW process and thought it

# Epilogue

would be similar. There, it turned out, my life changed again. In the ecumenical fracas of the last part of the century, with the movement toward closer relations with the Episcopal Church and the Reformed, I had to study ecclesiology, not my favorite topic in the theological encyclopedia. But there we were, poring over Luther, the Augsburg Confession, the Smalcald Articles, even the Formula of Concord, to understand Lutheran ecclesiology. From all that I could tell, Sverdrup was not far off from Luther, except for his language of the congregation being "the *right* form of the kingdom of God on earth."

When a merger of the ALC, LCA, and AELC was proposed by John Tietjen, president of Seminex, at a conference at St. Olaf, history began to rhyme. It was almost like the formation of the United Church in 1890 when, three years earlier, in 1887, the Anti-Missourian Brotherhood asked the Conference and Norwegian Danish Augustana Synod to merge. I naturally opposed the idea. As I said, I hadn't yet gotten over the 1890 merger. When the Committee of 70 planning the Evangelical Lutheran Church in America (ELCA) could not agree on a form of ministry, whether threefold, twofold, or onefold, they punted and compromised. A Task Force for the Study of Ministry would be formed from representative members of the new church, and it would negotiate the issue. This would be in the context of the proposal to adopt Full Communion with the Episcopal Church in America, which meant adopting their version of the historic episcopate, or threefold ministry. I was put on the Task Force to represent the tradition of the LFC!

It was a difficult five years. My parents were beginning to fail and needed me. My sister had breast cancer, and she and her children needed me. Flying to Chicago once a month, at least, took its toll. Furthermore, I had been chosen to represent Luther Seminary, an institution that was an object of criticism from the rest of the church partly, I think, because it still had a lively faculty with opinions and convictions across the board, including its pietism shaped by Hauge. He was always the piece that stuck in the craw of other American Lutherans when they spoke with us. For me, however, it was an added difficulty because some of my colleagues gave me the impression that I was not theologically qualified for the task—which, compared to many others on the faculty, I was not. Other colleagues were very supportive. On the other hand, few of the other members of the Task Force were theologians, except for Carl Braaten and John Reumann. Carl Braaten, whom I knew from my place on the *dialog* board, was among the most interesting in the group. I maintained good relations with him, even if he could be quite scornful of my lack of theological training and being what he thought of as a decadent liberal Protestant feminist.

In something of an act of self-defense, I wrote a long letter to the faculty every time I returned from a meeting. Sitting in Schaumberg, Illinois, a tony suburb of Chicago, in the new ELCA headquarters on Higgins Road, I had to represent the Luther faculty, even as I was representing the LFC. It was not pleasant, and the animus against me and my tradition, especially, was palpable, as though Sverdrup and Oftedal were ghostly presences in my flesh. Several others accused me of being a decadent American Protestant, individualistic and un-Lutheran. Nor was I liturgical enough for the liberals, who tended to be high church. It was a difficult time, and it sullied my reputation in the ELCA for good. I would laughingly accuse David Preus of ruining my life by appointing me to the committee. He would laugh heartily but also would wake up in the night, he told me, wondering what he could have done differently.

After the passage of Called to Common Mission in 1999, a group of us gathered and founded Word Alone, which in turn spawned Lutheran Congregations in Mission for Christ (LCMC), an ongoing church body today. In addition, Word Alone and others encouraged me to lead a group to make a hymnal. Knowing how exhausting that work could be, I resisted until a former student, Pastor Mark Luther Johnson, called and said let's do it. So, over the next few years, we developed the *ReClaim* hymnal, which is rather like the *Concordia Hymnal* I grew up with. The services are consistent with the Luther's theology of worship. We were advised by Dr. Oliver Olson, who had taught at St. Olaf, Luther Seminary, and Philadelphia Lutheran Seminary but did not receive tenure at any because of his notions about the liturgical revival. He ended up at Marquette University in Milwaukee. He was a Lutheran Free Church pastor's son who had gone to graduate school and found out, to his surprise, his father was right about Lutheran liturgy.[16] He argued, after his scholarship on Matthias Flacius (1520–1575), the quiet reformer from Croatia, that the liturgical revival out of Vatican II could not be Lutheran since it was rejecting the Lutheran understanding of the Lord's Supper as *beneficium* rather than the Catholic idea of *sacrificium*. It was Luther's reason for eliminating the eucharistic prayer.[17] During the compiling of the LBW, Olson had successfully gotten the eucharistic prayer deleted from one of the services of holy communion printed in the book.

*ReClaim* stands as one of the only things that witnesses to what we wanted to reclaim in our Lutheran church from Luther's clear revision of the medieval mass. A small irony and an astonishing kind of spiritual DNA appeared. As we were working on the liturgy, hoping to reclaim the traditional version, a debate over the words of absolution emerged. Would we use the conditional or the unconditional, as the most orthodox (known as *gnesios*) among us insisted? Shades of Pastor Ole Hersleb (1692–1760) and my eighth great-grandfather Tarald Olsen Gaupen (1691–1773) in Norway! The argument grew so fierce that the group commissioned Walter Sundberg, history professor at Luther Seminary, to write a book on the question, which he did—*Worship Is Repentance*. In it, he did the historical work, going back to Luther and Osiander and carrying up until today, that argued for our side: the conditional was used when it was spoken to large groups and the unconditional in private, where the pastor had heard the confession of a prospective communicant.[18]

## Passing Down the Tradition

Despite what my biography would have predicted, I flourished in the ALC and grew to love it. There are questions that now loom larger for me as I think about what Sverdrup and Oftedal stood for. Could something of their ideas still be kept alive? I brought their thoughts and traditions to almost everything I ever did in the church. As this narrative, I hope, shows, the LFC lived in my very being. It came with me to every position I had in the school and church.

As to the family story, the next generations are spreading around the United States, away from Minnesota, Augsburg, and the Lutheran church. Both of my siblings attended Augsburg, and all three of us were named Distinguished Alumni. My sister, LaRhae Knatterud, was elected student body president in 1969 during the centennial of Augsburg. She went on to become an expert in aging, ending her career as director of aging transformation for the Minnesota Department of Human Services. Her daughter, Liv Anda Asplund, teaches at a Catholic high school in the area, where her two children attend. Her son, Bryn Anders Knatterud, and his wife, Melinda, are faithful members of a local Assemblies of God Church in the neighborhood, sending their five children to the neighborhood Catholic school and Christian high schools.

Harald Theodore, my brother, a lawyer, served as chair of the Augsburg board for twelve years around the turn of the twenty-first century and brought to his work his sense for its history and his obligation to it as he labored to assure the church connection would still be there. He has continued serving the church and its charitable organizations. He served on the Good Samaritan Homes Board and is now on the Board of Lutheran Social Services. His older son, Karl Theodore, is assistant professor of security studies at the University of New Hampshire; his younger son, Erik Haakon, graduated from Augsburg and is a physician's assistant (PA) with two daughters.

One of my first cousins, Merrill Dean Ronning, served as a pastor in the ALC and ELCA, while his siblings were faithful laypeople in their respective congregations. Bradley Ellingboe, great-grandson of Bernt Sundal, a fine singer who sang the lead in the Hauge opera by Egil Hovland, *Fange og Fri* (*Captive and Free*), continues to compose beautiful choral pieces for church choirs. His brother, Craig, served as pastor in the ELCA until his retirement. Another cousin, whose husband bought the Tinseth farms, is a devout supporter of their church. Other cousins in their generation are raising devout children as followers of their great-grandparents and grandparents and parents. This is to name just a few.

One can also praise God for the fact that the mission in Madagascar that Grandma Jonette, and all of us, supported fervently has borne rich fruit in the lively Malagasy Lutheran church. One can see the prayers of Grandma Helga Kivle and Torbjør Tinseth coming to fruition in our lives: many faithful laity and many faithful missionaries, pastors, and seminary professors, especially in the Lutheran Brethren church, where Svein Kivley's family belonged.

What matters now to them and me is not keeping the LFC alive but that they share a living Christian faith with their children. Our heritage has fallen into pleasant lines with many of the children of the third and fourth generations but now without the institution of the LFC or Augsburg as the center of their spiritual lives. In some sense, that is the American story but also the modern story. Our little fellowship always knew our children would be in some sense lost to us once they abandoned the college and were educated elsewhere. One episode of *The Cosby Show* featured a moment when one of the kids decided to go to an Ivy League school and abandon the family tradition at a Black college. It plunged the father and mother into grief, not unlike that of my parents when they had to face that we might not attend Augsburg.

## The Tradition Handed Down

The institutional history, however, is mixed. Several questions have begun to haunt me as I was writing this. First, the general question of how a tradition lives and maintains its core over time. That can be asked of any institution in the world. The second, however, is more particular: whether Augsburg remained true to its heritage or even if it could. Was the merger necessary to preserve Augsburg? And if it was saved, how much of its original ethos remains? Has the spirit of the LFC endured in the ELCA, or could it? As I have marked here, both Sverdrup Jr. and Bernhard Christensen had to do some fast work to convince people that Augsburg was still the same when it simply wasn't.

Traditions can turn on a dime, although how that affects the laity is unclear. Changing a piety in midstream is not easy, something this era has done with abandon. The liturgical movement, with its change from emphasis on the Supper as repentance to a celebration of unity, confused people like my mother who were used to the very penitential nature of the sacrament. Once, after we had gone to receive the frequent distribution of the sacrament by intinction, now offered every Sunday and no longer taken while kneeling the way she had grown up, I asked her what she thought of communion now. Did she prepare as she had in the old days? She remarked flippantly, with her typical wicked humor, "Now I don't give it a moment's thought!" That was a serious change, one to be marked. The church has, I think, thoughtlessly tried to change pieties without regard for how deep they go in people.

**Figure E.3.** Harald Grindal in vestments with Jonette Grindal. Used by permission of the Grindal family.

This trend toward the middle is a tendency in all organizations, routinizing what was once spirit and inspiration against the ferocious forces of modernity. It is what happens, especially, to pietists as they try to pass on the faith to their children. One cannot tell the Spirit what to do, although we can pray for our children to be faithful. As the saying goes, God has no grandchildren. Each child must come to their own knowledge of salvation. Plus, pietists are known for not being builders of institutions that last over time. Their efforts are to inspire others with the word of God so that faith is born in them. They want to effect great changes in a people through the gospel of Jesus Christ. When they do, it can change individuals for life, but that cannot be handed down.[19] We can baptize our children, teach them in Sunday school and confirmation, and send them to church programs for children, hoping they will become living Christians. Those things often do spark a living faith in them but not always. What I often saw in my youth was that parents raising their children in a wholesome piety conveyed only the forms to their children, the rules of behavior, which became stifling and rigid to the second generation. They could not force their children to have a conversion.

One of the geniuses of the Lutheran Free Church was its youth program from my grandmother's time until the merger. Knowing that one could not force conversion, the leaders relied on teaching the faith in Sunday school and confirmation, which they did very well. The seed was sown thoroughly and responsibly, to grow during the lifetime of the child. It could be reawakened. The Luther League conventions, with their large attendances, inspirational speakers, and thrilling music, often brought teenagers to a moment in which they would commit their lives to Christ and did. Merton Strommen, the youth pastor of the LFC, created events and experiences in which youths might experience a reawakening of their childhood faith.

## The Historic Episcopate Wins

The leaders of the LFC in the 1940s and 1950s were aware what they were proposing in the merger was not consistent with the founding principles of the LFC but felt, for reasons I can understand, that a merger was the only way to go. At the same time, one wonders if it was the spirit of the times that also forced their hands. Not very many could be leaders at that time and not approve proposals for merger. It would have gone against the spirit of the age.

Given the origin of the Lutheran churches as ones with strong bishops in the Lutheran lands, even if only Sweden practiced the historic episcopate, this tendency was in Lutheran DNA. Although the Norwegians rejected the theology and practice of the historic episcopate, their practices remained the same as those of the historic churches: bishops were required to ordain candidates for the ministry after they had received a call. Even as the LFC maintained its theology of ministry, the practice of having the president ordain the candidates for ministry was restored in the 1940s. Until then, every annual conference had an ordinator, someone who was not president, ordain the candidates. When they returned to the practice of having the president do it, Burntvedt, for all intents and purposes a lifetime bishop, became a bishop as in the old tradition, necessary for ordination.

To say our theology was different was no help. The old rule that how we pray is how we believe—*lex orandi lex credendi*—ultimately kicked in. The worry of the sage Caspersen and Christian Ytrehus, that in fifty years the LFC would have bishops and the historic episcopate, came true for many old LFC congregations now in the ELCA.[20] Some fifty years later, in 1998, the ELCA agreed to full communion with the Episcopalians. Was such a thing in our DNA ready to emerge as the descendants of the first fiery rebels in the Friends of Augsburg lost their fervor?

These things happen. Can that be prevented? I don't know. The hankering to be bigger and more influential was almost like a drug, utterly in the spirit of the age. My mother, weary of the spiritual pride in being poor and the smallest, exploded against that now and then. In America, the temptation to be successful and impressive also worked against a main theme in the LFC. Many whom I quoted in previous chapters did exult in the smallness and thus faithfulness of the LFC over the larger church. In some regard, we were making a virtue of our necessity. Mother had suffered from the grinding poverty of our congregations but knew that Jesus tended to favor the little flock, not the approval of the world.

## Sverdrup's Dream Redefined

I cannot criticize the move from Sverdrup's dream of a seminary that would produce pastors without a sense of privilege into a liberal arts college that I attended and loved. His ideas attracted support from the constituency, who began calling Augsburg "our seminary" (*"vor presteskole"*). The congregation was at the heart of the matter for him. Pastors who understood their role as shepherds and servants of the congregation were the only kind who could help that idea flourish in the new land. The fight about that issue caused the LFC to be born when the Augsburg party could not accept the idea that St. Olaf should also be a college of the church, disrupting Sverdrup's idea of Augsburg as the pastors' school. That battle was the cradle of my ecclesiology, and especially the notion of the congregation. I also came to believe strongly in the liberal arts and valued my liberal education at Augsburg, as had my parents. There, in addition to having their faith nurtured and strengthened, they had their love of music and the arts awakened.

I taught a course with Professors Leigh Jordahl and John Bale at Luther College, the second course in the *paideia requirement*, the two courses required of all Luther students. The first included English and history, which all students took through the year, and in the second year, a semester-long course involved deeper immersion in such subjects.[21] Our class studied the liberal arts requirements of Luther and Augsburg. Sverdrup's proposal to have only one school—academy, college, seminary—and his denigration of humanism surprised me. Even if one could prove that he had adopted something of Grundtvig's notion that classical studies for Nordics should be the glorious tradition of the *eddas* and Old Norse, along with the Greeks, I could not quite be persuaded. I sort of understood his argument but was embarrassed by it in that context. I did not understand his reasons, as I do now.

As I have spent the next fifty years grappling with that, I have come to understand his point more clearly and see that he was right about creating an elite class of clergy. This was made especially clear to me in an article by Mark Granquist on Sverdrup.[22] On this matter, life experience has proven Sverdrup right. Sverdrup, as a man of his time, which idealized the common man and the democratic ideals of the West, saw the dangers of a leadership class, an elite so out of touch with its people that it began to despise them and finally lord it over them. This is what we see all around us today. Liberal education, to me, means engagement with the texts and ideas of the glorious past. Those ideas are for the common person at their best. On this, Sverdrup was prophetic and dead right. Hearing some of my colleagues at both college and seminary ridiculing "the folks" has been proof enough of that. I would sometimes note that the folks were paying their salary and they should be more conscious of their debt to such people, but the great unwashed seemed embarrassing to them.

Still, when George Sverdrup Jr. had to go against his father's dream of such a school to keep Augsburg alive, he knew he was betraying it at some level. He saved it by taking his father's brand of freedom, using it to describe the freedom of the Christian and thus the freedom of the congregation. He used the brand of freedom as the value of Augsburg College. When he preached to my grandmother Anda and her peers about the ultimate importance of the congregation, she wrote it down in her journal and believed it with all her heart, without really knowing that it was not the school her parents, Ole and Jonette Jacobson, had agreed to support. I don't think they would have minded if they knew the school was still teaching the faith as they knew it, but it would have sounded very different for them—in fact, not much different from St. Olaf, which in those days also did a fine job of teaching the Lutheran faith to its students through figures like F. Melius Christiansen with his great Christmas extravaganzas and his choral compositions using Lutheran chorales, Scandinavian folk hymns, and English hymns.

I am glad the younger Sverdrup introduced coeducation, and I understand the cost. At the same time, one could argue that the education of women at the time was to some extent focused on the woman finding a mate and becoming a good, well-educated mother, able to raise faithful and believing children. I approve of this. Men should also be educated to be good husbands and fathers as a part of their training in Lutheran vocation. Coeducation, inevitably, used almost the same curriculum for men and women, with the same expectations of a career for women as men. In fact, college and higher education has evolved to stress careers for both men and women over making citizens who can raise families and build the culture, to some extent the professed goal of the founders of these colleges. Was there something that coeducation missed, causing us to misrepresent God's intention for us as physical beings able to make families and raise children, that has not been salutary? That issue needs attention from the church in these days of uncertainty about our roles as men and women.

When Christensen in his inaugural address proposed that Augsburg was about educating laymen and women, free and living Christians, to support the congregations and not about being a *presteskole*, it was a direct attack on Sverdrup, which few heard. It was taken as a necessity once again. To read that, really for the first time, in the context of this book took my breath away. That may have surprised me the most. I do not at all disagree with the goal of educating young men and women for service—that is also deep in my blood as a daughter of an LFC pastor and his wife. Nor do I disagree with freedom as Sverdrup's great theme. It is the tradition taught to me by my parents and my education at Augsburg. Christensen shrewdly used the tradition against itself to save it.

Once, after Christensen spoke in chapel on education for service, I went directly to my father, who was waiting in the car to take me for summer job interviews. Ebenezer Home Society for the Aged needed workers. I said, "Take me there. I want to serve." After the interview, I was offered the job at ninety-five cents an hour because the head nurse told me they were a Christian organization. I took it and worked for a pittance over the next few years in the summers and on weekends. My experience there made it possible for me to get such a job in Oslo, Norway, during my year in the country, a life-changing experience for me, to be sure, and much more expensive for my father, who also revered Christensen and his message. He had to pay more for my education at Augsburg! But it made a difference to me throughout my life. I do not know whether that would be true for a student today at Augsburg regarding the Christian faith. There is still a Christian ministry at Augsburg, but its increasingly multifaith student body will make it complicated to maintain that tradition.

## Conclusion

As I have been writing this, I have been troubled by what I may have communicated about the LFC's betrayal of Sverdrup by those who succeeded him. They could not keep to his interpretation of the LFC principles. They can be defended for their efforts to save the institution of Augsburg, which they did. As I pondered this after completing the narrative, it occurred to me that on Sverdrup's main point, we have all gotten it wrong. Sverdrup's Principle 1 was not meant only to organize a church body, a model for people to follow when they are building a denomination. Sverdrup was simply describing what is true about the church from its beginning in Acts to now: there is no denomination without congregations. The LFC was frequently called a "fellowship" of congregations.

John Bunyan, the great Puritan writer of *Pilgrim's Progress*, after the Act of Uniformity of 1662 that forbade him from preaching without a proper ordination, is said to have recognized that wherever he went, the Church was a "fellowship of Believers."[23] He believed strongly in the communion of saints, "the apple of God's eye." No matter what the historical churches said, "the Church is no hierarchical institution; it is the fellowship of believers, but it is everywhere and inescapable. Christ and his Church are one."[24] For Bunyan, Wakefield argued, "Church fellowship rightly managed is the glory of the world."[25] Bunyan was preaching to the church, a congregation, a fellowship of believers, dissenters and others he gladly served.[26] These insights take on a kind of resonance for me as I consider how I fought the Act of Uniformity in our battle against Called to Common Mission, which essentially adopted the Anglican Act of Uniformity 1662, which adopted the threefold ministry that requires bishops in the historic episcopate to ordain all of its pastors.

In his foundational article "Do You Want a Congregation?" (*"Vil I ha menighet"*), Sverdrup makes it clear that congregations are formed by revivals when people, now living Christians, gather in fellowship. This makes them a congregation. They will call a leader to serve them. Revival is the spark that begins or reawakens congregations. Augsburg Seminary was devoted to providing pastors who could fulfill that call. My father practiced that notion of spiritual revival and awakening in the congregation and, as per Principle 4, always preached for the cleansing of the body. His emphasis was not just evangelism outside the church but also inside. But does that make Home Mission bureaucracies wrong? Can one establish a congregation from a bureaucracy? The Twelve Principles of the LFC go on to say that congregations can and should organize together to promote institutions like schools, hospitals, missions, and so on that one congregation could not support. That makes sense. Congregations are divinely instituted—Sverdrup believed this, as do most Protestants, but church structures are not divine. They are worldly institutions with a mission to serve the congregations by providing them with resources for their mission or the world on behalf of individual congregations.

There is some irony in this—many Lutheran church officials argued that churches should merge to make a reality of Jesus's prayer that they may be one. As many like Al Rogness, president of Luther Seminary at the time, pointed out, they already were one in Christ. The officials who argued that merger was necessary to make us one missed that and seemed to make the church a divine thing, sacramental, giving it spiritual value. This is the error of most Lutheran merger strategies. It confuses organizational union with Christian unity.

As we look at the situation today, Lutherans may in hindsight wish they had tried something else, organizationally speaking. Mark Granquist argued so in "The Urge to Merge" in the *Lutheran Forum*, holding up more modest ways of working together without destroying old alliances and fellowships in search of efficiency, hardly a Christian virtue.[27] Overlooking the power of relationships, familial or communal, to achieve efficiency for the sake of the Gospel does not appear to possess much wisdom, spiritual or human. Of course, tribal bonds are not spiritual and can be detrimental to Christian communion, but they should not simply be ignored. Loyalty is one of the better angels of our past. The merged churches we constructed are not a glowing testimony to the wisdom of breaking those bonds. Again, we see the modern drive to build and create also being destructive of what it wants to save. In fact, Lyle Schaller, on considering the cost of the merger that gave us the ELCA, opposed it. He noted that in twenty years, the merged church would be about the size of one of the merging churches. His prediction has proven to be accurate.

As I look back over the wrecks of time, now in my eighty-first year, I am grateful for my heritage and somewhat distressed by where we are now. Is it all over? Is there nothing here that we can bring forward into the future with us? Of course, Jesus Christ, the same, yesterday, today, and forever. But what about the spirit of the LFC? Were the leaders I quoted above right to say it would live on no matter what? And could it be revived? In a sense, Christensen and his contemporaries were correct in arguing that Sverdrup's dream had not ended with the merger. Unfortunately, they framed it in the notion that it would continue to live in the ALC through heirs of the tradition without assuring it be taught. There is also a piece of my disillusionment with what happened to the LFC that needs more clarity. Congregations have been established with success, thousands of times over the past millennia. Every time a faithful congregation of any stripe is formed, the kingdom of God is there. Finally, I have come to understand that Sverdrup's idea was not necessarily a plan for a particular church body. Sverdrup was simply describing the way the church had worked over the millennia.

To be sure, the Association of Free Lutheran Congregations has continued the tradition as developed by Sverdrup and operates with the Twelve Principles used by the LFC. Congregations that have joined it over the past few years join not because of their shared ethnic backgrounds but because they agree with the Twelve Principles and want to follow them. And to its credit, it has built an organization that works on and celebrates congregational freedom. Given my argument, whether they have built a church structure that is effective should not be the way to judge them as being successful—it should be whether the congregations are flourishing and have built institutions that help the congregations flourish. One can admire the starch the founders had when they shunned the merger with the ALC and set out on their own, with few pastors, but strong lay leadership from the Ose and Dyrud families in and around Newfolden, Minnesota, many of whom were in my classes at Augsburg, along with John

Strand, Fritjof Monseth, and others—plus the strong continuing leadership of Robert Lee, my classmate from Augsburg, have kept the church body and seminary afloat over the past sixty years, a commendable feat. Lee's genial spirit and strong convictions were clear from when I first knew him as a fellow student and continue to this day.

That story is not mine to tell, but it deserves to be marked as a communion that reveres and practices the theology and ecclesiology of Sverdrup and the LFC. The Sverdrup Society, established in 2003 and dedicated to the study and promulgation of his thought, has been a lively center for Sverdrup studies. The seminary and now college the Association has built seem to be doing that, but as the requirements of accreditation and scholarly standing encroach, it will be interesting to see if they can resist conforming to them.

What I have recounted in these pages is how Sverdrup's ideas were brought forward, first in the Conference, then the Friends of Augsburg, and finally the Lutheran Free Church, and how my family supported his idea, how it was imprinted on me, and what has become of it in my experience in the ALC and then the ELCA. I cannot follow those ideas into the AFLC or elsewhere. My history is complicated enough and shows, to my mind, that Sverdrup's dream for Augsburg Seminary, not the congregation, was, in effect, abandoned by the 1920s by necessity.

Sverdrup's First Principle, and all twelve that the LFC adopted, does not mean rampant individualism or congregationalism, something I was accused of touting when I quoted Sverdrup's ecclesiology during my time on the Task Force for the Study of Ministry. As I have said, I argued that I did not agree with the principle if it were required. However, it was, in fact, a description of the church, not just the LFC—a description of an ecclesiology that worked. I now see that I was partly misunderstanding it, too, and not fully understanding the truth of my assertion that it was a description, not a prescription. At his best, Sverdrup was not arguing for congregationalism. He was simply stating a truth: Congregations are essential. One cannot imagine a church body without the congregation. One needs gathered believers, wherever they are, to form a congregation. Far from being individualistic, Sverdrup realized that one could not be a Christian by oneself—one needed a congregation, a gathering of individuals to do the Lord's work of loving the neighbor. Rampant individualists would never join a congregation. The Christian faith requires submission of one's own will to the Lord Jesus and one's neighbor!

Sverdrup and his followers believed that the congregation was divine, birthed and succored by God. The church body was not. I agree with all my heart. We should take a higher view of his principle. It is much larger than the rules for a small, struggling church body on the Midwestern prairies. What Sverdrup was asserting in this first principle has been true since Acts 2: revival produces congregations. The entire book of Acts is a record of establishing house churches—congregations from Jerusalem to Judea to the uttermost parts of the world. As each apostle went forth to spread the good news, they went to preach the gospel to people who would establish congregations. The early church sent missionaries to all parts of Europe and Asia, and in each case, they sent priests to gather people by their preaching to establish congregations. The rules for priests setting up homes, or parsonages, as they settled in to serve the people with the gospel show this clearly. The word drew them together. One sent out missionaries, pastors, priests, evangelists, laypeople to preach the word and start mission sites, small groups, fellowships—congregations. Whoever preached the word was not essential, only that it was spoken.

I don't think Sverdrup would require that the congregation needed to resemble those in the LFC to meet his description. He believed in the freedom of congregations to determine how they would organize and worship. There are thousands of living and vital congregations around the world, from many different traditions, which remain vital and strong because their people are vibrant, living Christians. They are tended by priests, pastors, rectors, and lay pastors, who are themselves vital, living Christians. They know as they plan services and projects, dinners, Sunday schools, and youth events that Christ must be at the center and that where Christ is, there is truth and freedom. This is a fact.

Sverdrup had clearly reasoned, from Scripture, how the gospel works to change individuals who, on being awakened, gather to create communities of faith all around the world. While some, as in the Roman Church, sacralized the structure of the church, that does not contradict Sverdrup's position. Without faithful priests and faithful members in parishes large and small throughout the world, there would be no Roman Catholic Church. Somehow, the Roman Catholics and the Orthodox also landed on a structure that has made them the longest living organizations in the world. No other set of Christians has done that, and to some extent we all trace our origins to it.

We should take heart from the core of Sverdrup's message: the fellowship of believers, the congregation, is where it all happens. No organization of any church body can fulfill its calling without vibrant, living congregations. Even today, congregations are being formed around the world to drive the mission of Christ. Free and living congregations attract people who want to fully experience the joy of Christians here on earth and eternity. As Sverdrup once said concerning the common schools, their end is on earth; the congregations' end is in heaven. Parents should take care to see their children get an education in both but never forget that the more important and eternal of their missions is giving their children many chances to learn of and accept their goodly heritage and its saving promise of salvation in Jesus Christ.

# NOTES

## CHAPTER 1: LEAVING NORWAY

1. See the 1951 Annual Conference report of the LFC.
2. My father, who was never late, spent an anxious week driving Rossing around to speaking engagements in the congregations in the Rugby parish. When he finally left on the train, which they just barely made, he stepped into it as it was pulling out, turned around and smiled at my father, and said, "Vall, Harald, ve yust made it."
3. Jonette Grindal, *Lots of Sky* (Privately published, 1999), 2.
4. "Belle Fourche Plans Issuing Water Bonds," *Rapid City Journal*, September 5, 1952, 12.
5. Tor Mathisen, *Sømna: Gård og Slekt III* (Utgit Sømna Kommune, 1992), 31.
6. Joseph M. Shaw, *Pulpit Under the Sky: A Life of Hans Nielsen Hauge* (Augsburg Publishing House, 1955), 23.
7. *Electio*—believer is elected; *vocatio*—believer is called; *illuminatio*—illumined; *conversio*—converted; *regeneratio*—regenerated; *justificatio*—justification; *unio mystica*—mystical union with Christ; *renovatio*—renovation; *conservation*—conserved to the end; *glorificatio*—glorified with the Son.
8. See Martin Luther, *Works,* American Edition, vol. 44 (Fortress Press, 1966), 115 ff.
9. *Luther's Small Catechism Explained*. Adopted by the Lutheran Free Church, 1929 (The Messenger Press, 1929), 50.
10. Gerhard Forde of Luther Seminary, no fan of Pontoppidan's pietism, told me once that when he was considering a dogmatic question, he would recall the biblical citations from Pontoppidan, which he knew to be deep in the interpretive tradition.
11. Many jokes were told about this, like why are Baptists against sex, because it leads to dancing.
12. Shaw, *Pulpit Under the Sky*, 18.
13. Shaw, *Pulpit Under the Sky*, 18.
14. See Hans Nielsen Hauge, *Consideration of the World's Folly*, ed. Peter Tore Gabrielson, trans. Daryl N. Olson (Media Forlag, 2021).
15. Trygve Riiser Gundersen, *Haugianerne: Enevelden og undergrunn* (Cappellen Damm, 2022), 22.
16. Arve Bugge Amundsen, "Peder Hersleb," *Norsk Biografisk Leksikon*, https://inbl.snl.no/Peder_Hersleb.
17. Per Øverland, *Haugianerne i Norge*, as found in Tor Mathiesen, *Sømna: Gård og Slekt III* (Utgit Sømna Kommune, 1992), 31.

18. For an English translation, see Shaw, *Pulpit Under the Sky*, 201–210.
19. Shaw, *Pulpit Under the Sky*, 201–210.
20. Thomas Erastus (1524–1583) argued that the state should punish the sins of Christians.
21. Hans Nielsen Hauge, *Hans Nielsen Hauges Skrifter*, 5, 286, as found in Inger Furseth, "The Role of Women in the Hauge Movement," *Lutheran Quarterly* 13 (1999), 398.
22. *Indledning til virksomme Udøvelser af Patriotisc Meditations*, 1804, as found in Furseth, "The Role of Women in the Hauge Movement," 398.
23. Trygve Riiser Gundersen, *Haugianerne: Enevelden og undergrunn* (Cappellen Damm, 2022), 22.
24. The sons of one of the Jacobsons' neighbors, Arnliot Matthias Arnzten (1857–1934), editor of *Folkebladet* from 1887 to 1893, wrote a popular biography of Hauge, *The Apostle from Norway* (Wipf & Stock Publishers, 2011), that featured this scene on the cover.
25. See Johann Carl Keyser Preus, *Norsemen Found a Church: An Old Heritage in a New Land* (Augsburg Publishing House, 1953).
26. Augustana (Sioux Falls), 1860; Luther, 1861; Augsburg, 1869; St. Olaf, 1874; Pacific Lutheran, 1890; Concordia (Moorhead), 1891; Jewell, 1894; Waldorf, 1903; and California Lutheran, 1959, and the seminaries (Augsburg, 1869; Luther, 1876; Red Wing, 1879; United, 1893; and Luther, 1917). To say nothing of the many academies.
27. See Johan Oluf Evjen, *Scandinavian Immigrants in New York, 1630–1674* (K. C. Holter Publishing Company, 1916).
28. The most important and influential of these early letters was Johan Reinert Reiersen's *Veiviser for norske emigranter til de forenede nordamerikanske Stater og Texas (Guide for Norwegian Emigrants to the United States and Texas)* (Christiania, 1844).
29. The Augsburg Confession, *The Book of Concord: The Confessions of the Evangelical Lutheran Church*, ed. Theodore Tappert (Muhlenberg Press, 1959).
30. *Linka's Diary: On Land and Sea 1845–1864*, trans. Johan Carl Keyser Preus et al. (Augsburg Publishing House, 1952), 116: "I had become a minister; I had a congregation!" In his mind, the call made him a pastor; his ordination would simply be a public recognition of that.
31. While there is some controversy about whether she wrote it, scholars are unable to prove she did not.
32. In 1857, they had sent a delegation of Olaf Brandt and J. A. Ottesen to visit Concordia, Buffalo, and Capital in Columbus, Ohio, to check out the seminaries that would be most appropriate for their students to attend.
33. My father always said, "I am a Johnsonian, not a Haugian," as did many of his contemporaries who had read Johnson with appreciation while at Augsburg.
34. August Weenaas, *Livserindringer Fra Norge Og Amerika. Bibliotheca Norvegiæ Sacræ* (A.S. Lunde & Co.s, forlag, 1935), 113.
35. Weenaas, *Livserindringer*, 113.
36. August Weenaas, *Mindeblade: Otte Aar i Amerika* (R. P. Hjelles Forlag, 1890), 22.

37. To Mathiesen, *Sømna: Gård og Slekt III*, 31.
38. Ole Rølvaag, *i de dager*, 1925, *Giants in the Earth*, trans. Lincoln Colcord (Harper Brothers, 1927).
39. Johan Olsen, *Nogle salmer og leilighedssange* (Augsburg Publishing House, 1906). Translated by Gracia Grindal.
40. Marcus Lee Hansen, a Danish American scholar of emigration developed this theory in his book *The Problem of the Third Generation Immigrant* (Augustana Historical Society, 1938).
41. Fredrik Hansen Teigen, "Fra Chippewa County," *Nordisk Tidende*, August 18, 1869, 1.
42. *Nordisk Folkebladet*, 1868.
43. L. R. Moyer and O. G. Dale, *History of Chippewa and Lac qui Parle Counties Minnesota: Their People, Industries and Institutions*, vol. 1 (B. E. Bowen and Company, 1916), 227.
44. Carl Gustav Oluf Hanson, *My Minneapolis: A Chronicle of What Has Been Learned and Observed About the Norwegians in Minneapolis Through One Hundred Years* (Standard Press, 1956), 19.
45. Ole Paulson, *Erindringer* (The Free Church Book Concern, 1907). For an English translation, see https://dahlelawchurches.com/augsburg-seminary-minneapolis-history/pastor-ole-paulson-autobiography-introduction/.
46. August Weenaas, *Livserindringer fra Norge og Amerika* (A.S. Lunde & Co.s, forlag, 1935), 137.
47. In his report to the Conference annual meeting in 1871, Pastor Johan Christian Jacobsen describes his preaching using Finnish that was exactly spelled out for him even if he understood nothing of what he was saying. Johan Christian Jacobsen, "Indberetning fra missionspræst Pastor J. C. Jacobsen," *Beretning om 2det aarlige Konfersentsemøde, Konferentsen for den norsk=dansk evangelisk Lutherske Kirke i Amerika, afhold i den norsk=dansk ev.=luth. Trefoldigheds=Kirke i Minneapolis, Minn,; fra den 4de til den 13de Juni, 1871* (Konferentsens forlagsforenings trykkeri, 1871), 33.
48. See John Wilhelm Christian Dietrichson, *A Pioneer Churchman: J. W. C. Dietrichson in Wisconsin 1844–1850*, ed. E. Clifford Nelson (Norwegian American Historical Association, 1973).
49. Paulson, *Erindringer*, 32.
50. Paulson, *Erindringer*, 32.
51. Whether it was malaria cannot be determined, but an illness like it struck many in the north from Muskego to Kansas—it also affected Laura Ingalls Wilder's family. The Muskego area was a rather unhealthy region. Later Norwegian immigrants could not quite understand why the early settlers had settled there.
52. Paulson, *Erindringer*, 61.
53. David Hollatz, *The Evangelic Order of Grace: Or, How a Soul May Be Brought from Self-Righteousness to a Knowledge of Its Sinful Misery; and Thereupon Led to the Wounds of Jesus; and in This Manner, Through Faith, to the Forgiveness of Sins, and a Pious Life*, trans. Charles Erdmann (Pietan Publications, 2000). Hollatz's orthodox father, David Hollatz (1648–1713), is often confused with him.

54. Paulson probably knew this hymn in English written in 1835 or maybe Swedish. The Norwegian version of it was not printed until 1876. The stanza he refers to is unknown to me.
55. Paulson, *Erindringer*, 82–83.
56. Few books influenced Lutherans as much as this one written in 1605. While written some seventy years before the beginning of pietism, many feel it was a predecessor of it. Spener's book *Pia Desideria* in 1675 was the introduction to an edition of Arndt's book.
57. See M. Falk Gjertsen's *Hjemlandsanger*, 1877. More extensive information on this movement among Norwegians can be found in Gracia Grindal, "Keeping the Kids," in *Journal of the Lutheran Historical Conference*, ed. Mark Granquist (Lutheran University Press, 2018).
58. This is an interesting comment. Paulson is writing it long after the Muus marriage had fallen apart. These proceedings scandalized the Norwegian American community. Mrs. Muus probably came in for as much bad press as him. Neither escaped unscathed.
59. Paulson, *Erindringer*, 103.
60. Paulson says very little about his wife in his book except that he married her and that she frequently opposed his ventures, like being a colporteur, joining the army, etc. She must have grown up in Chicago since Erland Carlsson confirmed her. She was a native of Norway, and together they had nine children, two of whom died in infancy.
61. Paulson, *Erindringer*, 137.
62. Paulson, *Erindringer*, 141.
63. Paulson, *Erindringer*, 141.
64. Luther College taught music, and students sang together in a male chorus, but as far as I know, they did not tour until later.
65. I found the hymn in a songbook attributed to O. Paulson. It is very much influenced by the hymn "I am a stranger here / Earth is a desert drear, Heaven is my home." When my father heard a quartet sing it in a program at Luther Seminary, he wept. He knew it immediately and marveled that he should have heard it once again in his lifetime. So it must have been well known.
66. Paulson, *Erindringer*, 216.
67. C. G. O. Hanson, *My Minneapolis* (Privately published, 1956), 21–22.
68. B. J. Muus, "Correspond. fra Nordamerika til et norsk blad," *Lutherske Kirketidende*, December 9, 1866, 375.
69. Fra Studenter. "Ogsaa fra Amerika: et tilsvar i sandhedens Interesse," *Luthersk Kirketidende*, April 7, 1867, 210.
70. E. Clifford Nelson and Eugene Fevold, *The Lutheran Church Among Norwegian-Americans* (Augsburg Publishing House, 1960), 246.
71. Herman Preus, "Svar paa Stykket: Ogsaa fra Nordamerika," *Luthersk Kirketidende*, May 19, 1867, 307.
72. Preus, "Svar paa Stykket," 307.
73. Herman Amberg Preus, *Vivacious Daughter: Seven Lectures on the Religious Situation Among Norwegians in America*, trans. Todd W. Nichol (Norwegian American Historical Association, 1990).

Notes 519

74. "Gunder Larson Graven. Letter to Lars Holan," *From American to Norway: Norwegian American Immigrant Letters 1838–1914*, vol. 2, 1871–1892, ed. and trans. Orm Øverland (Norwegian American Historical Association, 2014), 47.
75. Weenaas, *Livserindringer*, 116.
76. Harkey left Marshall and had a distinguished career as pastor, teacher, and writer of hymn texts—mostly refrains—to well-known hymns. He served as president of the General Council for two years (1885–1887). Weenaas, *Livserindringer*, 118.
77. Weenaas, *Livserindringer*, 130.
78. Although there had been high hopes that the trains would go through Decorah, it was not to be. So Weenaas and his family had to take a local to Calmar, probably, and from there board the train to Minneapolis.
79. August Weenaas, "Fra Nordvestern, August 17, 1874, Benson, Swift County, Minnesota," *Lutheraneren*, August 1874, 278.
80. J. A. Bergh, "The First Home of Augsburg. Augsburg in Marshall, Wisconsin," *Augsburgian*, 1919, 23.
81. Andreas Helland, *Augsburg Gjennom femti Aar* (Folkebladets Trykkeri, 1920), 47.
82. Sven Oftedal, "Fra Prairien," *Folkebladet: Maanedsblad for Skolen og Folket*, November 1879, 1.
83. One of the most harrowing scenes in that story is when Per Hansa, trying to please Beret, who is going mad in their sod house, whitewashed the inside to make it more pleasant, but Beret gets angry at him since all she can see is white snow outside the house.
84. Bernt Sundal, "Mrs. Jonetta Jacobson Død," *Folkebladet*, December 20, 1922, 821.
85. Sundal, "Mrs. Jonetta Jacobson Død," 821.

## CHAPTER 2: AUGSBURG MOVES TO MINNEAPOLIS

1. Typhoid fever is caused by bacterial infection found in feces. Good sanitation is the best way to prevent it. The close quarters of the students at the school and the lack of proper sanitation made such an epidemic almost impossible to avoid once the bacteria infected the student body.
2. Paulson, *Erindringer*, 228. For an English translation, see https://dahlelawchurches.com/augsburg-seminary-minneapolis-history/pastor-ole-paulson-autobiography-introduction/.
3. J. Magnus Rohne, *Norwegian American Lutheranism up to 1872* (The Macmillan Company, 1928), 236.
4. Rohne, *Norwegian American Lutheranism*, 238–239.
5. Weenaas, *Livserindringer fra Norge og Amerika*, 46.
6. Weenaas, "Fra Amerika," *Luthersk Kirketidende*, August 31, 1872, 133–134.
7. Weenaas, "Fra Amerika."
8. Weenaas, "Fra Amerika."
9. Johan Arndt Bergh, *Den norsk lutherske kirkes historie i Amerika* (Augsburg Publishing House, 1914), 23.
10. August Weenaas, "Letter to Candidate P. Hærem," Marshall, Wisconsin, July 10, 1872, National Bibliotek, Oslo, Archives.
11. Weenaas, "Letter to Candidate P. Hærem."

12. Paulson, *Erindringer,* 226.
13. Bergh, *Den norsk lutherske kirkes historie i Amerika,* 24.
14. Carl H. Chrislock, *From Fjord to Freeway: 100 Years Augsburg College* (Augsburg College, 1969), 6.
15. Kap. 2, Art. 8, "Enhver af de af Konferentsens Pastorer betjent Menigheder have Ret til at sende en Delegat til Konferentsens Møder, men staa dog fri og uafhængige som saadan./Each of the Conference pastors serving congregations has the right to send a delegate to the Conference meetings but is entirely free and independent of it." This was amended to read "Enhver i Konfterntsens staaende Menigheder bør lade sig repræsenterer ved Konfentsens Møder ved at vælge og sende en eller to Delegater til disse./Each of the congregations that belong to the Conference should be represented at the Conference meetings by choosing and sending one or two delegates there." *Luthersk Kirketidende, Ny Række* 7, no. 9 (August 31, 1872), 132.
16. Paulson, *Erindringer,* 229.
17. My great-uncle Fred Tinseth told the story for many years about a man in Cyrus coming to him, pointing his finger at him, and saying "Fred, Fred, du blir shit out of luck." "Hvorfor?" Fred asked. "Du hører til Konfererntsen og jeg, jeg hører til S-s-s-ynoden." ("Fred, Fred, you are shit out of luck. You belong to the Conference, and I, I belong to the Synod.")
18. That it was the first seminary for Norwegian Lutherans in America became a matter of some dispute, which I first realized on rereading the first chapter of Helland's *Augsburg Gjennom Femti Aar,* in which he spends much time making the case that it was the first.
19. Kasseren. "Kasseren for Konferntsen for den Norsk-Danks Luth. Evg. Kirke i Amerika," *Lutheraneren,* September 1874, 144.
20. Kasseren. "Kasseren for Konferntsen."
21. Bergh, *Den norsk lutherske kirkes historie i Amerika,* 23.
22. Bergh, *Den norsk lutherske kirkes historie i Amerika,* 24.
23. Johan Olsen, "Formandens Aarsberetning," *Beretning om 4de aarlige Konferentsemøde af Konferentsen for den norsk=dansk evang. Lutherske Kirke i Amerika afholdt i Fort Howard (Wis.) norsk luth. Menigheds Kirke fra 10de til 18de Juni, 1874* (Konferentsens forlagsforenings trykkeri, 1874), 17.
24. Bernt L. Sundal, "Mrs. Jonette Jacobson er død," *Folkebladet,* November 1922.
25. August Weenaas, "Et Ord om Kvindeforeninger," *Lutheraneren* 5 (April 1871): 58–59.
26. The document histories are not easy to fit together. There was clearly a Norwegian Synod Lutheran congregation in the area from 1870 on. Brønø minutes record that the Conference congregation was formed in March 1873. The minutes of the congregation, sketchy as they are, begin in 1873, when Edward Eriksen arrived to help establish the congregation. The Chippewa County history book differs, but I trust them the least since they did not know Norwegian or Lutheran church organizations. For them, the Brønø congregation started in 1903, which Norlie says in

his comprehensive books on all the congregations and pastors of the Norwegian American Lutheran congregations. I will trust Sundal and the minutes for now. They are contemporaneous.
27. "Resultaterne af det 19de Aarhundredes Missionsarbeide," *Missionstraktat*; Georg Sverdrup, "Nu og for 100 Aar siden," *Gasseren* 1, no. 1 (1900): 89–90.
28. See L. DeAne Lagerquist, *From Our Mothers' Arms: A History of Women in the American Lutheran Church* (Augsburg Publishing House, 1987).
29. This is the origin of the name Karinsplass for the condos beside the Trinity offices on Riverside Avenue. Robert Lee, former president of the Association of Free Lutheran Congregations, told me once that someone who had observed them tear down the old main building noted there was not much of a foundation, just stones laid on the ground.
30. "Dedication of Augsburg's New Building," *Minneapolis Star*, November 1, 1872, 4.
31. Abner Batalden, ed., *Our Fellowship* (Messenger Press, 1947), 6.
32. Markhus served Norway Lake until his death in December 1885. His widow, Ingerid Egge Markus, a daughter of the Egge family, with whom the Korens stayed for some months before their parsonage was built, became a matron at Red Wing Ladies Seminary.
33. Minutes of Immanuel Lutheran Congregation, microfilm M678, reel 46, on file at the Minnesota History Museum.
34. Minutes of Immanuel Lutheran Congregation, microfilm M678, reel 46.
35. When my father arrived at a new call, one of the trustees had just left his wife and was having an affair with one of his employees. When my father asked the trustees whether they should ask him not to commune, the trustees were appalled and refused to discuss the matter at all, saying they were all sinners, somewhat missing the point. Of course, communion was for sinners, but the real question was whether or not it was for unrepentant sinners.
36. For a fuller discussion of the issues around this, see Walter Sundberg, *Worship Is Repentance* (Eerdmans Press, 2013).
37. E. Cliffort Nelson and Eugene Fevold, *The Lutheran Church Among Norwegian-Americans: A History of the Evangelical Lutheran Church* (Augsburg Publishing House, 1960), 247.
38. Jacobsen, "Indberetning fra missionspræst Pastor J. C. Jacobsen," 33. See also The Augsburg Confession, *The Book of Concord*.
39. August Weenaas, "Fra Nordvestern, August 17, 1874, Benson, Swift County, Minnesota," in August Weenaas, ed. *Lutheraneren* (Konferentsens forlagsforenings trykkeri, 1874), 278.
40. Weenaas, "Fra Nordvestern."
41. Weenaas, "Fra Nordvestern."
42. Christian Saugstad, "Missionsberetning fra Pastor Saugstad," *Beretning*, 1873, 66–67.
43. Saugstad, "Missionsberetning fra Pastor Saugstad."
44. Tor Mathisen, *Sømna: Gård og Slekt IV* (Utgit Sømna Kommune, 1992), 328.

45. Minutes, Saron Congregation, March 1874, microfilm M678, reel 46, on file at the Minnesota History Museum.
46. Minutes of Immanuel Lutheran Congregation, microfilm M678, reel 46.
47. Minutes of Immanuel Lutheran Congregation, microfilm M678, reel 46.
48. Weenaas, *Mindeblade*, 65.
49. Weenaas, *Mindeblade*.
50. Weenaas, *Livserindringer*, 151.
51. Weenaas, *Livserindringer*, 151.
52. Herman Amberg Preus, *Vivacious Daughter: Seven Lectures on the Religious Situation Among Norwegians in America*, trans. and ed. Todd W. Nichol (Norwegian American Historical Association, 1990).
53. Preus, *Vivacious Daughter*.
54. August Weenaas, *En kristenkvindes enfoldige liv og salige död* (den Norsk-dansk forlagsforenings trykkeri, 1873).
55. Andreas Helland, *Augsburg Seminar gjennem femti aar 1869–1919* (Folkebladetstryikkeri, 1919), 100.
56. Herman Preus to Johan Olsen, quoted in August Weenaas, *Wisconsinismen belyst ved historiske kjendsgjerninger* (Scandinavens Bog-og Accidentsstrykkeri, 1874), 87.
57. Helland, *Augsburg Seminar*, 99.
58. Sven Oftedal and August Weenaas, "Aapen Erklaring," in Helland, *Augsburg Seminar*, 442. For an English translation, see August Weenaas and Sven Oftedal, "The Open Declaration," in *Sverdrup Journal*, trans. Jan Horne (The Georg Sverdrup Society, 2006), III: 31–35.
59. Elisabeth Koren to Linka Preus (Summer 1874), Luther College Archives.
60. Herman Preus, *Professorerne Oftedals og Weenaas "Wisconsinisme" betragte i sandhedens lys, et gjensvar til Professor Weenaas* (B. Anderson, 1875).
61. Nelson and Fevold, *The Lutheran Church Among Norwegian-Americans*, 247.
62. Weenaas and Oftedal, "The Open Declaration."
63. Helland, *Augsburg Seminar*, 102.
64. Georg Sverdrup, "Alvorlig Strid, Alvorlig Fred," *Skandinaven*, December 7, 1874, reprinted in *Sverdrups Samlede Skrifter i Udvalg*, vol. IV (Frikirkens Boghandel, 1910), 169–179.
65. Weenaas, *Wisconsinismen*.
66. E. Clifford Nelson and Eugene L. Fevold, *The Lutheran Church Among Norwegian Americans: A History of the Evangelical Lutheran Church* (Augsburg Publishing House, 1960), 250.
67. Weenaas, *Wisconsinismen*, 38.
68. Helland, *Augsburg Seminar*, 118.
69. Batalden, *Our Fellowship*, 7.
70. Georg Sverdrup, "Fra Minnesotadalen," *Folkebladet*, August 16, 1883, 1.
71. Weenaas, "Fra Nordvestern," 278.
72. Weenaas, "Fra Nordvestern."
73. Rohne, *Norwegian American Lutheranism*, 242.
74. Sverdrup's suggestions for an agenda for these meetings. "Congregational Edification Meetings" can be found in *Sverdrup Journal* XVIII (2021): 90.

## CHAPTER 3: THE EARLY YEARS

1. See Andreas Helland, *Georg Sverdrup: The Man and His Message* (Messenger Press, 1947), 87–88.
2. Weenaas, *Mindeblade*, 83.
3. Weenaas, *Mindeblade*, 86.
4. *Lutheraneren*, 1874, 268. Found in Helland, *Georg Sverdrup*, 120.
5. Fevold and Nelson, *The Lutheran Church Among Norwegian-Americans*, 222.
6. Weenaas, *Livserindringen*, 159, as found in Fevold and Nelson, *The Lutheran Church Among Norwegian-Americans*, 222.
7. Georg Sverdrup, "Nøden i Grässhopper=Distrikterne," *Luthersk Kirketidende*, October 2, 1874.
8. Weenaas, *Mindeblade*, 87.
9. August Weenaas, "Augsburg Seminarium," *Lutheraneren og Missionsblad*, January 23, 1875, 61.
10. Weenaas, "Augsburg Seminarium," 60.
11. Andreas Helland, "Augsburg under skiftende Tider og Kaar," *Folkebladet*, October 7, 1942, 2.
12. Weenaas, *Mindeblade*, 89.
13. See *Elise Margreth Camermeyer Welhaven Gunnersen Memoirs, 1844–1904*, NAHA Collection Database P1532, St. Olaf College, Northfield, MN.
14. Georg Sverdrup, *Beretning*, 1875, as found in Helland, *Georg Sverdrup*, 54.
15. Georg Sverdrup's dedication speech, June 14, 1875, as found in Helland, *Georg Sverdrup*, 57.
16. Sverdrup's dedication speech, as found in Helland, *Georg Sverdrup*, 57.
17. "Dedication of Augsburg Seminary," *Star Tribune*, June 16, 1875, 1.
18. "Dedication of Augsburg Seminary," 1.
19. Lars Oftedal. His article on his travels that summer, "Report on the Trip to America/Beretning om reisen til Amerika," published by the Conference's printing press in 1876, gives interesting accounts of his experiences in many of the early settlements, which are still worth reading.
20. Weenaas, "Augsburg Seminarium," 198.
21. John Evjen, "Georg Sverdrup," in *Haucks Real-encycklopædia* (Leipzig). It can be found translated in Lars Lillehei's, *Augsburg Seminary and the Lutheran Free Church* (no publisher listed, 1928), 5–15.
22. Warren Quanbeck, professor at Luther Seminary, also noted, in his introduction to Melvin Helland's translations of Sverdrup's writing, that Sverdrup had the most trenchant mind of any of the theological leaders among Norwegian American Lutherans whose influence "might have helped prevent the excursion into scholastic and even fundamentalistic theology which blighted such Lutheran preaching and pastor practice in the next generations." Melvin Helland, *The Heritage of Faith: Selections from the Writings of Georg Sverdrup* (Augsburg Publishing House, 1969), 4–5.
23. L. R. Moyer and O. G. Dale, *History of Chippewa and Lac qui Parle Counties, Minnesota: Their People, Industries, and Institutions* (B. E. Bowen and Company, 1916), 387.

24. Sven Oftedal, ed., *Folkebladet: Maanedsblad for Skolen og Folket*, August 1877, 1.
25. Bernt Hanson's privately collected memoirs of his mother and his early life in Rosewood Township near Montevideo and Ethel Sylvina Jacobson, *History of the Ole Bjørge Jacobson Family* (Privately printed by Ethel Sylvina Jacobson and Bernt Hanson, 1980).
26. See Gracia Grindal, *Unstoppable: Norwegian Pioneers Educate Their Daughters* (Lutheran University Press, 2016), 181–182.
27. Martin Luther proposed that boys and girls needed to learn how to read and write so they could read the Bible and other edifying works. The Dano-Norwegian church required these skills for confirmation, which meant that the immigrants from Norway and all of Scandinavia were better educated than many other groups that came to America in the nineteenth century.
28. This caused them problems when they met the confessionalists of the Missouri Synod. Soon the Norwegian Synod had accepted them and others. President Hattlestad of the Norwegian Danish Augustana Synod had, unsuccessfully, demanded the Conference adopt the entire *Book of Concord*. Its failure to do so was one of the reasons for founding the Norwegian Danish Augustana Synod.
29. For a fuller discussion of Preus's proposal, see Grindal, *Unstoppable*, 163–185. There is a funny story in the tradition that tells of someone standing up at a meeting and saying, "I favor what God and the Preuses are for."
30. See Helland, *Georg Sverdrup*, 74.
31. *Beretning om 8de Aarsmøde afhold af Konferentsen for den norsk=dansk evang. luth. Kirke i Amerika i Willmar norskdansk ev. Luth. Kirke, Minn. Fra 2det til 8de juni. 1877. Udgiven af Konferentsens Sekretær* (Konferentsens Forlagsforeningns, Trykkeri, 1877), 99.
32. See my book *Unstoppable* (Fortress Press, 2016), 163–185.
33. Grindal, *Unstoppable*, 163–185.
34. Grindal, *Unstoppable*, 106.
35. Grindal, *Unstoppable*, 106.
36. Helland, *Georg Svedrup*, 74. Quoting Paulson's *Memoirs*, 235ff. Although I believe this account is true, Paulson's *Memoirs* do not include the prayer meeting. It does contain the sentence about the grasshoppers and debt disappearing. Helland may have heard the story from Paulson himself.
37. Helland, *Georg Svedrup*, 75.
38. Isaac Atwater, ed., *History of the City of Minneapolis* (Munsell, 1893), 153–154. Atwater, an early Minneapolis citizen, was obviously either quoting directly from Oftedal or had him write the entry himself, which is rather flattering to Oftedal.
39. Atwater, ed., *History of the City of Minneapolis*, 236.
40. Sven Oftedal, "Kvinden," *Folkebladet*, August 1880, 1.
41. Oftedal, "Kvinden," 1.
42. Oftedal, "Kvinden," 1.
43. Oftedal, "Kvinden," 1.
44. "Fra en Kvinde," *Folkebladet*, October 28, 1881, 1.
45. "Fra en Kvinde," 1.
46. This is one of the most astonishing discoveries I have made in my lifetime of searching the archives of Norwegian Americans.

# CHAPTER 4: TEACHING THE FAITH IN A NEW LAND

1. P. A. Rasmussen, *Lutheraneren*, 1880, 203–204, as found in Andreas Helland, ed., "A Serious Crisis," in *Georg Sverdrup: The Man and His Message* (Messenger Press, 1947), 91.
2. Helland, "A Serious Crisis," 91.
3. Georg Sverdrup, "Som Faar, der ikke har Hyrde," in *Fra Kirkens Arbeidsmark. Afhandlinger, Taler og Foredrag, Samlede Skrifter i Udvalg IV*, ed. Andreas Helland (Frikirkensboghandels Forlag, 1911), 247.
4. Helland, "A Serious Crisis," 91.
5. Sverdrup, "Som Faar, der ikke har Hyrde," 247.
6. In his *Memoirs*, 130, Weenaas praised the establishing of Luther Seminary in St. Anthony Park away from the city because it would keep the boys from women wanting to tempt them and trying to become pastors' wives. When I met his daughter in Oslo in 1965, she repeated his assertion several times!
7. Weenaas, *Mindeblade*, 79.
8. Weenaas, *Mindeblade*, 103.
9. The intricacies of this very hurtful and difficult period are too complicated to fit into this narrative, and a book could be written on it, but this is not the book. I have tried to make clear the more salient parts, but it is ugly, and despite their public apologies, which I am sure were heartfelt, no one comes out of it looking very good.
10. "Historical Background: The Sunday School Movement," The Sunday School Library Collection, McGill University Library Rare Books and Special Collections Division.
11. "De Scandinaviske Søndagskoler i Minneapolis," *Folkebladet*, January 6, 1886, 6.
12. What follows is taken from the visitation notes by Ole Paulson, which are from the microfilmed records of the American Lutheran Congregational records in the Minnesota Historical Society. Brønø congregation minutes, Microfilm No. 47/ALC 132 M678. Also Microfilm No. 144 for Brønø and 145 for Trinity in Montevideo.
13. From the microfilmed records of the American Lutheran Congregational records in the Minnesota Historical Society. Brønø congregation minutes, Microfilm No. 47/ALC 132 M678. Also Microfilm No. 144 for Brønø and 145 for Trinity in Montevideo.
14. Sverdrup, "Fra Minnesotadalen."
15. Sverdrup, "Fra Minnesotadalen."
16. Ole Paulson, "Fra den synodiske Slagmark: Smuler fra Willmar," *Folkebladet*, September 29, 1885, i.
17. Paulson, "Fra den synodiske Slagmark," i.
18. Johan Arndt Bergh, ed.,"Mødet i Willmar—Høyme—Koren—Resultat: Aabningstale af G. Høyme," in *Den Norsk Lutherske Kirkes Historie i Amerika* (Augsburg Publishing House, 1914). Bergh's book reflects on articles, speeches, minutes, and personal recollections that give us a richly textured sense of these meetings.
19. Andreas Helland, ed., "Years of Fruitful Progress," in *Georg Sverdrup: The Man and His Message* (Messenger Press, 1947), 112–139.

20. Helland, "Years of Fruitful Progress," 115.
21. Brønø congregation records on Microfilm No. 47/ALC 132 M678 in the Minnesota Historical Society Library.
22. Lloyd Svendsbye, former president of Luther Northwestern Seminary, who grew up on a farm near Tioga, North Dakota, told me once that the hardest things he had to get used to when he moved off the farm was that church services were held every Sunday.
23. For more information on how the various traditions addressed the education of girls, see Grindal, *Unstoppable: Norwegian Pioneers Educate Their Daughters* (Lutheran University Press, 2016).
24. See J. W. Richard, "The Liturgical Question, a Final Word," *The Lutheran Quarterly*, New Series—Vol XXI, ed. Philip M. Bikle (Gettysburg: J. E. Wible Pirnter, January 1891), 84-97.
25. Helland, *Georg Sverdrup: The Man and His Message*, 235.
26. Elisabeth Fedde, "Letter to Georg Sverdrup," as quoted in Gracia Grindal, *Elisabeth Fedde: To Do the Lord's Will* (Lutheran University Press, 2014), 204–205.
27. Helland. *Georg Sverdrup*, 241.

## CHAPTER 5: MERGERS, DISPUTES, AND THE FOUNDING OF THE LUTHERAN FREE CHURCH

1. William Jennings Bryan, "Cross of Gold Speech," Democratic National Convention, 1896.
2. Eugene Fevold, *The Lutheran Free Church: A Fellowship of American Lutheran Congregations* (Augsburg Publishing House, 1969), 53.
3. H. Bottelsen, "Reiseberetning," *Folkebladet*, June 25, 1890, 8.
4. "Smuler," *Folkebladet*, June 11, 1890, 3.
5. Helland, *Georg Sverdrup: The Man and His Message*, 143–144.
6. "Høyme's Address," *Saint Paul Globe*, June 13, 1895, 4.
7. Chrislock, *From Fjord to Freeway*, 48.
8. Fevold, *The Lutheran Free Church*, 62.
9. Ole Paulson, "Minder fra Festreisen," *Folkebladet*, June 16, 1890, 2.
10. Nils Christian Brun, ed., "Fest i Colisæet," in *Fra Ungdomsaar: en Oversigt over den Forenede Norsk Lutherske Kirkes Histories og Fremskridt i de Svundne Femogtyve Aar* (Augsburg Publishing House, 1915), 44.
11. Paulson, "Minder fra Festreisen," 2.
12. Paulson, "Minder fra Festreisen."
13. Chrislock, *From Fjord to Freeway*, 51.
14. "Nu gjelder det Augsburg Seminarium igjen," *Folkebladet*, January 28, 1891, 4.
15. "Nu gjelder det Augsburg Seminarium igjen," 4.
16. See Chrislock, *From Fjord to Freeway*, 52, footnote 16 for further documentation of this.
17. F. A. Schmidt, "Er de forberedende Afdelinger ved ugsburg (sic) Seminar en Bestanddel af den forenede Kirkes Presteskole?" *Folkebladet*, February 18, 1891, 1.

18. Urseth interview, Augsburg Archives website.
19. Chrislock, *From Fjord to Freeway*, 53.
20. As found in Chrislock from *Beretning den forenede Kirke, 1891*, 98–101.
21. Edgar Allen Poe's poem "To Helen" contained the often quoted line "the glory that was Greece, the grandeur that was Rome."
22. His skill with German is evident in a letter he wrote to the head of the Kaiserwerth Deaconess Home, Julius Disselhoff, January 14, 1891. Augsburg Archives.
23. The full breadth of his scholarship and writings is gathered together by Helland in the six volumes of Sverdrup's collected works, *Samlede Skrifter*. Nor was he a flabby sentimentalist. Many stories relate his trenchant humor in his interactions with overly pious students, as with one who announced when he arrived that God had called him to be a pastor. Sverdrup smiled and said, "That is for me to decide."
24. John O. Evjen, "What Is Lutheranism?" in *What Is Lutheranism? A Symposium in Interpretation*, ed. Vergilius Ferm (Macmillan, 1930), 9. As found in James Hamre, *Georg Sverdrup: Educator, Theologian, Churchman* (The Norwegian-American Historical Association, 1986), 209.
25. *Catalogue of Augsburg Seminary, Minneapolis, Minn. Twenty-Third Year, 1892–1893* (Augsburg Publishing House, 1893), 7.
26. For a discussion of Sverdrup and Grundtvig's thinking on this, see Jim Hamre's book *Georg Sverdrup: Educator, Theologian, Churchman*, 26–27.
27. Chrislock, *From Fjord to Freeway*, 61.
28. Chrislock, *From Fjord to Freeway*, 24.
29. Georg Sverdrup, "Menighedsmæssig Presteuddannelse," *Folkebladet*, May 18, 1892, 2.
30. Sverdrup, "Menighedsmæssig Presteuddannelse."
31. Sverdrup, "Menighedsmæssig Presteuddannelse."
32. Fevold, *The Lutheran Free Church*, 68.
33. Christian Saugstad, "Augsburg Historie," attached to the *Beretninger fra 1893–1901* (Oscar Lunde Trykkeri, 1893), 34.
34. "Norwegian Lutherans: Annual Session of the United Church," *Minneapolis Tribune*, June 8, 1893, 6.
35. Chrislock, *From Fjord to Freeway*, 71–72. While much of this is my own version of Chrislock, there is much that is directly taken from his language.
36. *Minneapolis Tribune*, June 14, 1893, 5.
37. *Minneapolis Tribune*, 5.
38. *Minneapolis Tribune*, 5.
39. *Minneapolis Tribune*, 5.
40. "Bone of Contention," *Minneapolis Tribune*, June 14, 1893, 5.
41. "Bone of Contention," 5.
42. "Bone of Contention," 5.
43. Helland, *Georg Sverdrup*, 149.
44. "Lars Swenson, the Treasurer of Augsburg Seminary," *Minneapolis Tribune*, June 18, 1893, 3.
45. "Meet Here Again, Augsburg Case Not Settled," *St. Paul Globe*, March 22, 1896, 4.
46. Fevold, *The Lutheran Free Church*, 74.

47. "The Fight Is Now On," *Minneapolis Tribune*, December 12, 1893, 8.
48. "A Star Attraction," *Saint Paul Globe*, December 15, 1893, 3.
49. "The Augsburg Seminary Case Still on Trial," *Saint Paul Globe*, December 14, 1893, 3.
50. "Can't Scare Them," *Saint Paul Globe*, December 17, 1893, 10.
51. "Prøver Aanderne," *Folkebladet*, December 20, 1893, 4.
52. "Surprise and Elation," *Minneapolis Tribune*, June 8, 1894, 8.
53. "Allies of Augsburg," *Minneapolis Tribune*, June 16, 1894, 1.
54. "Allies of Augsburg," 1.
55. M. Falk Gjertsen, "Festprediken: Den aabne Dør og de mange Modstandere, I Kor. 16:9," *Beretning om det 2det Møde af Augsburgs Venner og Augsburg Seminariums 25 Aars Jubilæum afholdt i Minneapolis fra 9de til de 12te oktober 1894* (O. W. Lunds Trykkeri, 1894), 22–23.
56. "A Day of Great Joy," *Minneapolis Tribune*, October 11, 1894, 5.
57. Sven Oftedal, "I Trefoldighedskirken om Aftenen," *Beretning om det 2det Møde af Augsburgs Venner og Augsburg Seminariums 25 Aars Jubilæum afholdt i Minneapolis fra 9de til de 12te oktober 1894* (O. W. Lunds Trykkeri, 1894), 24.
58. Oftedal, "I Trefoldighedskirken om Aftenen," 24.
59. Oftedal, "I Trefoldighedskirken om Aftenen," 24.
60. Oftedal, "I Trefoldighedskirken om Aftenen," 24.
61. Kapitel V., "Ordination," *Beretning om det 2det Møde af Augsburgs Venner og Augsburg Seminariums 25 Aars Jubilæum afholdt i Minneapolis fra 9de til de 12te oktober 1894* (O. W. Lunds Trykkeri, 1894), 87.
62. Martha Clausen, "Saa vil vi nu siger hverandre Farvel," in *Kirkesalmebog, efter offentlig Foranskaltning samlet og udarbeidet ved M. B. Landstad* (W. E. Fabritius & Sønner, 1869). 93.
63. Olaf Morgan Norlie, *Norsk Lutherske Menigheter i Amerika 1843–1916* (Augsburg Publishing House, 1916), 660.
64. "Are Still Hard at It," *Minneapolis Tribune*, June 15, 1895, 2.
65. Helland, *Georg Sverdrup*, 169.
66. Helland, *Georg Sverdrup*, 169.
67. Helland, *Georg Sverdrup*, 169.
68. "Are Still Hard at It," 2.
69. "Are Still Hard at It."
70. "Are Still Hard at It."
71. The Friends of Augsburg began ordaining candidates quite soon after they formed their group, aware that the United Church would discipline them. The first candidate who was ordained was S. E. Odland, which happened after he received a call to the Skjeberg, Oslo, and Two River congregations in Kittson County, Minnesota. See *Beretning om det 2det Møde af Augsburgs Venner og Augsburg Seminariums 25 Aars Jubilæum afholdt i Minneapolis fra 9de til de 12te oktober 1894* (O. W. Lunds Trykkeri, 1894), 87.
72. "Are Still Hard at It," 2.
73. "Are Still Hard at It." The nature of the insult eludes translation but means something to the effect that the person regards himself highly. Even the reporter used the Norwegian since the translation eluded him as well.

74. Sven Oftedal, "Fri Forbindelse mellem fri Menigheder: Indledningsforedrag ved Krikirkens først møde," *Beretning om Frikirkens Møde fra 9de til 13de June 1897* (Frikirkens Boghandel Forlag, 1897), 62–94.
75. "May Choose Harriet," *Minneapolis Tribune*, June 19, 1895, 3.
76. "May Choose Harriet," 3.
77. "May Choose Harriet," 3.
78. "Fra Mødet af 'Augsburgs Venner,'" *Folkebladet*, July 4, 1895, 4.
79. Han Adolph Brorson, "O Father, May Thy word prevail," in *The Lutheran Hymnary* #245 (The Committee, ed. Augsburg Publishing House, 1913).
80. See Robert L. Lee, *A New Springtime* (Heirloom Press, 1997).
81. Lee, *A New Springtime*.
82. "It Means Expulsion," *Saint Paul Globe*, April 23, 1896, 3.
83. "It Means Expulsion."
84. A. J. Flotre, "Kjære redaktør," *Folkebladet*, July 4, 1951, 3.
85. Georg Sverdrup, "Indberetninger fra Formanden for Augsburgs Venner, 1895–1896," *Beretning om det 4de Møde af Augsburgs Venner, afholdt i Fargo, N. Dakota fra 17de til 21de Juni 1896* (Frikirkens Boghandels Forlag, 1896).
86. "Høyme to Retire," *Saint Paul Globe*, June 4, 1896, 7.
87. "Augsburg Fight," *Minneapolis Tribune*, June 3, 1896, 5.
88. "Augsburg Fight."
89. "Augsburg Fight."
90. "Høyme to Retire," *The Saint Paul Globe*, June 4, 1896, 7.
91. "Augsburg Fight."
92. "Augsburg Fight."
93. "Refused to Hear," *Minneapolis Tribune*, June 9, 1896, 5.
94. "Refused to Hear."
95. Waldemar Ager, *Festskrift*, 296 as found in Dorothy Burton Skardahl, "The Scandinavian Immigrant Writer in America," *NAHA* 21:14, https://norwegianamericanhistory.org/pubs/nas/volume21/vol21_2.html.
96. Sverdrup, "Indberetninger fra Formanden for Augsburg Venner 1895–1896," 16.
97. Sverdrup, "Indberetninger fra Formanden for Augsburg Venner 1895–1896," 18.
98. Sven Oftedal, "Indberetning fra Formanden for Board of Trustees for Augsburg Seminarium," *Beretning om det 4de Møde af Augsburgs Venner, afholdt i Fargo, N. Dakota fra 17de til 21de Juni 1896* (Folkebladet, 1896), 34.
99. Oftedal, "Indberetning fra Formanden for Board of Trustees for Augsburg Seminarium," 34.
100. *Folkebladet*, August 1896.
101. Hans Villesvik, "Prestendstødelserne," *Folkebladet*, March 28, 1900, 4.
102. *Folkebladet*, March 21, 1900, 4.
103. Quammen, *Folkebladet*, March 21, 1900, 4.
104. Alpha Brevik Ovesen, "Kjære redaktør," *Folkebladet*, May 9, 1951, 6.
105. "This Time It Is Before the Attorney General," *Minneapolis Tribune*, July 24, 1896, 5.
106. "This Time It Is Before the Attorney General."
107. "That Augsburg Fight," *Minneapolis Tribune*, November 8, 1896, 7.
108. "Frikirkens første Aarsmøde," *Folkebladet*, June 16, 1897, 3.

109. "Frikirkens første Aarsmøde," 4.
110. "President Høyme's Report," *Saint Paul Globe*, June 17, 1897, 2.
111. "Budget of Expense," *Saint Paul Globe*, June 24, 1897, 5.
112. "Augsburg War Is On," *Saint Paul Globe*, September 16, 1897, 5.
113. "Ends Augsburg Case," *Saint Paul Globe*, October 19, 1897, 3.
114. Fevold, *The Lutheran Free Church*, 77.
115. "Control of Augsburg Seminary Try in Vain to Reach an Understanding," *Minneapolis Tribune*, July 21, 1898, 5.
116. "Control of Augsburg Seminary Try."
117. "Memorandum of Settlement," *Folkebladet*, July 27, 1898, 5.
118. "Nogle Oplysninger," *Folkebladet*, August 3, 1898, 2.

## CHAPTER 6: PASSING THE TORCH

1. *Lamberton Star*, September 29, 1897, 1.
2. Peg Meier, "Orphan Train," *Star Tribune*, November 21, 1997, 1.
3. M. Falk Gjertsen, "Et Besøg I Lamberton," *Folkebladet*, November 30, 1898, 5.
4. *Lamberton Star*, September 22, 1899.
5. Georg Sverdrup, "Forkyndelsen i Menigheten. Inledningsforedrag ved Frikirkens Aarsmøde i Montevideo, Minn. 1900," *in Beretning om Den lutherske Frikirkes 4de Aarsmøde afholdt i Montevideo, Minnesota fra 6te til 13de June 1900*, ed. E. E. Gynild and H. N. Hendrikson (The Free Church Book Concern Trykkeri, 1900), 102.
6. Sverdrup, "Forkyndelsen i Menigheten," 102.
7. Sverdrup, "Forkyndelsen i Menigheten," 102.
8. Iagtager, "Aarsmødet og Montevideo," *Folkebladet*, June 20, 1900, 4.
9. Iagtager, "Aarsmødet og Montevideo."
10. For a full account of this scandal and also a biography of the pastor, see Nina Draxton, *The Testing of M. Falk Gjertsen* (NAHA, 1988).
11. Sven Oftedal, "Indsamling til Augsburg," *Folkebladet*, July 17, 1901, 4.
12. Oftedal, "Indsamling til Augsburg."
13. Andreas Helland, ed., "A New Springtime," in *Georg Sverdrup: The Man and His Message* (The Messenger Press, 1947), 179.
14. Andreas Helland, ed., "Eventide," in *Georg Sverdrup: The Man and His Message* (The Messenger Press, 1947), 265.
15. A vivid narrative of this practice can be read in Ole Rølvaag's *Giants in the Earth* when Per Hansa visits the pastor to register for communion and tells him about his wife's troubles and his own, something the pastor responds to with a remarkable sermon.
16. "Rapport fra Frikirkens Liturgikomite til Aarsmødet 1901," *Folkebladet*, May 21, 1902, 3.
17. Letter from Svein Kivle to Harald Grindal, August 10, n.d., family collection.
18. En Frikirkemand, "Ny Menighed: Montevideo, Minn," *Folkebladet*, June 3, 1903, 2.
19. Helland, "Eventide," 271–273.
20. See also Sverdrup's letter "Et merkeligt Dokument," *Folkebladet*, December 26, 1906, 4.

21. Helland, "Eventide," 275.
22. Ole Paulson, "Smuler fra Fargo: Pigeskolen," *Folkebladet*, October 24, 1906, 2.
23. Paulson, "Smuler fra Fargo," 2.
24. O. L. Torvik, "Oak Grove Lutheran Ladies Seminary," *Folkebladet*, October 24, 1906, 4.
25. Torvik, "Oak Grove Lutheran Ladies Seminary," 4.
26. Torvik, "Oak Grove Lutheran Ladies Seminary," 4.
27. Carl S. Vang, "Dødsfald," *Folkebladet*, January 11, 1922, 29.
28. Vang, "Dødsfald."
29. "Pastor O. Paulsons Begravelse," *Folkebladet*, May 1, 1907, 4.
30. "Pastor O. Paulsons Begravelse," 4.
31. "Prof. Sverdrups Begravelse," *Folkebladet*, May 7, 1907, 1.
32. Fevold, "An Era of Transition," in *The Lutheran Free Church: A Fellowship of American Lutheran Congregations* (Augsburg Publishing House, 1969), 172–173.
33. Anda's diary, March 4, 1910.
34. Anda's diary.
35. A. J. Vigestad, "Ungdomsstevnet i Eidskog Menighed," *Folkebladet*, July 20, 1910, 3.
36. Anda's diary, November 22, 1909.
37. "Professor Oftedals Begravelse," *Folkebladet*, April 5, 1911, 1.
38. "Professor Oftedals Begravelse."
39. "Professor Oftedals Begravelse."
40. "Professor Oftedals Begravelse."
41. "Montevideo," *Folkebladet*, March 27, 1912.
42. "Til Sangkorene og enkelte Sangere i Willmar Kreds," *Folkebladet*, May 29, 1912, 6.
43. Letter from Anda to Amanda, July 12, 1912.
44. Anda's diary, January 22, 1913.
45. Ad, *Folkebladet*, March 27, 1912, 8.
46. Schaffnit, "Det lutherske Herberge og Hjem for unge Kvinder," *Folkebladet*, April 27, 1910, 2.
47. "Mission Society Labors to Aid Working Girls; Campaign for Fund to Lift Debt of Hospice," *Star Tribune*, April 24, 1910, 18.
48. Anda's diary, n.d. Family archives.
49. Anda's diary, January 23, 1913.
50. "Ole Jacobson Bjørge død," *Folkebladet*, February 4, 1914, 2.
51. Pedersen, "Ole Jacobson Bjørge død."
52. Andrew Olson, "Fra Willmar Kreds," *Folkebladet*, April 19, 1916, 363–364.
53. Andrew Olsen, "Ungdomsstevne i Willmar Kreds," *Folkebladet*, July 26, 1916, 701–702.
54. Olsen, "Ungdomsstevne i Willmar Kreds."
55. George Sverdrup, "Letter from Mahdi Muhammad Ahmad to General Gordon," *Journal of American Oriental Society* 31 (1911): 367–388.
56. Anda's diary, date unclear.
57. Anda's diary, date unclear.
58. From the *Citizen*, "Cyrus," *Morris Tribune*, January 3, 1919, 6.
59. Notice for Publication, "Fritjof J. Tinseth," *Chester*, October 22, 1920, 6.

60. Fevold and Nelson, *The Lutheran Church Among Norwegian-Americans*, 290.
61. The lodge question was a longstanding issue for Lutherans throughout the nineteenth and first half of the twentieth centuries. Freemasons at their beginning had been viewed as enemies of the Christian faith for their religious beliefs and ceremonies. While Eastern Lutherans tolerated the Masons in their midst, Midwestern Lutherans opposed them, and that became a strident issue in merger negotiations through 1960.
62. For an exhaustive study of this document and following ones such as the Minneapolis Theses, see Todd W. Nichol, "The American Lutheran Church: An Historical Study of Its Confession of Faith According to Its Constituting Documents" (Diss., Berkeley, 1988).
63. Minneapolis Theses III, 2.
64. Sundal, "Jonetta Jacobson Død," 5.

## CHAPTER 7: COEDUCATION AT AUGSBURG

1. "Another Word About Augsburg," *Folkebladet*, June 18, 1919, 454.
2. See chap. 1 where his speech is discussed.
3. Curt Brown, *Minnesota 1918: When Flu, Fire and War Ravaged the State* (Minnesota Historical Society Press, 2018), 4.
4. Alumni minutes, as found in Chrislock, *From Fjord to Freeway*, 144.
5. Alumni minutes, as found in Chrislock, *From Fjord to Freeway*, 144.
6. Birkeland's body was found in a Minneapolis massage parlor on December 1, 1925. A woman was charged for his murder, but it was never really solved to anyone's satisfaction. Most people believe that he had gotten into some kind of situation where his enemies drugged him and left his body in a compromising situation.
7. Oscar Mehus, "Augsburg's Three Needs," *The Augsburg Echo*, March 20, 1920, 13.
8. Mehus, "Augsburg's Three Needs," 13.
9. Mehus, "Augsburg's Three Needs," 13.
10. Christian Ytrehus, "Augsburg igjen," *Folkebladet*, March 9, 1921, 153–154.
11. Ytrehus, "Augsburg igjen," 153–154.
12. Claus Morgan, "The Fargo Conference," *Lutheran Messenger*, June 1922, 3.
13. Andrew Olson, "Vandret Hjem," *Folkebladet*, December 17, 1924, 818.
14. Oral histories, Gerda Mortensen, Augsburg website.
15. Carl Chrislock, ed., "Depression Decade," in *From Fjord to Freeway* (North Central Publishing Company, 1969), 163.
16. Chrislock, "Depression Decade," 163.
17. This argument was particularly anxiety-producing to the immigrant schools that were very sensitive about being other than American. I remember in 1968 when I was being oriented into teaching at Luther College, the head of student services, Clair Kloster, made the argument from tests that Lutheran students were no different from their counterparts in public secular institutions. I was appalled and protested, but my argument was from such another place that Clair did not even understand it. I was trying to say that if we argued that our graduates got a distinctive education at a Lutheran liberal arts college, qualitatively different

from secular public ones, we were defeating the entire argument with a test and argument like his.
18. Chrislock, "Depression Decade," 164.
19. Chrislock, "Depression Decade," 164.
20. Chrislock, "Depression Decade," 164.
21. Augsburg Archives.
22. Jana Nidiffer, *Pioneering Deans of Women: More Than Wise and Pious Matrons* (Teacher's College Press, 2000), 82.
23. See Qualben. "Før og nu," *Folkebladet*, June 6, 1928, 357.
24. Si Melby, *The Chief Fallacies of Dr. Qualben's "Bluebook,"* 15–16, n.d.
25. Chrislock, "Depression Decade," 167.
26. H. C. Caspersen, "Hvad skal faa aarsmøtet ta sig til?," *Folkebladet*, May 16, 1928, 112.
27. Lars P. Qualben and Claus Morgan, *Norsk luthersk kirkelig Forening* (Free Church Book Concern, 1928). I vividly remember my mother telling me how Sletten and Thor Quanbeck were always on the side of Oak Grove in any of these battles. Somehow, maybe from hearing about this moment, she had picked up Sletten's preference for Oak Grove over against Augsburg and thought it important to tell me.
28. Andrew Olson, "Har faat Hjemlov," *Folkebladet*, July 9, 1930, 439.
29. Chrislock, "Depression Decade," 169.
30. "Faculty Sketches," *The Lutheran Messenger*, 1933.
31. "Faculty Sketches."
32. "Den Lutherske Frikirkes aarsmøte," *Folkebladet*, June 25, 1930, 404.
33. "Den Lutherske Frikirkes aarsmøte," *Folkebladet*, June 25, 1930, 404.
34. O. N. Hem, *Folkebladet*, September 21, 1932, 613.
35. H. N. Hendrickson, "Review of the *Concordia Hymnal*," *Folkebladet*, March 15, 1933, 171–172.
36. Peder Konsterlie, *Folkebladet*, October 23, 1935, 43.
37. Peder Konsterlie, "Beretning fra Kweiteh og Ninging," *Folkebladet*, April 25, 1936, 239.
38. Mrs. Mattson, "Kvindernes Missionsforbund," *Folkebladet*, November 4, 1936, 707.
39. Gerda Mortensen, "Kvindernes Missionforbund," *Folkebladet*, November 4, 1936, 707.
40. Andreas Helland, "En velkommen bok," *Folkebladet*, July 8, 1938, 431.
41. Gerda Mortensen, "Church Extension Fund," *Folkebladet*, March 24, 1939, 180.
42. Jonette's diary, September 30, 1937.
43. Jonette's diary, September 13, 1937.
44. Jonette's diary, September 15, 1937.
45. Jonette's diary, November 11, 1937.
46. "Letter from LFC pastor in Seattle to Formand Burntvedt," May 26, 1938. Burntvedt collection. Luther Seminary Archives.
47. Anna Watne Grindal, "Letter to Harald," October 1938, private collection.
48. Grindal, "Letter to Harald."
49. Grindal, "Letter to Harald," 3.
50. Christopher Sverre Norbog, *Seksti selsomme år* (Cappelens, 1962).

51. Letter from Bernard Christensen to Burntvedt, Thursday, April 28, 1937, Burntvedt collection, Luther Seminary Archives.

## CHAPTER 8: A NEW AUGSBURG PRESIDENT AND WAR ON THE HORIZON

1. Marcy Ditmanson, ed., "Homecomers Fete Christensen," in *The Augsburg Echo*, 43 (Augsburg College and Seminary, November 17, 1938), 1.
2. Jonette's diary, October 27, 1938.
3. Bernard Christensen, *The Lutheran Messenger* (The Lutheran Free Church Publishing Company, May 1, 1933), 3.
4. Jonette's diary, January 1, 1939.
5. H. C. Caspersen, "Tilbakeblik," *Folkebladet*, January 4, 1939, 8.
6. Jonette's diary, January 1, 1939.
7. The Galesburg rule adopted by the General Council in 1875 stated that "Lutheran pulpits were for Lutherans and Lutheran altars for Lutherans."
8. H. C. Caspersen, "Tilbakeblik," *Folkebladet*, January 4, 1939, 8.
9. Caspersen, "Tilbakeblik," 8.
10. Members of the organized congregation are not, in every instance, believers, and such hypocrites often derive false hope from their external connection with the congregation. It is therefore the sacred obligation of the congregation to purify itself by the quickening preaching of the Word of God, by earnest admonition and exhortation, and by expelling those openly sinful and perverse.
11. Nils Nilsen Rønning, *The Boy from Telemark* (Friends Press, 1933), 5.
12. Jonette's diary, June 12, 1939.
13. "Kronprins Olav og Kronprinsesse Märtha av Norge og deres barn, Ragnild, Astrid og Harald," *Folkebladet*, June 7, 1939.
14. Bernard Christensen, "Greeting to the Crown Prince of Norway," *Folkebladet*, June 21, 1939, 194.
15. Bernard Christensen, *Annual Report of the Lutheran Free Church ... 1939*, 33–34, as found in Fevold, "An Era of Transition," 210.
16. Chrislock, *From Fjord to Freeway*, 189.
17. Christensen, as found in Chrislock, *From Fjord to Freeway*, 190.
18. Chrislock, *From Fjord to Freeway*, 190.
19. Jonette's diary, September 11, 1939.
20. Jonette's diary, September 12, 1939.
21. Jonette's diary, October 13, 1939.
22. While she doesn't say which song, I have an idea it was his soprano solo, "I have a song in my heart to sing."
23. Jonette's diary, October 15, 1939.
24. H. C. Caspersen, "Shall We Have Bishops?" *Lutheran Messenger*, November 28, 1939.
25. "Collegians Vote on Present Day Social Problems in America," *The Augsburg Echo*, February 29, 1940, 1.

26. T. O. Burntvedt, "Et Oprop til Bøn," *Folkebladet*, April 24, 1940, 1.
27. "Peace Drive Launched by Student's Society in Recent Meeting," *The Augsburg Echo*, May 29, 1940.
28. G. O. Oudal, "Bispenavn og bispeembede," *Folkebladet*, June 5, 1940, 189.
29. H. C. Caspersen, "Skulde en løsning være mulig?" *Folkebladet*, July 3, 1940, 216.
30. Caspersen, "Skulde en løsning være mulig?" 219.
31. Caspersen, "Skulde en løsning være mulig?" 219.
32. H. C. Caspersen, "Menigheten som den rette form," *Folkebladet*, July 31, 1940, 248.
33. P. O. L., "En bedre vei for Kristne," *Folkebladet*, September 11, 1940, 293.
34. Jonette's diary, September 12, 1940.
35. Jonette's diary.
36. Chr., "Nogen enfoldige ord om menigheten," *Folkebladet*, September 25, 1940, 305.
37. Chr., "Nogen enfoldige ord om menigheten," 306.
38. Chr., "Nogen enfoldige ord om menigheten," 306.
39. H. C. Caspersen, "Menigheted og ordinationen," *Folkebladet*, September 25, 1940, 312.
40. Jonette's diary, December 28, 1940.
41. Jonette's diary, February 7, 1941.
42. Jonette's diary, March 13, 1941.
43. H. C. Caspersen, "To Store Tanker," *Folkebladet*, August 27, 1941, 282.

## CHAPTER 9: A WORLD AT WAR

1. Grindal, *Lots of Sky*, 4.
2. H. C. Caspersen, "Den Lutherske Frikirkes 46de aarsmøte," *Folkebladet*, June 17, 1942, 5.
3. H. C. Caspersen, "De nye regler," *Folkebladet*, July 1, 1942, 5.
4. Garth Lean, *Frank Buchman—A Life* (Constable, 1985), 215–233.
5. Grindal, *Lots of Sky*, 6.
6. Begun in 1935 by the Roosevelt administration, it gave millions of unemployed workers jobs that helped them through the Depression. When World War II began, it ended because millions of young people joined the armed forces.
7. Grindal, *Lots of Sky*, 6.
8. Grindal, *Lots of Sky*, 6.
9. Ole Rogne, "Varme Hjerter," *Folkebladet*, September 9, 1942, 4.
10. Grindal, *Lots of Sky*, 12.
11. Grindal, *Lots of Sky*, 13.
12. Johannes Ringstad, "Ordination," *Folkebladet*, September 9, 1942, 9.
13. H. C. Caspersen, "Fra og om det nordvestre N. Dakota," *Folkebladet*, September 23, 1942, 5.
14. Caspersen, "Fra og om det nordvestre N. Dakota," 5.
15. Andreas Helland, "Augsburg under skiftende Tider og Kaar," *Folkebladet*, October 7, 1942, 2.
16. Grindal, *Lots of Sky*, 17.
17. Grindal, *Lots of Sky*, 17.

18. H. C. Caspersen, "The American Lutheran Conference," *Folkebladet*, November 18, 1942, 9.
19. O. H. Sletten, "The American Lutheran Conference," *Folkebladet*, December 2, 1942, 4.
20. H. C. Caspersen, "The American Lutheran Conference," *Folkebladet*, December 2, 1942, 8.
21. Caspersen, "The American Lutheran Conference," 9.
22. E. Cliffort Nelson and Eugene Fevold, "The Church Discovers Other Churches," in *The Lutheran Church Among Norwegian-Americans* (Augsburg Publishing House, 1960), 314.
23. Grindal, *Lots of Sky*, 17.
24. "Officials Forecast Joy and Woes in the New Year," *Minneapolis Star Journal*, January 1, 1943, 21.
25. Bernhard Christensen, "Julehilsener: Fra Augsburg," *Folkebladet*, December 16, 1942, 3.
26. Andreas Helland, "Hovedtræk i Professor Georg Sverdrups Religiøse Livssyn II," *Folkebladet*, January 12, 1943, 2.
27. Helland, "Hovedtræk i Professor Georg Sverdrups," 2.
28. "Annual Report...LFC," 1943, 104–105; Chrislock, *From Fjord to Freeway*, 196.
29. Grindal, *Lots of Sky*, 17.
30. Andreas Helland, "Hvori Bestod Forskjellent? I," *Folkebladet*, February 10, 1943, 2.
31. Georg Sverdrup, "Vil I ha' Menighed?," in *Samlede Skrifter II*, ed. Andreas Helland (Free Church Book Concern, 1910), 182–192. This chapter appeared first in four issues of *Folkebladet*, September 20, 1897, March 10, 23, 20, 1898.
32. T. Ostby, "Vil vi ha menighet?," *Folkebladet*, December 16, 1942, 12.
33. Chr. Ytrehus, "Nogen ord om den Lutherske Frikirke før og nu, I," *Folkebladet*, February 2, 1943, 1.
34. Ytrehus, "Nogen ord om den Lutherske Frikirke før og nu, I," 1.
35. H. C. Caspersen, "Noter," *Folkebladet*, February 24, 1943, 9.
36. Helland, "Hvori Bestod Forskjellent?" 2.
37. Chr. Ytrehus, "Nogen ord om den Lutherske Frikirke før og nu, II," *Folkebladet*, March 10, 1943, 2.
38. Ytrehus, "Nogen ord om den Lutherske," 2.
39. Andreas Helland, "Kirken og de kirkelige Samfund?" *Folkebladet*, March 10, 1943, 3.
40. Chr. Ytrehus, "Nogen ord om den Lutherske Frikirke før og nu, III," *Folkebladet*, March 24, 1943, 2.
41. Johan Rødvik, "Kirkelig forening," *Folkebladet*, April 7, 1943, 13.
42. H. C. Caspersen, "Ogsaa et missionsarbeide," *Folkebladet*, March 24, 1943, 8.
43. S. O. Sigmond, "Presidenter og moral," *Folkebladet*, March 24, 1943, 11.
44. H. C. Caspersen, "On Church Union," *Folkebladet*, May 5, 1943, 3.
45. Mrs. Karl Kleppe, "Litt om forening," *Folkebladet*, May 5, 1943, 16.
46. Johan Rødvik, "Om kirkelig forening," *Folkebladet*, May 19, 1943, 8–10.
47. Andreas Helland, "Den Lutherske Frikirke Kom," *Folkebladet*, June 2, 1943, 3.
48. Helland, "Den Lutherske Frikirke Kom," 3.

49. J. O. Hoyum, "Nogen ord om foreningssaken," *Folkebladet*, June 2, 1943, 7.
50. *Dannevirket*, "Henry A. Wallace om Fremtiden," *Folkebladet*, June 2, 1943, 14.
51. H. C. Caspersen, "Den Lutherske Frikirkes 47de aarsmøte," *Folkebladet*, June 16, 1943, 3.
52. Caspersen, "Den Lutherske Frikirkes 47de aarsmøte," 6.
53. Christian Ytrehus, "Kirkelig forening I," *Folkebladet*, June 16, 1943, 9.
54. Christian Ytrehus, "Kirkelig forening II," *Folkebladet*, June 30, 1943, 5.
55. Christian Ytrehus, "Kirkelig forening III," *Folkebladet*, July 14, 1943, 3–4.
56. H. C. Caspersen, "Sommerskolen iaar," *Folkebladet*, September 8, 1943, 8.
57. H. C. Caspersen, "Om kirkelig forening," *Folkebladet*, October 6, 1943, 8.
58. Caspersen, "Om kirkelig forening," 9.
59. H. C. Caspersen, "Lutherske redaktrørers møte," *Folkebladet*, October 6, 1943, 10.
60. Andrew Helland, "Missionær Ralph Mortensen vender tilbake til Kina," *Folkebladet*, October 20, 1943, 7.
61. Johannes Ringstad, "Ungdomsstevnet I Fergus Falls," *Folkebladet*, October 26, 1943, 3.
62. H. C. Caspersen, "Lutherske College-fakulteters krigstids konferens," *Folkebladet*, October 20, 1943, 7.
63. Caspersen, "Lutherske College-fakulteters krigstids konferens," 7.
64. H. C. Caspersen, "Kommissionen for social spørsmaal," *Folkebladet*, November 17, 1943, 8–9.
65. Sverre Norborg, "Det Norske folk slaar fra sig . . . ," *Folkebladet*, December 29, 1943, 2.
66. H.C. Caspersen, "Kristi legeme og de troende enhet," *Folkebladet*, March 22, 1944, 8.
67. "Northwest Pastors' Fellowship," *Folkebladet*, February 9, 1944, 10.
68. Letter from Clarence Olson to Harald and Jonette, April 2, 1944, Grindal family archives.
69. Letter from Clarence Olson to Harald and Jonette.
70. Grindal, *Lots of Sky*, 25.
71. Mrs. Ebertina Nordtvedt, "Allehaande," *Folkebladet*, July 26, 1944, 4.
72. Nordtvedt, "Allehaande," 4.
73. H. C. Caspersen, "Foreningsspørsmaalet igjen," *Folkebladet*, July 12, 1944, 8.
74. Caspersen, "Foreningsspørsmaalet igjen," 8.
75. H. C. Caspersen, "Spørsmaalet om luthersk enighet," *Folkebladet*, August 9, 1944, 8.
76. H. C. Caspersen, *Folkebladet*, July 12, 1944.
77. S. A. R., "En ting fattes dig," *Folkebladet*, October 4, 1944, 15.
78. H. C. Caspersen, "Fra Østen," *Folkebladet*, October 18, 1944, 4.
79. H. C. Caspersen, "Missourisk teologi og forening," *Folkebladet*, November 1, 1944, 9.
80. H. C. Caspersen, "Fra møtet I Milwaukee," *Folkebladet*, November 29, 1944, 11.
81. Olaf Rogne, "Victory Building Fund," *Folkebladet*, November 29, 1944, 13.
82. H. C. Caspersen, "Tilbakeblik," *Folkebladet*, January 10, 1945, 3.

83. Bernhard Christensen, "Concerning the Milwaukee Convention," *Folkebladet*, January 10, 1945, 3-4.
84. Christensen, "Concerning the Milwaukee Convention," 3-4.
85. H. C. Caspersen, "The A.L.C. and the Galesburg Rule," *Folkebladet*, January 10, 1945, 10.
86. H. C. Caspersen, "Home Mission Institutet paa Augsburg," *Folkebladet*, February 21, 1945, 4.
87. H. C. Caspersen, "Litt fra det sidste board-møte," *Folkebladet*, May 16, 1945, 2.
88. T. O. Burntvedt, "Den Signede Dag," *Folkebladet*, May 30, 1945, 4.
89. H. C. Caspersen, "Aarsmøtet," *Folkebladet*, May 30, 1945, 8.
90. "Choir Returns After Tour," *Augsburg Echo*, April 27, 1945, 1.
91. Gloria Greguson, "Notes from the Tour," *Augsburg Echo*, April 27, 1945, 2.
92. "Note," *Folkebladet*, February 7, 1945, 15.
93. "Minutes of the Home Mission Board of Directors," LFC records, June 9, 1945, Luther Seminary Archives.
94. Grindal, *Lots of Sky*, 33.
95. Grindal, *Lots of Sky*, 33.
96. H. C. Caspersen, "Den Lutherske Frikirkes aarsmøte," *Folkebladet*, June 13, 1945, 1.
97. A. H., "Et nyt arbeidsaar," *Folkebladet*, June 27, 1945, 5.
98. H. C. Caspersen, "Det nye fredsdokument," *Folkebladet*, August 8, 1945, 4.
99. Chr. Ihlen, "De Protestantiske Princippers Stilling I det Moderne Aandsliv," *Folkebladet*, October 3, 1945, 9.
100. Ihlen, *De Protestantiske Princippers Stilling*, 9.
101. Donald Ronning, "A Correction," *Folkebladet*, December 12, 1945, 15.
102. Grindal, *Lots of Sky*, 36.
103. H. C. Caspersen, "En forbausende erklæring," *Folkebladet*, February 6, 1946, 9.
104. H. C. Caspersen, "Den Lutherske Frikirkes aarsmøte, Fargo, N. Dak. 12-16 Juni," *Folkebladet*, June 26, 1946, 2.
105. Memorandum to the Campus Plans Committee Minutes, July 2, 1946, Board of Trustees Minutes, July 18, 1946, in Chrislock, *From Fjord to Freeway*, 201.

## CHAPTER 10: POSTWAR ECUMENISM AND ITS PROBLEMS

1. See *Fundamental Principles and Rules for Work*, esp. nos. 7-11. Fevold, *The Lutheran Free Church*, 307-308.
2. "Nyt og Noter," *Folkebladet*, February 20, 1946, 9-10.
3. H. C. Caspersen, "The Churches Are Undergoing a Change... Slowly," *Lutheran Messenger*, August 24, 1946, 13.
4. See Karl J. Mattson, "A. D. Mattson and Social Justice," Unpublished manuscript, Augustana Heritage.
5. "Growing Rugby," *Pierce County Tribune*, September 11, 1947, 1.
6. T. O. Burntvedt, "Annual Report... to the Lutheran Free Church," 1947, 4-7, as found in Fevold, *The Lutheran Free Church*, 227.
7. Burntvedt, "Annual Report... to the Lutheran Free Church," 1937, 7-8.

8. Bernard M. Christensen, "Concerning Candidates for the Ministry in Our Church," *Lutheran Messenger*, November 4, 1947, 1–2.
9. The American Lutheran Conference, "Overture Commission on Lutheran Church Unity," *Lutheran Outlook*, January 1944.
10. John Houkom, "Lutheran Unity," *Lutheran Messenger*, November 4, 1947, 5–6.
11. Houkom, "Lutheran Unity," 4.
12. Houkom, "Lutheran Unity," 4.
13. Houkom, "Lutheran Unity," 9.
14. Houkom, "Lutheran Unity," 9.
15. Kenneth Latourette, *A History of the Expansion of Christianity*, Seven volumes (Harper and Brothers, 1937–1945).
16. H. C. Caspersen, "Noter," *Folkebladet*, June 9, 1948, 10.
17. John Rimmereid, "Indtryk fra aarsmøtet," *Folkebladet*, July 7, 1948, 3.
18. Rimmereid, "Indtryk fra aarsmøtet," 4.
19. *Decorah Posten*, "Ikke nogen overkirke," *Folkebladet*, July 7, 1948, 6.
20. H. C. Caspersen, "Fra aarsmøtet," *Folkebladet*, July 7, 1948, 2–3.
21. Caspersen, "Fra aarsmøtet," 2–3.
22. Fred Ditmanson, "Brev fra missionær Fred Ditmanson," *Folkebladet*, March 2, 1949, 5.
23. Morris J. C. Vaagenes, "Fra arbeidet i Ampanihy district, 1948," *Folkebladet*, April 27, 1949, 6.
24. See June Chang, *Mao: The Unknown Story* (Random House, 2011).
25. Arthur Olson, "Brev fra Missionær Arthur S. Olson," *Folkebladet*, April 13, 1949, 6–7.
26. I know this through my parents' stories but cannot find printed evidence of it. I have no reason to doubt it.
27. Nelson and Fevold, *The Lutheran Church Among Norwegian-Americans*, 264.
28. "8 Lutheran Leaders Urge 'Closer Unity,'" *Star Tribune*, February 3, 1949, 7.
29. The Lutheran Free Church, "Annual Report of the Lutheran Free Church . . . Annual Conference," 1949, 30.
30. "Lutheran Unit May Study Federation," *Minneapolis Star*, June 10, 1949, 7.

## CHAPTER 11: A DECADE OF MERGER TALK

1. Sverre Torgerson, "Aarsmøtet stunder til," *Folkebladet*, April 26, 1950, 2.
2. "Fear of New War Decried," *Minneapolis Star*, June 15, 1950, 23.
3. "Unity Plan Backed by Lutherans," *Star Tribune*, June 16, 1950, 15.
4. Letter from T. O. Burntvedt to Harald Grindal, October 27, 1950, private collection.
5. Sverre Torgerson, "Theodore Tinseth," *Lutheran Messenger*, November 22, 1950, 9.
6. Sverre Torgerson, "Luthersk samarbeide," *Folkebladet*, November 22, 1950, 2.
7. Torgerson, "Luthersk samarbeide," 3.
8. Torgerson, "Luthersk samarbeide," 3.
9. Torgerson, "Luthersk samarbeide," 3.
10. "Lutherans Air Views on Unity Move," *Star Tribune*, November 10, 1950, 12.

11. "Lutherans Air Views on Unity Move," 12.
12. Mark Granquist, "The Urge to Merge," *Lutheran Forum*, Summer 2012, 20–23.
13. Grindal, *Lots of Sky*.
14. Sverre Torgerson, "Be for Aarsmøtet," *Folkebladet*, May 9, 1951, 2.
15. Torgerson, "Be for Aarsmøtet," 2.
16. T. O. Burntvedt, *Lutheran Messenger*, April 3, 1951, 14. As found in Fevold, *The Lutheran Free Church*, 274.
17. Fevold, *The Lutheran Free Church*, 276.
18. "United Testimony," *Handbook of the American Lutheran Church*, 1967 edition, 127–148.
19. Sverre Torgerson, "Et Velsignet Møte," *Folkebladet*, February 13, 1952, 2.
20. Torgerson, "Et Velsignet Møte," 2.
21. Torgerson, "Det Stunder til aarsmøtet," *Folkebladet*, May 21, 1952, 2.
22. "Continue Merger Talks, Church Asked," *Minneapolis Star*, June 11, 1952, 18.
23. "Continue Merger Talks, Church Asked," 18.
24. Torgerson, "*Folkebladet* gaar ind," *Folkebladet*, July 2, 1952, 2.
25. Caspersen, "Brudte Baand," *Folkebladet*, July 16, 1952, 4–5.
26. Willmar Thorkelson, "The Week in Religion," *Minneapolis Star*, August 30, 1952, 6.
27. Thorkelson, "The Week in Religion," 6.
28. Minutes, Joint Union Committee, November 10, 1952, 3–4; as found in Fevold, *The Lutheran Free Church*, 277.
29. Fevold, *The Lutheran Free Church*, n. 27, 278.
30. Fevold, *The Lutheran Free Church*, n. 27, 278.
31. "Committee Maps Government of Proposed Lutheran Merger," *The Minneapolis Star*, March 18, 1953, 27.
32. T. O. Burntvedt, "U.S. Urged to Identify Itself with Oppressed," *Minneapolis Star*, June 11, 1953, 30.
33. Burntvedt, "U.S. Urged to Identify Itself," 30.
34. Burntvedt, "U.S. Urged to Identify Itself," 30.
35. Fevold, *The Lutheran Free Church*, 278.
36. Clemmence Dyrud, "Dear Editor," *Lutheran Messenger*, February 2, 1954, 14.
37. Alvin Rogness, "Lutherans Are United," *Lutheran Messenger*, February 16, 1954, 6.
38. John Stensvaag, "Preface to the Union Report," *Lutheran Messenger*, April 13, 1954, 5.
39. Stensvaag, "Preface to the Union Report," 5.
40. Stensvaag, "Preface to the Union Report," 6.
41. Stensvaag, "Preface to the Union Report," 13.
42. Richard Torgerson, "A Thrilling Evangelism Experience," *The Lutheran Messenger*, April 27, 1954, 5.
43. Torgerson, "A Thrilling Evangelism Experience," 5.
44. "Appendix No. 1 Proposal of the Lutheran Free Church Committee," *The Lutheran Messenger*, May 11, 1954, 5.
45. Stensvaag, "Preface to the Union Report," 13.
46. "Appendix No. 1 Proposal of the Lutheran Free Church Committee," 5.

47. H. C. Caspersen. "A Word About the Question of Church Union," *Lutheran Messenger*, June 8, 1954, 10.
48. Oscar J. Johnson, "Light of Scriptures?" *Lutheran Messenger*, June 8, 1954, 10.
49. Johnson, "Light of Scriptures?" 10.
50. Fevold, *The Lutheran Free Church*, 281.
51. T. O Burntvedt, "Annual Message to Our Church," *Lutheran Messenger*, June 22, 1954, 9.
52. Burntvedt, "Dr. T. O. Burntvedt's Annual Message," 9.
53. Sverre Torgerson, "The Annual Conference," *Lutheran Messenger*, June 22, 1954, 3.
54. Agnes Tangjerd, "The Augsburg Library Rises," *Lutheran Messenger*, September 28, 1954, 7.
55. "A Message from the Second Assembly of the World Council of Churches," *Lutheran Messenger*, September 28, 1954, 4–5.
56. O. O. Aune, "A Layman Views the Merger," *Lutheran Messenger*, October 12, 1954, 5–6.
57. "Merger Forum," *Lutheran Messenger*, March 15, 1955, 7.
58. T. O. Burntvedt, "Facing Up to the Merger Question I," *Lutheran Messenger*, April 26, 1955, 4–5.
59. Gerda Mortensen, "Living That Is More than Shelter," *Lutheran Messenger*, April 26, 1955, 8.
60. T. O. Burntvedt, "Facing Up to the Merger Question II," *Lutheran Messenger*, May 10, 1955, 4.
61. T. O. Burntvedt, "Facing Up to the Merger Question III," *Lutheran Messenger*, May 24, 1955, 6.
62. Christian G. Olson, "A Changed Attitude Toward Merger," *Lutheran Messenger*, June 7, 1955, 12.
63. T. O. Burntvedt, "Annual Message to Our Church," *Lutheran Messenger*, June 21, 1955, 8.
64. Sverre Torgerson, "Now It Is Up to the Congregations," *Lutheran Messenger*, September 13, 1955, 3.
65. Fred Ditmanson, "Cooperation, Not Merger," *Lutheran Messenger*, August 16, 1955, 4.
66. Else Michaelsen and Katherine Michaelsen, "What About Merger?" *Lutheran Messenger*, July 19, 1955, 12.
67. Torgerson, "Now It Is Up to the Congregations," 3.
68. Leslie F. Brandt, "Hang Together—Or Hang Alone," *Lutheran Messenger*, September 13, 1955, 4.
69. Fritjof B. Monseth, "Shall We Vote Away Our Freedom?" *Lutheran Messenger*, September 27, 1955, 5.
70. "Church's 10th Anniversary Program Set," *Statesman Journal*, November 19, 1955, 7.
71. Sverre Torgerson, "Have Our Congregations Made Use of Their Freedom?" *Lutheran Messenger*, October 11, 1955, 3.
72. John Stensvaag, "Do You Really Want to Win?" *Lutheran Messenger*, October 11, 1955, 5.
73. Enoch Thorsgaard, "A Layman Speaks on Merger," *Lutheran Messenger*, November 8, 1955, 7.

74. Mrs. Karl Kleppe, "To Be or Not to Be—That Is the Question," *Lutheran Messenger*, November 8, 1955, 8.
75. Iver Olson, "Shall We Unite?" *Lutheran Messenger*, November 22, 1955, 5.
76. Olson, "Shall We Unite?" 5.
77. "Deadline Today in Lutheran Vote," *Minneapolis Star*, December 15, 1955, 16.
78. Willmar Thorkelson, "Prospect of Lutheran Center in City Dims," *Minneapolis Star*, December 22, 1955, 13.
79. "LFC Union Move Up to Parley," *Minneapolis Star*, December 30, 1955, 9.
80. "LFC Union Move Up to Parley," 9.
81. "Lutheran Body Picks City as Base," *Minneapolis Star*, March 13, 1956, 9.
82. Thorvald O Burntvedt, "President T. O. Burntvedt's Greeting and Report to the Joint Union Committee Meeting in Chicago," March 12-13, 1956. *Lutheran Messenger*, March 27, 1956, 5.
83. "Two Services Scheduled by Central Church," *Capital Journal*, January 5, 1957, 11.
84. "President of Free Church Re-Elected," *Minneapolis Star*, June 13, 1957, 14.
85. "President of Free Church Re-Elected," 14.
86. "New Merger Vote Authorized by LFC," *Minneapolis Star*, June 15, 1957, 12.
87. Daniel J. Hafrey, "Who Are the Lutherans?" *Star Tribune*, July 7, 1957, 21.
88. "Largest Crowd in American Lutheranism," *Capital Journal*, August 26, 1957, 14.
89. Don Brostrom, "New Liturgy Book Held Aid to Lutheran Unity," *Minneapolis Star*, August 16, 1957, 31.
90. "LFC Again Rejects Plan for Merger," *Minneapolis Star*, December 6, 1957, 53.
91. "Lutheran Unit Narrowly Rejects Merger," *Star Tribune*, December 7, 1957, 5.
92. Willmar Thorkelson, "Plea for 2 Mergers by Lutherans Beaten," *Star Tribune*, February 6, 1958, 58.
93. Willmar Thorkelson, "LFC Urged to Seek Closer Relations," *Minneapolis Star*, February 12, 1958, 19.
94. Daniel Hafrey, "Religion Plays a Vital Role," *Star Tribune*, April 6, 1958, 106.
95. John Stensvaag, "Future Relations with Other Lutherans," *Lutheran Messenger*, March 11, 1958, 8.
96. Stensvaag, "Future Relations with Other Lutherans," 9.
97. Stensvaag, "Future Relations with Other Lutherans," 10.
98. Stensvaag, "Future Relations with Other Lutherans," 10.
99. Luthard Gjerde, "The Contemporary Dilemma of the Lutheran Free Church," *Lutheran Messenger*, March 25, 1958, 6.
100. Gjerde, "The Contemporary Dilemma," 6.
101. Gjerde, "The Contemporary Dilemma," 7.
102. Gjerde, "The Contemporary Dilemma," 7.
103. Gjerde, "The Contemporary Dilemma," 10.
104. Gjerde, "The Contemporary Dilemma," 10.
105. "Echoes from Open Forum," *Lutheran Messenger*, March 11, 1958, 7.
106. Donald Ronning, "Our Spiritual Resources," *Lutheran Messenger*, April 22, 1958, 5.
107. Christian G. Olson, "A Plea to Congregations and Pastors," *Lutheran Messenger*, April 22, 1958, 6.
108. Merton Strommen, "Random Thought on 'Free, Living Congregations,'" *Lutheran Messenger*, May 6, 1958, 6–7.

109. Mrs. Karl Kleppe, "How Inconsistent Can One Be?" *Lutheran Messenger*, May 20, 1958, 5–6.
110. "Dr. Burntvedt Will Quit as LFC Head," *Minneapolis Star*, May 28, 1958, 15.
111. Richard Kleeman, "Augsburg President to Be Feted," *Star Tribune*, June 15, 1958, 23.
112. Kleeman, "Augsburg President to Be Feted," 23.
113. "Theologian Speaks at Augsburg," *Minneapolis Star*, August 27, 1958, 41.
114. "Retiring LFC Head Hailed at Dinner," *Minneapolis Star*, August 28, 1958, 45.
115. "Lutherans Pick Name on Merger," *Minneapolis Star*, November 14, 1958, 10.
116. "Meeting of 2 Major Lutheran Bodies Urged Before Mergers," *Minneapolis Star*, November 29, 1958, 7.
117. "Meeting of 2 Major Lutheran Bodies," 7.
118. "Report of the Committee on Polity and Organization," *Lutheran Messenger*, May 5, 1959, 7–9.
119. "Nature and Function of the Annual Conference," *Lutheran Messenger*, May 5, 1959, 9.
120. O. J. Haukeness, "Shall We Adopt the Representative System?," *The Lutheran Messenger*, June 2, 1959, 13.
121. Dr. John Stensvaag, "Annual Message to Our Church," *Lutheran Messenger*, June 16, 1959, 7.
122. T. O. Burntvedt, "Wider Horizons and Deeper Concerns," *Lutheran Messenger*, September 8, 1959, 3.
123. T. O. Burntvedt, "What About Evangelism?" *Lutheran Messenger*, October 6, 1959, 5.
124. Robert Paul Roth, "The Unity of the Church in Christ," *Lutheran Messenger*, December 15, 1959.

## CHAPTER 12: MERGER

1. "Lutheran Pick Name for Merger," *Minneapolis Star*, February 23, 1960, 9.
2. "Lutherans Study Combined Seminary," *Minneapolis Star*, February 27, 1960, 7.
3. Wallace Mitchel, "Religion Is 'Talk' in Wisconsin Race," *Minneapolis Star*, February 29, 1960, 7.
4. "Salem Greets Kennedy," *Capitol Journal*, May 18, 1960, 13.
5. When Colacci died suddenly in March 1968, he was replaced by a pastor from New York, William Rusch, later to become my nemesis in the ecumenical battles of the ELCA!
6. Mario Colacci, "Fixed Church Dogmas or Personal Commitment to the Bible?" *Concord III*, Easter 1960, 20.
7. Sverre Torgerson, "Impressive Ceremony Marks Formation of ALC," *Lutheran Messenger*, May 17, 1960, 3.
8. John Stensvaag, "Dr. John Stensvaag Brought a Greeting on Behalf of the Lutheran Free Church," *Lutheran Messenger*, May 17, 1960, 4.
9. Fredrik A. Schiotz, *Lutheran Messenger*, May 17, 1960, 4.
10. Sverre Torgerson, "The Annual Conference," *Lutheran Messenger*, June 28, 1960, 3.

11. "Report of the Committee on Relations with Other Lutheran Bodies," Annual Report of the 64th Annual Conference, Lutheran Free Church, 1960, 154.
12. "Report of the Committee on Relations," 4.
13. Theodore Blegen, "On Campus at Augsburg," *Lutheran Messenger*, June 28, 1960, 11.
14. Gordon Smedsrud, "The Congregation's Youth Program," *Lutheran Messenger*, July 12, 1960, 8.
15. "From Montevideo, Minn.," *Lutheran Messenger*, June 28, 1960, 12.
16. Arthur L. Bervig, "An Experiment in Sunday School," *Lutheran Messenger*, July 12, 1960, 4–5.
17. T. O. Burntvedt, "A Monumental Work," *Lutheran Messenger*, May 17, 1960, 10.
18. Amos Dyrud and Ovidia Dyrud, "Report of the Manasoa-Benenitra Districts," *Lutheran Messenger*, July 26, 1960, 7–8.
19. Morris Vaagenes, Sr. and Hanna G. C. Vaagenes, "Report from St. Augustine for the Year 1959," *Lutheran Messenger*, August 9, 1960, 5–6.
20. Sverre Torgerson, "Whither W.C.C.," *Lutheran Messenger*, August 9, 1960, 3.
21. Torgerson, "Whither W.C.C.," 3.
22. Torgerson, "Whither W.C.C.," 3.
23. "Four Lausanne Assembly Delegates Disagree with Us," *Lutheran Messenger*, October 18, 1960, 14.
24. "Four Lausanne Assembly Delegates," 14.
25. "Four Lausanne Assembly Delegates," 15.
26. James A. Bergquist, "The Lost Dimension in American Politics," *Lutheran Messenger*, August 23, 1960, 5.
27. Bergquist, "The Lost Dimension," 6.
28. Bergquist, "The Lost Dimension," 6.
29. Bergquist, "The Lost Dimension," 6.
30. Norman C. Anderson, "Writer Feels LFC-Augsburg Used to Further Roman Thrust for Power," *Lutheran Messenger*, October 18, 1960, 15.
31. Anderson, "Writer Feels LFC-Augsburg Used," 15.
32. Anderson, "Writer Feels LFC-Augsburg Used," 15.
33. Willmar Thorkelson, "A Son of His Time," *Minneapolis Star*, November 5, 1960, 9.
34. Byron Schmid, "Highlights of Europe Ecumenical Youth Assembly," *Lutheran Messenger*, November 29, 1960, 3.
35. John Stensvaag, "President's Message," Annual Report, *65th Annual Conference Lutheran Free Church 1961* (Messenger Press, 1961), 18.
36. Stensvaag, "President's Message," 18.
37. Stensvaag, "President's Message," 18.
38. Stensvaag, "President's Message," 38.
39. Donald Ronning, "A Plea for Unity," *Lutheran Messenger*, December 26, 1961, 4–5.
40. Victor Svanoe, "Christianity Requires Faith, Not Reason," *Augsburg Echo*, October 4, 1961, 4.
41. John Stensvaag, "Two Significant Statements," *Lutheran Messenger*, September 17, 1961, 4.
42. Carl. J. Carlsen, "Merger—The Better Alternative," *Lutheran Messenger*, September 17, 1961, 7–8.

43. This was a big issue around the church. There was a parody song written, "They're Dancing at Augsburg Now," that provided much merriment to us all.
44. Milo Bryn, "Dear Editor," *Lutheran Messenger*, September 17, 1961, 14.
45. Ingvald Norum, "Dear Editor," *Lutheran Messenger*, September 17, 1961, 14.
46. Merton Strommen, "Experiences Which Indicate Merger," *Lutheran Messenger*, October 31, 1961, 4.
47. "Students Favor Merger," *Augsburg Echo*, November 8, 1961, 4.
48. William Svanoe, "This We Believe," *Lutheran Messenger*, October 31, 1961, 6.
49. Viggo Dahle, "As We Have Opportunity," *Lutheran Messenger*, October 31, 1961, 6.
50. Mrs. Fredrick Kruse, "Dear Editor," *Lutheran Messenger*, October 31, 1961, 12.

# EPILOGUE

1. Marshall Berman, *All That Is Solid Melts Into Air: The Experience of Modernity* (Verso, 2010), 160–161.
2. Gracia Grindal, "Riding the Minneapolis Freeway Under the Place Where Trinity Lutheran Congregation Once Stood," private collection, 1968.
3. Berman, *All That Is Solid Melts into Air*, 333.
4. Bernhard Christensen, "The Fires of the Future," *Lutheran Messenger*, January 22, 1963, 2.
5. Christensen, "Fires of the Future," 15.
6. John Stensvaag, "And Jesus Was There," *Lutheran Messenger*, January 22, 1963, 5.
7. Les Dahlen, "And Then Shall the End Come," *Lutheran Messenger*, January 22, 1963, 8.
8. Glenn Nelson, my sociology teacher at Augsburg and colleague and dean at Luther College, told me this.
9. Leif. S. Harbo, "Augsburg Is True to Its Heritage," *Lutheran Messenger*, January 22, 1963, 6.
10. Paul Sonnack, "A Word of Gratitude," *Lutheran Messenger*, January 22, 1963, 16.
11. "Broad Is the Way That Leadeth to Destruction—Matt. 7:13," *Minneapolis Star*, February 2, 1967, 29.
12. The painting of Jesus ascending is now stored in the archives of Luther Seminary. It stood for many years in the basement of Trinity after it had been removed from the second building and replaced by the Grønvold painting of Jesus praying in the desert.
13. The story of how Gjertsen got the painting copied, paid for, and shipped to Minneapolis is covered in Nina Draxton's biography of Gjertsen, *The Testing of M. Falk Gjertsen*. The painting, whose subject was unusual for altar paintings, stood in the new Trinity church until it was torn down. After that, it was hung in the Augsburg Hoversten chapel, where the Trinity congregation would worship. After Augsburg took it down to replace it with a Jesus of color, it was given to Mindekirken, where it now stands.
14. Gracia Grindal, "Verge of Jordan, Views and Counterviews," *Dialog*, Summer 1975, 215–217.

15. See my book *Unstoppable: Norwegian Pioneers Educate Their Daughters* (Fortress Press, 2016), which is a history of Luther College and the Preus family, especially their grandmother Linka.
16. This was said by Walter Sundberg once describing to me what had happened to Oliver in his graduate school studied.
17. Oliver K. Olson, *Matthias Flacius and the Survival of Luther's Reform* (Harassowitz Verlag, 2002).
18. Walter Sundberg, *Worship Is Repentance* (Eerdmans Press, 2008).
19. For an exhaustive history of the Hauge movement in America, see Thomas Jacobson, *Pain in the Belly: The Haugian Witness in American Lutheranism* (Wipf and Stock, 2024).
20. H. C. Caspersen, "Shall We Have Bishops?," *Lutheran Messenger*, November 28, 1939, and Chr. "Frikirken og bispeideen," *Folkebladet*, January 31, 1940, 35.
21. Paideia was the Greek term for the educational program they gave their sons.
22. Mark Granquist, "Georg Sverdrup and the Purpose of Theological Education," *Lutheran Forum* 54, no. 1 (Spring 2020): 41–45.
23. *The Works of John Bunyan*, ed. George Offor (1852-3), 758.
24. Gordon S. Wakefield, "Bunyan and the Christian Life," *John Bunyan Conventicle and Parnassus: Tercentenary Essays*, ed. N. H. Keeble (Clarendon Press, 1988), 124.
25. Wakefield, "Bunyan and the Christian Life," 124.
26. Wakefield, "Bunyan and the Christian Life," 124.
27. Mark Granquist, "The Urge to Merge," *Lutheran Forum*, Summer 2012, 20–23.

# Praise for *What a Fellowship*

This is the book Gracia Grindal was born to write: a love story concerning the specific Lutheran group that gave her life and shaped her. We are fascinated reading about the characters within the Lutheran Free Church whom she brings so fully to life as Christians struggling to live out their callings. Beyond all the institutions, any such group is, at its core, the people who love it and fight over it, and who seek to pass its traditions on to future generations.
 —Mark Granquist, Lloyd and Annelotte Svendsbye Professor of the History of Christianity, Luther Seminary

In the genre of American Lutheran denominational histories, Gracia Grindal's *What a Fellowship* accomplishes something refreshingly unique. Not only does she tell the story of the Lutheran Free Church and Augsburg College and Seminary with skill and detail, but she does so as a part of her own family's history in this part of the American Lutheran experience. Filled with personal reminiscences, this book takes us back to an earlier time in American life amid changes and challenges from which everyone, both inside and outside of the Lutheran community, can learn.
 —Thomas E. Jacobson, pastor of Grace Lutheran Church, Thornville, Ohio, and assistant professor of history at the Institute of Lutheran Theology, Brookings, South Dakota

Gracia Grindal tells the story of the church she knew as home and continues to love. This detailed history sings like one of her hymns and creates images like her poetry. Some of these stories are held in her heart by lived memory. Many are drawn from interviews and church archives. Others bring back the voices of pastors and professors whom many today still hold dear. *What a Fellowship* helps the reader better understand the theology, ecclesiology, and culture of the congregations, communities, and educational institutions of the Lutheran church today. It is a story of faith in God's mercy and abiding presence in the church that can be, at the same time, both heartbreaking and home.
 —Dee Pederson, bishop, Southwestern Minnesota Synod, ELCA

In this remarkable book, Gracia Grindal weaves the story of her Norwegian immigrant family with the history of the Norwegian Lutherans who founded and led Augsburg Theological Seminary and the Lutheran Free Church for almost one hundred years. This is a love story, illustrating Grindal's deep appreciation for the life of local congregations, while at the same time naming the many cultural and theological forces that often warred against the intimate "life together" those congregations reflected. In the end, though Grindal admits her sense of betrayal of the tradition she cherishes, she nonetheless offers all of us a compelling narrative of how modern and postmodern forces have shaped our lives of faith in the world.

—Paul C. Pribbenow, president, Augsburg University

Behold a voice! Gracia Grindal recites how the Lutheran Free Church and Augsburg "lived in my very being." Her beautifully written narrative is "mixed, grateful, yet wistful," filled with leaders and losses amid institutional change, and testifies to God's saving presence in vibrant, diverse Christian communities.

—David L. Tiede, professor of New Testament and president emeritus, Luther Seminary, and author of *Prophecy and History in Luke-Acts* and *Luke* (Augsburg Commentary)

Gracia Grindal has written a lively and warm-hearted account of "ties that bind"—the story of the Lutheran Free Church. Her deep love for its people—saints and sinners galore—and the faith that sustained and nourished it are evident on every page.

—Mark D. Tranvik, professor of Reformation history and theology, Luther Seminary